THE DIARY OF
A. J. MOUNTENEY JEPHSON

EMIN PASHA
RELIEF EXPEDITION
1887–1889

HAKLUYT SOCIETY
EXTRA SERIES NO. XL

THE DIARY OF
A. J. MOUNTENEY JEPHSON

EMIN PASHA
RELIEF EXPEDITION
1887–1889

Edited by Dorothy Middleton

With Preface, Prologue and Epilogue
compiled by the Editor
in collaboration with
Maurice Denham Jephson

CAMBRIDGE
Published for the Hakluyt Society
AT THE UNIVERSITY PRESS
1969

Published by the Syndics of the Cambridge University Press
Bentley House, 200 Euston Road, London, N.W.1
American Branch: 32 East 57th Street, New York, N.Y. 10022

Library of Congress Catalogue Card Number: 68–23182
Standard Book Number: 521 01021 7

Printed in Great Britain
at the University Printing House, Cambridge
(Brooke Crutchley, University Printer)

PREFACE

The diary written by A. J. Mounteney Jephson between January 1887 and October 1889 contains as full a first-hand account as exists of the expedition led by H. M. Stanley to the relief of Emin Pasha, Governor of the Equatorial Province of Egypt, isolated in the southern Sudan from 1882 onwards by the rising and victory of the Mahdi. The disaster of the Rear Column is, indeed, only referred to incidentally, but the main course of the expedition and Jephson's own adventures on his special mission to the Equatorial garrisons is dealt with fully.

The complete diary, in two large and two small notebooks, runs to about 300,000 words, of which some 200,000 are printed here, with editorial narrative to bridge the omission of one or more entry, and dots to show cuts within one entry. Chapter headings have been introduced by the editor for greater clarity. The Prologue and Epilogue to the journal have been compiled in close collaboration with the late Brigadier Maurice Denham Jephson, C.B.E., the diarist's nephew, and incorporate details of family history from papers at Mallow Castle, County Cork.

Book 1 of the diary was begun when Jephson joined the expedition at Tilbury on 20 January 1887 and covers the voyage out to the Congo mouth by way of Zanzibar, and the journey up the Congo and across the Ituri forests to Lake Albert; it concludes with the meeting with Emin Pasha, the last entry being for 28 May 1888. The early part of this is abridged, but from Yambuya (28 June 1887) to the end is printed in full. Book 2 runs from 5 June to 31 December 1888 and tells the story of the mutiny of Emin's troops and the imprisonment of Emin and Jephson in the barracks at Dufilé; this section, in view of the fact that it was published by the author as *Emin Pasha and the Rebellion at the Equator* (1890), has been drastically cut. Book 3, from 1 January to 20 April 1889, covers the reunion with Stanley and the departure for the east coast, and is also abridged. Book 4, from 29 April 1889, covers the journey back, and is given in full. The last dated entry is 2 August, after which the narrative is continuous and undated (except for one entry), and peters out some time in October.

Books 1 and 4 measure 13 by 8 inches, with white card covers; these were the books brought from home by the diarist. Books 2 and 3 were given him by Emin from his store: 2 is 10 by 6½ inches, with squared paper and a green cloth cover, and 3 is bound in black leather and is only 7 by 4½ inches. The writing, in ink, is legible and uniform. Original spelling and punctuation have been retained, except for the correction of 'thier' to 'their' throughout.

v

Preface

The diary was discovered in 1955 in a cupboard at Mallow Castle by Brigadier Jephson who, as already stated, helped substantially with the Prologue and Epilogue. Its existence had been unknown, and no directions have been found to indicate the author's wishes regarding it.

Though Mounteney Jephson's diary may be described as the fullest account of the Emin Pasha Relief Expedition, it is by no means the only one. The official version is, of course, H. M. Stanley's *In Darkest Africa*, published in 1890. Events in which Stanley played no part are covered in Jephson's *Emin Pasha* and in the records of officers left with the Rear Column at Yambuya while the Advance Column, with Stanley, Jephson, Parke, Stairs and Nelson, pressed on to the lake. Herbert Ward and J. Rose Troup wrote books on their return to England, and E. M. Barttelot's and J. S. Jameson's letters and diaries were published posthumously, edited by their relatives. One other first-hand narrative, which deserves to be better known, is T. H. Parke's *My personal experiences in Equatorial Africa as medical officer of the Emin Pasha Relief Expedition* (1891); Parke, a humorist, wrote to Jephson: 'To me it reads simple magnificence and I get quite emotional over it—a good sign?' It also made him 'laugh like the mischief'. He explains that he has not asked Stanley to write a foreword as it might look as if the account was 'one-sided', but he had invited Mrs Stanley to do some pictures.[1] Casati's *Ten years in Equatoria and the return with Emin Pasha* (1891) includes time spent with Emin in Equatoria after the isolation of the garrisons; it is a disappointing book, lacking the power to evoke a scene. Emin's own diaries survive, with one important gap, and are the basis of *Die Tagebücher von Dr. Emin Pascha*, edited in five volumes by Franz Stuhlmann and published between 1916 and 1927. Unfortunately for our purposes, the material in vol. IV (1888–89) was reduced for reasons of economy, and vol. V (1890–92) never appeared, possibly owing to Dr Stuhlmann's death in 1928, and the diaries for those years have been lost. A new translation is being made by Sir John Gray of such portions of the diaries as refer to Uganda, and it is hoped this may throw some light, when complete, on Emin's relations with Stanley and the other members of the expedition.[2]

The exhaustive bibliography of Emin Pasha, compiled by D. H. Simpson and published in the *Uganda Journal* for September 1960, devotes two sections to the expedition and one to H. M. Stanley; there are 38 main titles under the heading 'First-hand accounts', 57 under 'Second-hand

[1] From letter dated 31 January 1891 among the Mallow Castle papers.
[2] These extracts have appeared in successive issues of the *Uganda Journal*, beginning with xxv, 1 (1961). 'Extracts, I' opens with Emin's first Mission to Buganda in 1877, and 'X', *Uganda J.* xxix, 2 (1965), recounts his first meeting with Stanley in April 1889.

accounts', and 27 relating to Stanley himself. Many of the items are, of course, articles in newspapers and periodicals, and an unexpectedly low proportion of the total represents straightforward narrative accounts of the expedition. The most succinct contemporary one (though it has *lacunae*) is A.-J. Wauters's *Stanley au secours d'Émin Pacha* (Brussels, Paris, 1890), by the editor of the geographical periodical *Le Mouvement Géographique*, who had close connections with King Leopold and others interested in the expedition. There is also a modern re-telling of the story, in popular style, in *The Remarkable Expedition* by Olivia Manning (1947), whose sources do not go beyond *In Darkest Africa* and Jephson's *Emin Pasha*. A select bibliography, including unpublished sources, is printed on pp. 437–9.

Although nothing positively new emerges from the manuscript of Jephson's diary, it is of great value to anyone interested not only in the Emin Pasha Relief Expedition but in travel and exploration generally. Primarily it has, of course, the obvious interest of an unedited and spontaneous account, uninhibited by considerations of what it was or was not proper to say about one's leader and companions on a long and difficult journey. It also provides useful verification of incidents and dates, not only where there was no intent to deceive, but where more than allowable poetic licence is in question. And it is particularly important that Stanley should be subjected to such a check, being a flagrant offender in this respect. Stanley is reliable over routes, places, dates, names and so forth; he was a great explorer. But he cannot be trusted when his pen runs away with one of his big set pieces; and where divergences between *In Darkest Africa* and the diary become outrageous, a footnote has been appended. It did not, indeed, require Jephson's modest pages to show up his leader's flamboyant journalese; Stanley is condemned out of his own mouth, so to speak, in regard to certain passages in his earlier *Through the Dark Continent* (1877). In his original diary, found among family papers and published in 1961,[1] an entry describes how certain chiefs on the Congo in 1877 objected to his writing in his diary, fearing magic. Stanley records briefly that he 'gave a sheet of paper scribbled over carelessly...which was torn and burnt' to everyone's satisfaction. In his published account, a far more dramatic scene is outlined in which Stanley sacrifices his pocket Shakespeare ('Chandos edition...my genial companion, which during many weary hours of night had assisted to relieve my mind when oppressed by almost intolerable woes...'), throwing it into the flames, 'heaping the brushwood over it with ceremonious care'.[2]

[1] Richard Stanley and Alan Neame, *The exploration diaries of H. M. Stanley* (London, 1961).
[2] Compare Stanley and Neame, entry for 4 June 1887 Zinga Falls (pp. 192–3), with Stanley, *Through the Dark Continent* (London, 1877), 2 vols., II, pp. 385–6, entry for 30 May 1877.

Preface

With the coming to light of the diary it may therefore be claimed that the documentation of the Emin Pasha Relief Expedition is as complete as it is ever likely to be, and more complete than any other of the great Victorian traverses of Africa. What would students of the period not give for such a journal as this written by John Hanning Speke as he and Richard Burton, barely on speaking terms, trudged home from Lake Tanganyika in 1859?

Adding enormously to the interest of the diary is its discovery in the lifetime of the author's nephew; and in acknowledging help and other facilities for editing the diary, I must first put on record the generous and self-effacing cooperation of its owner, Brigadier Jephson of Mallow Castle. He not only provided much useful background information, but gave me the freest access to family papers. His share in producing the printed edition of his uncle's journal goes far beyond his contributions, substantial as those are, to the Prologue and Epilogue. It is indeed tragic that Brigadier and Mrs Jephson should have lost their lives in an air accident over the Irish Sea on 28 March 1968, and that the owner of this unique document should not have had what would have been to him the supreme satisfaction of seeing it in print.

I also have to express my indebtedness to Mr R. A. Skelton and Miss E. M. J. Campbell, joint Honorary Secretaries of the Hakluyt Society when this project first came before the Council. I should like to thank my colleagues in the Library and Map Room of the Royal Geographical Society for help in my research. Thanks are also due to Mr Iain Smith, who is preparing a thesis on the Emin Pasha Relief Expedition, for some useful pointers in the course of my research; to Dr Roy Bridges of Aberdeen University for advice on my introduction; to Sir John Gray for his kind response to requests for information where his translation of Emin's diaries covered the period of the expedition. The maps are the skilful work of Mr Alec Herzer and a perfect typescript was made by Miss Diana Harding.

I also have to thank the publishers and authors of the following works for permission to quote them in the course of the Editor's Introduction:

Robert O. Collins, *The southern Sudan 1883–1898: the struggle for control.* Yale University Press, 1962, pp. 50, 51.

Ruth Slade, *King Leopold's Congo.* Oxford University Press, 1962, pp. 86, 87.

John Kirtland Wright, *Human nature in geography.* The Belknap Press of Harvard University Press, 1966, pp. 24, 26.

Alan Moorehead, *The White Nile.* Hamish Hamilton, 1960, pp. 357–8.

Chelsea,
June 1968

D.M.

CONTENTS

Contents

ILLUSTRATIONS AND MAPS

PROLOGUE

In order to present the reader with some idea of the diarist's antecedents, a brief outline of his family history is given here.

William Jephson obtained the Manor of Froyle in Hampshire from King Henry VIII in 1541. His son built Froyle Court, now Lord Mayor Treloar's College, in the year of the Armada. Of his two sons, William, the elder, was a prominent member of Parliament, knighted in 1603, and the subject of a eulogistic epigram by Ben Jonson. He died without issue in 1611, when the younger son, John, succeeded to the Froyle estate. John was a soldier. After service in the Low Countries, he proceeded to Ireland in 1598 in command of the Earl of Southampton's troop of horse. By 1603 he had been promoted to major-general, granted a knighthood and appointed a privy councillor in Ireland. Four years later, he married Elizabeth Norreys, god-daughter of Queen Elizabeth, and only surviving child of Sir Thomas Norreys, fifth son of Lord Norreys of Rycote by his wife Margery, daughter of Lord Williams of Thame. Sir Thomas was sometime Lord Justice of Ireland and Lord President of Munster at the time of his death. When the estates of the fifteenth Earl of Desmond were broken up after the Desmond Rebellion in 1579, he received the Castle and Manor of Mallow in County Cork, which passed to the Jephson family by this marriage. It has remained in their possession ever since, but Froyle was sold in 1651.

Arthur Jermy Mounteney Jephson, usually called Mounteney, was born at Hutton Rectory in Essex on 8 October 1858. He was the tenth of the twelve children, and the youngest son, of the Reverend John Mounteney Jephson and Ellen, daughter of Isaac Jermy, Recorder of Norwich, of Stanfield Hall, Norfolk. The murder of Isaac Jermy and his only son in November 1848 resulted in one of the *causes célèbres* of the century.

This was the cadet branch of the Jephsons of Mallow, deriving from the Parliamentarian colonel, John Jephson. The senior branch became extinct in 1911, and the last survivor appointed Mounteney her heir soon after his return from Africa. He never inherited the Mallow estate as he died in 1908, but his son succeeded in due course.

There is a strong clerical background to Mounteney's branch of the family. Colonel John Jephson's wife was the daughter of Richard Boyle, Archbishop of Tuam, and the five succeeding generations entered Holy Orders. There was also some tradition of scholarship and letters in the family. Mounteney's grandfather had been a prominent member of a circle of intellectual brilliance in County Meath in the early years of the nineteenth century, a circle which included such people as the Malones, the Edgeworths, Grattan and Curran. His great-grandmother was a sister of Richard Mounteney, a Baron of the Exchequer in Ireland, and author of *Demosthenes*. His great-great-uncle was Robert Jephson, the dramatist, and friend and correspondent of some of the literary giants of the late eighteenth century, such as Johnson, Horace Walpole, Goldsmith, Edmond Malone and Edmund Burke. During the last few years of his life, Mounteney's father had published three books. One, entitled *Shakespeare, his Birthplace, Home and Grave*, appeared in 1864 to commemorate the tercentenary of the poet's birth, and was a tribute to the almost traditional love the family entertained for Shakespeare's works, and with which Mounteney himself was in full accord.

Mounteney's father died on 1 January 1865, having just reached the age of forty-five. The family's financial situation, never very easy, now presented a serious problem to his widow. But she addressed herself to the task of bringing up and educating her numerous progeny with commendable results. The home provided the bare necessities of life. But in spite of the enforced frugality it was happy and tumultuous. The eldest son, back on leave from the training ship *Worcester*, walked round Fryerning, in Essex, to which village the family had recently moved, searching for the new home. Then he heard an unearthly screeching emerging from one of the houses. It was a well-known sound to him, just one child playfully torturing another. He turned confidently in at the gate.

Mounteney was educated at Tonbridge School. There are indications of some indecision in his choice of a profession. In the end he decided to follow his eldest and favourite brother into the Merchant Navy. He too went to the *Worcester*, and from there to the P. & O. Company, like his brother, as a cadet. But, before obtaining officer rank, he came to the conclusion that a seafaring life was not his *métier* and resigned from the company. During this period of training, however, he had learnt something which was to prove of great value in years to come: he could handle a boat and carry out running repairs.

While he was looking round for some more congenial employment, his cousin, the Comtesse de Noailles, urged him to come and help her with the many charitable activities in which she was forever engaged. Mounteney agreed; it seemed to him wise to be doing something while looking round for the right kind of work. In the event, he stayed with her for two years, moving between Eversfield Place, The Meads, Eastbourne, and her winter home, the Villa Montclaire, Hyères. He was active in looking after her varied interests, moved in high social circles, lived a life of ease and learnt to revel in luxury, a strange contrast to the austerity of his boyhood in Essex and the hard life of a Merchant Navy cadet. He was clearly popular and made many friends. But it was certainly not the life for a young man who was both physically active and mentally alert, and who ought to have been making his own way in the world. It is surprising that he should have resisted for so long the enervation such a life must inevitably have propagated.

But fortune was kind to him. Early in January 1887, H. M. Stanley, just appointed to command the expedition to relieve Emin Pasha in Equatorial Africa, called for volunteers to accompany him. Mounteney was then just over twenty-eight. After the soft living since he left the Merchant Service, it seems incredible that he should have even applied for an appointment which would necessarily demand a high state of physical fitness and ability to withstand the severest of privations. But the thought of such an adventurous journey fired his imagination. And Mme de Noailles was also deeply stirred by the romance and high ideals of the expedition. 'If I had a son', she said, 'I would send him on this expedition.' In his diary Mounteney records Emin's emotion when he told him her words. In any case, she strongly supported his wish to join the expedition, feeling, perhaps, some misgivings about the sort of life her young cousin was leading, and its possible effect on his will to find some work more fitted to his age and ability. He duly applied to the Relief Expedition H.Q. and the result can best be described by quoting Stanley's own words:

Our next volunteer was Mr A. J. Mounteney Jephson, inexperienced as yet in foreign travel, and quite unaccustomed to 'roughing' in wilds. On some members of the Committee Mr Jephson made the impression that he was unfitted for an expedition of this kind, being in their opinion of too 'high class'. But the Countess de Noailles made a subscription in his favour to the Relief Fund of £1000, an argument that the Committee could not resist, and Mr Jephson signed the articles of agreement with unshaken nerves. Poor young Jephson! he emerged out of Africa after various severe trials which are herein related.[1]

Stanley made no mention of Mounteney's ability to handle a boat, but this must have been taken into consideration, for he was put in charge of the *Advance*, the expedition's steel boat, with what effect the following pages will show.

One can detect a tinge of scepticism in Stanley's words at this first meeting with Mounteney. Later on in his book Stanley, waiting in anger and frustration for Mounteney to bring Emin to him at Kavalli's village, and keenly conscious of the heavy toll of lives and the sufferings the expedition had already incurred, referred to him with an ill-concealed resentment. He clearly held him responsible, in part at any rate, for Emin's dilatory progress. He labelled him 'a pronounced Eminist'. Other writers have seized upon these derogatory comments and given fresh publicity to them, expressing the

[1] H. M. Stanley, *In Darkest Africa* (London, 1890), 2 vols., I, 43.

opinion that Mounteney shared Emin's indecision and preferred the easy, listless life with Emin to the prompt performance of the task assigned to him. The reader must decide for himself whether or not these comments were in fact justified, and whether or not he acquitted himself with the courage, loyalty and selflessness such an assignment demanded.

But it is surprising that Stanley never altered these passages in his book before publication, for not only had he received Mounteney's official report of the period of his stay in the Equatorial Province, but he had had ample time during the long trek to the Indian Ocean to ascertain the true story in all its details. All through the expedition, however, Stanley seems to have been egocentric and coldly aloof from the happy camaraderie of his four subordinate officers. So the opportunities for clarification were lost. Yet he made amends a few months later for his lack of understanding when writing the Prefatory Letter to Mounteney's book:

There is within the covers of your volume much matter that is quite new to me, much that is extremely thrilling and exciting...When I despatched you...to convey my letters to Emin...I little dreamt that you would be subjected to a long imprisonment and to imminent risk at the hands of those misguided people you sought to save.[1]

All the same, it is surprising that he should have had to wait for Mounteney's book before becoming apprised of the real facts.

It will be noted that the diary was written under a variety of conditions. Sometimes Mounteney was fit, happy and at ease, but often he was weighed down by utter exhaustion, hunger, the ravages of fever and appalling weather conditions. The effort of writing must at times have called for great determination and strength of mind. Yet, whenever it was physically possible, he succeeded in faithfully recording the events of the day, and confided his innermost thoughts to the secrecy of the diary. His style is at times curiously stilted. The reader gets the impression that he wrote as though he was addressing himself to someone. And perhaps this was true, and he had promised Hélène de Noailles to provide her with a day-by-day account of his experiences. In estimating the fairness of the views he expressed, particularly those critical of his chief, it must be remembered that he wrote in a private diary, and at times under acute mental and physical stress.

Part of the interest of the diary, in fact, is that it gives an untouched picture of what actually happened from day to day on one of the most ambitious expeditions launched into Africa at a time when important events were taking place and the future shape of the continent coming into being. It illuminates the personal relations of the men taking part in a way no

[1] A. J. Mounteney Jephson, *Emin Pasha and the Rebellion at the Equator* (London, 1890), p. vi.

4

published book could do, inhibited as it would be at the time by Victorian codes of what might and might not be said. The image of Stanley is at times shocking, and clearly Jephson was himself distressed not only by Stanley's lack of justice, and even common sense, in moments of crisis, but by the brutality with which he battered his way through local opposition. These adverse criticisms of his leader might well have been modified if Jephson had published his diary in full. Hence, perhaps, the reason why he left no instructions regarding publication, preferring that the criticisms of his old chief should remain out of sight during his lifetime, and that thereafter posterity should decide. Those who read the diary to the end will observe that Jephson came to modify his views of Stanley, to value the forthright decisiveness when compared with Emin's vacillations, and to decide at some stage that, after all, Stanley was his ideal of a leader. He may have come to realize that Stanley's roughness and violence, his lack of consideration for his officers, and other aspects which jarred were due in part to a very real fear that failure was only just round the corner and that the outcome of the expedition was in doubt. Jephson's views were not necessarily confined to himself alone. The close friendship which existed throughout the expedition between the four officers of the Advance Column suggests the likelihood of some identity in the opinions they held. Afterwards, under the mellowing influence of time, and in conditions of physical and mental ease, there was an all-round reappraisal of the past. Stanley was unflagging in generous praise of his four officers as they, too, were of him, and he and Mounteney, so soon to be the sole survivors of the expedition, became ever more closely knit in friendship until death separated them. The overall picture is clear enough to anyone who has read their letters to each other after the return of the expedition in that all too brief period before death, which they had cheated so often and so narrowly in that hazardous adventure, overcame their vitiated constitutions. Stanley was their ideal of a leader, a man they would have followed eagerly again and again across the dark continent, a man whom in retrospect they never criticized. Not for nothing was Jephson's family motto *Loyalement je sers*.

Of Mounteney Jephson himself the diary conjures up a picture of a young man who, but for the understanding and generous action of Madame de Noailles, might easily have drifted into a life of *dolce far niente*, of ease, luxury and interesting social contacts, with some secretarial work which was a near sinecure. The expedition brought out in him all the latent virility in his character. He was shown to be impetuous and enthusiastic, with a tremendous sense of duty and fair play. He throve on hard work. He stood up well to privation, and trudged gamely along day after day when in high fever. He was bitterly disappointed when a heavy attack of malaria prevented him from joining Stairs in the ascent of Ruwenzori. Withal he was warmhearted and compassionate. There was nothing soft in his make-up except his heart.

Something of the impression he and his brother officers made on the men in his charge may be guessed from the nicknames the Zanzibaris, unable to pronounce the officers' English names, invented for them. Stanley's was, of course, Bula Matari, the breaker of rocks, the man nothing could stop—a sobriquet earned during his strenuous years founding the Congo Free State. Stairs, who was in charge of the Maxim gun, they called Bwana Mazinga, the master of the Maxim. Nelson, who was the tallest of the officers, was known as Pandalamona, the big, strong man. Parke was Bwana Doctori. Mounteney Jephson's name was spelt either Boubarika or Buburika: it meant cheetah, and was descriptive of his speed and impetuous nature. Jephson referred to these nicknames in his book *Stories told in an African forest* (1892), and added another instance which came to his ears. 'I remember hearing on the Congo,' he wrote, 'there was a white man who had rather a bad temper and used to make a tremendous noise when he blew his nose. Well, the Negroes immediately named him Barragourm, or the War Horn.'

From the diary there emerges also a picture of Jephson's attitude to the people with whom and among whom he was travelling. At first, it is difficult not to be irritated by his references to 'niggers' in the early part of his diary. One is reminded that those were the days when white men regarded themselves as the *Herrenvolk* of the world, and it was customary to think and talk in that manner. It was largely due to lack of personal knowledge of negro countries. Significantly, as Mounteney became better acquainted with the Africans with whom he served, his views changed, and in him and his brother officers there soon arose a very real respect and affection for the expedition's Zanzibaris. They got to know them by name, and it is clear that a genuine spirit of comradeship existed between the white officers and their African followers.

There are also passages in the diary to show that Jephson took an increasing interest in the native peoples among whom he found himself. His book contains a sympathetic study of the Bari tribe, and he paid much attention to the pygmies (or 'dwarfs' as he called them) whose camps they passed through on their way to Lake Albert. The political future of Africa engaged his thoughts, and the final pages of the diary describe his reading of books on the subject of Africa's future, and his discussions with the famous Uganda missionary, Alexander Mackay, with whom the expedition spent some weeks on their return journey. He was proud to record that Mackay had called him 'the friend of Africa and of the African'. His constant interest in the subject is shown by a correspondence in *The Times* to which he contributed on his return, and which is quoted in the Epilogue.

Prologue

The brief details given in this Prologue are intended to put before the reader some sort of picture of the traveller and the background against which he played his part in Africa. His later life and his sadly early death are the subject of the Epilogue, which deals with the aftermath of the expedition of which Jephson was eventually the sole survivor.[1]

[1] Details of Jephson's family background are taken from Maurice Denham Jephson, *An Anglo-Irish Miscellany: some records of the Jephsons of Mallow* (Dublin, 1964), chapter XVI, 'A. J. Mounteney Jephson'.

EDITOR'S INTRODUCTION

'The history of geographical discovery is a fabric into which many colorful threads are interwoven: threads of adventure and hardship, of military conquest and political intrigue, of commercial enterprise, of theoretical speculation, and of hard scientific thought.'

JOHN KIRTLAND WRIGHT

Human Nature in Geography (1966), p. 24

THE EMIN PASHA RELIEF EXPEDITION: HOW IT BEGAN

The Emin Pasha Relief Expedition was the last, as well as the most elaborate, the most controversial and the least successful of Stanley's invasions of the African continent. The word 'invasion' is used advisedly: beginning with the famous journey in search of Livingstone, all Stanley's journeys were on a quasi-military scale, designed to overcome resistance, whether from the terrain or from its inhabitants, and to come back with a trophy. In 1871 his achieved aim was the meeting with Livingstone at Ujiji on Lake Tanganyika, and the provisioning and cheering of the old hero, whose own friends had been unable to make a way through to him. In 1874–7 Stanley's trophy was no less than the discovery of the course of the Congo and the opening up of a whole new area of Africa. From 1879 to 1884 he was building the Congo Free State, and in 1887–9 nothing was going to stop his rescuing Emin Pasha, the last representative of orderly government in that part of Central Africa so painstakingly explored by Samuel Baker and where England's hero, General Charles Gordon, had lost his life.

To be understood, Stanley must be seen as a new kind of explorer, a principal player in the now discredited game in which European powers and interests 'scrambled' for Africa. It is one of the ironies of history that Stanley should have made a father-figure out of David Livingstone, whose outlook and methods belonged to a different and less acquisitive era. There can be no greater contrast between two men than that of the rough old Scots doctor, who held that to travel with a large retinue and bales of goods served only to 'excite cupidity among the tribes',[1] with the brash young journalist whose line of loaded porters, armed with Remingtons at the ready,[2] wound its way

---

[1] David Livingstone, *Missionary Travels and Researches in South Africa* (London, 1857), pp. 230–1.

[2] 'Boys, be firm as iron; wait until you see the first spear, and then take good aim. Don't fire all at once. Keep aiming until you are sure of your man. Don't think of running away for only your guns can save you.' Stanley, *Through the Dark Continent*, II, 271.

8

like a monstrous snake across Africa from east to west in 1874–7, and again from west to east to the succour of Emin Pasha in 1887–9.

Stanley did, however, genuinely believe that the exploitation of Africa by European interest was a good thing, an object on which a man might spend himself, for which it was worth while fighting a way across the continent, leaving the trail strewn with dead—not only the local tribespeople who had stood in his way, not only his Zanzibari porters, but white companions who had joined his army with a view to making a small name for themselves. In fairness to Stanley, it may be said that he came on the scene at a time when the sudden opening up of Africa, first by the ivory and slave traders and later in the interests of legitimate development and peaceful commerce, had bewildered and antagonized the inhabitants; Livingstone's early travels in South and Central Africa, with hand-picked followers among friendly natives, were no longer possible. But even allowing for more difficult conditions, Stanley did not make the best of Africa. He did not love the country and its people, confronting both with a dour determination to stand no nonsense. There are no passages in his books to match Livingstone's descriptions of those scenes which, 'flooded with bright African sunshine, and enlivened with the songs of the birds before the heat of the day becomes intense, form pictures which can never be forgotten'.[1] And though he established a relationship of a kind with his porters, and with the people whose country he passed through, he expresses none of the infectious enthusiasm of, for instance, his contemporary Joseph Thomson, who met with similar difficulties but contrived to avoid the use of force and also immensely to enjoy himself.

Elaborate and controversial, therefore, this last expedition of Stanley's was bound to be, but why was it the least successful? As regards its aim, it must be held to have failed, despite the acclaim which greeted the leader and his officers on their return, and the reasons for this are touched upon in the last section of this Introduction. It proved, in short, quite impracticable to remove an entire administration, keeping it in working order and good heart, from the territory being administered, and it was equally impracticable to carry in sufficient provisions and arms to maintain it effectively on the spot. That Stanley did manage to bring back to the coast the Pasha himself, his daughter and his European companions, and a ragged tail of some 6000 soldiers and camp followers was a remarkable feat, but hardly justified the enormous death-roll, the bitter controversies, the smell of scandal which persists to the present day. Yet the adventure is important, if only from a geographical point of view, for it cleared up the final mystery of African topography—the position and nature of the sources of the Nile.

[1] Livingstone, *Missionary Travels*, p. 441.

Moreover, it repays study because it reflected from several angles important contemporary movements. Relations between Europe and Africa entered a critical phase in the 1880s with the virtual completion of the primary exploration which had occupied the European mind for a century, and the actions of the expedition affected, or were affected by, these changing relations.

The story of Equatoria and the relief of Emin Pasha its Governor begins a long way back, as far at least as Mehemet Ali's conquest of the Sudan in the early years of the nineteenth century and the imperial ambitions of his successors. When, in 1862, Samuel and Florence Baker arrived at Gondokoro (modern Juba) at the navigable headwaters of the Nile, they found trade routes pretty well established into the interior, and regular caravans, to which, rather unwillingly, they attached themselves for convenient travelling. They reached Lake Albert two years later, and returned with stories of fine country between their lake and Speke's Victoria, ripe for development. In 1869 Baker accepted a commission from Ismail, Khedive of Egypt, to take a military expedition up the Nile to suppress the slave trade, and to annex the country south of Khartoum as far as the Equator for Egypt.

A masterful and self-confident man, Baker returned in 1873 claiming complete success for his mission, but, in fact, the problems of this primitive land, thrown into disarray by the random penetration of Arab traders and their private armies, were not to be solved in a four-year foray; and part of those four years had been spent in hacking a way slowly through the *sudd* which accumulates south of Khartoum, choking the Nile and bringing progress to a halt. Baker made a start, however, establishing at Gondokoro the capital he named Ismailia, and designing a chain of river stations through which to establish communications with Lake Albert. From Ismailia he meant to carry steamers either by water or in sections overland up to the lake but, falling foul of the Bari, the principal tribe of the Gondokoro region, he turned inland, crossed the Victoria Nile (which Speke called the 'Somerset' Nile) and invaded Bunyoro. Baker was impatient, too completely convinced of the advantages of the Western way of life to understand the suspicion and subsequent hostility of the young king Kabarega, and he had to retreat faster than he had come.

Later political development in Central Africa has been strongly influenced by the contacts made at this time with local potentates. The early explorers had a great enthusiasm for the able and astute Mutesa of Buganda, and a corresponding contempt and mistrust of his fellow monarch, Kamrasi of Bunyoro, who was succeeded in 1869 by his son Kabarega, with whom they were also at odds. Bunyoro had been, in past centuries, the senior kingdom, but by the time Speke, Baker and Stanley came on the scene it was playing second fiddle to its more powerful eastern neighbour. Baker never met

Mutesa, of whom he cherished an ideal picture. His relations with Kamrasi
had been put to the practical test of an actual meeting, and had not been
happy; he was standing no nonsense, therefore, from Kamrasi's son, Kabarega. When the King of Bunyoro prevaricated about accepting Egyptian
rule, Baker forced the pace, and hostilities broke out. Baker's fine station of
Masindi had to be abandoned in flames and the expedition, including Lady
Baker and their nephew Lieutenant Julian Baker, retreated northwards across
the Victoria Nile. Here, among the Acholi people, he built his fort of Fatiko,
not far from Gulu in modern Uganda, in country later vacated by Gordon but
which Emin, who had a station at neighbouring Fabbo, hoped to reoccupy.

General Charles Gordon succeeded Baker in 1874, and one of his first
acts was to move his capital from Gondokoro on the right bank of the Nile
to higher and healthier ground at Lado on the left bank. Baker had only
reached by water as far as the Bedden rapids, but with the interior in a
reasonably quiet state Gordon decided to persevere up stream, to establish
posts on the Nile as far as Lake Albert, and to launch Baker's little fleet.
He made friends with the blind chief of the Bedden Bari, with whom the
impetuous Baker had quarrelled, and was able to haul the boats up the
awkward rapids, and bring his supplies along to Kirri, where he built a
station. Into Kirri, on the high level of the summer Nile, Baker's steamer
the *Khedive* floated in July 1875, just two years after it had been assembled.
She stuck at the Yerbora falls, where Gordon built his next station of Muggi,
and was not afloat on Lake Albert until 1878. Gordon found that the seventh
(and last) cataract of the Nile, the Fola Rapids between the river Aswa and
Dufilé, was impassable and so it was decided to send the other steamer, the
Nyanza, direct in sections to Dufilé, to dismantle the *Khedive* and to take
her overland from Muggi to Dufilé. In March 1876 Romolo Gessi, Gordon's
able Italian lieutenant, was at Dufilé assembling not only the *Nyanza* but
two steel sailing boats which had formed part of Baker's original luggage.
In these, Gessi and a small party sailed up the last stretch of the Nile into
Lake Albert, and in July of the same year Gordon himself sailed through
from his new station of Dufilé to the Albert in the completed *Nyanza*.
Baker's largest steamer, the *Ismailia*, was assembled in Khartoum and made
her maiden voyage to Lado in October 1875.

Gordon ran the Equatorial Province and later the whole of the Sudan on
a skeleton staff recruited from the young men who found their way to Egypt
in the middle years of the century in search of employment, of wealth and
of adventure. Chief among them was his right-hand man Romolo Gessi,
who had served in Garibaldi's liberation army, and whose work in the Sudan
deserves to be better known. The Americans Colonel Prout and Lieut.-
Colonel Mason, out of work at the end of the Civil War, each acted for a

short spell as Governor of Equatoria. Rudolf Slatin was a Viennese army officer; Frank Lupton, an English merchant seaman. Among these diverse but recognizable types, one man stood out as an eccentric—the German doctor Eduard Schnitzer. Born in Silesia in 1840, Schnitzer had spent a number of years in Albania and Anatolia, where he had acquired a knowledge of the languages of the Middle East and a profound admiration for Islam. He changed his name to Emin and was thought by many to have become a Moslem, though he himself did not fully admit this. He was a remarkable linguist and acquired as time went by a European reputation in botany, zoology and ornithology.

Emin was appointed Chief Medical Officer in the Equatorial Province in 1876, and in the early years of his service undertook, with some success, diplomatic missions to Mutesa of Buganda and to Kabarega of Bunyoro. This was during a period when Gordon considered that the best chance of destroying the slave trade and bringing good order to the southern Sudan was by infiltrating the powerful kingdoms on the great lakes Victoria and Albert; Gordon's relations with Buganda, and Emin's important mission of 1876, are described a little further on.[1] In 1877 Gordon became Governor-General of the whole Sudan with his headquarters at Khartoum. After an interval partly filled by Colonel Mason and Colonel Prout, Gordon appointed Emin Governor of Equatoria. It was a depleted governorship, Egypt having abandoned the idea of expansion into Bunyoro and Buganda, and Gordon having withdrawn his garrisons on the Victoria Nile. But the stations of the Albert Nile remained the backbone of the province, and for thirteen years Emin lived in and around Lado, Rejaf, Kirri, Muggi, Laboré and Dufilé.[2]

Equatoria was always an isolated province, separated from the Sudan seat of government at Khartoum by some 1000 miles of difficult travel, mostly of desolate marshland, through which the steamers plied, slowly and infrequently, with supplies and news. For twenty months, from 1878 to 1880, Emin received no mail or supplies at all. Cairo lay over 1500 miles beyond Khartoum and the impact of events was diminished, not only delayed, by the immense distances and the uncertain communications. Writing to his friend Robert Felkin, in the enforced leisure of the years of isolation, Emin described something of the remoteness of his post, and the lack of any positive contact with the home Government after the flurry of activity which characterized Gordon's governorship. He enlarges on the restrictions imposed on him by the Egyptian Government, and his lack of resources compared with Gordon's:

They never gave me any power to use the ivory, indiarubber, oil, vegetable butter, sesame, skins, ostrich feathers, wax, etc. which I obtained for barter so as to pay

[1] See below, pp. 26–7.   [2] See map, p. 258 below.

my officials, discharge the cost of administration...I was ordered to send all the produce down to Khartoum where the same was sold by the local government, the sum being subsequently transmitted to me...I sent them down yearly 1200 cantars of ivory and they sent me 2000 dollars in two years, as well as a quantity of goods such as Khartoum merchants could not use, for me to divide amongst my people.[1]

He felt, he went on to tell his friend, that he could in fact become self-supporting, with a reliable route to the east and a small subsidy to tide him over. While, to quote Jephson, Emin's officers were 'always harping on Khartoum',[2] Emin himself seems to have dreamt of an independent province, with its links with the outside world of the east coast.

Events in Egypt mattered less than the daily routine of the Equatoria garrisons, and were noticed mainly as they affected life in the outposts on the Nile. Arabi's military revolt in 1881 was echoed faintly in Equatoria with the arrival of certain officers drafted to the southern garrisons as a punishment for having taken part in the mutiny. The British occupation of Egypt passed almost unremarked; the loyalty of Emin's troops was to the Khedive, who still nominally ruled in Cairo, and they could not know that when Britain took charge of Egypt's affairs, she rejected responsibility for Egypt's empire in the Sudan. This initial rejection was based on a realization of the immense resources in money and manpower needed to hold the Sudan, turbulent after 1882 with revolt; it did not take into account the extent of Egypt's commitment to her one-time empire, and so came Britain's disastrously partial acceptance of responsibility which was to send General Gordon to his death in Khartoum.

The emergence of the Mahdi was the most important in the chain of events which was finally to isolate Emin in his distant governorship and to make the relief expedition necessary. Mohammed Ahmed Ibn el-Seyyid Abdullah, a boat-builder on Abba Island in the Nile 150 miles south of Khartoum, in 1881 declared himself the Mahdi, reincarnation of the Prophet Mahomet, with the divine mission of cleansing the Sudan of the corrupt Egyptians. Contact with the north was disrupted by the operations of the Mahdi's Holy War, or Jihad, early in 1882, and the last dispatches to get through from Emin to Khartoum were carried by the *Ismailia* which, in April of that year, was the last steamer to navigate the upper Nile. It was left to Egyptian resources to combat the growing power of the Mahdi, resources finally exhausted by the annihilation at El Obeid in Kordofan of the expedition led by Hicks Pasha in November 1883.

---

[1] Emin to Felkin, 25 October 1887. There is a typewritten copy of the whole letter in the Mackinnon Papers (School of Oriental and African Studies, University of London) and extracts are printed in Felkin's Introduction to Georg Schweitzer (ed.), *Emin Pasha, his Life and Work*... 2 vols. (London, 1898), I, xvii-xliv.

[2] Diary, 13 August 1888.

The Hicks disaster precipitated the decision, reluctantly taken, by the British Government to become, after all, involved in the Sudan. In response to a popular campaign, stimulated as well as sponsored by such powerful papers as *The Times* and the *Pall Mall Gazette*, Gladstone, urged by those members of his Cabinet who favoured action in the Sudan, agreed to send for General Gordon. Gordon was empowered to go to Khartoum, to report on the situation and, if possible, to evacuate the Egyptian garrisons. He was at the time on the point of taking up an appointment offered him by King Leopold of the Belgians in the Congo Free State, as Stanley's second in command and probable successor, but he acknowledged the priority of orders from his own Government and in January 1884 was in Khartoum.

The Gordon story has been told many times, by many voices—as lately as 1966 in a film which was both popular and impressive. This is not the place to recapitulate the details, but the fact of the mission, and its ending in Gordon's spectacular and tragic death, lies at the heart of the history of the Emin Pasha Relief Expedition. Thoughtful people in Britain had a strong feeling of guilt over Gordon's death; they blamed their Government and felt the country should atone, so that when it turned out that one of Gordon's governors had miraculously survived the Mahdi's onslaught, it became a duty to rescue him. As one writer to *The Times* put it, 'Having betrayed the master, we might well exert ourselves a little to deliver his man'.[1]

Gordon was, of course, too late to evacuate the garrisons, though he put forward a plan soon after his arrival in Khartoum of withdrawing southwards, collecting Lupton in the Bahr el Ghazal and Emin in Equatoria with their people, and escaping by the Congo. The British Government vetoed such a venture as impracticable, as indeed by then it was.[2]

Slatin in Darfur and Lupton in the Bahr el Ghazal were attacked and, contending with risings of local tribes and mutinies among their own troops, were compelled to surrender: Slatin in December 1883 and Lupton in

[1] P. L. Sclater, F.R.S., Zoological Society of London, had been one of the first to urge relief for Emin in February 1883. This later letter, dated 1 November 1886, mentions the receipt of a letter from Emin containing interesting information on anthropoid apes, to be read to the Zoological Society at a forthcoming meeting.

[2] Lord Cromer, *Modern Egypt* (London, 1908), 2 vols., 1, 464. Part of Gordon's plan was to offer to King Leopold the provinces of Bahr el Ghazal and Equatoria, which had been renounced by both British and Egyptian Governments. Writing in the *Fortnightly* (December 1886), J. T. Wills, a Fellow of the Royal Geographical Society, lambasted the British Government for refusing permission and accused them of jealousy of King Leopold. 'There is little doubt', wrote Wills, 'that if Gordon with five steamers had gone up to Emin and Lupton in 1884, their provinces would now have been safe, under the jurisdiction of King Leopold.' There is no evidence that Leopold at that stage wanted so awkward a gift, and some that he did not: Père Ceulemans, *La Question arabe et le Congo (1883–1892)* (Brussels, 1959).

April 1884. A barrier of hostile troops now intervened between Khartoum and Emin at Lado. Slatin survived eleven years' imprisonment in the enemy camp and served again in the Sudan; Lupton died miserably in captivity four years later. Emin, who had been patiently waiting in Lado for reinforcements and reassurances from Egypt, was jolted out of all sense of security by Lupton's last message, which he received in May 1884; the Governor of Equatoria sought to gain time by sending messages of submission to Karam Allah, the Mahdi's general, and planned the withdrawal of all outlying garrisons. In January 1885 Khartoum fell and Gordon was killed. In March, Karam Allah captured Amadi, a key position on the way to Lado, after nearly three weeks' siege, at the end of which the Sudanese garrison slipped out of the town and escaped southwards. Pausing at the small station of Rimo in the Makaraka country, they were pursued by the enemy, on whom they inflicted a heavy defeat, from which the Mahdists fell back in some disorder. The breathing-space saved Emin and his garrisons.

The capture of Amadi and the defeat at Rimo had been costly; Karam Allah also had trouble with mutinous troops in the Bahr el Ghazal. By following his instinct to avoid rather than to cope with trouble, Emin put himself out of reach, slipping away to the south with his disordered battalions. By the end of June 1885 Karam Allah and the Mahdists had withdrawn from Equatoria.

THE GEOGRAPHICAL BACKGROUND: THE NILE QUEST

Although by the time the expedition set sail the outline of African topography was pretty well known, there were still blanks on the map which would have to be crossed by anyone trying to bring help to Equatoria. What then was the state of knowledge of the continent which Stanley called 'dark'? Africa was the last of the great land masses to be explored, and it was not until well into the eighteenth century that the discovery of Africa by Europe began in earnest. The African Association, founded in 1788, launched a number of expeditions to explore the western Sudan, ventures which were to lead to the discovery of the course of the Niger. John and Richard Lander's voyage down the river (sponsored not by the Association but by the British Government) cleared up the Niger problem, however, and in 1831 the Association wound up its affairs, making way for the more broadly based Royal Geographical Society. Attention now became concentrated on the problem of the Nile.[1]

[1] *See* Sir Harry Johnston, *The Nile Quest* (London, 1903), Alan Moorehead, *The White Nile* (London, 1960), for a general history of the explorations for the sources of the Nile; also, M. Perham and J. Simmons, *African discovery: an anthology* (London, 1942).

The sources of the Nile were the goal of one of those quests which throughout history have distracted man from the comforts of civilization and claims of human relationships. Cathay, Eldorado, the North-west and the North-east Passages, the North and South Poles, Everest, the Moon—the Nile Quest takes its place with these. The great river which brings life to Egypt has been the subject of picturesque rumours at least since the days of Herodotus, who came back from Egypt nearly 500 years before Christ with stories of four springing fountains far in the interior. Ptolemy drew a map in about A.D. 150 which showed great lakes and lofty mountains somewhere in Central Africa, and through the ages travellers and traders brought back tales of a great inland sea. More positive information came with the Portuguese Jesuit missionaries who were in Ethiopia in the seventeenth century. In 1615 Father Pedro Paez was shown the sources of the Blue Nile in the province of Gojam, and in 1622 Father Jerónimo Lobo left Lisbon on a journey which took him a year or two later to Ethiopa, and eventually to Lake Tana, the source of the Blue Nile. The Jesuits were followed by James Bruce, with whose journeys between 1768 and 1773 the modern, and most intensive, phase of the Nile Quest may be said to begin. Bruce claimed to have found in Lake Tana the main source of the river, but this, of course, lay far to the south beyond the vast marshes of the upper Nile. In the 1820s Mehemet Ali's conquest of the Sudan broke new ground, and was followed up in 1839 and 1841 by expeditions the second of which was to reach Gondokoro in north latitude 4° 42'. Gondokoro was to become the base from which the penetration of the southern Sudan was to be undertaken in the years that followed. Austrian missionaries established themselves there in 1850, but their work was short-lived. More enduring, unfortunately, was the work of the traders who followed, shattering the ancient seclusion of the Nilotic tribes, confronting aboriginal communities with nineteenth-century commerce in its most ruthless form. Arab merchants from Dongola pressed south, fanning out among the Dinka and the Shilluk, the Latuka and the Bari, hunting ivory and capturing slaves, accompanied by their own private armies and laying the land waste. Such invasions were not consciously part of the Nile Quest, but the traders blazed a trail which the explorers followed.

For the most part, however, the early seekers for the Nile sources worked inland from the east coast towards the fabled Central African lakes rather than from the north. In the 1840s German missionaries at Mombasa, notably Ludwig Krapf and Johann Rebmann, travelling into the interior, came back with stories, at first disbelieved, of snow-capped mountains on the Equator, which proved to be Mount Kenya and Mount Kilimanjaro. A colleague of Rebmann's, J. J. Erhardt, constructed, from local reports, a map of the inland 'Sea of Unyamwezi', shaped like a slug, as big as the Caspian, and corresponding roughly with Lakes Victoria, Albert and Tanganyika. The explorer Speke found this map on show at the Royal Geographical Society when he and Burton were being briefed for the expedition which left in 1857 under the Society's auspices, arriving at Lake Tanganyika in March 1858.[1] On the way back Speke made a detour to the north and reached Lake Victoria, which he boldly guessed to be the true source of the Nile.

The classic quarrel between Burton and Speke delayed for many years the acceptance of Speke's discovery, which he confirmed to his own satisfaction on his return to Africa in 1860 with James Augustus Grant. Working his way westward round to the north of the lake and into Buganda, he found what he supposed, rightly, to be the Nile pouring over the rapids which he named the Ripon Falls, but owing to the disturbed state of the country he and Grant were not able to follow the course of the river to where it was said to enter a second lake west of Victoria.

Meanwhile, Samuel Baker had set himself the task of attacking the Nile sources from the north. He and his gallant wife Florence met Speke and Grant at Gondokoro in 1862 and after comparing notes and maps worked their way south to the west of Speke's lake. In company with a band of Arab traders they passed through the kingdom of Bunyoro and reached a point near the south end of the lake they named 'Albert' in March 1864. Owing to the cloudy atmosphere which prevails in these equatorial latitudes, Baker failed to see the Ruwenzori mountains at the south end of Lake Albert, which he assumed to be much larger than it is, stretching far to the south. But he identified both the Victoria Nile entering Lake Albert at the northeast corner, bringing water from Lake Victoria, and the White Nile (sometimes called the Mountain Nile, or Albert Nile, at this point) flowing north out of the lake to Gondokoro and on to where the Blue Nile joins it at Khartoum.

Despite the evidence brought home by Baker in support of Speke's theories, the location of the true sources of the Nile remained a controversial subject for many years. Livingstone on his last journey wandered far to the south-west of Lake Tanganyika where the north-flowing Lualaba seemed a possible headwater of the Nile; yet he doubted, and feared that he might be following the Congo.[2] Turning south-east away from the Lualaba, Livingstone died, in 1873, on the shore of Lake Bangweulu, asking to the last whether any one had heard of the four fountains of Herodotus. Verney

[1] J. H. Speke, *Journal of what led to the discovery of the source of the Nile* (Edinburgh, 1864), p. 156. The original of the map is in the collection of the Royal Geographical Society.

[2] '. . .it may, after all, turn out that I have been following the Congo, and who would risk being put into a cannibal pot, and converted into a black man for it?': David Livingstone, *Last Journals* (London, 1874), 2 vols., II, 188.

Lovett Cameron, following in Livingstone's tracks, reached the Lualaba in 1874 and from there crossed to the west coast, collecting enough evidence to establish the Lualaba as the Congo, though it was left to Stanley actually to follow its course to the sea.

These diverse strands were woven into a strong rope by Henry Morton Stanley, in the course of travels which culminated in the Emin Pasha Relief Expedition. Back from the Ashanti Wars in 1873 to hear of Livingstone's death, his disciple (for so, all his life, Stanley regarded himself) determined to complete the task begun by the older man west of Lake Tanganyika. Equipped and financed jointly by the *Daily Telegraph* and the *New York Herald*, he set out in 1874 with a huge train of armed and loaded men from Zanzibar. He circumnavigated both Lake Victoria and Lake Tanganyika, establishing the former as the source of the Nile, and the latter as lying apart from the Nile system. He did not, however, visit Baker's Lake Albert, but skirted the south of the Ruwenzori range on his way between Victoria and Tanganyika. By his subsequent journey down the Lualaba to its junction with the Congo, and thence to the sea, Stanley once and for all established the identity of two separate systems—the streams flowing east and north to the Nile, north and west to the Congo. Important work in this connection was also done by Georg Schweinfurth, the German botanist who, in 1868–70, travelled across the Nile–Congo watershed from the headwaters of the east-flowing Bahr el Ghazal to the west-flowing Uele. Schweinfurth was the first traveller to bring back an authoritative account of the Congo pygmies. He was followed up by Wilhelm Junker, who played an important part in Emin's story. If one includes Livingstone's earlier penetration of the continent from the Cape north to the Zambezi, west across the Zambezi watershed to Loanda on the coast of Portuguese Angola, and then east down the Zambezi to its mouth at Quelimane in 1856, and his later expedition by the Zambezi and Shire to Lake Nyasa, it will be seen that, by the time Stanley returned from Africa in 1877, the main natural features of the continent were known. There was therefore a choice of routes for anyone wanting to penetrate to the centre of the land.

There remained one important blank still to be filled in on the map—the exact nature and position of the geographical features at the south end of Lake Albert. Baker's conception of a vast inland sea extending southwards of the point at which he came down to the water was inaccurate; he was, in fact, only a few miles from the southern tip of the lake, and what he took to be an expanse of water was the river Semliki flowing through marshy ground, on its way from what Stanley was to name Lake Albert Edward (now Lake Edward) further south, which lies at a higher altitude than Lake Albert. Baker's lake is not, strictly speaking, a source reservoir of the Nile; it receives water from the Albert Edward by means of the Semliki and from the Victoria by means of the Victoria Nile. The whole White Nile which flows out of the north end of Lake Albert owes its origin primarily to the Victoria, the highest of the three lakes. It was not till Stanley visited these regions on the Emin Pasha Relief Expedition, twenty-four years after Baker, that the whole Nile system was finally, and accurately, mapped out. In the interval, Romolo Gessi, Colonel Mason and Emin himself had been to the south end of the lake without identifying the Ruwenzori range, two peaks of which were seen by Jephson and Parke in April 1888 and by Stanley a month later, when the range emerged from the dense cloud which obscures it for most of the year. The 'fluffy, slightly waving strata of vapours of unknown depth'[1] which Stanley noticed around and over Lake Albert Edward, and which he described as typical of these latitudes and elevations, must have contributed to Baker's confusion of water with marsh and marsh with land.

THE POLITICAL BACKGROUND: THE 'SCRAMBLE' FOR AFRICA

Zanzibar and the east coast

It was certainly satisfactory to have established the lakes and mountains of Central Africa in their right places, but to do so was not the primary aim of the expedition, conceived originally as a straightforward rescue operation; only later was it bedevilled by political considerations and distracted by geographical curiosity. When the news filtered through to England of Emin's predicament, well-intentioned enthusiasts declared that he must be rescued, that by sending help to the last of Gordon's governors the disgrace of Gordon's death might be atoned for. But no sooner did the prospect emerge of a substantial expedition being sent into Africa than national and international interests were aroused, some of them connected only tenuously with the safety of Emin. J. K. Wright, one of whose observations heads this Introduction, has written in the same essay: 'The historian recognizes that the progress of exploration has been both the outgrowth and the cause of larger historical movements—colonial and commercial rivalries, politics and wars, missionary endeavors, the search for gold and slaves.'[2] This was peculiarly true of the Emin Pasha Relief Expedition, launched at a time when Africa was wide open to speculation and experiment.

Of the various points of entry to the African continent, Zanzibar was the most important in the great exploring years of the mid-nineteenth century. Travellers of all sorts were expected to ask the Sultan's permission and to

[1] Stanley, *In Darkest Africa*, II, 326.
[2] J. K. Wright, *Human Nature in Geography* (Harvard, 1966), p. 26.

receive his safe-conduct before setting off for the interior. Here in Zanzibar they recruited their porters, an élite which recalls the Sherpa porters of the Sola Khumbu who made the ascent of Everest possible. Headmen were passed on from one explorer to another; Speke's Bombay, Stanley's Uledi, Livingstone's Chuma, these were all personages in their own right. In Zanzibar the travellers bought their supplies and left their addresses. The island was the point of departure for the new penetration of Africa, for the attack on the slave trade, for the planning of commercial developments, and for the initiation of imperial schemes.

The opening of the Suez Canal in 1869 boosted the prosperity and importance of the island, where at this date Britain was the dominating foreign element, deeply committed to the extirpation of the slave trade in East Africa. Earlier in the century energetic action by the European powers, led by Great Britain, had brought to an end the old slave trade on the west coast and the export of slaves to the Americas. Slavery was abolished in 1834 in British colonies, and by mid-century the trade was thought to be dead. But when Livingstone returned in 1856 from his trans-African journey, he had a different tale to tell; the trade continued in Portuguese territories in West and East Africa, and the Arab merchants based on Zanzibar dealt widely in slaves. At much the same time, the Bakers travelled through an area where the trade flourished, conducted by merchants of mixed Arab and Turk descent up the Nile from Khartoum. Any enterprise launched by Europe in Africa from Livingstone's time onwards gave priority to action against the slave trade. Britain was, of course, as active in this new crusade as in the old one and, as has been said, the chief base of operations for the campaign was Zanzibar, whose Sultan exercised authority over the populous coastal belt of East Africa, and some sort of general influence for an unlimited (and undefined) distance into the interior; the Arab traders in this area were his subjects and to some extent under his control. British pressure was therefore brought to bear on the Sultan through her Consul in Zanzibar. From 1870 to 1886 this post was held by John Kirk, who had been on the Zambezi with Livingstone from 1858 to 1864 and had seen the slave trade at close quarters in one of the most exploited regions—south of Lake Nyasa on the Shire river.[1]

---

[1] Kirk's power and prestige were a dominant factor in Africa in the years he spent in Zanzibar, and his position is well described by Frederick Jackson, who went out to East Africa in 1884, towards the end of Kirk's time. 'John Kirk—his title was very rarely used by Swahilis—was known as a big man from the coast to the Congo and Uganda, and along the coast from the Zambezi to Mogadisho in Italian Somaliland. I do not think it is an exaggeration to assert that, even along the coast, he had more influence than the Sultan, Seyyid Barghash; and he was scarcely less respected and feared than that enlightened potentate. Up-country with Mirambo of Unyamwezi and

In 1873, the year of Livingstone's death, a treaty prohibiting the slave trade was signed by the Sultan, Seyyid Barghash, and by Kirk on behalf of the British Government, but the trade still continued under cover, supplying a greedy market in the Middle East, where domestic life could hardly be run without the time-honoured institution of slavery. It is not too much to say that in parts of the interior the trade not only persisted, it increased, becoming even more cruel and dangerous with the parallel increase of the trade in guns.

But Zanzibar in the 1870s and 1880s was not only important as a base from which to attack the slave trade; it was a commercial centre in which the nations of Europe and America were busily competing, jockeying for the Sultan's favour and with their eyes on the unexploited, or only partially exploited, mainland. It appeared a fruitful field to such merchant adventurers as William Mackinnon, who was to be so closely associated with the Emin Pasha Relief Expedition. Mackinnon was one of those hard-headed, high-principled Scots for whom the British Empire in its heyday offered endless scope. From a humble clerkship in Glasgow, first in a silk warehouse and later in a firm of Eastern merchants, Mackinnon went to India at the age of 24. In 1856 he founded, with a fleet of one ship, the Calcutta and Burmah Steam Navigation Company, renamed in 1862 the British India Steam Navigation Co. Mackinnon then 'developed and in many instances created a vast trade round the coast of India and Burma, the Persian Gulf, and the east coast of Africa, besides subsidiary lines with Great Britain, the Dutch East Indies and Australia'.[1] Mackinnon built his ships so as to be easily convertible into troop-carriers, having in mind the British Government's military commitments in India—a fact which was to come in very useful to the expedition, whose soldiers were carried to the Congo in a B.I.S.N.C. liner. In 1872 Mackinnon established a mail service between Aden and Zanzibar, and from then on began to turn an acquisitive, albeit benevolent, eye on the African mainland; for, to quote the *D.N.B.* again, 'his great business capacity did not impair the humanity of his disposition'. Mackinnon was a devout member of the Free Church of Scotland, a warm friend to missionary endeavour, and an ardent worker in the anti-slavery cause. In fact, as he became older, his humanitarian interests seem to have come first with him, and he never achieved the kind of success in Africa which made

Mutesa of Uganda, besides scores of minor chiefs, his influence, and their respect for him, were very much greater... Sir John's knowledge of what was going on, far and wide, was little less than downright uncanny. He knew everything of importance and worth knowing, and a vast amount that was trivial and unimportant; and it is only logic to infer that the accuracy of the former may be gauged from the accuracy of many examples of the latter, for which I can vouch' (Frederick Jackson, *Early days in East Africa* (London, 1930), p. 61).   [1] *Dictionary of National Biography.*

famous, in the southern part of the continent, his more single-minded contemporary Cecil Rhodes. The lack of support afforded to Mackinnon in his East African interests was not wholly due to the disinclination for imperial adventures characteristic of official thinking at the time, but partly to doubt of Mackinnon's effectiveness as a pioneer trader in the difficult and frustrating terrain of the African hinterland. It is not possible to say for certain at this distance of time how far these doubts were well founded. Mackinnon was a shipping man, unused to the peculiar problems of creating commercial openings in the interior of Africa; he was getting on in years, unprepared to go himself with his caravans, and possibly too inclined to combine philanthropy with trade. He had made his fortune before he came to Africa, unlike Rhodes, who arrived in the continent with his way to make and was not much concerned with such ancillary matters as spreading the Gospel and saving the Africans from themselves.

Whatever the reason, this lack of Government support was fatal to Mackinnon's East African ambitions. When in 1878 he had negotiated with the Sultan of Zanzibar a substantial concession on the mainland, including Lakes Nyasa, Tanganyika and Victoria, and extending to the borders of what was to become the Congo Free State, the scheme came to nothing.[1] It was after this setback that Mackinnon began to take an interest in West Africa, where King Leopold was inaugurating the schemes which led to the foundation of the Congo Free State. Nevertheless, in spite of this new preoccupation, there can be no doubt that Mackinnon felt considerable chagrin when the Germans, from 1884 onwards, moved into the area he had hoped to secure in the East, with the unequivocal support of their home Government.

Bismarck wanted an empire; Lord Salisbury did not, and nor did Mr Gladstone, and so Britain deliberately failed to take advantage of the favourable position established by British travellers and consolidated by a series of enthusiastic consuls in Zanzibar. The most notable of these, of course, was Kirk, who saw in the anti-slavery treaty of 1873 a step towards the spread of British influence in East Africa; Seyyid Barghash hoped it would lead to an era of safety and prosperity for Zanzibar under Britain's protection, and the two views were not incompatible. British travellers were ready to explore new routes and open up new areas, for although Britain did not join the International African Association founded by King Leopold in 1876,[2] she by no means withdrew from the field. So that they should not fall behind, the Royal Geographical Society in the same year inaugurated an 'Exploration Fund' with ambitious plans to try out a number of routes to

---

[1] See R. Oliver and G. Mathew (eds.), *History of East Africa* (London, 1963), I, 361, for details of the British Government's part in Mackinnon's discomfiture.

[2] See below, p. 30.

the interior, mainly concentrating on the Lakes.[1] Despite the Society's declared preoccupation with exclusively geographical research, the routes considered had a bearing on projects, in some of which Mackinnon was concerned, to do with transport and communications. The expense and difficulty of carrying all goods on the heads of porters, and the ravages of the tse-tse fly among pack animals, were impressing on everyone interested in Africa the necessity for better roads and for railways, and for these the accurate survey of known features of the land was as important as the discovery of new ones. Telegraph lines were also discussed. The activity of the Exploration Fund was, however, short-lived. The only expedition sent out was dispatched in 1878 under the leadership of Keith Johnston, after whose early death Joseph Thomson, then only 21 and a newcomer to Africa, took command. The route covered was from the coast due west to the north end of Lake Nyasa and thence to Lake Tanganyika; an attempt to investigate the Congo headwaters beyond was frustrated by unfriendly tribes, and Thomson returned to Zanzibar by way of Tabora (or Unyamyembe), the Arab trading post between Tanganyika and the coast. In 1882 the Royal Geographical Society sent Thomson to Africa again to prospect the shortest practicable route from the sea to the Nile headwaters, a way which Stanley, when asked his advice some years before, had maintained was barred by the warlike Masai. Thomson travelled from Mombasa by way of Mounts Kili-manjaro and Kenya and reached the north end of Lake Victoria at the present Kenya/Uganda frontier, having avoided trouble with the Masai by the com-bination of guile and good humour for which he was famous. In the years preceding the expedition, then, British merchants and British explorers were both in evidence in Zanzibar.

By the time the expedition was launched, however, British influence and the authority of Zanzibar had both been challenged by the growing power of Germany, represented by the adventurer Carl Peters, who in 1884 pene-trated as far inland as Kilimanjaro, where he persuaded (or coerced) the local chiefs to sign treaties accepting the protection of the German Coloniza-tion Society, and was vigorously supported by Bismarck. The British Govern-ment refused to interfere, ignoring the protests of the Sultan at what he regarded as violation of his authority, and the anger of Kirk at seeing Britain put at such a disgraceful disadvantage. Later Peters fell foul of the Arab and Swahili traders at points where he had established trading posts, and local wars broke out of which Jephson records the echoes in his diary; but this did not prevent Germany founding an East African Empire.

Britain's tolerance, if not encouragement, of German aspirations, is linked

[1] R. C. Bridges, 'The R.G.S. and the African Exploration Fund, 1876–80', *Geographical Journal*, CXXIX, 1 (1963), 25–35.

with events in the far north, with Britain's occupation of Egypt in 1882. Recent historical studies in depth of the years which contained 'the scramble for Africa' establish more and more convincingly the basic importance of Britain's occupation of Egypt in 1882. The abdication of the Khedive Ismail in 1879 did not stop the rot in Egypt's finances and when, under his son Tewfik, the position deteriorated further and the Egyptian army rose in revolt under Colonel Arabi, Britain moved in. Two main results followed. Britain became responsible for the country's government and, despite the reluctance of Gladstone's Cabinet for such a commitment, responsibility for Egypt's empire in the Sudan became difficult to avoid; hence the dispatch of Gordon to Khartoum, his death there, and the emotional involvement of the British public in his fate and the subsequent fate of Emin. Another consequence of the occupation was its bad effect on Anglo-French relations, and the necessity for Great Britain to conciliate Germany; hence the readiness with which Lord Salisbury's Conservative administration, heirs to Gladstone's problems in Cairo, were to allow the Germans to erode Britain's formerly predominant position in East Africa.[1]

In the 1880s, in fact, the old order in East Africa, based on the Sultanate of Zanzibar, was fast collapsing under the impact of the new men of all nationalities attracted by prospects of commercial and political power along the trade routes blazed by the Arab merchants and European travellers inland from the coast. The retirement of Kirk in 1886 and the death of Barghash in 1888 did not mean the end of Britain's presence in East Africa, but it took on a rather different colour.

Zanzibar's interests fell into the background, and Britain and Germany came to terms with each other. First, in 1886, spheres of influence were agreed, south of a line from the coast north-west through the Kilimanjaro region to Lake Victoria for Germany, and north of it for Britain, the two areas corresponding to modern Tanzania and Kenya. As for the Sultan, he was left with his three islands, Zanzibar, Pemba and Mafia, and a coastal strip 10 miles wide and 600 miles long where his authority was to be acknowledged. As a participant in the 'scramble' Britain was now as well placed as any other European power; in her old role as the doyen of the exploring fraternity and the protector of local African interests, she had lost prestige and authority.

---

[1] Since the publication of the late Professor Reginald Coupland's standard work *The exploitation of East Africa, 1856–1890: the slave trade and the scramble* (London, 1939) several important studies have appeared. The *History of East Africa*, vol. 1, ed. by R. Oliver and G. Mathew, contains valuable chapters on conditions in the interior in the 1870s and 1880s, and on penetration by Britain and Germany. Two more specialized studies are *Africa and the Victorians: the official mind of imperialism* (London, 1961), by R. Robinson and J. Gallagher with A. Denny; and *England, Europe and the Upper Nile* (Edinburgh, 1966) by G. N. Sanderson.

The political background

The way to the Lakes and the 'scramble' for Central Africa

North of the German sphere, on the other side of Lake Victoria, and north-west of the British, beyond hostile Masailand, lay the prosperous native kingdom of Buganda, which formed part of what we now know as the independent State of Uganda. Buganda lay outside the Anglo-German agreement of 1886, and was coveted by both parties. The British in particular had always been interested in the Central African kingdoms, of which Buganda and Bunyoro were the most important, since their own explorers, Speke, Grant and Baker, had made contact with them in the middle years of the century. As British influence spread in East Africa, Buganda became the promised land of explorers and businessmen alike, and the Royal Geographical Society expedition led by Thomson in 1882–4 had for its principal object the pioneering of a direct route from the coast to Buganda's eastern frontier at the north end of Lake Victoria. It was the strongest of the kingdoms lying between Lakes Victoria and Albert. Buganda and her rival neighbour Bunyoro lay at the mysterious heart of Africa in an aura of romantic legend: here Ptolemy had placed the great lakes which gave birth to the Nile, and those snow-capped Mountains of the Moon, which we know as the Ruwenzori, which Mounteney Jephson was the first European to see. Here could well be imagined the four fountains guessed at by Herodotus to be the sources, those magic and elusive springs Livingstone was seeking far away to the south when he died in the Bangweulu swamps. It was also reported that there was in Buganda a tradition of responsible government, a respect for law and custom, and civilized social habits, quite unlike what was to be found elsewhere in the unruly and exploited lands of coast and interior alike. Much of this was learnt from Arab traders who had penetrated to Buganda in about 1848, in the reign of Kabaka Suna, and had preached Islam and sold the lengths of cloth which the Buganda people had adopted for wear in place of their comely bark gowns. In 1857 Suna died and was succeeded by his son Mutesa, one of the key figures in this period of African history. Mutesa was at times both capricious and cruel, but he had a keen political sense and a capacity for imbibing experience which enabled him to preserve his kingdom at a difficult time when it was subjected to both alien and local pressures on all sides. In the north, Egypt had imperial ambitions, and two successive governors of the southern Sudan saw in such expansion the best means of defeating the slave trade. Baker was defeated in his attempt to annex Bunyoro in 1874, and Gordon made several abortive diplomatic sallies into Buganda. At the same time, British merchants and explorers operating from Zanzibar in the east saw Buganda as a desirable goal, while in the west there was intermittent warfare with Bunyoro.

The first European to enter Buganda was John Hanning Speke in 1862, on his second expedition to Africa in pursuit of the sources of the Nile. He came with Grant round the west of Lake Victoria and, leaving his companion sick at Karagwe, made his way to Mutesa's capital on the north shore of the lake at Rubaga. He found the Arabs well established, and Islam in the ascendant. Gordon's emissary, Colonel Chaillé-Long, was at Rubaga in 1874 and in the following year H. M. Stanley fell in with another envoy from Gordon, the Belgian Ernest Linant de Bellefonds. Islam's influence was in decline, Stanley thought, and Buganda and her rule ripe for the Christian message. He praised the land as 'the Pearl of Africa' and before continuing his journey wrote letters to interested bodies in England urging the dispatch of missionaries; Linant de Bellefonds took the letters back with him to Gordon and they were forwarded to England.

As a result of Stanley's letters, leaders of Christianity and commerce alike began to want to know more of this kingdom of Buganda. English evangelists of the Church Missionary Society were the first to respond to Stanley's dramatic appeal, and on the heels of the Protestants came the Catholics; urged by Cardinal Lavigerie, the White Fathers of Algiers, already busy on Lake Tanganyika, set up a mission. Mutesa welcomed the British, regarding them as envoys of the great English queen, and he welcomed the French also; so was laid the foundation of much future strife, for the two denominations were bitterly hostile to each other and their followers in time became identified with national interests. Both Protestant and Catholic missionaries were of course men of the highest integrity, but they clung strongly to those doctrinal points on which they differed rather than to those on which they agreed, and these differences puzzled Mutesa, who, for a time, showed tolerance to both. Towards the Moslems he blew rather hot and cold. At times he feared Islam as being increasingly identified with Egypt's imperial ambitions. Some of Egypt's military stations were uncomfortably near the Buganda frontier, and in 1876 Gordon went a step further in posting an officer, Nuer Aga, and 160 men inside Buganda's borders. Mutesa was already on the *qui vive*, in view of Baker's attack on Bunyoro's independence two years earlier, and of Gordon's subsequent suspicious interest in Buganda. Nuer Aga was politely invited to come to Rubaga, where he and his men found themselves cut off from their Governor, and in some danger. Gordon resolved the dilemma in designating as envoy to the Kabaka Dr Eduard Schnitzer, newly arrived in Khartoum and appointed Medical Officer in the Sudan administration. Even then enigmatically associated with Islam, and already calling himself Emin, this is the first important appearance of Jephson's Pasha on the Central African scene. Behaving with an admirable mixture of firmness and courtesy, eschewing force and disarming suspicion by devoting his spare time to botanical research, Emin secured the release of Gordon's trespassers, and there was no further question of annexing Buganda to Egypt. Emin paid another visit to Buganda in 1878, stopping in Bunyoro on the way and laying the foundation of a useful friendship with Kabarega.

Buganda was not, however, to escape outside influences, becoming in the 1880s a mission field where, despite early conflicts and the unrest which followed Mutesa's death in 1884, Christianity took healthy root. Mutesa was succeeded by his eighteen-year-old son Mwanga, who had nothing of his father's political acumen, intelligence or occasional clemency. Mwanga persecuted the Christians, only to see the number of their converts grow in circumstances which do the greatest credit to the teachings of the Catholic Father Lourdel and the famous Protestant pioneer Alexander Mackay. In 1885 the first Anglican bishop appointed to Buganda, James Hannington, set out for the interior by Joseph Thomson's route to the northern end of the lake, the route which, so a native legend ran, would one day bring a conqueror to the land. Mwanga sent orders for Hannington to be stopped, and he was murdered on the frontier. But the legend held true, for this was the road by which Gedge and Jackson, representing the Imperial British East Africa Company, entered Buganda in 1889.

Throughout Mwanga's reign a state of confused civil war existed in Buganda and in the territories on its borders, the Christian factions sometimes opposed to each other, sometimes combining against the Moslems, with the Pagans of the old religion also taking a hand. The details are unimportant to Emin's story, but the general confusion should be remembered as forming a barricade to any rescue attempts through Buganda; the few Europeans living there began to find conditions intolerable, and in 1887 Mackay moved out to the Protestant mission south of Lake Victoria at Msalala, near where Jephson describes finding him in 1889, just before his death.

Traders followed along the trail blazed by the missionaries. While the Emin Pasha Relief Expedition was struggling through the Congo forests, and later arguing with Emin on Lake Albert, commercial activity was being stimulated in East Africa by the conclusion of the Anglo-German treaty of 1886. In July 1887 Carl Peters signed an agreement with the Sultan of Zanzibar on behalf of the German East African Company operating along the old Arab trade route to Tabora and beyond; in the same year Mackinnon was back in the East African market and laying the foundations of the Imperial British East Africa Company, with a capital of a quarter of a million pounds, and was at last able to secure the official backing denied him in 1876. Motivated partly by a shift in Anglo-German relations, Lord Salisbury's Government agreed in September 1888 to the granting of a charter to the infant company, and plans were laid for an expedition to the interior, to be fitted out in Mombasa, where Mackinnon's East African agent, George Mackenzie, arrived soon afterwards.

The exact purpose of this first venture of Mackinnon's to the interior was never very clearly, or publicly, stated. It was led by Frederick Jackson,[1] then a young man keen on big-game shooting who had been introduced to the delights of the East African safari some years before by Rider Haggard. Jackson was invited to the London office of George Mackenzie in the autumn of 1888 and offered a place in an Emin Pasha Relief Expedition to be dispatched from Mombasa under the leadership of Captain Swayne of the Royal Engineers. Stanley's position was in doubt, and this was to be a supplementary effort to take the Masailand route and skirt round the north of Buganda with a view to making contact with Emin at Wadelai—the route, in fact, which had been rejected when it was suggested by Joseph Thomson two years earlier.[2] After several false starts, and the disappearance from the scene of Swayne (whose enthusiasm for the chase proved stronger than his interest in Emin Pasha or the Company), the expedition got off in the early part of 1889 and by July was at Machakos, 350 miles north-west of Mombasa, which Jackson described as the 'jumping-off base' for the interior. Jackson was accompanied by Ernest Gedge, who was to be responsible for map-making, by Dr A. D. Mackinnon, and by James Martin, who had travelled with Joseph Thomson. The expedition was to carry trade goods and to make trade treaties where appropriate en route.

No more is heard of Wadelai, but soon afterwards, in September 1889, Jackson was following orders 'to proceed direct from Naivasha to Lake Victoria, and there try and get into touch with Stanley, who with Emin Pasha was alleged to have reached Ururi at the S.E. corner of Lake Victoria. I was to assist him in any way I could with stores, etc., and incidentally hand over to him two cumbersome but light loads of pith helmets.'[3] Hearing no news of Stanley as they approached the lake, they turned north and travelled to Mumia's in Kavirondo, whence Jackson entered into correspondence with Mwanga at his new capital of Mengo (on the site of modern Kampala). Jackson states plainly that at this date 'my orders were that we were *on no*

---

[1] Sir Frederick Jackson, K.C.M.G., C.B. (1860–1929); Lieut.-Governor for East Africa Protectorate (1907–11), Governor and Commander-in-Chief, Uganda (1911–17). Jackson's *Early days in East Africa* is the source for this account of the 1888–9 expedition to Buganda. [2] See p. 45 below.

[3] Jackson, p. 181. See entry for 28 August 1889, when, on arrival at Mackay's mission station, Jephson is amused at the rumours of their whereabouts. A few weeks later, the American Thomas Stevens was writing from Zanzibar that Stanley was undoubtedly still with Emin in Equatoria and that news of his being at the southern end of Lake Victoria was 'moonshine': Stevens to Mrs French Sheldon, 21 October 1889 (Royal Geographical Society Museum, among other Stanley relics).

account to go anywhere near Uganda',[1] so he camped to await news and developments. The situation in Buganda was explosive; the English mission, then in charge of the Rev. E. C. Gordon, was, of course, hoping for the Company's entry into the country; Père Lourdel of the French mission favoured in general terms the neutrality of Buganda and the entrée for merchants of all nations, but as German interest in the region became more apparent he brought his influence to bear on their side; Carl Peters himself was determined to secure Buganda for the German East African Company. Jackson, unwilling to precipitate trouble, departed on 10 December 1889 for a reconnaissance-cum-shooting trip round Mount Elgon to the north,[2] leaving the situation to simmer.

On Jackson's return to Mumia's on 4 March 1890 he found that Peters had stolen a march on him, passing through some weeks before on his way to Buganda, and that he had opened the mailbag, which contained, among other correspondence, a letter from Stanley relating the relief of Emin Pasha, and one from Père Lourdel asking the British, after all, to come into Buganda. Peters had come up from the coast, through British territory, at the head of a German 'Emin Pasha Relief Expedition', with the ill-concealed intention of extracting a commercial treaty from Mwanga before the British could do so. The contents of Jackson's mailbag convinced Peters there was no time to lose, and he reached Mengo on 25 February 1890, where he won over the French mission and persuaded Mwanga to sign up with the German East African Company. Jackson hesitated no longer, and he and Gedge marched through Busoga, crossed the Nile into Buganda with no opposition and were in Mengo on 14 April. Although they came to no definite terms with Mwanga, the treaty with Peters became a dead letter on the conclusion of a further Anglo-German agreement, signed on 1 July 1890, definitely assigning Buganda to the British sphere. Jackson returned to Mombasa, leaving Gedge to safeguard the interests of the Company, and at the end of 1890 Captain F. D. Lugard arrived in Mengo as its official representative.[3] His subsequent pacification of the country from Lake Victoria to Lake Albert forms an important postscript to the Emin Pasha Relief Expedition, because he recruited into the Uganda service those of Emin's troops who stayed behind at Kavalli's on Lake Albert.[4]

[1] Jackson, p. 222.   [2] See below, p. 49.
[3] Lord Lugard (1858–1945), whose *Rise of our East African Empire* (London, 1893), 2 vols., contains the story of the Company's penetration of Buganda.
[4] See Epilogue below, pp. 423–4.

Editor's Introduction

King Leopold, the International African Association and the Congo

It may not seem at first sight that Zanzibar is on the way to the Congo, but it was from here that King Leopold of the Belgians took his first steps towards founding the State which was to play so large a part in shaping the fate of the Emin Pasha Relief Expedition. A big fish in a little pond, Leopold coveted empire and the wealth and prestige it would bring. For ten years or more before he appeared on the African scene, Leopold had nursed ambitions for a Belgian colony overseas, in the Far East, perhaps, on the pattern of the East India Company, and he had investigated possibilities in China, the Pacific and North Borneo; he had even considered a scheme to buy the Philippines.

In 1876 he invited leading European geographers to an International Geographical Conference at Brussels to discuss the problems of Africa. It was attended by a number of experienced African travellers, notably Verney Lovett Cameron and James Augustus Grant from Britain, and Drs Nachtigall, Schweinfurth and Rohlffs from Germany. William Mackinnon was also present. The Conference gave birth to the International African Association, an ambitious project designed to bring Western civilization to Africa and, an aim less overtly stated, to harness the potential of Africa's resources and her ample labour force to the commercial interests of the West. A series of stations was to be set up along the trade routes into the interior to act as staging posts for merchants, missionaries and the like from Europe, operating under an international flag. Side by side with the general object of spreading the light of European ways was the more specific design of destroying the slave trade.

Leopold's own first ventures in Africa were a series of East African expeditions which carried the Association's flag inland from Zanzibar, establishing posts on the way to the Lakes and a station at Karema on Lake Tanganyika. He had the enthusiastic support of William Mackinnon, who, as we have seen, had ambitious plans of his own for an East African trading company. Leopold also tried to enrol Gordon, recently retired from the Sudan, to oversee his plans, but Gordon was doubtful of the effectiveness of a private venture, albeit with a high-sounding international title, when it came to dealing with rival European enterprises with governments at their backs. A few years later, in 1883, he was to accept Leopold's offer of employment on the Congo where a recognizable State was coming into existence.

These first expeditions of Leopold's were planned to conform, superficially at least, to the programme laid down at Brussels: to spread civilization by the establishment of trading posts where missionaries too might operate. But in fact the King had other ends in view beyond mere philanthropy, and his imperial vision took on a national—not to say personal—form the more readily in view of the increasingly open nationalism of the other members of the Association. For the International African Association did not remain international for long. The Royal Geographical Society, speaking for Britain, withdrew from direct participation almost at once, because of a reluctance to become involved in schemes not primarily geographical. The Germans showed increasing enthusiasm and vigour over purely national projects for the penetration of East Africa. The Frenchman Savorgnan de Brazza, though travelling under the auspices of the French committee of the Association, was a patriotic imperialist of the first order and the founder of France's West African empire. Although Leopold sent off four expeditions in all from Zanzibar, one of them ambitiously (and unsuccessfully) equipped with elephants as pack animals, he could not but see that East Africa was inevitably going to fall to Great Britain and Germany; he began to focus his own eyes on the Congo. The Arabs had preceded him there; Zanzibar merchants all, they had penetrated far beyond Lake Tanganyika by the time Stanley reached the Lualaba in 1875, and, following in his tracks, the more adventurous of them were soon to be at Stanley Falls on the Congo. It was some such similar goal that Leopold had in mind when he staked a claim at Karema, but an alternative approach from the Congo mouth suggested itself when Stanley, in 1877, emerged at Banana Point from his tracing of the river's course. When the explorer reached Europe, he was met at Marseilles by emissaries from King Leopold, inviting him to Brussels to advise on the possibility of opening up the Congo basin.

Stanley, an idealist in his way, had hoped that the Congo basin might prove a fruitful sphere for British commerce, and before listening to Leopold's proposals he returned to England and tried to arouse interest in the business world and in Government circles for direct British involvement in the Congo. Only when the response proved lukewarm did he turn to Leopold, who, on the alert for his own sphere of influence in Africa, had recognized his opportunity in the Congo and his man in Stanley.

The early history of the Congo is only marginal to Jephson's story. Portugal, oldest-established of the European powers in Africa, had a special interest in the Congo in right of the first ascent of the river by Diogo Câo in 1485 or 1486 during the great age of Portuguese discoveries. Britain, in her self-imposed task of destroying the slave trade, was interested in the lower reaches of the river and had, in 1815, dispatched an unsuccessful expedition which it was hoped would penetrate far inland.[1] Portugal's claims to sovereignty over the Congo mouth were at first withstood by Britain, in

---

[1] Led by Captain James N. Tuckey, R.N. For the history of Britain's connection with the Congo, *see* R. T. Anstey, *Britain and the Congo in the 19th century* (London, 1962).

view of that country's long association with slave-trading, but by the time Stanley was completing his reconnaissance of the interior, the growth of French imperialism was threatening the upper Congo and Britain began to think of playing off Portugal against France. A treaty with Portugal was, in fact, signed in 1884 agreeing to her control of the Congo mouth, but it was not ratified and never came into operation. This was due partly to opposition in British commercial and humanitarian circles, but more specifically to King Leopold's energetic action in building up an empire throughout the Congo basin with claims to be not only active in combating the slave trade, but also a strong counterweight to growing French influence on the north bank of the river.

Political arguments about sovereignty and rival claims to 'spheres of influence' had not prevented traders from various nations becoming established at Banana Point, at the Congo mouth, where they had been busy for a number of years when Stanley emerged from the upper river at the end of his great journey. A French factory was founded in 1855, and the Dutch, British, Portuguese and Belgian merchants had followed. It was not this well-known region which Stanley wanted to offer to British enterprise, and which King Leopold sought for himself; Stanley's 'discovery' was the upper Congo, the rich undeveloped basin beyond the cataracts, and it was to exploit this virgin territory that the Comité d'Études du Haut-Congo was founded in 1878. The Comité was presented as an international undertaking, backed by funds from England, France, Germany, Holland and Belgium. William Mackinnon subscribed, as did his friend and business associate J. F. Hutton, who had a considerable interest in West African trade. Mackinnon's participation may be accounted for not only by his friendship with Leopold and his connection with the International African Association, but also by his disappointment in the failure of his East African plans.[1] In the following year, however, the Comité was transformed into the Association Internationale du Congo, under the sole control of King Leopold, who returned all foreign subscriptions. Nevertheless, Mackinnon and Hutton retained an active interest in the Congo's development because the return of their subscriptions took the form of interest payments on the profits of new trading concerns on the river, and hints were dropped of their possible participation in the building of a Congo railway. When the railway came to be built through the cataract region in 1884, Mackinnon and Hutton did their best to secure the contract for a British company, but it went to a Belgian one. The Association Internationale du Congo was the germ of the Congo Free State, recognized as independent by the Great Powers at different dates during 1884 and 1885. The U.S.A., represented by Leopold's

[1] Anstey, pp. 210–29.

32

friend General Sanford, a former American Minister in Brussels and a member of the Committee of the International Association, was the first to recognize the new State.

In 1879 Leopold sent an expedition to the Congo under Stanley. The international cover was maintained, but Stanley took his orders from the General Secretary of the Comité in Brussels, Colonel Strauch, and most of the officers were Belgians. His task was to establish stations on the upper Congo, the 1000-mile stretch of river from the top of the cataracts, where Leopoldville (renamed Kinshasa in 1966) was built as the State capital, to Stanley Falls, the site of Stanleyville (now Kisangani). Before Stanley could start on his stations he had to carry steamers in sections up the region of the cataracts from Boma to Leopoldville, a heart-breaking task before the days of road or railway. Stanley's story of the five years which followed may be read in his book[1] and also (in some ways with more illumination) in the letters he wrote to headquarters in Brussels which have only recently been published.[2]

The relevance of this period of Stanley's life to the fortunes of the Emin Pasha Relief Expedition is twofold. First of all it dictated the choice of a route. Stanley's previous knowledge of the Congo basin and his commitments to King Leopold influenced the decision to send the expedition through this way, over terrain so difficult as to make its success almost impossible. In more general terms, Stanley's earlier service in the Congo might be said to disqualify him from acting as leader. For years he was extended to the limit of his considerable powers, and his health and temper had suffered. He also acquired a mistrust, mingled with contempt, for European assistants. The untried young men posted to the Free State by King Leopold and his advisers were not an unqualified success, and Stanley's mounting impatience with them later recoiled on the unlucky heads of Stairs and Jephson, and disastrously on Barttelot. Stanley's letters to Colonel Strauch bristle with complaints of his underlings: Valcke is dilatory and unreliable, Lindner is efficient but has 'an unhealthy bad temper',[3] Harou only 'gets along so-so'.[4] At the same time he has difficulty in making headquarters understand that his Zanzibari porters and soldiers must be released punctually and sent home at the end of their contract; one of the counts against Harou is that he cannot manage Zanzibaris. And so when Stanley loses his temper at an early stage on the Emin Pasha Relief Expedition, and shouts to the men that they may tie Stairs and Jephson to trees,[5] years of pent-up rage and frustration are spilling over from the past. 'He was always', observes the temperate and

[1] H. M. Stanley, *The Congo, and the founding of its Free State* (London, 1885).
[2] Albert Maurice (ed.), *H. M. Stanley: unpublished letters* (London, 1957).
[3] Maurice, p. 109.   [4] Maurice, p. 83.
[5] See p. 99 below

tolerant surgeon Parke, 'inclined to favour the black man in preference to the white.'[1] Only by realizing something of what Stanley went through during the founding of the Free State can one understand his conduct during the later expedition; to excuse it is sometimes more difficult.

TIPPU TIB AND THE ARABS

Enough has been said in this brief survey to show that by 1887, when the expedition set sail, Africa had ceased to be the 'dark continent' from which individual travellers sought to lift the veil, and had become an open play-ground for the powers of Europe; governments rather than learned societies were now the arbiters, empire rather than discovery the aim, the whole influenced by relations between the powers, rather than by direct concern with Africa herself. But this was not all: another and more local factor was influencing events, namely the Arab penetration of Negro Africa.

Arab interests were of course active in the north at the headwaters of the Nile; indeed, the necessity for an expedition to rescue Emin Pasha arose from the establishment by the Mahdi of an Arab empire in the Sudan. Equally relevant for the fortunes of the expedition was the penetration of Eastern and Central Africa by those Arab merchants from Zanzibar who were pressing inland from the early years of the nineteenth century, on one well-marked route through Ugogo and Unyamwezi to Lake Tanganyika, or north to Lake Victoria, Buganda and Bunyoro; and on other routes, which do not concern Emin's story, south of Tanganyika and into Katanga, and yet further south to Lake Nyasa. By 1830 they had reached what was to become one of their most important depots at Tabora, earlier known as Unyamyembe, some 450 miles from the coast; by 1840 they had arrived at Ujiji on the eastern shore of Lake Tanganyika. They found the people of the interior eager for trade, and with a considerable aptitude for it. Indeed, much of the commerce of Unyamwezi became concentrated in the hands of Mirambo, the powerful Nyamwezi chief whose wars with the Tabora Arabs had blocked the road to Ujiji in 1867 when contact was lost with Livingstone. Stanley's success in getting through when supplies sent by Kirk from Zanzibar had failed to do so was the beginning of the bad feeling between Stanley and the Council of the Royal Geographical Society, who felt a march had been stolen on them.

The traders sought ivory from the abundant herds of wild elephants in the interior, and slaves from the tribes whose lands they invaded, the latter in demand both as domestic servants in Zanzibar, Muscat and beyond, and

[1] T. H. Parke, *My personal experiences in Equatorial Africa as medical officer of the Emin Pasha Relief Expedition* (London, 1891), p. 513.

as labourers in the clove plantations of the islands. Competition was keen, with a constant search for new hunting grounds, and by the middle years of the century caravans had crossed Lake Tanganyika and were ranging through the country beyond to the Lualaba river, and across the Lualaba as far as the Limami. When Livingstone reached the Lualaba in 1871 he found Arab traders established at Nyangwe, where he witnessed the massacre in the market-place which caused him such agony of mind.

Although the Arab traders have become labelled as slavers, the trade was by no means the only end they had in mind; the importance to them of the trade, and therefore its horrors, varied in different areas. Sometimes it was a business in itself, flourishing particularly on the upper Nile and round Lake Nyasa; sometimes the sacking of villages and enslavement of the people was a by-product of the more important commerce in ivory. Traders needed slaves as soldiers and servants to protect and staff their establishments, on occasions to act as carriers. Jephson nowhere mentions in his diary seeing slaves shackled and being marched to the coast to be sold as merchandise, but he often deplores the hard lot of local people, especially women, captured as slaves to wait on the merchants and their followers. Baker, on the other hand, during his brief governorship of Equatoria waylaid boats and caravans of men and women being dragged along the slave routes to Khartoum and the north, and Livingstone on the Shire and Lake Nyasa had some horrible tales to tell.

The fact that the better sort of Zanzibar trader, of whom Tippu Tib is a fair example, concentrated on ivory and treated their own slaves with reasonable humanity, encouraged, in the early days of European penetration, a hope that it might be possible to enlist the Arabs in the cause of civilization. Sir John Kirk was an exponent of this policy, and so was the missionary Captain E. C. Hore, working on Lake Tanganyika in the 1870s, but the dream faded, shattered by such scenes as the Nyangwe massacre, and the brutalities of which Jephson writes on the upper Congo. With the spread of guns in the interior the situation worsened, making tribal warfare more deadly. Guns and gunpowder became articles of trade, making the strong stronger and annihilating the weak.

The Arabs are a recurrent theme in the travellers' tales of the period. Sometimes they are the ruthless adventurers of the Nyangwe massacre. Sometimes they appear as good Samaritans in dignified garb, with courtly manners, the masters of prosperous and pacific settlements planted with flourishing crops, and tended by smiling domestic slaves. Both Jekyll and Hyde feature in Jephson's diary: Tippu Tib behaving with courtesy and dispensing hospitality to all who visited him; Kilonga-Longa's band being no better than bandits. Tippu Tib, whose real name was Hamed bin Mohammed, dominates the story of Emin Pasha. He was one of the most successful of the Arab merchants, and something more than a mere trader. Penetrating in 1870 or thereabouts into the Manuyema country west of Lake Tanganyika, he established an empire for himself with its headquarters at Kasongo. Tippu Tib's own story of how he secured recognition as ruler of the Manuyema by posing as the long-lost son of a local chief was a favourite anecdote, and is often repeated in the books of those travellers who were entertained by him. Jephson recounts it early in his diary on the voyage from Zanzibar to the Congo. The reality was not, of course, achieved solely by so simple an imposition, Tippu Tib having established himself king of the castle by *force majeure* expressed by the power of his guns. One explanation of his nickname is that his coming was heralded by the 'tip, tip, tip' of bullets; another, more likely reason is that 'Tippu Tib' described the nervous twitch of an eyelid which was characteristic of him. Despite the bloodthirsty progress described in the autobiography dictated by Tippu to the German Heinrich Brode, it must be conceded that his subjugation of the Manuyema tribes brought a certain degree of law and order to a troubled region, and accounts of Tippu Tib and his Arab partners and rivals are by no means entirely condemnatory. Ruth Slade, whose study of race relations in the Congo in the early days throws much light on this question, includes some interesting contemporary comments. The Belgian Jerome Becker, who served on two of King Leopold's international expeditions in East Africa, wrote of the 'happy, faithful and devoted slaves of Tippo Tib' and Adolphe Burdo, who was on the third Belgian east-coast expedition, admired the 'fertile rice plantations, the cultivation of wheat, lemons and guavas, and the splendid plantations of bananas'.[1]

Tippu Tib was on friendly terms with many of the European travellers of his time. He gave much-needed assistance to Livingstone when the latter found himself short of supplies in the neighbourhood of Lake Mweru in 1867, and when Verney Lovett Cameron was making his way across Africa in 1874 Tippu Tib entertained him hospitably at his capital of Kasongo. Intelligent and a thorough realist, Tippu Tib was invariably friendly with Europeans, admiring their superior equipment and convinced they had come to Africa to stay. He was a diplomat, keeping his ear to the ground, aware of developments and prepared to take advantage of any favourable to himself. Hearing of the Anglo-German agreement for the sharing of East Africa, he writes to his brother in Zanzibar asking him to report on the relative strength of the two camps, and to ingratiate himself wherever it may benefit the family fortunes;[2] apprised in 1889 of a plot against the Europeans on Lake

[1] Ruth Slade, *King Leopold's Congo* (London, 1962), pp. 86–7.
[2] See copy of a letter forwarded to the Foreign Office by the British Consul at Zanzibar, dated 31 December 1888, with the following note: 'I am to add that the contents of

Tanganyika, he warns the missionaries and defeats the attack; charged by Stanley with a breach of his contract with the Emin Pasha Relief Expedition, he defends himself stoutly and, it would seem from the abrupt withdrawal of the charges, with justice on his side.[1] Most relevant to Emin's story, however, was the original contact between him and Stanley. When Stanley reached the Lualaba in 1876, he persuaded Tippu Tib, with a gang of his men, to accompany him down the river into hitherto unexplored country north of Kasongo. Disputes arose as to the extent to which Tippu Tib had committed himself to the venture and eventually he turned back, leaving Stanley to make his way to the Congo and so downstream to the coast. Stanley later abused Tippu for leaving him in the lurch; Tippu maintained he had done all he had promised. The adventure was important, bringing the Arab into Stanley's calculations as someone to be used when occasion offered, and it introduced the Arabs into the Congo region, opening the way not only to Tippu but to the merchants of Nyangwe, with whom he was on more or less good terms according to the state of their respective fortunes. When, in 1883, Stanley was back in the Congo in the service of King Leopold and the Free State, he found Arabs established at Stanley Falls at the then extreme limit of Belgian penetration from the west. A year later George Grenfell, the famous Baptist missionary, met Tippu Tib himself at the Falls, which had by then become a prosperous trading centre.

A clash between the Congo Free State and the Arabs became inevitable, both parties depending, to finance their respective ventures, on the lucrative ivory trade; both sides needed to recruit porters from the local people and both needed to a large extent to live off the country. There was some ugly fighting at the Falls in 1886 when the Englishman Deane was driven out from the newly established Free State station by the Arabs, and his companions killed. Afterwards, an attempt was made to come to terms with the Arabs, to agree, in the European manner, on spheres of influence, to co-operate over trade, to make bargains which would stimulate commerce and yet bring an end to the slave trade. If the Arabs could be persuaded to send their ivory down the Congo through Free State territory instead of back overland to the east coast, the finance of the struggling infant administration might benefit considerably. At a still later date, interests and methods were found to diverge too widely, and all-out war ended in the expulsion by 1895 of the Congo Arabs, and the decline of Arab influence throughout Central Africa.

this letter throw an unfavourable light on the character of the writer.' Mackinnon Papers, School of Oriental and African Studies, University of London.
[1] For both these incidents, see article by Sir John Gray in *Tanganyika Notes and Records*, XVIII (1944), 11–27. See also pp. 54–5, 57–9 below, for the story of the Rear Column.

The Emin Pasha Relief Expedition was, however, deeply affected by the short-lived armistice between the Congo Free State, represented by King Leopold, and the Arabs represented by Tippu Tib—Stanley acting as go-between. Leopold, with his usual prescience, had early perceived that if the expedition passed through the Congo Free State it might not only help to pioneer an extension of territory to Lake Albert and into the southern Sudan, but might indeed add Equatoria as a new province, in working order, to his empire. He also saw the possibility of retrieving the situation at Stanley Falls, from where his agent Deane had been ignominiously chased two years before, and of coming to useful terms if Stanley would agree to make an ally of Tippu Tib. Such a project was discussed on one or both of Stanley's visits to Brussels before he left on the expedition, and the result was the appointment of Tippu Tib to the governorship of Stanley Falls. This was agreed in Zanzibar in February 1887 at the same time as the arrangement was made for Tippu to recruit porters for the expedition from the Stanley Falls region. Sanctioned as it was in Brussels, the arrangement was never fully explained to local Congo officials and the idea of turning the poacher into a gamekeeper produced misunderstandings. Out of it arose the long-drawn agony of the Rear Column, and the convenient allocation to Tippu Tib of the role of scapegoat for the numerous disasters which overtook the expedition as a whole.[1]

THE ISOLATION OF EQUATORIA

In the very heart of this intricate web of adventure, ambition and intrigue, lay the beleaguered Egyptian province of Equatoria. Emin's decision to withdraw to the south of his province in 1884 and to build a new headquarters at Wadelai at the head of Lake Albert was typical of his elusive cleverness, and saved the garrisons. In the years that followed he built two more stations south of Wadelai—Tunguru on an island in Lake Albert and M'swa on its west coast; it was at M'swa that Jephson and Emin first met. When the relief expedition arrived at Lake Albert, Emin was in nominal control of all his posts except Rejaf, just south of Lado, where the troops were in open revolt against his authority, and of Lado, which had been abandoned.[2] Emin brought with him on his retreat to Wadelai the Italian Gaetano Casati, who

[1] For this brief summary I have drawn freely on *La question arabe et le Congo* by Père Ceulemans, and on *Tippoo-Tib: the story of his career in Central Africa*, narrated from his own account by Heinrich Brode, translated by H. Havelock with a preface by Sir Charles Elliot (London, 1907).
[2] Emin to Felkin, Wadelai, 17 April 1887: quoted in Georg Schweinfurth (ed.), *Emin Pasha in Central Africa, being a collection of his letters and journals* (London, 1888), p. 510.

had come to Africa eight years before to help survey the Bahr el Ghazal, where his compatriot Gessi was then Governor. He had thrown in his lot with Emin, and Jephson observes disapprovingly that 'he had quite given up European habits, and lived almost like an oriental'.[1] Also with Emin when he moved south was Dr Wilhelm Junker, a German born in Moscow, who was exploring west of the Bahr el Ghazal, at the headwaters of the Uele, when he found himself cut off by the Mahdist rising. Striking across country he joined Emin at Lado, accompanied him to Wadelai, and eventually survived a hazardous journey through Bunyoro and Buganda during 1886 with news of Equatoria for the outside world. He brought with him Emin's valuable jewels for safe keeping, and letters to Emin's friends telling of his plight. Junker's difficulty in getting through by way of Bunyoro and Buganda was one factor in convincing the Expedition Committee that it would be very risky to send the relief by an eastern route, and inclined them to the Congo approach.

Emin had at his disposal something like 1500 regular troops, armed with Remington rifles, for the most part Sudanese but including about 40 Egyptian artillerymen. They were commanded by 10 Egyptians and 15 Sudanese officers. Divided into garrisons of one to two hundred men each, they were distributed among the stations on the Nile and Lake Albert. In addition there was, dispersed between M'swa and Tunguru, a community of Danaqla, people from Dongola in the northern Sudan, who had penetrated the south in considerable numbers as mercenaries and merchants in the prosperous trading days before the Englishmen came—Baker and Gordon—to put a stop to slave-raiding and to control the free-ranging Arab caravans. Jephson called them 'Emin's Irregulars'; as countrymen of the Mahdi (a native of Dongola) they and their leader Ibrahim Effendi were not popular with the troops, and they were later massacred in the confusion which followed Stanley's final departure from Lake Albert. The Egyptians included several officers who had taken part in Arabi's revolt, and who had been sentenced to service in the Sudan. Emin's deputy in the province was Osman Effendi Lateef, formerly head of the detective force in Khartoum, and each station had its commander. The most important of these when the expedition arrived was Hawashi Effendi, commanding the important garrison of Dufilé, an able man much disliked by his brother officers for his abuse of power and his greed for goods and women. Other names which come to the fore in Jephson's narrative, and who played an important part in the story of Equatoria, were Fadl el-Mulla, commanding Fabbo, who headed the mutiny of the garrisons and afterwards took to the hills with a body of troops as independent mercenaries; Shukri Aga, commanding M'swa, who remained loyal,

[1] Jephson, *Emin Pasha*, p. 196.

accompanied the expedition back to the coast, collected his back pay from the Egyptian Government and took service later with the Uganda forces; and Selim Aga, commander at Laboré, who did his best but was left behind with another group of men at the south end of Lake Albert, where he was found by Lugard in 1891 and joined his old companion in arms, Shukri Aga, in the Uganda army.

Although these were the troops and officers who caused Emin so much grief, Jephson so much exasperation, and Stanley so much trouble by the mutiny described in Book 2 of Jephson's diary, their earlier conduct had been impressive. The historian R. O. Collins points out that

although the Northern Sudanese and many of the native tribes in Equatoria had joined the Mahdists, just as their counterparts in the Bahr al-Ghazal had done, the Egyptian armed forces in Equatoria remained faithful to the Government and fought fiercely and loyally to support it. Certainly it was the admirable defense of Amadi which had forestalled the Mahdist advance, and it was their determination to carry on the defense of the province after the fall of Amadi that prevented the precipitous collapse of Emin Bey's Government at Lado.[1]

Mr Collins goes on to point out this was partly due to the fact that most of Emin's men were southern Sudanese, little affected by the Mahdist propaganda of the north; but, in addition, 'these southern Sudanese troops and particularly their Negroid officers had a profound loyalty to the Khedive of Egypt, whom they looked on with mystical awe, and there were countless incidents in Equatoria where their actions were based solely on a blind devotion to the Khedive'.[1] Certainly this loyalty, and the conviction of the officers that the Khedive would surely send them help directly from Khartoum if they only held on long enough, served to confuse the issue when Stanley appeared suddenly out of the forests of the Congo with proposals for them to march in the opposite direction. When Lugard reached Lake Albert in 1891, he was impressed by the reluctance of the remnant of Emin's forces to enlist under any but the Egyptian flag.

Emin's own household at Wadelai included his little daughter Farida, whose Abyssinian mother had died some years before, a Greek trader called Marco, and Vita Hassan, an apothecary from Morocco. The camp followers in the garrisons were so numerous that if the whole province—the Mudiria, or governorship—were to be evacuated something like 10,000 people would have to take the road with all their household goods.

These were Emin's people, and his feeling of responsibility for them is the most consistent and the most likable thing about him. That he kept them going in complete isolation in the heart of Africa for seven years was

[1] R. O. Collins, *The southern Sudan 1893–1898: the struggle for control* (New Haven and London, 1962), pp. 50–1.

something of an achievement, and he was slow to surrender the position. He had planted crops and encouraged industry; Jephson's amazement will be noted when he was given soap to wash with, new clothes to wear and an exercise book to use for a diary. How long it could have been maintained is another question. The grain-tax levied from the surrounding tribes was becoming more and more an excuse for looting the villages, and Jephson observed that the further the soldiers were from Emin at Wadelai the more oppressive was their rule in the countryside. The local people were very ready to join the Mahdi's troops when they invaded a few months later. An even more serious threat to Emin's Eden was that his own authority was failing. When Jephson was detailed by Stanley to accompany Emin on a tour of the garrisons, the 1st Battalion at Rejaf, the most northerly station still nominally under Emin's command, was openly refusing to take its orders from the Governor. Emin seems to have hoped to the last that, given fresh supplies, he might have been able to maintain his position. But reading of these events so many years afterwards, the impression is that the arrival of the relief expedition had the effect of the rush of fresh air into an ancient tomb— the fair exterior crumbles, the carefully embalmed body dissolves in dust. With Stanley's arrival, brisk, practical, urgent, albeit in rags and verging on starvation, the delicate psychological balance of Emin's government collapsed. The pity was that the resources of the relief party were by then so exhausted that no satisfactory alternative to the status quo could usefully be offered.

Although no official communication had been held with the north since 1882, in the years that followed rumours filtered along the troubled trade routes to the east, and an occasional letter from Emin himself got through to Mackay in Buganda. Letters survive, several to Robert Felkin, which tell of this tenuous contact with the outside world. In the October of 1885 Emin got into direct touch with Kabarega, with whom he had contrived to establish good relations on his way through to Buganda in 1877,[1] and it was decided that Junker should make a dash for the east coast. The German doctor, accompanied by Vita Hassan, landed at Kibero on the eastern (Bunyoro) shore of Lake Albert early in January 1886, and made his way to Kabarega's court. He was lucky enough to find there a party of Arab traders, among them Mohammed Biri, who was to be instrumental in keeping open communications between Emin and his friends in Europe during the next two years. Birri was an intelligent and well-educated Arab who had been in the service of Captain Raemaeckers at the International Association's Belgian station of Karema on Lake Tanganyika, and who had later established himself as a merchant with useful contacts in the mutually hostile kingdoms of

[1] See above, pp. 12, 26–7.

Bunyoro and Buganda. Knowing both kingdoms to be as suspicious of European and Egyptian infiltration as they were distrustful of each other, Birri was wary of becoming involved in Emin's difficulties, but he and Junker had private conversations which resulted in messages getting through to Mackay in Buganda. Some six weeks after Junker's arrival in Bunyoro, a number of letters were delivered from Buganda for forwarding to Emin, containing the first news of the outside world to reach Equatoria for three years. Having established this valuable link, Junker moved on, while Vita Hassan made his way back to Wadelai. With difficulty, Junker received permission from Kabarega to leave Bunyoro, and with equal difficulty permission from Mwanga to enter Buganda, and he arrived at the capital in March; but it was not until the end of July that the Protestant Mission was able to provide a boat in which he crossed Lake Victoria to Msalala on the southern shore, from where he announced his escape. Junker's letter dated 13 August 1886 to Georg Schweinfurth, then in Cairo, reached the coast in September, and by January 1887 Junker himself was in Cairo, where he met Stanley on his way to Zanzibar en route for the Congo.

The letters received by Junker in Bunyoro and sent back to Emin at Wadelai contained the Egyptian Government's official order for the abandonment of Equatoria, signed by the Prime Minister, Nubar Pasha.

'It is a cool business dispatch, in the fullest sense of the word,' wrote Emin to Schweinfurth, 'not acknowledging by a single word the cares I have borne for three years, my fights with Danagla and Negroes, my hunger and nakedness, nor giving me a word of encouragement in the superhuman task of leading home the soldiers, which now lies before me.'[1] Emin's first action was to strengthen his possible escape route by sending Casati to Bunyoro as his representative with Kabarega, and an early result of the contacts made by Junker was the arrival of the first cargo of supplies in Equatoria since the retreat to Wadelai. Mahommed Biri brought the goods to Kibero in October 1886, where he was met by Emin in the *Khedive* steamer. He brought another caravan through in July 1887, including cloth, which was especially welcome to Emin, for, as he wrote to Felkin, although they had learned to weave their own, this was better material and they could now have new clothes for holidays.[2] On the way back from this second journey Biri, pausing with Casati at Kibero, fell at last a victim to the cross-currents of enmity between Bunyoro and Buganda. Kabarega, alarmed by rumours of Buganda's designs on his kingdom, and suspicious of Casati's implication

[1] Emin to Schweinfurth, Wadelai, 3 March 1886, Schweinfurth (ed.), *Emin Pasha in Central Africa*, p. 495.
[2] Emin to Felkin, Wadelai, 25 October 1887 (typescript in Mackinnon Papers, S.O.A.S., University of London).

in a plot, arrested both the Arab and the Italian. Casati, as Jephson records, escaped with his life; Biri and his people were murdered by Kabarega's orders a few weeks later.[1] Emin's contacts were failing him. Already, earlier in 1887, his one friend at the disturbed court of Mwanga, Alexander Mackay, had found his position untenable and departed across Lake Victoria. With Mohammed Biri dead, his representative expelled from Bunyoro, and Mackay out of reach, Emin would have been cut off once more had it not been for the meeting with Stanley in April 1888.

THE PROPOSED RELIEF OF EQUATORIA

The interest aroused by Junker's dramatic appearance was not, of course, the first sign of concern over the fate of Equatoria. The plan initiated by Gladstone's Government, in the bitter aftermath of the fall of Khartoum and the death of Gordon, for a Suakin–Berber railway to restore contact with the Sudan was hailed by the humanitarian and anti-slavery lobby as a welcome act of atonement. Stanley, just back from the Congo in 1885, declared such a railway to be indispensable for the reclamation of the Sudan, and suggested the creation of a 'Gordon Association' on the Nile, on the lines of the Congo International Association, a scheme echoing suggestions already made by Georg Schweinfurth, and indeed by Gordon when the withdrawal of Egypt from the Sudan was under discussion. When the railway scheme fell through, the Anti-Slavery Association memorialized the Government in protest, and a cry arose for the development of the Sudan by the kind of private enterprise by which Rajah Brooke had brought prosperity to North Borneo—'Sarawaking the Sudan' was a popular catch-phrase. On 22 July 1885 a meeting was held at the Mansion House, where Stanley made a vigorous speech in favour of such private enterprise taking over the field pusillanimously abandoned by the Government, and it is of interest in the light of later events that he should have pressed for an effort by 'all who lament the death of Gordon' to sponsor an expedition to Equatoria by way of the Congo and its tributary the Aruwimi. The Mansion House meeting was followed up by the forming of a committee by Baroness Burdett-Coutts and Cardinal Manning, who invited Schweinfurth to lead an expedition by the Congo route. But public support was lacking, and the only attempts to reach Equatoria were on a less ambitious scale, concerned with the safety of Emin rather than with grandiose commercial and humanitarian projects.[2]

In the course of 1885 Junker's brother approached the German Consul

---

[1] For a definitive account of Mohammed Biri, see H. B. Thomas, 'Mohammed Biri', *Uganda Journal*, XXIV (1960), 123–6.
[2] Richard Gray, *History of the Southern Sudan 1839–1889* (London, 1961), pp. 186 ff.

in Zanzibar with plans for a rescue operation, and the German traveller Dr Fischer, then on the Sultan's staff, agreed to make an attempt from the east towards Lake Victoria along Thomson's route. At the same time, the Austrian Oscar Lenz, on the other side of the continent, had reached Stanley Falls in a steamer belonging to the Congo administration on what he hoped was the way to Wadelai. Fischer found his way blocked by tribal wars and got no further than the north-east corner of Lake Victoria; Lenz was unable to organize a caravan at all.

Wilhelm Junker's emergence reanimated the scene, and the first man to translate enthusiasm into action was Dr Robert Felkin of Edinburgh. Felkin has been the target of much undeserved censure. In his diary Jephson accuses him of misleading Emin's well-wishers by a too-optimistic view of the situation in Equatoria, and of an ill-judged and ill-founded admiration of Emin's personality. On the other hand, when Emin threw in his lot with the Germans, his countrymen (who had taken little interest in his plight up to then) taxed Felkin with being half-hearted in his support of the Pasha, and of having at first encouraged him to hope for help from Britain and then left him in the lurch. Felkin's own justification of the part he played in the rescue of Emin is dignified and convincing; it is contained in the introduction he wrote to the English edition of Schweitzer's biography of the Pasha.[1]

Dr Felkin first met Emin in 1878 on his way to Buganda with the first party of C.M.S. missionaries to establish themselves at Mutesa's court. The steamer in which Felkin and his companions travelled from Khartoum to Lado carried the official dispatch appointing Emin Governor of Equatoria, and Felkin was charged by Gordon with verbal instructions for the new Governor. Felkin had a fluent knowledge of German, and he and Emin took to each other at once. A year later ill-health obliged the Scotsman to return home, and on his way back through Lado he renewed the friendship with Emin which lasted through the years, nourished by correspondence as regular as the remoteness of Equatoria would allow. Felkin's knowledge of Emin's character and potentialities, therefore, belonged to the years of the Pasha's prime, and to a time when Emin was already an experienced African traveller and administrator and Felkin a newcomer. The older man taught the younger to draw an accurate map and, as a fellow doctor, gave him wise advice on African illnesses. Felkin's enthusiastic affection for his interesting friend may have misled him as to possibilities in Equatoria, but it was none the less sincere and well founded.

On 28 October 1886 Felkin received in Edinburgh a letter forwarded by Junker from Emin, written from Wadelai in December 1885, and on 23 November he put before the Council of the Scottish Geographical

---

[1] Schweitzer (ed.), *Emin Pasha*, I, xvii–xliv.

Society a statement of Emin's situation. The Society accordingly addressed a letter to the Secretary of State for Foreign Affairs in London, urging the dispatch of a 'pacific relief expedition' with aid for Emin, and suggesting Joseph Thomson as the leader.[1] Joseph Thomson was certainly ready for such a mission, having written to *The Times* with his plans.

This waiting policy might be understood if the relief of Emin required a military expedition such as we have been painfully familiar with in Abyssinia, Ashantee, and the Soudan; but when it means in reality nothing more than an expedition composed of half a dozen white men at the most, 400 or 500 porters, and from 50 to 100 camels and donkeys, that moreover, the cost would not exceed £30,000, then it seems to me that delay is inexcusable. I speak of the cost being about £30,000 on the supposition that no expense would be spared in hurrying on the expedition; otherwise £15,000 would be nearer the mark; but I think everyone will be agreed in considering promptness and rapidity as vital matters. To attain these objects the party should be no larger than I have sketched, and organized in the fashion of an ordinary exploring expedition. Then it is most important that the route chosen should contain as little as possible of unknown quantities—difficulties and obstacles to be met cannot be gauged and weighed. If these considerations are vital—and certainly to me they seem so—the possible routes are reduced to two—(1) the one which I explored through Masailand to the Nile in 1883, and (2) the old route by way of Unyanyembe, Victoria Nyanza, and Uganda. The Masai route presents the following advantages. It is the shortest and most healthy, the country presents no topographical difficulties, camels and donkeys agree admirably with the climate —a most important matter if a considerable quantity of ammunition has to be conveyed. Its disadvantages are the scarcity of food along some parts and, in a minor degree, of water also. The unknown quantity is the comparatively insignificant distance which intervenes between the north end of Kavirondo and the country of Kabrega.[2]

Thomson went on to discuss the route by Unyamyembe (Tabora) and Lake Victoria, and to dismiss it as being impracticable for pack-animals and too dependent on the goodwill of the King of Uganda. He did not, in the *Times* letter, explain how he proposed to get from Kavirondo to Bunyoro but, as Jackson and Gedge were to demonstrate three years later, there need have been no insuperable difficulty in arriving at Mount Elgon, where Thomson had been on his earlier journey, and then crossing the 200 miles or so to within reach of Wadelai.[3]

But Thomson was not the first in the field, which had been entered some weeks earlier by William Mackinnon. Bringing into consultation his old friend and fellow merchant J. F. Hutton, Mackinnon had approached Stanley early in October. Mackinnon's humanitarian instincts were aroused, of course, at the spectacle of the beleaguered Emin, but it so happened as well that the

[1] A.-J. Wauters, *Stanley au secours d'Émin Pacha* (Brussels and Paris, 1890), pp. 154–5.
[2] *The Times*, 24 November 1886.   [3] Jackson, pp. 240–1; see above, pp. 28–9.

call for help from Equatoria coincided with a renewal of his interest in the commercial possibilities of East Africa. Hitherto Mackinnon's African plans had been disappointing. In 1876, as we have seen, the British Government had failed to support him in his bid for a concession from the Sultan of Zanzibar. His enthusiasm for the International African Association and consequent friendship with Leopold had not greatly increased his profits even when, in 1879, he had begun to interest himself in the Congo. In the early 1880s he and Hutton had led the opposition to the treaty giving Portugal control of the Congo mouth at the expense of King Leopold and his infant Free State; and in 1884 they had made a strenuous effort to secure for British enterprise the contract for the Congo railway eventually built by Belgians. Now, in 1886, with a British sphere of influence agreed with the Germans in East Africa, Mackinnon saw prospects there brighten, and he and his old associates Hutton and Stanley laid their heads together.

They were greatly encouraged by Fred Holmwood, acting Consul in Zanzibar since Kirk's departure earlier in the year, who saw in Emin's situation the possibility of Britain's extending her influence inland. Why not, he suggested to the British Government, take the opportunity of sending an expedition into Buganda to avenge the murder of Bishop Hannington, thereby teaching Kabaka Mwanga a lesson and giving much-needed support to the Buganda missionaries? Such an expedition would then go on to rescue Emin and to establish Britain's claim to the headwaters of the Nile. Lord Salisbury and his Foreign Secretary Lord Iddesleigh showed themselves equally disinclined to meddle directly in the situation; the Prime Minister suggested that as Emin was a German he was the concern of the German rather than the British Government, and Lord Iddesleigh's reaction to missionary difficulties in Buganda was to advise these good men to abandon so perilous a post. If Emin was to be rescued it must be by private enterprise. Nevertheless, the British Government were ready to see the situation in Equatoria cleared up and Egypt relieved of any further preoccupation with the southern Sudan. The Government's benevolence towards an expedition extended thus far, with the useful result that Sir Evelyn Baring, Britain's representative in Cairo, was able to persuade the Egyptian Government to contribute £10,000 to the fund being raised by the Emin Pasha Relief Committee.

Already, with the participation of Mackinnon and Hutton the rescue of Emin was becoming something more than the simple 'pacific' venture envisaged by Thomson and his friends in Scotland. A number of proposals were mooted for making use, in the interests of British influence and commerce, of Emin's central position at the headwaters of the Nile. It was understood that Egypt relinquished the southern Sudan: Emin had been so informed; but to the eager philanthropists and merchants this implied that there was a vacuum to be filled rather than a hopeless proposition to be abandoned. The proposals which were now discussed were all based on the supposition, strongly supported by Emin's own letters to Felkin and others, that he wanted to remain in Central Africa provided supplies could be brought in and regular communication with the coast established. These letters are, not unnaturally, a kind of thinking aloud on Emin's part, and from them emerges the idea that he would on the whole like to get rid of his Egyptian officers who were themselves anxious to go home to Cairo, but that the Sudanese were more or less at home where they were and had accumulated household goods, women and children to an extent that would make it hard to shift them. Some attractive alternatives began to form themselves. Might not Emin remain, either in charge of an independent administration in Equatoria with which Mackinnon could open trade relations, or as an outpost of the British East African sphere, subordinate to the East African company that Mackinnon and his friends were then hoping to form? If, on the other hand, Emin wished to withdraw from Equatoria, he might be settled, with such of his people as did not want to return to Egypt, at Kavirondo, conveniently on the route which Mackinnon wished to open between the coast and Buganda. Side by side with these East African projects (in which Emin himself seems to have been most interested) was taking shape in Leopold's mind the possibility of extending the frontiers of the Congo Free State to absorb Equatoria with Emin as Governor.

Though no doubt discouraged by the failure of the Scottish proposals for an expedition led by Thomson from the east coast, Robert Felkin remained closely in touch with all these developments, and warmly recommended the plan of Emin setting up in business on his own in cooperation with Mackinnon. When the Imperial British East Africa Company received its charter on 3 September 1888, Felkin seized the opportunity of drawing up a formal agreement between Emin and the Company, which Felkin was to sign on his behalf, subject to confirmation when communication could be established. This contract was sent to Mackinnon in October 1888, and at the same time Felkin wrote enthusiastically to his friend explaining the alternatives proposed: 'One is for you to remain on your own feet (*selbstständig*) and agree with them to deal exclusively with them...or else you might, whilst retaining your personal independence and remaining Governor General of your own province, accept the British Protectorate.' 'I flatter myself', wrote Felkin in the same letter, 'that I have now carried out your instructions to the letter.'[1]

[1] A typewritten copy of this letter is among the Mackinnon Papers (S.O.A.S., University of London); there is no evidence of its dispatch or arrival.

Meanwhile, Stanley had arrived at Lake Albert and put to Emin the proposals evolved before the departure of the expedition: he might evacuate the province as advised by the Egyptian Government; he might form a settlement in Kavirondo; he might transfer his services to King Leopold. Taken together, these proposals suggest a surprising extent of cooperation between various personalities interested in the development of Africa and aiming at the hitherto unexploited, though hardly unexplored, regions of the centre round the Great Lakes. Felkin alone remained apart from these cross-currents, being single-heartedly committed to the dream of the heartland of Equatoria, financed by British private enterprise for the benefit of humanity, under the beneficent rule of Emin Pasha. He was strenuously opposed to any liaison with King Leopold, and believed the Pasha's own wish was to maintain his province with British financial help.[1]

The relationship between Mackinnon and King Leopold has been exhaustively examined and discussed recently by R. T. Anstey,[2] who concludes that, whatever the outcome, what may be called the East and West African parties had more to gain than to lose by cooperation; whether Emin chose to serve the Congo Free State, to forward Mackinnon's ambitions in Buganda and Bunyoro, or to maintain his independence, trading with both sides, political security and commercial success would be to the benefit of all. During the doleful retreat from Lake Albert, Emin came to feel that he had been made the pawn of the merchants and the empire-builders, and this was the line taken up by the Germans when Emin suddenly and (to the minds of his rescuers) unaccountably severed all connection with the British and took service with his own countrymen. But Felkin makes a good case for his having originally been in favour of the kind of solution outlined in the contract with Mackinnon which met him on his return.[3]

These were some of the motives behind the bustle which now began to get the expedition launched. The subscriptions came in, the largest single donation being the £10,000 promised by the Egyptian Government. A full and final list of the money received and of the expenditure is published in Appendix II giving £14,000 as the Egyptian contribution.

The money came in large sums from such interested parties as Mackinnon, J. F. Hutton and Baroness Burdett-Coutts. The Royal Geographical Society subscribed £1000, and Jameson and Jephson each paid £1000 for the privilege of coming on the expedition. Stanley promised to donate payments

---

[1] Schweitzer (ed.), *Emin Pasha*, Felkin's Introduction, pp. xvii–xliv.

[2] Anstey, pp. 210–29.

[3] See for Emin's later thoughts, A. W. Schynse, *A travers l'Afrique avec Stanley et Émin Pacha* (Paris, 1890), pp. 200–1. Quoted in footnote to entry dated 17 October 1889. For Felkin's exposition of his point of view, see Introduction to Schweitzer, *Life*, I, xvii–xliv

from the press for his articles, a sum amounting to £1350 in the final balance sheet, made up of fees from the *Daily News, Standard, Daily Telegraph, Manchester Guardian* and *Scotsman.* The Eastern Telegraph Company agreed to charge only half rates on telegrams from Zanzibar; Mackinnon was to help with transport in British India Steam Navigation vessels.

William Mackinnon was the Chairman and Francis de Winton the Secretary of the Emin Pasha Relief Committee, which was now faced with making a choice of routes to reach the isolated Governor of Equatoria. Many suggestions, some brighter than others, were put forward as to the quickest and safest way of reaching Lake Albert, coming down eventually to four possible ones. There was Joseph Thomson's preferred road through Masailand, and his second choice, the old traders' run into Buganda by Tabora and across Lake Victoria. A third East African route was from the coast to Msalala south of Lake Victoria, then to the west of the lake through Karagwe and Ankole into Bunyoro and thence to Lake Albert; this was substantially the way by which the expedition returned and it was the first choice of the Committee.

Stanley maintained that on all three east-coast routes desertions would be constant, that the first and second were barred by the disturbed condition of Buganda, and the first made more difficult still by the hostility of the Masai. Thomson did not, as his letter makes plain, mean to go through Buganda but, in fairness to Stanley, who has been much criticized for turning down the Masailand road, it should be admitted that Kavirondo to Lake Albert represented, to quote Thomson, 'an unknown quantity'. Emin himself made an occasional reconnaissance to the east of the Albert Nile, on which his stations were mostly located, with a view to reaching the coast by making a circuit round Buganda. Junker told Holmwood that 'the country to the east of the Ripon Falls has proved impracticable, and . . . Emin has lost many troops in endeavouring to open communication through it'.[1] Nevertheless, two years later, when Mackinnon had urgent business reasons for wanting to get through quickly to Buganda, he did not hesitate to send an expedition by this same 'impracticable' route.[2] Jackson maintained that the hostility had been much exaggerated, and that the tales of their bloodthirsty and rapacious ways were spread by Arab traders anxious to keep the region to themselves.[2] He and Gedge arrived at Mount Elgon with very little difficulty, and Jackson in his reminiscences expressed his surprise that the situation had been so misjudged by Stanley, and the Congo route preferred to that through Masailand and Kavirondo.[3]

[1] Quoted in Stanley, *In Darkest Africa*, I, 29.   [2] Jackson, p. 190.
[3] '. . . We were probably not more than 150 to 200 miles, if as much, in a straight line to Emin's outposts at Livem and Lobor, lying due east of Wadelai, and as we know

There was, of course, another objection to the Masailand route, though it remained unstated: it was peculiarly Thomson's own, and even if Stanley had been a man to follow in another's footsteps, he could hardly have done so when Thomson himself had offered to lead the relief expedition over his old ground. Stanley declares that after giving his opinion of the different routes to the committee, he told them, if he was not wanted: 'Let Thomson take his expedition through the Masai Land, and put me down for £500 subscription for it.'[1]

Against the third route Stanley advanced the argument that it meant travelling through the German sphere of influence, which might be resented, as at the time it might have been, so soon after the conclusion of the first Anglo-German agreement. He was, however, prepared to accept it and it was the route by which the expedition returned.

A.-J. Wauters claims to have been the first to propose the fourth route to be considered—from the west by the Congo; an article suggesting it appeared in the Brussels journal, *Le Mouvement Géographique*, of which Wauters was editor, on 5 December 1887. This was the way which Stanley made no secret of preferring. Here he would be on his own ground where, from the river mouth to Stanley Falls, he knew every inch of the way. River transport was faster, safer and more open than by land; the expedition would not only command the use of boats already plying on the upper Congo, but could take fifteen whale-boats with them. They would have water in abundance. There could be no desertions by the Zanzibaris, who could best get home by marching steadily towards Lake Albert. 'Food there must be',[2] Stanley decided in his impetuous way, thereby showing himself no less optimistic about 'unknown quantities' than Thomson. With equal enthusiasm

that Count Teleki was much nearer when he reached Ngamatak on the lower Turkwe, it shows how much Stanley was out in his deductions and estimates of the dangers and difficulties of the Masailand route, as compared with the Congo route he selected, and how mistaken the Relief Committee were in selecting him instead of Thomson for the undertaking. The latter, knowing the country as he did, would no doubt have selected Mumia's, with its unlimited food supply and most docile and friendly natives as a base-camp and not Baringo. Moreover, as events subsequently proved, he would, given the same resources and a real and effective backing by Sir John Kirk, General Lloyd Mathews, and Seyyid Barghash, the Sultan of Zanzibar, in place of promises by King Leopold and Tippu Tib, have relieved the Pasha, arrived at an amicable arrangement with him regarding his province, retired with him or without him, and returned to the coast within a year, leaving an open road behind him': Jackson, pp. 240–1. Gedge's sketch-map showing the relation of Baringo in Kavirondo to Emin's outposts is in the Royal Geographical Society Collection, to which it was presented by Mr H. B. Thomas in 1966. It is annotated, probably by Jackson, to show the area where Emin's troops were reported to have been repelled by Turkana tribesmen just south of Lake Rudolf in 1885. This map is reproduced as Plate II.

[1] Stanley, *In Darkest Africa* (hereafter cited as *IDA*), I, 33.   [2] *Ibid.* I, 34.

Stanley brushed aside the possible difficulties to be encountered in the un-explored stretch of the route from the Aruwimi junction to Lake Albert through the Ituri forests. All that was needed was to obtain the permission of King Leopold, and to order the whale-boats. The Committee, however, opted for the east coast route round the south of Lake Victoria, through Karagwe and Ankole, and Stanley was recalled from a lecture tour in America to command the venture.

King Leopold in Brussels was not unaware of the possibilities of the situation, being ready at all times to extend the frontiers of his Congo kingdom. He may also have seen that if the expedition was to pass by or near Stanley Falls the unsettled stiuation vis-à-vis the Congo Arabs might be stabilized; here enters the Tippu Tib element. Correspondence in official Belgian archives as far back as 1884 contains suggestions that Stanley might go to the help of the garrisons in the Sudan beset by the Mahdi; and when, two years later, the relief of Emin began to be discussed as an immediate practical problem, such ideas were revived. Colonel Strauch thought England might ask for a right of way through the Congo and suggested offering facilities; Leopold, as outwardly discreet as he was inwardly adventurous, advised a waiting game.[1] He allowed his hand to appear forced when even-tually Stanley, still nominally in the service of the Free State, asked for permission to lead the Emin Pasha Relief Expedition and was told that such permission could only be granted on condition that the expedition travelled through the Congo. King Leopold's letter laying claim to Stanley's services and stipulating the Congo route was received by him on 8 January 1887 when arrangements were already far advanced, and certainly too late to order the whale-boats which might have made the Congo a practicable route. There is, however, a slight mystification here: Stanley does not mention in his book that he had already visited Leopold on 30 December, when it may be supposed a private agreement was reached, and a possible discussion held on the proposal to enlist Tippu Tib's cooperation. He does state, how-ever, that he visited Brussels on 14 January to secure assurance that the State would put boats at his disposal. Taken together, the two visits, the first of which was kept out of the news, imply a closer degree of par-ticipation than was acknowledged by Leopold. Stanley's meeting with the King on 30 December is mentioned by A.-J. Wauters in *Au secours d'Émin Pacha*.[2]

Despite his enthusiasm for the Congo route, Stanley was not altogether happy about the question of transport, which was only promised 'inasmuch

[1] Ceulemans, chapter III, 'Au secours d'Émin Pacha et la réconciliation avec Tippu Tib'.
[2] Wauters, p. 163.

as it will allow the working arrangements of its own administration'.[1] He wrote personally to the philanthropist Robert Arthington of Leeds, who had presented the steamer *Peace* to the Baptist Mission on the Congo, asking for its loan. Mr Arthington was very averse to lending the *Peace*, considering that unless Stanley should 'repent and believe in the Gospel', delay would be more dangerous to him than to Emin.[2] Nevertheless, the missionary in charge on the spot, Mr Bentley, agreed to the loan on condition that the Zanzibaris 'behaved themselves'—a stipulation which much annoyed Stanley. As will be seen from the diary, the American missionaries refused the loan of their *Henry Reed*, which was only secured by the device of the State's commandeering it and leasing it to the expedition.

The last weeks of December and the first weeks of January were spent in preparations, not made easier by the final decision to switch the expedition from the east to the west coast. Details of supplies and of the recruitment of officers occupy the early chapters of *In Darkest Africa*: Burroughs and Wellcome presented nine medicine chests to the expedition, Benjamin Edgington supplied the tents, which, 'dipped in a preservative of sulphate copper', were still watertight when they were folded away for the last time three years later in Zanzibar.[3] Even after all the frustrations and disasters of the expedition, Stanley, writing the official account of the expedition, could dilate with relish on Messrs Fortnum and Mason of Piccadilly, who 'packed up forty carrier loads of choicest provisions. Every article was superb, the tea retained its flavour to the last, the coffee was of the purest Mocha, the Liebig Company's Extract was of the choicest, and the packing of all was excellent.'[4]

At last all was ready, and on 20 January the S.S. *Navarino*, of the British India Steam Navigation Co's fleet, sailed with the goods and officers of the expedition. The officers chosen in England were Lieutenant W. Grant Stairs of the Royal Engineers; John Rose Troup, who had been employed already in the Congo Free State; Major Edmund Musgrave Barttelot, 7th Fusiliers, who had served in the Egyptian campaigns; Captain R. H. Nelson of Methuen's Horse, whom Stanley describes rather patronizingly as 'fairly distinguished in Zulu campaigns'; A. J. Mounteney Jephson; James S. Jameson, who had travelled in Mashonaland and Matabeleland as a big-game hunter and naturalist; finally, William Bonny, recently retired from the Army Medical Department, of non-commissioned rank and engaged as medical assistant. The expedition doctor, Thomas Heazle Parke, sought out Stanley

[1] Comte de Borchgrave, on behalf of King Leopold, to Stanley, 7 January 1887; quoted in *IDA*, I, 43–4.

[2] Arthington to Stanley, 15 January 1887, quoted in *IDA*, I, 47.

[3] Sixty-six years later Edgington's provided the tents for the successful 1953 ascent of Everest.   [4] Stanley, *IDA*, I, 39.

when the latter arrived at Alexandria, and asked to join the party. Stanley told him to come on to Cairo to discuss the matter, and he was signed on there. Stanley did not travel in the *Navarino*, but went overland to Egypt, where he arrived on 27 January. He was received by Sir Evelyn Baring, British Resident in Cairo, with whom he discussed the plans of the expedition in relation to the Egyptian Government.

The first duty of the relief expedition was to carry letters from the Egyptian Government to Emin, confirming the earlier dispatch announcing their abandonment of the Sudan, and making clear the extent of their responsibility for the Equatorial garrisons. Letters signed by the Khedive and by Nubar Pasha were prepared and handed to Stanley. In them Emin was advised to take advantage with his people of Stanley's safe conduct to the coast, and to return to Egypt to receive their back pay; should they decide to remain where they were, Egypt would accept no further responsibility for them. The incredulity, resentment, misunderstanding and finally disillusionment caused among officers and men alike by these letters is the subject of many passages in Jephson's diary.[1]

None of this seems to have been foreseen during Stanley's short stay in Cairo, which was taken up in explaining the expedition's plans not only to the Khedive and Nubar Pasha but also to Schweinfurth and Junker, who were both in Cairo. All four were dubious of the Congo route, but Stanley was not to be dissuaded again from his own favourite plan and he overrode all objections. *In Darkest Africa* is particularly sarcastic about the suggestion made by the pacific Junker that the Emin Pasha Relief Expedition had been equipped to look more like a military invasion than a simple rescue party. It was indeed too late now to go back on the Congo decision, or to modify any of the ambitious preparations, and on 3 February Stanley left Cairo for Suez on the way to join the rest of the expedition at Aden, where he arrived on 12 February.

THE COURSE OF THE EXPEDITION

The expedition reached Zanzibar on 22 February, and here spent three busy days, which included the lightning negotiations between Stanley and Tippu Tib which were to be productive of so much trouble. Fred Holmwood was the go-between, and a contract was signed by which Tippu Tib agreed to provide porters for the expedition, to take over the loads when the expedition reached the limit served by the boats of the Free State administration.[2] The porters were to be recruited from Tippu's sphere of influence

---

[1] The full text of the letters is printed in Appendix III below, p. 430.
[2] Sir John Gray, 'Stanley *versus* Tippu Tib' *Tanganyika Notes and Records* XVIII (1944).

round Stanley Falls and were to be armed with guns and ammunition provided by himself, while the gunpowder and caps were to be supplied by the expedition. At the same time, Tippu Tib was offered, and accepted, the post of Governor of Stanley Falls under the authority of the Congo Free State.[1] In addition to these negotiations with Tippu, Stanley had to visit the Sultan with a letter from Mackinnon outlining the expedition's plans to return by the east coast route through the German sphere and the Sultan's territories. A letter was then dispatched to Emin 'by couriers overland, who will travel through Uganda into Unyoro secretly'.[2] Although this letter never arrived, an earlier one from Holmwood got through to alert Emin of the approaching expedition.[3]

On 23 February the expedition set sail and reached the Congo mouth, by way of the Cape, on 18 March. The timetable thereafter may be briefly given. They arrived at Matadi at the foot of the cataracts on 21 March, at Leopoldville on Stanley Pool on 21 April, and were at the navigable head of the upper river, and at the extreme limit of the Free State's authority, on 15 June. Here, at Yambuya, the Rear Column was to dig in to await supplies arriving from Leopoldville, on a second trip made necessary by the shortage of boats. From Bangala on the upper Congo, Barttelot had been detailed to accompany Tippu Tib to Stanley Falls to take up his governorship, and he rejoined the expedition at Yambuya to take over command of the Rear Column.

The decision to divide the expedition was, on the face of it, reasonable enough. The lack of adequate transport in the Congo Free State made it necessary for the steamers to do double journeys, and no concerted advance into the forest from the river-head on the Aruwimi was possible until Tippu Tib supplied the porters promised in the Zanzibar contract, from the region east of Stanley Falls. The Advance Column led by Stanley would blaze a trail through the unknown terrain between the Aruwimi confluence and Lake Albert, the essential loads being carried by the Zanzibaris, professional porters used to the work. The Rear Column under Major Barttelot, second-in-command of the expedition, with his friend Jameson as his deputy, was to await Ward and Troup, both experienced Congo travellers, who were coming up from Leopoldville with Bonny in the *Stanley*, bringing the less essential loads for which there had not been room on the first trip. The Sudanese soldiers, more suitable for garrison work than the Zanzibaris, would man Yambuya, together with those of the latter who were not fit to travel immediately. By the time all were assembled, probably by the middle

[1] Barttelot, Sir W. G. (ed.), *The life of Edmund Musgrave Barttelot...from his letters and diary* (London, 1890), pp. 402-3, Agreement between Mr Stanley and Tippu Tib.
[2] Stanley, *IDA*, I, 62.   [3] Diary, 27 April 1888.

of August, Tippu Tib would have had time to collect the 600 Manuyema carriers requested by Stanley.

Stanley's written instructions to Barttelot, dated 27 June 1887, are quite clear as far as they go; he is to start eastward after the Advance Column as soon as the porters are collected; if these are fewer than the number expected he is to start all the same, using his judgment as to what loads are to be left behind. There are no written instructions as to what he is to do if no porters at all turn up. *In Darkest Africa* contains the report of a conversation between Stanley and Barttelot on just this possibility, in the course of which it would appear that Barttelot was told not to wait indefinitely but to get the loads along as well as he could by making double journeys. But such a conversation is not mentioned by Barttelot, and frankly disbelieved by his brother who edited the diaries and letters.[1] There is no doubt that Stanley, who had had misunderstandings with Tippu Tib on his earlier journey through Africa, and should have been able to assess the uncertainties of the situation, left the Rear Column in an extremely difficult position. How difficult, may be understood by reading Parke's letter to Stanley of 4–6 November 1887 from Ipoto where they were left in a rather similar predicament.[2]

Stanley led the Advance Column out of Yambuya on 28 June 1887 with four officers—Stairs, Jephson, Nelson and Parke. He left Barttelot and Jameson with 45 Sudanese, an interpreter, 4 Somalis, 76 Zanzibaris and 5 boys; these had all been rejected by Stanley as sickly and incompetent. His last words were that he expected to be back in October. The supplies of the Rear Column were pitifully inadequate. For instance, European stores to be shared between Barttelot and Jameson and to last six months were listed by Barttelot as 'five 1-lb tins of coffee, three 1-lb tins of tea, two tins of salt, six tins of butter, eight tins of milk, one opening knife, one tin of sugar, six tins of jam, one tin of chocolate, three tins of cocoa and milk, three tins of sardines, four 1-lb tins of biscuits, one tin of red herrings, two tins of flour, four pots of Liebig, one of tapioca, one tin of sago'.[3] For the rest, they were to live off the country, making friends with the local people in order to do so.

The Advance Column's march to Lake Albert took five months, with fearful losses from disease, starvation, desertion, and in fights with the local people. They followed the line of the river, some using the boat (Jephson's charge) and some marching by land. Towards the end of August they came on the tracks of a band of marauding Arabs, who had penetrated from the south in the Manuyema country. On 31 August they reached the point

[1] Stanley, *IDA*, I, 114–29; Barttelot, pp. 114–16.
[2] Appendix IV below, p. 433.
[3] H. R. Fox Bourne, *The other side of the Emin Pasha Relief Expedition* (London, 1891).

where the Nepoko river flows into the Aruwimi from the north, after which the Aruwimi becomes the Ituri. On 17 September they reached the Arab camp, where one Ugarrowwa was in command, and here they left a party of sick men to be looked after. Marching along the south bank of the Ituri, they crossed the Lenda, and on 3 October were obliged to leave Nelson, too lame and ill to walk, at 'Starvation Camp' with a few more sick men. On 18 October they arrived at another Arab settlement, Kilonga-Longa's at Ipoto on the north bank of the Ituri, just beyond where modern maps show the Gayu flowing in from the north. From Ipoto Jephson was sent back to rescue Nelson, about which he wrote one of the most dramatic passages of the diary.

Dominated by the need for haste, Stanley now decided on another division of his force and a further lightening of their loads. The boat was to be left, the sections sunk by the river and the nuts and bolts kept carefully in camp; Nelson and Parke and those men who could not march and carry were to stay at Ipoto while Stanley pushed on to the lake, leaving the river and striking out across country. He and Stairs marched on 28 October, and were followed by Jephson on 7 November on his return from the relief of Nelson. Jephson caught up the main body of the expedition at Ibwirri, where they were later to build Fort Bodo near the edge of the forest.

From here to the lake (a distance of nearly 100 miles) the route lay roughly east. They no longer had the river to guide them, for here the Ituri makes a bend to the south, further than Stanley shows it on his map, and the landmarks in his and Jephson's narratives are not always easy to identify. On 30 November the forest which had hemmed them in so long began to open out and from a spur which Stanley called Mount Pisgah they could see the way ahead; next day they emerged from the trees onto the upland plain, and on 4, 6 and 7 December they made three river crossings, over what Stanley calls the West, Main and East Ituri. A week later they entered the district of Undussuma, and on this first passage of the region—which they were to come to know well, and feel at home in—Stanley fell foul of the local people under their chief Mazamboni, with whom they later made friends. Pressing on eastward through the territory of Chief Gavira (of the 'Bavira, or Bira people—more specifically, the 'Plains' Bira who still inhabit this area) they reached the lake shore on 13 December.

Here anticlimax met them; there was no sign of Emin Pasha and no means of going in search of him without the boat, left at Ipoto, or at least local canoes, which were unobtainable. Against Jephson's inclination, who thought they should have waited a little longer for Emin to turn up, the party retraced their steps to Ibwirri, and there built the camp they called Fort Bodo.[1] The

---

[1] 'Or the "Peaceful Fort".' Stanley, *IDA*, I, 327.

camp consisted of solid huts and was provisioned by sown crops; it became their base for the next few months and Nelson and Parke and their men from Ipoto joined them here. From Fort Bodo Stairs was sent to collect the invalids left at Ugarrowwa's, while Stanley, Jephson and Parke returned to the lake, carrying the recovered boat. On 20 April 1888 Jephson was sent off in the *Advance* to make contact at M'swa with Emin, from whom letters had been received at Kavalli's village above the lake shore. Jephson and Emin foregathered at M'swa, and returned to Kavalli's, where the meeting between Stanley and the man he had come to help at last took place, on 30 April.

The various proposals described earlier were now put to Emin: to follow Stanley to Zanzibar or to remain where he was, reinforced by the ammunition brought by the expedition; to transfer his governorship to the Congo Free State and take service under King Leopold; to settle in Kavirondo on Lake Victoria as an outpost of Mackinnon's projected East African trading company.[1] The unexpected vacillations of Emin now began, and he maintained that he could not possibly take any decision until he had consulted his people. Stanley, increasingly anxious about the lack of news from the Rear Column, decided to send Jephson with Emin on a round of the Equatorial garrisons, to read them the Khedive's letter and assess the feeling among the troops, while he himself returned to Fort Bodo and thence back on his tracks to find Barttelot.

Travelling light with a picked company of men, Stanley left Fort Bodo again in June 1888. He reached Banalya, just short of Yambuya, on 17 August, and found the remains of the column depleted and demoralized.[2] The story must be briefly told. Barttelot had spent twelve months at Yambuya, in constant expectation of Tippu Tib's porters. Relations with the local people had fluctuated, at one time being good enough for a fair supply of beans, bananas and fish to come into the camp, but at other times trouble broke out. Discipline in the camp deteriorated; frequent and increasingly brutal flogging was resorted to. Barttelot was a quick-tempered man, with no patience with and little liking for Africans, and he became more and more irascible. Constant visits to Tippu Tib at his Stanley Falls camp sapped the energy of the officers, and exacerbated nerves were stretched to breaking point by hope deferred. They all suffered much from fever. Nor was there unbroken harmony between Barttelot and his officers. In March 1888 Ward was sent back down river to the coast to get a message to the Committee in England asking for instructions in view of Stanley's continued absence;

---

[1] See above, pp. 47–8. The granting of a Charter to the Imperial British East Africa Company and Felkin's plans for Emin to sign a contract with Mackinnon were not then known to Stanley. [2] See Stanley, *IDA*, I, 467–519.

in May, Troup, weakened by fever, decided to leave the expedition. In June, a year after Stanley's departure, Tippu Tib sent 400 Manuyema porters, but before they could leave Yambuya there were complaints about the loads, which had to be broken up into smaller ones; then, of course, there were not enough men to carry them. In order to lighten loads, and to disperse what was lying at Yambuya in danger of deterioration, certain of Stanley's boxes were opened and some of the contents sent back down river. This action infuriated Stanley so much that it almost became his chief complaint against Barttelot's management of the Rear Column, though it would seem to have been done with the best intentions. More serious than the dispute over the loads was the discovery that 80 per cent of the caps supplied by the expedition, in accordance with the Zanzibar contract, for use with Tippu's guns were faulty.

On 11 June the expedition left Yambuya with Barttelot in command, Jameson as second, accompanied by Bonny, 22 Sudanese, 110 Zanzibaris, 430 Manuyema under the command of the Arab appointed by Tippu Tib, Sheik Muni Somai. On 15 June Barttelot pressed ahead, leaving Jameson to bring up the rear, and on the 24th he made a detour to visit Stanley Falls, leaving Bonny in charge with orders to go no further than Banalya. On 17 July Barttelot rejoined Bonny at Banalya, and on the 19th he was shot by one of the Manuyema in the course of a dispute over the drumming and singing in the porters' camp. Jameson died of fever on 17 August at Bangala on his way down river to report the news of Barttelot's death to the State authorities. When Stanley arrived at Banalya on 17 August, Bonny, the only surviving European with the Rear Column, was in charge.

Disasters demand scapegoats and the question of where to lay the blame for this one was fiercely debated at the time, and remains open today. *In Darkest Africa* contains an outright condemnation of the officers of the Rear Column, written without waiting to hear what Troup and Ward had to say, or to study the records kept by Barttelot and Jameson. Stanley's omission of even a conventional message of sympathy to Jameson's widow or to the Barttelot family counts heavily against him. He also instituted proceedings in the Consular Court of Zanzibar against Tippu Tib for breach of the contract signed at the outset of the expedition, on 24 February 1887. The posthumous papers of Barttelot and Jameson accuse Stanley of leaving the Rear Column in the lurch. More measured opinion concedes that Barttelot was not, temperamentally speaking, the best man to have left in a position requiring the maximum of diplomacy and patience. The imperfect state of the Congo Free State's transport and administration has also come in for adverse comment. But the most obvious scapegoat has always been Tippu Tib himself. Stigmatized in contemporary literature as 'the notorious slave trader', he was fair game. No doubt he was dilatory and, by European standards, uncooperative. Nevertheless, it should be remembered that the agreement he was accused of breaking was no one-sided affair. Tippu Tib certainly engaged to provide 'a number of able-bodied men' (the number 600, so constantly referred to in subsequent discussion, was not specified in the contract), each to be armed with a gun and bullets. But the gunpowder and caps were only supplied at a late date, and the caps were faulty. Moreover, Tippu Tib contended, with some show of reason, that without the active support of the Free State administration he was at a disadvantage when it came to recruiting porters and asserting his authority in the area of which he had been appointed governor. It is perhaps significant that when it became clear that Tippu was entering a strong defence in the case brought by the Emin Pasha Relief Expedition Committee, the case was withdrawn.[1]

Some space has been given to the story of the Rear Column because it is the one important aspect of the expedition which is not covered by the diary. The rest of the journey may be more briefly described. Stanley returned to Fort Bodo on 30 December 1888 with Bonny and the remains of the Rear Column, together with their Manuyema porters, and determined to evacuate the fort and march for Lake Albert with all speed. The speed was too rapid for the Rear Column survivors and for Nelson, who was again too lame to walk. What Parke called a 'Convalescent Home' was established in the open country on the side nearest Lake Albert of the Ituri river crossings. Here the three officers and the ailing men could stay to recuperate while Stanley and Bonny pressed forward. They reached the lake on 18 January 1889 to find letters from Jephson explaining that he and Emin had been detained by disaffected troops at Dufilé. The story of this

---

[1] A detailed, and probably definitive, examination of Stanley's charges (in the name of the Committee) against Tippu Tib may be found in Gray, 'Stanley *versus* Tippu Tib'. For a general account of the Rear Column, see Stanley, *IDA*, 1, 467–519; Parke, pp. 359–65. See also: Barttelot, 1890; J. S. Jameson (ed. Mrs J. S. Jameson), *Story of the Rear Column of the Emin Pasha Relief Expedition* (London, 1890); J. R. Troup, *With Stanley's rear column* (London, 1890); Herbert Ward, *My life with Stanley's Rear Guard* (London, 1891); J. R. Werner, *A visit to Stanley's Rear-Guard at Major Barttelot's camp on the Aruwimi with an account of river-life on the Congo* (Edinburgh, 1891). Jephson's comments, both in the diary (26 January 1889) and in *Emin Pasha* (p. 402) are confined to expressing the shock and grief he experienced on hearing of the death of Barttelot, who had been a friend before the expedition, and of Jameson, with whom he had found much in common in the early days on the Congo. He does not attempt the kind of assessment that Parke, a much less emotional character, includes in his *Experiences* (pp. 509–12). Stanley's harsh and unjust comments on two men whom Jephson had respected and liked must have set up a conflict of loyalties which led him to refrain from other than personal comment and to conclude that 'the whole story is a very dark one, as dark as any of the many dark stories connected with African travel' (Diary, 26 January 1889, p. 329 below).

'Rebellion at the Equator', as Jephson subtitled his book, occupies Books 2 and 3 of the diary. Emin and Jephson were at last liberated as a result of the panic caused by the advance of Mahdist troops from the north, and by March 1889 the expedition was reunited at Kavalli's.

There was still much discussion between Emin and Stanley as to what should be done. Emin found it difficult to make up his own mind, and his officers were mostly in a demoralized state and unable to join in any concerted course of action. Shukri Aga, commanding M'swa, had throughout adhered to Emin and continued to do so; Fadl el Mulla had remained with a still mutinous group at Wadelai; Selim Bey travelled to and fro arguing with his colleagues. On 10 April, however, the expedition marched out of Kavalli's. Emin had failed to rally his troops, nearly all of whom were left behind, but even so some 1500 souls—men, women and children—left for the east coast.

Retracing their steps to Mazamboni's, where they were delayed by Stanley's illness for a month, they finally took the road south on 8 May, crossing the Semliki on the 17th and 18th of the same month. Thereafter they skirted the western flanks of the Ruwenzori to Lake Edward, where they arrived a month later. They marched through Ankole, crossed the Alexandra Nile (on modern maps, the Kagera) on 25 July, struck the south-west shore of Lake Victoria, and on 28 August were received by Mackay at his mission near the south shore of the lake. They arrived at Bagamoyo on the east coast opposite Zanzibar on 5 December.

Jephson's diary ends some time in October, and the subsequent history of the members of the Emin Pasha Relief Expedition is told in the Epilogue (below, pp. 410–25).

SOME RESULTS OF THE EXPEDITION

This Introduction opened with the statement that the Emin Pasha Relief Expedition was, among other things, the 'least successful' of Stanley's expeditions, and gave a brief summary of why this was so. This summary needs to be slightly amplified before the diary can be read with full understanding. With so much goodwill and hard work, with ample finance and so many important and influential people interested, with the blessing of the British and Egyptian governments and godspeed of Emin's friends, the venture seemed certain of success. That it failed so signally to achieve any of its highly conceived aims, returning to the coast after nearly three years of suffering and repeated disaster, the rescuers and rescued barely on speaking terms, law-suits threatened in Zanzibar and in London, and ill-feeling of which echoes still persist, was due to an 'unknown quantity' much more disastrous than a mere lack of acquaintance with the way.

It was hardly possible, perhaps, to know either what Emin himself wanted or what he was in a position to do, but the misunderstandings which flowed from this lack of knowledge were fatal. Equally fatal was the misconception of Emin's character. He was a strange man, but he had, in his own way, achieved much in the years both before and after his isolation. Essentially a man of peace, long residence in the East had taught him a flexibility in dealing with African problems which, in happier times, might have given good results. The Westerner's regard for time, his preoccupations with cause and effect, were no part of Emin's make-up. He lived, metaphorically speaking, rather hand to mouth, deeply interested in his scientific pursuits, taking each day's events as they came. He had learnt to like African life; he enjoyed his position as Governor; he would, one imagines, have wished to stay where he was. But it would have been difficult for him to give any precise preference without knowing far more than he did, or could, of the Egyptian government's intentions and of events in the outside world.

Writing to Felkin on 31 December 1885, Emin debated the idea of sending his Egyptian officers off to the coast either north by Uganda or south of Lake Victoria through Karagwe, and staying at Wadelai with the Sudanese to await events.[1] A letter to Mackay of 6 July 1886 speaks of being 'in no hurry to break away from here, or to leave those countries in which I have now laboured for ten years'.[1] In *In Darkest Africa* Stanley quotes a number of passages from Emin's letters, to Mackay, to Felkin, and to Charles H. Allen, secretary of the Anti-Slavery Society. His comments on these extracts suggest that Emin had given a misleading impression of his situation; but, in fact, the impression, reading these letters now with the inevitable hindsight, is rather of indecision understandable in view of Equatoria's complete isolation. What does not fully emerge is that Emin's troops were getting out of hand, though there are hints for anyone who wished to take them of trouble at Lado and in the Makaraka country. That Emin was becoming, in his own mind, increasingly anxious about his position emerges from the diary entries in his *Tagebücher*.[2]

But it was not Emin's letters which sent the expedition off with falsely raised hopes of what they were to find. It was the impossibly ideal picture painted of the beleaguered governor by his friends Junker and Felkin,

[1] Quoted in *IDA*, I, 27.
[2] *Die Tagebücher von Dr. Emin Pascha*, ed. Dr Franz Stuhlmann, vols. I, II, II, IV, and VI (Braunschweig: Westermann, 1916–27); see Preface, p. vi. Translation of extracts relating to Uganda, by Sir John Gray: *Uganda Journal*, xxv (1961), xxvi (1962), xxvii (1963), xxviii (1964), xxix (1965), xxx (1966), xxxi (1967). Introducing Extracts VIII (July 1887–Jan. 1888), Sir John says that 'the general picture as at this date is shown by Emin's diary to be of gradual deterioration throughout the province': *Uganda Journal*, xxviii, 2 (1964), 201–12.

eagerly accepted and augmented by the humanitarian societies and individuals who had been so deeply shocked by what they regarded as the betrayal of Gordon. There is an exquisite symbolism about the fact that a suit of clothes taken out to Emin by the expedition had trousers six inches too long—they had expected a tall man. It was alien to the Victorian way of thinking that Emin should have kept his Governorship intact, and to a certain extent prosperous, by guile and by a fluid approach to problems which the typical hero of the time would have attacked with direct and uncompromising force. Emin cannot be held responsible for his rescuers' having envisaged him as possessing to a superlative degree the forthright efficiency of Baker and the religious devotion of Gordon. And it was not in the nature of Stanley to imagine anyone in a tight corner behaving other than he himself would do in similar circumstances.

When Stanley came to write *In Darkest Africa*, he recapitulated his impression of the situation in Equatoria and the views of those interested as they appeared to him after his visit to Cairo.

Junker does not think Emin will abandon the Province; the English subscribers to the fund hope he will not, but express nothing; they leave it to Emin to decide; the English Government would prefer that he would retire, as his Province under present circumstances is almost inaccessible, and certainly he, so far removed, is a cause of anxiety. The Khedive sends the above order for Emin to accept of our escort, but says 'You may do as you please. If you decline our proffered aid you are not to expect further assistance from the Government.' Nubar Pasha's letter conveys the wishes of the Egyptian Government, which are in accordance with those of the English Government as expressed by Sir Evelyn Baring.[1]

The Khedive's letters, however, frankly puzzled the officers, who expected to be ordered rather than consulted about their future, and who clung rather pathetically to the dream of a well-equipped military force from the north to carry them home by the only route they knew—the river to Khartoum. No one was much tempted by the offer of a free passage to Egypt, with back pay only up to the time of arrival; the Egyptians at least would be at home if they took the offer, but the Sudanese would be nearly as far from theirs as they were already. The Sudanese would have preferred Mackinnon's solution of a commercial settlement in Kavirondo. But, as will be seen, this and other practical solutions came to nothing in the general collapse of law and order which followed Stanley's arrival.

It seems to have been assumed throughout that time had stood still in Equatoria, and that on arrival the rescue party would have to treat with a well-based administration in good heart, needing only a few supplies to remain where they were, or a little man-to-man encouragement to march

[1] *IDA*, I, 58.

out in good order. It was evidently thought that cool consideration could be given on the one hand to the official intimation from Cairo that arrears of pay would be dependent on evacuation, and on the other that British merchants and the King of the Belgians expected them to stay where they were. That morale might have deteriorated and distrust developed between officers and men in the years of isolation does not seem to have occurred to Stanley. In his apologia, already quoted, Felkin writes of Emin's 'heroic struggle', of which 'the strain eventually proved too much for him, and . . . when at last the relief expedition arrived he was no longer, either physically or mentally, able to meet the difficulties of the situation.'[1] But it seems as if this took Felkin by surprise too. Emin himself wrote to Felkin on the last lap: 'All my hopes are shattered, and I return home half blind and broken down.'[2] With hindsight, and the modern preoccupation with personal relations and psychological attitudes, it is not difficult to understand how such splendid plans came to grief; the Victorians were less armoured against such disappointment. Stanley and his officers expected gratitude, or at least co-operation, and when the relief expedition emerged, starving and in rags, out of the unknown forests of the west, no one could understand the effect on the minds of Emin's isolated and basically ignorant soldiery. 'If we had arrived in smart uniforms, covered with gold lace, they would have kissed our feet and thought us something like deliverers,' wrote Jephson.[3] The forthright and open-hearted young Englishman did not perceive that in this fact lay most of the trouble. The Europeans with whom the men in the garrisons had been in contact in the past had always come to them well equipped and well clothed; they had known that Baker with his steamers and guns meant business, they had known that Gordon on his camel wielded authority—what were they to make of this tattered troop coming unexpectedly from the west and the feared and unknown lands of the Congo? Emin knew all this; when he repelled Jephson's well-meant, but perhaps rather often repeated, advice about dealing with his followers, he replied in some irritation that he had worked with them for 13 years and must know best. The tragedy of Emin is that he knew what was happening as his authority slipped away, as men he had trusted first insulted and then imprisoned him, even threatened to hang him, and he was powerless to stop it. Jephson's realization of this tragedy comes across movingly as day after day he observed Emin, noting the good and the bad, puzzled but always kindly.

[1] Felkin's Introduction to Schweitzer, xl.
[2] *Ibid.* xlii. [3] Diary, 14 October 1888, p. 294 below.

THE DIARY

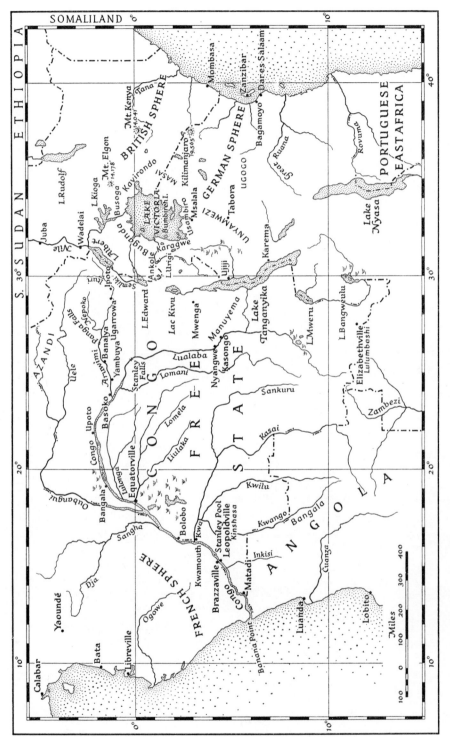

Map 1   The transit of the Emin Pasha Relief Expedition across Africa, from the mouth of the Congo in the west to Zanzibar in the east

CHAPTER I

TILBURY TO BANANA POINT

20 JANUARY–18 MARCH 1887

Mounteney Jephson commenced his diary on 20 January 1887, when he embarked on the *Navarino* at Tilbury. It would have been nice to know who were the people who saw him off, and what were his feelings on leaving his family and friends for an expedition of long duration and into parts of the world largely unknown and unmapped. But his thoughts were concentrated on the future and excited by the glittering prospects of the great adventure.

The day was bright and sunny, [he wrote] I hope it is a good augury. Stanley gone overland to Egypt & joins us at Suez, somewhere about Feb. 6th. Major Barttelot & Jameson also join us there. Lieut. Stairs of the Royal Engineers & Nelson, who has already travelled in Africa, start with me from London. The latter has been through the Zulu war & commanded a troop in Methuen's Horse in the Bechuanaland expedition & was also in the Boer War [that of 1880]. The vessel is bad, surprisingly so for one of the British India vessels. Stanley's black servant who will be useful as an interpreter somehow missed the vessel & after waiting over an hour we were obliged to proceed without him. It is hoped that he will join the vessel at the Isle of Wight or at Plymouth.

Stanley explained what happened in his book *In Darkest Africa*. William Bonny, who had recently left the Army Medical Department where he had been employed as a medical assistant, and had been accepted by Stanley to accompany the expedition in that capacity, had been put in temporary charge of the African boy, Baruti. He left Stanley's rooms in Bond Street with the boy at 8 a.m. to go to Fenchurch Street Station to catch the train to Tilbury. Having arrived at the station, he went off to the Tower of London, leaving the boy to his own devices. On return to the station, he was surprised that there was no sign of Baruti and he had missed the train. While he was away at the Tower, the boy had been found at Fenchurch Street, cold, hungry and deserted, by Colonel J. A. Grant and taken back to Bond Street. What Stanley said to Bonny about all this can best be left to the imagination. There is no record of any such act of lunacy on Bonny's part again, so perhaps it was as well that the lapse occurred when it did and not later on in Africa when the consequences might have been disastrous.[1]

From then on, the entries in Mounteney's diary are the usual reports of matters of importance to the passenger on board ship. He wrote on 21 January: 'Stanley is taking his donkey out with him on board, it is a fine bred looking beast, a good deal larger than the ordinary English donkey.' Little did he realize that he was

---

[1] Stanley, *IDA*, I, 48; see also pp. 106–9 below.

going to eat it later and be heartily grateful for the food it supplied! He recorded: 'Saw the last of England for many months to come.' It was actually three years before he saw it again! His diary for the 23rd records: 'At twelve o'clock midday, we passed a derelict vessel, a barque of about 500 tons, at about 30 yards distance. Her fore and main masts were broken off about 4 feet above the deck which was burst up: her lower mizen mast alone was standing. Name on her bows—Stormy Petrel.'

The following day he commented: 'It is interesting sitting smoking on deck & talking of the expedition, making all sorts of conjectures of possible routes & of our life on the march—probably most of them are wrong...This idle life on board ship is very irksome when one is longing for the real life to begin.' This eagerness to get started vented itself in criticisms of the slow speed of the *Navarino*, and scathing comments appear in the diary during the next few days, such as that on the 27th: 'Run 172 miles. What a slow old tub this vessel is.' Before the ship reached Port Said he had read the two books Stanley had published concerning his previous expeditions—*Through the Dark Continent* and *How I Found Livingstone*. He found much food for thought in them as it helped him to realize the difficulties which lay ahead and to be truly thankful that the expedition had a thoroughly experienced leader.

On 4 February they reached Port Said, fifteen days out from Tilbury. He wrote:

At once went ashore for a walk and to do a little shopping. Stairs & I stayed and had dinner at the New Hotel, where we got all the English papers up to 28th. January. In the *Graphic* was a long description of the Emin Pasha Relief Expedition with illustrations, & all the papers had something in them about it. We were able to get a fairly good dinner at the hotel & afterwards went to the El Dorado to hear some tenth rate music. Port Said is greatly improved since I was last there, two and a half years ago, though it is still the filthiest place I ever was in—there is still not the slightest attempt at making a road.

And this in spite of the fact that the Canal had been opened eighteen years earlier! The following day they only got as far as Ismailia, having had to tie up twice to allow other ships to pass. Mounteney commented on the amusement of passengers going east for the first time at reading the inscription on the Arab fruit-boat which came alongside—*Dingy boy gat frut.*

Off next morning at seven, they proceeded at full speed through the fifteen miles of Lake Timsah before slowing down to the regulation five miles an hour in the canal. They arrived at Suez at three o'clock, all agog to see Stanley embark. The diary reads:

Presently a little steam launch was seen puffing towards us & all the available glasses on board were turned towards it. We were soon able to make out Stanley seated amongst several gentlemen, one of whom was the famous Dr. Juncker who left Emin Pasha in January 1886 & was nearly a year reaching the coast, having arrived at Cairo only about two months

January–March 1887

ago. Stanley was accompanied by the missing interpreter, his German servant, Bonny the Hospital Sergeant, who is to accompany the Expedition as
assistant to the doctor, & Dr. Parke who is to be the doctor to the expedition.
He is an army doctor, quite a young man, & has been through the Egyptian
campaigns. He gives dreadfully sad descriptions of the carnage at Abu Klea,
Gakdul and Gubat Wells, & speaks enthusiastically of the firmness and
courage of the men. He, like most people who have been there, speaks of
the marvellous air of the Abyuda desert. We three of the Expedition, Stairs,
Nelson and myself, were at the gangway to receive our Leader, who after
greeting us very cordially introduced us to some of the gentlemen accompanying him. I had a long talk with Dr. Juncker, whom I was surprised to
see looking so well, after having read the descriptions of his careworn
appearance in the papers. He was quite unable to give one any idea as to the
probability of our being in time to rescue Emin Pasha. One can only hope
that we will be successful in our mission & save at least one of those abandoned by the Government. Dr. Juncker has given Stanley copies of his
maps and observations, but his explorations are I think too far north to be
of much use to him. Dr. Juncker is a short man, rather stout, with a very
pleasant face, but there is nothing remarkable in his appearance. He answered
all one's questions with the greatest good nature & seemed pleased to talk
about his travels. He speaks English very well, but with a strong foreign
accent. The usual motley crowd of dirty Arabs crowded on board, selling
cigars, cigarettes, Turkish Delight, figs, oranges & every sort and kind of
thing from a needle to an anchor, whilst a crowd formed round a conjuror
who did tricks upon the deck with a tame rabbit.[1] After waiting for about
half an hour sixty-three Soudanese troops we were taking with us came on
board. They are fine looking men dressed in brown khaki uniforms. They
are of the regular thick-lipped, flat-nosed type of negroes. They have the
thinnest legs I ever saw, but what they lack in calf they make up for in feet.
I never saw such enormous shapeless feet as they have. They very soon
settled themselves on the forward deck. At five we steamed away & were
tremendously cheered by the people from the steam launch as we moved
away down the Gulf of Suez.

The weather now got warmer, and the following day tropical clothes were taken
into wear. Stanley told Stairs to start drilling the Soudanese.

They are all in a very raw state with regard to drill and, as they have to be
taught through an interpreter, it is difficult work to get them into shape. It is
amusing to watch them at drill; they seem to enjoy it all like children &

[1] Evidently the forerunner of the 'guli-guli' man, the conjuror with his baby chicks,
who used to be a well-known figure in the crowds meeting the liners going to and
from India.

69

laugh at each other's awkwardness in the most good humoured way. The encampment on the forward deck is an endless source of amusement to the passengers; it is rather pathetic to watch these negroes, they are so like monkeys in all their movements and gestures. Many of them were in the expedition which started under Lord Wolseley for the relief of Gordon & some of them recognized Dr. Parke, having seen him at Metemmeh [about 100 miles down stream from Khartoum].

On 8 February Stanley started Mounteney off on learning to cipher and decipher the private telegraphic code the expedition was to use. He was glad to be useful, having been idle, he considered, much too long. Among the letters he had received at Suez was 'a very amusing and characteristic one from Lady Eldon'.[1] 'I had a letter of introduction also from Lord Salisbury[2] to Sir John Kirk, the English Consul at Zanzibar. Sir Rowland Blennerhasset[3] very kindly got it for me.'

On 9 February he entered in his diary:

It is delightful talking to Stanley—the conversation of a man who has seen and done so much could hardly fail to be interesting even if he did not possess that wonderful gift of word painting which Stanley has to such a degree— he seems to take you right away from your surroundings and you see the forests and rivers and lakes of Central Africa—he has, too, such a keen sense of the ridiculous which is nuts to an Irishman.

During these days the officers were getting to know each other. Mounteney wrote:

In talking to Stanley one is struck by the firmness with which he grasps an idea, and he explains it so clearly that immediately *il saute aux yeux*. Stairs keeps up drill for a couple of hours a day, it is wonderful how much the Soudanese are improving.

Early on 12 February they awoke to find themselves anchored off Aden. Lying a quarter of a mile away was the British India Steam Navigation Co.'s ship *Oriental* to which they were to tranship for Zanzibar. Barttelot and Jameson came on board and Stanley went ashore to breakfast with the Governor, General Hogg. Later the General visited the ship and was introduced to the officers of the expedition.

He is a fine soldierly looking man with very courteous manners. General Hogg came down on the forward deck to have a look at our Soudanese and thought them a fine looking lot of men. Stairs, Nelson and I then accompanied the Soudanese on board the *Oriental* in a lighter, after saying good- bye to all the passengers who were profuse in their wishes of success to the Expedition and in saying how much they would miss us on board, and a

---

[1] Henrietta Minna, wife of 3rd Earl of Eldon.
[2] 3rd Marquis of, 1830–1903, Prime Minister at the time.
[3] 4th Bart., of Blennerville, Co. Kerry, President of Queen's College, Cork.

variety of other things, which were all nonsense but were pleasant to hear. . .
We said goodbye and began another stage of our journey. The *Oriental*, a
steamer of about 1,000 tons, is not a bad little vessel but the cabins are small
and the accommodation bad and there is a perfect plague of rats and small
red ants, whilst the cockroaches, which abound in great numbers, are almost
as large as mice. The cabins are full of Germans, some going on a journey
of exploration, and others to colonise, so we are pretty well packed. Jameson
is my stable companion in a small cabin. The whole of the fore deck is taken
up by our Soudanese soldiers, twelve Somalis we took on board at Aden
to act as servants and a lot of Arabs going to Zanzibar. The whole place is
like a bazaar and smells horribly of natives, sheep and indifferently cured
fish.

They left Aden at 4.30 p.m. The following day all the members of the expedition
were vaccinated except Mounteney.

The doctor thought me mad and I got chaffed for being eccentric, but all
the same I refused and was firm in my conviction that it is a mistake. I
wonder what the result will be, for Smallpox is very prevalent all over
Africa. *Nous verrons.*

He was lucky.
During the voyage from Aden to Zanzibar they started to study Swahili, the
language spoken by the Zanzibaris who would be the porters of the expedition.
On 19 February they anchored off Lamu. Mounteney went ashore with Nelson,
visited the town, and had a look at a battlefield where in 1845 the troops of Said
Said, Sultan of Zanzibar, had fought the inhabitants of Lamu.

The ground—a narrow strand about 40 yards wide—between the sea
and some high sand hills, was for a distance of about half a mile literally
covered with the skulls and bleaching bones of the men killed in battle. It
was a very grim scene and not a very pleasant introduction to Equatorial
Africa. The Arabs had evidently been cut to pieces by the natives on landing,
for very few bones were seen on the sand hills.

Before sailing the following morning the Captain, Doctor and Jameson went
out shooting early and bagged three brace of red-legged partridges. They saw
several gazelle but could not shoot any. The next morning they arrived at Mombasa,
and Mounteney recorded the fact that Vasco da Gama had fought and defeated the
natives of the island in 1498. Zanzibar was reached on 22 February. Mounteney
describes the place as he found it, the people he met there, and the final preparations
for the expedition.

We anchored opposite the Sultan's new palace, a fine building just about
being finished; it is to be used for receptions only. The Sultan lives close to
it in another large palace, attached to which is a large building in which he
keeps his harem, consisting I believe of 170 wives. The Sultan's Prime

Minister came on board and we were introduced to him; he is a fine looking Arab with rather fine quiet manners. Several people came off to see Stanley, amongst others, Mr Holmwood, the acting English Consul, the Consul, Sir John Kirk, is in England just now.[1] We did not go on shore as we had to tranship to the *Madura*—the vessel which is to take us to the Congo. She is a fine vessel and the cabins 'are all very fine and large' and we each have one to ourselves, which is a blessing. The vessel is like a farmyard with our 60 donkeys, numerous goats and sheep, chickens and ducks. In the afternoon Stairs and I took up the hundred cases in which the powder is to be packed to take to Emin Pasha, to the Sultan's powder magazine about two miles along the sea coast. The magazine is a miserable mud built place with a dirty court in the middle in which two or three old men live and cook their food with a delightful disregard of the danger of lighting a fire with several tons of powder lying within a few yards of them. The country round is very pretty just here and is dotted about by the houses of the merchants who generally live in the country and have their offices only in the town. We got abundance of fruit on board, the finest mangoes and bananas I ever saw, and quantities of very good oranges, pineapples and small tomatoes. In the evening we had dinner on deck which was very pleasant.

February 23rd. We got up at five this morning and started off for the powder magazine to pack the two tons of powder into the small 45 lb. magazines for taking up to Emin Pasha. We took our luncheon and breakfast with us and worked the whole day long with our coats off. We were perfectly black with powder dust, even one's body got black all over through one's clothes. The Captain of the Turquoise, English gun boat, sent off men to help us, and we got the whole finished and got on board before dark. We found Mr Holmwood had invited us all to dinner at the English Consulate the next evening, which invitation Barttelot accepted for us. There are several German men of war in the harbour and their bands sounded very pretty across the water after dinner. One felt so well after the hard day's work—it is the enforced inactivity on board ship which is killing.

February 24th. This morning we went into the town to get a few things and to see the place. It is a wretched town with streets so narrow that it is impossible to drive a carriage through most of them. Most of the houses are mere mud huts thatched with cocoanut leaves, but all the consulates and some of the Arab houses are good, substantial, airy buildings. The Sultan's palaces are large, rather fine buildings, but are fitted up in a trumpery sort of way. He seems to spend his money in a childish sort of fashion; on bad electric lights, lighthouses which are never regularly lighted, clocks which do not go, and bells which ring cracked and untuneful peals. In front of the

[1] Kirk had gone on leave in 1886 prior to retirement; see Introduction above, p. 46.

palace are three large wooden cages in which are a lion and a lioness and a pair of small lynxes. I was surprised to see that most of the houses are roofed with corrugated iron—the heat in this climate from such a roof must be intense. The Sultan is very anxious to make a road along the sea front and there is some sort of a beginning made in front of the palace, but the work is carried on in such a desultory tropical kind of way that I should think there is little chance of its being finished in his time. The houses, as in most Eastern towns, are white and in this bright climate it is very trying to the eyes. Many of the Arab houses have the most beautifully carved doorways. We went and saw the Sultan's stables in which there were a great number of Australian and Arab horses, all of them seemed fairly well looked after— the stables had boarded floors and no stalls, the horses being just tied to posts with coir rope. We went and called on Drummond, the English Vice Consul, where we met a man named Goodrich who was Consul at Nyassa—he is rather a well known man about here and is well liked by the natives. He wanted to come with us but Stanley refused to take him on account of the extra expense. It was quite a sight to see our 620 Zanzibaris coming on board in lighters each containing 50 men. There must have been two thousand, or more of their friends and relations on the beach to see them off and there were dozens of canoes full of men and women paddling backwards and forwards to and from the ship shouting to their friends on board—the ship was a sort of pandemonium. In the evening we all went and dined at the English Consulate, where after dinner we were introduced to Tippu Tib, the king, prince and emperor of slave dealers. Having heard so much about him one was naturally very anxious to see him. Mr Holmwood brought forward and introduced to us a tall Arab dressed in the long white garment which Arabs commonly wear; his beard was slightly grey and there was nothing particular in his appearance to indicate in any way his being a remarkable man. However, we shall have plenty of opportunities of seeing him, as Stanley has persuaded him to come with us on the Expedition, so he and his eighteen wives come on board this evening. It is a wonderful piece of policy Stanley's getting him to come with us for on our arrival at Zanzibar he talked very big about stopping our going to Emin Pasha, so we have as a friend a man who threatened with his fifteen hundred armed slaves, to bar our way. Stanley has also made him governor of Stanley Falls station, the station from which he drove Deane and destroyed. It is a daring policy and reminds one of Gordon's request that he might be allowed to make Sebehr governor of Khartoum. Fortunately, in this case, Stanley has the Belgian and not the English Government to deal with, otherwise we should probably have had Tippu Tib's force to fight, in addition to those tribes who will oppose our passage to Emin. The news of our alliance with Tippu Tib was telegraphed to The Times, so I expect there will be a great excitement about it in England, and the philanthropists of Exeter Hall will be loud in their reproaches of Stanley's disgraceful conduct and will be dubbing him a fiend incarnate!! Tippu Tib will be of the greatest use to Stanley with his enormous knowledge of the country and I expect the prestige of his name will help us in many a difficulty and enable us to march unmolested through districts through which otherwise we should have to fight our way—it will therefore in many ways save great loss of lives and time. It will be amusing to get the English papers after the event is known. The Sultan sent us off a quantity of ice and several baskets of fruit and presented Stanley with a very fine diamond ring and a beautiful sword with a scabbard prettily worked in gold. The ship steamed out this evening and dropped anchor about three miles off the land to prevent desertions and to be ready to start on our voyage to the Congo at daybreak tomorrow morning.

February 25th. At daybreak we left our anchorage and steamed away South for the Cape distant 10 days' run. About an hour after we had started we heard a terrific noise going on forward and a Zanzibari came rushing aft to tell Stanley that the Soudanese and Zanzibaris were fighting. On going forward with Stanley it seemed as if hell itself was let loose—sticks, iron bars, coal and every sort of moveable thing were flying through the air, an indescribable scene of confusion and noise was going on—our men seemed transformed into devils and many were bleeding in their heads and arms. We went about the deck disarming the men and throwing their sticks etc. overboard, several of them were using spears. On seeing Stanley the Soudanese crowded around him, each man screaming out the cause of their quarrel and appealing to him to save them from being killed by the Zanzibaris, whilst the Zanzibaris on the other side, shouted out curses at the Soudanese as being the cause of the fight. Stanley's action in the midst of the babel of noises was theatrical and effective and much amused me. Placing his hand on his breast he told them to look at him and be reassured, he would protect them and see justice done, was he not their chief and protector! The quieting effect on them was wonderful and ordering the Soudanese into a separate place between decks aft, he soon restored order and quiet. The Soudanese were certainly the aggressors, and I was glad to see them get a beating for they are much too big for their boots and they require to be taught manners and have the conceit taken out of them.

Mounteney makes little mention of his part in the affair. But it seems to have impressed Stanley favourably. To quote from *In Darkest Africa*: 'I have been in the company of my officers since I left Aden, and I have been quietly observing them. I will give you a sketch of them as they appear to me now... There is a great deal in Mounteney Jephson, though he is supposed to be effeminate. He is actually fierce when roused, and his face becomes dangerously set and fixed. I noted him during the late battle aboard, and I came near crying out "Bravo, Jephson!" though I had my own stick, "Big as a mast", as the Zanzibaris say, to wield. It was most gallant and plucky. He will be either made or marred if he is with this Expedition long enough.'[1] The diary continues:

February 26th. Today the Chiefs were mustered on the quarter deck and six Chiefs with eighteen men under each, were given to each of us as a company. We also had given us two boys each to act as body servants and gun bearers—their duty is to fetch our tents, make our beds, etc.; they seem nice bright boys. The valiant Tippu Tib was sea sick today and did not appear. His wives have taken up their abode on the after part of quarter deck. Judging from his wives I should say either Tippu Tib is not a good judge of beauty, or that the Arab standard of beauty differs widely from the English—they are all perfectly hideous. Being officer of the day I had a good deal to do between decks, serving out rations and seeing the place cleaned up—the heat was intense.

February 28th. Today I had a slight touch of fever, but it was only very slight and soon passed off. I had a great argument with Stanley. He seemed to think that the only thing worth doing was to succeed, no matter how, in anything you undertook and that success was everything, whilst I contended that failure was sometimes a nobler thing than success—circumstances made it so. I think the argument started on the subject of Gordon's failure at Khartoum. Stanley seems to have no sort of patience with anything which does not succeed. Of course such a feeling is splendid, how could great things be done without a good deal of that feeling, still if one has *only* that feeling it leads to a great deal of injustice and intolerance towards other people who have not been so lucky in succeeding as he has done. He spoke very nicely about religion and how he envied people who still retained their childish faith and belief, how he wished he could have the same implicit faith that he had as a child, but that it was impossible. I can so well sympathise with the feeling for I have so often felt it myself and yet wishing to go back to the old feeling one cannot—evolution seems to be the only possible thing to believe in.

On 1 March they had a hard day's work repacking Remington cartridges. In spite of the heat Mounteney wrote that he felt much better for it. The next day the job was completed, but not before his hands were badly blistered. On 3 March they sailed out of the tropics into a cooler climate, but the weather deteriorated. Mounteney commented very favourably on the willingness of the Zanzibaris where work was concerned; he considered them much superior in this respect to the natives of India. He continued: 'Tippu Tib presented me with a smart pair of Arab sandals today. I suppose I must give him a present in return twice the value

[1] Stanley, *IDA,* I, 73.

of his; Stanley tells me it is the correct etiquette to be observed, in which case I trust I shall not get many presents.' Next day was fresh and cool, but an unpleasant swell necessitated the closing of portholes—'all the smell of the salt fish comes up from the hold and makes one's cabin perfectly unbearable.' The following day a strong head wind, added to the swell, whipped up a heavy sea. 'We are shipping a good deal of water which makes it hard on our poor donkeys on deck which get awfully wet—we improvised clothing by sewing blankets round their bodies.' That night the weather got worse and hatches had to be battened down: '700 men between decks and no air.' But the next morning, 6 March, was fine and sunny.

As we passed Port Elizabeth at about twelve o'clock a large sailing vessel with every stick of canvas set sailed out of the bay, it looked very jolly; one felt a longing to be on it instead of this beastly steamer, a sailing ship is so much nicer. It being Sunday, by Stanley's wish I read the service: why he chose me I can't imagine, for I've never done it before.

Two days later, 8 March, he wrote:

At daylight we were off Simons Bay but owing to the fog which came up we were delayed for an hour or two, but the fog soon lifted. It is splendid entering the Bay, the cliffs are so fine and bold looking. We dropped anchor off Simons Town at about half past eight. It is rather a nice looking little place, there are some nice houses close to the sea with very pretty gardens. There is a small dockyard very complete in its way. In the morning I went up to the Post Office with Nelson and found to my surprise that there was a long telegram for me from home, it was dated March 3rd.—I was so glad to get such recent news. In the afternoon several officers who are quartered here came off to see us and the naval officers sent a very civil note begging us to make use of their Club. In the afternoon we all went up to the Club and then went for a long walk right up and over the mountains. It was perfectly delightful being able to get a thorough good long walk. I came off to the ship at about half past six as I had some letters to write, but some of the others stayed and dined at the Club.

March 9th. This morning it was so rough that it was impossible for the coal lighters to come alongside with coal so we were obliged to leave for Cape Town at one o'clock and finish coaling there. Before leaving some of the officers came on board to say good-bye. Lady Hunt Grubbe and her daughters also came on board and went over the ship. They were very much interested in Tippu Tib and Stanley introduced them all to him. They made quite a fuss about him and finally asked for and got his autograph. They also inspected Tippu's wives. When we got outside the Bay we found there was a tremendous sea and a strong wind, half a gale, blowing. At about three we passed close to the Cape of Good Hope. I have been round it twice before but have never seen it and one could not possibly have had a better day to see it for the first time than today. It is a grand bold headland standing far out into the sea from a black iron bound inhospitable looking coast and has a lighthouse on the top. There was a tremendous sea and the breakers were hurling themselves at the foot of the Cape and throwing up the spray against the face of the rock, which looked quite black in the bright sunshine. The water all round was seething and boiling, the wind was piping loud and blowing the spray in sheets from the top of the waves, and huge breakers roared madly against the rocks whilst the Cape stood out grim and unmoved about the roar of the waters. It impressed me very much and made one feel small. Round the Cape on our way up to Cape Town the cliffs were splendid in the evening light. At about seven o'clock we dropped anchor off Cape Town.

March 10th. In the morning we went and breakfasted, Jameson, Nelson and I, at the Royal Hotel. Afterwards we did shopping and hunted the town to get some dogs to take with us. We got two fox and two bull terriers. In the afternoon a crowd of people came on board to see Stanley and the members of the Expedition. Tippu Tib was of course a great attraction, the old man seemed pleased at being made so much of—the ladies insisted on being taken down to the fore cabin to see his wives—they are queer creatures women. The deck was crowded up with people right up to the last moment and we were cheered by the people on the wharf as we steamed out of harbour.

Sailing north towards the Equator the temperature soon mounted again. On 14 March, Mounteney entered:

The other day I asked Stanley about Tippu Tib, what was his origin and how he became so rich and powerful—he gave me the following sketch of his life which I wrote down from memory thinking it interesting, and uncommon. Hamed bin Mahammed commonly called Tippu Tib, or as it is variously pronounced by the natives, Tipo Tib or Tibbu Tib, is an Arab of Zanzibar. He was formerly a small trader in Zanzibar, but having a speculative and adventurous spirit he borrowed £5,000 from an Arab[1] who was the Rothschild of Zanzibar, and equipped a caravan to trade in the interior of Africa, which was then considered by the Arabs to be a sort of Eldorado, a kind of paradise where ivory and slaves were to be had almost for the asking. He was not fortunate in his trading and made very little, but after three or four years of wandering he came to a large and important

---

[1] Mounteney could not remember the name, so left a blank space. Tippu Tib in telling his life story to Heinrich Brode of Zanzibar describes his first big journey into the interior as being financed by 'twenty creditors'; for a later journey, of how he played off against each other the wealthy banyan Ladda Damji and the merchant TariaTopan in order to secure substantial credits (Brode, pp. 12–23, 46–58).

village surrounded by a double stockade in the outer of which he encamped with his wives and 70 followers. The King of the village was rich and owned a large store of ivory. After remaining there some months and finding that he was not doing much in the way of trade and that the King was getting more outrageous in his demands for presents every day, he wished to leave the village and set out again on his search for ivory, but the King being anxious to get his whole stock of cloth and beads, invented pretext after pretext for keeping him there and secretly gave orders to his people to kill him should they find him alone outside the village. Tippu Tib, suspecting no treachery, was walking early one morning outside the village when three of the King's men attacked him with spears. Being unarmed he fled towards his camp pursued by the three men, one of whom flung a spear at him when he was just entering his camp and brought him to his knees. One of his wives happened to be out drawing water and hearing his cries for help ran swiftly into his tent and brought him his gun with which he shot one of the men and the other two seeing the fate of their comrade fled into the jungle. Tippu Tib's men hearing the shot seized their guns and flew to the spot. Seeing their master wounded and hearing of the treachery of the natives they immediately got ready for a fight. Meanwhile the villagers turned out in overwhelming numbers against them armed with spears, but the Arabs, maddened by their treachery, determined to destroy them—they were fearfully outnumbered but they had guns. After fighting for some time with desperate courage and firing the huts as they fought the ground inch by inch, the Arabs at last drove the villagers into the inner stockade and closed them in. Having them all so closely herded together their guns did terrible execution and they soon completely routed the villagers who fled leaving the dead lying in heaps. The King seeing it was all up, shut himself and his wives into his treasure house. Tippu Tib having beheaded him seized his ivory and treasure and after looting the village and taking a number of slaves, he started once more West—a rich man—collecting slaves and ivory as he went from the villages he passed until he had a very large caravan.[1] After travelling some years he came to Manuyema, about which there was a story that many years before its King and Queen had for some unaccountable reason left their country secretly one night taking their only child, a little boy, with them. The villagers sought far and wide for them but had never been able to hear anything of them again. Tippu Tib having heard the story determined to turn it to his own advantage. Having come upon one of the natives he told him that he was the son of their long lost King

[1] Brode recounts this story as having occurred in Itahua, between the south end of Lake Tanganyika and Lake Mweru. The chief was Nsama and the time 1867, or thereabouts. (Brode, pp. 29–36.)

and bid him go and announce to the people that he was coming. The people delighted at the news, turned out en masse to meet him and brought him in triumph to their village, where with one consent they made him King.[1] After safely installing himself he collected all the ivory in the country and taking with him what he had before collected he started off for Zanzibar to sell his enormous booty, having left enough of his followers to look after his interests in Manuyema. Thus after eleven years he returned to Zanzibar and realized over £70,000 for his ivory. It was shortly before he had come to Manuyema that he met and travelled with Stanley who was then on his famous journey "Through the Dark Continent". Since his return to Zanzibar he has settled in Nyangwe, the capital of Manuyema, where he has been growing richer and more powerful, making slaves and collecting ivory, until he has become the richest and most powerful man in that part of Africa. Some time after Stanley had founded the Congo State, Tippu Tib founded a colony on an island just above Stanley Fall station, but during his absence, owing to the interference of the Chief of the Stanley Fall station, there was a collision between the Arabs and the Europeans, and his people destroyed and burnt in the station.[2] Tippu Tib was on his way to Zanzibar when he heard the news of the fight and on arriving at Zanzibar and hearing a large expedition had been organised to start under Stanley for the interior he imagined it was coming to destroy his people. It was then Stanley assured him of the real object of the expedition and persuaded him to lend it his aid and come with us round to the Congo.

On the 15th a Zanzibari died of dysentery, and one of pneumonia the following day. Mounteney found that his baggage was overweight: he had not expected his camp bed and stool to be included in the allowance of 180 lbs. He had to discard several articles to reduce weight. On the 17th he discovered to his annoyance that his saddle had not been sent aboard at Tilbury. On 18 March the sea journey was completed, and the important part of Jephson's diary begins with the disembarkation at Banana Point at the mouth of the Congo.

[1] Tippu Tib's penetration of the Manuyema country and his annexation of Kasongo's territory occurred some years later. His capital was Kasongo, above Nyangwe on the Lualaba, see Introduction above, pp. 35–6.

[2] See Introduction above, p. 37.

CHAPTER 2

BANANA POINT TO STANLEY POOL

18 MARCH–30 APRIL 1887

March 18th. Arrived off Banana Point at 8 this morning, it is a pretty looking fresh place situated on a spit of land running out into the river, it is a good harbour & there is plenty of water for vessels of deep draught. Owing to the cable having broken somewhere off the mouth of the Congo Stanley's telegrams had not arrived & there were no steamers to take us up to Mataddi. It was a bad look out as it meant a delay of some days. However Stanley went ashore & saw the people at the Dutchhouse & arranged with them for one of their steamers to take 900 men & some cargo up to Mataddi whilst from the English house he got the Albuquerque, from the Portuguese the Serpa Pinto & the Heron from the Congo Free State. These vessels will all start tomorrow except the Heron which will start the day after tomorrow with Barttelot & I on board bringing up the rear. It is a very fortunate ending to what appeared to be the first hitch in the arrangements for the Expedition. Several men came off this morning & at dinner we had Messrs Dennet & Cobden Phillips, the latter being the Philosopher of the lower Congo & a well known character—& Messrs La Fontaine & Gray from the Dutch house. For men who had been so long in the place they seemed to be strangely ignorant of the Upper Congo—that 255 miles of unroaded country seems to be a terrible bar. In the afternoon the Portuguese Consul, Signor Carriolo [Queriolo] came off to see me, he had received a letter from Donna Maria Van Zellar telling him to do what he could for me & she had got the people at the foreign Office to communicate with him telling him to further the Expedition as much as possible.

Stanley does not mention this useful introduction, which led to a Portuguese gunboat, the *Kacongo*, being lent to the expedition. By 22 March, the whole party was assembled at Matadi, at the navigable limit of the lower Congo. Jephson travelled in the *Heron*, while Barttelot brought up the rear with his Sudanese contingent in the *Kacongo*. From Matadi to Stanley Pool the Congo is too broken by rapids for regular navigation, but the iron boat, named the *Advance*, was assembled with a view to ferrying stores over such Congo tributaries as might cross the expedition's path, and for negotiating stretches of the main river. Jephson records the important event:

March 25th. Marched out of camp this morning at about 5 o'clock & after a short march of four miles reached the Umposo river on the other side of which we encamped after crossing in our iron boat. We put her together on the bank & found she was a great success—she carried 60 men easily at a time...

Several days of painful uphill marching, the Zanzibaris 'literally groaning under their loads', took them into the deserted village of Congo La Lemba, where Stanley fell ill—according to his own account in *In Darkest Africa* from overindulgence in guavas. 'One could see by his temper—of which the natives have had some pretty strong evidence—that he was not well', wrote Jephson on 31 March, and later in the same entry: 'One has seen today when he is put out what a temper Stanley has & it is trying at the time & yet I know him to be one of the kindest hearted men possible & I like him extremely—he is most certainly never anything but nice to me & when he answers one shortly I answer as shortly too, perhaps more so—but I'm sure he likes me none the worse for standing up to him.'

Jephson was now to receive his first independent command and the diary records it fully.

April 1 [1887]. I am to march to the Congo, distant about nine miles taking the boat with me—get her put together at the river & go up the river over rapids about 65 miles to South Manyanga where I should take the boat to pieces & march to Lutete a three days march & wait there a day for Stanley & the expedition to arrive. I am very proud of being sent on a nine days trip by myself but am very anxious & nervous about it for it is all quite new to me—but as Stanley thinks I can do it I will do my best to succeed.

April 2nd. Started off with 100 men this morning in pouring rain it was very bad travelling along the wet path under dripping trees or with grass ten feet high on each side of the path which was about a foot wide—it was difficult to get the twelve boat sections along—it is a bad enough task at any time. Mr Richards gave me three men to guide me to the river. The road led through grass plains & we passed a good many villages on the way with their plantations of Manioc maize & ground nuts. The natives hang the dried heads of maize upon poles in front of their huts, for future consumption. At about half past four we came in sight of the Congo lying at our feet about four miles distant. On coming down the hill we had to pass through a large village where I found Walker,[1] whom I had sent on to look after the front & arrange the camp, had stopped & allowed the men to stop & cook rice whilest he collected guavas & other fruit. I found the men scattered about the village & one drunk, whilest their guns were lying about amongst crowds of natives—probably I shall find some of them are stolen. The whole caravan was halted & dispersed & the loads were just thrown down anyhow. It was quite heart breaking to find how hopelessly wanting Walker was in sense of decency & how little one could depend on him. I just swept through

---

[1] John Walker had joined the expedition at the Cape as an engineer.

the village with my small rear guard & drove the men down to the river which we reached just before dark. It is always hard work bringing up the rear & it was just maddening to find ones efforts stultified by the vulgar ignorance of a man who ought to have been a help instead of a hindrance. I made a vow never to work again with one of these middle men who are neither one thing nor the other but either work with people of one's own class or else with the very lower classes with whom one can get on perfectly —our reaching the river that night was imperative & yet this man who perfectly knew it, could have the stupidity & ignorance to stop & do his best to make me fail in reaching Manyanga in time. We found a comfortable place on the river bank to camp in—I of course had to arrange everything, Walker only thinking of his personal comfort.

April 3rd. At half past five I mustered the men & sent back 85 under two chiefs to join Stanley & carry loads whilest I with 8 Zanzibaris & 6 Somalis hurried up the river to Manyanga—distant four days. Having put the boat together & got the 42 loads into her we started off at about half past ten. It was peculiar what a feeling of hatred the river inspires one with. One hates it as if it were a living thing—it is so treacherous & crafty, so overpowering & relentless in its force & overwhelming strength. No two yards of its face are alike—here are whirlpools rushing round with horrid gurgles & there the water eddies up—whilest the river seethes & boils all round you—it is a bad river to navigate. The banks too have a dreary ghostly appearance, black jagged rocks stand out from the banks as if ready to devour anything that came near them & the very Kites & cranes seem to add to the inexpressible dreariness of the scene—it is all like a bad night mare. We heaved the boat over several rapids & worked our way slowly up—one has to cross the river from bank to bank to get out of the way on dangerous water, it is a constant fight a constant strain of watching the treacherous water. The Congo river god is an evil one, I am persuaded. At about 5 we camped on the south bank after having done a hard days work.

April 4th. We started off as usual at half past five. I had slept in the boat that night to see that nothing was taken out of it. We worked our way on over rapids with here & there a stretch of tolerably clear water, though there was a strong current against us all the way. The appearance of the river improved slightly today but it is still bleak & dreary to a degree. Walker was loud in his complaints that I would not stop to give him time to cook food in the middle of the day. We had tinned food & biscuits with us & yet it was not enough for him. This constant grumbling & sulking before natives, some of whom speak English, is very bad form & is most demoralising to them, for if they see a white man grumbling why should they not grumble, a thing they are always ready to do even without any encouragement. The result has been that I have had to deal with a discontented boats crew who were made so by the grumbling of this man who was sent to help me.

April 5th. We have had a bad day of it today. The rapids have been numerous & the progress necessarily slow. We came to one place where the river narrows terribly & flows round at right angles with overwhelming force & rapidity. On each bank are high dreary looking hills coming close down in cliffs to the waters edge—& standing right out into the river is the Castle Rock—a large rock with its face perfectly perpendicular to the water which is of great depth. Round this rock the water whirls with a rush & a roar & it was over this water that the boat had to be hauled. The whole face of the river was churned into foam & ones ears were confused by 'the voice of many waters'. It was a dangerous place to get the boat over but we managed it without any mishap but it took a very long time for the force of the water took the boat from side to side. In the afternoon a thunder-storm came on & drenched us & everything in the boat—I was obliged to stop against the bank till it was ended for we could make no headway against the current together with the storm of wind dead ahead. All the afternoon we pushed on in the soaking rain & encamped at about half past four, on the bank where a bend of the river formed an immense pool—we were all in a wretchedly dripping condition & all depressed & low. There were a great number of hippopotami disporting themselves in the pool & several of them came up quite close to the boat.

April 6th. We started off at half past five & had many weary rapids to haul over. Walker as usual keeping up a strain of grumbling & sulking. I cannot imagine anyone caring two straws for food, so that they had enough to get on with, when there is an object in view & that object is success in what one has undertaken. Walker was actually asleep when we were navi-gating the boat over some rapids this morning. It is hard to get natives to work & be sharp when there is a white man lying idly snoring in the stern sheets. The consequence was we were so slow that I had to keep the men on working till half past six—the last half hour we did was by bright moonlight. The river certainly looks less dreary now & there are people about. At every little causeway of rocks standing out into the river there are men fishing—they chiefly catch a sort of white bait in large quantities in large spoon shaped nets.

April 7th. This morning after navigating several rapids we hoisted our sail as there was a fair wind, & on swinging round a bend of the river we found ourselves in a long reach of water at the head of which stood Manyanga just below some big falls. We arrived at the Station at about 10 o'clock & found Troop, who is going with us on the expedition, was there waiting to send up the rest of the goods to the Pool. My Zanzibaris had not arrived to take the boat loads to Lutete, so there was nothing to do but to take the boat to pieces & wait for their arrival. Even here I had to do most of the work. Throughout the whole of the time I have been with Walker one would suppose that it was I who was paid for working & he who had paid over eleven hundred pounds for the pleasure of coming on the expedition. It is curious that the only two men of the expedition who are paid for their services are the men who take the least interest in their work & do least. This evening I got word from Stanley that I was to send Walker on to Stanleypool to get ready & patch up a broken steamer without delay. I was glad to see the last of him for a time though he did walk off with most of the food & left me nothing to live on for three days but some rice & a little Liebeg's beef tea.

April 8th. My Zanzibaris have not yet come, it is very annoying that I should have toiled to do my part of the agreement & that Stanley should fail to do his—however I can only wait & curb my impatience at being kept waiting as best I can. This afternoon I went out with Durnfeldt the Chief of the Congo State Station to shoot a large crocodile we saw sleeping on a rock in the river, he shot it but it rolled into the river. What a dreadful farce this Congo Free State is—one thing it cannot last much longer, it must come to an end soon.

April 9th. Still no news of my men—it is as well perhaps for I cannot move today. Last night I had a fearful night with cramps & dysentery, & today I cannot leave my bed. It is dreadful, this pain & nausea, one feels that the sight even of food would make one sick & yet I am fainting from having nothing. The lonely feeling of being left alone with nothing but native noises & native smells about one makes ones thoughts turn to home with the feeling of 'shall I ever see it again'. It is miserable, everything looks black & hopeless & useless—what is the good of doing anything, all is vain, all useless—why all this worry of oneself, why all this pushing forward, & the everlasting 'cui bono' repeats itself again & again in one's mind as one tosses backwards & forwards on one's bed trying to find an easy position & finding it nowhere.

April 10th. Today thank heaven I am better & all the gloomy thoughts of yesterday are departing. I got a letter from Stanley who is at Lukungu, he says he will be in Lutete in three days & is sending me my men for the boat, but for some unaccountable reason they have only just arrived (6 P.M.). I shall not be able to start till tomorrow. Stanley will be ahead of me, how I shall catch him up I dont know—it is a great shame to have left me in the lurch like this. I am still as weak as a cat & cannot eat anything, the very thought of food makes me sick.

April 11th. Got up this morning after a real good nights rest & everything seems bright again. I started on the march & had a delightful meal of fresh eggs lovely mellow bananas & tea before I started—this morning I felt fit for anything. Oh the relief it was to turn away from the treacherous river & from that fever stricken place Manyanga—five out of six of my Somalis are down with fever & one of my Zanzibaris—I intend to swear at Stanley for having kept me in that fever stricken place for such an unnecessarily long time. The delight I felt in hurrying along, at again being on the move & pushing forward. My little terrier 'Spot', a very handsome little dog given me by Tippu Tib, seemed to share in my good spirits & danced round me barking & jumping up at me—his absurdities amused me & chimed in with my mood, I felt inclined to run races with him over the grassy hills, but my prestige with my men, where would it be if I gave way to such boyishness before them! And yet I had not really any reason to be in such overflowing spirits, except that I was on the move & well again. The track which, for a wonder, was fairly good led through grassy plains & past one or two large villages, near one of which there was a most absurd grave— the grave of a chief. It was a sort of double mount some 10 ft long & 6 wide stuck all over with gin bottles, of the kind commonly known as 'square face', plates & tins were there in plenty, all stuck in rows, whilest on a narrow ledge to crown all was a row of common blue & white china pint pots. It looked like a sort of Tipsy cake with bottles & plates for almonds—I pre- sume the chief must have been fond of drink! On the road one of my boatmen fell with his load into a dry water course—I thought he was killed from the cramped huddled up position he was lying in when I came up. I poured water over him & whisky down his throat & I rubbed the back of his neck, on which he had fallen, with whisky & managed to bring him round & get him into camp. I camped at about one, on a hill just above the Kumbi Lake—a small, still lake swarming with crocodiles. As I am writing one has a fine view of the surrounding country. On the opposite hill is the Jouani village with its palms & bananas & to the right in the distance is a high hill, crowning which is a huge square rock—it looks exactly like a great Feudal castle with all its towers & turrets—whilest behind one gets a distant view of the hateful Congo & range upon range of hills stretching away into the blue distance. It is all so big & wide & open, & one can breathe—& feel what an atom one is amongst it all. After the heat & stuffiness of Manyanga it is delightful to see it lying eight miles off & hundreds of feet below one & to camp on the brow of a hill & take in great breaths of cool fresh air.

April 12th. I was up at four this morning & got the caravan started by twenty minutes to five—I was anxious to start early for I wanted to do a long march today & as some of the Zanzibaris & five out of the six Somalis were sick, it was as well to get on before the sun grew hot. One of the sick

Somalis had not come into the camp the night before so I sent the only one that was well to bring him on—he has just come in with the news that the sick man died on the way. It gives one a horrid feeling to hear a man with whom one has been working is suddenly dead but one is gradually becoming used to it, for many of our men are already dead & many are sick. It was a cool day & we were able to do the march well & get into camp by twelve. The track is better than it has been yet & the country is getting less barren— or perhaps I am becoming accustomed to its barrenness & notice it less. The track led past a great number of peculiar gorges & a great piece seemed to have been cut out of the hill, leaving a deep valley, the sides of which were almost perpendicular & the bottom two hundred feet below. In these ravines grew a number of trees—they grew so thickly it almost seemed one might leap in safety on to their tops, but their thickness & softness only served to hide the sharpness of the rocks below. There was a very striking kind of tree of the sort I had never seen before. It grew like a palm, with no branches on the stem & at the top were soft green branches growing quite flat like a mimosa & these were litterally encrusted with bright scarlet blossoms, it was one of the handsomest things I have ever seen. In a grassy plain a brace of guinea fowl got up right under my feet, but I had no gun with me. At the bottom of a piece of swampy ground we came to a small stream, on the banks of which were growing quantities of Osmunda Regalis fern—it is the first time I have seen it in the tropics. I camped in a deserted village about two hours march from Lutete called Baza Lutete. After I had been in camp about a couple of hours up came Tippu Tib, in clean white cloths & turban, with his smart gilt sword & light sandals & his servants following him. He nearly embraced me in the effusion of his greeting. I was surprised to learn from him that Stanley & all of them were on the road behind—I imagined he was in front of me & was well pleased to hear to the contrary. After a couple of hours Stanley & the rest of the Expedition came up. I was so glad to see them all again after being away nearly a fortnight—they all seemed pleased to see me too. They had not much news to tell one man had been shot whilest robbing a village & Stairs had to shoot his donkey which had fallen into a ravine & broken its leg—the Soudanese were nearly all sick & had given a great deal of trouble & the Somalis were all sick & so were a good many Zanzibaris. Stanley seemed pleased to find me there with the boat all safe & no serious mishaps to tell him of. In the evening he told me he wanted me to go on again ahead of him with the boat to the Inkisi river three days march off. I am to do it in three rapid marches, whilest he follows more slowly, & get the boat put together on the Inkisi river & have it in readiness to transport the Expedition across. I like being sent on like this, for one feels one is really giving some little help to the Expedition.

I & Barttelot had a long talk with him, in the evening, about the future movements & arrangements of the Expedition. He is still very close about telling us things, but as he very justly says circumstances might compel him to alter his programme & he does not wish to commit himself.

April 13th. Started off this morning before anyone else as I wanted to get my fifty men well ahead of the rest. The road was good though the high grass, about 8 ft high, on either side of the path—soon wetted one to the skin. Just before I got to Lutete a violent thunder storm came on & we arrived in Lutete in rather a pitiable condition. The people at the English Mission made me come in & change & have some breakfast. As the rain was still coming down I went in & had breakfast & then started on—Mr Davis, the Missionary, accompanying me a short distance on the road. He showed me the new mission house he was building & the kiln where he was burning his bricks—it is wonderful having bricks here & is a great improvement on the ordinary houses one has seen out here, which are either of mud or bamboo. The road led through the village of Lutete—which is about a mile from the mission house—the Chief of this village is the biggest chief on this side of the Lower Congo. The village itself is the largest I have yet seen & the most prosperous. It is extremely pretty & cool looking & there are groves of bananas & fields of manioc in plenty. What a lazy, easy, vegetable life the natives seem to lead—everything looks clean & prosperous, however, so I suppose the natives do work. We marched on to the Liassa river—a fair sized river, pretty, but rather swollen with the rains—& camped on the other side, on a bit of high ground above it. Stanley & the Expedition camp at Lutete mission tonight, so I am already well ahead of them.

April 14th. Up early & off in the cool of the morning it was lucky for the day is fearfully hot. The country is certainly getting better it is more wooded & there are the remains of a great many villages—all deserted on account of the policy pursued by the State. We crossed four streams & two small rivers at the last of which, the Ngoma river, I pitched my camp. I was delighted at seeing by some of the streams, about which were jungle, a profusion of Lycopodium Moss. It is of a kind I have not yet seen, it creeps up & over everything in great blue green masses, & it has almost leaves like a fern—it is quite the most beautiful Lycopodium I've ever seen—what wouldn't people give for it at home in their green houses. There were quantities also of Ribbon fern of the description usually grown by florists. After I had been in camp about a couple of hours Casement of the Sanford Expedition[1] came up & camped by me. We bathed & he gave me a very good

[1] The Sanford Exploring Expedition was the only company at this time to enjoy a trading concession on the upper Congo, otherwise reserved to the Free State. It was founded in 1886 by Henry Shelton Sanford, the wealthy American diplomat who had

dinner—he is travelling most comfortably & has a large tent & plenty of servants. It was delightful sitting down to a *real* dinner at a *real* table with a table cloth & dinner napkins & plenty to eat with Burgundy to drink & cocoa & cigarettes after dinner—& this in the middle of the wilds—it will be a long time before I pass such a pleasant evening again. Hearing Stanley was camped within an hours march of me, I determined to make an early start next morning to reach the Inkissi river & get the boat put together so as not to keep the Expedition waiting should he decide to cross it tomorrow.

April 15th. Got up at half past three & got my men started by four—it was moonlight & was pleasant marching. At half past five we got to the Luzardi river—a small rapid river with a very crazy old bridge across it. I saw a beautiful orchid near the river, there were clusters of great pink flowers with yellow centres—it had a very gorgeous effect. My men were going well & we were all in good spirits & I enjoyed the march with my compact little caravan of fifty men. Close by a market I came upon a man tied at the top of a high pole—he had been killed for stealing in the market place—it was a most ghastly object for the body was almost dry & mummified from the effects of the sun. There are certain fixed places—generally a clear space shaded by trees, in which a market is held once a week, & all the villagers from villages round bring their chickens, goats, plantains etc, for sale. Stealing in the open market is considered a heinous offence by the natives. The natives about here have a peculiar method to snaring birds. They put up high poles round any clump of jungle which is a likely place for birds, & pass a rope from pole to pole from which rope they hang running nooses made of fine twine & the birds flying at night become entangled in the nooses & are caught—in the distance these snares look like a

played an important part in Belgian affairs since his appointment in 1861 as United States Minister to Belgium. Sanford (frequently referred to by the courtesy title of 'General') was a delegate to the Brussels Conference of 1876 which created the International African Association, and was later elected a member of the Association's executive committee. Sanford was instrumental in securing recognition of the Congo Free State by the United States in 1884. The company founded settlements at Kinshasa, Matadi and elsewhere, and was the first to launch a trading steamer on Stanley Pool. In 1889 it was merged with the Société Anonyme Belge pour l'Industrie et Commerce du Haut Congo. For a full account of the company's history, *see* J. P. White, 'The Sanford Exploring Expedition', *J. Afr. Hist.* VIII, 2 (1967), 291–302.

At the time of the Emin Pasha Relief Expedition, Roger Casement was in the employment of the Sanford Exploring Expedition. He first visited West Africa in 1884 in a ship of the Elder Dempster Line, for whom he was then working, and took such a liking to the country that he made his career there for a number of years. When Jephson met him in the Congo he was 23 years of age. In 1892 he was appointed to a British official post as Acting Director General of Customs at Bakana, and from then on he filled a number of posts which combined, under different titles and in different towns, consular and 'intelligence' duties.

row of telegraph wires. At about half past eight we got to the Inkissi river—
a river of very considerable size—about the width of the Thames at Windsor
—but with a perfectly irresistable rush of water in it—it was moreover much
swollen by the rains. It is about four miles from the Congo, where we were
to cross, & the river at that point was 600 feet above the Congo—one could
hear the roar of the cataracts in the distance. At half past nine I began to
put the boat together & had her ready & in the water by midday. Stanley
however camped at a deserted village half a mile off & decided not to cross
till tomorrow. It took me the whole afternoon to get a cable across the river
—I managed it in a canoe. Once the rope broke & was swept down the
river & I did not leave off work till dark. There was a thunderstorm in the
night, the rain lasting off & on for about four hours—it came down in
torrents, & streams of water swept through my tent, for I was camped at
the bottom of a hill on the river bank. The unfortunate Zanzibaris were
just swept out of their grass shelters & spent the night huddled together in
a ruined hut. As for me, it was the most uncomfortable night I think I've
ever spent, & sleeping or waking I was haunted by the fear of the river
rising & sweeping the boat down the cataracts—I got up several times in
the night to see that she was all right—fortunately the river did not rise
more than a couple of feet so the boat was all right.

April 16th. Everything was in readiness when the Expedition arrived at
the river this morning, but Stanley on seeing the river & hearing that the
rope had broken once, dared not depend on it, but decided to trust to the
oars—it was a slower but much safer method of crossing. It took us the
whole day to get the Expedition across—I was at the landing place seeing
to the loading of the boat the whole day long, & got nothing to eat but a
handful of dates, I was thankful when it was all done & I & my men were
safe on the other side & the boat securely tied to the shore.[1] I camped close
to the boat, in the jungle—Stanley camped on the high land half a mile off.
In spite of the pouring rain I slept soundly & securely for I was perfectly
tired out by the hard work of the last two days.[2]

[1] Parke gives details of the operation: 'Reveille at 5 a.m. Jephson, who had gone on
ahead to launch the boat, was now ready to portage us across the Inkissi. Our boat
divides into twelve sections; and, plus the equipment, made loads for forty-one men
...Mr Stanley took great personal trouble in the crossing; remaining in the boat
during the whole time, and attending to every detail in the transit of men and goods.
The donkeys were also conveyed in the boat' (Parke, p. 43).

[2] Neither Parke nor Jephson refers to the quarrel described by Stanley: 'During
the ferriage some hot words were exchanged between Salim, son of Massoud, a
brother-in-law of Tippu-Tib, and Mr. Mounteney Jephson, who is the master of boat.
Salim, since he has married a sister of Tippu-Tib, aspires to be beyond censure; his
conceit has made him abominably insolent. At Matadi's he chose to impress his views
most arrogantly on Lieutenant Stairs; and now it is with Mr. Jephson, who briefly

April 17th. This morning at Daylight I began to take the boat to pieces & got it finished & the loads made up by nine o'clock, so I decided to hurry on & catch up Stanley today, though I was not supposed to catch him for three days. At about 12 o'clock I came upon Casement again, he was camping for breakfast beside a cool clear stream. I stopped & had breakfast with him—how I tucked into his oatmeal cakes! After remaining with him about an hour I started on & got into camp at about three o'clock. The country is getting much better & there are more villages to be seen, though all the villages on the road are deserted. We passed stream after stream of clear good water.

April 18th. Left camp this morning at daylight—it was funny being with the whole expedition, it is the first time I have marched with them for 18 days, it is not half so nice as marching with one's own 50 men. The Zanzibaris are going very well now & we got into camp by ten. There were a good many deserted villages on the road some of them must have been very pretty as there were some fine trees. Just before getting into camp we came upon the Congo again & one was struck afresh with its cheerless aspect—our camp is within half a mile of the river. This afternoon I went down to where the Inkalamo[1] river falls into the Congo—it is a beautiful fall one longed to be able to sketch it for it would have made such a pretty sketch—the river leaping in white foaming masses in a series of falls of ten to twelve feet each, from rock to rock, to the Congo which flowed a hundred feet below—a dark evil looking river all broken water & whirlpools, with its shores of black grim looking rocks, with heavy jungle covering the hills beyond. I climbed to a rock jutting out almost into the falls & sat there for over an hour, for I love to hear the roaring sound of water all round me—one seems so alone & away from all the little paltry bothers of the camp, & one thinks ones own thoughts & enjoys looking at the water, whilest gorgeous butterflies circle about one & sometimes even settle upon ones clothes. Stairs, who came with me, was poking about for specimens of gold bearing quartz, but I loved to sit alone & dream—rushing water always has the effect of raising my spirits. I like this life, I like the hard work & the constant moving & pushing forward, & I would not change it's hardships & unpleasantnesses for the ease of civilization. This evening a box of ammunition was found to have been lost on the march, so Stanley had some of the chiefs flogged & put in chains—it was rather an extreme measure but he knows best what to do I suppose—he is certainly fortunate in his treatment of natives. We reach Stanley Pool now in three days, I shall be glad

told him that if he did not mind his own business he would have to toss him into the river. Salim savagely resented this, until Tippu-Tib appeared to ease his choler (Stanley, *IDA*, I, 87–8).   [2] Stanley's Nkalama (*IDA*, I, 88).

when this part of the journey is over & we are clear of the Congo Free State. I picked up a piece of gum copal by the Congo, quantities of it, some pieces as big as my head, almost, had been washed amongst the rocks by the river. There are I believe in places enormous beds of it, but the natives will not dig it up for they believe if they do so there will be no rain—it is most valuable, from it is made the finest copal varnish which is so expensive at home.

April 19th. There was a heavy rainfall at night which continued in the morning & we were not able to leave camp till eight o'clock. At about half past ten we came to the Luila river, a small swift stream but so swollen by the rains that it stopped the expedition & I had to put the boat together. When I had almost finished it Stanley who had been exploring up stream told me there was a much better place above & that I must take the boat to pieces & get her carried to the place & put her together again there. It was very annoying but it could'nt be helped. We cut a path through the jungle & got the whole Expedition there—it was a kind of swamp through which the river ran & at this place was not more than thirty feet broad, but it was very swift & deep. It was three o'clock before the boat was ready & the ropes fixed for dragging her backwards & forwards—it was just dark when the last of the expedition with the donkeys & goats got across. I & my men were therefore obliged to camp for the night in the swamp—I noticed that the ground was covered with a sort of four leafed house leek growing perfectly flat on the ground & in the shape of a cross. Casement came up in the afternoon & being unable to cross with his caravan & heavy loads camped beside me. We sat outside the tents smoking & talking till eleven o'clock & could see Stanley's camp fires about half a mile off on the hillside above us.

April 21st. I woke yesterday after having passed a most uncomfortable night—the smells & mists that rose from the marsh were horrible & I got up feeling as if the damp had got into my bones & that all my limbs were made of lead. However I transported Casement's people & loads for him & got my own people across by seven. Then there was the boat to be taken to pieces & made into loads, all in the hot sun, while my head grew dizzier & my limbs more heavy. I got the boat started & sent the people ahead to catch up Stanley, for I felt I could march but slowly that day. I travelled slowly, each step being painful, & got about half through the march when I came upon Casement who was camping for breakfast in a deserted village. I could go no further for I felt the fever had me & I was fain to lie down in an old hut, whilest Casement got his bed made up & put me on it. For a couple of hours I tossed about in a half sleep dreaming that Stanley was far ahead & that I was struggling to catch him up with the boat & could'nt overtake him. Casement gave me ten grains of quinine & when it got a little cooler put me in a hammock & sent four men to carry me into camp. Stanley became anxious when the boat arrived & the men reported that I was not well. As I did not turn up he sent six chiefs back to fetch me in & they met Casements men on the way & carried me into camp. When I got into camp I was speechless from fever & pain—for the jolting of being carried on a rough track was awful—they undressed me & put me to bed & gave me more quinine. In a few hours the fever left me & I slept quietly to wake this morning feeling well except that I was weak & my legs did'nt seem to belong to me. For the first time I rode my donkey, which carried me splendidly. The road lay through beautiful country & the soil was rich & easy to work. At about eleven we caught a distant view of Stanley Pool lying burried in the trees—the sun was shining on it & it looked lovely. We camped on some high ground about half a mile from the Pool of which we had a lovely view. As we were to remain there some days we cleared about two acres of ground & had the camp made in lines with wide spaces of 10 ft between the huts— the tents were pitched in front.

April 22nd. Today was spent chiefly in improving the camp, making it clear & taking sanitary measures to keep it in good order & clean. In the afternoon all the surrounding chiefs with their wives & near relations began to arrive to pay their respects & bring presents of goats & fowls etc to Bula Matari—as Stanley is called by the natives,—it means the Stone Breaker— the great white chief who founded the State & made alliances & treaties with them. Chief amongst them was Ngeliamah whose village Kintamo lies about half a mile below us. He is a man with whom Stanley formerly had a great deal of trouble & was a long time teaching him to behave.[1] He is a great intriguer & is not even now to be trusted & still would give some trouble but that he has no longer the power to do anything. He really belongs to the other side of the Pool, but some years ago one of the chiefs gave him land for his village & he came over & settled at Kintamo, where by his self assertion & cleverness he has become thoroughly established & is now the richest & nearly the most powerful chief about here. Stanley called me to his tent & introduced me to him & his wife, who was dressed in a bright blue cloth & held a fan. Ngeliamah himself is a man of middle age, very ugly with his hair, or rather wool, dressed into a large chignon at the back of his head, while the front is kept short—most of the natives adopt this hideous fashion about here. He was dressed in an enormous dark blue cloth with a broad red border—it was rather handsome & trailed on the

[1] Stanley's negotiations with Ngeliamah form the key episode in his work for Leopold II in the early days of the Congo Free State. They resulted in the establishment of the State capital of Leopoldville on Stanley Pool, and are fully described in Stanley, *The Congo, and the Founding of its Free State* (London, 1885), *passim*.

ground in a sort of tail—his general appearance, especially when he walked & the tail was in full play was provocative of laughter—in fact to a person unaccustomed to the sight he was a ridiculous figure, a perfect fright. He had a way of constantly seizing Stanley's hand & murmurring the words 'Bula Matari' whilest he regarded Stanley with a sort of semi drunken leer—supposed to be expressive of great love & devotion. One had the feeling that one would like to knock him flat—he is a miserable humbug. Even after he had said good bye, having stayed about two hours in Stanley's tent, & had got a hundred yards out of camp, he rushed back to once more grasp Bula Mataris hand & breathe out afresh his assurances of love & respect for his dear 'blood brother'. I'm sure Stanley must have felt inclined to slap his fat face & send him about his business. Until night Stanleys tent was thronged with neighbouring chiefs, all of whom brought some present—they crowded to pay their respects to the great white chief & to see him after his long absence. It gave one an idea of the power he was & is in the country, his name acts like magic & to be one of Bula Mataris 'sons' means that you will always be treated with consideration by the natives. Stanley dismissed them at last & must have been very weary of sitting listening to them all day—but he had a friendly word for all & never ceased to be courteous to them in spite of the ennui from which he must have suffered.

April 23rd. Today I went down & got the boat put together, it took a good time for I had to do it very carefully & see that everything was tight & secure for the boat will probably be in the water now for the next six weeks or more. I had luncheon with the State people who have their meals all together in a large room. Leopoldville must in Stanley's time have been a pretty place & a great amount of labour must have been expended in making it, as it stands on an artificial plateau made by cutting into the hill-side. Rows of palms planted alternately between mangoes & 'sour sops' line the terrace in front of a long row of huts whilest fifty feet below, about 200 yds distance, is the Pool the space between being filled with groves of bananas & plantains & to the right lie the kitchen gardens & native village of the station. At the waters edge are the blacksmith's forge & carpenters' shops. All this in Stanley's time was kept up perfectly, the plantain groves were cultivated the terrace kept clean, no weeds were to be seen & there was an air of life & labour constantly going on. Today Leopoldville is a different place. It is a mere collection of tumbledown huts—grass grows on the once tidy terraces & chokes up the groves of plantain & pine apple, the blacksmith's forge is roofless, the paths are furrowed by the rain water, rotten doors hang creaking on their rusty hinges, all is neglect & decay. Sounds of life & labour there are none & the Kaffirs & Howzers[1] who belong

---

[1] Hausa soldiers recruited from Northern Nigeria.

to the Station have a half starved appearance & go about their with work a dejected deserted air. It must be galling to Stanley to see the enormous amount of labour he honestly expended in making the place so sinfully wasted & neglected. There seems to have been no idea of repair for years & the whole place has a forlorn appearance & depressing effect. It looked very well in the newspapers, the paragraph 'His Majesty the King of the Belgians has placed his whole flotilla of steamers at the disposal of Mr Stanley, thus the Expedition will be conveyed up river to a point only a few hundred miles from Wadelai'. On our arrival the 'flotilla' was found to consist of one steamer 'The Stanley' capable of holding two hundred men & 500 loads, a whale boat holding 50, & a small steamer, the En Avant, which has no engines & no paddles, capable of holding 85 men. Such a 'flotilla' is but of little use to an Expedition consisting of 800 men & 1000 loads. There are only two other steamers, the 'Peace' capable of holding 50 men & 100 loads belonging to the English Mission, & the Henry Reed, with the same carrying capacities, belonging to the American Baptist Mission. The former has been promised conditionally to Stanley, & the latter has been flatly refused.[1] On our arriving at Leopoldville there was a great scarcity of food in the country, so much so that the State & the Missionaries could hardly find food for their own people. With eight hundred people suddenly brought into the country & our provisions for them at an end, a long stay at Leopoldville meant not only starvation to our people but to the State & Mission people as well. Mr Billington the head of the American Mission knowing all this, & that as soon as our food was done nothing would keep our men from stealing, still persistently refused to let us charter his vessel, though Stanley sent Barttelot & I twice to try & get him to alter his mind— we sat & listened to a lot of pious cant for an hour but always with the same result—a refusal.[2] He was going down to Boma to be married & that was the reason why he could not go in the steamer himself & he said that to let the vessel go in charge of our or the State engineer was more than he dared do on his own responsibility, he had considered the matter 'prayerfully' & had come to this conclusion. Upon this Stanley sent me with some of our Soudanese soldiers to seize the 'Henry Reed' & Barttelot with some more to insist on the missionary giving up the parts of the boilers which had been

[1] Stanley says the *Peace* was available subject to repairs being completed. Barttelot states that Mission headquarters in England had refused permission to loan the boat to Stanley, but that Stanley (with the connivance of the State authorities) had the mail with the letter to this effect in it intercepted and held up until after the Expedition had left with the *Peace*. The *Henry Reed* was eventually secured by being leased by the State authorities and then lent by them to the expedition (Stanley, *IDA*, 1, 90; W. G. Barttelot (ed.), *The life of Edmund Musgrave Barttelot* (London, 1890, 2nd ed.), p. 87).

[2] Stanley's comment: 'Poor Major! Poor Jephson!' (*IDA*, 1, 90).

taken out of the vessel. Mr Leibricht the representative of the State also sent in a request for the Steamer to save the State people from starvation Mr Billington then gave up the Steamer & she was ours for the time being. I suppose about 50 days, for which we are paying £100![1] The Peace has finally been promised to us & a whale boat, the 'Plymouth' belonging to her, and Mr Swinburne the head of the Sandford trading expedition has lent us the 'Florida' a hull without any machinery in her, but she is a large vessel & will hold a good many men & will be towed by the 'Stanley'. Jameson went out in a canoe with some Bangalas & shot a hippopotamus which supplied the camp with food for one day. We had some of the meat which is really not half bad, it is not unlike beef...

Lack of steamers was to hamper the expedition's movements on the upper Congo, necessitating awkward double trips, and causing tension between Stanley and his officers when one or other of them was ordered to stay behind to organize loads while others had the honour of going ahead with the leader. Rose Troup, who, like Jephson, was a volunteer who had subscribed to the expedition funds, was left at Leopoldville to supervise packing while Ward, engaged by Stanley on their arrival in the Congo, was to accompany the advance party. Both Ward and Troup were later left with the unlucky Rear Column at Yambuya.

[1] Stanley's entry for 22 April quotes Jephson as saying, 'I vote we seize the *Henry Reed*', and himself as replying, 'No, my friend Jephson, we must not be rash; we must give Mr. Billington time to consider...' This exchange occurred at a conference between Stanley, Barttelot, Jephson and Monsieur Liebrichts, Governor of Stanley Pool district (Stanley, *IDA*, I, 90–1).

CHAPTER 3

STANLEY POOL TO YAMBUYA

1 MAY–27 JUNE 1887

From Leopoldville on Stanley Pool to what was to become Stanleyville at the foot of Stanley Falls, the upper Congo is navigable for nearly 1000 miles, and Jephson had some leisure to record what he saw.[1]

May 1st [1887]. Today at about ten o'clock we started up river. Stanley & Ward in the Peace carrying 50 men, & having in tow a lighter belonging to the State, carrying 50 men, & the missionary boat Plymouth carrying 35 men. The Henry Reed having Tippu Tibs men numbering 50 and towing the En Avant (a hull) with 50 men, & our boat, the Advance with 35. The Stanley with 168 men, with Stairs, Nelson, Jameson & myself on board, towing the Florida with 168 men & 9 donkeys. There were also 594 loads distributed amongst the steamers. We steamed up to the head of the Pool that day & camped for the night near a good sized village called Kimpoko. There is here an American Missionary station belonging to Bishop Taylor's mission. There are five missionaries in it & they do all their own work, they built their own house made & planted their own garden & depend entirely on themselves—they are very much to be admired—& are in consequence in much better health than most of the Europeans out here who do nothing or next to nothing. Coming up the Pool one got a splendid view of the Dover Cliffs. They are large white cliffs with patches of green on them & are not at all unlike the cliffs of Dover. They are of white sandstone & gleam & glisten in the sun. They are so unlike anything else round them that they have a remarkable appearance & in clear weather catch the eye at once even at a great distance.

May 2nd. The scenery coming up the river is grand & the river for the first time strikes one as being what it is a really fine & grand river I think it must be because there are trees in plenty right down to the waters edge & it gives it a clothed look.

They steamed slowly up the river, the *Stanley* keeping well ahead. They passed Kwamouth on 5 May, reaching M'swarte the same afternoon, where they found Barttelot and Parke with their men. On the way, Jephson had spotted seven new species of butterflies and made a number of observations on the people and the

---

[1] Leopoldville reverted to its old name of Kinshasa in 1966; this was the village out of which Leopoldville grew under Stanley's direction in the early days of the Free State. Stanleyville was renamed Kisangani, also in 1966.

vegetation. Steaming steadily up stream on 7 May, the *Stanley* ran on a rock and was so badly holed that engineers from the *Peace* and the *Henry Reed* had to lend a hand to help with the repairs. In the confusion of the accident Jephson fell overboard '& my watch got wet & has stopped, it is a horrid nuisance for one will miss it frightfully'.

May 9th. We got the holes in the vessel finished at last, but as the cement is a little wet we shall not start till tomorrow. The Peace & Henry Reed however left at about one oclock & will arrive at Bolobo tomorrow afternoon. We hope by starting early to get there too tomorrow, as we steam faster than they do. These delays are serious besides making us behind our time the expense is great. We were calculating the pay of our Zanzibaris today, not inclusive of their food & we found that it amounted to £21 a day. After Stanley left us two natives came on board for protection. A King of this district had died &—as is the usual custom—they were killing a certain number of men in honour of the event—in the present case they were killing fifty. The natives here are hideous & they are so lacking in intelligent looks—they grow a great deal of tobacco & brought down large quantities of it for sale, it is not at all bad but is badly cured & very strong. Jameson & I went out this afternoon & got a good many new butterflies. At about five o'clock we got the cargo & wood on board & had everything ready for an early start tomorrow morning.

May 10th. We had the men on board before daybreak & got started as soon as it was light enough to see our way up river. As we steamed up the river gradually widened out to a breadth of five miles, & was full of small islands amongst which we saw a great number of hippopotami—we counted seventeen on one small sandbank—& a good many spur-winged geese, they are fine large grey birds & when they are flying one sees a good deal of white on their wings. At one o'clock we caught up the Henry Reed & Peace—we shall probably get to Bolobo first after all. My dog is very ill today I think it is internal inflamation, I have done what I can for him, but the poor little beast suffers a great deal.

May 22nd. I got a place on my hand, which after a few days began to fester, it was a sort of blood poisoning for the whole hand & arm swelled up to a great extent causing me the most excruciating pain. I could neither sleep nor eat but lay awake all night in positive torture. I could not have believed such a thing could be so bad, one felt pain from it in one's back & legs—it has pulled me down very much. This is my first attempt at writing but my fingers are so stiff that it is a painful operation. It has been bad now for nearly a fortnight & has kept me from writing up my journal. We arrived at Bolobo on the 10th & were there four days—the boiler of the Peace broke down which delayed us longer there than had been intended. As soon as we arrived we cut wood & dispatched the 'Stanley' down to Kwamouth to bring up Barttelot & Parke together with the Soudanese and Zanzibaris with them—the Stanley returned with them on the third day. Bolobo is a very populous district—in it & the villages round about there are some 20,000 people. It is rather a nice village standing in a hollow near the river & shaded by numbers of palms & plantains. The people are rather fine looking but the men are very ugly & the women positively frightful & have nothing on but the very scantiest of cloths round their loins & even that is drawn as tight as it can be. The men paint themselves—their arms & breast—with white or red paint whilst a broad line of shaded green & white lines, like spectacles, round the eyes, seems to be the favourite kind of face decoration. The men also cultivate very long beards growing from one spot, about the size of a half crown, on their chins. These beards they carefully roll up into a little bunch so that it hangs in a small knot close to the chin. One old fat chief who was smoking a pipe with a stem five & a half feet long came up & made friends with us shaking hands & saying 'Botay' a great many times, 'Botay' literally means 'good' but it is their term of greeting to friends. By & bye he brought up a large calabash of palm wine, 'Molaffo' as the natives call it, & we all sat round with a lot of chiefs & drank it—in my opinion it is very nasty. I asked the chief to show me his beard, which I measured & found was four & a half feet long, he seemed highly delighted when I made a note of it in my note book. The beard consisted of only a few tangled hairs in some places & was encrusted with palm oil & the dirt of ages & my hands were horrible after touching it. All round the villages for miles are great fields of manioc—it is the first place where one has seen real cultivation & decent paths. The natives carry fine spears & have peculiar knives & battle axes. We reformed companies here, Stanley, Stairs, Nelson & myself each taking 85 men and as many guns. Stanley decided to leave Ward & Bonny in charge of 100 men here as he is unable to take them all up to the entrenched camp in the boats—they were both very disgusted at being left but it cant be helped. He has decided on taking the Soudanese on to the entrenched camp & to leave Barttelot & Jameson in command with 100 men under them, whilst he Stairs, Nelson & myself push on to Wadelai.[1] Of course I am delighted at not being left behind. A good many chiefs came down to see Stanley & hold a 'palaver' with him—how these people love talking—if they want to tell Stanley anything that is going on now, they begin right away back from the time when he first came down the river in canoe ten years ago & gradually work up to the present time.

May 27th. I have been prevented from writing up my journal from various reasons. Stanley has put me on board the Henry Reed where everything is

---

[1] See above, pp. 54–5, 57–9, for account of the Rear Column.

most unpleasant & uncomfortable. After leaving Bolobo, on the second day we landed the men in the evening to cut wood as usual. Near the landing place there was a small village. Stairs was ahead with the axemen when some of the Zanzibaris came running back saying the natives were unfriendly & meant to fight them. Stairs therefore thought it advisable to return on board & take some ammunition with him before going off into the bush to cut wood. Meantime the Zanzibaris & Soudanese made a rush into the village looting everything & setting a house on fire. It was all a hoax, the villagers were not unfriendly but were only afraid at seeing so large a force landing, it was however impossible to stop the looting altogether, though we did our best—the villagers all ran away directly they saw the Zanzibaris coming up. Next morning every man had an enormous bundle of loot consisting of food spears chickens etc. Stairs & I stopped each man as he came on board & made him leave what he had stolen—first because the men were packed as closely as possible on board & there would not have been room for it, the vessel would have been overloaded, & secondly we thought if they saw they did not benefit from stealing in a friendly country it would be a lesson to them that it would be useless to do so in future, & we should have no trouble in future. On arriving at Lukolela a village where there is a Baptist Mission & where we were to stop a day to allow the people to buy food some of the men went & complained to Stanley about what Stairs & I had done or rather to put it more exactly—what they said we had done, for of course they denied the stealing & said the food we took away from them was what they had bought. Stanley *apparently* at first believed what they said & it occasioned a scene in which Stanley, to put it mildly, lost his temper & said things which have cast a gloom over everything.[1] After two days steaming

[1] Stanley does not mention this incident in *IDA*, but Barttelot's journal (published after his death) records so serious a quarrel between Stanley on one side and Stairs and Jephson on the other that it is a wonder any of them were on speaking terms again. 'May 20.—The morning of this day was exciting to some of us—at least, for Stairs and Jephson'; then follows an account of the circumstances as told by Jephson, and Barttelot continues: 'Then Stanley turned round to the men, about 150, and spoke Swahili to the effect that the men were to obey them no more; that if they issued any orders to them they were to tie them to trees (referring to Jephson and Stairs), lastly offering to fight Jephson...I was astonished when Stairs and Jephson returned and told me about it, especially in Stairs' case, for no kinder officer to the men, or more zealous or hard-working officer is there in the Expedition, besides being most efficient and capable...On the way I met Parke, who told me that Stanley had called him on to the *Peace*, and opined that we were talking about him; that it was apparent to him that we had formed a compact against him and were tired of the Expedition, and only made a row to get sent back...I then saw Stanley, and told him I was sorry for what had happened, asking to know his wishes concerning Jephson and Stairs, whether they were really dismissed or not. He said they were...I went away, and Jephson and Stairs came over, at my advice, and saw him, and squared it' (Barttelot, pp. 96–8). Parke, on the other hand, makes light of the affair: 'Jephson and Stairs were both

we reached Equator Station, formerly a Station belonging to the State but lately made over to the Sanford trading expedition. Its chief Mr Glave a young fellow known as an energetic worker & good sportsman invited us up to dinner, which invitation we all accepted & took our plates spoons etc with us, for in Central Africa a man has not generally more than enough table things for himself, & perhaps an occasional guest. There is also an English Mission here, the last there is up the river. It was here that Stanley put me on board this boat, the Henry Reed which carries Tippu Tib & all his people, & a few of our own. The natives get more & more ugly they cover themselves with red paint & mark themselves all over with disgusting scars. They have fine spears with beautifully made shafts of a wood not unlike lance wood. Their shields are marvels of basket work. Jameson bought one for fifteen 'Matako' which was really most perfectly made. The ground work was white & the minutest patterns were worked in it in black, it was about 5 ft 9 in long by a foot wide. From Leopoldville pretty well all the way up to Stanley Falls 'matako'—brass rods, value in England about a halfpenny each,—are the current coin of the country. Empty bottles are however greatly in demand amongst the natives here & I believe at Bangalea a white glass brandy bottle is equal in value to forty 'matako'. Chickens here vary in value from three to five 'matako'. Matako at Leopoldville are 12/6 a hundred. The natives use the brass for ornamenting the stocks of their guns, shafts of their spears & the handles of their knives & sticks, whilst their women are decked with bracelets, anklets & necklets of brass these are often so heavy as to occasion boils & sores of all kinds to form underneath them. Some of these brass necklets I have seen weigh over ten pounds. It is a common sight to see women moving laboriously along under the combined weight of all their brass ornaments! The women, clothed with nothing but the scantiest of loin cloths, are the most hideous objects, with their long pendant breasts & colouring of red paint—the women accompanying Tippu Tib—natives of Zanzibar—are quite good looking compared with them. This vessel, 70 ft long with a 10 ft beam, is most uncomfortable. First of all the Captain—Captain Martin, a Dane—is a most unpleasant man & requires an immense amount of keeping in his place, he is a great contrast to Captain Shackleston—also a Dane—the Captain of the Stanley. The En Avant, one of the boats we are towing alongside, is occupied by Tippu Tib & some of his people, whilst the rest of them are on board here. It is impossible to keep these people from overunning everything. There is a small cabin of which Walker—our engineer—& I occupy a small part,

ailing; some feverish language followed, but after further explanation and apology the affair was smoothed over, and never once thought of again by either black or white' (Parke, p. 55).

the rest of it is curtained off & is occupied by some of Tippu Tibs women. They sit there all day long & chew tobacco or sugar cane & spit about the place in the most unpleasant way, & their food, of the most evil smelling sort, badly cured fish etc creates the most horrible smell. The dirt & filth & smells are most disgusting, & to make it worse lice are common & in plenty amongst them. One is obliged to endure it all, for Stanley is so anxious to keep in with Tippu Tib that one can do nothing to make it better for fear of making a row. Alas, I suppose there is another 25 days of it to be endured still, I shall be truly thankful when we reach the place of debarcation on the Arruwimi.[1]

May 28th. The river is enormously broad here & is full of islands, we have not seen the opposite bank for days, but keep along the South bank or thread our way amongst the islands wherever the channel goes, for navigation is difficult & there are many sandbanks. Today we passed a piece of jungle in which there were quantities of huge monkeys, one saw them in long processions leaping from tree to tree, & two great big red fellows sat on a tree at the water's edge and gravely contemplated us, whilst they passed all sorts of unpleasantly personal remarks to each other about us. There are quantities of guinea fowl, grey parrots & huge horn bills, the parrots & hornbills fly about in great numbers the former uttering their shrill cries to each other.

May 29th. For the first time I have noticed the famous orchilla weed. It hangs in great quantities from the high branches of the trees & looks like long grey green lichen, or moss. I have not yet been able to examine it closely, but shall try & get some this afternoon when we go ashore to cut wood. It is used for dyeing & is, I believe, supposed to be very valuable, though I do not know how it is prepared. We camped in the evening on a low swampy island covered with a dense growth of small palms bearing a peculiar kind of fruit upon which numbers of monkeys had been feeding, judging from the quantity of husks which covered the ground. The mosquitos & flies of all sorts were present in such clouds that one was obliged to carry a green bough to beat them off—they settled on one everywhere biting through ones clothes & thick stockings with a viciousness such as I have never before experienced—up to this time we have had wonderfully few mosquitos except during the few days I was on the lower Congo in the boat. In the night some of the Wangwana[2] set fire to a palm tree & this quickly spread amongst the others. The fire raging amongst the mass of dry sear branches had a splendid effect from the river the sparks soaring to a great

[1] Jephson had taken Parke's place in the *Henry Reed*: 'I am delighted at the change, but poor Jephson's olfactory and optic nerves will be ruined by having to sleep downstairs' (Parke, p. 56).   [2] Men from Zanzibar.

height. I had to get all the men out to stop it from spreading to the steamer. The captain was very nervous & wanted to put out into the river, but I assured him it was all right & finally I got it put out.

May 30th. Early this morning as we steamed along, the river became more & more populous with canoes, whilest on the North bank could be seen miles of banana plantations with huts dotted about amongst them— this was the beginning of the settlement of the Bangalas, the finest & most powerful of the tribes on the Congo, it was they who fought Stanley with such ferocity on his voyage of discovery down the river in 1877, & an account of them & the fight is given in his book 'Through the dark Continent'. The ease with which they manage their canoes is wonderful & the swiftness with which they make them travel is astonishing. A small canoe with three boys in it easily kept up with the steamers, & a large canoe with 10 or twelve men paddling passed all the steamers & sped on ahead of us to carry the news of our arrival to the State Station. On our arrival at the Station salutes were fired from the Krupp guns in honour of Stanley. The four white men, Belgians, came down to the bank to meet us & were astonished to hear of the object of the expedition having heard nothing of it before our arrival. This station, the last of the Congo Free State Stations, is, compared to the other stations, a good one, but that is not saying much, still there are signs of cultivation & care about it which are refreshing after the neglect & decay of the other stations. In the evening we all went up and dined at the Station— of which Mons Beart is the chief—& after dinner Stanley made an amusing little speech apropos of our seeing civilization for the last time for many months to come & finally proposed the health of the King of the Belgians.[1]

Early on the 31st Barttelot left in the *Henry Reed* to escort Tippu Tib to Stanley Falls, the seat of his newly instituted governorship; thence he was to make his way to the point on the Aruwimi river where Stanley had decided to build an entrenched camp for the Rear Column to occupy until the stores came up from Leopoldville. Next day the rest of the party left for the junction of Aruwimi where they would continue eastward by the lesser river to the tryst at Yambuya.

June 1st [1887]. The night has been rainy & the downpour of rain is persistent. The Wangwana arrived on board in a wretched plight but soon cheered up & made themselves quite comfortable—they are a wonderfully cheery people. The rain continued all day till about four when we stopped to cut wood for the engines. The island we stopped at was one large swamp covered by a dense mass of trees, palms, creepers & undergrowth. The smell

---

[1] 'This place was now a very large and prosperous settlement. There was a garrison of sixty men and two Krupps for defence. Bricks were made of excellent quality; 40,000 had already been manufactured. The establishment was in every way very creditable to Central Africa...Among the good qualities of Bangala, there is a never-failing supply of food' (Stanley, *IDA*, p. 105).

of dank mud & decaying vegetation was sickening, whilest one took in malaria at every breath.[1] In the evening I had an unpleasant touch of fever which was only what might be expected. Another Somali died the day before yesterday, this is two out of the thirteen who joined us at Aden, they are all in a wretched state of health & are very emaciated, they seem to be able to stand neither the climate nor food.

June 2nd. The forests we passed today are rich in orchilla weed, every other tree being covered with it, I cannot understand, if it is as valuable as Stanley says, how it is it is not collected & sent down for exportation—this country is, I see, marked in the maps as a gum copal district, but I have as yet seen no signs of it in the jungles. These Wangwana, some of them, work splendidly if they are well disciplined. Last night I had ten axemen out—to see these men at work, cutting up a long tree we had felled, was splendid. They were cutting it in lengths of two feet & as they stood in a row they all brought down their axes in time to a song they were singing, in which 'Congo M'to' came in very often. The chips flew as the axes came down, whilest they sang at the tops of their voices—their singing was not unpleasing at a little distance. Another Soudanese died of malaria. A Soudanese who has been sick for a long time died this evening—the weak men are gradually dying off, but the mortality has been small & we have lost very few comparatively.

The voyage from Bangala to Basoko on the Aruwimi was, on the whole, uneventful. Jephson was in the *Stanley* and they lost sight of the *Peace* among the islands in the twelve-mile-wide river, as they threaded their way from the south to the north bank. They camped at night in swampy, unhealthy sites, and by day Jephson studied both the natural scene and the strangely accoutred and painted villagers who appeared on the banks.

June 6th. Started off very early this morning as soon as it was light enough to steam. It is most intricate navigation threading one's way amongst the numberless islands, some of the channels being very shallow. At about twelve oclock we sighted Upoto, a long series of straggling villages situated on the slope of a line of hills—the first high & open land we have seen for some days, it was a relief to see it after the low swamps & dull jungle covered flats to which we have been accustomed for the last fortnight. There were no signs of the 'Peace', but as we approached the village we observed an unusual stir going on & soon the natives came running down to the shore all armed with spears & shields, shouting at the tops of their voices & by menacing gestures forbidding us to land. We however brought the vessel alongside the beach & having with us a Zanzibari who could speak the

---

[1] 'Malaria'—'bad air'; the mosquito had not yet been identified as the cause of the disease.

language sent him forward a few paces to talk with the natives. It was most amusing to see the gestures of innocence & friendship he made & to hear the soothing tones of his voice as he told the frightened natives we came only to buy food & not to steal or do any harm. Finally one of the natives came out alone to the distance of about twenty yards from our man & they held a long conversation together, the result of which was that the native said he would go to the chief & tell him the object of our visit. After a delay of something near an hour, during which time we could see the natives peering at us from the bushes on all sides, the man came back to say that if our chief would make 'blood brotherhood' with him we might land & buy goods & his people should not molest us, meanwhile if our people stayed on board, his men should bring us food & we should pay for it fairly, in earnest of our honest intentions. Little by little the natives approached & offered their chickens, manioc maize etc to our men, who paid for everything they got, & finally when the old chief appeared—trembling with fear—the performance of blood brotherhood was gone through by Stairs & the chief, & confidence was established & our men were allowed to land & buy food, of which there is abundance here. The ceremony of blood brotherhood is practised all over Central Africa. A small puncture is made on the arm of each of the proposed brothers until the blood flows, the two parts are then rubbed together so that the blood of each is mixed, whilst the men round chant a kind of song which exhorts the two brothers to be true to each other etc & the compact is generally sealed by a large jar or calabash of palm wine being drunk by the newly made brothers & by all the chiefs standing round. Little by little the natives mixed with us freely & brought down quantities of food & soon the women appeared loaded with manioc, chickens, palm oil, etc for sale. It was amusing to see the men who so short a time ago were all fire, shouting & brandishing their shields & spears at us, now bringing down all sorts of food & shyly offering it for sale. After waiting an hour or so to see that our people behaved themselves & that all was well, we went up the hills to cut wood for the steamer. There were a great number of small villages close together—they extended inland to a good distance. I was cutting wood near one small village & the natives all crowded round to see us & were greatly pleased & astonished at seeing our big cross-cut saws at work. In the afternoon the 'Peace' came up, they had been back to look for us & Stanley was very angry at the delay. The men here are finely built but are covered with tattooing, they paint themselves red & wear tall caps made of monkey or wild cat skin with the tails hanging down behind whilest the top is garnished with feathers. They wear very scanty & very dirty grass cloths round their loins—the women are absolutely naked, not a vestige of anything on most of them except a necklace of human or crocodile teeth.

These people are cannibals & have their teeth filed—I suppose to enable them to eat meat better—they string the teeth of the people they eat together & wear them as ornaments. I bought a necklace to send to Kerry Supple but I don't know if it will ever reach him. The shields & some of the spears are fine, the former having beautiful patterns in black & white. Gum Copal is found in quantities, judging from the amount of it one saw in the native huts. There is abundance of food here of all sorts & very cheap. One noticed, chickens, goats, bananas, plantains, eggs, manioc, chiquanga, palm butter, sugar cane, green Indian corn native spinach & a peculiar kind of salt made from burning grass. Matakos are still good money here, but cowries are beginning to be fashionable. Some of the earthen jars are well made & one saw nicely carved wooden scoops & manioc pounders, stools & wooden pillows. There were also small iron bells, not unlike sheep bells. The whole shore of the river was covered with empty oyster shells, oysters are evidently found in quantities here...

June 9th. There are great numbers of black, & red monkeys in the jungles, they look jolly leaping from tree to tree, they are very large & have enormously long tails. There are a great many villages, a regular series of them; as soon as you are clear of one you come on another, all are more or less friendly...

June 10th. Villages still line the banks, the natives all look much the same, though no doubt their tribal marks are different, but that one cannot see from the deck of the steamer. We camped this evening on a splendid grassy plain it was delightful to get into the open after the everlasting jungle & swamp—even the Wangwana felt the change & were delighted at camping once more in an open place. Even when one is out on the river one feels closed in & oppressed by the jungles all round & would give anything to get a distant view of the country, anything to be able to see through the dense curtain of trees that shut in everything, till one almost feels a difficulty in breathing—of course it is fancy but the feeling is nevertheless a strong one. This evening the grass caught fire near where we had been out cutting wood. The fire spread & swept down on the camp & we had to go & put it out—it was a fine sight as it swept crackling along with the flames leaping up to a great height.

June 11th. In the morning we passed close to a large village over a mile long which had been burnt & looted in the night, some of the huts were still burning...I have heard from Stanley this evening that he stopped to enquire about the burning of the village & learned from some of the natives amongst the ruins, that it was done by the people of the next village, with whom they were at war. We passed the village a few miles up river—it was one of the largest & most prosperous villages we have yet seen. It was situated very prettily & stood on a high bank twenty feet above the river, embowered in green cool plantain groves, whilest plantations of manioc & Indian corn waved behind it, there were great numbers of canoes on the river & a general air of plenty & prosperity about it. Some of the natives still had on their war paint & feathers—ugly under any circumstances, they look perfectly demoniacal in their red & white paint. Later on in the day we passed a smaller village whose people hid themselves as we approached, but it was amusing to see how valiant they became when we were passed, they rushed down to the waters edge brandishing their spears & knives shouting at us with contemptuous gestures—several of them turned their backs on us & slapped a certain part, in token of their contempt for us, a gesture not uncommon to the London 'cad' when he wishes to show his contempt for anyone!...

June 12th. We are to arrive at Basoko, at the mouth of the Aruwimi today. At one of the villages we passed the natives appeared to have the most enormous ears sticking straight out from their heads, they could hardly have been real ears for they were huge, but we were not close enough to see what it was they had on. It is curious lower down, where there are numerous buffaloes, the people do their hair like buffaloe's horns—here, where elephants are everywhere, one sees people with ears like elephants. I wonder whether the things really have any connection, at any rate the coincidence is curious. This afternoon we arrived at the mouth of the Aruwimi & ascended it as far as Basoko, opposite which we landed on the other side of the river to cut wood. Hundreds of canoes made off at our approach & disappeared up stream, a few however came near the 'Peace', & Baruti, Stanleys servant whom he bought years ago from Tippu Tib & who is a native of Basoko, spoke to the natives & told them who he was. Upon this the natives paddled back to the village & brought Baruti's brothers & sisters. They immediately asked if he had a mark on his arm where a crocodile had bitten him, upon his showing them the mark they were satisfied that he was their long lost brother & a good deal of weeping & kissing resulted. Baruti's father is the present chief of this strong & prosperous village. The people promised to bring over food to sell, but all night we heard the war drums beating which promised badly for our food tomorrow. The confluence of the Aruwimi & Congo is remarkably pretty, one sees up a long stretch of the Congo while at the mouth of the Aruwimi, which is here about a mile wide, are three small islands with fine trees on them, the effect is beautiful, for the banks are fringed with palms & large trees as well. Today my donkey died, it is a very serious thing for I shall now have to tramp on foot across Africa & most of my boots are riding boots which are unpleasant & tiring to walk in. We are now about 1350 miles from the sea & I have had two days riding out of the donkey, it is a dreadful piece of ill luck, just as I shall want him most on these forced marches. Lat of the mouth of the Aruwimi 1° 15 N. Long 24° 12 E.

June 13th. Today no canoes appeared with food, so at eleven oclock we started up stream. We had been out in the morning in small parties cutting wood & five minutes after the steamer left the landing place several natives came down to the waters edge & examined our camping ground. They had evidently been hiding in the grass & bushes watching us. I had wandered away into the jungle far away from the others looking for wood & had only one man with me armed with a Remington, whilst I had my large revolver which takes Winchester cartridges. It was a wonder we were not attacked—however with 15 rounds between us we could have made a good stand against spears. In the afternoon we passed another village & some men in hideous war paint warned us with furious gestures to keep off & as the steamer was almost passed more men appeared & a sort of war dance ensued, in which the contemptuous gesture, I have before mentioned, came in very often—there were many other gestures of contempt which are impossible to record. The river has now narrowed down to about 400 yds in breadth, it is wonderfully pretty & has a fine volume of water in it—the current is rapid & the water the same dark coffee colour as the Congo. We took possession of a small village & camped in it—there were no signs of natives, they had made off into the bush when we landed.

June 14th. Started this morning in a thick fog. I had a nasty touch of fever last night & still feel very bad, for the last three nights I have had a little fever—these slight fevers pull one down tremendously. We passed many large villages all more or less unfriendly. The banks are very high here & the villages, most of them, are in strong positions. Down with fever again in the evening. Just before stopping for the night we passed a huge village called Yambula it was quite three miles long & must have contained 3,000 natives. We camped on the site of an abandoned village—the bank was 20 feet high & rose almost sheer from the river, it was a regular climb for the men to get to the top. The Aruwimi is a really beautiful river, it is not too large to see both banks distinctly.

June 15th. We are I believe to reach the point of debarkation near the rapids today. With the exception of a delay of two hours to cut wood we steamed all day & arrived just below the falls, or rather rapids, as it was getting dark. On the south bank of the river was the large village, or succession of villages, called Yambuya, but we camped on the north bank & Stanley proposed having a palaver there tomorrow, apropos of being allowed to make the entrenched camp near & getting food for the men.

June 16th. Early this morning the 'Peace' steamed across the river & had a long palaver with the natives, we remained with steam up ready to cross if necessary—the signal that the natives were hostile was to be one long whistle from the 'Peace', we were then to cross the river & I was to land with my 85 men & extend them along the village, but Stanley had given me strict injunctions not to fire unless the natives actually attacked us. After about an hour & a half of waiting we heard the signal & crossed the river & I climed up a high bank about 40 ft high with my men. I extended them along the village but no natives were to be seen. Stairs & Nelson's men followed mine & formed a long line up the village & as no one appeared we took possession & housed our men in the huts. The natives had taken every bit of food with them & we only found pots & tools etc. in the houses. We pitched our tents & Stanley pitched his on the highest bit of ground in the village which he at once decided should be the site of the entrenched camp. In the afternoon Stairs & I got a zigzag road down to the river cut out & most of the men we put to cut down the bush all about the camp for 150 yards or so to prevent the natives from creeping up close to the village & surprising us. In the evening Stanley called us all together & told us what work we were to do tomorrow & gave us an idea of his plans. We shall remain here seven days to wait for Tippu Tib's men to come up & to make the entrenched camp. The huts here are quite different to any I have yet seen, they have high conical shaped huts roofed with the broad leaves of a plant which grows in great quantities in the jungle. The floors are earth raised a foot or so from the ground & the door ways are tiny & rounded at the top— they look like overgrown beehives with high pitched roofs.

June 17th. We were all hard at work today getting things in trim. Nelson cutting a road through the jungle, Stairs clearing the jungle round the camp, Parke exploring the position of villages & manioc fields all round, & I out cutting fire wood for the steamers. I was out all day getting wood for an immense quantity is wanted—we were cutting it in a manioc field acres & acres big, one could see no limit to it, the men who are left here should certainly not starve, for the begining of the manioc is not more than three minutes from the camp. A few natives came in today & sold food, we are still hoping they will come in in larger numbers by & bye with food to sell. We have come to our last goat & after that is finished I do'nt know what will happen. Large numbers of natives were seen crossing the river to this side this morning, it is supposed they are some of the natives belonging to this place who fled when we came. Baruti Stanley's boy, & a man & boy from the 'Stanley' ran away last night—it is thought they have gone down river in canoes to Basoko. Baruti took Stanleys revolver & hunting belt & the 'Stanley's' men stole guns from the steamer. It is most ungrateful of Baruti for when Stanley bought him years ago from Tippu Tib he was a bag of bones & he has trained him & been good to him ever since—but it is useless to expect gratitude from a savage, they *will* return to their old lives whenever they get the chance.[1]

June 18th. Out cutting wood for the steamers again all day, it [is] the most tiring & uninteresting work there is—we are to get ten days wood for them which will take us some days yet. There is the most extraordinary number of butterflies here all of them nearly different to those we have seen on the Congo, Jameson will be able to make a great addition to his collection here—one notices the butterflies in myriads in some places. Stanley wished to make me pay for my donkey again today—as it was put down by Col De Winton, together with the saddle, at £100 in my expenses, & I moreover paid for the saddle myself, it is a great shame his even thinking about it— I hate people doing those kind of things, it gives one a bad taste in one's mouth. The trench for the stockade round the camp is being dug today it will be a very strong place when it is finished.

June 19th. Still out cutting wood all day & have at last got enough for the 'Stanley', thank goodness, but we have still two small steamers to cut for, after that we can give undivided attention to fortifying the camp. I have been cutting wood for the last three days in the manioc fields in a different part every day & still I can find no limit to the field, it must be enormous, it is a great thing having it so near, for our people can feed themselves without the least trouble. As to us we have come to the end of our meat now & shall have to do without any, our salt also has run out, we certainly do have the most sickening food—one feels a perfect pig when one thinks of having good food again—the food question is terrible in Equatorial Africa. An old woman was brought in yesterday—she pretended that she thought it was all her people's fault that we took the village, she said they behaved very stupidly & badly, but that she would bring them to reason & fetch some of them in with her today. Stanley gave her presents & sent her away, but as he said she was an inimitable actress & took him in completely, for neither she nor the people turned up today—of course she was only a spy.

June 20th. The 'Stanley' left this morning. She will arrive at Leopoldville in twelve days from now—we took 46 days coming up stream, a slight difference. At the wood still; one is getting awfully sick of it, we have had such a dose of it for the last seven weeks. No meat today.

June 21st. Still out cutting wood for the steamers all day. This morning a native came in & proposed to Stanley that he should send over five Zanzibaris to the natives as hostages & the chief would then make blood brotherhood & peace should be concluded. Stanley of course promptly

[1] It was Baruti who was left to fend for himself by Bonny at Liverpool Street station at the outset of the expedition, see p. 67 above.

refused such a request, for the natives would never keep faith with us & would probably make a big feast off the Zanzibaris.

June 22nd. Wood! Wood! For ever cutting wood at this rate one will soon become a wooden machine. I got my last letters ready to send by the 'Peace' when she goes, it is really quite unsafe to send letters through the 'State' for the officers do not scruple to keep back & open any letters which they think will be interesting to them, & they would be almost certain to open letters sent by the officers of the Expedition for they are very jealous about Englishmen being taken & not the officers of the State through which the Expedition is to start.

June 23rd. Stanley was getting so anxious about the nonappearance of the Henry Reed that he decided on dispatching the 'Peace' with Stairs & 35 men on board to look for her tomorrow, but fortunately late in the afternoon she was sighted coming up the river. Barttelot & his Soudanese arrived all right having taken Tippu Tib & his people up to the Falls—he reports two or three collisions with the natives—one of Tippu Tib's women got her ear cut off. Tippu Tib has decided not to come with us himself but to send 300 men with one of his chiefs to accompany us to Wadelai—the men are to arrive in a few days. Tippu Tib has sent us two magnificent goats so we shall again have meat for a little & before this is finished I hope we shall be off & we shall have a chance of getting some—rice, cold beans & biscuits full of weevils may be nourishing food but they are not very appetising especially without meat or salt. Alexander the Syrian interpreter died today—he has been a very useless person throughout.

June 24th. The last day absolutely of wood cutting, the Henry Reed & Peace leave tomorrow. The natives come in in ones & twos with a few miserable fowls & Plantains but they still seem afraid to come over in any numbers. Jameson will be able to get a very good collection of birds & a splendid collection of butterflies here the latter are perfectly exquisite & so varied.

June 25th. The steamers left this morning & took the last of my letters I shall not be able to send any more now for months & months. Stanley promised the captain & engineer of the Stanley a present of £50 each when they returned in the Stanley with the rest of the men & loads from Bolobo & Leopoldville. I got the whole camp cleaned up this morning the place was in a horrid mess the Wangwana are not a cleanly people & just throw their refuse a few feet from their huts—the smell of one of our camps after three or fours days is—even with the care that is taken—is horribly strong . . . Stanley is leaving 45 Soudanese & 100 Zanzibaris as a garrison—they have in all 80 guns & Barttelot & Jameson have 4 beside. I got the boat out of the water this morning—it is wonderful how well she has travelled, the gutta percha between the sections is perfectly dry & in good preservation—this after being 50 days in the water is very good—it is well that it is so for Stanley was saying that in the journey to Wadelai she will save us 20 days march.

June 26th. Spent the morning in getting the boat into loads the oars, mast, bottom boards etc had all to be weighed & made up into 60 lbs loads. In the afternoon Stanley gave me the job of making a platform 9 ft square & 8 ft high with the sides defended so that 10 men can be stationed on it & can have a long look out & pot the savages in perfect security.

June 27th. Got on with & finished the platform today, it is a spendly strong place & is the admired of all beholders. It is very strong being supported by trees cut into 12 ft lengths & put 4 ft into the ground. Meanwhile the stockade is being got on with but is not quite finished, Jameson & Barttelot will be able to finish it in a couple of days. Tomorrow we start off on our march to Wadelai or rather to the Albert Nyanza. Stanley has sent up the order book with the orders for the march, I copy it as it will be interesting, also the letter of instructions to Barttelot & Jameson to regulate their movements.[1] Nelson & Jameson have been busy the last three days doing up & arranging loads & allotting provisions—Stanley certainly has a head on his shoulders it shows itself in everything even in all the little minutiae of loads, provisions etc—the European provisions are miserably inadequate, for instance an ordinary jar of salt has to last four men 6 weeks & tea sugar coffee & milk are on the same starvation scale. Today a chief came over & made blood brotherhood with Barttelot. This time an incision was made in the arms of each, & each sucked the blood of the other & then rubbed some blood on each others neck, a chicken was then killed & the blood strewed about & amid the chanting of the few assembled men the bond was complete. The chief at once asked to be allowed to come over & get manioc from the fields for his people, but this request was refused unless a present of a goat & some chickens was brought. We rearranged companies today; we each Stanley, Stairs, Nelson & myself have companies of 85 men each armed with Remingtons, we of course each have a Winchester repeating rifle & about 20 of Stanley's men have them as well. Stairs is down with fever & it is doubtful if he will be able to go tomorrow—it will be a great loss if he isnt for, after Stanley, he is the most valuable man in the expedition.

[1] No such copy is included in the diary.

CHAPTER 4

YAMBUYA TO PANGA FALLS

June 28th. This morning at about half past nine we got under weigh but took a long time getting everything 'en train'. The camp looked quite deserted & melancholy as we marched out, & Barttelot & Jameson felt very disconsolate at the prospect of their six months stay there with no prospect of anything to eat but rice & manioc. The men were in splendid spirits— Murabo, my chief, was a sight to behold in a gay handkerchief-turban, orange and green jacket, red shirt & blue loin cloth, he had a gorgeous appearance marching at the rear of my company. My boatmen—the best men I have—had painted their faces with red camwood & one of them, Ferhani, who was got up in the most extraordinary fashion & had a fillet made of shells round his head, executed a sort of war dance at an imaginary native in the bush, he didn't know a bit how to handle his gun & had he fired it in the position he was holding it, he would certainly have been knocked over. The men were all cheering at the prospect of the march but the difficulties they encountered with their loads on the path soon cooled them down. The jungle path, which was very narrow & bad, led up & down through ravines & streams in an ENE course along the South bank of the Aruwimi & in the course of the march we passed three splendid rapids where the river came down with a rush. At intervals along the path we got views of splendid reaches of water—it is a very fine looking river & widened to a breadth of $\frac{3}{4}$ of a mile as we left the camp behind. It was certainly very bad going & in some places the men carrying high loads had to go down on their knees to avoid the creepers which hung in tangled masses above the path—the natives had tried to hide the road by cutting intersecting paths & in some places had stuck small poisoned wooden needles in the path to lame our men—the boat was soon left behind for the men had the greatest difficulty in getting it on at all, every fallen tree & bush catching in it. At about half past four we heard the guns going ahead & knew that a fight of some sort was going on. The boat got on so slowly that we were benighted & did not get into camp till half past nine—fortunately there was a moon, but it was quite dark in the jungle & I had to go ahead & examine the trees with matches for Stanley's blazings to find the right road for there were many intersecting paths. As we approached the camp we heard the angry cries of the natives who had retired to an island a little way down the river. Soon we came to a village which had been burnt & was still burning & amongst the huts was a native who had been caught in the fire & the heat had burst his skull, it was a horrible sight—after passing through the village we came to another round which Stanley had built a boma with brushwood & was camping for the night. From him we heard that when the advance guard with himself at the head came up to the village the people appeared to be friendly but soon about 500 of them approached with menacing gestures & a spear & a couple of arrows wounded two of our men—Stanley then loosed off the 20 guns at them & they fled down the river in canoes, the guns raked the canoes, Stanley reckons there being 30 killed & numbers wounded. The huts were of a high conical shape & I slept very comfortably on a bed of dried palm leaves. I was sorry I had not been in the front to have seen the fight. The arrows were the smallest I have ever seen, they were very thin & only a foot long & feathered with a piece of palm leaf—the bows are on the same diminutive scale, made of cane 18 inches long with a bit of rattan for a bow string. The arrows were however poisoned & double barbed & would make a bad wound enough. The spears were magnificent. They had broad flanged heads quite 2 ft 6 in long sharp as knives & the hafts were bound & ornamented with brass & beautifully carved. Stairs being still bad was carried in a hammock.

June 29th. We got off at daylight without the attack Stanley apprehended being made. The road, whose general direction was SE, led first through large, half wild manioc fields, large trunks of fallen trees lay scattered in all directions across our path & made the travelling slow. Soon we struck the jungle again & came on a native path which led through a deep swamp ¼ mile long intersected by small streams. The unfortunate donkeys floundered about hopelessly & arrived at the other side exhausted & perfectly black. The donkey boys were often up to their waists in thin, black, unwholesome smelling mud. To add to the unpleasantness a perfect multitude of ants devoured one. I managed to get over it by swinging myself by the many creepers from island to island of firm soil. At about 10 we got across the swamp & stopped in a small clearing to get some coffee made & something to eat. At eleven we started on again & at about 12 arrived at a deserted village in which Stanley decided to camp, as the people were very tired after yesterday's march—we had only marched about 3½ miles today. There are numbers of villages all round whose people have all deserted them on our approach, after having stuck the paths full of poisoned spikes and broadened them near the villages so that they could see down them & not be taken by surprise. The men managed to get plenty of sugar cane, manioc, plantains & gourds in the surrounding villages. Stairs is still being carried and is very much pulled down. Parke is also down with fever—I with a little, but not much. In passing through the swamp this morning our men & the donkeys stirred up the mud & decaying vegetation which emitted a very unpleasant smell, one felt as if one was drinking in malaria, one could taste it at every breath one took—I am sure it is the cause of Parke's & my fever. I took 20 quinine & arsenic pills to try & drive it away. I have found this a most valuable medicine. Sir Francis De Winton recommended me to take it with me & it has been very useful to me on the Congo for checking malarial fever. It is very jolly stopping in the middle of the day for after making the boma round the village I have had plenty of time to get a good bath, & write up my diary. I got a splendid hut & had a bed again of dried leaves.

June 30th. This morning Stairs seems free of fever but is terribly pulled down & weak & has still to be carried. The road, whose general direction was E by N led through half cleared jungle with dense undergrowth, & was almost blocked in places by fallen trees. The going was very bad, first we came to a long swamp with foetid black mud which delayed us a good deal & then the front guard clearing ahead had a lot of work cutting & still further delayed us. At one place for the distance of about a mile the road got broad & the ground was just like heath land, so soft & springy, the trees met overhead & we marched along in twilight on the soft ground in perfect silence there was not the slightest sound heard, it had a most soothing effect on one's nerves after the constant noise of the men—the men themselves even seemed to feel it a relief for they were perfectly silent, which is not usual. We soon got into a chain of villages whose people had left them hearing we were in the neighbourhood, they had as usual spiked the paths near the villages. We did not touch the huts, but the Wangwana put a fire stick into every war drum they saw, they delighted in doing it. The shape of the huts changed slightly, instead of the high conical huts being only seen others the shape of a round haystack were mixed among them. The natives had left their beds chairs cooking pots etc just as they were but had cleared out every goat & chicken. The beds were just 5 lengths of cane nailed together & a piece of wood nailed across the end with wooden pegs for a pillow, they were simple but very neatly made & the patterns cut on the pillow were in good taste. To each village there was a look out place in a high tree with steps made of rattan up to it. In the afternoon we came to a shallow stream about 30 yds broad flowing rather rapidly in a Northerly direction over a bottom of snow white sand—the sort of stream one longs to bathe & splash in. After leaving this river behind we noticed the path & trees on one side were much splashed with blood & on getting into camp at half past five we heard from Stanley that when he & the advance guard came to the stream they saw three natives & shot one of them who was throwing a spear, he was hit in the side but though two of the front guard pursued them for some distance along the road they managed to get their wounded companion away & disappeared into the bush. Our camp was in a tiny village with just five huts. In the middle of the night a lot of savages came within a hundred yds of the camp & sang. Their song in the middle of the night sounded very weird, it's tones expressed hate for us, one felt as if the words must be words of hate & fury against us—after a little they went away singing as they went, in the distance their singing sounded sad & pathetic, particularly when one remembered how perfectly impotent the poor people were against us.[1] I am still very feverish. Distance marched today 10 miles.

July 1st [1887]. The road lay, in a general direction E by S, through a dense undergrowth 12 ft high, there were as usual numbers of trees again across the road. After passing through a chain of villages all deserted we came to dense forest jungle in which were trees with straight huge stems like columns with branches growing from the top only. Some of the trees which were blazed emitted a strong smell of garlic. After passing through a long swamp in which I saw a filmy fern growing in profusion—it was exactly like the rare & much prized Trichomanes Radicans, commonly known as the Killarney fern—we came to a shallow stream 20 yds broad flowing N & we again came to a chain of villages—this part is for Africa pretty densely populated. For the last two days we have noticed that the trees in our road have blazings some months old whilst most of the villages have been burnt—this is the work of Tippu Tibs slave & ivory raiders. At noon we got into a real open forest with undergrowth but not much & the trees reaching high & closing the sky from our sight, it was like going into black darkness—it reminded one of the forests one read about as a child, in which Kings sons used to get lost & have all sorts of adventures in robbers castles. After going till four we made a small round boma & camped in the forest. The lay of the land in the forest is nearly level, & may be described as flat. Our scouts went out from camp to a distance of a couple of miles & came upon four natives eating elephant meat who took to their heels as they came in sight. The evening I feel really bad with fever, it has been hanging about me now for three days.

[1] Stanley describes the camp being woken before dawn by horn-blowing and howls, and by a 'Speaker and Parasite' declaiming:

> 'Hey Strangers, where are you going?'
> 'Where are you going?'
> 'This country has no welcome for you.'
> 'No welcome for you.'
> 'All men will be against you.'
> 'Against you!'
> 'And you will surely be slain.'
> 'Surely slain!'   (Stanley, *IDA*, 1, 140.)

July 2nd. Today as we are in a regular forest with no prospect of food ahead Stanley decided to send 170 men back to the nearest manioc fields to load themselves with roots & bring them into camp for the people. 170 men were accordingly sent off at daybreak & returned at half past one with sufficient manioc roots to last the entire people for four days. The rest of the people remained in camp & I was very glad of the rest for I got no sleep in the night from fever & was able to sleep this morning. When the men went to the manioc fields they captured two women two small boys & a little girl & brought them up before Stanley. There was one of Stanley's boys Kassim who knew Basoko & through him Stanley got answers to his questions, he asked them of the people & country but what the answers were Stanley did not tell us. They were perfectly calm & did not seem much frightened— poor creatures I pitied the women who were so ugly & wretched looking, one of them was holding a baby to her poor withered breasts & looked very downcast & anxious. Both women were perfectly naked. As Stanley is going to return this way he has decided on keeping them all & leaving them at their village on the way back in hope that some of the men will pick up their language. At 2 o'clock we started off for a short march of about three miles. I rode Stair's donkey as I was very weak after the fever. We camped at 5 o'clock near some swampy ground in which were marks of rhinoceroses in plenty. The general direction of the march was E.S.E. Stairs getting slowly better but still being carried.

July 3rd. Today we are nearly retracing our steps & are marching in a NNW direction. We soon came into a tolerably clear part of the jungle & struck a broad smooth elephant path—for about half a mile it was as good going as on a turnpike road. The whole forest was crossed & recrossed by elephant tracks they must be here in swarms. Some of the trees are really magnificent I never saw such huge straight stems, it was a pleasure to look up their great grey smooth trunks into the mass of foliage branching out 100 feet above. One, especially, was much larger than any of the others & was an immense height, its head was covered with a profusion of ferns & orchids—it was like a great tower built up. As we came to swampy ground the marks of elephant, rhinocerous, & bush buck became very plain. Parke & I couldn't catch up the front guard so made tea in an old milk tin which we used as a kettle & cooked some manioc in the embers of the fire—it is very good done so & is not unlike baked potatoes. Soon we came to a vast swamp upwards of two miles long through which we floundered for about three hours—it was terrible getting the boat through it. When we got to the end of it we were caught in a thunderstorm, the little slave girl who had nothing on was awfully cold & shivered & looked so wretched I felt almost inclined to give her my waterproof but a wetting after the fever would probably have brought on a really bad fever, & after all what was the value of that poor little life. However I got one of the men to give her a cloth. We were soon benighted, but after groping along we heard two guns fired in the camp ahead to let us know the direction of the path & in about half an hour we came up with the rest of the column—it was then half past seven, so we had been going for 13½ hours, which is rather much considering we have no meat, & what food there is is poor & in small quantities. Everything in camp was drenched—the ground wet, no bed, no food ready—pleasant after a long march. I put down my waterproof sheet & slept on the bare ground—I was so dead tired I managed to sleep well.

July 4th. Started this morning in an almost Northerly direction. At 9 we heard the guns going ahead. When we got up to the front we found we had again struck the Aruwimi. Stanley had seen five canoes loaded with food going down stream & had fired on them, four got away, but one put into the opposite bank & Stanley sat down & kept firing on the canoe to keep the natives from removing the provisions from it. Meanwhile I got the boat put together & Stanley crossed in her & towed the canoe across to us. It contained a goat, native cloth numerous jars & pans & 13 large jars of palm oil, we kept the goat for ourselves & distributed the rest of the things amongst the Wangwana. Stanley then went up the river to explore, whilst we stayed & got the camp ready for the night. It was a blessing to have meat after being without it for 10 days. After all these days marching we are only 15 miles above the camp at Yambuya, we have been coming wrong. The river runs in the direction we want to go so Stanley intends following it tomorrow.

July 5th. Stanley sent me in charge of the boat today to row up river & meet him at his camping place. He sent twenty men with guns & Uledi[1]—the coxwain. After pulling up river for about three miles we came to a series of rapids over which we had to haul the boat with a rope. After passing the rapids we saw a lot of canoes at the bank on the other side of the river & on crossing over & landing we came on a native encampment. The natives had only just arrived for a good many of the canoes, of which there were twelve, we[re] still unloaded. I with 10 men landed & scouted round the encampment, & finding no natives returned to collect the manioc, of which there was a great quantity lying about, just thrown down in a hurry as the boat came up, we also got four chickens. Numerous beds chairs, cooking pots native cloths etc were left behind & as we were collecting these we heard a shot

[1] Uledi was Stanley's coxswain on the great journey across Africa (1874–7) which concluded by boating down the Congo. He was an able and reliable man, despite some unpleasantness towards the end of the earlier expedition when he was caught out stealing beads. (Stanley, *Through the Dark Continent*.)

fired in the jungle. We instantly made off in the direction it came from & found that one of my scouts who had not come in with me had seen two natives running away & had shot them both—I was awfully angry with the man for shooting men who were merely taking the liberty of running away from us in their own forest. One was shot in the side, the bullet entered at the top of the thigh & had come out through his stomach, the main artery was severed & he was fast bleeding to death—the other, an oldish man, had his leg bone broken & would probably recover. Poor old fellow he looked so emaciated & thin & wretched. Both looked at me with doglike eyes, like suffering animals, I felt sickenly sorry for them & awfully choky. It was such a cruel ruthless, unnecessary thing, for neither were armed & both were running away, & here they were lying all huddled up & bleeding to death, all we wanted was the food & that we could take—unjustly enough, though necessary—without shooting them. I left them there, for as soon as we had left their people would find them & do the best they could for the poor fellows. I couldn't get the look in their eyes out of my mind. We took what food we wanted & towed 11 canoes across to the other side of the river, for Stanley wanted them & then landed & waited for Stanley to come up. I sent out three men to see if they could come across him & after an hour & a half they returned saying we were on an island. We accordingly took to the boat again—we had to leave the canoes for they were too heavy for us to tow—& rowed up stream & got into camp at half past 5. Stanley was camped in a large deserted village—the people from whom we took the canoes were probably the inhabitants of the village who had fled on hearing of our being in the neighbourhood. Stanley had marched about 8 miles today.

July 6th. This morning Stanley sent me back in the boat to fetch the big canoe we left yesterday with the others. We started at half past 6 & got back to camp at 8.30. Stanley intends putting loads in it & sending it up river. All the morning we were getting the guns cleaned & started off on the march at one o'clock. Stanley went in the boat & took Stairs with him. I was doing front guard work today so I went ahead of the column with the men clearing the track. The road lay in a NE by E direction by the river bank the whole way. There were several deep creeks to cross & one deep river at which Stanley had stationed the big canoe—it was about 60 ft long & just reached across the river so that we walked across the river on a floating bridge—it is a fine broad deep canoe & made a capital bridge. The road was entirely through jungle. At half past three I came upon Stanley who had landed from the boat, & got the boma made. The butterflies were in the path in clouds they settled all over one even on ones face.

July 7th. Stanley went in the canoe today—he looked very comfortable in his armchair seated in the stern. Parke was front guard & led the way—

the road ran at first by the river & was intersected by streams & creeks—after a bit we left the river to find a ford in a large deep stream & Parke cut the path all wrong so that we wandered about all the afternoon in the manioc fields going in any direction but the right one, & at last at half past five we struck the river again & got up to Stanley & made a hasty camp before dark. The butterflies are still the greatest nuisance & settle all over one. In the morning we passed through a fine stockaded village—the huts were well made & placed with great regularity on each side of a broad street.

July 8th. Stanley again in the canoe—Stairs in the boat. There was no road to start off with & it had all to be cut through dense undergrowth—the front guard left the camp at 6 oclock & the rear guard did not leave till half past nine, the men ahead had so much cutting to do. Nelson was leading today. River running in a NE direction. The butterfly plague continues—I noticed one or two new sorts today. We passed two very large & fine stockaded villages within a few hundred yards of each other, they must have held over a thousand people. There were large groves of plantains all round & a good many in the main street, which gave it a pretty shady green appearance. The men brought away a great many plantains & bananas. Got into camp in the forest at half past four. From the villages one got the most lovely views of the reaches up & down river, which is very beautiful here—the Aruwimi is certainly a beautiful river. In one place in the manioc fields the road led over a series of great mounds of oyster shells, they must have been the accumulation for generations from some village formerly existing near by, they were large shells with particularly pretty green & pink tints in them.

July 9th. Stanley in canoe. Stairs in the boat. I in the front guard. Road good at first & we got to a fine large stockaded village at about 10 o'clock. The road was above the river which looked lovely today. One got beautiful views of long reaches with trees over hanging the water—the Aruwimi strikes one as being so bright & pretty looking after the Congo. At one place the whole of the undergrowth in the jungle was covered by huge spiders webs hanging in great curtains from tree to tree. The webs were peopled by innumerable black & white spotted spiders about the size of an ordinary garden spider—the spiders were in no want of food for the butterfly plague continued today & there were myriads caught in the webs. We passed through large manioc & indian corn clearings, the men walked into the latter pretty considerably. At half past three we camped in a small village for the night. Stairs is now much better & it is now only a question of getting up his strength again. Today we have all of us found small ticks on ourselves they are horribly painful but the idea is the nastiest part about it. The men tell me it is a sort of tick with which elephants get covered, it comes out of the grass & bush. In the morning we had occasion to leave the river as the path stopped & led up a small stream over which we crossed & recrossed. There was not much undergrowth but the trees met overhead & we walked along in half darkness—it was the wildest looking spot. The stream wound about, flowing over a bed of white sand, great moss grown trunks lay across it, whilst the roots of fallen trees upreared themselves to a great height & over hung the path, everything was covered with moss or ferns, there was a deep silence & in the half light one half expected to see some supernatural fairy sitting on a stone dangling her feet in the clear stream— it was so exactly like the pictures in fairy tales.

July 10th. This morning I was rear guard & as the road was bad to start off with the rear of the column was some time in getting off. Murabo, my chief, amused himself & the men by putting a huge earthen crock he found in the village on a fire one of the men had lit in the middle of the main street. He put all sorts of things in the pot & hung clean eggshells & every sort of thing round the fire, & dressing himself in plantain leaves began a sort of war dance with a spear, I couldn't understand the words of his song, but it caused the men great amusement. He is a queer fellow & gets into violent rages out of which he slides into laughter with marvellous rapidity & ease. After travelling along the river till ten oclock we left it & went inland on account of there being no path. We passed through great numbers of villages —all deserted—& Parke who was leading led us again most erratically— some of the chiefs said to Nelson & me 'when either of you two white men lead us we go straight but when the "Doctari" leads us we go round & round'. We struck a broad elephant track which led us into some wild looking places—there were several trees on the track which were evidently the favorite scratching posts of the elephants, for they were quite shiny & greasy from being scratched against. In the afternoon we came upon some of the finest & cleanest looking villages I've yet seen, the huts were beautifully built & each had its canework door way & cane ornaments at the apex of the hut. The river here is perfectly lovely & from the villages one got the most exquisite views of where it came down in rapids among tiny islets & boiled over big boulders below. Some of the men disappeared as we were passing through a village & kept me waiting nearly half an hour, I was furious, but could'nt for the life of me help laughing at the appearance they presented as they came out of the bushes. Their blankets were full of indian corn, they had tied their shirts round the waist & had stuffed them full. Indian corn cobbs were hanging from every available part of them, they were litterally bristling with it—they are real born theives the Zanzibaris & would much rather have to forage for & steal their food than have it given them. I threatened to have them up before Stanley & have them punished & all sorts of things, but in the middle of a furious tirade I couldn't help laughing & let them off eventually. At four o'clock we camped in one of the many villages which line the river bank here. It is opposite a very large rapid over which the boat will have to be hauled tomorrow. There is abundance of vegetable food here for the men—indeed it is one of the reasons why Stanley sticks to the river,[1] for we are not quite going on our right course, plantains, gourds, several kinds of spinach, small native tomatoes peppers & manioc. We have no meat & fill ourselves with manioc fried & native spinach.

July 11th. Today we only marched to the next village half a mile off & camped there for the day. It was a splendid opportunity of getting ones clothes washed & dried. Last night one of the native women we had captured & taken with us ran away & a little girl as well—the woman left her baby behind her strange to say. Stanley had it left in the village saying the natives when they return will find it—poor little thing it looked so happy as we left it sitting by the fire with its hands full of corn cobs—the natives will certainly eat it. We now have only one woman left—she is very hideous, a mass of skin & bone & perfectly naked. The men for the last few days had been bringing me nasty cooked messes of manioc, vegetables or Indian corn, it is very good of them but I can't possibly eat them & it is embarrassing for one does not like to hurt their feelings. The river is flowing now very well for us & goes S of E which will counteract all the Northing we have been making. Yesterday we got another canoe which will carry twenty loads & so relieve the expedition of them—it was in a bad condition & Stanley sent me down to the river to repair it. It took me the whole afternoon to do it, I had to brace it together with rattans, as it was slightly split, caulk several places with native bark cloth & put three patches in her—I've managed however to make her water tight & I think she'll carry very well. Parke went out & shot a few pigeons so we shall have meat of some sort tonight.

July 12th. Today we have done a very good march & the river runs well in our course. We marched through jungle all the morning & stopped for coffee in a village surrounded by Indian corn—the men were able to get a good supply. Stanley came up in the canoe & stopped as well. The canoe I mended yesterday made a good deal of water, but not enough to matter much. It is an amusing sight to see Munia Pembe, one of the chiefs, leading along the native woman we captured. He is always dressed rather well & is rather portly—he moves about with a very important air & has a great

---

[1] 'By the river I could assist the ailing and relieve the strong. The goods could be transported and the feeble conveyed...I felt that if the river ascended as far as $2°$N, it was infinitely preferable to plunging into the centre of the forest' (Stanley, *IDA*, I, 152).

presence. The woman is oldish, nothing but skin & bones, & perfectly naked. Stanley gave her over to him to look after & he seems to think it quite beneath his dignity to have such a job. The old woman goes in front carrying his food & he walks behind holding the rope by which she is tied, he tries to look as if he had nothing whatever to do with her, & he has a sort of expression on his face as if she were a bad smell. I always laugh when I see the pair coming along & the men chaff Munia Pembe tremendously about his old woman. We camped in the jungle at four o'clock—it is very unpleasant after camping in an open village to camp in the damp dark jungle.

July 13th. We started today with a very bad road leading through jungle & swamps—most of the road was elephant tracks & these always lead to swampy ground we were constantly up to our ancles in mud, or had to be carried. Stanley went ahead in the canoe & camped in a village so far ahead that only two thirds of the expedition arrived there, the rest were benighted & had to camp, as best they could in the huts they came to. Nelson & I who were in the rear toiled along hurrying the men up. At about half past five the most furious thunderstorm we have yet experienced burst upon us. The thunder & lightening seemed to be instantanious the rain came down in sheets whilest the wind howled & lashed the trees so that branches were constantly coming down across the path. It was a sight to see the men with their loads crossing a small river. It was almost dark & the flashes of lightening showed the men wading across with the water up to their shoulders & their loads held as high above their heads as possible—some climbing up the opposite bank & some clambering into the river on this side & others in the river staggering to keep their feet, which was a difficult thing to do in the current & deep mud. Nelson & I managed to cross in an old canoe full of water, but we got wet nearly up to our waists. We got the men along in the dark as well as we could picking up loads which men had left in the grass when it got dark—I myself picked up three guns which the men had thrown away, it is fatal to us to loose any guns—& at about eight o'clock came to a small clump of huts, it could'nt be called a village. Here without any fire we had to stop & get the loads put into the huts. We were both so tired we just sat down outside a hut & lent our backs against it & went to sleep wet & cold as we were. My matches were all wet & we could not get any fire to warm us but at about 10 o'clock one of the men got a light by firing a gun into some dry tinder & the men then made large fires round which we sat & tried to dry ourselves & get warm. When the fires were lighted by good luck we discovered a box of provisions which we opened & got a tin of biscuits a tin of meat & some beef tea. We sat at the fire till after twelve & heated our food & got some coffee made—I do'nt think I have ever enjoyed food more for we were awfully cold & had had nothing since half past five in the morning, except some coffee & biscuit at half past ten. We then lay down in one of the huts, they were all very damp, on some wet ammunition boxes for a bed, but did not get much sleep for we were deadly cold & wet & had nothing but our wet mackintoshes to wrap ourselves in. In the early part of the night we could hear the signal guns & bugles going in the camp but they sounded a long way off. We had sent forward three chiefs to try & find their way into the camp & brings us a lantern but they returned a little after twelve saying they could not find their way & that there was a river to cross.

July 14th. At daybreak we were up, & an indescribable confusion of loads, boxes, guns & packages met our eyes when we came out of our huts, all were lying about any how in the wet for men had come in in the night bringing their loads with them attracted by the light of our fires—to make things worse a second thunderstorm came upon us but fortunately did not last long. I went back with ten men as far as the last river to pick up any loads we might have left the night before. It was fortunate we did so for we found our only medicine chest abandoned in the grass. I then went back to our encampment where Nelson was stopping with the loads & we started off for Stanleys camp where we arrived at about nine oclock. It would have been impossible to have attempted the road the night before for it was very bad & winding & we had to cross two small rivers. On arriving in camp we counted over the loads & found that we had lost none—it was quite wonderful. The day was wet & Stanley decided not to march today but to rest the tired people. We spent the morning in patching up two rotten canoes which the natives had left. In the afternoon I had a violent fit of internal cramp, the result of last nights wetting, but I got a dose of brandy & chlorodyne & lay down & slept it off. This is a splendid village, the huts are all conical shaped & are planted close together with here & there a large square left. In the centre of it stands a large open hut in which the natives sit & talk & decide upon their affairs.

July 15th. Left camp this morning with a bad head ache which in an hour developed into a nasty attack of fever—the result of sleeping in my wet clothes. I caught up the Doctor at eleven & he gave me a dose of quinine, he took my temperature which was over 101°—he wanted me to ride or be carried but the very idea of the jolting made my head worse so I preferred going on marching. It was very bad toiling along especially where we emerged from the jungle into open places, the sun was strong. We stopped for the night in a very fine stockaded village—I felt awfully bad & went to bed as soon as it could be made up.

July 16th. Being unable to march this morning I went in the boat. We had hardly left the village before several canoes full of natives shot out from the opposite bank & began to shout at our canoes, Stanley, who was ahead turned & fired a couple of shots at them, which silenced them & sent them flying. All day long we could see canoes ahead crossing & recrossing the river, the natives were very much terrified & hardly seemed to know what to do, we harrassed them all day & Stanley pursued a canoe with four men in it—he shot one of the men & the other jumped ashore & got off. We towed the canoe to the other side of the river with the wounded native in it, but he bled to death before we reached the bank & the men threw him overboard. He had been shot in the thigh. The men then washed the canoe which was covered with blood & we manned & put loads into her. We camped at night in the jungle & a thunderstorm came on & saturated my blankets, one could wring water out of them in the morning, it was very bad for my fever.

July 17th. I was again in the boat today very weak & feeling wretched after the wetting last night, it was raining all the morning so we did not start till late in the morning 12.30. I was in the boat again. We camped in the jungle & I had to sleep in my wet blankets as I could not get them dried.

July 18th. Today will I hope be my last day in the boat & tomorrow I shall be able to march. The river is full of islands & one saw canoes slipping in & out amongst them. Stanley pursued some of them, but they all got away. The people are getting hungry for we have not seen any manioc for three days & they are so improvident that they do not carry much with them. Stanley is very anxious about it for we have not come on any villages today. He stopped & camped at three & sent me over to a village on the other side of the river to get any food I could. I brought back a quantity of Indian corn. We had gone so far that none of the land party reached us but camped in the jungle lower down the river. I had my tent in the boat but nothing else so I slept as I was with a mackintosh over me. I had only a hand full of biscuit & a little beef tea & as the fever had left me I was frightfully hungry.

July 19th. In the morning Stanley went off reconoitring at seven oclock. The land party turned up between 9 & 10 oclock & Stanley came in a few minutes after having struck a village ahead. We got some breakfast & then started off & got in a little after one. I was able to get all my wet things dried in the sun. The men went off after food & struck some manioc fields but they were a long way off. I am looking forward to a good sleep in dry blankets after being without them for three nights—when they have been in the sun they are always much nicer to sleep in the warmth of the sun seems to stay in them much longer than the heat from the fire.

July 20th. This morning after a short march we arrived at a deserted village in which we camped. Opposite was a little island with a village on it & there were villages on the other side. The river ran in a series of rapids here. The men went off, a good many of them to forage for food & brought in quantities of manioc. In the afternoon the 'Mashenzie' (savage) boy we had with us called to some natives in canoes & after a good deal of calling 'senneneh', 'seneneneh' 'sen-nen-nen-nen-nen-neh' they were induced to approach the shore & make blood brotherhood with Uledi, the coxwain, whose hat, a bright red fez they took a great fancy to & finally received as a present. They then brought over twelve fowls which we bought from them for one matako each. It was a great god send getting them. The natives were fine looking men but very wild & savage looking. In the evening it was found that two of the men had not returned—they had been out foraging for food & had got stuck by the natives with spears. They have been repeatedly warned not to go out except in parties, but they take no notice & trust to chance & this is the result.

July 21st. Again we marched a short distance of four miles & camped in a large village. The same natives who had sold us the fowls yesterday came again & brought more. From them we learned that the Arabs have lately cut their way up here & are encamped some way ahead in a strong 'boma'. The river has for the last few days been running in a Northerly direction & Stanley is very anxious to get away from it but hesitates, as it means leaving a country where we can get food, for a jungle in which there is in all probability nothing & where he is certain to lose a lot of men from hunger. We are too far North & shall however be obliged to leave it soon if it continues to run North. I forgot to mention further back, that Tippoo Tib did not keep his promise of sending men with us. He has behaved very faithlessly after his being conducted to his own country at the expense of the expedition. It is only another proof of Arab faithlessness. Not one of his men turned up & we had to start without them. As I am writing the natives are calling across the river to us & are cautiously putting off in canoes but are afraid to come very near even after they have seen that we do no harm to the canoe that has come over. Three more men have not turned up tonight, it is feared they also have been caught by the natives. Stanley spoke to the people & gave an order that no men were to leave the camp on a foraging expedition less than ten in number—he says he has on his former expeditions lost more men in this way than in actual fighting.

July 22nd. The three men returned late last night having followed an unknown track & been benighted. They were all three well flogged & put in chains. Today we did a longish march, the path was fair in the morning but in the afternoon we had to cut every foot through the jungle, it was very tedious & slow work. This morning in passing through a marsh the whole caravan was attacked by hornets. There were two nests of small, long black, waspish looking hornets & some of the men must have shaken the tree to which they were hanging, for the hornets attacked us with the greatest fury & simply routed us, we had to turn back & go round & join the path ahead. I myself got fearfully stung, two stung me on the eye & bunged it up, I had seven or eight on the face & numbers on the back of my neck & in my hair, my hands & arms were also much stung. For about a couple of hours the pain was really horrible, one kept finding hornets in different parts of one's clothes for an hour after. The advance guard came upon some natives picking manioc leaves, they managed to capture a woman with a baby & brought her up to Stanley. She was quite nice looking, though perfectly naked. Stanley was anxious to catch one of the natives to get information from them about the river & tribes living inland—he will probably let the woman go tonight.

July 23rd. Today I was at the head of the column. The road led through jungle, I was some way ahead of all the men & came upon a very neatly made fence about two feet high running from the river into the jungle, there was a small opening left through which the path led. I examined the fence & quite unsuspectingly walked through the opening, & immediately the ground gave way underneath my feet & I fell into a long wedge shaped hole about 8 ft deep, it was so narrow at the bottom that I was completely jammed & could not move without going deeper. I called to the men who came up soon after & pulled me out amid much laughter at my mishap.[1] The natives dig these holes to trap elephants, the small fence being sufficient to lead them up to the trap. The sides of the hole were cut perfectly smooth in the clay & an animal falling into it would be perfectly unable to get out & would probably break its legs in the fall—the natives cover these holes so cleverly that it is quite impossible to tell where they are, but I ought to have suspected something when I saw the fence, however we live & learn. At 9.30 we came to a large village surrounded by a deep shady grove of plantains & amongst the huts we found a poor wretched little thin boy seated on the ground eating manioc, he did not seem the least afraid of us & we left him sitting there. At eleven we came upon Stanley who had landed at a village from the boat & was stopping to have coffee. He had captured another canoe & had found in it the broken end of a sword, which shows that the Arabs have been here, though whether the sword was broken in a fight or whether the natives picked it up of course one cannot tell. In the afternoon the track led inland through a chain of small villages & I had to

[1] Mary Kingsley, travelling in the French Congo a few years later, maintained that her long stout skirt was a great protection when she fell into a similar trap, but there were spikes in hers. Stanley describes Jephson, 'with his usual free, impulsive manner, and with a swinging gait. . . crashing through the jungle, indifferent to his costume, when he suddenly sank out of sight into an elephant pit!' (Stanley, *IDA*, I, 157).

cut my way through dense scrub till I got into an elephant track which led us to the river. Soon we came to some land lying 50 feet above the river & below it was a large grassy flat through which ran a small river which was unfordable at the point we struck it. We had to follow it up to try & find a ford. The elephant tracks were innumerable & led up & down ravines with sides as steep as a house, how the elephants managed to get up & down is extraordinary, in places they had regularly ploughed up the ground with their feet—many of the tracks were only a few hours old. As I was stopping & debating with the men as to whether we could cross the river at a certain point I saw a native with a big head dress of feathers & a boy coming along the track. I shouted & went for him but he doubled & made off as hard as he could with me after him twice I almost had my hand on his shoulder & just missed him, he ran down a steep bank towards the river & turned head over heels & at the same moment my foot caught in a root & I fell close to him, his spear was broken in the fall, but he held on to the blade of it & could easily have stabbed me had he turned, but I fired my revolver at him & he made off across the river. I cut my forehead badly in the fall & the blood almost blinded me so he got away—however he had showed us where the ford was & we were able to cross with the water only up to our knees. When the men came up & saw the blood streaming down my face they thought I was wounded. I don't know where the boy went to, I think he must have hidden in the grass. After a couple of hours hard marching along elephant tracks we came upon Stanley who was camped for the night on a small grassey flat, it was the longest march we had yet made & as it was in the right direction, the river here running ESE, Stanley was very pleased, he told me I had made the two longest marches we have yet done.[1] The savages here are regular cannibals & look like man eaters the way they look at you as if you were meat is very creepy, & they have a peculiar smell about them which is also suggestive of man eating.

[1] 'On the 24th Mr. Jephson led the van of the column and under his guidance we made the astonishing march of seven and a half geographical miles—the column having been compelled to wade through seventeen streams and creeks. During these days Jephson exhibited marvellous vigour. He was in many things an exact duplicate of myself in my younger days, before years and hundreds of fevers had cooled my burning blood. He is exactly of my own height, build and weight and temperament. He is sanguine, confident, and loves hard work. He is simply indefatigable, and whether it is slushy mire or a muddy creek, in he enters, without hesitation, up to his knees, waist, neck or overhead it is all the same. A sybarite, dainty and fastidious in civilization, a traveller and labourer in Africa, he requires to be restrained and counselled for his own sake' (Stanley, *IDA*, I, 157).

There is no knowing at what stage in their acquaintance Stanley wrote this eulogy of Jephson, much at variance with his description of Jephson's character recorded by the latter later in his diary (see p. 229). Perhaps Stanley's lecture on this later occasion was part of the restraint and counsel of which he suggests Jephson stood in need!

July 24th. Today Stairs was leading & we did a very good march along elephant tracks. The banks of the river are very high here & the whole jungle bears signs of numberless elephants, by the innumerable tracks & broken trees, I wish we could stop a day or two & get a shot at them. We crossed today over seventeen small rivers & at one we all had to strip & wade across, the water was up to my neck. We camped in the jungle in a very uncomfortable place. We marched about 9 miles & all in the right direction, Stanley is very pleased at the progress we have made in the last few days.

July 25th. Today as there were so many rapids ahead Stanley ordered me into the big canoe to superintend getting the canoes, of which we have six, over the rapids. After going about half a mile we had to unload the canoes & haul them round a very bad point & after paddling a bit we came to a great number of small rapids through which the canoes had to be got with great care. At about 11 we came to a good sized river & Stanley had the whole expedition transported by the boat & big canoe, it was past one oclock by the time I had got all across. After leaving we soon came upon a long series of rapids some of them very bad, once I thought the big canoe was done for, the 35 boxes of ammunition it contained, besides other sundry boxes & bags would have been a terrible loss. The current drove the big canoe down stream & wedged it between two large boughs of a tree, it was as nearly done for as possible, if the canoe had been the least rotten, it must have gone down. The boat led the way & as they were getting up between the mainland & an island & were hauling themselves up by the boughs they were attacked by a nest of hornets exactly like those which stung me so terribly a few days back. We could see Stanley & all the men in the boat tearing at their hair madly beating themselves with cloths & boughs as if they had gone mad. The hornets began to come down to us 50 yds below so we all sheered off as fast as we could & came up the other side of the river. After hauling up a great number of rapids we arrived at a large village in which we camped for the night. I had had a very hard days work in the canoes & my clothes were torn to pieces. Stanley told me when I got into camp that the hornets had punished him fearfully so we were well out of it in crossing over.

July 26th. In the night a thunderstorm came on & the rain has been falling heavily all day, off & on. We are staying in the village today to let the people get a supply of food for themselves as there is not a village to be seen ahead up river. It is wonderful how the natives clear out from every place before us. Opposite my hut is a large dead bough stuck in the ground & garnished with skulls & bones, some of them are not picked clean, the natives have not eaten all the meat off them—it is not a pleasant idea. The village is several inches deep in clayey mud, churned up by the numbers of our men passing backwards & forwards all day long, it is rather depressing to sit in one's hut & watch the rain & listen to the roar of the rapids below. Some of the natives came over from the other side & examined us carefully in canoes from a distance, they all have the same repulsive looking faces. We tried to make some manioc bread this afternoon but it is a failure— one's food of rice manioc & weevelly biscuits is most nauseous & disagreable.

July 27th. An uneventful march. The road had to be cut through solid jungle but we struck elephant tracks in the afternoon & got along pretty well—we camped early in the afternoon in the jungle.

July 28th. I was leading today & started off with a splendid path expecting to make a long march. The path however ran inland & I had to leave it & cut my way back to the river making use of elephant tracks when they ran in the right direction. The natives thinking we were following the river bank had all gone inland & we came upon several different lots of them—we came upon them before they heard us & had several chases after them for Stanley always gets natives when he can, to get information from them, he puts them in chains for a few days & when he has got all the information he can out of them lets them go. We caught one man & a boy, the former lay down & refused to move, neither arguments & assurances of friendship nor strong pursuasion from a stick could move him, so we had to let him go— I took a very fine knife from him. The boy we brought along & Stanley managed to get quite a lot of information out of him, he was a bright little lad & did not seem the least afraid. From him, & another native Parke captured, he learned that four days march ahead a large tributary joins the Aruimi & runs from the SE out of a large lake,—possibly Muta-Nzigi,[1] if so it will be a great find—it is probably true, as a river is down in Stanley's map at about that point, put in from the report of natives. He also learned that two days march from the river is a great plain with high grass & no tracks. We came on party of six natives who ran when I came up, we were quite close on them & I made sure of catching one, he turned & threw a beautiful spear at me but it hit the bushes & fell close to my feet, I am ashamed to say I fired at him, however it did not matter as I missed him—it was impossible to get a good shot running as he was along a winding path

---

[1] 'Muta Nzige' or 'Luta Nzige' seems to have been a pretty general name for any large lake in Central Africa. Speke first heard of the lake to the west of his own Victoria under this name and gave particulars of its whereabouts to Samuel Baker when the two men met at Gondokoro in 1862. Baker reached this second lake in March 1864 and called it the 'Albert'. The same name, however, was applied to the lake to the south of the Albert, on the other side of the Ruwenzori. Stanley named this lake the Albert Edward (see p. 376 below), after the Prince of Wales, but its current name is simply Lake Edward. There is, in fact, no river flowing out of Lake Albert into the Aruwimi as Jephson was given to believe.

among trees & bushes. Jumah, a lad who was ahead with me, threw his bill hook at one of the men & hit him in the back, the native thought it was a spear & howled as if he was nearly killed & staggered in such a ridiculous way that we both had to stop from laughing & the man disappeared in the bushes. We came across several large paths all leading inland from the river, which is an indication that there are many villages a little way inland, & it bears out the report we got from our captives in the evening. There are no villages on this side ahead but numbers on the other side of the river—our men are getting short of food & we are all looking anxiously for manioc & Indian corn fields. We got into camp in the jungle early having marched nine & a half miles. I have kept the spear as being the first spear ever thrown at me. Poor devils, I pity these savages, but they are such cowards & smell so nasty one cannot look on them as human beings hardly, besides too one would fare badly if one got into their hands, one feels less pity for them too when one knows they would eat you if they got the chance—they all have their teeth filed.

July 29th. We only did a short march of 6 miles today as heavy rain was threatening all the morning. We got into camp at 1.30 & just had time to get the tents up when the flood gates were opened & down came the water, it was too heavy to be called rain. After it was over the natives came over from the other side where there was a very large village & sold us a few chickens & some Indian corn & manioc. At about 5 the rain came down again & lasted all the evening.

July 30th. We remained here today & gave out matakos & cowries to the men to enable them to buy food from the natives when they came over in canoes. It had rained all night & lasted till 9 oclock when the rain ceased, but the day was foggy & damp & we could get nothing dried. It is miserably damp & cheerless in the jungle with the trees dripping & the ground saturated with rain. The natives brought over food in the morning, but wanted ex-horbitant prices for it, so that the people could not get much.[1] In the afternoon Stanley took one of the natives & had him brought up to his tent to get what information he could out of him, upon which the rest of the natives shoved off their canoes & fled with angry cries across the river. The river about here is quite beautiful, it winds about in short sharp curves & the banks are in many places very high & finely wooded. From the native we learned that the name of the Chief of the village was Maguai & that the people & village are called Maguai also. They are the most powerful people about & have driven several peoples from the villages about & destroyed

[1] Stanley's party having arrived first had had the best of the deal here: 'When the land column arrived, prices advanced somewhat owing to the greater demand' (Stanley, *IDA*, I, 161–2).

them. In the evening Stanley went over in the boat to tell the people he was not going to hurt the man & would give him up for three goats, but on the boat approaching the shore she was greeted with such a shower of arrows that Stanley fired on them & knocked over two or three, all the rest ran in terror from the guns which they had never heard before.

July 31st. Today half the expedition went over to Maguai & brought back quantities of manioc from the fields at the back of the village. Nelson followed on the track of some men with goats but did not get them—he came however upon villages with quantities of Indian corn done up in baskets & brought it all into camp—it was good food for the men & the unfortunate donkeys who have lived upon leaves for the last month were given a good feed.

August 1st [1887]. We buried the ivory in the river intending to get it on our return. One of my men died & I buried him much against the will of the other men who said the natives would only dig him up & eat him— they wanted to throw him in the river—for my part I do not see that it matters much whether one is eaten by men or crocodiles.[1] We only did a very short march today & camped in the jungle. I had to report two of my men absent but they came in later on & Stanley gave them 180 each, they had gone away in search of 'm'boga'—which is anything in the shape of vegetables—& had got lost.

Aug. 2nd. Marched through jungle on & on until it was dark without coming up to Stanley & the canoes so we stopped & camped. Fortunately the baggage was all up so we had blankets & could change our clothes which had got wet from crossing streams & from the heavy rain which had fallen in the afternoon. We had a few damp matches with us & I lit a bit of tinder from my flint & steel but the firewood & everything was so wet that we were nearly an hour getting a fire lighted—our agony lest the fire should go out when the matches were finished was ludicrous & I tore up a book & was recklessly extravagant with the leaves & finally we managed to get a fire—to camp in a dripping forest without a fire to sit by or cook one's food is highly unpleasant. We opened a tin of Leibig's beef tea—which is perfectly invaluable out here—& made some soup & got rice cooked & managed fairly well. I rigged up a sort of tent with a boat awning & slept very comfortably in my clothes though it only covered my head & shoulders.

Aug. 3rd. After marching for about half a mile we came upon Stanley's camp, we had fired signal guns the night before & it was extraordinary that being so close he should not have heard & answered them, but the noise in

---

[1] Stanley records his death on 2 August: 'The first death in the advance column... the 36th day of departure from Yambuya, which was a most extraordinary immunity' (Stanley, *IDA*, I, 163).

the camp I suppose prevented his hearing them. We marched on & camped in the jungle opposite a large village whose people cleared out, as usual, when they saw us.

Aug. 4th. I was in the front today & reached Stanley by 12 o'clock. He was camped opposite a village called Panga, which is on a large island below a huge cataract extending right across the river. He had captured twelve goats! This cataract is the largest we have yet seen. A crescent shaped dam of rocks covered with grass & small shrubs extends right across the river & in the middle through a very confined channel the river rushes as through a huge flood gate in a fall of between six & seven feet. It looks very fine from the river, one gets a full view of it from the boat. The great yellow coloured stream rushes down with a roar & hurls itself with a roar against the rocks below & covers the river below with flakes of foam for a distance of a couple of miles. Close below the cataract is Panga a large settlement whose people live to a great extent upon fish. In the morning Stairs two canoes which were lashed together & about 15 boxes of Maxim & Remington ammunition went to the bottom all our cowries, head necklaces, beads & copper wire also went down & 13 rifles. The canoes had been carried down a rapid & struck against a protruding tree some 40 feet from the bank, one canoe with the ammunition was smashed to pieces & the other after turning over & being carried down stream was recovered. Stairs got the canoe tied over the place where the ammunition went down & got a Somali to dive for the boxes. The current was tremendously rapid & the water 12 feet deep so that it was no easy task to get up the boxes, he managed however to get up 5 boxes & 4 guns by giving the Somali a rope when he dived to tie round each box, whilest another rope was fastened round the man's waist to prevent his being swept away. When Stanley heard of the accident he sent me down with the boat to help & we got five more boxes & two more guns. The scenery going up river is perfectly magnificent as one rounds each curve & bend of the stream some fresh beauty delights one, one is never tired of the river but is struck afresh each day by its beauty.

Aug. 4th. Stanley sent me down again today in the boat to try & get up more boxes, but I only managed to get up one gun & two boxes of ammunition, though we were all day long fishing for them, the current was so strong it had swept the boxes into deep water. None of the necklaces etc were recovered which is a very serious loss as we are now without money, with the exception of brass rods which are not accepted as money about here. It is wonderful how ravenously one devours meat after being without it for five weeks, it makes one feel a different person for our fare of plain rice & manioc was quite insufficient to satisfy hungry men at work all day in the open air. The people have had no food except green stuff they pick up in the jungle for the last three days so Stanley distributed eight goats amongst them. Nelson & Parke went out to forage for food but could only find green stuff & plantains, there is no manioc whatever about here.[1]

Aug. 5th. We cut a large broad track today & got the canoes dragged over land for about half a mile & put in the river above the rapids. The boat I took out of the water & carried with 60 men just as she was. In the afternoon I had to patch up & lash my two canoes together. In the middle of the river about a mile above the rapids is a small round island perfectly bare with its banks rising sheer 7 or eight feet from the water & on it is a group of some 15 or 20 huts which cover it entirely, it has a most peculiar appearance & looks like a round fort such as one sees off Portsmouth. There is not a herb of any sort to be seen on it. We captured two women but could not get much information out of them, except that there was another large cataract a day higher up the river.

Aug. 6th. After we had been marching about a couple of hours I heard shouts ahead & on running up found that one of my canoes had been swept against the large branch of a tree sticking out into the river & had been upset. Very fortunately there were no loads in the canoes, but eleven rifles had gone to the bottom. Stanley was close by in the boat & we at once set some men to dive for them, the current was very rapid but as the water was only 6 feet deep we recovered 9 in a couple of hours & then marched on to camp at the foot of the cataract about which the natives had told us.

Aug. 7th. Got a track 12 feet broad cut through the solid jungle for about three quarters of a mile & dragged the canoes over it & got them into the water above the cataract. It was frightfully hard work for the track was most uneven & sharp pointed sticks & branches cut the mens feet badly, I got cut above the ancle by a pointed stick whilest I was superintending the porterage of the boat. In the afternoon when I had got the boat into the upper water Stanley started off in her to explore up river & returned in the evening having captured 8 goats & 5 kids besides a quantity of knives & spears & ivory horns. The kids & three of the goats were given to the men.

Aug. 8th. Short march & camped in the jungle. The country must be swarming with elephants one passes their tracks all day long, in fact since we have left Yambuya we have never marched a day without coming on their tracks.

[1] Jephson dates two entries running 'Aug. 4th', and his Aug. 6th, is Aug. 7th in *IDA*. By Aug. 10th (see next page) the diary and *IDA* are once again in agreement.

CHAPTER 5

PANGA FALLS TO UGARROWWA'S

Aug. 9th. March today through the jungle & came to a small stockaded village, there were no people in it but there were goats & chickens running about. We captured 10 goats—eight of which were given to the men—& several chickens. It is most difficult to catch the goats they run off into the jungle & are very wild.[1] There was only one conical shaped hut in the village all the rest were oblong & had small square yards made of cleft logs of wood in front of them, they looked like large pig styes, only that they were clean & comfortable. Whether these yards are for defensive purposes or merely to make the huts more private one cannot tell; if for the former they were but poor defences.

Aug. 10th. Stanley sent out three foraging parties today to get food for the people who are getting terribly weak from want of food, some of the men are mere walking skeletons & all are suffering from hunger, if this scarcity of food goes on for many days more we shall lose a lot of men. Stairs went ahead & returned having found nothing but he captured an old man & woman, husband & wife who were very communicative—Stanley christened them Ananias & Saphirah—& they promised to lead us to a village the next day where they was plenty of food to be got in the shape of goats. From them we learned that the name of this village is Uteri & that yesterday its people went out to fight another village & killed five of its people, they were returning in the evening triumphant, when they found we had occupied their village. Nelson went across the river & brought back a goat & a few bananas, besides ivory hammers knives & spears. These hammers are made of the small end of the tusk & are used for beating bark into cloth. I went back upon yesterdays track & followed a big path into the country. We came upon a stockaded village which we surprised but we could not get through the stockade quick enough & the natives got away with the goats. We got a large quantity of plantains & vegetable & I loaded up 80 men with them. One of my men got an arrow through his throat but it is not a dangerous wound.[2] I was disgusted with the cowardice of the four men with

---

[1] Parke records: 'One goat is made to supply six of us for two days. I am now mess caterer and have to bear a great deal of grumbling, as I have reduced the rice-ration to half' (Parke, p. 89).

[2] The man died, however, a few days later (Stanley, *IDA*, 1, 169).

him they ran away from one native with a bow & arrows when they were armed with guns—I felt inclined to shoot them. I captured a little girl who did not mind being captured, but was miserable & made a great fuss when her necklace of teeth was taken from her as a curiosity.

Aug. 11th. We started off this morning with the two natives as guides. They turned off at right angles to the river & led us right inland but after marching about 5 hours we came most unexpectedly on the river, it took a sharp curve after leaving the village & we had cut off the corner. We passed through groves of oil palm trees & finally came on a string of four villages the inhabitants of which had got wind of our approach & had fled taking everything with them. After marching about two miles further we halted in the jungle for the night. Stanley was left behind in the boat & canoes as we had cut off the curve & he had 19[1] rapids to pass which made his progress slow. We had the old man & woman up after dinner & learned from them in what direction the food lay & then agreed to send off men in the morning in search of it. Just as we were going to sleep the men of one of the canoes came in saying Stanley was camped about 3 hours down the river.

Aug. 12th. Stairs & Parke started off early with the old woman as guide, & 170 men in search of food. Stanley & the canoes turned up at about nine o'clock & camped for the day. If the men bring back plenty of food Stanley intends to stay here tomorrow to rest the people who are in a very sick & exhausted state from want of food—Stanley reports the rapids below as having been very bad. In the afternoon Stairs & Parke returned with very little food nothing but plantains & green stuff & reported a great scarcity of food, no signs of manioc. We seem quite to have got out of the manioc country & the people live entirely on plantains, apparently, with a few goats & chickens. Coming back from foraging for food one of our men was murdered by another man, there had evidently been a quarrel & the murdered man had been shot through the head. We were unable to detect the murderer.[2]

Aug. 13th. Today I was bad with fever & went in the canoe. At midday we reached a village in which we camped, we captured a woman & she told us the name of the village was Aveysheba.[3] We had not been camped very long when we heard firing going on & on going down to the small river 100 yds from the village we found that the natives had mustered on the other side in fairly large numbers & were shooting a perfect shower of poisoned arrows at our men in the boat some of whom were already hit. We all went down to the stream & fired at the natives wherever we could get a shot, but it was difficult to hit many as they were all firing from the bushes

---

[1] Figure difficult to decipher; could be 12, but 19 more likely.
[2] According to Stanley, it was Engwedde, a Zanzibari (Stanley, *IDA*, I, 170).
[3] Stanley gives Avisibba.

& kept out of sight. Poor Stairs got a poisoned arrow between the ribs & unfortunately it penetrated very far & the end broke off in the wound. After firing for some time the natives retired shouting angrily & carrying away their dead & wounded with them. The doctor hopes to pull Stairs through, but it is bad that the arrow head is still in the wound & he dare not probe for it as it is so near the heart.[1] Two of my men turned up in the evening with 7 goats, they had actually followed the natives alone & had come up with them as they were carrying away their dead with wailing cries & had fired on them & shot two more, the natives thinking we were following them in numbers fled & the two men went on to one of their villages & brought back the goats. Stanley gave me orders to build a 'boma' with brushwood round the village fearing there might be an attack that night. The bows are the most contemptible looking little weapons & yet they are most dangerous & the arrows penetrate very deeply. The bows are only about 2 ft long & the arrows about 18 inches, but the points are thickly encrusted with a black sticky poison. They are feathered with a small triangular shaped bit of leaf inserted in a slit at the end of the arrow—for a distance of 2 inches from the point the arrow is in different places partly cut through, so that the point readily breaks off in the wound, there are no iron tips, the wood is merely sharply pointed. We tried some of them at a saddle & found they penetrated the thick leather saddle flaps & when shot up in the air they went an immense distance. It is a curious sensation being shot at by arrows, one sees & hears nothing but the 'pit, pit, pit' of the arrows as they strike the brushwood round. I have got a sore place on my ancle from the sharp bushes striking it & I fear it will turn into an ulcer. A great number of our men are suffering from deep foul ulcers which come from merely a scratch & penetrate in a few days to the bone.

Aug. 14th. Today Stanley sent out 200 men to forage for food & to burn the villages round. As we were mustering the men the natives again attacked us but we very soon drove them off. We shot one man who came out into the open & I went to look at him. He had a most low, villainous face & looked capable of anything. These bushmen are I should say a very low type of men, their food is poor & that generally means a poor race of men.

[1] 'As the arrow was a poisoned one I regarded suction of the wound as offering the best and only chance of his life; for the point had penetrated much deeper than a caustic, applied externally to the wound, could possibly reach. Acting on the idea, I at once sucked the edges of the wound; till I felt sure that I had extracted the greater part, if not the whole, of the adherent poison. I then dry-cupped—by forming a partial vacuum; washed out my mouth with a weak solution of carbolic acid, and injected the wound with the same, touching the edges finally with lunar caustic. I applied carbolised dressings to the wound and bandaged the whole securely. He was now very faint; and, of course, very anxious; so I gave him half a grain of morphia by hypodermic injection' (Parke, p. 91).

The men brought in very little food nothing but plantains. At night the sky was lit up by the villages they had burned.

Aug. 15th. As we were starting this morning 7 men were reported as not having returned the night before. Stanley decided to wait a few hours & sent Nelson with 50 men to look for them—he brought them in having found them at a short distance from camp & we started off at 12 o'clock with the native woman as guide—I was leading. We passed a dead native in the path about 300 yds from the village, one of our men had shot him the day before. Stanley told me to stop at 2.30 on the river, but the native woman led the way & I went on till nearly 5 oclock & never reached the river. We passed through plantations of the finest plantains I've seen—they are of a yellowish colour inside & are almost like bread when baked & there has been no manioc since Maguai's village the people seem to live entirely on plantains. We passed through three villages close together & surprised the natives who fled to the jungle uttering angry cries. There were a great many chickens in the villages & the men got a good number of them as well as a great many of the big yellow plantains. We passed through the villages & could see the warriors with their feather head dresses disappearing into the jungle as we marched on down a track which I thought would lead to the river. Soon we came upon great wedge shaped holes, many of which were fully twelve feet deep, cut in the paths for purposes of defence. There were some 10 or 12 of them—they were evidently cut with a view to preventing a night attack on the villages. I marched on till 5 oclock & camped in a village. As half the loads did not come in I took some men & made large torches of dried stalks taken from the roofs of the native huts & started off in search of the men, for the thought of the deep holes I had passed made me very nervous & I imagined all sorts of accidents happening to the men & loads. I managed to get all the loads into camp except one or two & got out as far as Nelson & Parke whom I found camping for the night round a large fire they had only tea & plantains to eat, but as they had so many sick men with them they decided to remain where they were & come in in the morning. I got back & had something to eat & went to bed at 12 or so thoroughly worn out & disheartened & depressed at missing Stanley. Baroko one of the men leading heard two guns in the S Easterly direction, they must be signals from Stanley so I hope the river is not far off.

Aug. 16th. Nelson & Parke came in in the morning at about 7 o'clock, I had a good breakfast ready prepared for them & left them to eat it while I started off in the direction in which Baroko had heard the guns—he had heard & answered them again this morning which made us doubly sure we were not far from Stanley. After marching a couple of hours we came on another village & made a rush at the natives who all fled as hard as they could. As we were evidently still far from the river I determined to reach it by as short a road as possible & took a track which led in a Northerly & afterwards a North Westerly direction. Very soon a violent thunderstorm came on which wetted us to the skin & depressed the spirits of all the men. After marching till ten oclock we came on a good sized, deep, rapid river. Baroko & the men leading declared this to be the Aruwimi & the land on the other side an island—on looking at my compass I found it was flowing from the SE & might therefore be the river so I took their advice and followed it up. After marching till 12.30 we found it was not the river for I crossed on a large fallen tree & found it was the mainland. I recrossed & stopped for Nelson & Parke to come up & we decided to cross the river by the fallen tree & camp in a village on the other side not far off & to start again tomorrow in a North Westerly direction. By this time my mind was worked up to the highest pitch of anxiety at still being away from Stanley & the rest of the expedition & I was in an agony of suspense for Stairs was in a very precarious state when we left him & Parke & the medicine being with us may be a very serious matter—there were a good many sick left in camp, two of whom were cases of arrow wounds.

Aug. 17th. I started off in the morning in a N Westerly direction which brought us to the river we had crossed the night before. It was bad going, however we followed the river the whole morning & must have been near the Aruwimi when Nelson came up & said both he & Parke thought it advisable to retrace our steps to the village where we parted from Stanley & to follow the river till we reached him. I wanted to go on as I was certain we were near the river, but I agreed to follow their advice & we halted for lunch. While we were at lunch we heard shots ahead & started off thinking they were Stanley's signals, but soon found it was Sartato[1] one of Stanley's men & coxwain of the big canoe, with six men whom Stanley had dispatched to find us & lead us back to where we started from, we therefore recrossed the small river by a log & camped in the jungle ready for an early start in the morning. It was a great relief to have the responsibility of leading taken off one's shoulders, but I regretted having to go all the way back when we were so close to the river. Sartato said Stairs was all right when he left, which was good hearing.

Aug. 18th. The first thing in the morning I dispatched six men with a note to Stanley saying we were all right & gave them orders to reach him as

[1] 'Saat Tato' or 'Three O'clock' the hunter is described by Stanley as 'a good soldier who had seen service in Madagascar and with Sultan Barghash [the Sultan of Zanzibar] as a sergeant, but who, from his habit of getting drunk by the third hour of each day, was nicknamed "Three O'Clock" and dismissed. He was an excellent man, faithful strong and obedient, and an unerring shot' (Stanley, *IDA*, 1, 250).

soon as possible. Led by Sartato we started off at 7 oclock on our way back. Shortly after we started a furious thunderstorm came on & soon drenched us, it was the heaviest rain we have yet had & lasted till 12 oclock—we were a dreary procession marching back in it. At 12.30 we reached the group of three villages in which we had surprised the natives the day we left Stanley & I camped in the farthest which was the only stockaded one. The loads came in fairly well & the men were able to go out and get large quantities of enormous plantains which grew near, but Parke & Nelson did not get in till nearly 5 o'clock & reported one man having died on the road from cold. They had carried four men who were sick & who arrived in camp stiff & speechless from cold. I had them brought to my hut where there was a fire & gave them hot tea & soup & soon had the satisfaction of bringing them to life again. One goat had also died on the road from cold & we had it cut up & distributed amongst the sick. As the stockaded village was too small to take in the whole of the men about a third of them camped in the next village about 100 yds off. In the evening one of the chiefs came in to tell us that one of his men had been shot by a poisoned arrow in the stomach whilest he was out looting in a village close by—the man died a few hours afterwards. In the night I heard a noise of shouting & on going to see what it was saw the village in which the rest of the men had camped was in flames. Nelson immediately went down & managed to get the fire down before it had destroyed the village—one of the men had made too large a fire & after feasting on chickens & large plantains had fallen asleep by it & it had caught the nearest hut & quickly spread. By the time the fire was got under it was four oclock & Nelson & I sat round the fire & had some coffee & talked over our misfortunes & the general gloominess of the last few unfortunate days.

Aug. 19th. We were now on the first day's track & after marching along it for an hour & a half Sartato struck off to the right & we reached the river an hour later. How delighted one was to catch sight of its silver gleam through the trees after searching for it for three days. There was no path along the bank but we cut our way along & soon arrived at Stanley's camp & found to our surprise he had gone on up river. It was a great disappointment for we had all counted on reaching him today—there seemed to be a fate against our rejoining him—we camped on the site of his old camp.

Aug. 20th. Started off in the morning & had to cut a road the whole morning, at 10.30 we got to a large village in which I stopped for lunch. In the afternoon we reached the small river which we had been following two days before—it was fearfully flooded by the rain of the day before yesterdays & there seemed no chance of our getting across without canoes. We fired signal shots which were answered & soon Uledi the coxwain came down in the boat & from him we heard that Stanleys camp was about a mile off on the other side of the river, so that had we gone on the day Sartato found us we should have reached him on the third day after we missed the river, as it is this is the 6th day & we have had to return over a day & a half's march & have gone in a circle almost—it is just in keeping with the rest of this unfortunate march. We crossed a good many of the loads but could not get them all over before night & Nelson & Parke camped by the river whilest I went on to Stanley's camp which I reached after it was dark. I expected to be met with reproaches & by angry words but Stanley was very quiet & nice about my having led the expedition astray.[1] My story which was hard to tell under any circumstances, was however made harder by the perfect tissue of lies which Baroko, the man who was leading—had told Stanley. Stanley believed him or appeared to do so, so that one could only be silent though one was inwardly fuming at listening whilest all the blame was laid on me whilest Baroko represented himself as being a martyr to my obstinacy—of course according to his account we should have reached the river half a dozen times if I had only followed his advice. I found poor Stairs installed in the back of Stanley's tent amongst boxes of ammunition, a most dreary place, without a light or bed—he had had a most uncomfortable time but was much better.

Aug 21st. In the morning Stanley sent me down to Nelson in the boat & canoes to tell him before bringing the men on to take them all to the village near by & collect all the food he could—Parke went back to camp to look after the sick & reported favourably on Stairs condition. Two of the men sick from arrow wounds died of lock-jaw today from the effects of it—they were hit on the same day as Stairs. One man with us had died the day before yesterday from the same thing. It is evidently the thing to be feared from these wounds. The patient apparently gets along fairly well for some days, when he is suddenly struck with pains in the back & back of the neck & dies of lock-jaw in great agony.[2]

Aug. 22nd. Today the expedition marched out of what Stanley calls the 'Dismal Camp' the camp in which he passed six days of torturing anxiety about the fate of the expedition. As there were rapids ahead the loads which go every day in the canoes & boat were left in camp under my charge until the canoes were over the rapids, the crews then returned & brought them on to the canoes & took them on to camp. I remained in the 'dismal camp' till one o'clock & then marched on to camp in a violent storm of rain. Strange to say it was fine as I neared camp & when I got in I found they had had had no rain but that it had been bright sunshine all day.

[1] Stanley makes remarkably little of this anxious episode, merely recording: 'At 5 p.m. the caravan arrived. Its sufferings have been great from mental distress' (Stanley, *IDA*, 1, 182).

[2] Parke records that he gave 'small but repeated enemas of a strong infusion of tobacco to the case of incipient tetanus' (Parke, p. 97).

Aug. 23rd. Before starting today Stanley made us fall all the men in & report on their condition.[1] They are all very poor from hunger & want of food for so long, for we only get food now by fits & starts, but apart from the want of food there is very little real sickness & disease in camp, it is only hunger that has brought the people down & reduced them to such a state of weakness. A great number have large foul ulcers on their feet & legs. These come generally at first from a scratch & the man neglects it & does not wash it until it festers & then his blood being in a poor state it gradually develops into an ulcer which in a few days eats its way to the bone. This bush is very trying to the mens feet, we have numbers lame from the sharp sticks penetrating their feet.

Aug. 24th. Before starting in the morning violent rain came on which prevented our starting till past ten. I started ahead but had to stop very soon to get the loads out of the canoes at the foot of a bad rapid, we had them carried past the bad water & camped near a village about which the people got a good many bananas of the big yellow kind. Stairs complained of bad pains in the back of the neck & Parke was terribly nervous about it as it is the first symptom of lock jaw coming on. Stanley sent me after dark with ten men to launch a new canoe one of the men had seen up river, we went after it but were unable to get it into the river, & as it was only just finished & had never been in the water it was harder to move. We came back by moonlight to camp & had to cross a deep stream on a very slippery log.

Aug. 25th. Stairs was much better this morning, the pains had gone, it was a great relief to us all, as Parke really had grave apprehensions about him the night before—it is a great thing that he is able to go in the canoes & get rest & quiet. We did a very fair march today, just off the river there were a good many villages & the men got plantains & indian corn in them. The donkey which Stanley brought out from England with him has been failing for some time & today he crept along so slowly I was obliged to leave him behind. I left him by the side of a small river in a little grassy clearing, a pleasant enough place to be left in. This hard life with little or no grass is a great change for him after the pampered life on board ship where all the ladies fed him with apples & sugar, or after his easy life at Mr Mackinnon's place. One of Stanley's two donkeys & Stairs donkey are also dead—they died of want of food & the hard travelling, the constant crossing small rivers, sometimes as many as 15 in a day, has been very trying to them, they get stuck in the mud & have to be pulled out, poor beasts.

Aug. 26th. About ten o'clock we heard a large rapid ahead & expected to have to take the canoes & boat out again but on arriving opposite we found it was a large river which joined the Aruwimi at right angles in one huge rapid.

[1] 'Healthy 316; dead 16; sick 57' (Stanley, *IDA*, 1, 184).

This is the 'Nepoko' of which the famous Dr Juncker wrote as joining the Aruwimi in all probability, he crossed it about 120 miles north of its junction with the Aruwimi. At the rapid it is about 300 yds wide & pours an immense volume of water into the Aruimi, it runs from due North almost while the Aruimi flows on—a considerably diminished river—from the SE. Opposite this fall are great numbers of villages connected by good broad cut tracks, the best we have yet seen, village after village run inland in a long chain with only about 50 yds between each. There must be a population of some thousands of natives here but we drove them all out as we approached. There is food here in great quantities, plantains of the largest & best kind, manioc, & chickens, so Stanley decided to camp here & remain for a day or so to let the people get a real good feed. The village we camped in had three stockades & was surrounded by a dense grove of plantains, the street ran straight down hill to the water's edge exactly opposite the cataract & one got a splendid view of it from the bottom of the village. We were all very seedy here, it must have been something we had eaten. Stairs is much better, he, Nelson & I each had a hut opening into a large covered in place, it was very comfortable & made a good place to have our meals in. In the evening we had quite a good dinner off chickens, bananas, vegetables & manioc & for pudding a large pot full of porridge made of indian corn with some condensed milk—it is quite the best dinner we have had since leaving Yambuya. Late at night one of the men, 'Katembo' brought in seven chickens & the news that there was a new canoe of monstrous size lying ready to be put into the water five villages off inland, it was, he said, so large that if you sat in it you could not see over the side.

Aug. 27th. Early this morning Stanley sent me off with a hundred men to drag the canoe to the river. I was much amused to notice that this morning Katembo's description of the canoe got less & less large until on arriving at the place where the canoe was lying we found only a decently large canoe, not so large as the one I got down river & not so well cut. We were the whole day getting the canoe along, the road ran through a chain of villages & as the streets were not straight we had to pull down numbers of huts to make room for it—it was 56 feet long & $4\frac{1}{2}$ ft broad. We had at last to leave it at the top of the village in which we were camped for it was five oclock & the men were tired out. In the afternoon one of the men Jumah was brought in by a couple of men, one of the two had by mistake shot him badly in the foot & Parke was obliged to amputate it.[1] Stanley got a photograph of the fall this morning but he has not yet developed it.

[1] The patient recovered completely and it seems to have irritated Stanley, who paid him for a year's stay with the Arab trader Ugarrowwa, that he arrived back in Zanzibar 'as fat as butter' (Stanley, *IDA*, 1, 187).

Aug. 28th. Early this morning we had the whole force out & ran the canoe down the street into the river. Stanley gave her over to me to carry some of my loads & sick men in, so I discarded the old rotten one I had before. She is a fine canoe but very badly cut, the bow & stern being depressed instead of raised, she will however take a good many loads & sick men. At 10 oclock we started off, Parke leading, & soon lost our way inland—there was a violent thunderstorm all the morning but it cleared off before noon. At about half past one I went ahead & persuaded Parke to return to our starting point & follow the river on path or no path, I had a lively recollection of the time we were lost & the feeling of anxiety then—Parke agreed to return & we retraced our steps & reached the river in a couple of hours. Some poisoned arrows were fired at us on our way, they had peculiar shaped iron heads & were smeared thick with poison—fortunately they did not hit any of our men. We passed through huge groves of plantains for a distance of a mile—food is so plentiful here it was almost a pity we did not stay another day to let the men pick up a bit. We followed the river Parke leading & I in the rear, Nelson & Stairs both being in the boat with Stanley today so that there were only us two with the land party. We were very much delayed at the river & I did not get up to where Parke camped till long after dark. Our camp was in a large village for we could not reach Stanley that day.

Aug 29th. We started off early expecting to reach Stanley's camp in an hour or so but we were again delayed by a river which was too deep to ford & we had to cross the expedition in a small rotten canoe the natives had left half sunk. Once the canoe upset & 6 rifles went to the bottom but the men dived & got them all up, the crossing took us four hours & when we reached Stanley's camp of the night before we found he had gone on & we had to follow not expecting to reach him again. However at about five we reached his camp as he had camped early so as to let us come up with him.

Aug. 30th. Started leading today & did a long march not reaching Stanley, who had camped at the foot of a bad cataract, till 5.30, Parke who was in the rear did not reach camp till seven oclock. The men were terribly tired & knocked up by the length of the march. Today for the first time for a long time we saw two hippopotomi, I hope it is a sign that this awful bush is going to end, hippopotomi are never found where there is no grass so one hopes grass country is at hand. Stanley tried hard to get them, for they would be a real boon to the men who have had no meat for so long, but was unable to get a good shot.

Aug. 31st. In the morning Stanley took his company & cut a track up to a place above the rapids & we got the boat and canoes transported over it. It was hard work getting the boat carried for it was a quarter of a mile to the head of the cataract & the road was up & down amongst rocks & roots.

Towards evening we heard shots close to camp & in half a minute a party of 20 Zanzibaris burst into the camp followed by our men cheering at the tops of their voices. The strangers rushed up to us & shook hands violently all round. Stanley who was a little way out of camp soon arrived & was presented with a beautiful fat goat which we were pleased to get as we had had no meat for some days. They turned out to be a party of slaves out foraging the country for ivory & belonged to a company of Arabs who had a permanent camp some 20 marches up the river. From them we learned that the bush extended for a distance of 40 marches ahead & that the river was broken up continually by rapids & cataracts. They said there was a fair amount of food ahead in the shape of plantains, & one could well believe it for they were all so fat & well fed looking & were a great contrast to our wretched thin men, some of whom are worn to skeletons from want of food & hard work. After talking for about an hour they took leave of us—we expect to reach their camp tomorrow. It is wonderful how meeting these people in this wilderness had cheered the men up & even ourselves too, anything to break the dull monotony of this march through the bush, besides there is something definite to look forward to ahead.

September 1st [1887]. Here we are in September & miles from our destination yet. In London Stanley said he would reach Wadelai by Aug 15th—it is much more likely that Nov 15th[1] would have been nearer the mark. We started off expecting to reach the Arabs by evening but after a few hours marching we came to a string of large villages one of which had evidently been their camp, but they had left it the night before. We found some native children lying dead about the village, the Arabs had speared them from sheer wanton cruelty—one poor little boy was still alive though his entrails were protruding from a spear wound in the stomach. Our men who were suffering badly from hunger were able to get quantities of huge plantains at a little distance from the village. We got into camp at 4.30 much disheartened at not seeing the Arabs who must have had some reason for leaving so suddenly & getting out of our way. The men were all terribly disappointed & two men deserted that evening one taking a box of ammunition & one our only box of salt, the latter a fearful loss as we shall be without it now for weeks, with them, they have evidently followed the Arabs track which led away from the river in the hope of catching them up. Stanley sent 12 men after them in the evening to try & catch them but I do'nt expect it will be much use.

Sept. 2nd & 3rd. Today Stanley hearing the roar of a cataract ahead decided to take the boat out & abandon the river. We remained in camp all day & I got the boat taken to pieces & made up into 32 loads. The men Stanley

---

[1] In fact they reached the south-western shore of Lake Albert on 13 December.

sent out in search of the deserters came in this evening, they had followed the Arab track for a long distance but had not come up with the deserters. Stanley was very despondent about these desertions for he says they are only the first of a good many for when Arabs are near men always desert to them, they like the lawless thieving life even though without much pay much better than the steady work & steady pay they get under a European. This camp which is surrounded by swamps is very unhealthy & we all have fever & diarhoea—Stanley is very seedy indeed & is nervous about himself.

Sept. 4th. We marched today a short march & camped about a mile above the cataract, over which the canoes have been hauled. Carrying the boat was very hard on the men, for the bush is dense here & a track has to be cut for it. I was much surprised & very glad when Stanley told me he had decided on having the boat put together again as the water was smooth ahead. The men who had to carry the boat were of course delighted. Three more men have deserted tonight taking with them their guns a box of ammunition & a bag of Stanley's clothes. One man was caught trying to desert with a box of European provisions—Stanley wished to hang him as an example to the rest but the chiefs would not hear of it & he was only put in chains. If I were Stanley I should hang the man whether the chiefs wished it or not, he will never stop desertions till he does.

Sept. 5th. Today to prevent men from deserting Stanley had the breech blocks taken from the guns of all those men who were suspected of wishing to desert thus rendering their guns useless, it is hoped that the knowledge of this will deter them from venturing to leave the expedition unarmed. We only marched a couple of hours this morning & camped in a beautiful grassy place dotted about with palm trees. The men were able to go out & get some bananas, which will pull them through till the day after tomorrow. The boat went ahead up the river & brought back two goats & two kids, these are a god send to us for today we have only had 5 bananas each which is starvation.[1]

Sept. 6th. We were delayed by the rain & did not start till past eight. Last night one of the donkeys got loose & got among the tent ropes & pulled down the tent in which Parke & I sleep, I was pulled out of bed onto the grass & could'nt help laughing at the way in which the donkey frightened at what it had done gallopped off amongst the grass huts of the men knocking them down as it went, it woke all the men up & the whole camp joined in the hue & cry after it. After a very hard wet days march I arrived at a large open place at the head of a huge cataract where Stanley had camped. It was a splendid place for a camp & one got a beautiful view of the cataract foaming below & views of lovely reaches of water two miles each way above

---

[1] Parke's record for 5 September begins '*We are all without food*' (Parke, p. 105).

& below the cataract. The river poured itself over a narrow ledge of rock in a fall of from 7 to 8 ft at the side was a large plateau of smooth rock over which we shall have to haul the boat & canoes tomorrow. I went down & examined the place with Stanley & found it will only take us a few hours tomorrow to get the boat & canoes over, as we shall not have to haul them for more than a couple of hundred yards across the rock. It is the finest looking cataract we have yet seen, that at Panga is not near so fine & one could not get so good a view of it.

Sept. 7th. The first thing this morning we had all the men out to cut down trees to act as rollers to haul the boat & canoes over the rock. We got the boat & canoes over & floated in calm water above the cataract by 12 o'clock. The men being very short of food Stanley sent us four Europeans over to the other side of the river, where there were villages, with 70 men. There were three villages with peculiar stockades of broad flat boards round each hut, they were situated very prettily amongst groves of plantains & palm trees & there were open patches of short grass here & there, it reminded me very much of the country one sees going up the Hoogley to Calcutta. Led by one of my chiefs we went a long way inland to some plantain groves but we did not get very many, but it will be enough to carry us on for a day or two.

Sept. 8th. Made a short march today with Nelson leading, the road was very bad & the men ahead had to cut a track nearly the whole way. We passed through so[me] pretty bits of open where there had evidently formerly been villages. In the afternoon heavy rain came down & we had to pitch the tents in the dripping rain. Being awfully hard up for food we opened some of our European provisions & found that several things had been stolen by the men who had forced open the box. It is a great loss for our European provisions are so absurdly few that we can only afford to open a tin now & then.

Sept. 9th. There being rapids about another hours march ahead we had to carry all the loads ahead of them & put them into the canoes. We then did a fairly long march & camped in a nice piece of open jungle opposite some villages on the other side of the river. As we got into camp by two oclock the men were sent over to get plantains & returned in the evening with a pretty fair supply, they brought over large quantities of native tobacco & dried caterpillars which latter they ate with great appetite & told us they were very good, they looked & smelt horrible & Stanley told us they were very bad indeed & would make the men ill, they have a peculiar result of making the muscles of the stomach relax & for some days the men are useless. They brought a little honey over with them, it is the first we have tasted—it was not bad, but had a sort of fermented taste about it, we ate it with some banana cakes & it went very well with them,—out here anything that is not actually nasty & nauseous seems good to us. Some of the men went up a track inland & brought back most beautiful huge plantains, it is a pity we cannot stay a day & load up the men with them.

Sept. 10th. At one, we came to a place where the river suddenly narrowed down to a width of 80 yards & came down with a tremendously rapid current, it must be very deep. Ahead we could hear the roar of a cataract. The river presented the appearance of a huge torrent with rocky sides & ran in the direction of due N & South. Stanley had gone on ahead to reconoitre & we all made up our minds that we should have to abandon the river. Word came back in the afternoon that we were to go on to camp ahead & that the boat & canoes with their crews were to camp at the bottom of the cataract. I was to remain & take the boat to pieces ready to carry to camp next morning & put in the water above the fall. I got the boat to pieces by dark & Nelson—who was also left behind—& I camped at the fall & had a good dinner off baked ripe plantains, they are like a vegetable batter pudding, we seldom get any ripe as they require keeping so long. The river falls almost straight down over a rock through a very narrow opening a height of 17 or 18 feet, this is the highest fall yet.

Sept. 11th. In the morning Stanley came down with his company & got a road cut to carry the boat up to camp. I had only taken the boat into 5 pieces instead of 12 & each piece was carried by 12 men, being so broad a large track had to be cut. He gave orders to Nelson & I to fill up the canoes with stones & sink them in still water as we are unable to drag them over this fall the distance being too far. By doing so we shall be able to find them on our return journey & use them going down river. After sinking the canoes, Nelson went back to the last camp to look for his donkey which had strayed away the night before & I went on to camp to get the boat put together. Camp must have been a mile from the fall & the road lay through villages all of which had been burnt by the Arabs. The camp was splendidly situated in a burnt village which sloped down at right angles to the river. I got the boat put together & into the water by one & Stanley went up the river to see what was ahead, he came back & reported a rapid ahead & he also captured three canoes, they were short but immensely broad & will be very useful & safe to carry the boxes of ammunition in. I was able in the afternoon to get a lot of my clothes mended—they are getting very ragged—this stuff I got from Stanley is comfortable, but very unsuited to this hard rough work & is always getting torn, I do'nt think my clothes will nearly last me till I can get some more. Nelson returned in the evening without having been able to find his donkey, this is the fourth donkey that has gone since we left Yambuya, three have died & one been lost—Parke & Stanley are now the only two who have donkeys.

Sept. 12th. The first thing this morning all our companies were fallen in & Stanley had an inspection of the sick—some of them were a sorry looking lot having been brought down almost to skeletons from hunger & dysentery. We left camp at 9 led by an old native woman we had captured the day before, we left 4 men who were almost dead in the camp with a little food & water with them, they were quite unable to move & were bound to die in the next 24 hours. The old woman led us so badly I took the lead out of her hands, she led us right away from the river until the men got so angry they gave her each a shove as she passed them to go to the rear guard, one could hear her scolding, as she went down the line, at the top of her voice. There were some bad rapids & Stanley took the loads out of the canoes & boat & had them carried some distance by land. In the afternoon we were just abreast of Stanley when we heard his big elephant rifle going ahead. A large elephant had been seen by him, in the boat, throwing water over itself & playing in the water, he was able to get pretty close to it & fired hitting the elephant in the head, it turned sharp round & waded across the river, which was on an average 6 feet in depth, at a great rate chased by the boat. Stanley said he put 6 bullets into him but the elephant clambered up the opposite bank & got away.

Sept. 13th. Stairs leading this morning: we did a fair days march & reached a large cataract at 3 pm. It was a very long cataract the fall from the top being 30 feet, the water coming down in a series of four steep rapids. Stanley went on and pitched camp a quarter of a mile above the rapid & sent me back to take the boat to pieces ready for transporting her tomorrow. I got her ready by dark.

Sept. 14th. The first thing in the morning we all went down with the men to get the boat & canoes over the cataract. Stairs cut a road through the jungle & I got the boat up & put her together at the still water & we had the boat & canoes ready at the camp by 12 o'clock. The men were allowed to go out & get food after work was done. Some of them came back & reported a large track running parallel with the river inland the road was blazed & in one place there were 15 natives lying dead, shot by bullets—this is evidently the work of the Arabs. Men have day after day been deserting in the hope of joining the Arabs & I'm afraid this new report about there having passed near so recently will lead to fresh desertions. Stanley is getting quite low about the number of men who have deserted with their loads. A couple of my sick men were lost on the march yesterday, they must have gone into the bush & lay down & the column passed them & left them behind.

Sept. 15th. We did not start till after breakfast today owing to the heavy rain. Stanley sent for Stairs & I & we had a long talk about the possibility of reducing the numbers of loads & leaving all the sick men if we could come across the Arab settlement & the Arabs would undertake to look after them. He had out the maps & showed us where we were & talked of what the country would probably be like ahead & how the river probably would run. He pricked off a spot equidistant 90 miles from Albert Nyanza & Muta Nzigi & said if the river ran as it has been running some time it would cut that spot, here he would leave some loads & sick men & start across country with reduced loads to Albert Nyanza. He asked what I thought of leaving the boat behind & trusting to getting canoes at the lake, I was of course against it, though it is my company that has to carry the boat, Stairs was also against it, as was Stanley himself. The lake is a stormy one & progress in canoes would be slow & risky & Wadelai would not be reached in a quarter of the time if he went in a canoe. The point at which he proposed leaving the river is about 40 geographical miles from here. Some of the chiefs came to the tent too & he told them what he proposed doing & talked of the distance being very short but in the state in which the people were from hunger & sickness we were only able to go a few miles a day. After breakfast we started off & camped about four miles ahead.

Sept. 16th. Started off in the morning with Parke leading. As Stairs & I were stopping at eleven to get some coffee we heard guns going ahead, regular volleys from the small sharp crack of a Winchester to the heavy report of a large elephant rifle. We could not imagine what it was but we hurried on & after marching for a couple of hours we came to a largish river where we found Parke & nearly all the men & loads had stopped, & two of the canoes were there ferrying the people across. Parke told us we had struck the Arabs at last & that the firing we heard was their saluting Stanley who had gone ahead & pitched camp about a mile up river. On reaching camp we found that the Arab settlement was a couple of miles ahead on the other side of the river, but that the Arabs were coming down to see Stanley today. In about half an hour we heard drums beating & horns blowing & soon six canoes came down river full of people & landed just opposite Stanley's tent. The head Arab—whose name is Ugarrowa—landed first & took his seat in silence, on a mat already placed opposite Stanley for him, whilest his inferior officers took seats on one side of him inside the tent. Behind him in four rows were seated his guard of honour & on the other side six or seven very fat, but rather nice looking, women, whose faces were smeared with a white paint of some sort, these women were accompanied by all the drummers & hornblowers who sat behind them. When all the people were seated, all being done in perfect silence, the presents, three goats, 8 chickens, 40 lbs of rice & ripe plantains were brought to Stanley, Ugarrowa's snuff box was handed to him & he took a big pinch of snuff & the women struck up a song accompanied by two men & drums, it was a sort of whining song sung all in 'tremolo' & suddenly ending with a loud bang on the drums. After singing five or six of these songs, all very much alike Ugarrowa began to talk to Stanley & to ask him who he was & what was the object of his expedition. Stanley told him all about it & Ugarrowa told him then about himself.[1] He was a native of Zanzibar who had left Manyama two years ago, he had been settled here a year having driven the natives from a village & planted his settlement on it. He had with him 80 guns & three hundred people in this settlement; a settlement inland & another on the river 20 camps ahead with 40 guns. There was not, he said, much food ahead but plenty at & beyond his settlement ahead which was at the end of the bush at the edge of a grassy plain where there was abundance of cattle & game & sweet potatoes & matamah in plenty. Ugarrowa is a nice looking man of the regular African-Arab type & speaks in a quiet, well mannered way. After remaining about an hour talking with Stanley, who showed them their position on the map, which greatly delighted them, they left & went up river to their village. We promptly got the goat killed & some of the rice cooked, the food was a God send for we were at a very low ebb—we Europeans are begining to feel the result of the poorness & scarcity of food. Tomorrow we are to march two miles up river & pitch our camp opposite the Arab settlement.

Sept. 17th. This morning at about three oclock we were wakened by a violent thunderstorm, the rain came down like a water spout & in a very short time the tents, which had been pitched in a hollow, were over a foot deep in water. The tent in which Nelson & Stairs are sleeping was lowest & had most water in it. Stairs who has a camp bed was just out of the water though all his boxes & clothes were under water, Nelson who was sleeping on a bed of leaves & grass was driven out & spent the rest of the night in a mackintosh sitting out in the pouring rain. Parke had a bed & was all right though all his boxes were soaked. I came off best as my side of the tent happened to be on the slope & I was just out of the water but some of my clothes were in the wet. It was a melancholy sight to see the tents in the morning standing in a lake of muddy water with clothes & blankets etc floating about. Nelsons watch compass & aneroid were under water & had to be fished up, they were quite ruined & Stairs' watch & compass as well. At about 9 o'clock we started off, I leading, the whole place was like a marsh after the nights rain. We camped at a place where there was a good landing place just opposite the Arab settlement which is a collection of large mud & wattle buildings. Ugarrowa soon came over & all the same ceremony as yesterday was gone through. After about an hour he returned & in the

[1] The history of the Arab penetration of Africa from Zanzibar and the east coast is a story to itself. The chief points are summarized in the Introduction above, pp. 34–8.

afternoon Stanley made a return visit of ceremony in the boat, with the Egyptian flag flying at the bow & all the boatmen in clean white dresses. We were occupied all the afternoon in trying to get our clothes dried. The Arabs men came over with plantains ripe & green to sell & very nice flour made of dried plantains pounded up fine; they also brought chickens & Indian corn. We had no cloth & were unable to buy anything. In the evening Ugarrowa sent over a lot of curry & rice for Stanley & he gave us some of it for dinner—it was very good, & moreover it had salt in it which was a great treat.

Sept. 18th. Early this morning all the companies were fallen in & Stanley & Parke had an inspection of the sick. Eleven were taken from my company, in all there were 54 sick to be left behind with the Arabs, including all the four Somalis. Fifty guns with the breach blocks taken out of them were also left with the Arabs, we shall pick up the men & guns on our return journey. The sick men were a miserable sight going over in two boat loads, most of them were mere skeletons & had huge ulcers. Many of the men looked at them with envious eyes & would have been glad to have been left too & to have done with this hopeless, or rather what must appear to them, a hopeless march. In the afternoon Ugarrowa came over to see the working of the Maxim gun which was to be fired for his edification. He & all the Arabs were astonished & delighted with it & as each volley of shots struck the water half a mile down stream they laughed aloud & pointed out its effect to each other & to their slaves. In the evening more food came over to Stanley, which we did *not* see any of.[1] We had nothing allowed us to buy plantains, but fortunately we had some thirty odd Matako left from our Congo allowance & with these we bought plantains enough for two days.

Sept. 19th. Before marching this morning Ugarrowa came over to say good bye, he brought with him again a large amount of curry & rice for Stanley, which again we did *not* see anything of, he accompanied the canoes some way up the river with his canoes blowing horns & beating drums. We had a very bad march; the road was full of elephant holes &, as there had been heavy rain last night, the mud was frightful. In the evening one of Ugarrowa's canoes came up to our camp with three men who had deserted to him that morning when we left, he had given them each fifty & had sent them on bound together to Stanley. He told me to tie them to trees & he would deal with them in the morning.

---

[1] Stanley writes of 'large trays of exquisitely cooked rice, and an immense bowl full of curried fowl, a dish that I am not fond of, but which inspired gratitude in my camp' (Stanley, *IDA*, I, 198).

CHAPTER 6

UGARROWWA'S TO IPOTO

20 SEPTEMBER–18 OCTOBER 1887

Sept. 20th. After giving out the loads Stanley had the men fallen in in companies & told them these three men had deserted to the Arabs & he intended to hang them, one was to be hung today, one tomorrow & one the next day & so make an example of them & stop desertions in future. He then took three pieces of paper of three different lengths & the man who drew the shortest was to die now the man who drew the next shortest tomorrow & so on. The man who drew the shortest was one of Nelson's men belonging to the company from which there have been most desertions. The noose was then put round his neck, a rope passed over the bough of a tree & the end given to the deserters in chains who were made to pull the condemned man up & make him fast. He died very easily & was left hanging as a warning to other deserters. We only marched about 5 miles for the road was very bad. On arriving at camp one of the men saw an elephant in the river & Stanley & Nelson went after it in the boat, they put a couple of shots into him but did not bring him down.

Sept. 21st. In the morning it was found that one of the two condemned men left had got away in the night. However after the loads were given out the men were fallen in & the noose was put on the neck of the condemned man left. Just before he was swung up the chiefs all came up to Stanley & begged him to let the man off as the first man's being hung was a sufficient example to the men. Stanley therefore let him off & then gave the men a long oration.[1] We marched today through a series of villages with curious bomas 15 feet high made of boards, round them, they had all been deserted for some months & many of them were partly burned. After passing through several we came to one on the top of a rise which had been completely burned, from it one got a lovely view of the river which opened out here into a kind of pool. There were large banana groves on the other side but

---

[1] In a typically 'written-up' passage in *In Darkest Africa* Stanley describes himself as interceding with the head chief, Rashid, for the man's life; three pages conclude with a scene of wild enthusiasm among the men, crying, 'Death to him who leaves Bula Matari!' (Stanley, *IDA*, I, 201–6). See Preface, p. vii, for comment on such scenes as described in print by Stanley, and in diaries by him and others. In this instance, Parke records that Stanley privately suggested to the headmen that they should intercede for the deserter, and that Stanley should then make a ceremony of pardoning him (Parke, p. 111).

there were no plantains at all, the Arabs evidently come up here & take them all as soon as they get large enough. At one o'clock we came to a large river flowing from the S, the Arabs told us it was the Lenda, we crossed it & camped on the other side, on the site of a burned village. The Aruwimi is now a small river compared to what it was for the Lenda brings in a volume of water equal to the Aruwimi as it is now. The camp being in such an open place we were able to get all our things out & dried.

Sept. 22nd. Left camp this morning with no food, I was leading & we came along a fairly good track but all the men are perfectly spiritless & dejected from want of food & we do not go along with any elan. We got no food in the middle of the day either & one felt in reality the gnawing pain of hunger, we have been feeling it a good deal lately & are likely to feel it pretty often ahead—one feels now more than ever how inadequate & what a farce the 'European Provisions' are, meanwhile the seven chickens continue to go one by one into Stanley's tent & we have seen nothing of them. At about one oclock I reached Stanley who had camped opposite a plantain grove. He sent the men across to try & get some plantains. The men returned with a few but all so small & undergrown that they are but poor & sickening food.

Sept. 23rd. Today I was rear guard. After five hours marching, during which time we had simply to drive the men along so weak are they from hunger we came upon large banana groves, there were not many plantains but my chief Abdullah brought me some very fair plantains, some of which I got cooked at once as I had to wait for men who had gone to look for food. How good they were after the scarcity of any food for the last two days, & yet these plantains which I thought so good now would simply be nauseous to one at home. After getting the men together who were out looking after plantains & making them take up their loads I marched on about 2 hours into camp, which was at the foot of a very large cataract.

Sept. 24th. Early in the morning most of the men were sent back to the banana groves we had passed through the day before to get food. Stanley & I got a road cut through the jungle to the head of the cataract & a large place cleared in which to put the boat together. The natives had evidently been accustomed to drag their canoes over as there were still some rollers left in the track. The cataract consisted of two falls, the lower one was like a huge stair & the upper in the shape of a horseshoe. There were a good many snipe flying about among the rocks & trees in the middle of the fall, but it was of no use firing at them for we could'nt have got any of them. In the afternoon I got the boat to pieces ready for transporting to the head of the fall. The day has been just like a summer day at home & there has been a fresh breeze blowing off the river & the birds singing.

Sept. 25th. The men returned from the plantain fields yesterday evening with a good many plantains but all so small & ill grown that they are hardly worth carrying. The first thing this morning I got the boat carried up & put together at the head of the fall, I then got my own canoe dragged up & Parke, Nelson & Stairs got the other five up. We were a very long time over the work, for the men are all weak from hunger & work in a miserable dejected way. This hunger is terrible & it is terrible to see its ravages on the men & to feel its effects on oneself. I have been suffering horribly for the last few days from diarhoea & this joined to want of food has made me very weak & ill. After getting the boat & canoes into the water we marched on a couple of miles into camp which was in a marshy place on the site of an old native settlement, I could hardly get along I felt so weak & went to bed directly I got into camp.

Sept. 26th. This morning I was leading. After marching an hour we came to a bad rapid & the loads had to be taken out of the canoes & transported to the head of the rapid. Stanley & the other officers stayed there for coffee & were fortunate enough to knock over a Guinea fowl which came in very opportunely for lunch. Stanley told me to go on as he believed there was another rapid ahead, he told me to examine the rapid & if it was very bad to stop the caravan & cut a road to the head of the bad water. On coming to the rapid I left a chief to stop the people & await Stanley's arrival in the boat & canoes whilest I went on & got the road ready for bringing up the loads. I found a very good road leading along the river bank, but found to my great annoyance 'Baruku', who was one of the men cutting the road behind me & with whom I had had trouble the time I lost Stanley further back, had led the people by an inland path & they had all missed the rapid. I had to go on & send them all back making them leave their loads by the side of the road in charge of a chief. Stairs came up & we had infinite trouble in getting the people back & getting them to take the double loads into camp which was about a mile & a half ahead. 'Baruku' had the impertinence to lie to Stanley to excuse himself for the trouble he had given, he had the effrontery to tell Stanley I lost the road, whereas my road lay close along the river bank & was used by Stanley who camped on it. This man will play a trick on Stanley himself someday & he will then perhaps see how foolish he has been in trusting him as he does. I have had fever & ague all day & when I got to camp just threw myself down on some boxes, I felt unable to do anything. The people are daily getting weaker & weaker from hunger, for the one day on which they got a full stomach they starve for three or four, & the consequence is they are going down hill very fast. The river here for the last two miles is broken up by rocks & rapids & as far as we can see ahead it is much the same. Nelson is very seedy now & has to go in the canoes, he has a skin disease called 'Psoriasis' & it has broken out on his feet & he is quite unable to march.

Sept. 27th. Today as there was no food in camp & the people had been starving for two days Stanley decided to stay a day in camp & send the people across the river to look for plantains, we could see signs of plantain clearings a little way down—the people returned in the evening with a goodish lot of very fair bananas enough to last them the next day with a good meal this evening as well, they were very welcome to us as well, for we were almost starving too. All day I lay on my bed of branches in a high fever, my bones aching in every joint. Stairs started off early in the morning up the river track, to see if he could see any signs of the Arabs ahead & to report to Stanley what the river was like. He came back in the evening saying the river was still broken up into a series of rapids he had seen no signs of food or of the Arabs ahead—we are getting very anxious now about the state of the people. He shot at two elephants & one charged & very nearly killed him, all the five men he had with him ran away, on hearing the elephant trumpeting when it was hit, except my chief 'Murabo' whom I had sent with him. Murabo told me Stairs was within an ace of being killed the elephant charged at him & he shot behind a tree but got caught among the creepers & the elephant just shaved him with his tusks. The river is running in an ESE direction.

Sept. 28th. We only put a few loads in canoes & boat today as there were so many rapids, & starting off with the rest of the loads at 6.30 we had orders from Stanley to get on as far as ever we could & act independantly of the water party. We got on about 8 miles when we came upon Stairs who with the whole column was halted & hidden by the jungle were watching a village on an island about 50 yds from the bank in which the natives were all working away & laughing & talking in happy ignorance of the 250 odd enemies watching them at so short a distance. We heard the sound of numbers of people pounding what we though was Indian corn & the hungry column was eager to get food. As the boat did not come up & it was getting late we decided to fire a volley into the village hoping to scare the natives so that they would run, & leaving their food behind them we could get it when the boat & canoes came up. As we fired a volley two men fell & Parke shot two who were escaping in a canoe. The people fired very wildly many of the bullets striking the water half way only between us & the island. The natives made off escaping in canoes over to the main land on the other side of the river. One fellow kept firing arrows at us from behind a hut but Stairs put a bullet through the hut & he thought discretion the better part of valour & disappeared into the canoes. When the natives had cleared out, six of our men swam over to the island—they did not find much food except a little dried elephant's flesh, it was cut up in small squares & dried in the sun. We pitched the tent & formed camp but Stanley did not turn up that night.

Sept. 29th. At about 10 in the morning Stanley the boat arrived with Stanley—Nelson turned up at about 2 pm having experienced great trouble in getting over the rapids. As all the men nearly had gone inland to look for food Stanley pitched his tent & waited for the day the men returned in the evening having found nothing.

Sept. 30th. Started off Parke leading, Stairs & I in the rear. My little fox terrier 'Spot' has been getting thinner & thinner & a few days ago he got a large ulcer on his neck which dragged him down still more, today when we had gone some distance I missed him, he was evidently so weak he was unable to follow & has lain down somewhere on the road. I shall miss him very much for he was such a faithful affectionate little dog & always kept close to me on the march, I expect Stanley's fox terrier will not last much longer on this poor food. We are all very much in want of food, especially meat which we have not now had for a good many days. As we we[re] marching along Stairs said to me 'I'll just go up this hill away from the track & see if I can't get a shot at something' he had not gone six yards away from the track when he shouted to me he had found a deer in one of the pits which the natives dig to catch game. We drew it up & found it was a gazelle a little smaller than a goat. It was a tremendous find, we made a fire & had a shoulder cooked at once on the hot ashes, it was very good eating. At about 2 o'clock we heard guns firing ahead & on reaching Stanley found he had camped in an old native camp & had been met there by 10 or 12 Manyema men belonging to the Arab settlement ahead. They brought us nothing to eat except a few plantains which we had to buy from them, they told us the Arab camp was four good days march ahead but that there was no food to be got on the way—this was not pleasant hearing as we were out of food. They said Ugarowa's far camp which we were anxious to reach, as there was plenty of food, & it was on the edge of this interminable bush, was five days march beyond their camp. They left us that evening to return to their own camp. They were all the same fat looking well dressed men as Ugarowa's slaves were, many of them were natives who had been caught as children & trained up by the Arabs, they all spoke Swahili, but the natives spoke it with the same singing intonation that one notices when they speak their own language.

October 1st [1887]. Stanley sent large parties out on both sides of the river to search for food but they returned the greater part of them before dark with very little food except green stuff & a few plantains, however at about 9 o'clock in the evening two men returned laden with very fine bananas & reported there being great quantities of them far away down the river, this decided Stanley to stay here another day & send all hands down the other side of the river to get a good supply of food for the four days wilderness between us & the Arabs.

Oct. 2nd. This morning Stanley sent a large party of men over the river with Stairs & Parke—Nelson & I remained in camp, Nelsons feet are very bad now, he can hardly walk, I had fever rather badly & lay on my bed for the greater part of the day. In the evening Stairs & Parke returned with the men who brought in large quantities of very good plantains, of which each of the Europeans got a share sufficient to last four days. We had a big feed of plantains for dinner this evening & went to sleep thankful for small mercies.

Oct. 3rd. I was leading this morning & started off in good time. After marching along a fairly good track we came to high hill over which we made our way with great difficulty. We came upon the traces of a deserted village on the top of a very high hill—one comes on such traces very constantly when there are any Arabs in the neighbourhood; it is extraordinary how wanton & destructive they are. We found it very hard marching but finally I struck a small track which led us down to the river on to a narrow flat between the river & hills. I stayed an hour here for coffee & a rest & had my fire made on the bank of a beautiful clear gushing stream which rushed over huge boulders down from the hills. After resting I started off along a very good track on the flat but after going a mile or so the flat ended & we had to ascend the hills, the sides of which were so rocky & steep one had almost to go on one's hands & knees to get up them. The rocks here are covered by a growth of moss and magenta coloured balsams which has a very cool & pretty effect. On the top of the hills, which are here about 500 feet above the river, the bush is thinner & we made our way pretty easily through it, but towards the afternoon the bush got tangled & thick & we laboured along but slowly. At five o'clock we cut our way through dense bush down to the river & camped on its bank. There was hardly a level place to be found & we could only pitch one tent, in which we all slept, amongst the rocks. There were no traces of Stanley & Nelson in the boat & canoes. The river was very narrow & rapid here & presented the appearance of a large mountain stream.

Oct. 4th. In the morning Stairs started up river with a couple of men to see if he could cut a road along the river bank for a mile or so to see what the river was like ahead. At about then Stanley turned up in the boat & told us he had had great trouble in getting over the rapids the day before—Nelson & the canoes arrived an hour or so later. After waiting in camp about an hour Stanley decided to cross the whole expedition to the other side of the river as he thought there was likely to be a better track. We got the men, loads & two donkeys all across by two o'clock. It was very bad crossing as

the river was so rapid & there was a large broken rapid 100 yds below—
one canoe full of men & loads through the carelessness of the coxwain,
Hatibu Khamis, missed the landing place & was swept over the rapids below,
it just missed striking the rocks in the middle of the rapids by a few inches,
everyone held their breath for had it struck the rocks it would have been
smashed into a hundred pieces & the loads & men lost, the canoe reached
the opposite bank after being swept half a mile down stream. We got all the
loads started off by 2.30 & marched till 5 along the side of the hills or rather
it would be more correct to say we scrambled on till 5 oclock & camped on
a little platteau against the hill side. How the two donkeys managed to get
along was a marvel they seemed to hold on to sloping slippery rocks like
cats, twice they rolled over & we had to haul them up again & a dozen times
I thought they would roll over the precipice into the river.

Oct. 5th. Parke led this morning & we left the river a little & ascended
the hills the top of which were almost flat & we found a splendid track.
We got along till ten very fairly well until we heard the boom & roar of
a huge waterfall ahead. When we got nearly abreast of it Stairs & I made
our way down to the river's edge right to the foot of the fall. The whole
river dashed through a narrow chasm 150 ft above & tumbled in a series of
three falls into a broad basin below, out of which it rushed through a
narrow opening in great brown foamy waves. The basin was surrounded by
high rocky cliffs from which hung balsams & vines & orchids & mosses of
several sorts all kept green & dripping by the spray which rose like a cloud
from the fall & on which one could see a rainbow. One stood still & regularly
feasted one's eyes on it all. After a bit we climbed up to the hill track again
& reached Parke & were just agreed on sending back to Stanley to tell him
of the fall, when a messenger came from Stanley saying the river whose
banks we were following was a large tributary of the Aruwimi & we must
return with the messenger to a place where Stanley was waiting to ferry us
across. We reached the place by two oclock & the whole expedition was
across by half past three. Both rivers ahead being all rapids Stanley told me
to take the boat to pieces ready to carry by land. That evening we found
our box of plantains had been stolen & most of the few European provisions
we had left had gone also. What we shall do now for food I've no idea for
we are without food almost & are in the middle of a wilderness & don't
even know how far ahead the Arabs may be. We all sat round the fire till
late that night & talked over the grim outlook—we allowed ourselves a
small modicum of brandy all round, out of the 6 bottles we four left Yambuya
with we have only drunk one & a half.

Oct. 6th. I finished getting the boat to pieces & we all got our companies
fallen in to see what available men we had for carrying loads. I found, out

of my 88 men with whom I left Yambuya I could only muster 42 men who were fit to carry loads & many of these were so worn out by starvation that their loads would have to be of the lightest. Neither Nelson or Stairs companies could take all their loads either & as Nelson's feet were so bad he could not march Stanley decided to leave Nelson in charge of the sick & the loads we could not carry & start on & try & reach the Arabs & send back relief to Nelson as soon as possible. It was a terrible position for Nelson to be left in, he had food for only 2 days & will have to exist on what he can pick up in the shape of fungus & roots, or if there are any fish in the river he may be able to get a few, meantime we are going on with an exhausted & starving column to try & find food in a trackless wilderness. Stanley called us all up & told us what he intended doing & asked us if we could make any further suggestions as to his plans of proceding, he also called up all the chiefs & told them his position & asked them what they had to say. After a good deal of talking it was decided that five chiefs should at once start ahead & try & reach the Arabs or food & return with help as soon as they could. Raschid the head chief was told to choose his chiefs—he chose Khamis Parry one of his own, Khamis Kururu & Alsasi wadi Simba chiefs of mine & Munia Pembe one of Nelson's chiefs to go with him—we shook hands with them all & wished them good luck & they started off at once. I found with my 42 men I could only just manage to carry the boat & I had to leave some of the boat boxes containing extra bolts etc & 23 boxes of ammunition. Altogether 81 loads & 60 sick men had to be left behind with Nelson. We had great difficulty in getting the men to take their loads & I had a perfect fight to get some of my men to take the boat sections, one man, Nasibu Maquelah, was so troublesome I had to knock him down & then he was so mutinous that it was only by our threatening to put him in chains that we brought him to his senses & made him take his load. Stanley had marched off with his loads without hardly taking the trouble to say goodbye to Nelson & left us to look after the loads as best we could—he certainly never troubles himself to say a good word or a nice thing to us & gives his orders with a kind of snarl, which is highly unpleasant, especially to men like ourselves who have worked hard for him & have had little food & no pay & are putting up with hardships & privations merely for the love of the thing.[1] We got off by about two oclock & said goodbye to poor old Nelson very sadly, for his position is very precarious & our chances of relieving him slight, he has worked with

[1] Stanley's description of the leave-taking: 'I consigned the fifty-two men, eighty-one loads, and ten canoes in charge of Captain Nelson—bade him be of good cheer, and hoisting our loads and boats on our shoulders, we marched away' (Stanley, *IDA*, 1, 211).

159

us in good fellowship all these months & now we are practically abandoning him. Stairs Parke & I marched along rather silently at the rear of the column, urging on the people with the boat, Stanley had hardly cut any road & we had fearful difficulty in getting the boat along one could hear the sections bumping along ahead against trees & rocks. We only managed to get about three miles & camped just before dark—Stanley & the main column had camped on ahead, we had only the men carrying the boat & tent with us our boxes & blankets were on ahead. We had a plateful of tapioca boiled in water & some coffee—not much of a meal for three hungry men.

Oct. 7th. Had a very hard day urging the men forward with the boat. They are so worn out they carry the boat along for a bit & then sit down & have a long rest, or go from the track to search for fruit or fungus. After travelling for a couple of hours we came down from the hills & struck the river just above a large cataract. The river here is broad again & comparatively free from rapids & looks as if it were going to be navigable, the land on the river bank is flat & the path good. We finished our tapioca this morning & now only have a tiny tin of arrowroot, some of which we had for dinner tonight. We ate fruit such as it is, & fungus during the day.

Oct. 8th. My 29th birthday—this day last year was spent on the Downs, a great contrast to this. After marching along till ten o'clock I got a note from Stanley telling me to put the boat together & go over to an island opposite his last nights camp & look for an elephant he had shot the day before, it was badly wounded & had got away on to the island only probably to die, the men were greatly relieved to think they no longer had the boat to carry. I got the boat ready & put into the water while Stairs & Parke marched on to camp which was a couple of miles further on opposite a village on a small island. After searching a couple of islands & finding no traces of the elephant we turned the boats head up the river towards camp. There was a large long rapid between us & camp & we did not get in till long after dark—past eight. We found Stanley & most of the people down on the river's bank anxiously waiting our arrival firmly expecting we had found the elephant & were bringing them food—their disappointment was great when they found we had none—the people crawled back into camp more dejected than ever. Stanley had captured a canoe & the men had crossed over to the island they shot three men & captured a lot of women & children who had hidden themselves in the mud. They got a little Indian corn & some black beans of the former Stanley gave us a very small share & all of the latter he kept himself. The captured women were nearly all dwarfs[1] some of them with babies were only 4 ft high—a few of them were not bad looking. I sat over the fire with Stairs till late that night & we had

---

[1] They were now marching through the Ituri forest, home of the pygmies.

a little brandy to cheer us up—our brandy has been a great thing for us, since we have been on starvation diet we have allowed ourselves a few sips every night after dinner. My dinner was three quarters of a cup full of Indian corn made into porridge.

Oct. 9th. Stanley sent all the people out on both sides of the river to look for food but they returned with only a little fruit they had picked up in the jungle & some fungus, the latter is not bad eating but awfully indigestable. In the afternoon Stairs & Parke took their guns & went out & tried to get a shot at something, but the men who were out scouring the jungle for something to eat had frightened all game away. The canoe was sent over with 3 men to a small grassy island to cut grass for the donkeys; as they were cutting it a native sprang out of the grass with a large knife struck one of the men Feruzi Ali, one of our best men, over the head, the other two men seeing the struggle going on jumped into the canoe in the most cowardly way deserting their comrade & called to the people in camp for help; Feruzi after struggling some minutes managed to get off into the canoe. He was frightfully cut about, two cuts on the head & two on the arm & shoulder. Parke examined the wounds & said that one on the head would probably prove fatal in a few days. The boat immediately went over to the island & the boatmen shot the native & captured 13 women & children. Some of the women had rather pretty necklaces on made of shells cut into little discs; all were naked & had their lips pierced with elephant hairs which stuck out like cats whiskers. The women were full of information but as nobody understood a word of what they said it was not of much use. Today we had a cup full of Indian corn & now have nothing but what we can pick up; we have been eating a sort of large flat bean which drops from the trees, it has a very unpleasant taste like a horse chestnut.[1]

Oct. 10th. Most of the men who went across the other side did not return last night but determined to sleep there & go further afield today so we had to wait in camp for them, Stairs & Parke went out with their guns to try & get a shot. I stayed in camp & mended my clothes which are getting into a very tattered condition. In the afternoon Stairs & I fished & caught after a couple of hours patient fishing, '3 small fishes'. Ah for a miracle worker now to feed the multitude with them! We gave one of the fish to Stanley, for however unfairly he divides the food, at least we will treat him fairly. We had the two fish, each about 6 inches long for dinner with some of these nauseous beans. This hunger is terrible & we are all getting very weak & drawn looking. As we were sitting round the fire after finishing our poor food, with our stomachs still pinching us from hunger, the boat was hailed

[1] Stanley 'found it sufficiently filling, and about as palatable as a mess of acorns' (Stanley, *IDA* 1, 215).

from the other side of the river & it at once went over to fetch the people back from foraging.[1] They had got a fairish amount of bananas a quantity of native tobacco very well cured & packed & a good quantity of fungus & green stuff. They gave us a share of bananas some of which we had cooked at once—it was hard to keep ourselves from devouring them in quantities but we had to think of the days ahead before we should get food. They brought in reports of there being signs of Arabs in the shape of blazed tracks etc & thought the Arabs could not be many days ahead. One went to bed with one's hunger allayed a little but still one was famishingly hungry.

Oct. 11th. Started off this morning with Stanley leading. We were all so weak that the slightest exertion makes ones head go round & one breaks out into a perspiration. The boat followed with only ten loads in her to make her way after us over the rapids. The state of the people is frightful & the groans one heard in camp last night were most distressing, the people are dropping loads right & left & many will be lost today I fear. In the afternoon Stairs & I saw an elephant feeding on a small grassy island about 150 yds off. We crouched down & Stairs hit a bullet into his head which brought him to his knees, he got up & turned slowly round & as he turned Stairs put two more into his head but he slowly waded off to a large island to die. If we only had a canoe to go & cut him up what a God send the meat would be, but we have no canoe & the boat is at the foot of a large cataract & cannot possibly get up till tomorrow & the island is in the middle of a bad rapid & the men could not attempt to swim across. He was a splendid fellow coloured yellow with huge white tusks, he looked very happy standing knee deep in grass eating to his heart's content & whisking his tail & enormous ears. In the evening at 6 o'clock we reached camp having marched 7 miles. One of the boat men came in sometime later saying that three or four bolts had given way in getting the boat over a cataract & that it was waiting at the foot of another to get new bolts put in before the men dared attempt the ascent. Stanley therefore told me I must return tomorrow & mend the boat & I must catch him up as best I could. It is terrible this having to return & catch Stanley up when one is so weak one can hardly go forward even.

[1] Stanley does not mention the fish. He says: 'The officers Stairs, Jephson and Parke, had been amusing themselves the entire afternoon in drawing fanciful menus, where such things figure as:—
Filet de bœuf en Chartreuse
Petites bouchées aux huitres de Ostende
Bécassines rôties à la Londres
'Another had shown his Anglo-Saxon proclivities for solids such as:—
Ham and eggs and plenty of them
Roast beef and potatoes unlimited
A weighty plum pudding' (Stanley, *IDA*, 1, 216–17).

Oct. 12th. In the morning Stanley held a consultation, or 'Shauri' as they call it, with all the chiefs & people as to whether we should go on or cross the river this morning; the people were anxious to cross as they believed they would find more food on the other side. On the other side we could see a canoe tied against the opposite bank & a man tried to cross the river on a raft made of some of Stanley's bamboo tent poles & an inflated water-proof clothes bag to get the canoe but he had to turn back, as the current was too strong. The attempt was therefore abandoned & Stanley decided to go on & wait for the boat to catch him up & then cross the river. At about 8.30 I started back taking with me 10 men & my chief Rajab bin Lumah, he is the best man of my four chiefs & I always keep him with me; he has been with Europeans before & speaks a little English, he is a very good fellow, quiet, well mannered & dependable—I wish I could say the same of his brother Yuseph who is one of my servants & is rather a scoundrel & not always civil. Rajab is always civil & quiet however impatient & unjust one is with him & I'm afraid I'm both too often—one feels he is a friend & is always loyal. I found the boat at the foot of a large cataract, she was in a very bad state & leaking fast, four top bolts had given way in one section & it was a wonder the boat had not foundered. I got her mended up & started the men up the cataract. I got my 10 men to carry the loads to the head of the fall & sat down & had some tea made & waited for the boat to come up. While I was waiting I got the men to scrape some beans for me as I have seen the native women doing. It makes a sort of brown flour & this mixed with water & made into a rough paste & then wrapped up in large broad leaves & baked on the embers makes cakes which are quite palatable &, though they are not very sustaining they have not the same nauseous horse chestnut flavour that the beans have—the men poor fellows live on nothing else now, they make the flour into a sort of thick porridge & have a meal of it night & morning with a little fungus to give it a taste. I waited on till nearly three oclock reading my little Shakespeare which I always carry about with me in my pocket, when the boat came up. The men were litterally tired out with the hard work of getting the boat over the rapid, which was a very bad one—it is a marvel to me how they managed to get it up at all especially as they are utterly worn out with want of food—had it not been for the unflagging energy of the coxwain Uledi nothing would have been accomplished. I managed to urge the men to go on a bit further & sending my 10 men on to catch up Stanley, which they will probably do tomorrow, I got into the boat & decided to take charge of her myself till we reached Stanley. After pulling for a couple of hours & only making a mile & a half against the strong current there is here, I ordered the boat to put into the bank & the men to camp. Fortunately I had brought my bag of blankets with me or I should have been badly off as I had no shelter of any kind. I had a large fire made & cooked the last of my bananas—now I have nothing more to eat—& rolling myself up in my blankets & waterproof sheet slept soundly till morning.

Oct. 13th. Made an early start but got on very slowly as the river is all broken up into rapids we sighted three elephants & got up quite close to them before they deigned to move off. In a wild state they look huge creatures feeding or wading about in the rapids. After pulling some time we saw a canoe ahead tied near two or three huts on an island, we made for it & the men sprang ashore & ransacked the huts in which they found a small basket of beans two large baskets of beautiful Indian corn containing about a peck & a half each, several finely cured gazelle skins some native cloth, & some 15 or 20 large packages of native tobacco well cured & beautifully packed. The mens joy at the sight of the corn was delightful after the dejection one has been seeing for the last few days—they raised their hands & faces up to heaven & said 'Allah be praised'. At 11 I ordered a halt for coffee & divided the corn & tobacco among the men—I reserved one basket of Indian corn for Stanley & ourselves also, 4 packages of tobacco, & divided all the rest among the men; they had a good feed then & there. We saw two of our men lying dead by the side of the track near where we stopped, one was one of Stanley's men & one was one of mine, they both died from hunger & dropped down as they were following the column; one man crawled up on his hands & feet & I gave him a little food & took him on in the boat. All day long we were fighting our way up over the rapids & in the afternoon got amongst a network of islands with rapid channels rushing amongst them. Here we came upon a most extraordinary sight, some 50 natives, men, women & children were in the rapid clinging to rocks & the boughs of trees—they evidently thought the boat would come up the other side of the island & had thought they would hide themselves from us in this way. They were ducking & dodging behind the rocks with just heads above water trying to hide; their terror was great as we approached, women abandoned their children & made for the shore, it was piteous to see small children & babies swept past us in the rapid, one saw tiny hands & feet appearing for an instant above the rushing water & then disappearing for ever over the cataracts below. We captured one man only; though we could have captured numbers, I shall take him to Stanley who will get what information he can out of him. After going another couple of hours we came to the foot of a large cataract & I ordered a halt for the night as it was nearly five & a violent thunderstorm came on which soon drenched us all. As I was trying to get a fire lighted two of Stanleys men came up who told me Stanleys camp was only half an hour ahead. I therefore decided to go on to camp at once & take the Indian corn with me as their food in camp must be nearly out & I dare'nt trust it out of my sight in the present hungry state of the people. I took the native I had captured with me & the Indian corn & got into camp in about half an hour. Stanley & the others were astonished & delighted with the corn so much so that Stanley actually had the grace to say a good word to me—he said 'that's the second time you've done us a good turn you've brought us food now & you captured that large canoe for us down river'. I asked Stanley at once if I might divide out the corn then & there as we were all famishing, he said 'Yes'. I asked on purpose for I knew if I did not see it shared out we should never get our fair share, Stanley never gives it us & we should not otherwise have got it this time even though I myself brought it in. Our share was 36 cups of corn, with care we three can make this last 7 days, of course one will always be hungry but we can exist on it. The tobacco I divided between Stairs Parke & myself. The people are in a perfectly rabid state from hunger & we shall have to carry the corn ourselves on the march for fear of its being stolen. One of our best men was drowned today trying to swim across a rapid to get a canoe.

Oct. 14th. At about 8.30 the boat arrived at camp & later on in the morning Stanley crossed the entire expedition over to the other side. We have heard no tidings of the Chiefs yet so before starting across the river Stanley blazed the trees all round & cut arrows pointing across the river—on one tree he wrote a few lines to Khamis Parry who understands English that we had crossed on Friday 14th & that the chiefs were to follow us if possible. We also stuck in a high pole with an arrow pointing across the river—they cannot fail to understand all these signs. On crossing we camped by the river side & sent the people out to look for food but they came in in the evening reporting, as is usual now, there was none.

Oct. 15th. Stanley had another rubbishing Shauri this morning in which every one gave his opinion & a good many suggestions made as to our plans & much valuable time was wasted in talk which led to nothing as far as any of the suggestions made being followed.[1] Stanley had the previous day sent out Baruku & a party of six men to scour the country & search for the Arab

---

[1] It is a great feature of Stanley's own accounts of his travels that such conferences are described at length and an impression of democratic discussion given. Of this 'shauri' he writes: 'Many suggestions were made by the officers and men, but Uledi of "Through the Dark Continent", always Uledi—the ever faithful Uledi, spoke straight to the purpose. "Sir, my advice is this. You go on with the caravan and search for the Manyuema, and I and my crew will work at these rapids, and pole, row, or drag her on as we can. After I have gone two days up, if I do not see signs of the Manyuema I will send men after you to keep touch with you. We cannot lose you, for a blind man could follow such a track as the caravan makes." This suggestion was agreed by all to be the best, and it was arranged that our rule of conduct should be as Uledi sketched out' (Stanley, *IDA*, I, 219).

track which Stanley was sure lay inland. At last it was decided that we should march on a little way & see if it was possible to come on traces of the Arabs; we accordingly left camp at about 10 o'clock & marched in a Northerly direction away from the river. It was hard work getting the people to take their loads & the road proved very bad & hilly, we got along slowly however, the people picking up a good deal of a certain sort of red fruit—I think it is a kind of cardimon. At about 4.30 we reached Stanley who had struck upon a native camp & had pitched his camp there. He had captured a little Indian corn of which our share was 6 cups, this ensures us three another day's food & is a great catch when we do not know how many more days we may be finding food. Seeing the state of the people Stanley determined to kill his donkey & give the people some meat all round. The donkey was therefore shot & there was a great dividing up of meat amongst the companies; it furnished each man with a fairly good size piece of meat. We Europeans had the hind leg & had soup made & a big stew; the meat was'nt really half bad & we devoured it eagerly though it was a bit tough & queer tasting. At any rate we went to bed that night having had a really satisfying meal for the first time in many days. The men were so starved they fought for the entrails & cleared away every vestige of them. That night two of my men followed the natives & have not come back, my company is now so diminished I hope they will turn up some time or other. Late in the evening Baruku came in & reported finding a large track with blazings on it running parallel with the river. I forgot to mention that on the march today one of the men who had gone up a high tree to get fruit fell down on two other men & crushed them tremendously. The fall was a good 60 feet & the man got a slight concussion of the brain, but after lying senseless for half an hour he was able to stand up & talk—all three men walked into camp afterwards, it was marvellous they were not all killed. Feruzi Ali the man who was cut over the head died this morning of compression of the brain.

Oct. 16th. We started off this morning hoping to reach the Arab track today; the men with this hope before them & feeling the effect of the feed of meat last night marched slightly better than yesterday. I had very bad fever & ague & could hardly get along at all, the men got quantities of red fruit of the wild cardimom & I got a lot—it is very juicy & refreshing & I felt better after eating some of it. We stopped at 11 for coffee & cooked some steaks of donkey meat on the fire—it was very good. At about 12 Stanley sent back word to us that he had come upon the Arab track & was following it up & we hurried on as fast as we could after him. We struck it at about 2 pm & reached Stanleys camp shortly after four. Stanley was very glad about the track & was confident that we should reach the Arabs in two days time. During all this time Stanley's anxiety has been frightful, for the success of the expedition has been & is indeed hanging in the balance.[1] Here he has a starved & worn out people with no food but these miserable beans; Nelson & 60 people with 81 loads are left behind & their chances of relief are daily growing less; the five chiefs who went ahead to look for food have not been heard of; Uledi & the boats crew are on the river making their way up in search of the Arabs & food; 50 sick men are left behind with as many guns at Ugarowa's settlement, & Barttelot & the rest of the men, officers & loads are probably now working their way on after us & will experience all the same troubles about food as we have. The expedition is in fact entirely split up & God only knows whether it will ever be united again. He has been very despondent & low & at times talks about it all in a very hopeless manner. My two men have not yet come in & people drop out & die daily on the road now from hunger, our numbers are getting daily less & less. We had the last of our donkey meat for dinner tonight & we all feel stronger for the four meals of it we have had but it will take us some days of rest & good feeding to pick up for we are still very weak.

Oct. 17th. My fever is very bad today & every bone in my body is racked with pain I have had great trouble in getting along & keeping up with the column. The track to start with was very good but towards the afternoon it got so bad & tangled that we feared lest we had lost it. In the morning the whole column was routed by a nest of hornets who stung the men most frightfully; they threw their loads & ran & it was two hours before the last of the loads was got on again, one poor old man of mine who is nearly dead from starvation must have had at least fifty stings on different parts of his poor thin old body. He plunged into a stream to escape from them & I should say the starvation, the stings & the cold will about do for him. Another man fell from a high tree whilst getting fruit & we left him for dead in the road. In the afternoon a heavy thunderstorm came on & all the men were in a shivering state, this will do them more harm in their present state than two days marching. We reached camp very late & pitched our tent on the dripping drenched ground, for though the rain had ceased everything was very cheerless & wretched. My fever got slightly better this evening.

Oct. 18th. Stanley started off in good time, we were kept behind a bit as we had to investigate a stealing case. Some of our precious corn had been stolen the previous evening from the tent & Yuseph one of my servants & Parke's servant were suspected we investigated the whole thing & Yuseph was found guilty of the theft & got 50 lashes whilst Parke's servant got

---

[1] Much of Stanley's bad temper and ill-considered dealings with officers and men alike should in fairness be attributed to his anxiety—a mitigating circumstance of which Jephson himself seems to have become increasingly aware.

25.[1] We were just starting ahead when we heard volleys of guns a very little distance on & knew at once that Stanley had at last found the Arabs. It was a great relief to us for there was food & rest for the starving people & ourselves. We all hurried on & soon emerged from the interminible, hateful bush & came into great open fields of rice & Indian corn at the far end of which rather more than a mile off we could see the Arab village. This one clearing must be at least 700 acres in extent & one can see another stretching further away still.[2] On reaching the village we found Stanley seated on a skin in the verandah of the chief's house with all the chiefs round him, we all took our seats round & there was a long talk during which a present of three goats & some hundreds of heads of Indian corn were presented to Stanley. The Village & settlement turned out to belong to an Arab of Manyema[3] named Abed bin Salim & the chief here whose name is Khamis is only a slave & acting for him; none of the people here are Arabs but are slaves of Abed bin Salim; they are all of the fat sleek type of Manyema men & are dressed in very pretty clothes made of different coloured fibres of the palm leaf, all are woven here by the women. Khamis gave Stanley a house to live in & one for our three selves, I say a house, but it is merely a hut made of leaves & rough boards with two small rooms, very low & an uneven mud floor. A share of goat was given to us by Stanley & 27 heads each of Indian corn—we had some goat & corn cooked at once for we were ravenous. In the afternoon the people brought us baskets of beans, Indian corn, bananas & chickens to sell but as we have no cloth & they do not care about Matoka, which is the only money Stanley has, we had to buy things with our clothes. In the evening we all went down & had a talk with Stanley. Four heads each of Indian corn was issued to the men & with this miserable allowance they will have to be satisfied today until Stanley has made some allowance with the Arabs for feeding them. This settlement is only seven months old & the rice has not yet come to maturity, but there are five crops of it which will be ripe in another month. Stanley sent us each 27 heads of corn & we had $\frac{2}{5}$ of a goat to last us two days.

[1] Parke records that he lay awake all night listening for the corn 'crackling while being toasted (or "popped") on the fire...I gave my faithful Achates "twenty-four" for this work of supererogation.' He also tells how they tried to keep going on 'forced march tablets', but that they derived no benefit from them. 'We have a little stock of brandy, which we gradually help ourselves to during these days, and it certainly has proved beneficial' (Parke, p. 123).

[2] The name of the settlement was Ipoto, often called 'Kilonga–Longa's' after the trader left in charge by the Zanzibar merchant Abed bin Salim. Stanley describes Kilonga-Longa as 'the slave of Abed bin Salim', and the Manyuema headman Ismailia (Jephson's Assimaili), Khamis and Sangarameni as 'the slaves of Kilonga-Longa' (*IDA*, 1, 338).

[3] More usually spelt Manyuema.

CHAPTER 7

IPOTO WITH KILONGA-LONGA AND THE RESCUE OF NELSON

19 OCTOBER–5 NOVEMBER 1887

Oct. 19th. We just stayed in our hut all day & rested. Nearly all day we were bargaining with men women & children for beans, Indian corn, flour etc for which we gave clothes, bottles or any little thing which struck their fancy.[1] We ransacked our boxes & bags & sold every available thing we could, for we can plainly see that we shall get no food to speak of from Stanley but will have to buy it all ourselves if we want to eat, & after our weeks of starvation we must try all we can to pick up our strength. It is a great shame that we who have worked hard for nothing & have never complained should have to sell what poor clothes we have to get food. We bound ourselves to accept any post under Stanley he chose to give us & to serve him loyally, in return for this he was to feed us & give us a share of native provisions this he is not doing & had we no clothes to sell we might be almost starving in the midst of plenty. It is perfectly scandalous the way he is treating the men— all sorts of promises of food when we reached the Arabs were held out to

---

[1] Lecturing after his return, Jephson was able to make a funny story of their privations at Ipoto: 'Stairs would be holding up a red flannel cholera belt before some fat, well-fed Manyema slave, hoping that its brightness might tempt him to buy it for his wife, with some beans or Indian corn. I would be holding up an old, tattered flannel shirt without any sleeves, and trying to get some sort of bid for it, while Parke, dear soul, with an insinuating smile, which would have charmed a bird off a twig, was trying to get a basket of beans from a woman, by offering her an old pair of duck trousers, which he said was sure to fit her husband beautifully. He was holding them, I remember, and trying artfully to hide from her the fact that they were patched in the seat with a piece of old blue and white checked coverlet. But it was of no use; the sharp eyes of the Manyema spied out all the rents and holes, and we had to lower our prices in the most heart-rending manner...Before leaving England a lady had presented me with a housewife in which there was a remarkable variety of bodkins and needles of every size and shape. The Manyema women bought these eagerly, and those needles alone kept me and my fellow-officers and our servants in food for three whole days. Bottles too were in great request. We had four empty brandy bottles, which, by the way, contained all the brandy we ever had on the expedition. These, Stairs, who had a mania for storing up rubbish, had fortunately kept. For the first bottle we asked the modest sum of six cobs of Indian corn. This was paid at once, and seeing that bottles were so much in demand, we at once raised our prices, and for the fourth bottle got the surprising sum of twenty-five cobs of corn and a small basketful of beans' (printed lecture, undated, among the papers at Mallow Castle).

169

them to urge them forward when we were in the wilderness without food &
now they have only had from him 4 heads of corn for two days. In the evening
Stanley told me that the day after tomorrow I am to return to bring Nelson
& the 81 loads back with me. I am to take 10 of our own men & Khamis will
send some of his Manyema men to take the loads. They propose to reach
Nelson in 5 days, remain one day & return in 5—in all 11 days. Nelson looked
for relief on the 9th day after we left him & this will make it 19 days; I doubt
if we shall find him there, certain it is that 50 per cent of the sick men we
left with him will be dead when we reach him. Stanley I'm afraid means to
leave me behind here with the loads & sick men if I bring Nelson back with
me, I simply hate the idea of staying here but want to get ahead & Stanley
from what I can see would just go off & leave me here without making any
arrangement with the Arabs about supplying me with food etc & I should
just be stranded here a dependant on the charity of slaves.[1] Of course after
bringing Nelson & the loads up here I could follow Stanley with the 10 men
& catch him up, as we could travel without loads three times as quickly as
he could. The prospect of remaining here has made me feel very low.

Oct. 20th. This morning all the companies were mustered in front of
Stanley's hut & a strict investigation of the rifles & ammunition was held.
It was found that some of the men's guns had disappeared in the night &
it was supposed that they had been sold to the Arabs for food—many of the
men were flogged who were suspected of being concerned in the disappearance of the guns. There was general discontent in camp about there
being no food given out & the wholesale flogging. In the afternoon some
men were convicted of selling their rifles & one of them was hanged & the
rest tied up. Whilst all rifles were collected & given over into the charge
of Stairs Parke & I & Stanley made the Arabs give up all the rifles they had
bought at which they were highly indignant. Late in the Afternoon there
was a great firing off of guns among the Arabs for the native chief—Sultan
they called him—of all the land & natives about here had come to make
friends with their enemies the Arabs & had brought in a present of two tusks
of ivory. In the evening I went round to Khamis's hut to see the old savage
chief. He was an awfully ugly old chap; he was sitting or rather squatting
in the verandah of Khamis' hut on a gazelle skin smoking a long pipe. He
was dressed in a spotted deer skin & had an old tin crown on his head; he
had no nose whatever & his bleary old eyes were in a constant state of
running, he spoke in a wheezy old voice & was altogether a disgraceful old
object. His followers sat round him & were rather fine looking men, all had
their faces tattooed & examined me & my clothes in astonishment for I was

---

[1] The position in which Nelson and Parke found themselves. See Appendix IV below,
pp. 434–6.

the first white man they had ever seen. There is some hitch in the arrangements between Stanley & Khamis as to the Manyema men being sent back for Nelson, so I shall not after all start tomorrow.

Oct. 21st. Some of the boat men came in saying they had brought the boat up to a landing place on the river 2 hrs march from here—this is the nearest point from here to the river—they have seen the chiefs who will come up tomorrow, this is a double relief to Stanley as he did not know what had happened to either of the two parties, the men report a large cataract ahead & no food on the river. Stanley will have the boat taken to pieces & left here with the loads. No satisfactory agreement can be come to with Khamis as to sending back to Nelson or for feeding the people—Stanley is afraid he is playing a deep game & is trying to induce the men to desert. He is very low & despondent about the position of the Expedition & talks of returning & going up the Nepoko, but it will not we trust come to that for it would mean we should take months more in getting to the Lake & we are now only $82\frac{1}{2}$ geographical miles from Kavalli the point Stanley wants to strike on the Albert.

Oct. 22nd. The Chiefs came in today they are all very much weakened & pulled down by the starvation they have experienced on their wanderings, my little chief Alsasi wadi Limba is quite changed, he started off a bright cheerful strong little chap & is now pulled down & weak & wretched—I am very sorry about it for he was very useful to me & now I'm afraid he's done for & will have to be left here with the sick. The chiefs have been a long way up the river & report, no food of any sort, the country is evidently a complete wilderness; Khamis told me his people were hungry for two months when they first came here. We did nothing today but rested. Stanley is still negociating with Khamis in the hope of bringing him round, but it is slow work. In the evening he told us he had at last come to an understanding & that I could start off in a couple of days if a party of men whom Khamis had sent out to search for ivory came in—they are expected in tomorrow.

Oct. 23rd. This morning the ivory party came in bringing with them 16 tusks of ivory & a lot of chickens & food, so now I suppose the day after tomorrow I shall start off. It is not a pleasant mission I have on hand for there is no food going or coming & we shall have to travel very fast & I have a bad foot which gives me great pain when I walk, (Agricultural Distress!) I shall go with men whom I know nothing about & they may give me a lot of trouble, still when one thinks of poor Nelson one hardens one's heart & makes up one's mind for the best, at any rate I shall have 10 of my own men with me & with them alone I could relieve Nelson though I could'nt carry the 81 loads. Today we managed to buy some sweet potatoes, a few eggs

& a little honey, they were great luxuries to us. We see very little of Stanley, he stays in his hut all day & we remain near to ours. This evening he came up whilst we were at dinner & remarked that we seemed to be doing very well in the way of food, we told him that except the coffee everything we were eating we had bought with our own clothes—he turned the subject violently.

Oct. 24th. This evening Stanley sent for us all to come to his tent, he then told us he had decided to leave Parke behind here instead of me & that after relieving Nelson I was to hurry after him & catch him up as soon as I could. Of course I was delighted at the change in his plans though I was very sorry for Parke who naturally took it very much to heart. He asked Stanley how long he was likely to be left & Stanley said perhaps three months, perhaps longer, he could'nt say, it all depended on how things turned out. Parke asked if he had made any arrangement about feeding him, Stanley said, the second chief Assimaili had promised to look after him & Nelson, he must 'make love' to Assimaili; a great deal could be got by smiles & then added 'why I smile a dozen times a day'. So all the money Parke has to pay his way with is 'smiles'. Stanley said he did not intend to return this way but to go down the Nepoko & try to get Emin Pasha or his men to come here & get the rest of the ammunition left here or to send men of his own to bring it on with Parke & leave Nelson here till Barttelot came up bringing with him the bales of cloth, for Stanley had promised the chiefs a present of a bale & a half of cloth so Nelson would be a hostage in the hands of the Manyema until the cloth was paid; this may mean a stay of nine months here for Nelson, for goodness knows when the expedition under Barttelot will be able to get up here, if we have experienced such frightful difficulties & troubles under Stanley, the troubles of the expedition under Barttelot will be ten times as great as he has no experience of the country & the men will not be likely to have the same faith in his leadership that they have in Stanley's. Parke's lookout here is certainly not very bright, it would be much better if there were some real Arabs here instead of there only being these Manyema slaves. Poor old Parke takes it very badly indeed & cannot make up his mind to the inevitable, though I must say that it is hard to do so under the circumstances. Stanley has not even made any arrangement about getting Nelson & Parke a hut to live in. We sat up over the fire talking it all over till very late that night.

Oct. 25th. I was to have started today but Khamis came up & told Stanley that he was expecting his big chief in today & the people wanted to see him & the people before starting back with me. Of course Stanley could only say 'why certainly' so I shall not leave till tomorrow—Stanley proposes starting the next day. Meanwhile I have been buying all the meal &

beans I can afford to buy with my clothes to last me on the road for there is no food & I do not expect Stanley will give me very much. The expedition which came in today turned out to be one from the Lendi river—the same people we saw down river—& not the one Khamis expected so we might have started after all today, they were only an ivory hunting party who brought in very little ivory but great quantities of chickens Indian corn banana's etc.

Oct. 26th. Stanley had all the men fallen in early this morning—the men who were considered to be too sick to go on, 28 in number, were picked out & the remaining men—145 in number—were formed into two companies one for Stanley & one for Stairs—I expect when I catch up Stanley I shall have to look after his company, a by no means pleasant job—Stanley picking out all the best men left in Stairs' Nelson's & my companies & leaving Stairs the worst men. Khamis only brought 30 men instead of the 80 he had promised to send back with me so Stanley gave me 40 men out of Stairs & his companies. He expected me to be back in 11 days & gave me 110 heads of Indian corn to last me that time, but half of these were so small & unripe that the number might be put down at half. He then gave me Nelson's food for 6 days—a good sized plateful of coarse hard flour & one small chicken.[1] When this was brought in he remarked that it was an ample allowance for that time. I said nothing but I think my face must have expressed the disgust I felt at the scandalous smallness & meanness of the allowance for a few minutes after the food was taken away to my hut he sent another small chicken for me to take on—it was very fortunate for me & for Nelson as well that I had sold my clothes for food, we should have been on short commons indeed had we depended entirely on Stanley. The fact of having 40 of our men will I'm afraid make me much longer in getting back here as they are worn out & will give me much more trouble than the Manyema who will be managed entirely by their own chiefs. The Manyema men got off by 10.30 & were soon followed by my own men—I got off by about one o'clock & reached the river & got across to camp by 4.30. Before starting Stanley sent for me & told me what to do in case Nelson had died before I reached him—he seemed to be very much affected at the possibility of such a thing but I cannot believe it was real. Arrived at camp I served out 100 rounds of ammunition to the men & pitched the fly of the tent after putting the bag containing Nelsons & my food in a safe place. I do not expect to catch Stanley under 30 days.

[1] Stanley's account of supplies for the relief party is rather different: 'For some fancy articles of personal property I succeeded in purchasing for Mr. Jephson and Capt. Nelson 250 ears of India corn, and for 250 pistol cartridges I bought another quantity, and for an ivory-framed mirror from a dressing-case purchased two baskets full; for three bottles of ottar of roses obtained three fowls, so that I had 1000 ears of corn for the relieving and relieved parties' (Stanley, *IDA*, I, 237).

Oct. [*26*]*th.* I got men started off early & followed in rear of all closely following my man carrying the food. The road was bad & muddy & there were a great many rivers to cross, all of which I just waded through. We reached the camp where we had crossed the river at 11AM. The arrows on the trees were still very plain pointing the way across the river, but Stanley's directions to Khamis Parry which were written in ink on the blazed tree were hardly legible now from rain & exposure. Soon after this a tremendous thunderstorm came on which made the road very bad & one constantly sank up to one's knees in the thick mud in which elephants & hippopotami had been wading & as my right foot was so sore I was only marching in a slipper sort of boot I could not get on very fast. I reached Stanley's next camp at 3 o'clock & found all the people had stopped there on account of the rain, I wanted to go on but the Manyema were so averse to going on & said they were so cold & wretched from the rain that I was obliged to stop much against my will & camp for the night. We are now three of our marches from Nelson's camp, I hope to reach him by tomorrow evening. A second thunderstorm came on & soon put out my fire but I just managed to get my porridge & beans cooked but I had to eat them in darkness in my tent in cheerless dampness with the rain dripping & splashing round me & turning the camp rapidly into a swamp.

Oct. [*27*]*th.* The rain had made the track very bad & there was mud up to ones knees in some places. The Manyema promised to go far today but at a place near where I had before returned to mend the boat when I was nearly dropping from hunger they all stopped to go up the trees to hunt for fruit, the consequence was I pushed on with five or six men & left the people to follow. I got to the Starvation camp opposite the island where we captured so many women & where poor Feruzi Ali got his death wound at about 12 o'clock only, the Manyema & Wangwana coming up half an hour after. I was so hoping to get to Nelson today & now I cannot possibly reach him till tomorrow morning & all through the laziness of the Manyema. I had gathered a lot of fungus on the way & had it & the few bananas I had left cooked. The old camp looked very dismal indeed, we had spent three miserable days of hunger & uncertainty there with the men lying in their shelters at night groaning all round us. I never expected to see it again—this going over the scene of one's sufferings when the remembrance of them is still so vivid in one's mind is very depressing, the more so that I am going on a mission which may turn out to have a very sad ending & we are not safely through our prospects of starvation yet. At this rate I shall never catch up Stanley. I had my food cooked just where Stairs & [I] had cooked our food & talked so dismally over the fire on the night of my birthday which was about the most miserable one I've ever spent—we had talked of the poor chance Nelson had yet awhile of being relieved yet awhile & yet we neither of us expected his relief would be so long in coming. As I come along I make all sorts of conjectures as to whether I shall find Nelson all right in camp. After remaining an hour I started on with my tent bag & bag of food, I could not get the Manyema to move as they said there were still some of their men behind, I said, very well I shall go on & you can follow. They followed shortly after but soon complained of being tired & wanted to camp, so much against my will I was obliged to camp at 3PM, only 1½ hrs march from Starvation camp. It is a ridiculously short march & I am furious about it, our tired & starving people did very nearly the same march in the day & they were carrying loads, I can see I shall have many difficulties with them on the return journey when they have loads, in fact when I think of all I have to get through before I leave the Arab camp I feel a despair of ever catching Stanley up. Im quite sure I shall have a lot of trouble in getting up the boat to the camp & a great many desertions before getting clear of it; if Stanley had difficulty in getting the people out, how much more must I expect to have & yet I know Stanley will make no allowance for those difficulties even if he allows there are any, he always slangs one indiscriminately so one must just make up one's mind to grin & bear it.

Oct. 28th. Before starting this morning the Manyema brought one of my men up before me & complained that he had stolen their corn in the night, I could do nothing to the man though it was quite clear he had stolen from them, I merely told them to keep a better look out for their corn & to shoot any thief they detected in act of stealing just as they do in their own camp— this is the second instance of stealing which has occurred since I started. After settling the case after a great deal of talk, I started off with one man only determining to get to Nelson's camp that day & decide the question as to whether he was yet alive or what had become of him. I soon passed the Manyema & Wangwana who had gone ahead & was soon far beyond any one. How vivid every incident of that miserable march appeared as I passed place after place where I had had difficulty in urging forward our starving people who were carrying the boat. Here was the stream which had taken us so much time & trouble to get the boat sections across & here was the bank up which we had to drag up the boat & cut a way through the bush. On the road were three skeletons of our men who had just fallen down & died from sheer starvation. We had passed some further back on the road, they were grim reminders of our days of starvation when we were wandering hopelessly on in search of food; until one saw these proofs of our hunger one hardly realised how bad had been our case & how narrowly the whole caravan had escaped anihilation. The man with me was one of those very men who had helped to carry the boat & at several bad places he said 'Look

Master do you remember the trouble we had here'. All was passed by rapidly today. As I hurried along I picked up any fungus or fruit I saw & carried it along with me for I did not know if every atom of food I could get would not be wanted for the starving people in camp. As I said before Stanley had provided me with no food for the people left in camp & only the very smallest amount for Nelson, so small an amount that I wonder he was not ashamed when he handed it over into my charge. As I neared Nelson's camp my anxiety to know Nelson's fate became intense & I hurried along through bushes & streams utterly regardless of anything so that my clothes were soon split & torn & my knickerbockers hung in tatters from my knees. As we were hurrying along within half a mile of Nelson's camp we suddenly came on a half starved man wearily searching for fruit or fungus, he was one of the sick men left with Nelson. In great excitement I plied him with questions & learned that Nelson was alive but was in great straits for food & was much pulled down from hunger. Without waiting to hear more I pushed on & soon got to the camp. As I entered it not a sound was to be heard except the groans of two dying men in a hut close by, the whole place looked woebegone & deserted. I came quietly round the tent & found Nelson sitting there—he started up with an exclamation of astonishment, we clasped hands & then poor old chap he turned away & sobbed like a child & muttered something about being very weak, twenty two days of hunger & torturing anxiety with the suspicion that we had abandoned him had brought him down in body & mind—as for me with an hysterical gulpy feeling I rushed off & began to prepare some food & after putting it down to the fire I returned to the tent to hear Nelson's experiences during the 22 days he had been left.[1] Seventeen men had died, Jumah Unyamwezi, Stairs chief, with ten men, of whom two were my boys Almas & Nasibu who had been so pulled down that I left them with Nelson, had stolen the big canoe & had deserted & gone down river in the night. Omari, Nelson's chief, & twenty men had gone off in search of food & had not yet returned, they had been away twelve days & I am inclined to think they have deserted, but Nelson has great faith in him & does not think so, especially as Omari went away before & was eight days away before he returned & brought a small supply of dry bananas into camp. The 20 men with Omari were all in the last stage of starvation so perhaps some catastrophe has happened to the party & they have not been able to get back. Suédi who stole Stanleys box of clothes &

[1] After his return to Cairo, Stanley reported on the conduct of his officers: 'Like the Roman soldier at the burying of Herculanaeum, under the fires of Vesuvius, Captain Nelson remained at his post.' And as for Jephson, 'The relief of Captain Nelson at Starvation Camp is a striking example of indomitability of spirit, courage and celerity of movement'. (Stanley to the Committee of the E.P.R.E., Villa Victoria, Cairo, 25 March 1890. Mackinnon Papers, S.O.A.S., University of London.)

Rehani who stole Parke's clothes on the way to the Arab camp had come into Nelsons camp at night & after making an attempt at robbing the tent had jumped into one of the canoes—the large one I had dragged down to the river at Nepoko—& had gone down river taking with him five or six men from the camp. Others had deserted at different times & out of 56 men left with Nelson only 6 men were left, two of whom were in a dying state & the other four so reduced by illness & hunger that only two would be able to drag themselves after me to the Arab camp. Nelsons two boys Osmani & Fickerini had kept him alive, they went out every day & brought in fungus & Mabungu, the latter is the fruit of the india rubber vine, a pleasant enough fruit but not one that one could exist on very long & Nelson could only get it in limited quantities. Nelson's despair at being left in this way with men daily dying round him & other deserting with no food hardly & lastly the feeling that something had happened to the expedition & that Stanley had been obliged to abandon him must have been terrible. He told me he was unable to sleep at night from anxiety. Omari had tried to persuade him to leave the ammunition as Stanley was evidently unable to relieve him & to go down river to where there was food; Nelson was sorely tempted to do so but felt he could not leave his post. Poor old chap he looked terribly haggard & pulled down & there were deep lines round his eyes & mouth which told plainly of starvation & sleepless nights of anxiety & care. He looked altogether shrunken & small & much older & moved about very painfully. His feet & legs had been bad some days before we left him & since we left him he had had no less than 10 small ulcers on them, five of them have got well, but he is only just able to get on a large shoe & to walk. It did one good to see how he enjoyed the porridge, chicken & beans I got ready for him. We sat up till late that night for there was much to tell him of our experiences since we left him & of Stanleys plans. He seemed quite resigned at the idea of being left with the Arabs, & indeed he could not go on with us in the weak state he is in & his feet are not likely to get well for some time yet, particularly if he is obliged to march. He was very much interested in hearing all about our difficulties before reaching the Arab camp & was much amused at the idea of our eating Stanleys donkey. As he was unable to sleep at night from excitement he woke me up at about 12 oclock & we sat round the fire smoking & talking for a couple of hours.

Oct. 29th. This morning I was up early to get the loads given out & the men started off, for I was anxious to lose no time in returning as there is no food to be got here & I have much to get through before starting after Stanley. The Manyema exclaimed at the weight of the loads & as some of them were mere boys & five of them women it was not to be wondered at, though I noticed the women took their loads without a word & started off with them, poor things I expect they have a rough time of it. They carry their loads as I have noticed all the natives about here do, suspended on their backs by a band passing across their foreheads. Of the 30 sent with me only 24 were able to take loads & as I had to put two of my own men on to one load the consequence was I was obliged to leave 13 boxes of ammunition & some other loads all of which I buried—Parke will, I hope, be able to get some men & return for them bye & bye. I started the Manyema off first but it was 12 oclock before I had got the last of the Wangwana off & had buried the loads. Nelson started off an hour or so before me & got on wonderfully well considering. I came on him sitting down resting by the way & started on for camp to get food & a bed ready for him when he arrived. The men had gone further than I expected & had reached my camp of the day before, that was two of Stanleys marches & as we had not left Nelsons camp till 12 it was very good going. I had not expected them to get so far & was not surprised when a man brought me word from Nelson that he was unable to reach camp but had camped in the jungle further back; he had food & all that he wanted so it did not much matter though I was sorry to be seperated from him again so soon, I sent a man back with a note to him saying I would wait for him in the morning after sending on the loads.

Oct. 30th. Last night there was another case of stealing from the Manyema they made a devil of a noise in camp & brought the man up before me, I should like to have flogged the man but thought it better policy not to as the men are only too ready to have an excuse for deserting. About an hour & a half after I had started off the loads Nelson came up, but as he said he thought he would be able to go well today especially as he had the whole day to reach camp in, I started off almost at once. On reaching the camp where we had spent the three memorable days of starvation I found to my disgust that the Manyema & some of my men had got up the canoe we had sunk near the river's bank & a good many men & loads had already crossed intending to go back to the Arab camp by a road on the other side of the river, whilest three of the Manyema had gone on with their loads by the road by which we had travelled on our way to Nelson. It was my intention to have returned by the same road as I came for the boat was ready to take us across & we knew the road, besides too I was to have left my chief Rajab bin Jumah to take the boat to pieces whilest I hurried on to the Arab camp with the loads, I should have returned the next day with men to take it up to the village & have thus saved a day. Entreaties or commands were useless, the Manyema were determined to cross & said if I insisted on their going by my road they would throw their loads. As I was entirely in their hands I was obliged to submit which I did with a very ill grace. We accordingly all crossed, but the canoe was so small & the river so rapid just here that it was nearly three o'clock before we all got across. When we got across the road was by no means good & as it led away from the river & the Manyema had hardly blazed it at all we had great difficulty in finding it, it was the harder to find being intersected by innumerable elephant tracks. After going for about two hours we had to camp with only about 10 men with us, the rest of the Wangwana & all the Manyema had camped further on. We had just finished our dinner of porridge & beans when a furious thunderstorm came on & as we only had the fly of the tent pitched gipsy fashion we spent rather a damp night—my bag with clothes & blankets was far ahead.

Oct. 31st. Nelson was for recrossing the river & going up by my road, but I was against it & the men also so it was decided we should follow the Manyema tracks as best we could. After following it with difficulty, for there were very few blazes, in a northerly direction we came on their camp from which they had started off this morning in a Southerly direction. Yesterday they told me there was a village they were going to where they would get food & I fancy that after coming so far & finding no regular track, they got frightened & returned, at any rate they returned almost on the same track they travelled yesterday & then turned off in a South Easterly direction along a track parallel to the river but a good way from it. The road taking it altogether was not bad, but it certainly did not justify the expectations of it that the Manyema had raised, moreover there was no more food than there was on my road. Several times during the day we missed the track for they were continually blazing the track & then returning & taking another. We came on a poor little native child lying in the road, it was mere skin & bone & emitted a faint cry only when I lifted it up—of course we had to leave it on the road, probably some of its people will find it & bring it along. I stopped in the middle of the day to give Nelson some food & a rest & we got his hammock slung between two trees & he was able to get a good hours rest while I got some porridge & coffee made for him. Leaving Nelson to follow slowly I hurried on to try & catch the Manyema & most of my men who had gone on with them & get them to camp & wait for Nelson to come up, besides I did not want them to get right away from me. I went on till half past three & as I could not come up with them I was obliged to camp & get the tent up & my bed ready for Nelson who I was sure would be done up as we had come a long way today. He came in at 5 oclock utterly worn out & almost speechless & just lay down on my bed exhausted—I was quite alarmed by his looks, he looked so haggard & wan. The rain which lasted nearly all night came down soon after in torrents, but the boys had rigged up a sort of shelter & were able to cook us a good dinner of beans & porridge. My chief Rajab bin Jumah did not come in tonight I hope he is not lost, he will probably turn up during the day.

November 1st [1887]. Leaving Nelson to follow with the loads I started off with one man only hoping to reach the Arab camp in good time today. After going for about an hour we lost the road, for the Manyema had made no blazes & the rain of the night before had washed out all their foot marks. It was all dense scrub & we wandered about for nearly 3 hours trying to find the track & I was finally obliged to cut my way through the bush with nothing but a large knife I had borrowed from one of the men. I soon came upon large clearings in which were quantities of recently planted bananas & I finally came upon a collection of half ruined native huts where the Manyema had camped the night before—here I found two of my men with loads. As it was nearly 12 oclock I waited for Nelson to come up & we got some coffee made & then I started on expecting to reach the Arab camp in the course of an hour or so, but to my astonishment & disgust after going for an hour I struck Stanleys old road 1½ marches from the Arab camp. I went on till four & camped about 5 miles from the Arab camp just at the place where one of our men had fallen from a high tree when we were on our wanderings for food. Nelson came up worn & tired out, it will be a good thing for him when this marching is done for it knocks him up terribly every day & he cannot go on much longer. He wanted me to leave him behind to follow & go on ahead to look after the loads & get my work done so that I could follow Stanley quickly, but I do not like to lose sight of him & now I've brought him out of danger I wo'nt let go of him until I've landed him safely with Parke. He is a tremendous drawback for I can only make such limited marches with him, but tomorrow I shall reach the Arab camp for certain as I know exactly how far it is—the Manyema will just about reach camp today. Rajab bin Jumah has not yet been heard of, I most sincerely hope he is not lost for he is most useful to me & is such a nice fellow, Nelson saw him yesterday not far from camp going up a tree to get fruit, it is possible he may have had a fall.

Nov. 2nd. Got off as early as possible leaving Nelson to follow. I knew every foot of this last march for I had travelled along it so slowly, dragged down by hunger & starvation & racked with fever & ague. I passed three skeletons of our men in the track within 200 yds of each other—the ants & birds had eaten them quite clean & what poor clothes they had on them were left untouched—they were fresh proofs of the trials through which we had gone, looking back on it all from the time we left Nelson on Oct 6th till the time we reached the Arab camp Oct 18th it seems like a bad nightmare, a hideous dream, except that these skeletons on the road & those we left in nearly every camp prove that our sufferings were grim reality. I got to our last camp at about 9 oclock & reached the Arab village at 10. There was a great air of quietness in the village when I got there for all the people nearly

were out working in the fields, it was a great change from the time when
we were they when all was bustle & confusion. Our hut looked very lonely
& deserted; Parke was sitting in front of it & was very much surprised at
seeing me back so soon—Stanley had given me 11 days to do the trip in &
I have been only 8 even with the drawback of having been obliged to come
by a longer road & having Nelson with me—& was still further surprised
that Nelson was only a few hours behind. The Manyema had as I expected
come in last night & three men who had gone by my road & crossed the
river in the boat had come in on the evening of the day before yesterday
thus doing the whole trip in 6½ days. Parke told me some of the boxes of
ammunition carried by my men had been tampered with & some of the
Matako I was bringing with me had been stolen but all the rifles had come
in all right & all the people had come in except those behind with Nelson.
Stanley will be very mad about the ammunition being stolen. Parke was
strong in his expressions of disgust at the way in which Stanley had left him
without any proper arrangements being made with the chiefs of the Manyema
for feeding him—last night he had only one head of corn for dinner, ever
since Stanley left it had been a struggle to get food—Stanley left on the 27th
the day after I started off to relieve Nelson, he had allowed Stairs no food
for the road & had given the men none, fortunately Stairs was fairly well
provided as he had sold a large part of his clothes for food—Stanley himself,
so Parke tells me, took quantities of food & great numbers of chickens.
He did not even take the trouble to say good bye to Parke when he went,
which to put it mildly was ungracious. It is really quite wonderful how little
Stanley seems to care about the welfare of his officers, he seems to take no
interest whatever in what they do or how they manage to get on. I think it
is a mistake his having European officers under him, he should merely have
Zanzibar chiefs & see to all the work himself. He expects his officers too
much to understand what he wants done without telling them & is constantly
giving orders to the men without letting the officers know that such orders
are given, the result is often an absurd confliction of ideas & Stanley gets
furious & completely loses his head & says things which he must sincerely
regret saying when he comes to his senses. He has left Parke & Nelson
entirely dependant for food & housing on the charity of the three Manyema
chiefs who are themselves merely the slaves of Abed bin Salim a Zanzibar
Arab who is now in Mecca. They are a very low class of men, so the white
men's look out is not a pleasant one whilest they stay with the Manyema,
which I'm afraid will be for a good many months to come. On hearing of
the poor state of Parkes commissariat I at once sold a shirt for a couple of
chickens & one of the bottles out of my dressing case for some Indian meal
& beans so that Nelson might have a good meal when he came in, he had

expressly asked me to tell Parke to have a good dinner ready for him & I did not want him to be disappointed—poor old Nelson he's a terrible one for his food! I have now only two shirts left, but I was awfully sorry to have to sell the dressing case bottle. I hope if this journal is ever read by the giver of the dressing case, I shall be forgiven.[1] I found that Khamis the head chief & one of the others together with a good many of the minor chiefs had gone away two days before on a round of visits to the native camps for miles round which were all under the old native Sultan who came in some fortnight since. He had been fighting with the Arabs for 5 months & had just made friends with them & this round of visits which Khamis was making was an earnest of his friendship, he is to be away two months. All my arrangements therefore will have to be made with Assimaili who is second in command. At about one oclock Nelson came in & was welcomed by Parke, he was very much done up; it is a very good thing for him that this marching is done. His frame is greatly shrunken & he is just like an old man, he is terribly irratable & quarrelsome but one knows he has been through a great deal & is really in need of rest, he is unable to sleep at night & that is always an excuse for any amount of irratability. Assimaili came up to see Nelson & brought him a present of a small basket of coarse meal & two small dried fish. We sat round the fire till pretty late talking over Nelson's experiences & Stanley's arrangements or rather lack of arrangements for Parke's & Nelson's feeding whilst they stayed in the Arab camp.

Nov. 3rd. This morning I intended to take a few men down to the boat to take her to pieces & get her ready to bring up to the village tomorrow, I could however only get together three men all the rest had gone out to work in the fields for food & were skulking amongst the network of huts & one could not get them out. It was of no use going down with three men only as Parke had let Uledi the coxswain & 6 sailors go off with Khamis to get food & though they had promised to return in two days they had not yet turned up, there were only 4 men left down at the boat & they were insufficient to drag her out of the water & bring up the seats bolts etc to the camp, I was therefore obliged to give up the attempt today on the under-standing that all would turn up tomorrow & get her up. Their complaint

[1] When very ill with fever on the way back Jephson made a will (dated 11 May 1889, see Plate 13, between pp. 256–7). It was written in pencil on a half-sheet of paper. He asked Stairs to take charge of his effects, after him Parke and after him Nelson. His journals and agreement with Stanley were to go to the Countess de Noailles, and his dressing-case to Miss Blennerhasset. She was the sister of Sir Rowland Blennerhasset, Bt., and they lived in Ireland not far from the Jephson property at Mallow. Miss Blennerhasset had a remarkable career as a nursing sister first at Johannesburg and later in Rhodesia, in Mashonaland. She helped to set up the first hospital in Umtali. Can one assume that she was the donor of the dressing-case?

was that they could not work without food & it was a just one, as Stanley had made no arrangement for feeding the men during their stay here, I saw I should be obliged to give them food if I wanted them to work & therefore went to Assimaili to see if I could get any food for them. He wanted 300 Remington cartridges for 350 head of corn & as he would not come down in his price I was obliged to let him have them—the price is of course preposterous. Probably Stanley will be very angry with what I have done, but here are the men come from a hard march with no food & then expected to do hard work immediately again without food. Nelson & Parke had interviews with Assimaili on the question of his feeding them & their three boys, he said that when he ate they should eat, but judging from the amount he had hitherto sent Parke one can only come to the conclusion that either Assimaili does not do what he undertakes to perform or that he has a marvellously small appetite, & as he is very fat & well nourished one cannot think it is the latter—the boys he utterly refused to feed. Nelson afterwards had a further interview & presented Assimaili with his cavalry sword & the result was that he said if Nelson wrote to Stanley & got his written promise to give Assimaili two bales more of cloth when Barttelot's carravan came up, Parke & he should be fed better & their boys should also be fed. Nelson therefore wrote a letter to Stanley giving a description of all that had occured since he was left in camp upon Oct 6th & a complete list of all the men who had died or deserted, he also told Stanley the state of affairs in the Arab Camp & enclosed a paper agreeing to pay the Committee in London the sum of £50 or any further sum demanded if Stanley would send two bales of cloth to pay for his & Parke's maintainence whilest staying in the Arab camp—it is of course scandalous that Nelson should be obliged to do this— the value of a bale of cloth at home is probably £4 or £5. I am to be the bearer of Nelson's & Parke's letters & they hope to get an answer by the Manyema guides who accompanied Stanley, if I can catch him before they leave, which is doubtful. If they cannot get an answer from him their position for some months to come will be anything but enviable. It is an awful shame that they should be treated in this way after having worked hard for the expedition all these months & having gone through hardships for the good of it perfectly uncomplainingly, it is surprising that Stanley even little as we know he cares about our welfare should care to leave them in such a dilemma. Today I began to buy food for the road as Stanley has made no provision for me. I sold anything I could—one of my blankets had to go to Assimaili for Indian meal—I regret the sale of this very much for I fear when we get near the lake at the higher altitude & in the open plain I shall need all my blankets to keep me warm at night, I had also to sell a lot of needles & thread & a pair of scissors to the women for a small amount of Indian meal & beans. Tomorrow I hope to get the boat up & start after Stanley the next day, for I shall be absolutely cleaned out of clothes if I stay here much longer.

Nov. 4th. On attempting to fall the men in to go down to the boat I experienced much the same difficulty as I did yesterday, but with the help of Assimaili I managed to get together 11 & with them I went down to the river to get the boat taken to pieces. On the way down I came upon one of our men dying in the road, he was one of the men who had deserted with his load when Stanley left here. I could not find his load but took away his rifle—it will be a salutary lesson to the men who are with me not to run away unless they want to die of hunger. On getting down to the boat I found the sailors in a very poor condition they were quite different men from what they were when they rowed me across the river a fortnight ago; they had been living on tree beans & fungus & had not apparently thrived on such poor fare. I got the boat taken to pieces & carried up to camp. The boat sections I had to put in a large open space in the jungle about 20 yds from the river & well above high water mark ready to be carried up to the village, though I'm afraid that work will have to be done by Assimaili's men & Stanley will have to deduct the price of the work from the mens wages. I got the loads carried to the village by one oclock & stowed them away in Parke's hut, there is nothing left out in the open of the boat that can spoil, but it is a great source of trouble to me that I ca'nt get it up as Stanley told me. The men got afraid of it when they had to carry it those days when we were all starving & the badness of the road & the logs we have to climb over seem to have completely funked them.

Nov. 5th. This morning I was determined to give the men another chance to get up the boat & to give Uledi & the 6 sailors another days grace, I therefore decided not to start till tomorrow though it was much against my will to remain here another day, for Stanley will be getting too far ahead of me if I do'nt look out. The men did not turn up & as I could not get them together they simply ran away into the fields when they knew I was coming, so I could only abandon the idea of getting up the boat & get the loads ready for starting tomorrow morning. Of Uledi & his men nothing has yet been heard. Poor Rajab bin Jumah I'm afraid he has met with some accident he has not turned up & I fear he is done for. I'm awfully sorry, apart from his being a most useful man one had quite an affection for him for he was always so nice & obliging & civil; he always went with me wherever I went & always looked after me & carried me across streams etc, he used to say he was going back to England with me & had in fact quite attached himself to me. I shall miss him horribly & he will be a great loss to the Expedition.

CHAPTER 8

IPOTO TO LAKE ALBERT

6 NOVEMBER–11 DECEMBER 1887

Nov. 6th. This morning the men turned up readily enough & I issued rifles to them & gave them out their loads 17 in number putting two men to each load so that they can travel quickly. Parke had an inspection of all the sick Stanley had left behind & pronounced 8 of them fit for marching, they will accompany me. I gave out Indian corn to the men who had gone down to the boat with me, to the sailors & to the 8 men Parke was sending, to those men who did not come down to get the boat up I gave no corn. It took some time getting all this done & I did not leave the village till 12 o'clock. I went ahead & Parke promised to follow in the rear to some distance to see all the men safely out of the village. I reached Stanleys first camp in three hours & decided to stay there the night & do two of his marches tomorrow if possible, I did not like to press the people too much on the first day particularly as the men Parke is sending on are far from strong yet. Stanley's camp was by some ruined native huts & I got my tent pitched & the loads put inside in good time. I felt sorry to part from Nelson & Parke, I had just relieved Nelson from starvation & I should see neither he nor Parke for many months to come—perhaps never. We had lived & worked together & had been thrown closely into one anothers society for the last nine months & had always got on excellently well it is melancholy too that the Expedition should be broken up in this way.

Nov. 7th. I started off in good time but did not go as fast as I should have liked, many of the men had bad feet & the road in many places lay through half deserted native fields & there were logs to be climbed over in the track constantly & often it was just climbing from trunk to trunk sometimes one was 10 feet from the ground. At 11 we reached Stanley's second camp close to more ruined huts in the middle of half deserted native clearings. Here I found the men in front had managed to get a good many bananas & the natives were bringing them in in the most friendly manner—all the natives for days ahead are under the Manyema. I stayed here for two hours to enable the men to get a good supply of food, but on attempting to start them on found they were anxious to remain there for the night, as the natives had told them Stanley remained there two days, this I do not believe for Stanley told me he intended to travel as quickly as possible to get out of this starvation country. I told the people if we only made one march to Stanley's one we should never catch him up, so I said I should go ahead & started off with one man & my boy. The road led through half deserted native fields for about a mile & a half over logs & then we struck the jungle again. There were huge plantations of plantains but none were fit to eat as far as we could see, Stanleys people must have cleared all out that had been left by the Manyema, there were also quantities of sweet potatoe vines & the remains of Indian corn & manioc, but all had been cleared out months ago by the Manyema. After going for about 2½ hours I camped & lit a fire, I had neither tent, blankets, or my bag of food; I had picked some fungus on the road & fortunately had a few head of Indian corn which I divided between myself & the two men with me. None of the people turned up at all. I had my dinner of fungus soup & roasted corn & wrapping myself in my mackintosh I lay down on my bed of leaves beside a huge fire & soon fell asleep. At about 12 oclock a furious thunderstorm came on & I sat in front of the fire in the pelting rain for two hours watching it being slowly put out, fortunately the boy had piled quantities of wood on it & the rain stopped before it was quite out. He soon made it up again & I lay down wet as I was & slept soundly till morning.

Nov. 8th. Up early & got some tea made & some tree beans roasted—the Zanzibaris call them Quemma. After waiting for a couple of hours the first of the loads came up & amongst them was my bag of food, this I stopped and got some porridge made whilest I waited for the rear guard to come up. The last of the loads did not turn up for another two hours & I waited impatiently till near 10 o'clock to see the last of them go by & then started off after them. We went a good long march before we came to more deserted native fields in which there were great quantities of bananas & sweet potatoes but all in so immature a state as to be of no use. In the middle of the fields was a small deserted native village where I arrived at about 2 o'clock, here Stanley had camped & here I found all the men as yesterday had stopped & were unwilling to go on. I stayed about 20 minutes & got a few bananas cooked which the men gave me & then started on leaving the men to follow or not as they pleased. I took good care however this time to take the two men carrying my bag of food & tent with me. I went on for about 2 hours & camped in the jungle & got my tent pitched & food cooked before dark. I had some fungus & beans boiled together, it is really a splendid dish, the soup tastes exactly as if it was made with meat. I cannot understand why the men are behaving in this way, none of them have followed me on to camp, they all say they are anxious to catch Stanley & yet when they have done one of his marches they say they are tired & want to stop; they quite understand that if they do only one march to Stanley's one we shall never catch him up still though they quite see it they say they are tired & can't go on, it is like talking to a brick wall. The chief Khamis Parry is a horrid fellow & is worse than useless for he is a bad example to the men, he just gets to Stanley's camp & lies down & cooks his food & no arguments or commands will move him to do anything. One decent chief would take all this trouble off my hands, he would speak to the people & they would all go on. If only Uledi had been with me there would be no worry, I wish he would catch me up, if this state of things goes on much longer it may be disastrous. It is partly Stanleys fault he never does act as he says he will, he told me when I left to go down to Nelson to bring on only two boxes of ammunition & on my return I find orders to bring on nine, of course when forced marches have to be made 7 extra loads make a great difference.

Nov. 9th. This morning I started off with my boy & the three men with me leaving the people behind to follow. I shall now go ahead of the men every day & see if that has a better effect, of course it would be the right thing to do if I had any trustworthy chief behind to bring up all the loads, but I'm afraid I shall lose some of the loads by doing so, at any rate it does not much matter how I lose them for I feel sure some will be lost either way, Stanley will have to settle up with the people when we catch him up if we ever do catch him that is to say—it looks very doubtful. I feel as if I had fever coming on I suppose it is the result of sleeping out in the rain the night before last & sleeping last night without blankets—I was very cold last night—my quinine is behind in my box I would give a good deal to have it with me. The road is fairly good but very muddy in places, it is much better than the road near the river, there are not those continual creeks to wade through & rivers to cross, all these jungle streams are shallow & gravelly. I stopped at 10.30 to get tea made & the men caught me up & went on to Stanley's camp & made preparations for stopping the night. I spoke to them again & told them the folly of doing this every day & after talking with them for a quarter of an hour I started on saying I should go on till 3.30. The result was a good many men brought on their loads & camped near me in a deserted native encampment. I was very bad with fever & ague & lay down as soon as my tent was pitched, it was most fortunate my blankets were with me & my box containing my quinine came up soon after—I took 25 grains at once.

Nov. 10th. I had a very bad night of it, my head & limbs were racked with pain & I could get no rest, this morning before starting I took 12 more grains of quinine to try & get rid of the fever. As I went along I could hardly see from the combined effects of the fever & quinine, the rain of the night before dripping from the bushes as I went along the track soon wet me through & did not improve the fever. Stanley has done fairly long marches I am surprised that his people should march so well, I did not reach his camp till 12 & I was gong fast the whole time. At 11 I came on large half deserted native fields & after going through them climbing over logs etc I came on a native village which was the site of Stanleys camp I found 6 or 8 men had come on the day before with their loads & had slept here, so much for my speaking to them, this is two of Stanleys marches that they have done, now that the ice is broken I hope the people will make the two marches every day. In the village there were five or six natives who were friendly enough, they were armed with arrows & bows the arrows had enormous barbed iron heads. The chief had a large round shaped hut in the centre of the village with a doorway at each end. The natives about here when they wish to show they are friends call out 'Borrdu, Borrdu; Brenda, Brenda' & one answers them in the same way, though they repeat it dozens of times over. This form of greeting corresponds to the 'Sen. nen. neh' of the Aruimi & Upper Congo & the 'Botay' of the Lower Congo—The Aruimi is called the 'Ituri' for some miles below the Arab camp up to its source. They dwell on the *r* in saying Bordu & draw it out to a great length. These natives are as a rule short & thickset & strong looking though they look a very low class of people; they are tremendously decorated with iron bracelets, & anklets made of elephant hair, they have better clothes than some of the bush natives & the women are not entirely naked as they were a little lower down. All the fields & villages for miles round have been devastated by the Manyema of whom the natives are in great dread & are now subservient to them—they call them Wa-tamba-tamba. Their villages of which this is a fair sample are built in a long street of huts all joined together like a terrace & the huts have a sort of lean-to roof. They are made of rough poles & are thatched & closed in with banana leaves the sides are further covered with rough planks. In the middle of this village is the chief's hut an enormous high beehive shaped hut about 35 feet in diameter with a neatly rounded doorway & porch at each end. All these villages are in a semideserted state & half the huts are in ruins, the natives though they own the supremacy of the Manyema are only half assured & are very shy of returning to their villages—the Manyema have cleared out all their ivory & most of the goats & chickens. No doubt they will become gradually reassured & will return & cultivate their clearings & pay the Manyema what tribute they ask in goats chickens & corn. The huts were so dirty that I slept in my tent, I had had enough of the hut in the Arab village—it was swarming with vermin & we had all got covered, it is impossible to get them out of one's clothes, I shall have to get all my clothes boiled to get rid of them. In India or out here too, I used to be astonished at the rapt way in which the natives pick themselves over, they seem for the time to see & care for nothing else but the objects of their search. I can understand it better now. After the first feeling of repugnance & disgust is over one sets about getting rid of these creatures & there is a certain keen feeling of satisfaction in following up a fellow & catching him just as he disappears one takes the greatest interest in it & really thoroughly enjoys the pleasures of the chase! When the rest of the men came in with the loads I found that three of the boxes of ammunition had been split open & some of the cartridges stolen, this shows a very bad state of affairs, the spirit of lawlessness is rampant amongst the men, starvation demoralised them & the Manyema did the rest. I can do nothing with the men until I reach Stanley & if the men who stole the ammunition do'nt run away before we reach him, he will make it pretty hot for them.

Nov. 11th. Got the loads off after a good deal of trouble, three days of fever had played the devil with my temper & at last I simply took up my stick & beat the last of the men out of the village, one of the men refused to take his load & I just gave him a good thrashing & at last split his head open with my stick, it was of course a mistake my doing so but I was so angry I didn't much care where I hit him. For five days I have been patient with them & have not touched any of them, I told them I saw talking was no use & that now I should use the stick & freely too if I had any more trouble with them. My outbreak was really perfectly justifiable for I have been very patient with them ever since I started to relieve Nelson & they have been very troublesome. At any rate several of them went off with smarting backs & the result is we did two of Stanleys marches today. Our camp was in a deserted village & the men got a good many bananas in the clearings round.

Nov. 12th. This morning the rain came down in a steady downpour so that I was unable to start, it lasted till nearly 12. Some of the people, the weak men not carrying loads did not come in last night so I decided to remain the day here & sent all the men out of camp to get a good supply of bananas for the road. Some natives came in & sold the men Indian [corn] & chickens. You may strip a Zanzibari of everything he's got & still he'll find something to buy food with. I thought the men were pretty well cleared out by the Manyema & yet they have found something to buy Indian corn & even chickens with—perhaps they bought food with some of the cartridges they had stolen, they will be perfectly useless to the natives, but they may have been taken with the brass cases. I passed the day very impatiently; I hate these delays, I really dont know where we shall catch Stanley. A good many of the people have not come in by this evening they must have stayed behind in Stanley's last camp.

Nov. 13th. I could not wait this morning for the rest of the people to come in so when I had given out the loads I started off with 5 or 6 men leaving the rest of the loads to follow. After marching for a couple of hours we came to more half deserted native fields & from them could see high forest covered hills ahead half hidden in clouds & mist & after going for another couple of hours we began to ascend. The road was very bad all up & down & slippery from yesterday's rain. We came on four natives carrying bananas & after the usual 'Borrdus' had been exchanged we managed to make out from what few words we knew of the language & a great many signs that Stanleys camp was not far ahead. We went on & were soon hailed by another native who led us to Stanleys camp close to a small village. We went on to another village a short distance off in which was an old chief & two or three other natives. There were only four or five of the loads up so I thought it best to stop for camp, but after we had been here a couple of hours 5 of the Manyema came in saying that Khamis, one of the minor chiefs who had started a couple of days before me to catch Stanley & act as a guide, was in a village an hour ahead & hearing from a native I was so close was waiting for me to come up. I therefore started off following the Manyema up hill after hill, through huge clearings of bananas over logs & down ravines, up banks & slippery places until after one more long steep climb we came upon a village at the top of the highest hill in which Khamis & his men were camped. There were a good many natives in the village & amongst them the old chief of this district, an ugly old fellow with a stiff head dress of red bristles which stuck out straight from his head like a bottle brush. He was brought up to me, by Khamis, & introduced to me & his men brought me a present of two splendid branches of bananas, a chicken & a basket full of ants—the ants are the winged ants which are found in the colonies of white ants, they come out in clouds after a heavy rain & the natives collect them & set great store by them as a great delicacy. They certainly are very good to eat, one just roasts them over the fire in an earthen crock until they are crisp, they taste like the most refined mutton fat & smell awfully good when they are being cooked, in fact they are among my pleasantest experiences of Africa. Khamis said he would stop another day until all my people came up & then start ahead with me to catch Stanley. I trust the people will come up for this is a good chance of getting them on. Stanley according to Khamis stayed here two days & has left 5 ago if the men would only go we should catch him in three days, it is most provoking. Khamis tells me five months ago the Manyema fought & conquered all these people & got a good many tusks & great quantities of goats & chickens. There are huge clearings here of plantains & sweet potatoes. Now all the people round are friendly & submissive to them & each village has a high pole in its centre with the tattered remnant of a flag to show it acknowledges the supremacy of the Manyema. I am the more anxious to start with all the people & accompany Khamis as he tells me we are now on the confines of the country conquered by the Manyema & the natives ahead are likely to be troublesome. Only the few men with me, two loads, my tent & blankets & food have come in all the rest of the people are behind, & my boy with my cup plates cooking pots etc has not yet turned up. When the Manyema were having their food Khamis sent me some, it consisted of bananas boiled & mashed up into a good stiff pudding & some ants boiled & pounded with salt & pepper—it was very good. The view from this village is splendid it is in the middle of a group of high hills & is built on the highest of them. One can see all round for miles in every direction except towards the East in which direction our path lies. One can see the forest stretching away for miles undulating like a great green sea till it is lost in the distance. It is splendid to be right high up on this great breezy hill & to be able to see all round into the distance after being shut up in the bush for so long, one breathes again & takes in great breaths of fresh air.

Nov. 14th. Khamis came to tell me this morning that some of the Wang-wana were in the village below stealing from the natives & getting into mischief so I sent one of my men & five of his to bring the offenders in, they turned out to be the men carrying loads & came in with Khamis' men. All the rest of the loads were there except two but the rest of the people not carrying loads are far behind. I waited all day in camp for them to come in but they did not turn up, at any rate I shall start tomorrow without them.

Nov. 15th. The rain came on in the morning early & Khamis did not want to start so I remained another day here. Early in the afternoon a native came in from Stanley's camp, he had only started yesterday morning, he said Stanley was camped in a village & was going to wait till I came up. I am astonished at hearing he is so close, only three camps, we ought to reach him the day after tomorrow at the latest. He said that the Manyema & some of the Wangwana had been out foraging & had fought some of the natives & had captured a lot of ivory goats & chickens—three of the Manyema had been killed but our men had all got off Scot free. Khamis sent me some of his food this afternoon & some more this evening as my boy had not come in to cook my food, these people certainly know how to make palatable menus.

Nov. 16th. After giving out the loads I started off with Khamis & his men expecting to reach Stanley's camp tomorrow. We travelled very fast through the bush almost at a jog trot. There were six natives leading & they went along beautifully easily in & out amongst the trees, one found it awfully difficult to keep up with them with boots on, if one delayed an instant one was left behind & had to run after them & blunder through bushes & creepers—my clothes got terribly torn for the track was not a very good one. We passed through two deserted villages which had been burned some time

since by the Manyema. As we were going along in the jungle we came upon
a party of natives belonging to Killimana they had been ahead with Stanley's
Manyema guides & were returning laden with chickens corn beans etc.
They were driving a herd of 13 goats along with them. This represented a
part of the loot which the Manyema got when they made a raid on the
neighbouring villages with our men—the Manyema in Stanley's camp had
still a great many goats & chickens with them so they must have made a
pretty good haul. These natives had started the day before from camp &
as they had large loads Khamis thought we ought to be able to reach Stanley
today if we went fast, we accordingly started on at a great pace & did not
stop till past 12 for something to eat. The people had no fire & were at a
loss how to get some food cooked they always carry a smouldering log
with them but this had gone out. I said I had fire, & taking out my flint &
steel struck a light at once on the tinder & gave it to them, their faces of
astonishment were a study, after looking at each other for a few seconds
they all burst into a roar of laughter, they seemed to think it was magic.
We went on & on until I got very foot sore, we passed three of Stanleys
camps & at last got into some big clearings & reached Stanley's camp at
half past three. As I came up the village all the Wangwana ran up to me &
shook my hand & some of them even raised it to their lips I was quite
surprised & very pleased for one never expected such an effusive greeting.
Stanley was surprised at seeing me so soon & said I had gone very well,
he would not believe I had come from Killamana that morning.[1] He said it
was 21½ miles & as I did not start till past seven, had stopped nearly an hour
& a half in the middle of the day & got in at 3.30, it was very fast travelling
for the bush. Stanley was relieved to hear that Nelson was safely installed
with Parke in the Arab camp & one gave him an account of all Nelson's
experiences, & mine since I had left him—I had been away just three weeks
& expected to have been away a month at least. It was a great relief to get
rid of the responsibility of the loads & men under my charge & to get back
to the main column under Stanley, the loads will I expect get in tomorrow
some time. I was glad to be with Stairs again & to hear all about his experiences. The amount of food here after the starvation rations we have been
on is simply bewildering. The villages all round are like huge granaries of
Indian corn, the clearings are all full of splendid bananas, we have as much
goat meat & chickens as we can eat, flour & beans in plenty; such abundance
I never dreamed of. This is the first village[2] beyond the country conquered

---

[1] 'At 3 p.m. on the 16th Mr. Jephson appeared, having performed his mission of
relief most brilliantly' (Stanley, *IDA*, 1, 258).

[2] This was Ibwirri, the region where Stanley was later to construct Fort Bodo as a
base camp.

by the Manyema so the bad effect their presence has in the country may easily be imagined, directly one gets beyond their influence there is abundance of food. Stanley has been here 7 days & the men even in that short time look quite different, they have nothing to do here but to eat & sleep, & they get through a pretty good share of both. The village is on the top of a small rise & one can see large clearings full of bananas all round & outside the clearings in jungle. The Manyema caught the King of a very large village next to this, about 40 minutes off & brought him in here intending to cut his throat, but Stanley hearing of it had him brought up to his tent & tied up & told him he should have his freedom if he led us to the open country, the old man says the plain is not far off, but these natives are such liars one can hardly ever believe their reports—he says there are quantities of cattle. Stairs told me Stanley had had a row with the Manyema the day before I arrived. He had agreed with Khamis, the head chief of the Manyema, to pay him so much for sending his men to lead him for a distance of 15 marches. They have only come 11 & want to return, Stanley objects & says they must stick to their agreement & suspecting they meant to flit in the night he took their rifles & ivory away from them, saying they should have them back when they should fulfil the agreement. It is a pity there should have been any unpleasantness, but Stanley is of course in the right, he allowed them to send their goats & chickens away to Killamana yesterday—they were the goats & chickens we saw under the charge of natives today when we were in the jungle. Stairs & I have a huge big hut, it is so large that the cook & the two boys sleep in the other end of it & cook our food there. Stanley sent for me after dinner & we had a long talk about various things connected with the expedition.

Nov. 17th. Early this morning Stanley had all the men fallen in & sent Stairs off with 30 to find the path to the open country, the old Sultan was tied to a rope & was led ahead to lead the way. Stairs was to go two days journey & two days were allowed by Stanley for him to return in, he was to be away altogether 4 days. I was sent with the rest of the men to clear an open space all round the village & to build a boma. In the morning early the Manyema all quietly cleared out of the village, we all thought they had gone out to make a raid as usual on some village near, but Khamis Parry who came in early in the afternoon reported having met them all on their way to Killamana. They had told him a wonderful story of how Stanley had taken their guns & ivory & they were evidently terribly afraid of him, so they were just clearing out & going back to their settlement. This is a very serious state of affairs, for should they go back with this story the loads left in their camp may be seized & even the lives of Nelson & Parke may be endangered. Stanley decided to send them all their rifles & ivory to show them he wished to do them no harm. In the afternoon Simba one of the men came in with two arrow wounds, one arrow had hit him on the collar bone & the wound was not serious but the other arrow had hit him in the stomach & as it was doubly barbed it was impossible to extract it without cutting away the muscles in which it was imbedded. The man would not hear of its being cut out so Stanley could only secure it in such a way that it would not penetrate any further & send him to his hut to lie down. The man carrying my box came in & I delivered Nelson's & Parke's letters to Stanley. Nelson's letter in which he spoke very strongly about their position in the Arab camp & the lack of arrangements for their feeding made Stanley very angry & he blamed me for allowing Nelson to write such a letter, he spoke in very strong terms about Nelson & his officers, & all before Khamis Parry it was a great mistake & I told him afterwards, when he had cooled down a bit, that I was sorry he should have spoken in that way of us before him. He blamed me very much for putting my name as a witness to Nelsons signature in his agreement to pay the Committee £50 if Stanley would send two bales of cloth to pay for his & Parke's feeding. I told him if Nelson asked me to do the same tomorrow I should do so for I saw no harm whatever in it. Stanley then wrote a letter to Nelson & enclosed an agreement to send Khamis, or rather Assimaili, 2 bales of cloth. The letter was to be given to the men returning to Killimana who were returning the Manyema their guns & ivory. Whilest Stanley was talking to me we heard a shot fired & on running out to see what it meant we found that Simba, the man who was shot by an arrow had committed suicide by blowing out his brains—the head was completely severed right down the middle, it was a horrid sight. I stayed up till very late talking with Stanley.

Nov. 21st. In the last few days nothing eventful has happened. The men have just had to get their guns cleaned & put into perfect working order. They have had all the rest of the time to themselves to eat & sleep as much as they like they are sleeping & making flour all day long & it is surprising even with the unlimited amount they have how quickly they are getting fat, a few days makes quite a change in their appearance. Stairs returned at midday with his men; he had gone about 38 miles in the two days under the guidance of the old Sultan 'Borio'. He had seen no signs of the open country, but said the track was good ahead & that there was abundance of food, for the road ran through a chain of villages all of which were stored with beans & corn & had a wealth of bananas all round them, there were numbers of goats & chickens & the men had had as much as they could eat of both—Stairs brought a great many goats & some chickens back with him, he was terribly footsore & tired out after four days hard going—all the natives had cleared out as soon as they caught sight of our men.

Nov. 22nd. Stanley sent me today with a lot of men to cut a good track round the fallen logs wh^ch lay between here & Ibwiri, which is the name of Borio's village, about 40 minutes distant. The rest of the day was given to getting ready for the march tomorrow.

Nov. 23rd. Stanley decided not to march today but to give another day's grace to my chief Alsasi & 5 men with him who had not yet come in, they had been loitering fearfully on the way for I have already been in 6 days. They came in at midday & all got soundly flogged for loitering behind & delaying the expedition. I forgot to mention that Uledi & his men turned up three days ago.

Nov. 24th. We started off in good time this morning, we were all in good spirits & the men are in splendid condition for going. They had large supplies of flour, corn, bananas, sweet potatoes etc, enough to last them 5 or 6 days. We did a march of 9 miles the men went well & the rear guard got into our camp in the jungle by three oclock. Stanley thinks we shall get to the Lake in eight days but he is only going by native report for he suspects his chronometers are considerably out, which will put him considerably out of his reckoning, they got a terrible bumping during our days of starvation. How different it is marching with the column now to what it was when I was last marching with it, then we were all half skeletons & in the lowest spirits now we are all fat & have plenty of food, & are eagerly pressing forward to reach the Lake.

Nov. 25th. Today we did another march of 9 miles & camped in a village in which Stairs had captured great numbers of goats & chickens—the village itself was a mere collection of filthy huts, but there were still quantities of corn in all the huts & bananas in plenty growing all round. Stanley was very unwell this evening & complains of having felt bad for the last two days— I hope it is not going to be anything serious. The road lay all through the jungle but was fairly good & even for a bush track. The people are divided into two companies only now, one of which Stanley has & the other Stairs so that I have no regular duty now—I do'nt like it at all, one feels quite shelved.

Nov. 26th. We did a march of 11 miles today & reached the village belonging to Borio's brother; we found the natives had burnt it & the village next it, to the ground & it was still smouldering when we arrived. I suppose he imagined we might settle ourselves into it for some time & raid the country all round, & so determined to outwit us by burning it down. We camped in it for the night & pitched out tents among the ruins.

Nov. 27th. After a march of 8 miles we came to a very large village consisting of one long straight street. The natives most of them had already cleared out but there were still a few & our men shot four & captured a woman who were carrying away corn. The huts had a large quantity of corn in most of them & also large quantities of beans & green corn. Stanley decided to stop here tomorrow & has fortified the place in case of attack. The village being a long continuous row of huts on either side with no inlet except the two ends, he has made it perfectly impregnable by stopping these up by two bomas & building sidings of boards to flank them. The native we captured is a very fine looking woman, Stanley had her brought to his hut in the evening but did not get much information out of her. This village is as far as Stairs got, so we do not know anything of the road ahead, & as Borio the old Sultan managed to escape last night, we must now go on our own hook & find the road for ourselves.

Nov. 28th. Stanley sent me ahead today with a party of 30 men to find the road ahead. I took as guides the woman we captured yesterday & one that Stairs had captured previously. Between them they made a mess of it & led me too far South. We followed on the track of the natives who had fled from the village we were occupying, they made the most wonderful round temporary huts to sleep in, they were made of small pliant saplings & covered in with large leaves of a plant which grows in the jungle—judging from the size & number of the huts there must have been several hundred natives. We followed their track until we came to their camp of last night, here we got a lot of chickens & tobacco & as they went in a Westerly direction I gave up following them & struck a large track leading in a South Easterly direction to a village called Interpasi. After following this track till past 12 & not coming to the village I was obliged to return as Stanley had told me to get back that same night. On getting back I found Rashid one of the chiefs had also been out looking for a road—he had not found a satisfactory one but had brought in a lot of goats. Stanley decided to take the left hand path tomorrow the one which neither Rashid nor I had tried, we both thought it led too far North.

Nov. 29th. The track Stanley chose turned out to be a very good one. It gradually led round in a SSE direction & at 10 oclock brought us to a village prettily situated in a valley with hills rising all round. The natives had only just gone & the men got quantities of bracelets, knives, shields, skins, ripe bananas, & castor oil—the latter is a very good find as we were wanting oil badly for the guns. There was abundance of food in the village & in the villages all round. In one of the huts we found a long arrow 2 ft long made of a reed like bamboo & feathered with a bit of hide, round the feathering there were very pretty patterns worked. It is quite a different style to the bush arrows to which we have been accustomed, they are only 18 in long, are made of wood ornamented with iron, & are feathered with a bit of leaf—this is a sign that we are near the plain. We struck a track leading

NNE through the jungle & camped in a very dirty village—there are more bananas & of a finer sort round this village than I've seen yet.

Nov. 30th. Found a good track leading ENE. At 10 we came out into a large new clearing surrounded by high hills & after clambering over logs for about half a mile we saw villages on the hills to the South & Stanley led the way for them. After ascending about 200ft we came to the first of a chain of villages which led up to a height of 500 ft above the clearing & in the highest village of all Stanley had camped. On looking round one got a splendid [view] & to the east one could see the open country at last at about a distance of 4 hrs march.[1] It is a glorious sight after being accustomed to the jungle for 6 months to see a splendid grassy plain dotted about with clumps of trees like a park, it looked almost as if it might be a distant view of Kent. Stanley decided to stay here for the night & sent out foraging parties to look for a road. The view from our hut was beautiful, it was lovely just to sit and look at the open country—the men cheered when they saw the plains & are immensely delighted at the idea of having finished with the jungle for a while, after dinner they came & executed a sort of war dance which lasted nearly an hour, they went through all sorts of antics supposed to be a representation of their fighting the natives, they sang all the time, accompanied by two drums they found in the village.

December 1st [1887]. We started off this morning in an ENE direction & after marching for a couple of hours we came to a high ridge of hills over which we crossed & descended the other side & came to a large dirty village at 11.30. We could see no signs of the plain from the hills as they were densely covered with jungle. Yesterday according to Stanley's reckoning we were only 15½ geographical miles from the lake but he is almost certain his chronometers are out. At 2.30 we came on Stanley who had camped in a small collection of huts, today we have merely been wandering about looking for a path leading us out into the plain. Some of the men brought in a lot of goats & chickens. This morning on starting 4 men were missing so

[1] Stanley's entry under 30 November reads: 'This then was the long promised view and the long expected exit out of gloom! Therefore I called the tall peak terminating the forested ridge, of which the spur whereon we stood was a part, and that rose two miles E. of us to a height of 4600 feet above the sea, Pisgah,—Mount Pisgah,—because after 156 days of twilight in the primeval forest, we had first viewed the desired pasturelands of Equatoria.

'The men crowded up the slope eagerly with inquiring open-eyed looks, which, before they worded their thoughts, we knew meant "Is it true? Is it no hoax? Can it be possible that we are near the end of this forest hell?" They were convinced themselves in a few moments after they had dropped their burdens, and regarded the view with wondering and delighted surprise.

'"Aye, friends, it is true. By the mercy of God we are wellnigh at the end of our prison and dungeon!"' (Stanley, *IDA*, 1, 267–8.)

Stanley sent Rashid & 10 men out to look for them—they have not yet come in.

Dec. 2nd. At muster this morning a man came in with the report that he had gone out yesterday afternoon & had come on a large village in which there were a great many goats, close to the open plain. We started off with the man leading but he led us all wrong & at 1.30 we came to a small collection of huts where we captured 4 goats & a lot of chickens. The plantains here are splendid, we got a lot of green Indian corn in the clearings. The huts here are quite different to any we have yet seen, they are round & neatly thatched & covered in with grass, the roof is made of long thick reeds something like bamboo. On striking SE we came to a big patch of long grass & then into the jungle again & struck a village in which we camped. We found the new style of huts very comfortable & roomy & the clearings of plantains splendid. We captured an old woman, a perfect old fiend with a voice like a man, we had to tie her hand & foot for she bit & kicked everyone who came near her, it took four men to tie her up & then she bellowed like a bull in the night & had to be gagged. It was hopeless to try & get information out of such an old harridan. She was quite the ugliest old woman I've ever seen—she was perfectly naked to begin with & her dull old skin hung about in lappets all over her, her nose was dreadfully flat & her upper lip was stuck out by a large round piece of wood inserted in it, she had a voice like a man & claws like a bird & was altogether a most disgusting old object.

Dec. 3rd. After marching for about an hour this morning we came upon a good sized river about 35 yds wide which is either the Ituri[1] or a branch of it, not finding a place to cross & there being no canoe to be got, Stanley returned to where we camped last night & camped, sending me out with a party of 20 men to search for a place where the native track led down to a crossing or canoe. He told me to go back to a village we passed yesterday & then to strike North until I came across a track leading to the river. I went about 6 miles up & tried three roads but none of them led to the river, so early in the afternoon I returned to camp. Stairs & I then went out & followed a small stream, not far off, down to the river & here we found it was fordable. We took off our clothes & crossed over with one man, leaving the rest of the men on the other side, the water was about up to one's chest & the current pretty strong but the caravan can cross all right. When we got on the other side we followed an elephant track & after going about 300 yds struck the open plain which is all quite short grass just here. It was splendid to be out in the open again at last & to feel grass under one's feet

---

[1] Stanley calls this the West Ituri; they reached the main stream on 6 December (see below, p. 200).

& hear it rustling in the breeze. We should have made a very good subject for a picture in a comic newspaper entitled 'How we found the open country'. Both Stairs & I had only our shirts on, our clothes & boots were on the other side of the river, we were carrying our guns in our hands & were treading most gingerly to avoid thorns, & were followed by a perfectly naked Zanzibari carrying a stick & a helmet. We must have presented an absurd appearance as we emerged from the bush. We went out into the plain for a little way & sniffed the fresh air for a bit & then returned & got into camp well before dark. Rashid, who had gone out the day before yesterday to search for the four missing men, returned this afternoon with them, he brought back about 20 goats, & Stanley had 13 killed & distributed amongst the men, so tonight they are having a regular Hondo (feast). He gave Stairs & I 3 milch goats, it is the first milk we've had since we left Yambuya—we have quite a flock of goats now.

Dec. 4th. I started off this morning at the head of the carravan to show the way to crossing & out into the open country. Stanley fired at an Eland he hit it but did not kill it & it got away—it is a splendid looking beast about the height of a good sized pony & is the largest of the African Antelope. During the morning we came upon a herd of buffalo & a herd of Springbok —Stanley broke a buffaloe's leg but it went off at a tremendous pace on three legs & soon disappeared. We went in an ENE direction the plain was so jolly fresh & dewy & one could see the caravan winding along after us, it was so different to the bush where everything was stifling & we could only see a few men before & behind. We went about 11 miles & camped in a wooded hollow with a good clear stream running through it. A good many of the men returned to a village we had seen in the distance to the south of us & came back at dark with quantities of ripe bananas, Indian corn & beans. The natives had left it the day before. The men reported having seen fields of Metamah (Dhura) growing but it was not in a very advanced state.

Dec. 5th. There was no sun & travelling was very pleasant, every thing was cool & fresh. After going for some time we struck some scrub with a plentiful under growth of huge thistles & mimosa bushes. In one of the ravines we came upon the track of a lion, it was a huge big foot print & was very clearly defined in the mud. At 9.30 we came on a small village sur-rounded by fields of Dhura & bananas in which the men captured a woman & her three children & got quantities of ripe bananas, chickens & goats. Afterwards we came on great plantations of Dhura, millet, bananas, Indian corn & beans amongst which large beehive shaped huts made of grass were dotted about. Each hut has its little cooking hut close by & also a rather prettily shaped granary made of grass & standing on a small platform a couple of feet high. There were chickens & goats in plenty, but we marched straight through & camped in the last collection of huts. One man came in wounded by an arrow & early in the evening soon after dark a good many arrows were dropping into camp shot by natives who had crept up close hidden by the long grass or Indian corn. The men had built a light boma round the camp & fortunately only one man was hit. The arrow penetrated his thigh to a depth of 6 inches & though it was badly barbed Stanley managed to tear it out. The sentries fired a few shots among the long grass & the natives dispersed.

Dec. 6th. The rain came on in the morning & we did not get off till 10 oclock. We found quantities of arrows sticking in the banana trees close to where the men had their fires, a good many of them must have had a narrow escape. We found one arrow sticking in the small boma I built before the entrance to our tent—it was lucky I thought of building it. At 11 we came to a large river about 80 yds wide running in a Southerly direction, this Stanley at once pronounced to be the main stream of the Ituri. We fortunately found a small canoe but it took us till dark to get the whole carravan across— I had to superintend this work, it is awfully tiring standing there all day directing the men. The natives gathered on the hills on both sides of the river & parties had to be sent out to disperse them. Stanley formed a circular camp on a grassy hill close to the river—the men always build grass huts at night & these, built in the shape of a circle round the tents & loads, form a very good boma.

Dec. 7th. After marching till 10 we came to a valley in which there were a good many villages & in passing through one of them the rear guard was fired on with arrows. At 11 we came to a large tributary of the Ituri over which there was a narrow swinging bridge made of creepers suspended from trees on each side of the river. It was so rotten & narrow that only two men could cross at a time & it took us till after dark to get the carravan across, I had to look after this work as yesterday. The natives gathered on the hills in our rear as they did yesterday but a few shots dispersed them. This afternoon when Stairs was pursuing a party of natives he saw a cow & calf in the distance, this is the first indication we have yet had that we are in the cattle country. In crossing the river different parts of the bridge kept giving way & I was constantly at work mending it up with fresh creepers—we lost one load of ammunition in consequence of one of the ropes giving way just when a man was in the middle. Camp in a circle on a hill above the river.

Dec. 8th. Directed our course this morning in a SE direction making for some high hills about 10 miles off—on the other side of them Stanley thought must be the Lake. At 9.30 on getting to the top of a low range of down like hills we saw lying beneath us a long broad valley, watered by a wide clear stream stretching away to the hills. Almost the whole valley was under cultivation. There were great fields of Dhura, millet, bananas, sweet potatoes, Indian corn & beans reaching far up the hill sides—it was a very land of Goshen. We could see groups of huts dotted about amongst the fields, but very few natives were in sight, they were probably hiding in the Dhura. Broad cattle tracks led from the plain to this settlement which is probably a very rich & strong one. Stanley halted the carravan, for he dared not venture into the fields of Dhura with so small a force, 173 only, all told, we certainly looked a mere handful of men as we halted at the top of the hill & looked down on this huge populous valley. He decided to skirt round the edge of the valley & cut across it to the hills where it was narrowest & most open. We managed this most successfully without firing a single shot, we skirted along the edge of the plain & were across the valley & into the open again by 1.30. Here the plain was lovely—it was exactly like meadows one sees in Kent, dotted about with hawthorn trees. Soon we came to another settlement even larger than the first, but as our road lay right through it & there were mountains on either side there was nothing for it but to bore our way through as best we could. The natives gathered on the hills on either side & shouted & yelled at us & we had to keep up a brisk fire to prevent their closing in on us, at one place they came very close, but Stanley fired at a man about 350 yds off & killed him—this checked them a bit for they were evidently astounded at the distance at which our weapons could kill, & whenever a gun was fired, no matter in what direction, all the natives ducked their heads with one accord. By this time the natives had gathered in large numbers from all sides & the shouting & yelling across the valley began to get unpleasantly loud. We saw a collection of huts up a gully between two low hills & made for it, the natives who were occupying it cleared out before us & we at once began to build a boma whilest Stanley sent men to occupy both hills & to keep the natives off by firing at them whenever they came within range. After the boma was built round the camp Stairs & I built a small one on each of the hills & these were filled with sentries. Stanley says we are almost certain to be attacked tonight. This is the first real opposition we have yet met with from the natives, I mean to say the first determined opposition. Our position is in about the middle of this large valley & as far as we can see both ways & on the hill sides are great fields of Dhura, Indian corn etc. & villages in numbers. If the natives are really determined it will take us all our time to keep them out of the boma, I'm afraid our men in a night attack would shoot very wild in fact they would simply shoot each other—their shooting in the day time is wild enough in all consience.

Dec. 9th. Stanley determined not to move until either the natives made friends with us or we gave them a good licking, for he considered it would be dangerous to venture through the rest of the settlement until something was decided for the natives with increased boldness & augmented numbers would only follow us & harrass us in the fields of Dhura & Bananas where they shoot their arrows at us unseen. Besides too these hill men in the plains have a much better idea of warfare than the bush niggers we have been accustomed to hitherto. They understand manoeuvering & taking advantage of positions & the lay of the land, whilst the bush nigger thinks only of cumbering the ground with pitfalls & nasty spikes which lame people, they shoot their tiny poisoned arrows from behind trees & never come on with a rush. These people have long strong spears & large bows & stand up & shoot their long reed unpoisoned arrows like men & have some courage about them. In fact they think & move in larger circles; the distant wide views they get from their native hills & the strong breezes they inhale seems to make them freer & gives them a more enlarged view of things in general, both in their systems of cultivation, warfare, & way of living; whilst the poor unenlightened bush nigger shut in for ever by a thick wall of jungle, has his vision cut off & moves in semi darkness & in the twilight of ignorance. He is content with his badly cultivated field of manioc, pea nuts or bananas, his few chickens & goats, & lives in happy ignorance of there being any other way of living. Today therefore we stayed in camp & waited to see what the day would bring forth. First of all we strengthened & enlarged the three bomas & had fresh sentries posted, we got this all done before the natives appeared for here the nights are so cold & the mists in the morning so chill that the natives do not leave their houses until the sun is well up. At about 9 they began to gather on the hills & to shout & jeer at us, but as yet made no attempt to molest us & all that was needed was a good look out kept. In the afternoon one of our men,[1] who was brought up in Unyoro, on the east side of the Lake, understood what some natives who were shouting to each other across the hills said, & he instantly spoke to them & found they spoke the Unyoro language. The result was a long conference he stood at the foot of the hill & a native on the top & they shouted to each other. The native said the people wanted to make friends with us they we[re] so afraid of those, 'tubes which threw out fire & smoke at them & wanted us to take them away'. Stanley told the native he was willing to make friendship with them & sent a piece of fine red flannel & a matako as specimens of the present he would give the chief when friendship was made & sent me down to the foot of the hill to make blood brotherhood with the chief, or Sultan as they called him.[2] I was obliged to leave my gun as the native would not

[1] His name was Fetteh (Stanley, *IDA*, 1, 292).

[2] Stanley says he ordered Stairs to step out and show himself to the tribesmen; he does not mention Jephson at this point. He adds that the Chief was to make blood brotherhood with him, Stanley (*IDA*, 1, 293).

approach if I had one in my hand, I had my little 'Bulldog' revolver however in my belt & was quite ready with it if he ventured to play any games. I walked out to the foot of the hill accompanied only by our interpreter, & asked the native several questions, the name of the district we were in was M'Somboni[1] & the chiefs name was Mazamboni; he said we were three days from the Lake—but that I dont believe, these strong cold winds come from the Lake & it cannot be more than a day or so off; he did not know Kavalli or said he did'nt. Kavalli is the point on the lake for which Stanley is making, Mason has it on his map as a collection of villages or small district about 12 miles from the South end of the Lake. After talking some time the native said if I would deposit a piece of the flannel & a matako at the foot of the hill & then retire to some distance he would come down & take it to the chief & would then bring him down from the hills to make blood [brother-hood] with me—I went away & the man came down & took the flannel up to the people who were all this time gathered on the hills watching & listening to the conference. It was now evening almost, so I returned to camp, there is not the slightest chance of the chief coming down tonight.

Dec. 10th. At about 9 oclock hundreds [of] natives were gathered on the hills all round, all were armed with immensely long spears, bows & arrows, & had on their war feathers they began shouting to each other across the valley & were apparently shouting to each other the signal to begin for they were evidently bent on war. Stanley had the people mustered & sent me to occupy a small village below the camp with 40 men, whilest Stairs was in readiness with another party to sally out if the natives should attack from the other side. They sent a man down into the valley to reconoitre & he was instantly chased by 5 of our men & shot. The natives then began to descend from the hills with tremendous shouting & Stanley gave the order to burn all the villages round. Simultaneously Stairs & I sallied out he with his party went along the North side of the valley whilest I swept round the south burning everything, huts, granaries etc as we went. We met at the top of a sort of watch hill at the West end of the valley & looking back could only see clouds of smoke from the burning huts between us & the camp. The natives were so astonished & scared with the quickness of the whole thing that they all took to their heels & disappeared over the mountains—. In one place Stairs & his party had a pretty thick shower of arrows falling amongst them but only one man was slightly wounded. In the afternoon Stairs & I were again sent out to burn the huts on the other side of the camp, whilest Uledi with another small party went up the hills & burned 8 villages & cattle Kraals. We so completed the work that no huts were to be seen on either side of the camp as far as one could see. The men got quantities of

[1] Undussuma in *IDA*; see entry for 15 April 1888 below, p. 237.

food in the shape of chickens, goats, beans, corn etc, but we could find no traces of the cattle, the natives must have removed them all yesterday. The men killed one cow only & found another which had been burned to death in one of the huts, they brought the meat into camp & had a good feast.

Dec. 11th. In the morning some natives on one of the hills began to get rather noisy so Stanley sent Stairs & I by different roads up the mountain to give them another lesson. We burnt about two dozen villages in the valleys amongst the hills & captured a lot of chickens & goats. On reaching the top of one of the highest ridge of hills we saw laying below us another large settlement, several hundred acres were under cultivation, chiefly Dhura & bananas. Our appearance at the top of the hills caused a great stir below for we could see the people who looked mere dots in the distance hurrying backwards & forwards & we could hear them calling to each other & could just distinguish the lowing of cattle. It was too late to descend & try & get the cattle, so we returned to camp. During our absence a native had come down to one of the hills at the foot of the mountains & had begged Stanley to desist, they had had more than enough, they had been kept up in the mountains for three days, their houses had been burned & their food taken, & we had killed many of their people. They had indeed taken our present & then made war, but it was not the chief's fault, but that of the young men who were anxious to fight, if we would now desist from fighting them they would submit tomorrow morning & would bring in presents of cattle.

CHAPTER 9

LAKE ALBERT AND THE RETURN
TO IBWIRRI

12 DECEMBER 1887–6 JANUARY 1888

Dec. 12th. This morning without waiting to receive the natives presents we left camp & marched on through the now desolate valley & were clear of it before any of the natives appeared on the hills. We burned our camp on leaving it & the village we had occupied below & left the head of one of the natives we had killed suspended from a tree close to camp, as a warning to the natives to behave themselves when we return this way. Stanley did not care to waste any further time in making friends with them, we had given them such a lesson that our rear guard was safe from being harrassed by them & that's all that we wanted. Our track was directed towards a rocky mountain about 17 miles distant & Stanley was certain that the Lake lay beneath it. We passed through a lot of scrub intersected by numbers of lovely little creeks with clear sparkling water, the rocks at the side of one of these were covered with maidenhair fern drooping over the stream, it was quite lovely & looked so cool & fresh. Towards 2 o'clock we were in another settlement & the natives as before gathered on the hills & shouted & jeered at us. They were very afraid of our guns especially as Stanley killed a man on the hills at a distance of full 600 yds, but they followed closely on the rearguard & began to get very bold. Stanley moved the column rapidly across a deep ravine &, ordering the men to put down their loads, turned on them suddenly & having driven them away to some distance burned all the huts rounds & so quieted them. We then marched on & camped in a small village at the top of a hill & got a cheerful view of the burning huts below. The wind this evening is strong & intensely cold & in spite of our having a large hut to sleep in Stairs & I were very cold & put on big coats, it is now I feel the want of the extra blanket I was obliged to sell to the Manyema for food. We are now regularly in the cattle country, for all the huts, nearly, have Kraals attached to them, the huts are very large & are littered with grass & the cows evidently share them with the natives. This settlement especially has not much cultivation about it but evidences of abundance of cattle.[1]

Dec. 13th. Today is a day to be marked in red letters for today we have at

[1] They were now among the Bavira (or Bira), and the settlement was 'Gavira's', called after the local chief, whose name appears also to have been Mpinga.

205

last seen the Lake. After marching for a couple of hours the natives as usual began to gather on the different hills & gradually to unite & follow us shouting & annoying the rear guard, whilest another lot made a feint of attacking our flank, in front there was a small round hill behind which about a hundred natives were hidden, the front guard doubled round this & dislodged them & Stanley sent me with the front guard to pursue them across the plain. The natives ran like deer & we could not get near them, in the mean time Stanley had repulsed the party attacking our flank & Stairs, who is always with the rear guard, had driven the natives in the rear away, so we were left to have our midday rest & coffee in peace, the natives watching us from the distance. After 'terokeso' we marched on & were soon on the top of a sort of low ridge & in five minutes came across a small stream running *East*. We were standing exactly between the watersheds of the two greatest African rivers, the Congo & the Nile—five minutes before all the streams were running into the Atlantic, now all were running into the Mediteranean, it is curious that such a small gentle slope should at this point be the division between two of the greatest rivers in the world—what an enormous tract of country is drained by the Congo.[1] We could see nothing before us but a mile or so of smooth plain with small 'doddered' bushes dotted about it & then it suddenly seemed to end in the clouds—Stanley turned round to me & nodded his head. In ten minutes cheer after cheer burst from the men ahead & several of them rushed madly up & down shouting out 'Nyanza, Nyanza, cheer for Bula Matari'. On coming up we found we were on a tableland, & there 2500 feet below us lay the Lake glittering like silver in the sun. Sheer below us lay a large plain about 9 miles broad & about 15 miles long, on one sided bounded by the mountains on which we stood & on the other by the Lake. We could see villages in the distance on the shore of the lake & could see the boundary of the South end—Stanley had struck the exact place, Kavalli, he had been trying for, we could see the path winding down the mountain side below us. To the south of the lake stretches a broad flat plain studded with dwarfish trees & in the distance one can see Gebel Agif rising sheer up from the plain; to the East one sees the beautiful cliffs of Unyoro with the lake coming right up to their feet—it was there that Sir Samuel Baker[2] was very nearly drowned, almost

[1] Jephson's deductions were not correct here, the watershed of the Congo and the Nile lying considerably to the north of lat. N. 1° 23′ 00″, Stanley's calculation of the point where they had their first view of Lake Albert. Any east-flowing stream in this locality would flow into the Mediterranean by way of Lake Albert. Stanley does not mention this east-flowing stream in *In Darkest Africa* though it may well have been noted in his original diary.

[2] In March 1854 Samuel and Florence Baker reached Lake Albert at a village called by them Vacovia, on the south-east shore of Lake Albert, calculated as being on lat.

exactly opposite here, for the Albert is a dangerous lake & very subject to sudden squalls, I suppose on account of the mountains lying round it; today it lay placid & smiling below us as we stood feasting our eyes on the welcome sight & sniffing the fresh sweet breeze. To the North one could see nothing but a broad stretch of calm blue water. To say one experienced a feeling of relief or even of joy on at last seeing the Lake would hardly describe what one felt. The Lake had ever been the goal held up before one's eyes since we had left Yambuya, nearly 6 months ago. In our first dark days we had always looked to it as the haven where all our troubles would end. We had pored over our maps day by day & when our position was determined every day at noon had measured off the distance we had yet to go with the greatest interest & anxiety. To the men too it had always been looked forward to as a place where there were cattle & food in plenty & where their marching & load carrying would be ended for a while, & there would be little to do & lots to eat. Then when the black days of starvation & exhaustion came on, our chance of ever seeing the lake seemed to grow less & less until they had receded into the far distance & we would only see & think of the miserable blank Present. After a bit the expedition was again split up, Nelson & Parke were left behind with men & loads & we struggled on a small handful of men until we came to a land of plenty & were obliged to stop for 16 days to let the men get back some of their strength. From this time our spirits gradually rose as we marched on day by day, until at last we suddenly came on the Lake lying below us & one felt a warm glow, almost a feeling of triumph & mixed up with it a feeling of thankfullness & gratitude, it was as if one had wakened out of a bad dream—& the waking was very pleasant. We had left Yambuya with 389 men & arrived on the shores of the Albert Nyanza with 169 only,[1] the difference between the two numbers speaks for itself & will testify to the difficulties & trials we have gone through. Of these 389 men, 56 were left behind, too sick to move, with the Arab, Ugarawa, 24 were left in the Manyema settlement, reduced to skeletons from starvation, 20 men are missing, & from death & desertion we have lost 120 men. That is, that for every 100 men who left Yambuya 45 only reached the Lake. Stanley Stairs & I sat on a group of rocks at the head of the gorge, down

---

1° 14' 3". Baker's great-nephew, Dr John Baker, has gone over the ground and identified this with the modern village of Bukobya, N. 1° 14' 37". The Bakers embarked in two canoes and spent thirteen days rowing to the north end of the lake, and were nearly drowned in a violent storm. Indeed, they suffered from rough weather throughout their journey, their rowers were inexperienced and they had to use Baker's Scotch plaid as a sail, while the poultry running loose in the bottom of the boat 'bothered us dreadfully'. S. W. Baker, *Albert Ny'anza, Great Basin of the Nile* (London, 1866), chapter XII.

[1] Jephson's rough notebook gives a later comparison of figures: 'Left Zanzibar 708 strong; arrived at Zanzibar 210.' (Mallow Castle unpublished papers.)

which the path wound which led to the Lake, & he pointed out to the men who all collected round us, the direction in which such places as they knew lay, Uganda, Ujiji, Unyanyembe Muta N'Zigi & so forth. We had the map out & examined it to see if Mason had got the shape of the South end correct, we had a splendid bird's eye view of it & found that he had traced each small bay & island most correctly. Stanley must have felt a feeling of triumph at having led us through an unknown country of some 600 miles of bush & landed us in spite of the many difficulties, & his chronometers being 30 minutes out, at the exact point for which he had been steering. After halting an hour we started off on our descent into the plain. Some of the men unfurled the big Egyptian flag & carried it at the head of the column, whilest another man carried the pennant of the Yacht Namouna. Gordon Bennett[1] the owner of the yacht & proprietor of the New York Herald had asked Stanley to carry it across Africa. The last of the men had no sooner begun the descent than the natives who had been lying hidden in the long grass appeared & began shooting their arrows at our men from behind rocks, they were so quick in their movements & took every advantage of the cover of the rocks, that it was almost impossible to get a good shot at them. They wounded one of our men in the leg & were so determined that it was as much as the rear guard could do to keep them from closing in on them. They followed us half way down the mountain harrassing the rear until we gained an open place into which they dared not follow us as there was no cover. We got to the bottom of the mountains & into plain below at 3.30 & after marching for about an hour camped on some low sand cliffs above a small clear gravelly river. We had hardly camped when we saw our friends the natives peering at us from between the bushes on the other side of the river, Stanley fired a shot at them & I think hit one for they all disappeared, though they came early in the night & fired arrows into the camp, but the sentries who fired rather wildly dispersed them. Towards evening flocks of Guinea fowl came down to drink at the river.

Dec. 14th. We left camp & marched along towards the lake, at midday we came to a small village[2] & sent our interpreter on to say we wished to make friends, the natives retired at a distance at first but gradually became reassured & approached us. The whole carravan sat down at the entrance of the village with Stanley in front while the Interpreter Faiti & two or three men went forward a few yards & mixed with the natives. They told us there was no food in all this big plain between the mountains & the Lake but what small number of inhabitants there were supported themselves by

---

[1] It was Gordon Bennett who gave Stanley the order to 'find Livingstone' and so launched him on his career as an explorer.
[2] 'Katonza's', called after the local chief.

fishing & making salt from the earth of the plain; the fish & salt they sold to the natives on the table land above who came from long distances to buy it & brought them in exchange, beans, corn, potatoes etc—there was absolutely no sign of cultivation about the village. The chief of the village after a lot of talking consented to make blood brotherhood with Stanley & he & his chiefs were all sitting round Stanley ready & the knife was prepared for making the incision in their arms when suddenly some controversy arose amongst them & the upshot of it was that they said they were afraid & wished to send for the chief of the district who lived in a village close by. Stanley said very well & the chief was brought, he was a very fine looking man—as indeed are all the natives here—& after a long talk he said he was afraid & did not wish to make blood brotherhood with us he had heard our guns yesterday & knew we were fighting with the natives of the table land above & as they were his friends he did not wish to make friends with us but he did not wish to be our enemy & would send some of his men to show us the way to Kavalli, but he said there was no food to be got there. Stanley thanked him & accepted his offer of sending 8 of his young men to show us the way. We marched through the village the natives examining us, especially the white men, very closely. The guides led us for about a couple of miles & then left us telling us we could not miss the road. They were all nice looking strong lithe looking men armed with long strong spears with out any attempt at ornamentation & bows & arrows; their shields were very long & broad & of great thickness & strength, they were made of a sort of rattan woven together very skillfully, one or two of the men had beautiful shields of an oval shape with a large spike standing out from the middle. Stanley told me all the shields in Uganda were of this pattern & these are evidently copied from them. The shape is like the pictures one sees of the old Grecian shields even to the spike, all the cooking pots & water jars too are made in beautiful classical shapes. Most of the men had bead necklaces which they probably got from trading with the people of Unyoro where ordinary English & American beads are the current coin. The plain is perfectly lovely & is just like a great park, it is full of antelope of all kinds within a short distance of each other we passed herds of springbok, Kuddu & hartebeest, the latter are splendid great animals of a sort of sable colour. Under the shade of a tree near the shore of the Lake, Stanley halted for our midday rest & coffee, & for the first time we drank the waters of the Albert. After we had finished our lunch Stanley called Stairs & I & put before us the position in which we were now in. We were here on the shores of the Albert in a plain in which there was no food we had not our boat with us & from what he could see would not be able to get a large canoe, as all the trees were small probably a small fishing canoe would be all we should be able to get & in that it would be dangerous as it could only hold three or four men. His plan, as we knew, had been, on arriving at Kavalli, to send men in the boat—if we had it with us—or in a large canoe, to Kibero, at which place Dr Juncker had told him Kasati[1] an Italian explorer had been living for some years unable, like Emin Pasha, to leave the country, the Nile road being closed & that through the Masai country being unknown & the people hostile & also that through Uganda, whilest the West side of the Lake, the road by which we had come, was peopled by hostile tribes & believed to be impassable. The boat would then go to Kibero & take the information to Kassati that an expedition for the relief of Emin Pasha had arrived at the South West end of the Lake. Kassati was a friend of Kawarago the powerful King of Unyoro & Kawarago[2] who was a friend of Emin Pasha's would send a fleet of canoes up to Wadelai & give Emin Pasha the letters Stanley would send & he would bring down his steamers to Kavalli & take his ammunition & stores on board. Thus we should be saved the labour of marching up the Lake through hostile tribes & much time & loss of life would be saved; indeed this road was also closed for Emin Pasha was unable to get out by it. The whole question then lay with communicating with Kassati. We could not march round the South end of the Lake & up through Unyoro for though it was a friendly country one would have to pay ones way or starve & all our money in the shape of beads & brass wire had been lost below Panga in the river when Stairs canoe upset & we had no more until Barttelots carravan came up. One of the plans suggested was to seize a canoe however small & go round to Kibero, I volunteered to go with three men, but Stanley said it was too risky & besides he did not wish to incur the hostility of the people on this plain for we were enemies of the people on the table land above & Stanley thought the two would be too strong for us. We should therefore have to turn back after having seen the Lake. Stanley called all the chiefs & people up & held a large 'Shauri' & a good many opinions were given on our case. Stanley himself said as far as he could see there were only three plans which we could carry out. First, tomorrow we would try & buy a canoe from the natives & after having given the men & officer a supply of food enough to last five or six days start the canoe off for Kibero whilest the column would return up the mountain & build a strong boma on the table land above & there wait for the return of the canoe. There is plenty of food up above but the people would have to make raids & fight for it. If we failed in getting a canoe the second plan was to return to the Manyema camp, a distance of 28 marches, & bring on the boat to the Lake, launch her & send a party round to Kassati. The third plan

---

[1] Captain Gaetano Casati; see Introduction above, pp. 38–9, 42–3.
[2] Jephson has a variety of spellings for the King of Bunyoro, usually spelt Kabarega in modern books.

was to return to Barttelot & bring up the whole carravan to the Lake taking along on our way the men left at Ugarawa's & in the Manyema camp, together with the loads & boat which we had left there. The last plan was universally considered to be the best, should the first plan fail. If we returned to the Manyema camp & brought on the boat it would probably take us altogether four months & after that we should have to return & bring up Barttelot who we should probably find had not got far from Yambuya, for Tippu Tib is certain not to turn up with his people to help him with the loads. We have already left Barttelot nearly 6 months & it will take us probably four or five months to reach him now, & if another four months were added to this—the time we should take to get the boat up from the Manyema—we should probably find when we reached him eventually that nearly all his people had deserted & we should never be able to get the loads up to the Lake. It is considered that it will take us 10 good months to return to Barttelot & bring the whole carravan on to the Lake. This added to the 11 months we have already been out from home, make it a year & nine months till the entire expedition will reach the Lake, then with the communicating with Emin Pasha & the delays on the return journey to Zanzibar we shall not reach England till three years after the time we left it. It is a dismal look out, for three years of this life is too much, absolutely cut off as we are from the civilized world, especially as we all expected to be only half the time—people at home will wonder what has become of us & will give us up for lost. After every sort of plan had been talked over & discussed, & every sort of suggestion made, it was decided that if tomorrow we were unable to buy a canoe there was nothing for us to do but to return & bring on Barttelot & reunite the whole expedition. We then marched on for an hour or so & camped in a beautiful part of the plain. In the evening Stanley called Stairs & I into his tent & he opened a couple of bottles of champagne. We talked over our position & the plans we had made & later on he called some of the chiefs in & we discussed a plan Stanley started of bringing Nelson & Parke, together with the boat & Maxim gun on from the Manyema camp & establishing an entrenched camp at Borio's village Ibwiri[1], leaving with them our present loads & what sick men we have, starting off for Barttelot empty handed. After discussing it some time & calculating the time taken etc, this plan was accepted & decided on in connection with our plan of returning to Barttelot.

Dec. 15th. In the morning Stairs with a party of 40 men started off for the village of Kavalli to try & make friends with the people & buy a canoe from them. I stayed in camp & mended my clothes, for I have arrived on the shore of the Albert in a very tattered state. At midday Stairs returned,

---

[1] See entry for 16 November above, p. 192.

he found that the village of Kavalli which was large was on an island, & was called Kassinyeh, about half a mile from the shore. After hailing the island some time a fisherman had appeared in a canoe & told him that if he would go in the afternoon to the landing place about a mile off people would come in canoes & talk with him. Stanley sent me off with the men after lunch & I made my way to the landing place through more than half a mile of swamp, then after a walk of a couple of miles the track led round to a broad spit of sand covered with reeds & mimosa bushes & at the end of this spit was the landing place for the canoes from the island. There was nobody to be seen but after we had been hailing the island for about half an hour three canoes shot out from the other side of the island, one, containing one man only paddled away up the lake & the other two, with two men in each, made towards us & stopped at a distance of 200 yds from the shore & began to talk with us. I asked the people or rather the man who acted as spokesman, if he knew of a white man (Misungu) at Kibero in Unyoro, he said he had heard of him. Then if he had heard of Emin Pasha, a very big white man, with plenty of soldiers & steamers, who lived at the North end of the Lake; he said he remembers a white man who came in a steamer, when he was a little boy, to Kavalli; he had stayed one day & had shot a hippopotamus & had then gone away, but that since then he had heard nothing of a white man at the North end of the Lake. The white man he speaks of is evidently Mason[1] who was a surveyor travelling in the employ of the Egyptian Government, he was at Kavalli about 10 years ago. I told him we were come to see the big white man at the North of the lake but were friends with the white man at Kibero (or Kiberi as he called it) & wanted to communicate with him, could any of the men of Kavalli take a message or letter over to Kibero for us. (Kibero is about 35 miles off across the Lake); he said that nobody would undertake it for us. I then asked him if he would sell us a large canoe or if they had none a small canoe & we would go over to the white man; he laughed at such an idea & said they had no big canoes & did not want to sell any small ones which were all like the canoe he was in, (capable of holding about four men) that all the people on the island were afraid of us & nearly all of them had run away to the bush & he did not want to have anything to do with us. With this both canoes heads were turned from us & the natives

---

[1] Lt.-Col. Mason was an American who took service under Gordon on the latter's appointment as Governor of Equatoria in 1872. Part of Sir Samuel Baker's plan on being appointed to the governorship in 1869 had been to launch steamers on Lake Albert, but he was not able to get them so far. Gordon brought them partly over the rapids, and partly in sections by land, launching the *Nyanza* in 1876 and the *Khedive* in 1878. Both were in use on Lake Albert when Jephson arrived there, having been used extensively by Emin in the years between. (See Introduction above, pp. 11–12 also p. 208 above.)

paddled off to their island. The water between the island & the shore is very shallow & I fancy if we wished we could wade across to it, I sent a man out to a distance of 350 yds & the water was nowhere up to his waist. The whole shore & all the mud huts are swarming with birds, they are there in thousands. Swans geese, curlew, plover, snipe, ibis, duck & half a hundred other sorts of birds whose names I do not know—there were whole flocks of duck on the shore & one could get within 30 yds of them, they did not seem to know what fear was. I did not like to fire at any of them for fear of frightening the natives. Anything like the beauty of this end of the plain I never saw. The grass is all cropped short by the numberless herds of Springbok, Kudu, Elands, Hartebeests etc & up every glade one sees some of these beautiful antelope or a herd of buffaloes. Large clumps of trees are dotted about the short sweet grass & form the most lovely glades & nooks, in the shade of which the game shelter itself from the midday sun. It is exactly like a beautiful park at home, the nearest thing I've seen to it is the park at Powderham Castle, near Teignmouth. The game is all so tame & has evidently been little hunted by the natives, it would be easy to supply the whole expedition with meat here. On my way back to camp a large flock of guinea fowl ran along ahead of us for some distance, they seemed to be very little wilder than ordinary guinea fowl at home, this place is a perfect paradise for hunters. When I got in to camp I found a small party of the natives who had acted as guides to us yesterday had come into camp & had advised us to leave the plain soon or we should starve. Stanley on learning the non-success of my mission said there was nothing for it but to return. I suggested that as a last resource we should return four days march to where the natives did not fight but cleared out before us, then march North till we were opposite Kibero, strike the Lake at that point, try & seize a canoe from the natives & I would go across the Lake in it & take my chance of reaching Kassati. Stanley said, No, it would not do. I said let us try anything rather than turn back when we were on the eve of success.* However Stanley was against it, though Stairs was on my side so we must make up our minds to the return journey. We held more consultations with Stanley & the chiefs in his tent that night, but all followed his opinion that the only thing to do was to return. I thought, no, we ought to try more before giving it up. Stanley has of course immense experience & marvellous powers of resource & I was rather astonished that with his resource he could not hit upon a feasible plan.

Dec. 16th. Stanley thought it would be dangerous to start off & attempt the ascent of the mountain on to the table land above today as the natives on the plain would give information of our coming to those above & they

* Had my advice been followed we should have reached M'swa Emin Pasha's most southerly station, for M'swa is exactly opposite Kibero & we should have saved 4 months.

would gather in numbers at the top of the gorge & would have us at a great disadvantage, whilest the natives of the plain would probably follow us & harrass the rear. He decided therefore that we should march out of camp at the usual time, go for a couple of hours & then stop till 6 o'clock, retrace our steps till we got to the path leading up the mountain, follow it in the dark & camp at the foot of the mountain & make no fires. In the morning we could start off early & be halfway up the mountain before the natives of the plain knew where we were & it would then be impossible for them to get before us & give information to those ahead of our coming. We left camp at about 8 o'clock & marched on till 10 & then stopped in the most beautiful part of the plain; that part through which I had passed yesterday— both Stanley & Stairs were greatly struck as I was yesterday by its extra-ordinary beauty & by the quantities of game. Stanley shot a Kudu & 'Sar Tato', the hunter, a large hartebeest, both were cut up & divided amongst the men whose stock of food was now nearly exhausted. In the afternoon 6 natives came upon us suddenly & fired some arrows, we thought it was a regular attack & men were quickly posted to guard the loads whilest Stanley & Stairs with the greater part of the men scoured the plain in the direction in which the natives had gone. It turned out that there were only 6 men & these were probably spies sent out to watch our movements. The game was so plentiful about us that as Stanley said it was quite bewildering, no sooner were you following one herd than another appeared & you hardly knew which to follow, our men were all scattered about laughing & talking, but the game was in no wise scared away. We sat on the grass & had our midday meal & another meal at 5, as we were to get no food cooked when we got to camp; the men were scattered about us in the shade of the clumps of trees, cooking their food, & the whole thing seemed like a big picnic & would have been very enjoyable but for the thought of our return after having achieved nothing, which hung like a cloud over us. At 6 o'clock we started back struck the path leading to the mountain path & followed it in silence. It was pitch dark & we missed the way & after marching till about 10 we came to halt & lay down just as we were, the men with their loads sleeping round us. We pitched no tents but spread out a part of them & just slept on them.

Dec. 17th. Before daylight we started off & reached the foot of the mountain by 9 o'clock, here we halted for an hour & got some food cooked & then began the ascent. The rearguard had hardly got half way up the first spur of the mountain, when we saw a party of natives bounding along to try & get ahead of us, but it was too late they could not get in front of us & were only able to follow & annoy the rear guard. One man Bamazan was sick & would not attempt to move from the place he was lying so he had to be left & no doubt the natives made short work of him—two men were lost last night, they had missed the path & wandered away in the darkness & will probably be killed by the natives today. We got to the plain above in about three hours without the natives knowing we were coming so that Stanley's plan was a complete success. When we got to the top Stanley stationed a few men behind some rocks to wait for the natives who were following us to come up; when they got pretty close they got a good volley of bullets & some of them were wounded & the whole lot made off down the mountain & disappeared. We halted for a hour on the spot where we had halted four days ago when we first saw the Lake. How bitter it was to be sitting there knowing that we were returning & that all our work & labour had been in vain. Four days ago we had been standing there looking down on the Lake with feelings of triumph & relief, now we were looking on the Lake which we should lose sight of in a few minutes with feelings of utter dejection & bitter disappointment. We marched along feeling as if we were going to an execution or a funeral. How miserable one felt as one turned on the top of a small hill to take a last look of the Lake before it disappeared from view, all spirit all interest seemed gone; one had nothing to look forward to but a long dreary march dragging all the loads back over the ground over which we had toiled with them so short a time ago. We must leave this open country where one could see & breathe & plunge once more into the darkness & starvation of the bush. We had not been marching more than an hour when the natives began to gather on the hills from all sides & close in on our rear. A large party of them with shouts & waving of spears came on with a rush & made as if to attack the rear. Stanley stepped out & taking a good steady aim with his Winchester Express fired at a native 550 yds distant & shot him through the head. The natives all rushed up to the body & were so utterly thunderstruck at the possibility of our being able to kill a man at such a distance that they took to their heels as hard as they could pelt & a body of our men pursued them till they were out of sight. Stanley had the dead native cut up, the Zanzibaris mutilated the body in a horrible way. He said it was the only way to put fear into the natives so that they would cease to attack us & was the most merciful way for otherwise we should have to kill a great many before they would see it was best to let us alone. Of course it is horrid to our ideas to mutilate the dead, but I believe Stanley is right. We marched on & camped early in a small collection of huts at the top of a hill & the men went out & brought in abundance of food.

Dec. 18th. Today we stayed in camp & Stanley sent out two parties of men to forage for cattle. Stairs & I were occupied the whole day making boots out of hides we had picked up in the villages: the natives wrap them round their bodies for shields. Our boots were all worn out & our feet are in a terrible state from marching in patched & tattered boots with no soles to speak of. At four oclock the men returned bringing in 16 cattle, some goats & quantities of chickens & food of all sorts. Stanley had seven cattle killed at once & distributed amongst the men, who sat up nearly the whole night feasting & talking. Three of the cattle are milking cows so now we have a fair supply of milk, of course these cows do not give a sixth of the milk that English cows do; Stairs & I got 3 cups of milk between us this evening.

Dec. 19th. As we were leaving this district the natives gathered in large numbers on a hill & the chief began talking to us. He said 'we do not wish to fight, the whole country is at your feet; but if you would pursue & kill the man who first made war on you you would do us a favour'. Afterwards they said they wanted to come close & look at the Inkama (chief) & see our faces. Stanley told them he had no wish to make war on them, they had followed & attacked us, & that if they wished to see our faces six of them might come down & look at us, provided they laid aside their spears & bows; they said they were afraid, so we passed on. In the afternoon as we were passing through another settlement, the natives became troublesome, so after camping in a small village at the top of a hill Stanley sent two parties of men to punish them, they shot two natives & brought back quantities of chickens & food from the villages round. They brought in the head of one of the natives they had shot & it was stuck on a pole close to our camp as a warning to the natives to behave themselves in future.

Dec. 20th. This morning we passed through the settlement where we had stopped four days & had burnt all the villages. Small huts had been built in the place of those we had burned but they were all mere temporary affairs & very small. We could see a few natives watching us from the hills, but this time they made no noise, most of them had hidden, & there was silence throughout the whole valley, & we marched through the settlement un- molested; so much for the lesson we had given them. We also passed through the large settlement which had so excited our admiration on our way to the Lake & through which Stanley had considered it unwise to pass. Except for a party of about 20 natives who came & shouted at us after we had passed, we were quite unmolested, the bulk of the inhabitants being silent & unseen. The men got a good many chickens & seven or eight goats which they found tied up in the M'tama. The goats were all gagged so that we should not hear their bleating. We camped in a good sized cattle Kraal.

Dec. 21st. Leaving camp in good time we reached the river over which we had before crossed by a ricketty native bridge, at about 9 oclock. This time we marched up river some distance till we came to a ford which one of the men knew of, here we crossed & camped in a small settlement close to the bridge. In crossing the river some of our cattle came near drowning.

Dec. 22nd. Today we stayed in camp & Stanley sent out two parties of men to forage for cattle—they returned very soon bringing in 17. Today Stairs was very sick with an attack of bilious fever & Stanley also so I had to look after the camp & post the sentries. Most of the day I was mending my clothes & boots, I manufactured a splendid suit of clothes out of a set of pyjamas! Two cattle were killed for the men in the afternoon.

Dec. 23rd. We made a short march today & camped on the bank of the main stream of the Ituri. We found the canoe we had crossed the river in on our way to the Lake had been removed by the natives. Stanley sent parties of men up & down the river to search for canoes, but the natives had taken them all away hoping to stop our crossing. Rashid brought word that there was a bridge over the river a little way down but that the natives had cut it in two that morning. A good number of natives came down to a low hill above the river & Stanley offered them a cow & calf & said he would march through their settlement without molesting them in any way if they would lend us a canoe. They said they did'nt want us or our cow & shouted & jeered at us so Stanley fired a shot & dispersed them & promised to punish them for their stupidity when we did get across.

Dec. 24th. We started off & marched to the broken bridge for Stanley decided to get it mended up & cross the caravan by it. He set me to work at it with Rashid & some of the men & after a good deal of difficulty we got it mended up sufficiently to send over a party of 15 men to reconoitre. They found the bridge took them only on to a large island & that there was another channel to cross—some of the men managed to swim over with their rifles & found that the natives had left the two villages opposite & had all retired on to a large island lower down. I was the whole day at work at the bridge & got it finished & ready to cross the caravan early in the afternoon. Stanley told me I should have to swim across the river tomorrow & get a raft made of banana stems so that we could get the men & loads across the other channel. The men found eight goats tied up on the island. In the afternoon a most furious hailstorm came on; the hailstones were the largest I've ever seen & most curious in shape—the wind was so strong for a short time that it almost carried the tents away.

Dec. 25th. A curious Christmas day with plenty to do, my last was spent in idleness at Eversfield Place,[1] & the possibility of my accompanying this Expedition was being discussed. Early in the morning I swam across the river & we began to make a raft & I got it finished by ten o'clock. I spent the whole day half in & half out of the water looking after the people & loads crossing, I had on only a shirt & pair of knickerbockers. We got two thirds of the men & all the loads crossed before dark. Stanley

---

[1] With the Countess de Noailles.

camped for the night on the island whilest Stairs & I camped in the village opposite. Our Christmas dinner consisted of goat meat, ripe bananas, green corn, & milk & after dinner Stairs produced from a mysterious box, a medicine bottle full of Whiskey & we had a good stiff jorum each & drank to those at home.

Dec. 26th. We went down & got the rest of the caravan & the cattle crossed & then remained in camp. Stairs was sent out with a party of men to burn the villages round to punish the natives, he got in early & all of us were hard at work making & mending boots—some of the boots I have manufactured would surprise & disgust Mr Moykopf, if he could see me wearing such boots I doubt if he would ever consent to make for me again. In the afternoon Hamis Kururu one of our biggest chiefs, formerly in my company, died. He was buried that afternoon & the men sang rather a pathetic sounding chant over his grave. One will miss him very much for he was a nice cheery old fellow & there is not too much of the cheerful element in this expedition. Some cattle & calves were killed & distributed amongst the men, there is great abundance of food here & they had a regular feast.

Dec. 27th. We stayed in camp & the men feasted & stuffed on meat, ripe bananas, green corn, & porridge. Both Stairs & I had slight fever, mine probably came from spending nearly the whole of Christmas day in the water.

Dec. 28th. Today we started off by a different road to that by which we had come on our way to the Lake. We passed through rich fields of M'tama & plantains & at 10 o'clock came on a large settlement hidden away from the plain in a patch of bush. I never before saw such abundance of ripe plantains, the huts were full of them, we also captured goats & the men got great bundles of sugar cane. Late in the afternoon we camped in a collection of dirty huts in the middle of a large settlement. Two more cattle were killed for the men; there is such abundance that they literally gorge themselves with food & they carry the meat till it is so putrid that the smell of the column as we march along in the hot sun is almost unbearable— In camp the smell is frightful.

Dec. 29th. Today we struck our old path & reached the bush at 10 o'clock; we passed a large herd of springbok & another of buffaloes, but we had so much meat it was not worth while killing any. Now we have seen the last of the plain for many months. No more herds of buffaloe or antelope, no more large breezy views, nothing but the everlasting semidarkness & monotony of the hateful jungle. We crossed the river & camped in our old camp early in the afternoon, when more cattle were killed for the men. One feels this return from the Lake more & more every day.

Dec. 30th. This morning Stanley tried a new road as our old road for two camps ahead was very bad; we got on to a much worse one & wandered about in all directions in the bush, we finally struck our old camp, which was a collection of huts but we found that the natives had burnt them all to the ground.

Dec. 31st. We started off on a new road in order to avoid going over the mountain as we did on our first journey. It was a good path through a very dry jungle & we camped late in the afternoon in the bush. The men went out & got food in a village not far off & captured a woman & child. This is the last day of 1887, it has been a year of very curious experiences for me.

January [1888]. An additional plan had been adopted in connection with the plan to return & bring Barttelot & the rest of the caravan on. About 40 minutes march this side of the camp where we had rested for a fortnight after leaving the Manyema there is a large village called Ibwiri, the Sultan of which we had captured & had made him act as guide to Stairs when he went ahead a two days journey to look for a road leading to the open country —the Sultan whose name is Borio escaped the night after his return with Stairs.[1] Round this village were great plantations of plantains & numerous other villages round about had also their plantations & abundant supplies of Indian corn & a good many sweet potatoes. Here in short was a plentiful supply of food & a village both from its size, position & water supply eminently suited for a standing camp. It is about 18 days march from the Lake & 9 good marches from the Manyema settlement. Stanley therefore decided that instead of carrying all the loads back to Barttelot he would form a standing camp in Ibwiri & fortify it strongly. He would wait there himself with all the loads & send a party down to the Manyema settlement to bring back the boat, Maxim gun & all loads of amunition, together with Nelson & Parke & all the sick men left with the Manyema. On their arrival he would start off empty handed with the greater part of the men & return to join Barttelot & bring him along, leaving officers & a sufficient number of men—men who were the least able to travel—to garrison the place. By this means he would be able to travel faster, being unencumbered with loads & sick men, meanwhile the sick men would be getting well & the loads would be safely bestowed at a convenient distance from the Lake. Everyone at once saw the advisability of this plan.

Jan. 1st. We marched through the bush & camped early in a good sized village which the natives had deserted some weeks before, probably when we were on our way to the Lake. Here I had a very bad touch of fever in the afternoon and all night.

Jan. 2nd. The fever was so bad today I could scarcely drag myself along

[1] See entries for 21–28 Nov. 1887, pp. 194–6 above.

the road was bad & led over a high hill at the top of which were poised in the most extraordinary positions huge rocks which looked as if a slight push would send them bounding down the hill. After doing a good long march we came to a village in the middle of plantain plantations which the natives had begun to destroy. Here we camped & I half blind with fever just threw myself down in the shade until a hut & bed could be got ready for me. Fever is a terrible terrible feeling; the feeling of misery & utter prostration which accompanies it is unequalled.

Jan. 3rd. The fever is much better this morning, but one feels very shaky & weak in the joints. Stanley got an attack of it today & had to be carried in his chair, it is wonderful how he gives way when he has the least illness & how anxious he becomes—perhaps the latter is not so much to be wondered at, seeing that he has so much on his shoulders.[1] We passed two burnt villages & camped in one which the natives had half destroyed. As Stairs says, ones feelings of anxiety when Stanley falls ill are greatly relieved on seeing the large plates of food which go into his huts & the empty plates which come out of it.

Jan. 4th. We stayed in camp today as Stanley was still unwell.

Jan. 5th. At 10.30 today we struck our old road & camped late in the day at a village where we had camped on our way here—I should say rather on the site of the village for the natives have burnt it. Our march to the Lake seems to have destroyed the whole chain of villages on the way, the natives doubtless feared we were going to settle as the Manyema have done & thought thus to deter us from doing so.

Jan. 6th. We passed the skeleton of one of our men today in the path, he was a sick man & had been unable to keep up with the column. He had evidently, finding he could not keep up with us, decided to return to the Manyema settlement & the natives had killed him on the road, there was a good sized bag of decaying beans & corn lying close to the skeleton so he had had plenty of food with him. It is quite wonderful how foolish these people are. He thought that because we a large body of men were able to get along all right, that therefore he by himself would be able to traverse the 90 miles of bush between here & the Manyema in safety. We camped today in the jungle a little beyond our old camping place & were nearly flooded out of our tents by a violent thunderstorm.

---

1 From now on Jephson's bitter criticisms of Stanley abate somewhat; he seems to be considering the strain on the leader, and coming to depend more and more on Stanley's brute strength.

CHAPTER 10

FORT BODO

7 JANUARY—1 APRIL 1888

Jan. 7th. At noon we reached Ibwiri & found that it had been burnt, with all its supply of corn. This was of course a nasty slap in the face for us, but Stanley with his usual determination began at once to build a boma & to clear away all scrub & bush about us so that the natives should have no cover to shoot at us from. In a hut near by in the bush about half a ton of corn was found which had not been burnt. The boma is being built of rough planks such as the natives use in building their huts, we have found a good many of these planks lying near in the jungle.

Jan. 8th. Hard at work all hands, as soon as the sun rose, some building the boma, others at the houses for Stanley & ourselves, others clearing the bush round the boma. From 6 till 6 we were all hard at work with only an hours rest from 11 till 12.

Jan. 9th. Today one of the men came in with the report that about $1\frac{1}{2}$ hours off there was a large camp of natives in the jungle & there was a plentiful supply of Indian corn in it. The man had shot two of the natives & the rest had fled leaving all their corn behind them.

Jan. 16th. We have been at work so hard that it has been quite impossible to write up one's journal. We got in about 8 tons of Indian corn from the native camp the men discovered in the jungle—it is not to be given out to the men but we have free access to the store & take what we want, so that we have an unlimited amount of porridge & banana puddings. We have got the boma finished, it is a peculiar shape. We have made five mud houses for Stanley & ourselves, & two houses for certain of the chiefs, inside the boma, also two goat houses & a kitchen. There is one gateway only & from this the mens houses stretch in two lines in the shape of a wedge & the tower on the gateway commands the space between. At the same time we have been clearing ground about the boma for planting Indian corn—which only takes 3 months to ripen from the time it is planted. Work goes on from morning till night. Some men out in the jungle cutting trees for building, others cutting leaves for thatching the houses; some digging clay to build with, others fastening the frame work of the houses together; one party clearing the ground for planting, whilst another gets the logs together to burn; parties are coming & going on reconoitring expeditions or carrying rough boards or corn from the deserted villages round—all is noise & bustle

221

& all hands are hard at work every day. Thus at the end of 8 days the work is sufficiently far advanced to admit of a large party being sent down to the Manyema camp to bring back Nelson & Parke, the men left with them, the boat & Maxim gun & all the loads of rifles & ammunition. Stanley had all the men mustered & asked who would volunteer to go down & fetch the boat & loads. The men not volunteering very readily, Stanley promised every man who helped to bring the boat here, 10 Dollars, & every man who brought a load, 5 Dollars. The inducement being given a good number volunteered, 88 in all, but not enough to bring all the loads. Stanley then asked the men to choose whether they would be accompanied by Stairs or by me, & they chose Stairs; so I stay here & help Stanley with the work whilest Stairs goes down to the Manyema camp—the journey there & back will in all probability take him 25 days. Stanley sent two large parties out to forage but they returned with very little they say that the villages all round have been burnt & the natives have decamped into the jungle. The two days before Stairs started, work was stopped & all hands were put on to prepare food, flour etc for the men returning to the Manyema camp, for there will be no food to be got either on the way or in the Manyema settlement. Stairs was busy patching up his shoes & making others out of raw hide; he & I are simply without boots except what we have made ourselves, he also got his tattered clothes patched up a bit.

Jan 17th. Stairs started off this morning with a goodly supply of food,[1] the men had big loads of food for the journey but they are so improvident that it will probably be finished by the time they reach the Manyema & they will have nothing for the return journey but what little they can pick up. There are not many men left now in the fort—Fort Bodo[2] as Stanley calls it—about 80 only & everything is very quiet after the noise & bustle of the larger force.[3] The men still bring in Indian corn in small quantities,

[1] 'Three cows were slaughtered for meat rations for Stairs' Expedition, each man received 120 ears of corn, goats, fowls, and planters were taken for the commander and his two friends, and the party set off for Kilonga-Longa on the 19th' (Stanley, *IDA*, I, 331).

[2] Or 'Peaceful Fort'. (Stanley, *IDA*, I, 327.)

[3] Stanley gives the following table:

Stairs' part at muster consisted of:—	The garrison numbered:—
88 men	60 men
6 chiefs	3 cooks
1 officer	4 boys
1 boy	3 whites
1 cook	——
1 Manyema	70
——	
98	

(Stanley, *IDA*, I, 331)

they find it in the fields or old deserted native camps. The good bananas which were so plentiful at first are getting more scarce, but there is still abundance of inferior bananas sufficient to insure us from want.

February 7th [1888]. Tomorrow or the next day Stanley expects the caravan with Nelson Parke & Stairs to come in, but if the loads come in, I consider it will be impossible for the boat to come in for another 4 or 5 days, considering the numberless native clearings through which the path leads & the miles of logs & encumbrances which have to be climbed over in those clearings—it will be very hard work getting the boat on at all. Since I have been here alone with Stanley I have been out at work from morning till night & begin to feel rather done up, the sun is terribly hot & one feels it more when one is standing about than one does on the march. Several times I have been obliged to go into my hut & lie down in consequence of one's head reeling & turning from the heat of the sun & once I thought I was going to have sunstroke for I felt just as I did before I got a sunstroke in Ceylon. We have with immense labour, cleared & planted four & a half acres with Indian corn & interlined it with beans. These beans are a sort we brought with us from the plain & are much liked by the Zanzibaris; they are about the size of French Kidney beans but are black & yellow speckled. The men eat them when they are dry & ripe, but I think they are nicest when eaten as French beans. Inside the boma we have improved the houses & have whitewashed them with white wood ash, it makes a capital whitewash & lightens up the houses wonderfully.[1] Stanley's house which has two good sized rooms in it is very comfortable. Ours is a long house 33 ft by 14 ft in which four of us are supposed to live. It is not bad but Stanley has not taken much trouble about it & the roof is so flat on the top that it leaks like a seive—I have got four beds built in it, one in each corner & have put up a table in the middle, this last is a great luxury after being 8 months without one. All the sanitary arrangements of the camp Stanley gave me to do, & I think I have made them very complete. Broad roads have been made at the ingress & egress of the camp to some distance & will be a great help to the boat as many logs are cleared by them. The defences of the camp have been strengthened by 'banquettes' being made nearly all round on the inner side of the boma. In the clear space in the middle of the boma a good sized granary has been built standing on legs which raise it

[1] 'On the 28th, headquarters was ready for occupation. We had cleared three acres of land, cut down the bush clean to the distance of 20 yards from the fort, chopped the logs—the lighter were carried away, the heavier were piled up—and fire applied to them, and the next day folded the tents and removed to our mansions, which, as Jephson declared, were "remarkably snug". There was at first a feeling of dampness, but a charcoal fire burning night and day soon baked the walls dry' (Stanley, *IDA*, I, 332).

about 9 ft from the ground, this is done to keep the corn from the rats which abound here & eat up everything & bite holes in one's clothes at night. In the very centre of the boma a high flagstaff is put up & our big Egyptian flag floats over us, it is a flag I hate—albeit a very pretty one—& dislike serving under, I would much sooner see the dear old Union Jack up there it would remind one more of home. Ah home! shall I ever see it again, it seems so far off & distant. It will be still two years and a half before we can get back to England & when one thinks of the fevers etc before us one trembles a bit for one's chances of ever seeing dear old England again. Stanley lent me 'Sartor Risartus' & the Bible to read, both very interesting books. Poor old Teufelsdrockh he was very nice & had splendid thoughts & ideas, but I do'nt wonder at the 'Bluniene' thinking it impolitic to marry him, Mrs Teufelsdrockh would have had a bad time of it, for however fine & splendid his thoughts & ideas were the man himself reeked of beer & stale tobacco. It is wonderful after being on the plain amongst people who live among their flocks & herds how one can see exactly Abraham & Isaac & Jacob as described in the Bible, as one reads about them things one saw on the plain are constantly rising up & one says to oneself, 'that description is exactly what we saw'.—Parties of Ruga Ruga[1] have been sent out from time to time to forage & have brought in three or four goats only. Baroko,[2] my old enemy, generally heads these expeditions. He brought in a woman & child from one of these expeditions & after a couple of days the woman ran away leaving the child, who is about 2 yrs old. Baroko's treatment of this child is simply diabolical, he beats it starves it & throws it about the hut, so they tell me. I ordered my boy to feed it with my food & to see that it got plenty to eat. Finally Baroko took the child away into the jungle & left it there, but the unfortunate little creature found its way back here & in the middle of the night I was wakened by strange cries & moans & on getting up found that Barokos little child had fallen into a deep pit outside the boma & had broken its arm & leg. Baroko came & took it back to his hut where it dragged on a miserable existance until at last he again took it out into the jungle & left it; this time he probably knocked it on the head as it did not return. Stanley would not allow one to interfere as Baroko denied the ill treatment in spite of the accusations of the Zanzibari, though Stanley admitted Baroko had done many a cruel deed on the road. It is terrible how cruel these people are.

Feb. 8th. At about 10.30 we heard guns & drums, & shortly after Parke appeared with the front lot of the caravan & said Nelson & the rest of the men carrying loads would be in shortly. He gave me a note from Stairs in which Stairs told me that finding the boat got on so slowly he had sent

[1] 'Freebooters' or 'guerillas'. [2] See p. 140 above.

Nelson & Parke on with the loads & would probably reach this place in another 4 days—I had judged exactly right in saying it would take him 25 days in spite of what Stanley had said—in his note Stairs asked me to send him food as his was nearly finished. In two or three hours Nelson turned up with the rest of the loads. He looks wretched & thin & ill & is hardly able to walk, he went to bed at once. They have had a fearful time of it in the Manyema camp—Stanley desired Parke to write an official letter giving an account of their stay there, this letter I copy & it will tell its own story.[1] This letter is only a short & mild description of what they suffered during their stay & numberless more cases of theft, annoyance & even insult could be cited. I sent Stairs a supply of food in charge of 10 men under Baroko & hope it will reach him before his is all finished. Stanley tries to make as little as possible of what Nelson & Parke suffered & talks about their expecting to find themselves in an hotel.

Feb. 10th. This morning at 5 minutes notice Stanley sent me off with 32 men on a foraging expedition of 5 days.[2] I took nothing with me but my waterproof coat, not even any food trusting to what I could pick up. We started off at about 7.30 & Stanley told me to try & find the river Ihuru & go in a Northerly direction. I went along our old road for nearly two of our former marches & then turned off to the North by a big track which crossed ours at right angles. We followed this for about an hour & then came suddenly on a party of natives who ran as soon as they saw us throwing some of their loads of food as they went—their baskets chiefly contained yams & dried ripe bananas these last are very good & taste when roasted on the fire like dried figs. After going till about 3 oclock we came upon banana plantations & signs of where natives had been recently working & in another hour we had crept up to a village in which we could hear the natives working. I collected all the men silently & we made a rush into the village. Every man woman & child left everything & ran as hard as they could leaving bows, arrows, knives everything they possessed just as they were, the cooking pots full of bananas yams etc were left on the fires so that one had a dinner ready cooked if one cared about that sort of food. We chased the natives from village to village—there was a perfect net work of

---

[1] See Appendix IV below, pp. 434–6 for the text of this letter. Despite Stanley's apparent brushing off of the complaints, he acknowledges in *In Darkest Africa* the severity of the ordeal suffered by Parke and Nelson at Ipoto. He prints Parke's report in full, and comments: 'The stay of these officers at the Manyuema village required greater strength of mind and a moral courage greater than was needed by us during our stormy advance across the grass-land' (Stanley, *IDA*, I, 338).

[2] Parke describes Jephson's departure, 'taking nothing but what he stood up in, with the addition of an old mackintosh. He wore boots of his own manufacture, of the fashion of Veldtschoons, which in all probability will be left buried while crossing some muddy marsh, where elephants love to wallow' (Parke, p. 197).

them—& drove everything before us. One man only made a stand & shot one of our men through his shirt but he paid dearly for it for a bullet through his head gave him his quietus. The natives are building several new villages all together it is a very large settlement. They are evidently the natives whom we have driven out of their villages about us who are building here & have all united together for safety against us—it is rather a shame that they should get no rest from us. I fixed upon a small village for our camp as it was easily fortified by building a boma of boards at each end. The men then went out to loot all the villages close by. They brought in all sorts of food in the shape of ripe bananas yams chickens goats etc. There were quantities of goats but the men shot at them & they became so wild that it was almost impossible to catch them & they only brought me 4 live ones—Chickens they brought me in plenty. One of the men Markatooboo who was by way of looking after me spatched me a fat chicken by the fire & brought me dry ripe bananas very well cooked, so I had an excellent dinner although I had nothing but my fingers for I had brought no plates knives forks etc & ate my food on a green plantain leaf & drank out of a gourd. I slept on a native bed with fresh plantain leaves on it, it was not very comfortable for native beds are always so short that ones feet stick out a foot beyond.

Feb. 11th. Today I decided to wait in camp & send the men out to try and catch goats & chickens. There were quantities of goats all round but I only managed to get thirteen & about sixteen chickens to take back to camp with me. The men got quantities of goats judging from the great heaps of goat flesh drying over every fire on kind of tables made of sticks, there were quantities of chickens too in various stages of drying & cooking. The men brought me in numbers of beautifully made little bows ornamented for the most part with monkey skin & sheaves of perfectly made arrows with the most wonderful variety of iron barbs, they also brought me iron bracelets & necklets & lip ornaments, the latter are this shape[1] the small iron peg at the bottom being stuck into a hole in the lip, it wags about when the wearer speaks & gives her a most absurd appearance. They also got numbers of very pretty little knives some of them of the most fantastic shapes. It is very interesting going on a foraging expedition on account of the curious things one sees, but the cruelty of these Zanzibaris sickens one. As I was strolling about from village to village, a guard of men being with me, I came upon several small children huddled together in huts all more or less bearing marks of violence on their faces which had been inflicted by my Zanzibaris, poor little things they screamed out as I approached, I found one little boy speared to death in a hut. Of course if I see any cruelty going on I put a stop to it at once, but it is impossible when the men are out of my sight. They cap-

---

[1] There is a drawing in the MS.

tured five or six women, this I do'nt mind as the women always get away after a few days & from them the Zanzibaris are able to pick up a few words of the language which is useful.

Feb. 12th. I started off this morning to find the river & was reluctantly obliged to leave 16 of my party of 32 to look after the goats etc whilest I & the remaining 16 went off to try & find the river. I gave them strict injunctions to remain in camp & not to scatter about for the natives are about in great numbers. We started off on a road leading due North & after travelling along it all day & not reaching the river we were obliged to camp in the jungle for the night.

Feb. 13th. We returned to yesterdays camp where I found everything all right the men all there & the goats chickens, axes hoes etc, which we had taken from the natives, all correct. I got everything packed up & got ready for an early start tomorrow.

Feb. 14th. A most violent thunderstorm came on just as we were starting & we were unable to start till 8.30. It was very wretched travelling through the jungle after the rain, every hollow was a swamp & every stream a rushing torrent. We travelled hard all day & got up to our settlement just before dark. My men shouted & blew horns as we approached & all the Zanzibaris came running up the track to meet us & take their friends loads— every man with me was loaded with as much dried meat & chickens as he could carry & they had also knives, tobacco, ornaments, native cloth etc. One marched in triumphantly & told Stanley all there was to be told—he was very much disappointed that I had not come across the river. I found Stairs with the boat had got in on the 12th i.e. 25 days after he left here which is exactly what I said he would take.[1] I was very glad to see him again & to hear his news. He told me Stanley wanted to go back to the Lake & was waiting till I & my men returned to hold a big 'Shauri' on the subject. Of course Stairs I & were both for returning at once to the Lake & when Stanley asked Stairs yesterday about it he told him that he knew I wanted to return.

Feb. 15th. This morning all hands were mustered & every Tom, Dick & Harry were on parade, & it was (almost unanimously) decided that we should return to the Lake. Meanwhile a party of 20 men was to be dispatched down river with letters of instructions to Barttelot telling him to come on as fast as he could & warning him of the places where there was no food & telling him of those places where there was plenty—Stanley gave him a short account of our experiences since we left him & we all wrote. Stairs was to accompany the men as far as Ugarrowas settlement from which he would return here with all the men & guns we had left there. Stanley promised

[1] Stanley gives the distance from Fort Bodo to Ipoto as 158 miles the 'round trip' (Stanley, *IDA*, I, 341).

each of the men £10 if they reached Barttelot & brought back a letter from him. A garison of 40 men was then chosen of the worst men to remain here with Nelson & Parke. In a few days Stanley & I go on to 'Imandi', a colony at the edge of the plain, we shall reconoitre all the country there & I shall get the boat in the Ituri ready to cross the whole expedition. Stairs & his men from Ugarrowa's will according to Stanleys calculations catch us at Imandi by March 25th, but I think he will take longer, & we shall then proceed to the Lake & put the boat in the water & build our boma at the top of the pass leading down to the Lake plain. These are now our plans which are of course subject to slight alterations if necessary.

Feb. 16th. Stairs accompanied by Rashid & Khamis Parry, who will return with him, & the 20 men going down to Barttelot started off this morning. Stanley is unwell, he has something the matter with the glands of his arm.

Feb. 17th. Early this morning at about 4 am Stanley sent for Parke to come to him as he felt very ill.

Feb. 26th. Stanley has been dangerously ill, he had an attack of 'gastritis', he has had two attacks before at home & has been three months on his back from them, he is much better now & I hope will get well soon. His plan of going to 'Imandi' has been put off & it [is] just possible when Stairs arrives he will find us still here for the illness has been dangerous & Stanley will take some time to recover; to make things worse he had fever with the gastritis & his arm is still bad; two days ago it was nearly well but in one of his ungovernable fits of rage—which by the way are of very frequent occurrence—he hit his German servant[1] across the head with a stick & it has made his arm really bad, for matter has formed among the glands & it will be an affair of many days before it gets well. Parke & I have been sitting up by his bedside on alternate nights, he hardly sleeps at all but sits up in bed & talks a good deal between the intervals when one is putting hot stoups & poultices on his body & arm & giving him milk, which latter he takes frequently in small quantities.[2] A few nights ago, by way of amusing himself

---

[1] William Hoffmann, who is hardly mentioned in any account of the expedition. His own book, *With Stanley in Africa*, was written many years later, and is not to be relied upon. Though Hoffmann was in constant and close attendance on Stanley—he witnessed Jephson's contract when the latter joined the expedition—he was not *persona grata* with the officers. See Epilogue below, p. 420.

[2] 'Dr. Parke has been most assiduous in his application to my needs, and gentle as a woman in his ministrations. For once in my life every soul around me was at my service, and I found myself an object of universal solicitude night and day. My faithful friends, Parke and Jephson, waited, and watched, and served' (Stanley, *IDA*, I, 345).

Parke, who describes the course of the illness in detail, declares that Stanley was very near death. The anxiety of the men for their leader, and the constant enquiries of the headmen, give the lie to those critics of Stanley who maintain that he misused his porters. (Parke, pp. 198–206.)

he gave me a sketch of my character as he had observed it. He began by saying that my enthusiasm led me to exaggeration (perhaps that's true) & that I was full of cracks & prejudices, & in fact made me out to be a perfect fiend to all of which I listened with a smile. But the thing he laid most stress upon was my 'overweening pride—pride of birth & pride of self'. To the latter accusation I remarked that I did not see where my pride came in, for I had had many jobs to do since I had accompanied the Expedition, such jobs as are usually given to the very lowest & I had done them all without a word & without even thinking them derogatory. He said that perhaps I had but that in doing them I had shown pride in every movement & turn of my body, though he admitted I had done them properly & well—& so on until he had contrived to paint a very nasty character. He said that at the age of eighteen had I been sent out for three years into a very tough life, say, three years before the mast in a coasting vessel I should have bourne the impress of it all my life & it would have improved my character to a very great extent. He said I had only seen the soft side of life—there he made a very great mistake, but I did not contradict him but smilingly asked if he had any other unpleasant traits to add to my character, upon which he said No, but added from what he had seen he had very great hopes of me & thought that I should return from this expedition greatly improved, which I thought was just as impertinent as his tirade against my character. He then gave me a sketch of his own character, he told me he had been just as impetuous & rash as I am when he was my age but that time etc had taught him to curb himself & a whole lot more rubbish. He made himself out to be a St John for gentleness, a Solomon for wisdom, a Job for patience & a model of truth. Whereas I do not suppose a more impatient, a more ungentle, a more untruthful man than Stanley could exist. He is most violent in his words & actions, the slightest little thing is sufficient to work him into a frenzy of rage, his sense of what is honourable is of the haziest discription & he is certainly a most untruthful character—'Oh wad some power the giftie gie us'.

March 6th [1888]. Stanley is now convalescent & is able to sit out most of the day but great care has to be taken of him still & his arm is most painful. Parke & I no longer sit up with him at night, although one sat up with him most willingly it was a great tax upon one for I have to carry on the entire work of the camp every day & keep 140 men at work from 7 AM to 5 PM at various things building cutting a trench etc & have 36 hours right off without any sleep, at times even at work I found it hard to keep awake. A few days ago Stanley was carried round to look at the works to see how they had got on during his illness—he had no fault to find so I conclude he was satisfied with what I had done. Uledi the coxswain & 30 men went out on a foraging expedition & returned in 4 days with a good many goats & chickens & loot of all sorts, but they had had a good fright from the natives who came & fired arrows into the camp at night & so frightened the men that they precipitately left the village in which they were camped & returned here.

March 18th. Stanley has been getting slowly better but his arm has been keeping him back very much & has given him constant pain. Some days ago Parke lanced it & a great quantity of matter came out & relieved the pain very much, since then it has been getting rapidly well & he is now able to get about & sleep well. There is nothing now to prevent our starting for Imandi, but Stanley expects Stairs back every day & has decided to wait for him & start altogether. Some days ago 7 men arrived from the Manyema camp they are those remaining men who did not come on with Stairs before as they were away with some Manyema on a foraging expedition. They were perfect skeletons. They told us that Stairs had been unable to find a road to the Ihuru[1] from Killimani & had gone by way of the Manyema camp had crossed the Ihuru lowerdown & so on to Ugarrowas. Chilongalonga[2] had given him two men as guides & he was to get there in eight days from the Manyema camp which makes it 15 days from here to Ugarrowas. Stanley was very much vexed that Stairs had been unable to find a road to the Ihuru & go down the route he had planned for him. Another party under the chiefs Hari & Munia Pembe went out foraging last week. They were to go to the place which I looted & were to go on & try & find a road to the Ihuru & bring a report to Stanley of the river & probable roads on the other side of it. They returned after an absence of 7 days greatly dispirited. Munia Pembe was carried into camp with a poisoned arrow wound in his leg & he & Hari brought us the bad news that Salimini & Kamweia, two of our very best men had been killed by poisoned arrows wounds, both had been shot in the stomach. Hari told his story in a very disjointed manner & I was certain he was not giving a true account of what happened—afterwards I questioned Munia Pembe who gave a different story. Hari's story was, they had reached the place that I looted & led by a native woman had reached the river the next day. Here they came on a large village whose inhabitants had deserted it & in it they camped. The next day the natives had come in great numbers from across the river in large canoes & had attacked them, meanwhile numbers of natives from another village attracted by the sound of guns came & attacked them in the rear & they were all these days trying to get back. They brought in 4 goats & 3 chickens which they said they found in a canoe. They said they had got little or no food, but when I had occasion to go into some of the mens huts I saw a plentiful

---

[1] Ihuru river is the Epulu on modern maps.
[2] Kilonga-Longa, chief Arab of Ipoto, see p. 168 above.

supply of fried meat, which fact did not fit in which Hari's story. Munia Pembe told me they built no boma at night & the men scattered about so that had the natives made a determined attack they would have fallen an easy prey to them. It is always the same thing, these men are like children; they never think & it is marvellous with their stupidity how often they have escaped. Nelson is now considerably better & comes out & looks after a small section of men in a desultory sort of way. The corn we planted a little more than 6 weeks ago is now in flower & is as tall as I am, it will be a wonderful crop. Another 2½ acres have been cleared & planted & will be up in a few days.[1] A broad ditch with earthworks has been dug round two sides of the camp, another wattled boma has been built round the entire settlement & I have just finished building some fine large new houses for the men, so that the camp & its defences are now completely finished & there will be little left for the men who remain here to do except planting & clearing. Now that Stanley has been ill he wants to take the doctor on with him, but is very nervous about leaving Nelson in charge of the Fort lest he should get ill again & let things go to ruin. He wants to start on Wednesday but I do not think Stairs will arrive till Thursday at the earliest. I have had a good deal of fever lately & shall be very glad to get away from this place.

March 25th. Stairs who was expected to arrive any day last week has not yet turned up, Stanley is getting rather anxious about him, he has had to go through a country where there is no food for 15 days & we are afraid he is experiencing great trouble in getting the men along for 12 of them are Somalis & Soudanese & they are bad marchers & knock under very quickly. This week we have been doing up roads & clearing the stream etc. I have just finished a large high tower to flank the outer boma & command the road & bridge over the stream, it also flanks the ditch & earthworks & is higher than any of the other four towers. There is also another clearing of 3 acres nearly cleared & ready for planting, we shall soon have quite a considerable acreage under cultivation. The men now have a sort of service every morning & evening among themselves in camp. They have built verandahs to my new houses & all sit there & read the 'Koran' in a kind of singing droning voice & write prayers on small boards smoothed & whitened for the purpose. Sali, one of Stanleys boys, was telling me the story of Mahomet, which I had never heard before, I do not know if it is

---

[1] 'During my convalescence I have been supported each afternoon to the centre of a lofty colonnade of trees, through which our road to the Nyanza leads, where in an easy chair I have passed hours of reading and drowsing...As the sun appears low in the west, and lights the underwood horizontally with mellow light, my kind doctor assists me to my feet and props me, and I wend to the Fort, my corn with dancing motion and waving grace bidding me farewell' (Stanley, *IDA*, I, 347–8: entry for 25 March, 1888).

the correct history[1]...Stanley is almost quite well & goes & looks after the work—he has an enormous appetite.

April 1st Sunday [1888]. Stairs has not yet returned, he has now been away 46 days so Stanley has decided to go on without him, we start tomorrow for the Lake, the pleasure of again being on the march & returning to the Lake is greatly damped, for me, by Stairs' nonappearance. First of all he is most useful to the Expedition & carries things on well; then again we have in consequence of his not returning less men than we had before & now every man will have to carry a load & no allowance can be made for the sick, he himself will be wretched at having missed going back to the Lake & will be fretting his life out here, if indeed he ever reaches this place, for we do not know what may not have happened to him; & I shall miss him terribly for we always get on so well together,—in fact I am terribly sorry about it. Yesterday we got all loads etc ready & had them told off to the different men to carry. I had previously got the boat all done up ready & had mended various things that were broken, had made five new oars to replace those lost & broken, had made a new tiller & a variety of other things, so that the boat & its effects were all in readiness. Stanley sometime ago decided on sending me up to Wadelai in the boat to communicate with Emin Pasha. Directly we get to the Lake the boat is to be put into the water & I with a sufficient number of men, probably from 15 to 20, together with Faiti the man who understands Unyoro & Binza, Dr Juncker's servant who has been to Wadelai, will start & skirt the Lake to Kibero & communicate with Kassati who will tell me whether Emin Pasha is at Wadelai or not. If he is there I shall go on, probably taking Kassati with me, to Wadelai & shall deliver over to Emin Pasha all the letters we have brought him & letters from Stanley as well. He will then come down in his steamer & take over the ammunition & outfit we have brought him from Egypt & will tell Stanley whether he will come out with us or not. It is a splendid mission to be sent on & I am of course delighted at being chosen to undertake it, at the same time there is a good deal of danger about it, &, as Stanley says, I shall have to be awfully wise, one will go into it in fear & trembling lest by an error of judgement one may not be successful in reaching Emin Pasha. Stanley has decided to form a camp in the village of Kavalli, on the island in the Lake, instead of building a boma at the top of the gorge leading down into the plain as he formerly intended, this probably is on account of our greatly diminished number. Nelson with about 45 men is to be left alone at the Fort which we have made perfectly impregnable, he ought to be able to hold it easily in case of attack, though an attack is extremely probable. Parke, the doctor, comes on with us.

[1] Sali's story is omitted as containing nothing of special interest.

CHAPTER II

RETURN TO LAKE ALBERT AND CONTACT WITH EMIN PASHA

April 9th. We started last Monday & have been coming along very fairly, the men are in good spirits & carry the boat over all the difficult places most cheerily. We found all the villages we passed through burnt & where formerly there was shelter every night & heaps of corn there is now nothing but burnt village & bananas. It makes the journey not nearly so pleasant especially as it is now the rainy season & we are flooded regularly every day. This morning we reached Imandi[1] but as the logs were so bad & the brushwork had grown up to such an extent Stanley decided to pass by the villages without going up to them & in a few minutes we struck our old road by which we had left Imandi on our way to the Lake. We came over a ridge of hill as before but Stanley struck a big path to the right leading in SE direction & in half an hour we came upon a small village in which we camped for the night. From this village we catch glimpses of the plain through the trees, the grass looks very long. Stanley hopes to cross the Ituri below the two branches we crossed on our way before & thus make one crossing of them all, this we can do now as we have the boat, it was different before. The men captured a woman here & led by her a party of them soon reached the river & came back with the news that all the natives in the villages on this side of the river had crossed over to the other side & were in some large villages there. They report the river as being the main stream of the Ituri & being rocky & many cataracts & rapids in sight but they say the boat can cross easily—the natives have taken all the canoes over to the other side they will be considerably astonished when they see the boat put together & crossing the river; there will be plenty of work for me tomorrow. The men say that a number of women came down to the river's edge & turning their back on them they slapped a certain part in derision—they were quite naked.

April 10th. We reached the river, which is very broad here, at about 9.30. There were numbers of natives gathered on the opposite shore at a landing place where there were two large canoes tied up to the bank, Stanley fired a shot from his 'Express' & the ball went through one man & wounded another, instaneously there was a great blowing of horns & beating of drums

---

[1] The region lying between the eastern foot of Mount Pisgah and the Ituri river.

& the natives, of whom there must have been some hundreds to oppose our crossing, gave tongue like a pack of hounds—it was a horrid sound & made one's blood run cold. However Stanley's shot had the effect of dispersing them very expeditiously & when the first boat load of our men was landed there was no one to be seen, but there were tracks of blood where the wounded natives had made off. The boat took some time to get together as I had fixed everything up so snugly for carriage, but when she was once in the water she landed the whole expedition, men & loads, on the other side in forty three minutes. Stanley decided to camp on the river bank as there was a nice clear space while I set to work at once to get the boat taken to pieces & made up into loads ready to start tomorrow. It has been a hard days work for me, but a very satisfactory one as everything has gone off well & there has been no delay with the boat. The men who went out to forage came in in the evening bringing in goats fowls, ripe bananas etc & great quantities of tobacco in great bushel baskets. They report there being numbers of villages in the neighbourhood. Parke made a great find in the shape of about a peck of very good salt, but he very weakly handed it over to Stanley to divide & the consequence was, as I foresaw, that we got only about a thirtieth part sent round to us in the evening. The want of salt, as I think I have frequently said before, is our most pressing want, people at home, to whom salt comes as a matter or course, could hardly believe how terrible it is to be without it, the very animals even feel it & frequently eat a certain sort of earth which has a slight taste of salt about it. Parke & I had a regular feast tonight.

April 11th. Started off early & passed through a very large settlement there was a perfect network of villages or rather collections of huts. There must have been several hundreds of inhabitants & the banana plantations stretched far away to our right. After passing through the settlement we came to the jungle & came out onto the open at about one o'clock. It is needless to repeat how delighted one was at once more being able to breathe again after being shut up in the jungle.[1] The grass on the plain is very much higher than when we were here before owing to its being now the rainy season. The boat which is so difficult to carry in the jungle now goes along

---

[1] Emergence from the jungle caused Parke 'to quiver with delight. Deep draughts of champagne could not have painted his cheeks with a deeper hue than did this exhilarating prospect' (Stanley, *IDA*, 1, 354).

'It *did* feel as a deliverance,' wrote Parke, and later: 'Last night Jephson and I gormandized on a real aldermanic dinner of goat, chicken, and beans. We smoked our native tobacco, in order to complete our happiness; but we soon grew pale, and became very faint and sick, the dose was stronger than we had calculated it to be; this pure native growth being much more potent than that which we have recently been accustomed to' (Parke, p. 210).

capitally & without the least stoppage, the men felt the difference at once & delight in the change. We camped early at 2.30 in a patch of wood with a cool stream flowing near by.

April 12th. We camped early today in a large settlement, the men went out to the neighbouring villages & a good many shots were fired, it was evident there were a great many natives about, one of the men, Iohari, came in bringing the head of a native with him. It was not a bad face & from the size of the head must have belonged to a very big man. Early in the afternoon one of our men, Faiti, was shot close to the camp, the arrow penetrated just below the breast bone to a depth of about three or four inches, Parke gives little hope of his recovery, but he can hardly tell yet. If he dies he will be a terrible loss for he is the only man who can speak the Unyoro language & was to have gone with me in the boat to interpret for me. He also understands the language of all the natives up to the Lake—he is one of the men we can least afford to lose just now. Stanley got in a great rage with the men today & as they were not working as well as they might he fired at two of them, he just grazed the heel of one of the men & took a piece of the skin off about the size of a sixpence, a quarter of an inch more would have shattered the bone of the foot & made him lame for life; Stanley really is not responsible for what he does when he gets into these fits of passion, & yet to hear him tell one how completely he has his temper under control—!

April 13th. There was no attack last night as we expected, & this morning we marched out of the settlement unmolested. Faiti is better this morning, he is being carried in Stanley's litter, every hour he lives now adds to his chances of recovery. After marching for four hours we could see the mountains surrounding the settlement we burnt on our way to the lake. The natives here began to gather on the hills but did not molest us in any way. At 1.30 we camped in a small patch of wood with a good sized stream running through it. Some natives came to the brow of a hill close by and watched us so I went after them with a couple of chiefs, they ran away & we followed them but about a mile from camp they were joined by several more natives & I thought it prudent to desist in the pursuit. Just as I had gone to bed we heard a native calling out to us from the long grass near by, he asked us where we were going & what we were going to do. We were all in readiness expecting an attack but the night passed quietly without anything happening.

April 14th. We left camp & marched towards the settlement we had burnt, the natives following us in the distance. We stopped for lunch at the top of a large settlement whilst the men went about foraging in the villages close by. In the village in which we stopped there were large heaps of M'tama covered over with plantain leaves, the M'tama had been damped & left to shoot & ferment, in fact it was a primitive way of making malt, from this malt the natives make a kind of thick muddy looking beer which is intoxicating & not very good to taste, but the natives & Zanzibaris are very fond of it & drink it in great quantities. The natives gathered about us & came so near that we had to fire a few shots to keep them at a respectful distance. As we marched on we saw a good many natives ahead & Stanley fired at them, however they followed us & came pretty close to the rear guard, of which I am always now in charge, & shouted out to us not to fire for they wanted to make friends, the men wanted to fire, but I ordered them not to do so, but made signs to the natives to follow. Yesterday I discovered that one of my men understood the Unyoro language some of the men told me of it & I went & spoke to the man 'Mabruke' about it, he seemed very shy & said he did not understand it well but when the native came last night & spoke I had 'Mabruke' up & he answered the native very well. It is most fortunate as Faiti is not likely to be well enough to accompany me in the boat even should he recover, which is still very doubtful. We entered the settlement we had burnt at about 2 oclock & gained our old camp at 4. Most of the huts had been built up again but the M'tamah was all gathered in & stored so that the whole appearance of the valley was altered. But the most remarkable difference was in the behaviour of the people. On our former visit the hills were all covered with men who shouted & howled like a pack of wolves the noise was so great as to be quite bewildering. Now not a sound was to be heard & only a few natives were to be seen timidly peering at us from the hill tops & we camped quietly & sent Mabruke down to answer a small cluster of natives who were gathered on a low hill near the camp & said they wished to talk with us. The result of his mission was that he brought four natives into the camp who said that the whole country wanted to make friends with us. They told us amongst other things that about a month after we had gone a white man came down the Western side of the Lake & told them he was looking for his brother who was coming to him with a large number of people. The natives told him we had gone about a month & after ordering the natives to let him know if they should see us again he left having only stopped a couple of days. It is evident that it was Emin Pasha & that he has got Stanleys letter which was dispatched from Zanzibar & which we thought had miscarried—his disappointment must have been very great at finding we had gone. Of course we are greatly pleased with the news & feel nearer success now, the faces of the men too when they heard the news expanded into a broad grin of delight. With all the pleasure & relief one feels at this news there is a sort of selfish disappointment mixed with it in my mind, for though probably I shall go in the boat to Wadelai just the same and I shall see Emin Pasha first, still we know now that he is there & I shall not have the pleasure of bearing the news of his being there to Stanley—though the mission in the boat will still to a certain extent be dangerous, it will not be quite the same as if I was going & nothing was known. Stanley got a good deal of information from the natives about the district & people round. Three of the men who came in are oldish & small & ugly but one is a fine looking fellow with a particularly nice face, his features are clearly cut, almost like those of a European, & there is nothing hardly of the thick lipped, flat nosed negroidal type about him— one of these men is chief of the next settlement to this, one that we burnt when the natives attacked us. The natives left camp just before dark & said that all the natives round were coming in to make friends & bring us goats tomorrow.

April 15th. This morning the natives began to come in all without their bows or spears & many of them having cinctures of cloth round their temples as a sign of peace. Deputations from all the settlements & villages round came in until there must have been some hundreds of men in & round the camp. They were all unanimous in saying they wished to make friends with us, the country was ours & they wanted Stanley to be their Sultan & not Kavereega, King of Unyoro who was their nominal Sultan. Stanley of course refused the honour saying he did not want their country he only wanted to pass quietly through it & when he had done his work he should return. All the different chiefs brought a few representatives & had their say; they were coming & going right up till dark some of them have very fine faces; these belong to the Wa-tossi[1] people who are supposed to be descended from the Gallas, they are of royal blood & their sole occupation is to look after cattle. They told us quite readily how many men we had killed, I forget the number but it was sufficiently large to make them very anxious for our friendship. Stanley later in the day made a present of a very nice Scotch plaid & 20 matakos to the Sultan of the whole district who then made blood brotherhood with me.[2] It was a most uncomfortable perform- ance. First of all we were seated close together on a mat, he then put his two legs round me & I had to do the same to him, we then had to rub each others sides violently & two incisions were made in his leg & mine & after salt had been rubbed in, his blood was rubbed into my leg & my blood was rubbed into his leg. During the performance I laughed outright but the natives evidently saw nothing laughable in it but talked away at the top of their voices exhorting us to be true to each other, the chief then took off an iron bangle & put it on my wrist & one of the men gave me one to clasp on his

[1] Correctly Watusi.
[2] This was Mazamboni, chief of the district called by Stanley 'Undussuma'; see above, p. 203 (entry for 9 December 1887).

arm, after this the brotherhood was complete. In the afternoon I cut upon a big flat stone at the top of a hill near camp.

E.P. Expn
Dec 11th. 87

If any white man comes this way in after years the natives will probably point it out to him as the white mans stone. The Sultan brought us presents of goats, chickens & a heifer which latter was killed & distributed amongst the men. The whole day long Stanley was sitting in his chair receiving & talking with the different chiefs, some of their faces were nice looking & taking, & some looked awful scoundrels. It was amusing to watch the different bearings of the chiefs, some were apparently indifferent to what was going on & allowed their followers to do the talking, whilst others were intensely eager & interested in everything that was going on, the big Sultan[1] of this district showed a supreme indifference to everything except his long pipe; he sat there a long time smoking in the most impurturbable manner—this manner was of course adopted for the occasion, it not being etiquette for him to show much interest in anything. His pipe stem was of wood about 3 feet long & the bowl was made of a pretty shape made of black clay & worked with a nice pattern round the rim; it was the size of a tea cup & held about 2 ounces of tobacco. They are all great smokers & brought numbers of these pipes with them passing them on to each other to pull at. Whilst Stanley was talking to the chiefs rather an amusing incident took place, the heifer which had been tied to one of the iron boat sections suddenly took fright at something & dashed off, careering up the hill side with the section behind it, which clattered over the stones & sounded like a big drum, it was pursued by our men & a lot of natives & was brought back to camp with great shouting & laughing. I was glad when the evening came & the natives left, for one was awfully tired of sitting there the whole day.

April 16th. Today at day-break numbers of natives came into camp & a small party of them, headed by a young fellow with beautiful features, volunteered to be our guides to the next settlement & show us a good path, Stanley accepted their offer & we set out. On the way numbers of natives came out to see us pass & a good many followed us, they all wanted to see the face of the Inkama. At one time there were a great number following us in the rear so I turned round & told the interpreter who was with me to tell them if they wanted to follow us they must lay aside their bows & spears or I should consider them as enemies & shoot them, this they did quite readily & sent men back with their bows & spears, however as we got clear of the settlement & into the open country they left us altogether. One

[1] Mazamboni.

man came running after the rear guard saying he wanted to look upon the face of the Inkama, 'there he is' said the men pointing to me; upon which he came up & made his salaams & presented me with four chickens. The natives are all very respectful now; the contrast between our last visit here & this strikes one more & more, the last time we were greeted with nothing but shouts of hate & defiance at about one oclock we were in the next settlement, it was one that we had burnt as the people had attacked us furiously. The huts are now all built up again & we marched up to our former camping place in a cluster of huts at the top of a hill. A number of natives came in & brought a good quantity of pombe or m'tama beer with them, they presented me with a large jar full, but a couple of mouthfuls of it was quite enough for me & I gave it to the men who drank it up at once. It is very thick & has a sour taste about it & a purplish red colour. At night the wind was strong & intensely cold & we had a big fire in our hut.

April 17th. Stanley stopped here today as there are chiefs & deputations coming in from all round, the chief Sultan, Mazamboni, came in & brought presents of chickens & goats & a splendid fat cow which Stanley told me to slaughter & distribute amongst our men. Great numbers of natives came in & all sat in camp & about the houses, these are far finer looking men than those in the last settlement many of them have very fine faces, not the flat noses of the negroes, but the finely cut features of the Wa-toosi.* In the afternoon two natives arrived from Kavalli, the village on the Lake we are going to camp in, saying that the white man had left a letter with the chief for us, he had come down in a steamer a month after we had left saying he had heard from the natives that there had been a white man looking for him & that if he returned the chief was to give him the letter & take him by both hands, which means be as friendly as possible. The two men told Stanley if he would march to the top of the plateau above Kavalli they would send down to the chief of Nyamsassie for the letter & ask the chief if he wished us to stay there or to come down to Nyamsassie. Of course we are greatly excited about the news, but I have a terrible feeling of disappointment, it would have been so splendid to have started not knowing anything & to have found Emin Pasha there & brought him down. Stanley said to me after we had got the news 'Well Jephson I'm afraid you've lost the chance of the prestige you might have gained by going up to Emin Pasha & being the first to find him'. Perhaps, even, there will now be no need to send the boat at all. This is just what Emin Pasha should have done for when we get to Nyamsassie tomorrow his letter will no doubt tell us what to do. We

* The Wa-toosi *or* Wa-homa—Wa signifies people & Toosi or Homa Strangers. Wa-Homa is the Uganda & Northern name, Watoosi the Southern & Western name.

are all anxiously looking forward to reading the news the letter will contain. The natives tell us that the people at the edge of the plateau where Stanley shot a man & had him cut up will not make friends with us but intend fighting, they are very foolish to take this attitude for assuredly they will get severely punished & will be houseless for we shall burn all their villages. Further news came in that Kaverragga's scouts to the number of 300 had come over from Unyoro & were foraging the country ahead & had burnt one of our enemy's villages, the very one we were going to camp in tomorrow. Stanley therefore by the advice of the natives (our friends) intends marching to a place just above Nyamsassie about 8 miles North of the path by which we descended into the plain on our former visit. If we come across Kaverregga's men there will be a pretty stiff fight, for they have guns & are more than double our number.

April 18th. It rained tremendously nearly all night & the wind drove it through everything almost, it was delightful to lie in a nice dry warm hut on a comfortable bed & hear the wind whistling outside, outside it was intensely cold. The natives gathered in the camp this morning to see us off but did not, with the exception of a party of guides with Stanley, follow us very far, but as we passed village after village the natives followed us to the number of some hundreds, & some of them even carried some of the men's loads. We got into camp which was in a large collection of huts at 1.30 & here we were to wait for the coming of the chief of Nyamsassie with the letter. The country here is a splendid cattle country & the natives evidently trust us implicitly, for they have not driven their cattle away but there are numbers roaming about the plain & there are quite a flock of calves running about near the huts. I got a splendid basket here it is most beautifully woven & is immensely strong, I shall use it for carrying my plates, food etc. It is so closely woven that it holds water, I used to read in books of the Africans weaving baskets so closely that they held water & always thought it must be a traveller's exaggeration but I've seen numbers of natives bringing water in these baskets. Parke & I were sitting in our hut when we suddenly heard the Zanzibaris calling out in great excitement 'Burruwah, burruwah',—'the letter, the letter', & on going out found them crowding round Stanley's hut, we went in & found he had got Emin Pasha's letter which he handed me to read. It was as follows;[1] It was addressed to Stanley so he has probably got the letter which Stanley wrote from Zanzibar. We are now certain of reaching Emin Pasha & the men are all very pleased & delighted at the prospect. Many different chiefs came in to see Stanley during the day. The

[1] The letter was not copied into Jephson's diary, but it may be found in *In Darkest Africa* (1, 367–8). It instructed Stanley to stay where he was and the Pasha would make his way to the end of the Lake.

chief here whose name is Kavalli is our host & is behaving very well he tells his story nicely & quietly without any long preamble such as the natives love. He sent Stanley in a large quantity of milk in the evening in a most beautifully shaped wooden vessel something of this shape, if I could only draw it properly. The wood was of a dark rich brown & beautifully grained, the handle on the top of the lid was a sort of compromise between a cross & a fleur de lis, but it was so beautifully cut & polished.

April 19th. This morning the natives have been bringing in large quantities of food in the shape of goats, cattle, chickens & flour. The flour I had put in an enormous pile & distributed amongst the men, by Stanley's order I also had a cow killed & divided amongst the men. A good many more chiefs came in to pay their respects to Stanley & to bring presents. Stanley told me in the course of the day that tomorrow I & Parke were to start with 60 men, carry the boat to the shore opposite the island of Nyamsassie put her together & I was to start with 13 men & two native guides for Emin Pashas settlement which according to the natives I should reach on the fourth day. Parke would return with the rest of the men & he Stanley, would expect me back on the sixth day & would post sentries on the plateau to be on the look out for the steamer, when they sighted her he would march down to the shore of the lake & deliver over the loads of ammunition to Emin Pasha. All day nearly I was mending up my clothes to make myself as decent as possible, but still I shall look a very ragged & patched object. Nampiga, the chief of Nyamsassie, has not appeared, it was to him that Emin Pasha delivered the letter, but he handed it over to Kavalli to give us. It is quite wonderful how friendly all the natives are, they come by fifties from the neighbouring villages to look at us & give us presents, there are some hundreds of them in & round the camp. Amongst them are a great many Wa-tossi with their tall figures & fine faces, a great contrast to the rest of the natives here.

April 20th. We left camp early with the boat loads Parke leading and I as usual bringing up the rear. Led by 'Jadeau', the native of Kavalli's village who is going with me in the boat, we seemed to go straight away from the Lake, but after going till ten we came to the top of the table land & came in sight of Nyanza lying beneath us. We stopped for half an hour at the top of the gorge & the natives from a village near came to see me & brought me a goat & some chickens. We began the descent to the plain at 10.15, & reached the bottom by 1 o'clock having stopped an hour on the way down for coffee & a rest. This path is only about 3 miles north of our former path but is much better than it, it is a good deal longer, but the descent is much more gradual, there are not nearly so many rocks & it is less of the nature of a watercourse. The plain at this point is very pretty but stiflingly hot. I found Parke had stopped in the middle of a good sized village under the shade of a large tamarind tree, the inhabitants had all collected round & asked me to stop there for the night, and as all the men were tired out I consented though it was only 1.30. The chief gave Parke & I a large dirty hut to sleep in, full of rats & mosquitos. The village was very prettily situated—a circle of round grass huts built on a large grassy lawn—whilest the plain all round is best described as being park like. The natives were not living in their huts but in a small patch of bush not far off. Kaveragga's bandits had visited the village only three days ago & had taken away a large amount of plunder, & they were afraid they might return & rob them of what they had left. They were, however very generous & brought us two goats & a good many fowls & a good many eggs, most of which had young ones inside. Parke & I had a splendid dinner off some mutton, the first we have tasted since we left the sea. Kavalli had presented us with a fat tailed sheep, it was very good & a great treat to us after the everlasting goat meat to which we had been accustomed so long. The mosquitos in our hut are so overpowering & the stuffiness so unbearable that we had our beds made up outside.

April 21st. We were up by 4 A.M. to get our breakfast & to have everything ready for an early start. The mosquitos had simply eaten us up in the night & we got little or no sleep, the men made hardly any attempt at sleeping but sat up round their fires all night. My face was much swollen & painful from the attacks of the mosquitos in the night. At daylight we started off & should, according to the natives, reach the Lake by nine o'clock. We passed through a very pretty part of the plain which was swarming with game, Parke told me he saw forty head of buffalo & innumerable hartebeest, Kudu & springbok & a good many Guinea fowl. We reached the Lake opposite the village of Nyamsassie, a small village on an island which gives the name to a good sized district. We were about 5 miles north of Kavalli,[1] the island on which was the large village where I had tried to buy a canoe on the occasion of our first visit, Kaverragga's bandits had visited it lately & had burnt it to the ground. At this point the lake is swarming with crocodiles, Parke hit several but the bullets from our little Winchesters have no effect whatever on their tough hides. I began to put the boat together almost at once, got her ready by 1 P.M. & started off by 1.30 amid the cheers & hearty Goodbye's of the men who had carried the boat & escorted us to the edge of the Lake—they return with Parke today to Stanleys camp at the top of the table land. The boatmen[2] pulled well & we must have gone quite

[1] Not to be confused with 'Kavalli's', the village on the hill above the lake.
[2] The improvement in Jephson's relations with Stanley must have been accelerated by the fact that the latter had detailed his best men to accompany Jephson on this mission. In his account of this mission in *Emin Pasha and the Rebellion at the Equator* (1890), Jephson writes: 'My crew of fifteen consisted of the best men in the expedition, as

12 miles by the time we reached camp at 5.30. We pulled all along the edge of the lower plain which was very pretty & fresh looking, we passed a number of herds of hippopotami playing & plunging in the water, some of them indeed were unpleasantly close. We passed by the districts of the chiefs Kanama, Kumbu & Nampigua (Nyamsassie) & reached a good sized village at the end of the plain by 5.30, it was right under the mountains which arose 2,000 ft above it, its people got their living by fishing. The chief whose name was Waju came down to the beach to receive us, he was a most villainous looking old fellow with a face deeply marked with small-pox & only one eye. The greater number of the men slept by the boat in order to look after it & I went up to the village & slept in a hut at Vaju's request, I took six men with me but he took me to a hut so far from the boat that I felt quite uncomfortable at first, especially when I looked at Vaju's villainous old face. He brought me some fish & he & a great many of his people came & sat round me as I ate my dinner, and stared at every mouthful I took, they were evidently very much astonished at my plates, knife, fork, spoon, etc, & could not understand how it was I did not touch any food with my fingers.

April 21st.[1] I was up by 4 o'clock & was down at the boat by 5.15. Nothing happened during the night & the natives came & helped us in great numbers to put the boat into the water. All day the scenery was much the same, high mountains rising up straight from the Lake, covered with grass & small trees. Here & there were cascades of beautifully clear cold water dashing down into the Lake below. Most of the larger cascades had formed a flat piece of land, sometimes as much as two acres in extent, these jutted out into the lake & were covered with grass & small mimosa bushes. On

Stanley had allowed me to choose my own boat's crew. I had chosen those who from time to time had rowed the boat up the Congo and Aruwimi, and who were all tried men, and thoroughly at home in the boat. The faithful Uledi was coxswain, and Murabo and Sudi, who had both been with Stanley on former expeditions, were pulling the stroke oars. The rest were fine active men, and all young' (pp. 3–4). He describes the start of the voyage in Stanleyesque style: '"Now boys", I said, turning to the crew, "pull as you never pulled before, and Inshallah we shall see the Pasha, whom we have already toiled so long to reach, in two or three days." They responded with a shout of "Inshallah, Master!" and, bending their backs to the oars, sent the boat flying gaily through the water. Murabo struck up one of the crooning but not inharmonious songs which the Zanzibar boatmen usually sing when rowing, and to which they keep time with their oars. He sang of the forest and the troubles we had gone through, of praise of our great chief, Bula Matari, of the miles we had marched to help the Pasha, of our nearness to him now, and of our troubles ended. The crew joined in a chorus in which the names of Bula Matari and the Pasha were mingled' (p. 4).

[1] This looks like an error for 22 April, and the dates from now on until the end of the month would seem to be one behind. They are given as Jephson wrote them, as also on pp. 267–9 where 11 and 14 July are each entered twice in one day's entry.

all these small plains natives had built their villages & lived chiefly by fishing, these little settlements were very pretty & peaceful looking, each had its flock of goats grazing on the smooth green lawn, & its plantation of bright green banana trees, some of the natives were lying idly among their goats smoking their pipes, whilst others paddled about in their tiny one-man canoes & looked after & set their fishing nets, they looked so happy & contented, these were regular little Arcadias where one might peacefully dream away one's life. The sun was very hot & it was almost intolerable sitting without shelter in the boat, every iron plate of which was burning hot. I got my water bottle constantly replenished from the cascades, for though the water of the lake is as clear as crystal it is lukewarm & has an unpleasant soft, soda like taste & a draught of it seems neither to refresh or satisfy one. The men declare it is salt & will not drink it. The water from the cascades is cold & aerated & beautifully refreshing. We passed numbers of huge baboons sitting or walking about unconcernedly on the beach with their tails held aloft in the shape of a crook which gives them a very comical appearance. They took not the smallest notice of us but just blinked at us as if we were an every day sight—the natives, I am told, hold them in great fear. I shot one enormous fellow who was sitting on a rock about 80 yds off, he had a beautiful skin & I should have liked to have got it, but the shore was very rocky & I was afraid of landing for one cannot play tricks among the rocks with these thin iron boats you knock a hole in them before you know where you are. In one of the villages, in Bonganza's district, we picked up Mogo, one of Emin Pasha's chiefs, he had brought Emin's letter to Nampigua chief of Nyamsassie, who had given it over to Kavalli, from whom Stanley received it on our arrival at Kavallies five days ago, he was on his way back to Emin Pasha so we took him on with us in the boat. He was a queer ragged looking fellow with a bright red handkerchief round his head, a necklace of big opal coloured beads round his neck & an enormous brass bracelet on his wrist. A girdle of large iron beads held together his dirty ragged clothes of goat skins & his long hair was fantastically plaited up, a bow & arrows, a pipe & crooked walking stick, all huge of their kind, completed his get up—like 'Nanki Poo' he might be described as 'a thing of shreds & patches'. We camped at 4.30[1] at one of the villages such as I have described, & from it we could see Emin Pasha's settlement about 19 miles off. At one side of the village was a large sandy flat upon which we all camped. The chiefs son, Kajalf, came down to receive us on the beach, he was a particularly nice looking young fellow; he wanted me to come up to the village & sleep in a hut, but I preferred sleeping in the open near the boat; the huts are so awfully stuffy & full of vermin. After dinner I had my

[1] Jephson, *Emin Pasha* (p. 10), gives 5.30.

chair brought down to the beach where a narrow spit of land ran out into the lake, here I sat down in the bright moonlight with the waves lapping up at my feet. It was so peaceful sitting there smoking my pipe with the cool breeze of the Nyanza playing round me & the voices & laughter of my men reaching one faintly across the water. Here I was within sight of success after toiling for it for over 15 months, I alone had been sent forward & would be the first to see Emin Pasha & bring him our news, & what with thinking of this & then of home, with the Nyanza gleaming in the moonlight at one's feet like a silver carpet one got quite sentimental & felt inclined like Silas Wegg to drop into poetry & exclaim with Tom Moore's Peri, 'Joy joy for ever my task is done, The gates are past & heaven is won'.

April 22nd. We started off at 6 A.M. & I had our big Egyptian flag hoisted at the mast head, the men pulled like madmen & we reached Emin Pashas settlement or station,[1] I should say, at a little before 10 o'clock, where a guard of honour was drawn up to receive me on the beach. They gave me a grand salute & then with bugles sounding & flags flying they conducted me up to the station which stood on the top of a low flat hill about a quarter of a mile from the Lake. The station is made entirely of grass & bamboo & is exquisitely neat & clean & the houses are all cool & airy. I was shown into a large 'barrazan' or receiving room, in the East there is always one of these rooms to receive deputations in. There was a couch with a Persian carpet on it & pillows for me to recline on & chairs were placed near it, whilest my Zanzibaris were accomodated with a mat to sit upon behind me. Gourds of m'tamah beer were brought in for them & a large vessel full of snowy curds & whey were brought in for me of which I drank most gratefully. Well after a bit I thought this is all very fine but it is not the sort of reception I like from one white man to another in the very heart of Africa one would prefer something more warm & unceremonious. Presently Shookri Aga, the chief of the station came in; a tall Nubian in a smart Egyptian uniform, & after talking a bit told me that Emin Pasha was not here but was at Tunguru, an island higher up the lake, with his steamer & that the name of this station was M'swa & had been built in July when Emin first got news from Zanzibar that an expedition was being despatched for his relief. I would have gone on in the boat to Tungaru but Shookri Aga told me he had heard from the natives last night that I was on my way here & he had early this morning sent messengers to Emin Pasha telling him to come down at once in his steamer & he said that Emin Pasha would arrive here tomorrow at midday, in which case I considered it best to stay where I was & await his coming here. It was of course a great disappointment finding him away & accounted for my very ceremonious reception. I however

[1] This was M'swa, the station commanded by Shukri Aga.

dispatched a note myself to Emin Pasha & had it sent off by two men in a canoe. It is always so, as someone once said to me 'you are lucky but there is always ill luck in your luck', it is quite true, I am lucky in being sent on this mission but unlucky in finding Emin Pasha away just at this moment. I sat in the barrazan & talked with the people for some time, they all looked so smart & clean compared with us who had arrived in rags we looked as if we were in want of relief far more than they, I felt awfully dirty in my old worn out suit of Tweed beside the smart Nubian officer & even beside the servants who were all dressed in suits of fresh white cotton cloth which Emin Pasha's people weave. Finally I was shown into a large lofty hut about 28 ft square made of bamboo & grass, it was beautifully cool & airy. They brought me an enormous omellette & some delicious bread for my midday meal. I was very tired & after luncheon lay down on my angarep (bed like a sofa with the bottom made of strips of cowhide neatly woven across & across) & slept for 4 hours. I found that while I was asleep they had brought me a large round iron sponge bath full of water a round piece of Soap, which Emin's people make here, & an Egyptian Loofah, I had not ordered the bath so they must have thought I looked dirty. How delightful the bath was: how I soaped—(I had been without soap for five months) & scrubbed myself with the Loofah till my skin was almost worn into holes & for the first time since we started from Yambuya I felt really clean. One quite hated putting on one's old patched & worn out clothes, they had been patched & washed & worn till they were quite thread bare. In the evening another deputation of people came to talk with me, they told me Emin Pasha had got a letter from Consul Holmwood 5 months ago telling him Stanley was coming & on its receipt had done everything he could to find us & was most anxious about our coming, one fellow said 'He wo'nt sleep tonight when he hears you are here'. They told me of many atrocities Kaveregga had committed & how he had expelled Captain Cassati after having stolen all his goods had thrown him perfectly naked on to an island in the Lake. The news had been brought to Emin Pasha by a native & he had gone immediately in his steamer to the island where he found Cassati hiding in the grass, he had been there naked & without food for three days. In the evening they brought me a most elaborate dinner on two great brass trays. I did not eat much meat but ate quantities of white bread & took great draughts of new milk, one wished one had ten mouths to feed & ten stomachs to fill, it was so good after not having had a decent meal served in a civilized manner for so long.

April 23rd. I had a very bad night the mosquitos came in swarms & devoured me. On getting out of bed I stepped into my bath with a feeling of delight & after finishing my very simple toilette ate a smart breakfast they brought me with a very good appetite. After breakfast a good many people came to see me & a great many chiefs from the country round came to shake hands & to sit & gaze at me, as all natives seem to love to do when a new white man comes into the country. I am waiting most impatiently for 12 o'clock when Emin Pasha is supposed to arrive. Last night I went round to see that my boatmen were well looked after for I had asked the chief here to see that they were well fed. I found they had been lodged in a boma all to themselves with 5 or 6 large huts in it, a bullock had been killed for them & numerous dainties supplied, they were highly delighted with the treatment they had received & welcomed me clamourously, each man had had a nice new cow hide presented him to sleep on, but they were most delighted because their food was cooked for them by the women belonging to the station. I wrote a letter to Stanley[1] telling him we are delayed but that we have reached Emin Pashas settlement & are waiting for him here, I shall dispatch this letter by two men in a canoe tomorrow; it will allay Stanley's anxiety about us, meanwhile there is nothing to be done but to wait. Yesterday when I was shown my room I was very much amused, my luggage consists of a few old tattered clothes in a tent cover, a basket containing two or three very black looking cooking pots, my plates etc, some potatoes & a goat skin containing beans, in short it would be hard to describe more disreputable looking baggage. This baggage was brought in by two smart looking Turkish servants in snowy white clothes & deposited reverentially as if it contained the most valuable jewels. What a contrast we are, I & all my men are in rags & are a dirty looking lot whilest the people we have come to relieve are all beautifully clean looking & neat.

April 24th. No signs of the steamer & no books to read, how shall I pass the day! I [was] lying on my angerep when at 1.30 Binzer who was Dr Junckers servant, & is acting as my boy, came to tell me a messenger had arrived with a letter for me from Emin Pasha & presently Sulieman Effendi, one of Emin Pasha's officers was ushered in & handed me a letter. He was dressed in a spotless white uniform & spoke a little French but only of the feeblest kind. Emin Pasha's letter was very cordial, he got my note yesterday, but the steamer is away, he has sent for her & hopes to be with me tomorrow. Sulieman Effendi sat & talked with me a long time & afterwards I walked round the settlement & inspected everything attended by him, Shookriaga— the commander of the station—& a lot of other officials. They have some hundred of cattle, sheep & goats & abundance of vegetables such as onions brinjales etc, whilest the natives supply them with corn & fish so that they live in plenty here. There are large fields of cotton & one sees numbers of people going about with little distaffs making the raw cotton into thread.

[1] Dated 23 April (see Stanley, *IDA*, i, 373, entry for 29 April).

They took me into a large open hut where there was a spindle of the most primitive kind for weaving the cotton into cloth. Emin Pasha has instructed his people how to weave & they make large quantities of loose strong cotton cloth. The spindle was very simple & was worked very quickly by an intelligent looking Nubian lad. The goats here are of a huge size, some of them almost as big as a good sized calf. There is a large parade ground for the soldiers & this divides Emin Pasha's own boma from those of the men. It is wonderful with what love and affection his people speak of him & how they all look up to & revere him—what a difference from our leader with whom things are done by sheer brute force only. Murabo my chief amused me very much yesterday, he said 'the Bwana M'Kubwa—Stanley—is half a white man & half an Arab'. That describes Stanley very well. All the falseness & double dealing, the indifference to breaking his word, the meanness, brutality & greediness, are the Arab side. The wonderful powers of resource, the indomitable energy & strength of mind, the dogged determination to carry through to a successful issue all that he takes in hand, his cleverness in mapping, writing, conversation etc, all belong to the European side. He has two distinct [characters], one cannot be too much admired & praised the other is contemptable in the extreme.

April 25th. The steamer has not turned up today. In the evening I called my Zanzibaris together & asked Sulieman Effendi to come to my house. I then spoke to my men & told them I was tired of waiting & that I proposed starting off in the boat for Tungaru tomorrow. The men agreed it would be good, but at the urgent request of Sulieman Effendi I agreed to remain here one more day before starting after Emin Pasha. Sulieman said he was quite sure the steamer would arrive tomorrow & begged me to cut his throat if she didn't!

April 26th. I had quite given up hope of seeing the steamer today when they came to tell me at 5 o'clock that she was in sight. I came out to look & saw her just rounding a rocky headland about 5 miles off. The soldiers all turned out & the officers put on their best uniforms & the little cannon was got ready to fire a salute. The guard then marched down to the shore with two Turkish flags, followed by my men marching two & two, carrying the big Egyptian flag, after a bit I went down to the shore to await the steamer's coming, my men begged me to allow them to fire a couple of salutes when Emin Pasha landed. It was almost dark before the steamer had dropped anchor & the boat was pulled ashore. As the boat touched the sand Emin Pasha leaped out & welcomed me with both hands, he kept repeating expressions of welcome & cordial greeting as he held both my hands in his; one really felt that the welcome was from the bottom of his heart. He introduced me to Captain Cassati who was with him, but, as Cassati spoke no English & did not understand French, I could only say a few words to him through Emin Pasha, he is a thick-set middle-aged man & not very prepossessing in appearance. After this Emin Pasha put his hand on my shoulder & we walked up to the station together followed by all the officials. We sat outside in the bright moonlight & talked till late about many things. We remain here tomorrow & then go down in the steamer to Nyamsassie where Stanley & the people will meet us with the loads & impedimenta.

April 27th. Early this morning a cup of delicious strong sweet coffee was brought me served in a very pretty dainty little cup on a brass tray. Before I had finished dressing Emin Pasha came into my room & sat on my bed & talked to me as I dressed. We then went out & sat in the cool breeze & I brought out my maps & showed him our route up the river. He was much struck by the position of the Nepoko river & the point where it fell into the Aruimi, he at once said what a good road might be opened up that way if he formed a station in the Mangbattu[1] country, through which the Nepoko runs, & transported his Egyptians & ivory down the Nepoko to its junction with the Aruwimi, then down the Aruwimi to the Congo, & so on. He was all for Stanley's returning that way to fetch up Barttelot & the rest of the goods. I pointed out to him the immense difficulty of such a route, the numberless rapids & cataracts in the river, the starvation & want of food on the road etc, but of course Stanley will be able to tell him the pros & cons of such a route better than I. I gave him a sheet of the Graphic newspaper containing an account of him & his work, by Dr Felkin, & numerous illustrations of the scenes & people in his province, he was much amused by them. Emin Pasha is not very much like his picture in the Graphic; his face is much shorter & he is altogether a smaller man than his picture would lead one to suppose; he is very foreign looking, speaks English very well but with a strong foreign accent. All my men came up to pay their respects to him & he asked me to tell them that he would give them cloth to cover themselves with, for the poor fellows were but scantily clad. They were delighted at the idea of getting cloth. There is an apothecary, a Tunisian— Signor Vitta[2]—a very decent little fellow & very useful to Emin Pasha, he was sent out some eight years ago by the Egyptian Government when Emin Pasha applied for a doctor, he is now his apothecary, store keeper, general helper. After breakfast Emin Pasha presented me with a cigar, a real beauty, Dr Juncker when he was here three years ago left him this cigar & he said he had kept it all this time in case of a festival & produced it, it was splendid to be smoking a good cigar again, Signor Vitta also brought me two

[1] More usually Mangbetu, see below, p. 288.
[2] Vita Hassan.

cigarettes & I sat & puffed myself into Paradise. Seeing my tattered state, clothes were brought me by Emin Pasha's orders, two coats & a pair of trousers & the tailor was called in to take my measure for four pair of knickerbockers, & the shoemaker was called to take my measure for 5 pair of shoes, whilest a quantity of red cloth was delivered over to my servants to put in my bag. Emin Pasha then sat down with his note book & insisted on my telling him my wants. With much hesitation & a good deal of shyness, at begging in this wholesale way, I told him the following things would be most acceptable, salt, soap, & a note book, all of which he wrote down & gave orders that they should be put in my house, grumbling all the time at the smallness of my demand. He enumerated several things he could give me & which I should awfully have liked to have, but I said, no I was quite ashamed of asking for anything at all, for his kindness is quite overpowering & his manner paternal, one's heart really goes out towards such a man for one feels he is really sincere. It is such a pleasure to get someone quite new to talk with & that person such a clever & intelligent man. Afterwards Emin Pasha asked me to tell him of the origin of the expedition & how it was got up & about all the officers & their names & how I became connected with the expedition, I told him all about it & could not help telling him when speaking of myself, how Madame de Noailles had said, 'If I had a son I would send him on this expedition', the tears started in his eyes & for a moment he turned away, & then he took my hand & said 'How can you thank me for the few things I have given you & be shy about taking them, if I lived for a hundred years I could not thank the English people enough for their disinterested kindness in sending me help when I have been abandoned by my own government for so many years'. He had never received Stanley's letter from Zanzibar but had only received a short one dated Feb 7 '87 from Holmwood, the acting Consul, telling him that an expedition under Stanley would start up the Congo some time in March, & that he was expecting Stanley to arrive in Zanzibar in a fortnight's time to get his men together & to start for his relief. The two letters written to him by Holmwood & Stanley are probably still in Uganda, for there are courier loads of letters waiting for us, Kaveregga will not permit them to pass through his country & has sent them back to Uganda, there are also many things for Emin Pasha waiting in Uganda for Kaveregga will allow nothing to pass through his country to Emin.

April 28th. We got off in the steamer at about 8 o'clock, she was like a small farm yard for we had quantities of cattle, milch cows goats sheep & chickens, whilest the hold was filled with grain for our people. The steamer, the Khedive, is one which Sir Samuel Baker had brought out when he was Governor of this provice, she was built by Samuda in   , is   ft long &

has   ft beam.[1] It is quite wonderful that she is in such good order; Emin Pasha has taken very great care of her. Her boilers are however getting rather worn, though her engines are still in very good condition, & they dare not force her to go more that 6 knots an hour. We reached our anchorage opposite the place where I had put the boat together at about seven oclock & found that Stanley had marched down to the Lake that day & was encamped about three miles down the shore a little way inland. Late as it was Emin decided to go & see Stanley that night. All the Zanzibaris came rushing down to the shore to greet us, firing off their guns & shouting in the maddest manner. We sat & talked till past ten & Stanley brought out three bottles of champagne after which we went back to the steamer, Stanley having delivered over the mails to Emin Pasha & Cassati. When we got on to the steamer Emin opened the bale of letters & books—the letters, some of them, were hardly legible they had got so rubbed & damp on the road. He was so interested in them we did not sit down to dinner till past one.[2]

April 29th. This morning Stanley & the people marched up to the steamer & he went on board & told me to take the people on & find a good camping place as he had promised Emin Pasha to stay 10 days with him. I marched on about 6 miles & then pitched camp in a splendid place where the plain suddenly rose to a height of 50 ft above the lake, it was all beautifully grassy & there were a great many trees of acacia & tamarind scattered about. Stanley came up some time after & we formed our camp. Emin Pasha camping below us at a little distance here we shall probably remain ten or more days.[3]

April 30th. Today large rations of corn were given out to the men, sufficient to last them ten days.

May 2nd [1888].[4] The steamer returned to Wadelai today she will bring back some things Emin Pasha has written for, more grain for the men, cattle, milking cows, goats, vegetables etc, & some things such as shoes, cloth & honey for us. Emin Pasha offered to send to Duffile station & tell his people to collect 130 natives to act as porters to accompany Stanley & help him with the loads, Stanley accepted the offer, so a message has been sent & the porters will be here in about 14 days, this will be a great help to Stanley & it is well worth waiting a few more days for the carriers to come up.

[1] There are blanks in the diary, but *Emin Pasha* (pp. 28–9) gives the following details: 'She was built by Samuda and was still a fine strong boat, some eight-five feet long, with a beam of eighteen feet. . . He had besides this another small steamer, the *Nyanza*, and two large whale boats, all of which were brought up by Sir Samuel Baker.'
[2] Stanley describes this meeting in his entry for 29 April, and the visit aboard the *Khedive* under 30 April (Stanley, *IDA*, I, 373 ff.).
[3] Nsabé was the name of the camping place.
[4] This date seems correct, tallying with Stanley, *IDA*, I, 383.

May 7th. One of our men has been fearfully torn & lacerated by a buffalo, he was brought in in a terrible state with frightful looking wounds all over him. Three of our men went out & shot a couple of buffalo, this man M'bruki Kassim shot another, but only wounded it. They had been warned never to follow up a wounded buffalo for it is dangerous in the extreme for they turn upon you like lightening & literally trample & pound you to death. Nevertheless these men followed the wounded animal until they lost sight of it. On coming up to a clump of trees & bushes M'bruki, who was the only man who had any ammunition left & he only had one cartridge, went up to the clump of trees to look for the buffalo, there was a rush & a bellow of rage & the buffalo burst through the bushes, the man threw down his gun & ran, but the buffalo caught him on his horns & tossed him twice & then tried to trample & gore him to death. M'abruki seized the beast by the horns, but the blood was flowing so freely that his strength was soon gone & the buffalo gored him fearfully, three times it left him & three times it returned to gore him afresh. Meanwhile one of his two companions—both of whom had climed up trees—, Sar Tato, managed to creep up & get M'bruki's gun, which contained the only cartridge they had amongst them, with this he shot the buffalo & released poor M'bruki. It was two & a half miles from camp but Parke went out & brought him in. It is perfectly marvellous how he can live for he appears to be covered with wounds. Three or four ribs are broken, one of his thighs has three fearful gashes in it, there are two deep wounds in his side, his shoulder blade is broken & the side of his cheek is gashed up & one eye almost gouged out, besides all these there are quantities of small wounds in different parts of his body & the whole flesh is trampled & contused. He told me afterwards when I went to see him that he did not feel much pain, but he said 'Little Master never go after buffaloes, they are very bad animals, when the buffalo seized me I caught him by the horns but it was awful to see him standing over me snorting & feel him pounding me to death & after a little I lost my strength & could hold his horns no longer & his horns ploughed my flesh & I cried out for Sar Tato to come & help me, but he was far away, Master it was awful'. Parke says he is likely to live if he can just rest still & doesn't get exhausted before his wounds are healed. Poor M'bruki he was a very good fellow & one of my best boat carriers. I hope Stanley will forbid men who know nothing about shooting buffaloes going out, for they are so stupid. The idea of three men, all indifferent shots, following up a wounded buffalo with only one cartridge!

May 12th. We are still here at this camp, the name of the district we are in is N'ssabe. Stanley asked Emin Pasha to get him some carriers, so he has sent down to the chief of Duffile station to procure him 120 natives of the Madi tribe to accompany Stanley back & act as porters, it will keep us waiting here some time, but it will be well worth it—Four or five days ago I went out shooting with Parke, but before I had gone three miles I was seized with a fit of ague & fever & had to drag myself back to camp, my temperature went up to 107 degrees, but fortunately it did not last long at that temperature or there would have been little left of me. Emin Pasha told Stanley that his officers were exceedingly sceptical about our coming here & in the far stations hardly yet understand that we have arrived & will not believe unless they see some proof. He also says he will come out but he is not at all sure if his people will be willing to come to Egypt, the Egyptians he thinks will, but he is not sure about the Soudanese, they have so many wives & children & are thoroughly settled in the country, if they do not go out he does not think they will allow him to go. His people including the women & children are likely to amount to over 8,000 souls, this will be an enormous undertaking to get them all down to Zanzibar. He says he cannot give Stanley a decided answer whether he will come out or not until he hears what his people have to say to the Khedive's proposals. He has therefore asked Stanley to leave one of his officers with him until Stanley's return here with the rear column, he would wish this officer to be his guest & to go round with him to all his stations in the province & to address the people & read to them the Khedive's letter & a proclamation from Stanley telling them he has come here to bring them help in the shape of ammunition for their guns & will bring them down to Zanzibar by a safe road & then transport them to Egypt. The people would all be drawn up to hear what is said & could ask the officer any question they pleased about the road etc & he could answer them. Emin Pasha thinks that this alone will satisfy them & it could then be seen whether the people were willing or not to come out & if in the event of the people refusing to leave & he comes out with us, it can never be said of him that he deserted his people. Stanley said he would leave an officer with him & nominated me. He then came over to my tent & told me Emin Pasha had asked for an officer & he had named me & asked me if I would accept the post. I said I would think about it, for though it was doing work for the expedition, still I did not like leaving the expedition for so long a time (probably for 9 or 10 months) especially as there was such a lot of work to be done yet & I did not want to get out of it. He said I could help him very much by getting things ready so that he could start for Zanzibar with as little delay as possible on his return; however I said I would see Emin Pasha first before I gave him my answer. I went & saw Emin Pasha & had a long talk with him, he repeated to me more or less what he had said to Stanley & begged me to remain with him & told me he believed I should be doing a most important work for the expedition by going round his country with him & speaking to his people. I therefore said I would stay with him until Stanley's return & in the evening I told Stanley my decision. Of course it will be delightful to travel about this most interesting country where there are half a dozen different peoples & tribes, & where there is so much which is interesting in different ways, then again too the shooting (!) besides this, all in the company of a man of Emin Pasha's description. Against this, there is the return journey through the hated jungle, lots of work & hardships & long months of toiling at uninteresting work, but there is the meeting with the officers of the rear column & their news. I am strongly drawn towards the return journey & would elect to return with Stanley if it rested entirely with myself, but Stanley wishes me to stay & Emin Pasha urges me to remain, so I must remain, & so it is decided, & if by going round and addressing the people I can induce them to come out with us I shall have done good work. Two men got shot yesterday, they were out looting in a village in the mountains. One man, Mibi M'bari, a very good fellow was shot dead but the other man made his escape & got back to camp he is likely to recover all right. Parke went with a party & burnt the village & killed three men.

May 22nd. The last two days I have again been laid up with fever. This morning we sighted Emin Pasha's two steamers in the distance & on their arriving found they had brought us 120 carriers of the Madi tribe, Stanley is greatly pleased & will start the day after tomorrow. I am very glad, for I'm awfully tired of staying here doing nothing. The carriers are fine looking men armed with bows & arrows, but they are perfectly naked.

May 24th. Everyone was busy yesterday packing up for an early start today. Stanley got off by about 6 oclock A.M. At about 4 o'clock in the afternoon Parke came in with a party of men with the news that all the carriers with the exception of 21 whom they were able to capture, had run away. They were going quietly along when at a signal all the carriers suddenly plunged into a thicket & disappeared, one of them fired an arrow at one of our men who instantly shot him dead. On hearing the news Emin Pasha sent out scouts, but with no success. The reason of this sudden flight cannot be understood for the men had marched all the way from Duffile to M'swa of their own freewill & now on the eve of starting they have run away. Emin Pasha thinks they were frightened at being so far from their country, & going with a stranger like Stanley proved too much for them. Just at evening time at about 6 PM a messenger arrived in a canoe from M'swa station saying 80 more carriers had just arrived, Emin Pasha there & then decided to send the steamer off to M'swa to bring them, the steamer started at midnight & by going night & day (there is a bright moon) can be back here by 9 P.M. tomorrow. Parke sleeps here tonight & returns to Stanley tomorrow &

will get him to stop where he is tomorrow & to wait for the fresh lot of carriers.

May 25th. Parke started off to Stanley this morning & men returned with a letter from Stanley in the evening saying he would wait for the carriers. The steamer returned at 9.30 PM with the 80 carriers, who were at once on landing tied together with thongs of cow hide in parties of 10 men, each ten men being guarded by two of Emin's soldiers, they will be conducted to Stanley & handed over to him. He will keep them tied up until he has gone some days march & placed two or three hostile tribes between them & the Lake, return will then be impossible for them & they will be obliged to follow him or be cut to pieces by hostile natives. The native carriers landed at about 10 o'clock P.M. & by 11 PM they were marched off in gangs to join Stanley who is camped in a village at the foot of the mountains some 10 miles distant, it is bright moonlight & they should reach Stanley's camp by daybreak easily.

May 26th. This morning I went out after butterflies for Emin Pasha & was able to secure him a good many that he had not yet got in his collection. He has large collections of birds, beetles, butterflies, human & animal skulls & all sorts of things, these from time to time he dispatches to Europe when a chance offers itself. His last collection he sent to the British Museum where it was received with great interest & appreciation. He has made quite a name for himself in the scientific world by the interesting & rare collections he has sent to Europe, & the letters we brought him contained several from different well known societies telling him they had enrolled his name among their members. His face quite lights up with pleasure if one brings him some beetle or bug of an uncommon species! In the afternoon the soldiers returned with a letter from Stanley saying the carriers had arrived safely. He also confirmed a discovery I had made some time ago, at the time I told him of my discovery he had laughed at me & pooh poohed the idea.[1] When I was marching down from Stanley's camp on my way to the lake with the

---

[1] The identification of the Ruwenzori range south of Lake Albert undoubtedly belongs to Jephson and Parke, not to Stanley as claimed in the past. Parke records this first sight fully, and later it was confirmed (see diary for 2 April 1889 below, p. 341):

'April 20.—Jephson and myself were sent by Mr. Stanley this morning to bring the boat and launch it on the lake; preparatory to sending Jephson, accompanied by the boat's crew, to go on a voyage of exploration, and, if possible, find the Pasha...On the march we distinctly saw *snow* on the top of a huge mountain situated to the south-west of our position. As this was a curious and unexpected sight, we halted the caravan to have a good view. Some of the Zanzibaris tried to persuade us that the white covering which decorated this mountain was *salt*; but Jephson and myself were quite satisfied that it was snow...

'April 22...I reported to Mr. Stanley that I had seen a snow-clad mountain. He was a good deal interested' (Parke, pp. 217, 220).

boat when I was sent forward to find Emin Pasha, I suddenly on rounding a mountain saw in the far far distance a high snow capped mountain towering above the plain. The men with me at once exclaimed 'why that's just like Kilimanjaro' & I told them they were quite right it was undoubtedly snow. However on my return to Stanley with Emin Pasha when I told him of my discovery he laughed at the idea & said it was only mist. But he now writes Emin Pasha word that at a distance of 4 miles from the Lake he 'discovered' a snow capped mountain, the first he has ever seen in central Africa & from its position it must be Ruenzori & that 'its altitude is immense', & as it is some 40 or 50 miles distant it must be a very high mountain for us to be able to see it in this plain with mountains of 2,000 ft high rising up all round us. He says nothing of Parke & I having seen it more than a month ago & having told him about it, but he makes it out to be his discovery.

May 27th. Today we started off in the steamers for M'swa station but as we did not start till 9 oclock we shall not get there till late at night. The two camps looked very deserted as we steamed away from them, we had been more than three weeks there.

May 28th. We did not get to M'swa last night but stopped at Mugunga where I had formerly stopped on my way here in the boat. We did not sleep on board the steamer but had our Angareps brought on shore & after having had a large fire lighted rolled in under our mosquito curtains & went to sleep. Alas! at 12 oclock down came the rain in a good steady downpour & soon wetted our blankets through, without shelter we sat in a dripping state & were glad when morning came. We got to M'swa station at 10.30 & here begins my stay with Emin Pasha & here also ends my journal. I have yet another but it is with Barttelot & will not be up for months. I shall have to do the best I can & try & get from Emin Pasha some paper or something to make one. We have now been just a year & four months out from England & what prospect have we of getting back for another two years & more? There must be a great lot of nonsense in this journal for one has kept it in just a helter skelter kind of fashion putting down facts in a disconnected way without much regard to grammar or spelling I'm afraid. It must be recollected however that it has been written under very trying circumstances, often I would much sooner have laid down & slept after a long & fatiguing march than sit up & write my journal. I have however kept it pretty regularly thus far, & hope it will answer it's purpose which is to tell a true & exact story of the expedition, of how we found & relieved Emin Pasha & of the trials & difficulties we met on the road & how through the strong determination of our leader & the hardiness of our Zanzibaris we over came them all & arrived a small handful of men on the shores of Nyanza & reached Emin Pasha after fourteen months continual marching.

A. J. Mounteney Jephson
Oct: ?/94.

1   Portrait of Jephson (photograph of an oil painting at Mallow Castle)

2(b) Surgeon T. H. Parke

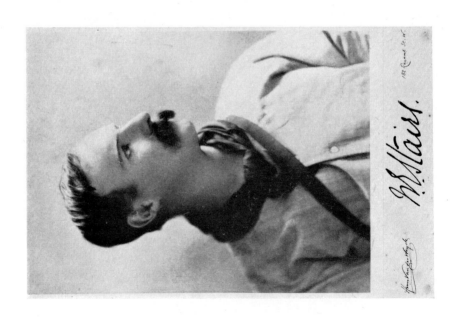

Lieutenant W. G. Stairs

Emin Pasha
Photographed in the Equatorial
1889. Province

3 (b)   Emin Pasha

Robt. H. Nelson, 8th Contingent
Africa 1887 8. 9.   May 5th 1890

3 (a)   Captain R. H. Nelson

Photo of 1896. Oct.

To the gallant Buburika from Bula Maturi

Henry M Stanley

4   Henry Morton Stanley

April /87

for him & got my own kettle across by seven. Then there was the boat to be taken to pieces & made into loads, all in the hot sun, while my head grew dizzier & my limbs more heavy. I got the boat started & sent the people ahead to catch up Stanley, for I felt I could march but slowly that day. I travelled slowly, each step being painful & got about half through the march when I came upon Casement who was camping for breakfast in a deserted village. I could go no further for I felt the fever had me & I was fain to lie down in an old hut, whilst Casement got his bed made up & put me on it. For a couple of hours I tossed about in a half sleep dreaming that Stanley was far ahead & that I was struggling to catch him up with the boat & couldn't overtake him. Casement gave me ten grains of quinine & when it got a little cooler put me in a hammock & sent four men to carry me into camp. Stanley became anxious when the boat arrived & the men reported that I was not well. As I did not turn up he sent six chiefs back to fetch me in & they met Casement's men on the way & carried me into camp. When I got into camp I was speechless from fever & pain — for the jolting of being carried on a rough track was awful & they undressed me & put me to bed & gave me more quinine. In a few hours the fever left me & I slept quietly; to wake this morning feeling well. Except that I was weak & my legs didn't seem to belong to me. For the first time I rode my donkey which carried me splendidly.

5   Page from the diary, showing part of the entry for 21 April 1887

6(*a*)   The south end of Lake Albert, 13 December 1887.
(From Stanley's *In Darkest Africa*)

6(*b*)   The *Advance* on Lake Albert. (From Jephson's *Emin Pasha*)

7(a)   Entry into Dufilé, 20 August 1888. (From Jephson's *Emin Pasha*)

7(b)   Emin arranging his specimens. (From Jephson's *Emin Pasha*)

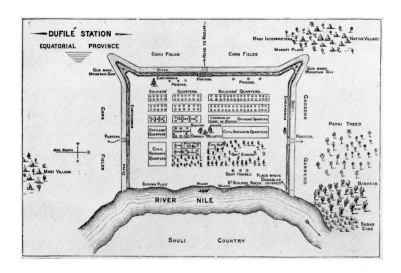

8(a)   Plan of Dufilé. (From Jephson's *Emin Pasha*)

8(b)   Harbour at Dufilé, 1966

8(c)   Ditch and bank at Dufilé 1966

9 (*a*)   'Our prison at Dufilé.' (From Jephson's *Emin Pasha*)

9 (*b*)   The flight from Wadelai, 5 December 1888. (From Jephson's *Emin Pasha*)

10(a) 'News from Stanley at last!' 26 January 1889. (From Jephson's *Emin Pasha*)

10(b) 'I rejoin my leader', 6 February 1889. (From Jephson's *Emin Pasha*)

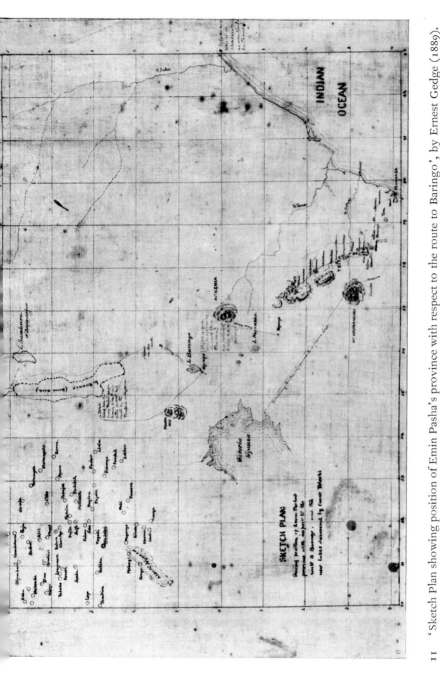

11 'Sketch Plan showing position of Emin Pasha's province with respect to the route to Baringo', by Ernest Gedge (1889). Annotations (in red on the original) are probably by F. J. Jackson with whom Gedge travelled to Uganda in 1889–90. The note west of Lake Rudolf reads: 'Teleki heard here of Emin Pasha's people having come to raid cattle in 1885 but beaten by the Tourkana or Elgourma'

January 1889

anything moreover to eat. However I reserve my judgement of the whole until I hear the story from Bonny, the sole remaining European of the rear guard. Stanley's stories are never very just in matters of this kind & I suspect there is a good deal more in the real story than meets the eye in his letters. Immediately I had communicated with the Pasha we told Casati of the news & spread it also in the station. Poor Barttelot's death is most tragic & sad, & will create a profound sensation at home where he is fairly well known. Poor fellow he was so bright & full of life & go — indeed the whole story is a very dark one, as dark as any of the many dark stories connected with African travel. Ward's having returned to St Paul de Loanda & set such news (false news) afloat is very bad & will have a very bad effect in Europe. No doubt my

January 1889

people will all consider I'm dead — Well I should be no great loss that I know of. Immediately on receiving the letters I sent for Saleh Aga & told him I must have carriers ready to start tomorrow morning for M'swa from which place I shall proceed in canoes to M'sala & from thence ascend the mountains to Kavalli's there to await Stanley's return from the Ituri river. In the evening the steamer came in bringing Hawashi Effendi & a lot of clerks & refugees, it was sent from Wadelai. It was decided therefore that I should go in the steamer to M'swa & perhaps on to M'sala in her if the steamer's people would take me. We sat up till late talking over the awful news Stanley's letters contained & the method of imparting that news.

January 27th People have been out all day getting wood & yet they have only brought in enough to carry us to the

May 11th /89

If I die before I reach ~~England~~ ~~to~~ ~~me~~
England I leave every thing I possess
absolutely in charge of
Mr S. Stairs Lt R.E. with the exception
of the following things which he will
~~take~~ ~~charge~~ ~~of~~
take charge of & deliver in England
to the people I have named

All my journals (4 books) & my outfit
~~account~~ with Mr Stanley

To: the Countess de Noailles
        The Mead
        Eastbourne

My dressing case to Miss Blennerhassett
        Mildros Park
        Shrewsbury

I ~~wish~~ leave ~~to~~ & Stairs my field classes
& some ~~lines~~ which are in my dressing case
The letter he finds in my ~~dressing~~
~~box~~ addressed to people at Zanzibar

---

he will ~~deliver~~ ~~it~~ those & send by
post to their addresses. All other letters
he will burn.

~~the~~ ~~watch~~ ~~key~~ ~~for~~ ~~the~~ ~~watches~~
My clothes boxes & every thing remaining
I would wish him to divide between
Dr Parke, Capt Nelson & himself
~~share~~ Lt. Stairs & ~~Lt. Stairs~~ gives ~~each~~

to act in the same exactly the
same way, my chattels
being divided between himself
& Capt Nelson
Should Dr Parke not reach
England I appoint Capt Nelson
to act in his place & he receives
all my things all the ~~above~~
mentioned ~~letters~~ etc

A J Mounteney Jephson

---

13   Jephson's draft Will, 11 May 1889

S. and A.I. (from right), Nelson bov, Stanley, Stairs, Jephson

MR. JEPHSON. LADY BURTON.

MRS. H.M. STANLEY. SIR. RICHᴰ. BURTON.

MR. H.M. STANLEY.

15   Reunion in Switzerland: the Stanleys, the Burtons and Jephson, October 1890

16   Memorial window to Mounteney Jephson in St James's Church, Mallow

CHAPTER 12

KAVALLI'S TO WADELAI

28 MAY–28 JULY 1888

Emin's first action on arrival at M'swa on 28 May was to order a punitive raid on Kibero on the eastern shore of Lake Albert, an important centre for the collection of salt, where Captain Casati had been living for eighteen months as the Pasha's representative in Unyoro. Relations, formerly good, with Kabarega, had soured, and the people of Kibero had attacked and robbed Casati, leaving him tied naked to a tree, a predicament from which he had hardly escaped with his life. The soldiers returned triumphantly with a fine haul of salt, as scarce as it was prized in Central Africa, and a collection of weapons and ornaments for Jephson. Casati later declared in his book[1] that the raid had degenerated into a massacre, and he rejoiced at the escape of the local chief, Kagoro.

At M'swa all was peaceful, not to say Arcadian. The station commander, Shukri Aga, was a reliable Sudanese, on good terms with the local chief Mogo, and the first entry in Book 2 of the Journal reads:

June 5th [1888]: I have been all round the native fields and villages and have brought in some butterflies for the Pasha's collection. This is a most wonderful place & with careful cultivation might be made to support some thousands of people.

A local chief, Ouma, came to visit Emin and presented his friends with 'a lovely leopard skin'. They arrived at Tunguru on 6 June, but Jephson's first entry at this station is dated eleven days later. In all the months he spent in Equatoria he was never to be free of fever for very long, and his visit began inauspiciously in every way.

June 17th. Almost every day since I've been here Tunguru I've had fever & have been able to do but little. The chief of the station Sulieman Aga is away, he has been away some time on the table lands collecting the grain tax, & I have been waiting till his return to address the people. On arriving here the Pasha was told by his people that the Egyptians had been preaching treason amongst the people. Amongst the people whom Emin Pasha brought down to our camp at M'sabe[2] there were two Egyptians viz a clerk & his Adjutant,[3] an officer who had been with Arabi during his rebellion. These

---

[1] Capt. Gaetano Casati, *Ten years in Equatoria and the return with Emin Pasha.* Transl. Mrs J. R. Clay and I. W. Savage Landor (London, 1891), 2 vols., II, 164. See also Gray, 'Diaries of Emin Pasha, Extracts XI', *Uganda Journal*, XXX (1966).

[2] Jephson often writes M'sabe for the more correct Nsabé.

[3] Casati names them as Abdul Waab Effendi and Ahmed Mahmoud and writes: 'Stanley listened to their complaints and counselled them to wait patiently for his

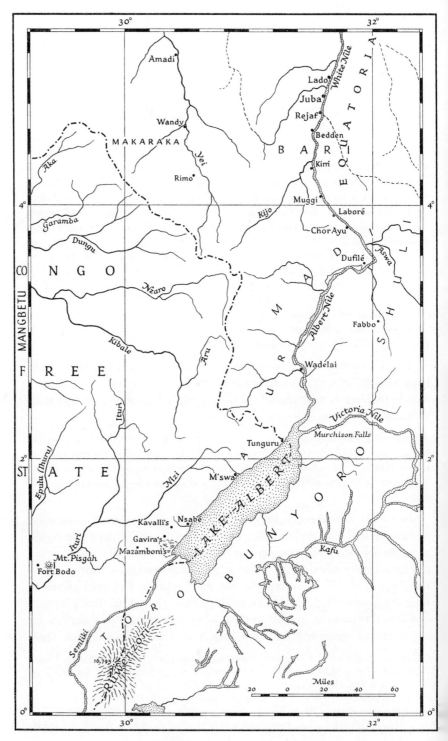

Map 2   The Equatorial Province and the area round the Albert Lake
where the expedition found Emin Pasha

two men, it appears, went to Stanley & complained of Emin Pasha's having treated them hardly & so on. Stanley merely told them he had nothing to do with their complaints, if they had any thing to say, they must say it when they reached Egypt & so dismissed them, but did not say anything to Emin Pasha as he should have done & so put him on his guard. After the people Emin Pasha had brought with him had remained some few days he sent them back to this station to await his coming, he had only brought them down to the camp so that they might see Stanley & the expedition in general. But they began at once to make mischief. The first thing they did was to tell the Madi[1] men who were going down to act as porters for our goods, that Stanley intended to kill them when he had got some distance from the Lake, hence the sudden flight of our porters is accounted for. They then began to rail against Emin Pasha & said they would light a fire from here to Redjaf which would not be easily put out & they induced two other Egyptians to join them, Sulieman Aga, who is chief of the station, being away they had it all to themselves & spoke to the people & sent letters to all the stations & in fact made up quite a nice little plot. The Soudanese

return, begging them also to persuade their comrades to concord and obedience, and to turn their attention to carefully preparing for the departure to Egypt. He, prudently and with much sense, thought it would not be wise to speak to the Governor about the denunciation he had received, lest it should cause fresh complications, and interfere with military discipline.

'Hardly was Stanley gone, when Emin heard of this circumstance, and was so full of anger and indignation that he could not pass over the matter; wounded to the quick by the confidences made to the leader of the Expedition, self-love moved him to an infraction of military discipline...

'I had attentively followed the spirit of general discontent that afflicted the Province for some time, and had several times persuaded the Governor to adopt a more conciliatory policy, that might avail to maintain the crumbling edifice in tolerable condition till the time of our departure. Rigorous measures that in former times would have been of use in consolidating authority, had then no probability of success, in consequence of the general alienation of the people's minds. This course was naturally repugnant to Emin, but force of circumstances exacted it, because he had himself brought on the situation by his own actions; but once more, instead of accepting my prudent counsel, given in a cordial spirit of friendship, he gave himself up to a policy of repression and rigour, supported by the heated encouragement of Jephson who, relying on the principle—not denied by any one—that energy produces salutary effects, even advised that the two culprits who had complained to Stanley against their own Governor, should suffer the extreme penalty. He did not know the political condition of the Province, nor did present circumstances lead him to modify the ideal that had been engraved on his heart and mind in England, where he had heard the praises of the prisoners in Equatoria sung. However, a lighter sentence was passed: the captain was reduced to the rank of second lieutenant, the secretary was put in irons, several of the other officers were reduced in rank, and the Vice-Governor, Osman Latif, was deprived of his office' (Casati, II, 166–8).

[1] Tribesmen from further north, round Dufilé.

who are perfectly loyal did [?not] however enter into their plot. On our arrival all the officials came, as the custom is, to kiss the Pasha's hand & to assure him of their loyalty & devotion, these Egyptians also came with un-blushing faces & made the usual salute & compliments. The next day how-ever the Soudanese officials came & told the Pasha what had been going on during his absence & then everything came out. The chief offender, the clerk, was sent down to Duffilé to be kept a close prisoner under the charge of the chief of that station until Stanley's return, the other three officers were degraded & confined to their houses & suspended from duty. Emin Pasha then addressed his soldiers & told them of the punishments he had awarded to the conspirators & enjoined the soldiers not to be led away by such people. The soldiers answered him enthusiastically. These Egyptians of whom there are some 56 have been a terrible nuisance always complaining always intriguing & getting into mischief. The trouble at Redjaf amongst the sol-diers is entirely owing to an Egyptian officer who had stirred up the people till they are in a half rebellious [mood], he was one of Arabi's people who was sent up here for punishment instead of being shot, & he said to the people 'Why should you fear to oppose Emin Pasha, we in Egypt were not afraid to oppose the Khedive himself'. Lying & treacherous, false & cowardly they look down with contempt upon the Soudanese who are infinitely their superiors, it is hard to find one good quality. These Soudanese as they are called are for the most part men belonging to the Dinka, Madi, Boru, Shafalu, Maru Maru, Bongo, Makraka, Mongbutee or Moru tribes, tribes whose countries are included in Emin Pasha's province, they have heard of Egypt, but know but little of it, they have heard of the Khedive also, but know nothing of him & care less, why should they he has never done anything for them & has not even paid their wages. They only know Emin Pasha, the man who has looked after them all these years & clothed them & pro-tected them & their families from slave raiders, therefore if they are luke-warm about going down to Egypt it is not to be wondered at, especially as the Khedive only promises them their pay until the time they reach Egypt and says nothing about giving them employment after that. Two or three days ago Sulieman Aga returned to the station & I sent for him & spoke to him about leaving the country, he said 'Where our Pasha goes, my soldiers & I follow', he put his two hands together so as to form a circle & said, indicating his hands 'These are my soldiers & the Pasha goes in the middle, that is the way we will travel, by whatever road the Pasha wishes' . . .[1]
I have been out shooting birds for the Pasha's collection, this is a splendid place for shooting, there are abundance of geese, duck & painted snipe, the two latter are very good eating. The Pasha has a wonderful collection of

---

[1] Excisions include two manuscript pages missing from the original MS.

stuffed birds all ready packed in skin covered boxes ready for sending to the British Museum, he has already sent out several collections & one he was sending to the British Museum was in Captain Casati's charge when he was driven out of Unyoro, it was of course lost. The people bring me wonderful curiosities in the way of native ornaments household utensils etc but I'm afraid I shall never be able to get them carried to Zanzibar. One of the officers brought in three beautiful leopard skins—they are very common here—I shall have them made into a covering for my Angarep. One cannot help noticing how all the good & lasting things were brought into this country by Sir Samuel Baker, one often hears of him from the people & particularly about Lady Baker to whom all seem to have been devoted. Sir Samuel was very hard with the natives, & she always tried to mitigate their sentences. There is a story that a soldier, who had twice deserted, was at last condemned to be shot, & at the last moment she prevailed on Sir Samuel to reverse the sentence, she arrived on the scene just as the soldiers were taking aim at the man, who was tied to a tree, she moved swiftly forward & raised her hand & ordered the deserter to be unbound & released, he threw himself at her feet & from that moment there was no more faithful & devoted follower. It would make rather a pretty picture, the swarthy negroes about to fire at their comrade bound to a tree, & the beautiful fair haired woman coming up with uplifted hand to rescue him.[1] The natives of Unyoro, in admiration of her fair-haired beauty, called her Myadue, or the Morning Star, by which name she is known to this day—they called Sir Samuel Baker, M'bidzu or the Bearded One.

Tunguru is built on a narrow spit of sand which runs out some mile or

[1] Jephson names this man later (see below, p. 266) as Faratch Aga, and he would seem to be the same as Ferritch Ajoke, of whom Baker writes in *Ismailia*, but without the picturesque details quoted by Jephson. On the way to Gondokoro in 1870, Baker's flotilla stuck fast in the Nile *sudd*, demoralization set in among the soldiers and Faratch Ajoke, captured after deserting, was sentenced to death. Lady Baker wrote in her diary: 'Sam had all the troops out about 11.30 a.m. to condemn the soldier who ran away yesterday to be shot. Sam said that it looked very sad to see that poor fellow led to his death although he stood it like a man; when he was led to the spot, and had to kneel down and a soldier came to tie his eyes up and they were prepared to shoot him—Sam went up to him and called him, and asked him how long he has been in the service, the poor fellow answered only four months—that he was taken to Khartoum from Fashoda of course as a slave. Sam took great pity on the man and told him that this time he shall be spared, as he is still very young; but if he will do it again of course nothing can save him, but this time he shall be let off with 50 lashes. Poor fellow he was so very grateful and thanked Sam very much for his great kindness to him. He is only 19 years old and has only served a short time in the army'. (S. W. Baker, *Ismailia* (London, 1874), 2 vols., I, 82–4; Lady Baker's unpublished diary, in the possession of Mr Valentine Baker, entry for 18 April 1870.)

so into the Lake, the Lake is sinking so rapidly that in the course of a year Tunguru which was formerly an island is now joined to the main land & has become a peninsular. The country on the mainland just here is a large flat plain reaching away to Wadelai, the mountains which have hitherto come right up to the lake gradually trend towards the West, thus forming a large broad plain between them & the Lake...

The question of the best route out from here is rather a vexed one. The route Stanley proposes is to go South from here to the N. Eastern corner of Mutan Ziga[1] skirt down the Eastern shore & then make across in an easterly direction & strike the Victoria Nyanza at somewhere about opposite Ruwondo island, then to march round the Southern shore to M'sallila & so to Unyanyembe or rather Tabora & on to Zanzibar. Or if the new country is to be formed at Kavirondo, to march round from M'salala to Kavirondo, on to Killaman Jaro & Mombassa. Emin Pasha rather leans towards a shorter route, which is, to proceed from here to M'ruli on the Victoria Nile or Somerset River, cross the river at that point & then skirt round the Northern end of Usoga & so on to Kavirondo. It would be a much shorter route but there would be fighting to a certainty there will probably be a good deal of fighting also by Stanley's route...Emin Pasha has some thousands of tusks of Ivory if he goes by Stanley's route these will have to be abandoned & many thousands of pounds lost, for we cannot carry them, if he goes by the shorter route it will be possible to transport a good deal of the ivory, which he wants for his people, to buy them clothes etc...

June 22nd. Friday. This evening at 4.30 at my request Emin Pasha ordered all his people to be fallen in, in order that I might address them & read to them the Khedive's & Nubar Pasha's letters & also Stanley's address to the soldiers. The people were all drawn up in a long line, their guns were all bright & clean & they all had on their smartest clothes & were really a very fine looking lot of men. The whole thing looked very well, there were five Turkish flags flying & the trumpeters standing together in their bright red suits gave the whole thing a very gay appearance. As Emin Pasha & I approached the flags were dipped & the trumpeters played the Khedivial Hymn. I then spoke to them & made them a short address & told them how the Expedition was got up & a few of our experiences on the road, & the reason why Stanley had sent me to speak to them & so forth. I then called upon the clerk of the station to read the Khedive's & Nubar Pasha's letters which were in Arabic & after he had finished reading them, I read them Stanley's letter[2] & then spoke to them again, numbers of the men made short speeches all expressive of their loyalty & devotion to their Pasha.

[1] Lake Edward, south of the Ruwenzori (see map, p. 66).
[2] See Appendix III below, pp. 430–3, for text of all three letters.

The burden of their song was always the same 'We will follow our Pasha wherever he goes'. They all spoke most respectfully of 'Effendina' (the Khedive) but he was only to them a person in the clouds. They are told he is their Sultan & that the flag they are so fond of displaying on every occasion is his, but to them he is only a Mythical person who sends them fine words, but through all these years has neither helped them nor sent them their pay. That's all very well but they want some tangible, real person to look up to, a person who will clothe them & give them food, that person is Emin Pasha, & I must say they seem to look up to him with both loyalty & devotion...

Before being dismissed three cheers were given for the Khedive by the Pasha's order & the Khedivial Hymn was again played, & the people were then dismissed. The Khedivial Hymn is very pretty I wonder that I never should have heard it before, it is rather a pathetic tune & sounds very well when it is played by five or six trumpets in unison especially if you hear it across the water.

On the journey here, Mabruki, the man who was wounded by the buffalo at our camp at M'saba, died of exhaustion, his wounds were terrible & were long in healing & he would not eat, so the consequence was he became like a skeleton & died of exhaustion. Yesterday the steamer came in from Wadelai & amongst other things brought a quantity of tomatoes of the big red kind & also a small yellow sort, they are grown in the Pashas garden. On the 25th we start for Wadelai & travel by land sending our baggage round by steamer, the Pasha wants to take observations on the road, I shall enjoy the two days march very much, it will do me a lot of good.

June 23rd. Saturday. Today I had all the chiefs of the people up before me to get their answer as to whether they wished to go to Egypt or not. First I had Sulieman Aga a huge enormous Soudanese who is the picture of strength & has a neck like a bull, he is the head of the Regulars here, he brought with him his lieutenant & six non commissioned officers & they unanimously said, in answer to my question, as to whether they had made up their minds, 'We will follow our Pasha'. I then talked to them & told them it was all very well for them to say that now but would they be prepared to say the same thing when it was time to start & they had to leave their houses & a great many of their things, they said 'Yes'. I also told them the road would be long & difficult & probably at times we should suffer from hunger but they said they had thought about it all & were prepared to carry out their words. Ibrahim Aga, the chief of the Irregulars came next with his lieutenant & non commissioned officers, these people are regular Soudanese & come from the country about Dongola.[1] Their answer was

---

[1] These people belonged to a group very active in the southern Sudan from the early days of Egyptian foreign penetration to the lands of the upper Nile. The early traders

precisely the same as that of the Regulars. Then I sent for the clerk & civil officers of the station & they returned the same answer as their predecessors. It is plain therefore that the feeling in the station is not for going to Egypt. I am glad it is not for it augurs well for our Kavirondo plan. I have however done my best to persuade them to go to Egypt...

July 2nd [1888]. On the 25th we started for Wadelai, the Pasha riding a donkey took observations with a prismatic compass every five minutes, he is anxious to lay down this road in his map of the country & so to complete the system of roads connecting his stations. I rode an Abysinian mule which was lent to me by Signor Vita, the Apothecary. It was a handsome looking little animal like a black Shetland pony & carried me very well. The country we passed through was a fine open plain, dotted here & there with trees & flowering shrubs, after going for a couple of hours we came to a fine patch of jungle, very dark & abounding in game, this we skirted & then the plain became more thickly covered with trees & shrubs. Here we saw flocks of Springbok & quantities of Guinea fowl & signs of big game in plenty, all along the road in the soft mud one saw numerous fresh foot prints of leopards, hyena etc. At about ten o'clock we got out again into the open plain where there were a good many villages dotted about, & large herds of goats might be seen feeding in different parts of the plain, each herd being attended by two or three natives fully armed. Round each village, or more properly speaking, round each circular group of huts, was a boma or fence of mimosa branches, but these branches were so covered by a complete network of cobwebs that it seemed as if each village was encircled by a curtain of the finest white gauze. The huts in this country are very untidily made; the natives plaster the inside to a height of some three feet with a mixture of mud & cow dung, thus forming a sort of dado all round the hut. With the exception of a few small patches of ground planted with potherbs, there are no signs of cultivation near the villages. The natives fear the raids of Kaberega's people & have their fields of M'tama, Indian corn etc. in the distant hills, keeping a small quantity only for present use in the different graneries in the middle of the villages. We stopped for half an hour under the shade of a large banyan tree close to the principal village belonging to Boki, the chief of this district. The natives brought quantities of cold clear water in large earthen crocks for the men & brought me a good sized bowl of curdled milk which was very refreshing. From here we got a good view of the end of the Lake which gradually narrowed into the river, which flowed, a good

enlisted them in their private armies and many of them settled in the south, as merchants, artisans or simply adventurers. Coming from the Mahdi's homeland their loyalty to the Egyptian Government was suspect, and the Danagla provided an uncertain element in the southern Sudan for many years after the fall of Khartoum. See Introduction, above, p. 39.

sized stream, towards the North & one could see it in the far distance winding like a silver thread through the plain. To the East one got distant views of some splendid mountains in Unyoro, three sharply defined peaks which must have been 7,000 ft high. On the opposite side of the river, which was some two miles distant from where we were seated, was the site of the station of Magungu, abandoned three years ago on account of Kaberega's hostility. A pleasant breeze came up from the Lake & stirred all the leaves of our tree & gave one a delightful feeling of fresh coolness which was most grateful after a ride of three hours in the hot burning sun. Soon however we started again for we had a long way to go till we got to our camping place... The plain now became thickly covered with acacias & jasmine, the former is covered with long sharp prickles growing out of a sort of roundish shaped hollow ball in which small black ants made their nests, the acacias grew close to & over the path in some places, & pricked one fearfully, they do not grow into trees, but grow only to a height varying from eight to twenty feet. They have a white feathery blossom which has a very good smell & with it, & the smell of the jasmine, the whole air was heavy with perfume. Numberless butterflies flitted about from tree to tree, but I was not able to stop to catch any specimens much to my regret... At 3.30 we reached Okello's village he had been told of our coming & had prepared a cluster of huts for us. Tomorrow we send the natives we had engaged as porters back to Tunguru & Okello gives us porters to carry our things to Wadelai, he is a fattish, jolly old man, but his eyes are very dirty & he has a bad smell. We dined at six o'clock & turned into bed early, for we were very tired, having come 16 miles that day.

July 3rd. Early next morning we started off before daylight; it was beautifully cool & fresh. The country we passed through today was very pretty but there was no water so at 8 oclock we stopped at a village of which Amadje was chief & he gave us carriers to carry large vessels of water to give the people a drink on the road. The road was on the low hills running parallel to the river & the country was like a large Park & through the trees one got occasionally lovely views of the river. We got to our camping place early & the men made us large grass huts in an incredibly short time. Innumerable mosquitos & insects of all sorts drove us to seek refuge under our mosquito curtains at an early hour.

July 4th. The next day after going for a couple of hours we came to a group of villages the chief of which, Wadelai, was waiting with some of his chiefs to receive us. He was an enormously fat old man & was dressed in a long & very dirty robe like a night gown, I have never before seen a native so fat; ordinarily they are quite thin. It is from this chief, who is chief of all the country round here, that Emin Pasha called his station Wadelai. After stopping a few minutes to speak with the natives we started on & soon got a distant view of Wadelai station on a top of a hill, almost the only hill to be seen near the river...At 10.30 we reached Wadelai. All the soldiers were drawn up to meet us & the Khedivial Hymn was played. Here the people are dressed much better than at most of the stations, & the soldiers looked very well drawn up in line. We walked through the station & on into Emin Pasha's divan which was nicely furnished & had a very homelike air about it—I was glad to see two book cases full of books. Here all the officials, civil & military, came in to greet Emin Pasha & myself, a long line of them entering at one door & going out at the other. This ceremony being finished Signor Marco, a Greek Merchant who came up to trade some years ago but is now an enforced resident here, came to pay a visit, he is not at all dark coloured & seems a very decent old fellow. My hut is very nice & comfortable; it is built in the same court yard as the Divan & in front of it is a pretty garden planted thickly with lime, orange, pomegranate & custard apple & papai trees, all of them in full bearing. Wadelai itself is a very large station with fine broad street & the whole surrounded by a ditch, at each corner is a small fort flanking the ditch, each fort being armed with a mountain gun, in these forts there are sentries day & night. The station is built on a hill which rises abruptly from the river, which is here divided into two chanels by a large island. The country opposite is a fine looking country all grass but well wooded, it slopes gently away from the river till it forms a long ridge of low hills beyond which one cannot see. The people all round Wadelai belong to the Loor race—Loor is pronounced very long. On the opposite side of the river between it & the hills is still the Loor race but beyond the hills are the Shulis...

July 7th. Today the Major of the 1st Battalion of the Regulars with two officers & two non commissioned officers arrived from Rejaf. These are some of the rebellious officers who for three years have defied Emin Pasha & who never would believe an expedition, a year ago when Emin told them an expedition was coming they wrote back that he was lying to suit his own purposes, but hearing from the people that an expedition actually had arrived and that I was here they came in all humility to beg Emin Pasha's pardon & to see me. The Major Hamad Aga has always been obedient & loyal, but has been quite unable to stop the tide of rebellion stirred up by the Egyptians. Faratch Aga,[1] his captain, is the man whom Lady Baker saved from being shot, he has been completely led away but is now apparently deeply sorry for what he has done & prays for pardon...I told Faratch Aga that Lady Baker would be certain to hear of his bad behaviour when we returned to Europe & he was dreadfully overcome, it is his vulnerable point, for he is

[1] See above, p. 261.

devoted to the Bakers & is horrified at the idea of their hearing he has been in rebellion against his governour.

July 8th. Today Hamad Aga and Feratch Aga paid me a visit in my house & asked me about the expedition etc. I told them all about it & of our experiences on the road & several things connected with it. Feratch Aga had evidently been thinking of what I had said yesterday for he begged me when I got to England not to tell the Bakers of his bad behaviour, he would rather anything than that, I told him it depended upon how he behaved himself in future, so now I hope I have a sort of moral lever which can be used to induce him to behave well. Afterwards I asked them to come with me & see the Pasha, as we had arranged a little farce together before hand. The Pasha received them very coldly & then gave them a long talking to & upbraided them with their treachery, he told them that they had disobeyed his orders & had refused to help him for three years & now when he no longer had need of them they came to beg his pardon. . . Of course eventually the Pasha will forgive them, but it is as well for him not to forgive them at once but to humble them in the dust a bit first & they will be brought to see their behaviour in a stronger light & will value their pardon accordingly. I am told that last night Hamad Aga told his people they were not to drink (a most common failing amongst the Soudanese), for it would be terrible for the Christian (that's me!) to see them in a drunken state. Poor simple man if he only knew the enormous proportion of Christians that do get drunk ! . . .

July 10th. The Pasha has been very seedy all day & has been now for a good many days, it is his heart, he is, as he says, utterly worn out with the work & anxiety of thirteen years in the country, particularly the last five years since he has been abandoned & left to his own resources. He is very low about himself and says he has but few years more to live unless he can have rest in a cooler climate. I have been into the storehouses to see the ivory, there are some tons of magnificent tusks, it will be a great pity to be obliged to leave them, & this is only a small portion of the ivory in the country.

July 11th. This afternoon all the people of the station were mustered at my request in order that I might speak to them & read them the Khedive's, Nubar Pasha's & Stanley's letters. . . The people formed a large semicircle, & after the Khedivial hymn had been played & three cheers given for the Khedive I began to speak to them & told them the object of the expedition etc, then read them the three letters & then explained their contents, just as I did at Tunguru. I told them I would like to see their officers tomorrow & hear what decision they arrived at etc. The people having given three cheers for the Khedive then dispersed. . .

July 11th. This morning Kodi Aga, the chief, came in with all his officers, two of whom were Egyptians, they all gave the same answer as the people at Tunguru, 'We will follow our Pasha'...After I had spoken with the officers at some length, all the noncommissioned officers came in to speak with me. There were over 30 of them & there was hardly standing room in my hut. I spoke long with them & at different points of my speech which pleased them they testified their approval by the most lively exclamations, which were perfectly deafening & threatened to take the roof off the house, they all spoke at once & each endeavoured to make himself heard when I had finished speaking to them, the result was a deafening uproar in which I could not hear a single word for sometime. However I managed to quiet them & said 'I gather, from what few words I have been able to make out that your answer to me is that you do not care to go to Egypt you only care to follow your Pasha; if he goes to Egypt you will go; if he stays here you will stay & if he wishes to stop by the way you will stop, do I understand your wishes aright?', a deafening 'Aywah' was the answer; which was quite convincing; I told them I should write down their answer in my note book & that I should give it to Stanley, who would give it to the Khedive as their final answer, they replied, that was what they wished. Then came all the clerks, a motley crowd of Egyptians, Circassians, Khartoumers Soudanese & half breeds, they gave the same answer, however I told the Egyptians that it was an understood thing that they would return to Egypt & in speaking to the people generally what I said referred chiefly to the Soudanese who had no ties in Egypt...

July 13th. The last two days have been taken up with getting ready for the journey to Regaf. One can only go as far as Duffilé by steamer for below Duffilé are large cataracts & the whole river between Duffilé & Regaf is so confined between two ranges of hills that the river is narrowed in & consists of a long series of rapids which are so studded with rocks as to be quite unnavigable. We therefore had to make considerable preparations for a march of 75 miles to Regaf.

July 14th. Early this morning we started in the steamer for Duffilé which we shall probably reach at mid-day tomorrow. The river here is very difficult to navigate, it divides into innumerable channels forming islands overgrown with reeds & papyrus. Here & there it broadens out into large lagoons several square miles in extent, in these lagoons are to be seen numberless herds of hippopotomi plunging & diving in the water & sending up large jets of spray from their noses. Lately during the last few days there have been heavy rains in the upper waters of the river for the stream has risen considerably & has become of a thick chocolate colour, the whole face of the stream is covered with floating vegetation, some of it forming small floating islands on which birds may be seen seated, it is this floating vegetation which causes the well known blocks in the river which in former times, when steamers were running between Khartoum & Lado, used to stop navigation sometimes for months...We had to stop in the middle of the day to take in wood, we stopped near a village & the natives brought in loads of wood, they were strong well developed men & were perfectly naked, not a stitch or a rag of clothing, the country all round was covered with Palmyra palms, all bearing quantities of a large orange fruit, which has a very good smell like a melon & not a bad taste, consists of an orange stringy flesh with a large kernel inside which the natives make into flour for bread making the whole afternoon we steamed past huge swamps covered with Papyrus & camped at 8 PM on the first solid ground we came to. Here the mosquitos abounded in such numbers & were so fierce that we were glad to retire behind our mosquito curtains as soon as we had finished dinner.

July 14th. We steamed on & reached Duffilé at mid-day. The numerous channels joined the main stream some ten miles above Duffilé & the river again became broad & fine looking...On landing at Duffilé all the soldiers were drawn up & one received the usual salutation, with however an additional ceremony, as I landed on the wharf the throat of a cow was cut close to me & the blood was allowed to flow all over the path, this ceremony the pasha told me was to welcome me into the country. This station is by far the finest in the country, it is one of the oldest stations & has a well established air about it. One lands on a large open place from which a small wharf runs out into the river for the steamer to lie against, from this open place, in which are the boat building sheds, a broad street runs right through the station & terminates in a large postern gate at the other end of it, this street is shady with large trees which in some places meet above it, & the Government gardens give it a particularly cool & fresh appearance. In the very centre of the station is a good sized square in the middle of which is a clump of three enormous trees, of the fig tribe, with great gnarled trunk, under these trees is a sort of raised platform of earth like a bandstand enclosed by thick walls about a foot high on it are chairs & this is the general gossip place for the officers of the station. On one side of the square is the Pasha's compound, on the other the compound in which strangers stay whilest visiting the station, on the third side is the Chief of station's compound, which is full of beautiful orange & lime trees full of fruit & on the other side is the river which one sees through a sort of arch of green trees. Under these trees Baker, Gordon, Gessi, Juncker, Prout & all the celebreties of the Equatorial provinces have sat & talked & had their coffee & cigarettes as they settled the affairs of the Province, the Pasha has many an interesting anecdote to tell of the conversations he had with Gordon as they sat together under these trees, of his plans & ideas, many of them romantic, highflown & impossible, but all with the stamp of genius upon them, in listening to his description of some of them, one involuntarily thinks of what some old fellow said 'Great wit to madness nearly is allied'. On this platform we rested for half an hour to receive the officers, soldiers & civil servants who all came up to kiss one's hand, a horrid ordeal and one which one would gladly dispense with, I would be pleased to shake hands with all of them, but to have ones hand kissed by a lot of perspiring negro *men*, Ugh! it makes one creep. . . After one had received all the people & had drunk the inevitable sherbet lemonade & coffee we retired to our houses. The strangers compound being so large & having so many houses in it I preferred to stay with the Pasha in his compound. The houses here are very nice all built with bricks, they have regular doors & windows & are whitewashed inside, they are like a better sort of barrack room, which for this country is something very superior. I have a very nice airy house opposite which are two tall Palmyra palms on which numbers of herons roost & quarrel at night they rather disturb one with their angry croakings. In the cool of the afternoon I was taken all round to see the station & gardens. The former is beautifully kept, all the streets are swept twice a day, & everything is well ordered & clean. From the main street, which I have before described, other streets at regular intervals branch off at right angles & terminate in a broad road which runs round the entire station, the whole is enclosed by a broad ditch twelve feet deep & earthworks, it would be utterly impossible for negroes ever to take the station; it is impregnable. All the government buildings are built in a firm solid style & the mosque is really quite a triumph in building for this barbarous country, it is a large square building neatly finished & white washed & carpetted all over with a very nice kind of matting which is made in the country, it is further decorated with numbers of ostrich eggs suspended in mid air from the roof, the apex of the roof outside is also decorated with ostrich shells, I believe ostrich eggs are the recognised decoration for mosques. We visited the Pasha's pets, an elephant & a giraffe, they are perfectly tame & rove about the station as they please; they go out in the morning with the cattle to feed & return with them at milking time. The gardens are well tended & are very extensive; they lie immediately outside the station. There are large gardens belonging to Hawashi Effendi, the chief of the station, who is an Egyptian with the rank of Major, containing a big patch of peas, beans, onions, garlic, balmias, endive & spinach, & dotted about are a great number of orange, lime, pomegranate, prickly pear, custard apple, guava & papai trees, all bearing freely. Along the river's edge are plantations of bananas. For a radius of two miles round the station are fields in which the people grow different kinds of corn & ground nuts: millet, tullaboon, red & white m'tama & Indian corn are the chief kinds of corn which are grown rice also grows well & wheat fairly so, but of these two latter there is but little grown in the country. All about the station are villages belonging to the Bari tribe who live under the protection of the station & act as porters or interpreters when their services are required...

July 15th. This evening we have an invitation to dine with Hawashi Effendi, these people eat with their fingers & the dinner is served a la Turque. Hawashi Effendi, like all the Egyptians, is a great scoundrel & was sent up here as a criminal; but unlike all the other Egyptians he works & makes his people work therefore the Pasha forgives a good many of his short comings. There is something most amusingly cynical in his scoundrelism; he is not the least ashamed when he is found out, but says, 'Oh that's nothing you know, all Egyptians are scoundrels'. As we were sitting together this afternoon under the trees, Hawashi Effendi began to compare the Egyptians with the Soudanese, he began by saying all Egyptians were scoundrels. The Pasha remarked 'And you'. 'Oh' said Hawashi Effendi 'I'm the biggest scoundrel of them all'. He then went on to say 'If a Soudanese comes at you with a loaded gun & from the other side an Egyptian comes towards you with a carpet, go towards the Soudanese, he with his loaded gun will do you less harm than the Egyptian with his carpet & friendship'. In the evening we went & dined with Hawashi Effendi. The dinner was served on a splendid large round brass tray & we all sat round & ate out of the dishes with our fingers. The most striking dish was a goat roasted whole & stuffed with onions ground nuts & beans. Hawashi Effendi seized it in his hands & wrenched the legs & shoulders off, he then broke its back & emptied all the stuffing out onto the dish, it was rather a nasty looking operation for the grease oozed through his fingers as he tore the goat to pieces, but this dish I found very good eating & particularly the stuffing of ground nuts. There were a great number & variety of dishes some of which were rather liquid & I being unused to this style of eating found some difficulty in getting the food to my mouth, the great fault was that everything was swimming with butter & oil, & one was obliged to eat of every dish for nothing is considered such bad manners as not to eat freely of your host's dinner. The consequence was, the dishes being so numerous I rose from dinner with the feeling of being perfectly stuffed!

July 16th. I had an awful time of it last night, the result of Hawashi Effendi's hospitality, I shall think twice before again accepting an invitation from these people. We started off early this morning for a march of ten hours to Hor Ainu [Chor Ayu] a small station some 16 miles distant... The plain was freely dotted with trees & shrubs chiefly of the acacia tribe & intersected here & there by small mountain streams which cut deep beds in the rocky soil, we soon came upon numberless signs of elephants, in the shape of broken trees, torn up soil, grass beaten down, etc & in a few minutes we saw a sight such as I have never seen before, close to us to our left & moving parallel with us was an immense herd of 200 or 300 elephants. People who have never seen a large number of elephant gathered together can form no idea how impressive such a sight is. This great number of huge black bodies moving slowly along with their long white tusks gleaming in the sun seemed perfectly overpowering, wherever one looked for the space of half a mile one saw nothing but elephants marching sedately along, the very face of the plain seemed moving. Occasionally the ranks were broken by the rather clumsy gambols of a little elephant who broke from the herd & performed a series of stupid looking plunges in the open. I noticed that a very large elephant, a perfect mountain of flesh, kept some 30 yards ahead of the herd, by its self, so I mention this to the Pasha who told me that when a herd of elephants is travelling the largest female always goes in front. The men on seeing the elephants, some of which were not more than 200 yds distant, all began to whistle, it appears that they do this in the belief that it will prevent the elephants from charging, for they believe that the sound of whistling or of a cock crowing is particularly offensive to them & they invariably make off when they hear it. It is strange that a female elephant should act as the pilot of the herd of elephants. In the case of a herd of horses or buffaloes a male always goes ahead, there are a great many wild geese here which always go about in pairs, & the Pasha tells me that either swimming or flying the female always goes ahead, it is curious there should not be one general rule in the case of all animals. At midday the mountains gradually closed in & ran parallel with the river not more than a quarter of a mile distant from it & the path lay close along the river bank. On the opposite bank the mountains rise sheer up from the river which being thus closed in is very narrow here & rushes along in one long series of rapids. The country is perfectly beautiful & of a wild park like description; small valleys run up into the mountains full of fine trees, whilest the little plain between the river & the hills is covered with short cropped grass & dotted about with large finely shaped trees, there is an air of quiet & peacefulness about it, you are shut in on all sides by the mountains which gives a feeling of security & retirement. At four oclock we reached Hor Anu a small station close to the river surrounded by large fields of corn & ground nuts. Owing to the post having miscarried in some way our huts were not got into very good order for us, but I was still very seedy & was glad to lie down in any sort of hut. Khamis Aga the chief of the station came in to pay his respects but was very coldly received by the Pasha who was very much displeased with the state his station was in.

July 17th. Somewhat late we began our march for Labore station distant two hours & a half. The character of the country was much the same as yesterday but the narrow plain between the two stations was almost entirely under cultivation. At 10 o'clock we arrived at Labore a good sized station on the top of a high rocky hill overlooking the river, our compound was on a narrow flat between the station & the river. Selim Aga the chief of the station came to pay his respects & his people brought the usual offering of sherbet & coffee. The huts here are very nice & cool, the sides being formed of basket work of split bamboos. In the cool of the afternoon we went up & paid Selim Aga a visit in his house & drank coffee, & then went over the station. It is very rocky & uneven & is surrounded by a thick dry stone wall which is suppliemented by a thick hedge of thorns. I am trying to buy cotton cloth, the cloth they make here in the country, but it has been a bad year for cotton & cloth is scarce & very expensive which is most unfortunate as I arrived in the country with one tattered suit only & two torn shirts & have to set myself up completely in clothes sufficient to last me for eighteen months.

July 18th. Leaving Labore station we started for Muggi a seven hours march distant. The mountains again receded from the river & the path lay through a fine broad plain some distance from the river. My riding donkey is not a good one he does nothing but bray & does not go so I walked most of the way. We are now out of the Madi country & are now in the country of the Baris. The country is pretty but nothing much, but there are numbers of birds one quite longed to take ones gun & go after some of them. The Pasha is imbuing me very strongly with his taste for ornithology; I find it a most interesting subject. There were numbers of brilliant scarlet weaver birds, & steel blue Lamprocolu flitting about in all directions in the long grass, as we got nearer Muggi there were very extensive Bari cultivations on both sides of the road & large numbers of Guinea fowl & geese might be seen running about the fields. There were a great many women working in the fields, perfectly nude with the exception of a sort of apron made of bright rings of iron, like a coat of mail, they also had long tails of string hanging down behind which are useful to them when they are kneeling which is their usual posture whilest working in the fields . . . The Bari woman, while working on her knees perches her baby on her back, it has a queer effect on entering a Bari field to see ten or a dozen women on their knees each with a little round, fat, shiny piccaniny on her back. The chief crops are M'tama, ground nuts & beans. On arriving at Muggi we did not enter the station but went at once to our compound some distance from the station & right on the bank of the river which comes down at this point in a good sized cataract, the rush of water so close is very pleasant, it is a sound I always like. Abdullah Aga Manzal the chief of the station & one of Emin

Pasha's best & most loyal officers appeared with the coffee, he was very anxious we should stay seven or eight days on our return. Abdullah Aga strikes me as being more intelligent than most of these people...

July 19th. We made an early start for Keri distant 4½ hours march. The country is poor but very pretty all up & down with gullies & streams, & hills covered with short grass there are in places circles & squares of stones marking the site of what were once extensive Bari villages. The Baris have abandoned them & built their villages inland behind a low range of hills, Emin Pasha's soldiers occasionally made too free with their goods so they decided to move their residence somewhat further from the path. For some distance there are curious geological phenomena, natural terraces all lying so evenly in one direction that they look as if they had been built, there are also strange upheavals & subsidences in the rocks, & curious strata such as would delight the heart of a geologist. Early in the day we reached Keri a small station rendered smaller by the number of desertions amongst the soldiers who under the influence of the Regaf faction deserted to a station they had made in the Makraka country. Bacheet Aga the chief of the station remained loyal to the Pasha but was quite unable to check the desertions, he is a very decent sort but is rather a drunkard. Our compound is away from the station & close to the river, this was Gordon's favourite spot, he used, whenever he was able to get away from Lado to come here, & like Gladstone, used to amuse himself with cutting down trees. When his soldiers first saw him cutting away at a large tree with an axe they couldn't understand it & the chief of the station approached him & said 'Why should your Excellency trouble yourself in this way, permit me to bring ten or fifteen soldiers & I will clear the tree away at once'. Gordon turned on him in a towering rage & asked him how he dared to presume to accost him & told him to return to his station & mind his own business! Bacheet Aga in order to make our huts extra nice had had the floors plastered with fresh cow dung, this if left for some days makes an excellent floor, but it had not had time to dry, so much to our annoyance we arrived to find our huts perfectly untenable, however numbers of Bari women were called in & soon gave the huts a completely new flooring of clean sand, & the huts were then fumigated with a kind of gum which is found extensively in this country it has a smell like pastilles when burnt...

CHAPTER 13

THE REBELLION AT THE EQUATOR

28 JULY–25 OCTOBER 1888

Emin now decided to call a halt, sending Hamad Aga on to Rejaf with orders to the rebellious 1st Battalion to come south to Kirri and make their submission. If they continued to defy his orders he would evacuate the southern stations preparatory to leaving the country with Stanley, and leave Rejaf to its fate. Having issued his ultimatum the Pasha returned to his bird collection while Jephson nursed a fever and a bad cold.

On 28 July they learnt that the Rejaf officers refused to come to Kirri without consulting with Ali Aga Dgabor and Mahommed Effendi el Ademi, two of the insubordinate officers who had set up the station in the Makraaka country mentioned in the entry for 19 July. Hamad Aga was virtually a prisoner and had smuggled out the letter with this news by one of the boatmen who were 'the only loyal people amongst all these men...this speaks well for sailors.' Emin and Jephson decided to stay at Kirri and await developments in Rejaf, and on 29 July Jephson addressed the garrison. Though Bacheet Aga, chief of the station, was known to be well affected, there were doubts about the loyalty of the others, and Jephson was greatly surprised when he was visited early next morning by the officers, N.C.O.s, clerks and boatmen, who all declared their intention of following the Pasha. They were assured that they would be allowed to bring their wives and families

and in the cool of the afternoon the soldiers had great rejoicings in the station on account of the news we had brought, they had horns & drums going & the Pasha & I went up to see them dancing...

Their troubles were not over, however, for on returning from the celebration Emin was handed a letter from Hamad Aga, again smuggled out from Rejaf by one of the boatmen, begging the Pasha to keep away. They had better, it was decided, return to Muggi, and Emin made a half-hearted attempt to dismantle Kirri before they left. An undignified wrangle took place over the ammunition which the soldiers refused to pack up and hand over to be taken south.

Kirri abandoned, the garrison once more in open revolt, Emin fell back on Muggi, 'the most loyal station on this side of Duffile', in whose commander, Abdullah Aga, the Pasha had great confidence. Once Abdullah Aga and his people began to pack up and move south for Dufilé, it was hoped the others would follow suit except for the rebels who could stay where they were and make their own plans. In a long entry outlining the situation, Jephson considered the Pasha's plight with typical sympathy.

August 2nd [1888]. It will be a great relief to the Pasha when this is done & he is clear of them; they have been a source of endless trouble and annoyance to him for over three years. I feel ashamed of having been angry & impatient at his not having acted more promptly about the ammunition the day before yesterday. He has been over ten years in Turkish service as a surgeon & most of that time has been spent, he tells me, in very hot climates, Syria & different parts of Asia Minor, Armenia, Persia, Arabi & Tripolis, after that he entered Egyptian service & has remained in this country whose climate is most trying to Europeans, for 13 years with all the anxiety of its government on his shoulders. He has with dispair & indignation seen all his best efforts for the good of his province clogged & nullified by the shameful policy of his government at Khartoum & for the last five years since he has been cut off from Egypt it has been all he could do to hold his own against his enemies & to clothe & look after the people under his care & to rule over the teeming millions of negroes who inhabit his province. He is now in such a state of nervous exhaustion that he is unable to sleep & his heart gives him a great deal of trouble and anxiety. Unless he goes to a colder climate he says he does not give himself more than three years of life—he is now only forty eight. He has the character for being reserved but he has spoken to me quite openly about himself. It is only at times when the troubles of his province, his sleeplessness, & anxiety about his work combine to make his burden seem almost heavier than he can bear, that he gives way to melancholy & to a feeling of despair as to who will take up his work should he be obliged to relinquish it. Such fits never last long & as a rule he is cheerful & busy, his one recreation is in his ornithological researches, for which he has a passion, his hunters go out daily & bring him in many rare specimens of birds, & in his leisure time he may be seen measuring & classifying his birds with all the fresh ardour of an amateur ornithologist. His valuable collections he has given & from time to time forwarded to Professor Hartlaub of Bremen & to the Vienna Museum, his last two collections he has however given to the British Museum. A brave man bearing up against his trials and unhesitatingly giving up the best years of his life for the good of his people whom he rules justly & beneficiently, beset with troubles from within & without, he must be to everyone who sees & knows him an object of admiration & sympathy; whilest his kindness of heart, unselfishness & courtesy make those who know him intimately sincerely attached to him.

There follows an account of Emin's career and accomplishments, his years in Turkey and later in the Egyptian service, his scientific skill and his mastery of languages. 'Such a man' concludes Jephson,

would have risen to emminence in whatever capacity he was acting, it is a pity that the country he has been governing all these years has not been under a better home government for he could have developed the country to an enormous extent & could at the same time have paid a large yearly revenue into his government.

From now on the situation became increasingly confused. A party of soldiers came in from Rejaf, protesting loyalty to the Pasha, and Emin sent them hopefully north again to persuade their mutinous companions to return to their allegiance— a vain exercise, Jephson thought. Meanwhile, the evacuation of Muggi continued, and Jephson passed the time shooting both for the pot and for Emin's collection of birds. He was surprised, and rather amused, at Emin's alarm when he did not return at the exact hour he was expected one evening, for he was

so accustomed to being out late & often sleeping out in the jungle with Stanley that one had got to think nothing of it & was surprised to find that one was considered a sufficiently important person to warrant the sending out of two search parties for my recovery, Stanley never did such a thing & used to show a supreme indifference when we did not reach camp at night.

One day, 11 August, he had a pleasant excursion after pig and antelope which led him into a Bari village where the inhabitants

were very friendly & invited me to come in & inspect their huts & household goods, which I was very glad to do, for since I have been amongst them I have been collecting a variety of facts about them & was pleased at having an opportunity of extending my knowledge of them.

Soon, however, they were on the move again.

August 12th. We started off this morning & reached Labore by midday, tomorrow I speak to the people & next day we go to Chor Aiu where we stay for a few days. I had bad fever & had to lie down all the afternoon. Selim Aga sent down word & assured us all the soldiers were ready to start for Duffile whenever they were ordered. Seeing this part of the river which is entirely unnavigable owing to the many rapids & cataracts, had set me thinking of a plan I had thought of on the Congo when I was sent by myself to navigate those rapids between Manyanga & Isangila. The plan was, where there was regular traffic, to have two long chains fastened to rocks or piles about the cataract & fastened in the same way below, at the foot of the cataract was to be an iron float like a boat, only completely decked in & so completely protected that rocks could not injure it. On this float were to be two windlasses one on each side worked by handles & the two chains were to run round them, just in the same manner as a horse ferry is used in England for ferrying carts & horses across a river, the boat or nuggar coming to the foot of the cataract would be closely attached to the stern of the float, the crew would then go on board the float & work the windlasses & haul the float & nuggar over the cataract. It would be utterly impossible for the nuggar to be wrecked, as is so often the case, & an immense amount of time & labour would be saved. In the same way & by the same float nuggars might be lowered down the cataracts in perfect safety. I was telling the Pasha about it, for these rapids reminded me of it, he listened gravely & made one or two objections to it, which objections were upon mere matters of detail which I could at once see a way of overcoming, so he made the grand objection, which is by far the most aggravating of all objections, namely, that several very clever men, Gordon, Mason & so on had tried to find a way of getting over the cataracts satisfactorily, but had failed, & therefore he did not think my plan would be likely to succeed. But I argued, Gordon's plan was a chain of steamers working between the cataracts, Mason's was a system of locks, & Ismail Pasha's was a railway, & though their plans would, if carried out, make the river a more complete high way than mine would they all three failed on the subject of the enormous outlay of money, an outlay which Egypt could not, & nobody else was prepared to, make. They had never tried to utilise the existing means which nature had given them & which they could take advantage of with a comparatively small outlay. He said yes but they were clever men & were engineers, upon which I said that generations of Naval & Mercantile seamen of the highest intelligence had tried to invent a more safe & less cumbrous anchor than the one which originally existed, they had failed, & it had been reserved for an old fool like Trotman to invent an anchor which had now been adopted by all mercantile nations of the world. If I had the place & means I warrant I would make my idea a perfectly feasible & workable one, it is awfully annoying when you see an idea as clear as light before you to be told that you are not likely to succeed because cleverer people than you have failed. Now Stanley is a man who at once sees what is valuable in a suggestion; he tells you what he thinks bad in it, but encourages you to improve & develope what is good, & even makes suggestions himself, it is one of the things which makes him such good company; if anything strikes him as good he pushes you to go on with it...

August 13th. This afternoon I went up to the station with the Pasha to address the people & read the letters to them, I noticed several of them appeared inattentive & spoke in an undertone to one another & when I had finished speaking & the Pasha addressed them, one of the soldiers suddenly fell out of the ranks & exclaimed in a loud tone of voice that he did not want to go away, that they knew of but one road & that road was by way of Khartoum, if the Khedive really wanted the people to come let him send up his steamers & they would go down to Khartoum. (Were there ever such fools as these people, always harping on Khartoum?) As for the other road we spoke of they did not know it & would have nothing to do with it & that we were telling the people lies & that the Khedive's letter was a forgery, for if it had come from him he would have *commanded* them to come down & would not have said they might stay here if they liked. The Pasha at once siezed him by the throat & wrenched his gun away from him & ordered him to be put in prison, then rose a scene which was most unpleasant, the soldiers rushed at us with loaded guns, they were sixty odd & we were eight & were not armed—they seized their companion & bore him off in triumph amid howls of execration at us & drew themselves up round the store houses which contained the ammunition & levelled their guns at us, the officers did what they could to stop the mutiny but their efforts were of no avail for the soldiers were for the moment perfectly mad, Selim Aga entreated the Pasha to go out of the Station & go to his house, but I said I would try & speak to the soldiers first & endeavour to calm them down, I took Binza only with me to act as interpreter, on approaching the soldiers I was greeted with howls & yells & some of them ran away, but only a few, the religious old orderly, who had prayers with the boys, was perfectly drunk & rolled up whilest I was trying to quiet the people & began laying about him among the en- furiated soldiers with his gun, they wrenched it away & threw him on the ground & trampled on him, I most sincerely wished they had killed him, I called up one of my own orderlies who dragged him away. After a minute or so of trying to reassure the soldiers they were sufficiently calmed down to listen to me, & I told them they were very wrong & foolish to act in this way, that the object of the expedition was only to help them & not to force them to leave the country unless they wished to, I had told them to come to me on the next day & give me their answer & that then they could have said what they pleased to me, they all exclaimed that the Pasha had no business to seize the soldier & take away his gun in that way, to which I answered that they were soldiers & not savages & must know that when a soldier steps out of the ranks & openly defies his Governour he must be imprisoned, they said the soldier was wrong but that the Pasha was wrong too & finally told me they would consult amongst themselves & would speak to me afterwards as I told them I was their friend & wished them well. Whilest I was speaking with them two or three people came up to me & entreated me to come away, but after the first rush there was nothing to fear, for I said to the people when I came up to speak to them 'You see I am alone & am not afraid to come among you because you are soldiers & not savages' & they lowered their guns & said 'No you have nothing to fear from us'. After speaking to the soldiers for some minutes I rejoined the Pasha & his people who were waiting under the tree where we had addressed the people & we went down to our compound. Had one of these guns, which the soldiers were brandishing about cocked & loaded, gone off, there would have been a general massacre for if once a gun was fired there would be no stopping the excitement which would have followed & down we should have gone. The demeanour of some of the Pasha's people during the first few risky minutes which followed the first rush, was somewhat amusing. Ragab Effendi the Pasha's secretary hid behind the tree & his knees gave way under him from sheer terror; Araf Effendi a clerk a most peculiar looking little creature, rushed into the chief of station's kitchen when he howled & wailed at the top of his voice accompanied by all the black sluts in the house; Hassan Aga the Pasha's hunter ran about exclaiming 'we shall all be murdered & we have nothing to defend ourselves with, Allah be merciful to us' etc. The Pasha's four orderlies & my three who were the only people of our party who had guns, all behaved very well & did their best to pacify the people. This evening the soldiers have put eight sentries at each gate of the station & allow no one to enter.

August 14th. This morning early, the chief of station sent down word that the soldiers were all drawn up & would like to speak with me, I went up to the station accordingly, accompanied only by Binza to act as interpreter for me. The Pasha wished me to take some people with me & the orderlies all came up & said they wished to accompany me, but I preferred to go alone, when people are excited nothing pacifies them so much as to go amongst them by yourself & show them you have no fear of them, however I took my little revolver in my pocket for fear of mishaps. I spoke some time with them & told them the whole fault lay with the soldier who had stepped out of the ranks & as much as told us we were liars, I told them the Pasha could not have done otherwise seeing that the soldier had spoken such words before him who was their Governor. I then said they had known their Governour for thirteen years & asked them if they had ever known him do a bad action towards them, they replied, that on the contrary he had only done good by them, well, I remarked, if for 13 years they had only known him do good why did they think he was going to turn against them now, they repeated it was because he had seized the soldier. They then told me that he was their mother & father & that they were perfectly willing to follow him anywhere provided he did not throw away the people in Regaf, I told them it was the people in Regaf who had refused his aid, which I could see they didn't believe. However I told them they were perfectly free to act as they wished & to profit by, or refuse our help as they pleased, I told them we had come many hundreds of miles to help them & had fought a great many enemies in the way, but that never with all the fighting against enemies had I had so many weapons pointed at me as yesterday when I came amongst the people whom we wished to help & whom I had imagined were my friends. They seemed very much ashamed at the whole thing & saw that they had acted stupidly, so I wished them Good morning & left the station...At midday we started for Chor Ayu, the little station between this & Duffile. The soldiers by way of showing their repentance for what they had done yesterday begged to be allowed to fall in & salute the Pasha as he left the station, but he refused to allow them to do so, & said he did not wish to see them. However eight of them insisted on acting as an escort to our carriers to Chor Ayu, & on our arrival there the non commissioned officer who was in charge of them came to the Pasha & asked him to give him his discharge from the Labore company, for he would not stay with the people there after what had happened, the Pasha therefore gave him his discharge & he & his family come here tomorrow; no doubt others will come in after a bit.

August 15th. Yesterday evening, late, a messenger came in from Hamad Aga in Regaf saying Ali Aga & Mahomoud Effendi the two chief mutineers had just arrived from the Makraka country & said that they would not come & see the Pasha but that he might come & see them—which was extremely kind of them. So this morning by the Pasha's advice I wrote to Hamad Aga saying it had been my intention to come down to Regaf to speak with the people & read them our letters, but that they had behaved in such a way as to make it impossible for us to come down, I however enclosed the Khedive's letter which he would read to the officers now they were all assembled, & I requested him to tell them what I said in my letter & that anyone who wished to see me now must come to Duffile. The Pasha is inclined to think that when the chief rebels hear we are moving the stations, & particularly after they hear the news from Labore, that they will come down & remove all the stations up to Duffile by force. Things really are getting very serious & from the first the Pasha said the Khedives letter would have a bad influence, he ought either commanded them to go to Egypt or to stay here, anything rather than leave it to the people to decide, but they are his orders & they must be carried out. At any rate the Pasha says had we arrived six months later he would have been lost, he could have held out against the natives, perhaps for another year, but when his people at Regaf turned rebels it was the hardest blow he had yet received...

August 18th. This evening late a letter came in from Hawashi Effendi saying that rebellion had broken out in Duffile. Three officers & 60 soldiers had arrived today from Fabbo station, they had liberated all the prisoners, seized the store houses & spoke to the soldiers who joined them readily enough. They said that the people were fools to listen to those letters of the Khedive, Nubar Pasha & Stanley, that the road we wished to go was a false one & would not bring them to Egypt, there was only one road & that was Khartoum & so forth. Hawashi Effendi they have confined to his house, but have not otherwise illtreated him, all the Egyptian officers of Duffile

281

have made their submission to the Fabbo people. This is terrible news for here we are caught in a trap completely. Regaf at one end, Duffille at the other & Labore between, it is quite possible & indeed probable that we shall be made prisoners by these people & sent down to Regaf, & if they take it into their silly heads to march down to Khartoum our fates are not likely to prove pleasant... The Pasha has at once sent for Selim Aga & Surore Aga the chief officers of Labore to come at once, they should be here by daybreak tomorrow & we shall then start at once for Duffile in spite of its being the great Mahommedan feast, Id el Kebir...

August 20th. Sunday. This morning early we started for Duffile, there were not sufficient carriers to carry all our luggage so we had to leave a good deal of it behind... One was struck even more than on our journey down by the inexpressible loneliness & solitude of this huge rocky waste of uninhabited country. No sort of cultivation or signs of habitations are to be seen for miles, nothing but dreary stretches of quartzy plain, broken only by huge masses of rock torn & upheaved in all sorts of curious shapes, some looking in the distance almost like ruined castles & the whole studded about with dwarfish shrubs & mimosas, to the West is a long line of high rugged & inhospitable looking mountains whilst to the east the barren looking plain stretched away as far as the eye could reach into the distant Shuli country. The sight of this plain recalled very forcibly to my mind some words which I had read somewhere—I think in Scott—which as far as I can remember were as follows: 'It is a remarkable effect of such extensive wastes, that they impose an idea of solitude even upon those who travel through them in considerable numbers; so much is the imagination affected by the disproportion between the desert around & the party who are traversing it. Thus the members of a caravan of a thousand souls may feel, in the deserts of Africa or Arabia, a sense of lonliness unknown to the individual travellers, whose solitary course is through a thriving & cultivated country.' At about 3.30 we entered Duffile, it is now the four days holiday & a great many people were lounging about, but the soldiers were not drawn up as usual with their officers to salute their governor, nor did anyone come forward to greet us in any way, though numbers of people came to look at us to see what would happen. The only person who ventured to come & kiss our hands was a poor little Circassian tinker, who in spite of the frowns of the people round came forward to greet us, his poor little white peaky face was puckered up with crying, he could say nothing for sobbing but could only hold our hands & kiss them. As soon as we entered our houses eight sentries were posted at the gate of our compound so we are now prisoners. All the people with us are also prisoners & Hawashi Effendi as well. Only our own boys & a few other people are permitted to go in & out. Selim Aga whom the Pasha had brought with him from Labore to act as a sort of go-between for him & the mutineers went over to consult with Fadl el Mulla[1] & the officers to gather what news he could. He came back in the evening saying he had been with them for a couple of hours, the one eyed clerk Achmet Effendi who had gone to Stanley & whom the Pasha had put in prison was one of the prime movers of the mutiny. They told Selim Aga that one of the chief reasons for the mutiny was Hawashi Effendi whom everyone hated, but hitherto they had been afraid to say anything as he was always upheld by the Pasha. Another was that they would not go to Egypt, they were unwilling to leave this country for they would never be able to carry away all their wives children & goods with them & they knew nothing of the road to Zanzibar except that it was long & that there would be great dangers & difficulties in the way. There were a variety of other small things, they all professed a strong dislike of Signor Vita, the Tunisian Apothecary, & all said they had no word to say personally against the Pasha. For myself they said I was perfectly free to do whatever I pleased & to go where I liked, no one would hinder me. The mutineers had sent for officers from Regaf, Muggi, Labore Wadelai & Tunguru & when they had arrived a council would be held & their complaints laid before the Pasha, until these officers arrived nothing could be done, so we must wait patiently in our houses & let things develope themselves...

The days passed slowly; Fadl el Mulla's soldiers from Fabbo were on guard over the prisoners who were allowed to see only their own servants. The boys smuggled in an occasional note from Hawashi Effendi with their food. On the 29th, however, the monotony was broken by news from Shukri Aga at M'swa and Kodi Aga at Wadelai, which threw the camp into a ferment: it was rumoured that Stanley had arrived at the south end of the lake. Jephson determined to make every effort to rejoin the expedition, and if he was prevented from doing so to contrive for a letter to be taken by the captain of the *Khedive* to Shukri Aga, the only really staunch man among Emin's station commanders.

August 31st. This morning at midday the people from Regaf have come in. There are Ali Aga Djabor, Faratch Aga Adrok (who sent me a present of a beautiful piece of Monbuttu work) Ali Aga Shaumru, Dau el Beyt Aga, Shiek Moorajau (a scoundrelly priest) & a clerk from Regaf—from Muggi Bacheet Aga Ramadan—& from Labore, Surrore Aga. They marched into the station with flags flying & trumpets playing & all the soldiers were drawn up to meet them:—it was a great contrast to our lowly entry! The officers are now shut up together in the Fabbo mutineers compound; they are consulting & we are awaiting our trial. They brought sixty soldiers with them, drawn from the different stations...

---

[1] Commanding Fabbo, one of the few inland stations, east of the Albert Nile.

September 1st [1888]. Saturday. This morning Bacheet, one of my three Soudanese orderlies, came to me & told me that the rebel officers had sent for him & Abdullah another orderly of mine & wished them to go over & speak to them, I at once said, yes, & told the two to be careful what they said, & to tell them to say everything as it has happened, & to come & report to me on their return. After half an hour they returned, saying the officers had asked them whether they really came from Egypt & on their saying that they were the Khedives soldiers & were sent by him to accompany us, they told them they were liars & that they would put them in chains, that Stanley had picked them up on the road only & that they were no real soldiers, to prove this one of the officers put them through a short rifle exercise, &, seeing that my orderlies were well up in their drill they permitted them to return here. After a short interval they sent for my boy Binza & he returned & said they would be glad if I would go & see them, upon which I answered I was quite ready to come & speak with them, but that it was not the thing to send such a message to me by my servant, if they wished me to go to them, they must send an officer over to invite me to come & to accompany me to the council. They at once sent over Ali Aga Shamru who came to my house, where I shook hands with him in the most affable manner & accompanied him to the rebels with a feeling that everything depended on what concessions I could get them to grant. Binza acted as interpreter, I spoke to him in Ki-Swahili & he spoke to them in Arabic. On entering the house where some 22 of them were assembled they all rose quite respectfully & I shook hands with such officers as I knew, & Ali Aga Dgabor & Fadl el Mulla Aga came forward to shake hands with me. I told them they had sent for me & I was here to hear all that they had to say—after a long silence they began. First they all hated Hawashi Effendi who was a seducer a robber & a scoundrel & that their Pasha was wrong to have made intrigue with him & to uphold him in everything he did & they were greatly incensed against him for having done so, except for this they had nothing against him, except that in moving the boxes of ammunition from Muggi up to this station he had done very wrong & had arranged it all with Hawashi Effendi & the plan was to take away all the ammunition & to leave them 'planté' here in the country at the mercy of the natives. I told them the people of Muggi said emphatically they wished to leave the country & I had told them to at once begin to move their things for if when Mr Stanley returned and they were not there he would most assuredly start without them, for he could only wait a short time. I then gave them the Khedive's & Nubar Pasha's & Stanley's letters, written in Arabic, & told them from them they would see it was not our wish to take them from the country unless they wished. They believed the Khedive's letter was a forgery & sent for some of their Brevets to compare his signature in the letter I brought with those in their Brevets. After examining it for a long time they said they were unable to say whether it was a forgery or not as the letter I brought was so effaced by the damp. After a long long talk during which time I could hardly sit up for I had a bad attack of fever, they said their plan was to send the steamer down to Stanley with some of their officers & soldiers & to invite Stanley to come up with his officers with them to Duffile & they would then hold a consultation with him. I told them that it would be of no use for the first thing Mr Stanley would say was 'Where is Mr Jephson, why have you not brought him with you, if you were friends you would have done so' & so forth. I then asked them to let me go down & to take the Pasha to Wadelai, if they did not wish him to go to Mr Stanley, this they refused to do. I then upbraided them & told them here was I a guest in their country, I had come by myself because I trusted them & had gone amongst them freely without fear because I was their friend, & now they had made me prisoner & had refused to let me go & join my people. They protested they wished to do me no harm & that I was free to go where I pleased, only that they wished to see Mr Stanley before they sent me to him. I said again it was useless to attempt to see Stanley without me & by dint of hammering this into their heads & taunting them with treating me, a guest in their country, in such a shameful manner, some of them began to come round, for these people have in them a kind of rough chivalry; it is rough, but it is chivalry, & the bitterest thing I could say to them was that they had treated their guest badly. I then said I had finished talking to them, but I would for the last give them a piece of advice, which was that if they did not wish to lose sight of their Pasha let him rest where he was, but let several of them go in the steamers, take whom they pleased & I would go with them & do my best to bring Stanley down here with me & if they wished to give him any letters to Egypt I would hand them to him; these were my last words...

Up early on the morning of 3 September, Jephson had his things taken on board, and after an argument was allowed to take the *Advance*, having to look sharp to see the oars and rowlocks were not left behind. The voyage was intensely uncomfortable, the steamer overcrowded by eight officers and some 65 soldiers, in oppressive heat which turned next day to drenching rain. Sleeping on deck for the sake of fresh air, Jephson was soaked to the skin and the result of the wetting was:

Sept. 4th...this morning I had such a fearful fever I was hardly able to stand up when we reached Wadelai. On arriving I at once went to the Pasha's house where I established myself & some well affected people came in to kiss my hands & hear the news. Signor Marko a Greek merchant who looks after the Pasha's house when he is absent & the Storekeeper were quite overcome when I told them the story of our troubles & the tears ran down their faces as they listened. All the Pasha's boys came in to me to make their salutations & to assure one of their loyalty. For the last two days it has been impossible to eat & I staggered off to bed at an early hour with one of the worst attacks of fever I have yet had. I found poor little Fareda Emin well but very anxious to hear where her 'Baba' was & why I had come without him...

Next day the fever had abated and Jephson set about packing the Pasha's bird collection to take south to Stanley and safe keeping. The people of the station avoided him, especially the supposedly faithful commander, Kodi Aga. Jephson brooded on Emin's plight.

September 6th...What must not Emin Pasha be feeling now, shut up in Duffile, with all those semi-savages around him thinking only of what fresh concessions they can wring out of him, each night the same drunken scenes going on in the rebel leaders compound & not knowing each night whether in their drunken state they may not commit some deed of violence & plunge the whole station into wholesale riot & bloodshed. He has given up so much for these people & held so faithfully to them, hoping against hope, thinking only of holding his people together, the people whom he has ruled over for twelve years, throwing away every opportunity of leaving the country & returning to a more congenial life, where he could indulge in the luxury of living & conversing with clever & scientific people. And with what result? Are not such men as Gordon & Emin too good for such a useless sacrifice? You Exeter Hall & Anti Slavery party, are these people worth the trouble you take about them? I do not believe it. Ignorance, fierceness, love of war, & cruelty may be eradicated, but treachery never...

September 8th. Left Wadelai at about half past seven, Kodi Aga coming with us, this makes it evident that he is in league with all these people, otherwise he would not have left his station, he looked very shamefaced when I looked at him, but avoided meeting my eye. I am very sorry to see that Kodi Aga has not held out against the rebels, for if everyone is against the Pasha it is a bad look out.

September 9th. The morning was very rainy & bitterly cold for there was a strong wind blowing. The river is very wide & gradually widens out until it reaches the Lake. For the first time I saw wild giraffes, they are the queerest looking beasts, when one sees them in the distance they are like bare trees, they have a curious way of straddling their forelegs wide apart when they want to eat anything off the ground, for long as their necks are, they are not long enough to reach the ground owing to their being so enormously high in the withers. Their motion is most peculiar when they trot & to see a lot of them making off is a most laughable sight. On arriving at Tunguru we found the little steamer there & Sulieman Aga to meet us on the beach. He had been drinking & after shaking hands wished to embrace me, but I managed to avoid it. The soldiers were drawn up & saluted me as I passed, & many people came up to greet me. I walked on to Cassatis house & he welcomed me rapturously, & was most anxious to hear my news. He was very much down when I told him all that had happened & handed him over a letter which Signor Vita had given me for him. From Cassati I learned that they knew nothing further about the people who had arrived according to native report[1] . . .

September 10th. It is splendid to be here on the lake again & to hear the waves lapping against the shore when one wakes up in the morning & feel the cool breeze against one's cheek, if I lived in this country I should always like to live on the lake. . .

The human scene, however, was not so lovely at Tunguru; the Egyptian officers curried favour in a way that outraged Jephson, and the looting of Hassan's house set the station in an uproar. It became increasingly clear that Stanley had not arrived at the lake, and rather than endure another steamer journey, Jephson decided to stay at Tunguru while the rebel officers visited M'swa—accompanied, he was sorry to see, by Kodi Aga on apparently friendly terms. But who was on whose side became more and more difficult for a straightforward Englishman to make out, and the following is a typical entry:

September 13th. This morning at about half past seven the steamer started for M'swa. Sulieman Effendi came in to see me & talked a great deal of his loyalty etc. I rather shut him up, for I told him, I knew him to be a liar & I considered him, in addition, a fool. . .Abdullah Vaap Effendi came in shortly afterwards & brought me a present of three wax candles he had made for me. He talked a great deal about routes etc & seems very anxious to get out. The truth of it is, this storm has been raised chiefly by the Egyptians, & now they are in mortal terror of what they have done, & are awfully afraid of the Soudanese & want to cry off, so the Soudanese, who hate them, will have nothing to do with them & as they have estranged themselves from the Pasha by their disloyalty, so now they find themselves fallen between two stools & they are most anxious to get on our side so as to profit by Stanley's coming & go out to Egypt with us. I do'nt pity them in the least & I hope the Soudanese will be very hard on them. The people who do

---

[1] 'At about 3 p.m. on 9 September, the steamer *Khedive* entered the bay of Tunguru. An unusual bustle enlivened the soldiers of the garrison, who, having put on their dress uniforms, were drawn up by the landing-place. A short time after, Jephson came to my residence and sorrowfully related the sad events with which he was associated. I should have reproached him, although in friendly terms, for not having given due consideration to my words as to the doubtful condition of the Province, but a genuine pity overruled all my feelings, and I promised my full support, encouraging him with hopes of a brighter future' (Casati, II, 178).

the most mischief are the Egyptian clerks, they have just a little education, which gives them a sort of ascendancy over the more ignorant Soudanese, yet they have not enough education to use that ascendancy properly, but use it for the vilest ends.

September 14th. Today I have had to keep my bed, for the last two days I have had an attack which threatens to end in dysentry unless I take very strong measures. It has made me so weak & miserable that I have not been able to leave my bed. It is at these times that Africa is so terrible, when one can only lie down feeling miserable & ill & think, all sorts of horrors rise before one & it seems as if one never will get out of the country.

He made himself as comfortable as he could, attended by Hassan's servants, and with Casati for company. The Italian was full of grievances and his conversation not very amusing especially as his 'French is execrable; compared to him I speak like a native, & it is painfully difficult to follow what he says; indeed in an ordinary way it would be quite impossible were it not for the telling gestures in which he indulges & which help one to understand what he means'. He told Jephson stories about Romolo Gessi, at whose invitation he had originally come to the Bahr el Ghazal to survey the Province of which he had been appointed Governor by Gordon. Casati had a grievance here too, regarding himself as having been abandoned when Gessi left the country and died on the way. He spoke grudgingly of his fellow Italian: he was 'by no means a Gordon' and though he did well in the war against Zobeir, 'he had no powers of organization in the time of peace'. They talked too about the pygmies or, as Jephson calls them, the dwarfs of Monbuttu,[1] about whom Casati really did know a good deal. But the two men were not in sympathy. After a bout of fever, Jephson struggled out for fresh air:

September 16th. This evening I went for a walk with Cassati across the plains, he has an immense idea of his own opinion and yet he is a person I should never like to be guided by, he thinks he knows a great deal about this country & the people, but I do'nt think he does, nor can I see how he can, for he never leaves his own house, hardly, which is a filthily dirty place. And there he sits all day & smokes, he has no books, he does not write or even keep a journal, I ca'nt imagine how he can pass his time...

At about one o'clock the steamer came in from M'swa. The officers have brought with them the 31 boxes of ammunition we brought for Emin Pasha &, I hear, Stanley's two boxes of Winchester ammunition which was given to the Pasha to keep till our return...

---

[1] Monbuttu, or Mangbetu, to the north-west of Lake Albert, was a part of the Equatorial Province which Emin had only just begun to explore when he had to withdraw to Wadelai. Jephson and other writers of the time use the word 'Monbuttu' indiscriminately for the Bantu tribes, akin to the Azande, or Niam-Niam in the old travellers' tales, and for the pygmies, more correctly described as the M'buti. A recent study of these pygmies in the Congo forests is *Wayward servants: the two worlds of the African pygmies*, by Colin Turnbull (London, 1966).

September 17th. We start for Wadelai tomorrow, the boats have all gone to the forest to fetch wood . . . This evening I went round to see the officers & to insist on Stanley's two boxes of ammunition being handed over to me & without much difficulty I got what I wanted, the boxes were sent to my house & in the evening I sent them over to Cassati & they will remain in his house till I want them.

September 18th. We started early & reached Wadelai late this evening. Cassati came with us as the rebels wish him to join in the big council at Duffile, he has gone to stay in Signor Marko's house, so that I am alone in the Pasha's house, Cassati is always more at home in the houses & companionship of inferior people. We did the voyage very quickly, in an ordinary way, it takes a day & a half . . .

September 22nd. We started from Wadelai this morning at 6.30 & tied up against the bank at about sunset. The steamer is fearfully crowded & this day's voyage beats all the others for general nastiness, stuffiness etc . . .

They arrived back at Dufilé on the 23rd to find the Pasha unmolested but very dejected. On 24 September the Council began its deliberations and its composition and proceedings are described more fully in Jephson's book than in his diary.

'It was composed of between sixty and seventy officers, clerks, and employés from every station in the Province. Most of the officers were Soudanese, but the clerks were chiefly Egyptians, Copts, and Khartoum people or half-breeds. The Council met under the trees in the middle of the square, and a sort of divan was formed by seats being placed upon the raised platform of which I have before spoken. On these were seated the principal members of the Council, while the lesser members found places on a large semicircle of seats below the platform. Beyond these were drawn up the non-commissioned officers, who were not considered members of the Council, but who were occasionally appealed to by their officers. The whole of the large square was crowded with people, who pressed round the outer circle to hear the proceedings. A non-commissioned officer and a large number of sentries were always on duty to bring up the witnesses and to keep order. The first meeting lasted from eight in the morning till four in the afternoon, but afterwards these sittings generally lasted from eight till one.'[1]

The Council were concerned principally, of course, with determining the fate of their Governor and with deciding what to do with themselves when they had deposed him. Secondly, and hardly less important, was a paying off of old scores concentrated in the indictment of Hawashi Effendi, commander of Dufilé, long the Governor's right-hand man and favourite. There were charges against Vita Hassan, the Moroccan apothecary who was much in Emin's confidence, and Casati came in for a certain amount of censure, but there seems to have been no ill feeling

[1] A. J. M. Jephson, *Emin Pasha*, pp. 210 ff.

against Jephson, who had constant access to the officers and was asked from time to time to attend the Council, as was Casati. The two Europeans lost no opportunity of pleading Emin's cause, and urged that should the Council persist in deposing him, he might be sent back to his own house at Wadelai to rejoin his daughter. Casati, indeed, came well through this difficult time and although Jephson could never find him congenial, his natural fairmindedness led him to write in the diary (for 27 September): 'Perhaps I was unjust about Casati, he really is a very good fellow and is doing all he can for the Pasha amongst the rebels, but he *is* so dirty and has such nasty ways about him.'

There was little either of them could do for Hawashi Effendi; Jephson pitied the old soldier as he recorded that 'indictments were read against him which contained accusations of his having acquired goods, women, money, cattle, etc by unlawful means, & a storm of abuse was hurled at him, everyone had something against him and some insulting epithet.' His women were beaten and his servants bullied as the hunt went on for the concealed wealth Hawashi was known to have hidden away. The cries of the women made Jephson's 'blood boil'.

As for Emin, he sat grieving in his prison, meekly signing the paper from the Council stating that he was to be deposed, and worrying only about where they might decide to send him. When it was eventually decided to pack him off to Rejaf the relief of knowing something for certain temporarily raised his spirits, but they were dashed again by his servants being sent away to Wadelai, and by the final insult of a decision to search his house there for Government property. On 6 October a party left on this mission, accompanied by Casati who had insisted on going to see fair play, and who secretly carried letters for Shukri Aga at M'swa to be forwarded to Stanley. Emin made his will and asked Jephson to act as guardian to Farida, and to hold in trust what was left from the savings of his years of service. Jephson agreed, suggesting that Felkin should also be appointed Farida's guardian.

After seeing Casati off to Wadelai, Jephson took a walk round the compound and paid a visit to Osman Effendi, Emin's second in command or vakeel. Osman had been a detective officer in Cairo and was on the whole well affected to his chief in the present predicament. He had, at an early stage of the mutiny, jumped into the river in protest over the treatment of the Governor, and there had been some argument between the two factions as to whether or not he should be fished out. Casati suggests he was under a cloud earlier in the year (see p. 259 n) but Jephson does not say so in the entry for 6 October. He found him seated on a mat in his compound teaching his four little boys to read & write.

October 6th [1888]...He was very low about all that was happening here & said he had told people that if they did harm now, they would have to suffer for it hereafter. He was anxious to know, if things came to the worst, whether I thought England or Egypt would send an expedition to avenge these outrages, I said 'possibly they might', which seemed to give him great satisfaction...He begged me to be sure & put down all that happened in the book in which he had heard I wrote every day—these people always have a great idea of anyone's journal. He offered me a very nice pair of European boots, which I refused, as I do not like taking presents from these people, though I should have very much liked to have had the boots. I do not like Osman Effendi he is altogether too complimentary & cringing, & though he has behaved well in this mutiny & has strongly espoused the Pasha's cause in the face of all the rebels, I know it is only because he thinks it will benefit him hereafter, & he does it for love of his old mother & his children, to whom he is greatly attached, & not for love of the Pasha, against whom formerly he behaved very badly. One is down on their faithlessness & ingratitude, & after all is one quite just? They are here in this country, an ignorant lot of semi savages & they see the Pasha's chances of ever getting his head above water gradually growing less & less every day, & so to save their houses & wives & children, or rather, I should say, their means of supporting their wives & children, they declare for the rebels & go against their Governour, they all admit he has been a father to them all, but they shrug their shoulders & say 'what are we to do?' Whenever some very outrageous piece of ingratitude, on the part of someone whom the Pasha has invariably befriended, comes to light one feels furious & says there is not a single good quality in these people & repeats the old cut & dried phrase of travellers, who say that 'Africans possess neither love, gratitude nor affection', but are civilized people much better in proportion, is it not self interest that governs savages & Europeans alike? It is not perhaps therefore to be wondered at that every day we hear of fresh instances of desertion to the rebels & ingratitude & deceit, & yet though it may not be wonderful, at the same time it is very sad to see the disappointed & down look of the Pasha when fresh instances of the defection one by one of his few most trusted people comes to his ears, he only shakes his head sadly & his eyes seem to say 'Et tu Brute'. . .

The diary for 7 and 8 October records an abortive attempt by the rank and file to have the Pasha reinstated, a movement quickly quelled by Fadl el Mulla, backed by the hitherto faithful Selim Aga, who was now pressing for Emin's removal to Rejaf. Jephson begins the entry for the 8th:

My birthday. This day last year found us in the middle of starvation, & now we are in the midst of rebels, of the two I would sooner have to fight the former.

Later in the same entry he considers Emin's position:

If he is taken away to Regaf I'm afraid Stanley will never be able to extricate him from the country, in case he goes to Regaf I shall go with him, if I am allowed by the rebels, for I cannot desert him, & I shall probably be in the same box. We hear that there are secret orders to bring the Pasha's house & people back in the steamer & his little girl as well. He declares he will not go to Regaf he will shoot himself sooner & this he has firmly made up his mind to do. He has spoken to me about it & tells me that it means starvation of him to go to Regaf, as there is nothing there, & if he is once there neither he nor his little girl will ever get out, & therefore to save his girl he will destroy himself, for if he is dead the rebels will allow me to take his little girl with me. I promised him I would do all I could, & I am sure amongst my friends at home, I shall be able to find someone who will be kind to the little Farida. As far as right & wrong goes, I think a man is perfectly justified in committing suicide if he pleases & no one can say it is wrong. Life is forced upon us whether we will or not, we do not agree to accept it, therefore I think we are quite justified in putting an end to it when we no longer desire to live—Carlyle himself was of this opinion. Of this I am quite certain I would sooner die than remain a prisoner at Regaf without any hope of being able to get out, & to dail bey subjected to starvation & insults & if the Pasha intends to destroy himself I would never put any difficulty in the way *if I thought things were hopeless for him* though on the other hand, I would never counsel him to do it. . .

Towards evening I went & paid a visit to Hamed Aga & Bacheet Aga & Moorajan Aga—the latter a Muggi officer—were with him. Hamed Aga is dreadfully distressed at what is happening & says, though he is, as I know, the nominal head of the present government, he never leaves his house hardly, & strongly expresses his disapproval of what is going on to the officers, but he is powerless to do anything. To Bacheet Aga I talked a long time, he was the chief of Keri, & was sent for the other day by the rebels, together with Abdullah Aga Manzal, chief of Muggi—they are both devoted to the Pasha. I told Bacheet Aga it was useless to attempt to reason with the rebel officers; they were too far gone in this enterprise to listen to anything but treason, but if he & Abdullah Aga Manzal would go amongst the soldiers, as they are both well liked by them & tell them actually what our wishes were about them & that instead of wishing to take them all out against their will, all our wish was to take those who wished to go to Egypt & leave those who desired to remain. He said he would do so. . .

I spoke to Hamed Aga about sending us meat of some sort for we have nothing, the rebels are apparently anxious to starve us, both he & Bacheet Aga were terribly distressed that he, their governor, should be without food & I, his guest, should have to come & beg for it. . .

October 9th. I went this evening to see Abdullah Aga Manzal, I wished to speak to him & get him to talk with the soldiers—with whom he has great influence—& to get him to rouse them up a bit by telling them that what the officers have told them is entirely false. There were so many people that I was not able to speak to him much on the subject, but talked to him only on indifferent subjects, I got some fresh information about the dwarfs in Monbuttu. . .

October 11th. Far away in the forest we have constantly come upon traces of the dwarfs & have from time to time captured some of them, though chiefly women & boys. Since I have been here I have also seen a good many living in perfect goodwill with the soldiers. These have been captured in raids & are mostly women & children. I have got what information I could from them, but they are rather reticent & shy, a great contrast to the people round about, who tell you all about themselves with the greatest volubility.

October 12th. Today a large council was held under Hamad Aga, the officers wish to remove soldiers from the Northern countries & bring them here & make stations to the East in the Shuli country.[1] This was a measure the Pasha has been trying to carry out for the last three years & the people would not hear of it, now they see the necessity of it, for there is no food whatever in Regaf & the road out from here lies to the East, though most of the people still hold to the road to Khartoum. Hamad Aga told Ali Aga Djboor that all the officers had decided on erecting stations to the East & ordered him to go to Regaf & bring down soldiers, Ali Aga refused & finally ran away from the council & went to his house. The people now have become completely demoralised, each has an idea of his own & nobody obeys orders from anyone; it is all anarchy & confusion...

October 14th. Nothing has happened today, rumours go about the station continually but they are not worth recording. The Apothecary made me very angry today & I flew at him promptly, I record it because what he said is only what has been said by so many of the people, to me, here & it never fails to make me furious. He began asking me if Stanley was able to get us out from here, how many porters could he give him. I told him, not many if any at all. He remarked '& my women'? 'They must walk'. 'And my children'? 'They must walk too unless your boys can carry them'. 'And our food'? 'Your food is on the road & you & your people must forage for it as we do' 'And our cooking pots & all our boxes, chairs beds etc'? 'Well you must throw most of them away'. After which conversation he looked very blue & thought it was a great hardship & was a very hard case, & a whole lot of other nonsense. Upon which I flew at him & told him what I thought about him & all those people who asked such questions & thought it a hardship. These people who are the very scum of the earth & in their own country live a life of poverty, give themselves airs as if they had been accustomed to be waited on by troops of people all their lives. Here each person is accustomed to have as many carriers as they please & carry about with them all sorts of rubbish, with one man to carry his pipe, & another his washing basin, & so on & now they expect to travel in the same way to

[1] This was where Baker built his station of Fatiko after his retreat from Bunyoro in 1872: Baker, *Ismailia*, II, 83 ff., 389 ff.

Zanzibar & want to carry all their worthless trumpery & rubbish with them, & think it a hard case if they have to throw away some of their things, & think it terribly hard to have to use a box for a chair, & another for a table, & have to sleep on a bed made of grass or boughs, instead of carrying a bed stead with them. They also want all their women to be carried (which means 8 men every day to every woman), these women, of whom each man has 4 or 5 & sometimes more, & who two or three years, or even only a few months ago were only savages who were captured in raids & who never in all their lives have been carried. There are perhaps some 8,000 people in all in this province of Hatalasteva, so how many porters would be required to carry all these people chairs, tables, women etc to Zanzibar? The country could not support us, & we should be old men before we reached the coast. It makes me quite mad when I think of the utter inability of these people to understand that if they want us to help them, they must help themselves as well. Here are these people to whom it is a matter of life & death to get out of this country (I am speaking of the Egyptians, Jews & Greeks who will assuredly be massacred if the Pasha leaves the country) & who one would imagine would do anything to get out of it, grumble at having to throw away or sell their few paltry chairs, beds, etc. What a contrast to our officers, who have all been gently nurtured & are not accustomed to hardships, who have come out here to work & have borne all sorts of trials & unpleasant-nesses merely for the sake of helping people they have never seen, all has been borne with a cheerful & uncomplaining spirit...If we had arrived in smart uniforms, covered with gold lace, they would have kissed our feet & thought us something like deliverers...

Next day brought an abrupt change in the situation. A soldier arrived from Rejaf with the news that three steamers[1] and nine boats, loaded with people, had arrived at Lado from Khartoum. The hope that this was a rescue party from Egypt was quickly dispelled by the arrival in panic-stricken Dufilé two days later of emissaries from a Mahdist force led by Omar Saleh.

October 17th. The people are all becoming paralized with fear & know not what to do. In the afternoon, three peacock dervishes arrived with a letter to the Pasha, which Fadl el Mulla at once confiscated. The dervishes

[1] The *Talawhin*, the *Safia*, and the *Mahomet Ali;* the *Bordein* and the *Ismailia* were said to be on their way from Khartoum. The *Bordein* and the *Talawhin* were the two steamers in which the vanguard of the expedition to relieve Gordon, commanded at this stage by Sir Charles Wilson, arrived before Khartoum and, under heavy fire from the Mahdist troops who had occupied the city after Gordon's death, were withdrawn down stream. Lord Charles Beresford came to Sir Charles Wilson's aid in the *Safia*. Jephson has some caustic observations on the attempts to sabotage the steamers before they were abandoned to the enemy; 'it seems a pity they were not rendered useless more completely' (Jephson, *Emin Pasha*, pp. 257–8).

are the most curiously patched looking people. Their white coats are patched all over with black, green & red patches, they all have big rosaries, & a large many coloured shawl wound round their heads. Each carries a long sword & three spears. When asked what they came here for, they said they came to conduct us by the true path to heaven & to teach us to pray, as they, the true believers, the true Mussulmen. There was a great controversy as to what should be done with them, some were for putting them in chains & sending them to Fabbo, others were for killing them out right. However they have been confined in a house in the soldiers' quarters . . .

These heralds of the enemy's approach caused a sharp rally in favour of the deposed governor. On the 18th he was waited on by a delegation of officers led by Fadl el Mulla, who brought with them a letter addressed to Emin as 'Mudir of Hatalastiva' [Arabic name for Equatoria] from Omar Saleh, commanding the Mahdist forces, which exhorted Emin and his people to surrender. The letter also recalled the events which had led up to Emin's isolation in the Province, and the fate of those who, like Gordon in Khartoum, had presumed to withstand the will of God as expressed by his servant the Mahdi. Unwilling to take charge of the rapidly deteriorating situation, Emin was persuaded by his panic-stricken officers to give a few words of advice. His counsel was that they should speed up the evacuation of the northern stations, bringing out the women and children and leaving only a fighting rearguard with plenty of ammunition. He also advised fortifying Tunguru, the island station which could be cut off from the mainland and held indefinitely provided the steamers were kept running to bring in supplies. But Jephson noted with dismay the inertia which succeeded this energetic burst of consultation. Fadl el Mulla was constantly drunk, and the only matter receiving urgent attention seemed to be the dividing up of Hawashi Effendi's fat-tailed sheep among the dissident officers. Emin begged Jephson to try and make his own getaway and rejoin Stanley, but 'that I don't wish to do &, with the Pasha here, if I left it would savour too strongly of what Gordon called "ratting out"'.

On 21 October refugees began to pour in from Laboré with alarming stories. The Mahdist forces had attacked Rejaf and the officers and men in the other stations were falling back on Muggi. Native interpreters and other camp followers were deserting daily. Grilling the Dervish emissaries brought no satisfaction to the increasingly menaced garrison at Dufilé. 'This evening', runs the entry for 21 October,

the rebel officers had the three Dervishes up before them & told them they were liars that they had come with friendly messages to them & now their people were attacking, so they would kill them. The Dervishes did not seem much to mind & said 'If you kill us it does not matter, it wo'nt help you to escape, & do you think that one of you officers will escape? You will all be cut down, but the soldiers who are acting under your orders will be spared'. They were finally put in chains and put in prison . . . Meantime nothing is done here, no preparations are being made to receive the enemy; they are not even collecting wood for the steamers so that they can ply between here & Wadelai without delay & get away the women & children...

On 22 October came news of the fall of Rejaf. The 'Donagla', as Jephson invariably describes the Mahdist forces, had encircled the fort, cut off all retreat and slaughtered the garrison except for a lucky few who had escaped and were flying towards Makaraka. The women and children were taken captive and removed to Khartoum. The local Bari were joining the enemy in large numbers, led by Chief Befo of Belinian. Jephson watched with dismay the disorder into which bad news was throwing the garrisons, and on the day the news came from Rejaf he wrote:

Should the people all combine & place the Pasha at their head, & act strictly under his order, all might yet be well, for a time, but I fear they are too much resolved on following the headlong course they began two months ago & now have become too demoralized to return to the right course again...

October 24th. The chief clerk & Ibrahim Effendi Ellam went this morning down to Labore to try & persuade the officers not go down to Regaf & to try & retake it, but to concentrate here. This move was in consequence of our having heard last night that the officers in Labore had made up their minds to try & retake the station. The artificers have been at work all day making silver bullets to fire at the Khartoumers. They have taken a hundred dollars from the money they took from Hawashi Effendi & each dollar makes a bullet. They do this because they believe the Mahdi's people are some of them impervious to ordinary bullets, but silver bullets will kill them, if they were the devil's own people. It seems rather queer that such beliefs should hold in the nineteenth century, but when one comes to think of it, it was not so long ago that the belief held in Scotland, I believe Claverhouse was considered proof against bullets & was finally supposed to have been killed by a silver button used as a bullet, & that was as late as William & Mary's reign. The belief in the efficacy of silver bullets holds, I am told, over the whole Orient, even to this day.

October 25th. The officers here have been torturing the three dervishes to make them give them information. They twisted split bamboo round their heads & then twisted it up, like a switch, until their skulls nearly burst. It is shameful, for the unfortunate men came as messengers & trusted themselves amongst these people of their own free will. I went out this morning & walked round the station & amongst the gardens & then came back round the station. I found the soldiers were busy at work deepening the ditch—it is about time they began to do so—as I was watching them Selim Aga, Osman Effendi & Mustapha Effendi came up & asked me to come & sit in the gate House & talk with them. They told me they intended keeping the dervishes until Stanley came & handing them over to him. Whilst I was talking, two of the Dervishes came by, they were heavily ironed & there were marks round their heads where the torture had been applied which sickened me, the vile Egyptian officers pointed to them & grinned. They had such a down look & kept their eyes fixed on the ground:—poor devils my heart ached for them. They did not look at me, except by a sort of side glance, but I cant get their miserable tortured look out of my head. Their patched & tattered coats made them look all the more pathetic, especially when one knew that the torture had wrung no information against their people from them, & one admired their courage & felt ones blood boil against the foul, cowardly, abject Egyptians who were pointing to their poor crushed heads in derision. Enemies as they were they were brave, & what they did was for their religion, & as they passed slowly staggering under their heavy chains I felt much more friendly to them than towards my so called friends the Egyptians, & I would gladly have struck off the Dervishe's chains & set them free, & as gladly I would have put a bullet through the head of every grinning, jeering Egyptian. Their swords are ordinary long straight double edged swords, with leather scabbards decorated with iguana skin, but the spears were immensely long, with the most enormous iron heads, which were about 18 inches long & as broad as an ordinary shovel. After a bit I went to Fadl el Mulla, who asked me if I wished to retire South by the next steamer & get out of danger, I told him of course, I had no wish to run away when danger came, that I was in the same box with them & was perfectly ready to fight along with them & that it was'nt usual for Englishmen to clear out when fighting was expected.

CHAPTER 14

RETURN TO WADELAI

26 OCTOBER–31 DECEMBER 1888

Confusion mounted in the days that followed: there were rumours from the north that the soldiers at Muggi and Laboré were rallying to Emin, and Casati, arriving in the big steamer from Wadelai, declared that 'all the soldiers in the Southern stations are displeased at the Pasha's deposition & great confusion prevails no one obeys orders & the soldiers do not work'. Shukri Aga, remaining true to the Pasha at M'swa, was avoiding contact with his brother officers at the other stations. Fadl el Mulla, seeing the tide turning against him, could do nothing to control a situation rapidly getting out of hand, and when Bacheet Aga, 'the best fighting man there is in the country', came in from Laboré and declared for the Pasha, he was put at a further disadvantage. The diary entries for the first few days of November give an idea of the last phase of Jephson's and Emin's imprisonment.

November 1st [1888]. This morning the first steamer load of refugees started from here for Wadelai. They were the families & people of six of the clerks, together with all their property, & a good many other people of various denominations, boatbuilders, nondescript Government servants & others. The steamer is not likely to be back for another six days, so that at the present rate it will take at least six weeks before the station is cleared of all but the fighting people, & if the Donagla intend attacking this station, which they most decidedly do, they will be here long before that time.

November 2nd. The small steamer the Nyanza arrived this morning & starts the day after tomorrow for Wadelai with a load of refugees.

November 6th. There has been no news whatever & nothing has happened during the last four days. The Nyanza is still here & remains for five or six days—it is really disgraceful how these people waste time—she is waiting for Sulieman Aga who has gone to Fabbo to fetch his wife & children & is to take them back to Tunguru—he has sworn to the officers he will not leave the station unless the Pasha goes to Wadelai, but I dont know if it will have any effect. Yesterday the big steamer came in from Wadelai—she took a load of women & clerks in her—she starts the day after tomorrow. Several letters were brought in to the Pasha secretly from some of the faithful at Wadelai. The clerk of M'swa station is at Wadelai & returns to his station almost immediately, he wrote & asked the Pasha & I to write letters to Stanley & he would forward them by Shookri Aga to Kavalli if possible. I wrote a long letter telling him of the position of affairs in this country & of the coming of the Donagla & begged him to be careful how he approached the

298

country. It is certain if he does not come soon we shall be taken by the Khartoum people. I have no fancy for becoming a Mahomedan & going about the streets of Khartoum as a Dervish. One is beginning to feel rather low & worried: I feel as if some awful catastrophe was impending, perhaps it is because I have been writing to Stanley & telling him of the position here & it has made me more alive to the seriousness of it. Cassati & I had quite a quarrel last night because I would not accept some presents that were sent to me from some of the rebels in Wadelai, he brought them in & I told him I would neither accept them, nor give those people my hand to kiss, which they are very fond of doing. He told me I was a fool for we were prisoners & must accept any thing they chose to send & appear friendly with them. I told him I did'nt care if we were prisoners; I would not smile & accept presents from people whom I knew were doing every thing they could to make things bad for us & the country, it might be more politic but that I could not bring myself to do it however much it might bring me into trouble, though I do not believe such a thing would bring me into trouble, I've no notion, because one happens to be down in the world, why one should thank everyone for the kicks one receives & smile & look as if one liked it. I know these people always do it, but I do'nt a bit believe they respect you a bit for doing it, for they must know one hates them. An Arab Oriental will appear to be your greatest friend & will wait for years till he can take a thorough revenge against one, one of their best known sayings is that 'vengeance is a dish to be eaten cold'. I dislike going out in the station, even, for these people always come & take one's hand with every appearance of friendship, they may feel it for all I know, but when one knows what thorough-paced scoundrels they are, one feels inclined to knock them down. The weather is most extraordinary, this is now the dry season & yet there are torrents of rain every day & at night as well, whilest in the rainy season there was the greatest scarcity of rain. The people here say that the coming of the Donagla has brought it.

November 9th. Absolutely nothing has happened in the station for the last four days. Rumours from the people at Muggi have come in, but none of them are reliable, they seem to be waiting and just doing nothing...

November 13th. There is really hardly anything to write about these days. No news comes in & nothing is stirring in the station. Hawashi Effendi & all his people went in the small steamer to Wadelai. The large steamer came in the day before yesterday & brought a good many notes for the Pasha from the faithfuls there. Kodi Aga, the chief of Wadelai station, wrote to Selim Aga begging him to send the Pasha, for the soldiers in the station are getting insubordinate & he cannot manage them, & that unless the Pasha is sent nothing will quiet them. Sulieman Aga has returned from Fabbo & has brought his wives & children with him. He has been reinstated as chief of Tunguru, but swears he will not go unless the officers allow the Pasha to go with him, so now great discussions are going on about it. He comes in to see the Pasha & tells him he will be certain to get his way in the end, but I doubt it, though the bulk of the officers wish the Pasha to go, the clerks are doing all in their power to prevent it. Fadl el Mulla Aga says he does not object, but he is afraid that the officers down at Muggi will be angry with him, Sulieman Aga, who is his brother by the way, says that the real reason is that he is afraid if the Pasha got into power again he would be one of the first to suffer punishment...

I got a place on my heel more than a month ago & it is still very bad, I am not even yet able to put on a boot & have to get about in a slipper, I suppose one is in a bad state from being shut up here so long & consequently it will not heal...In the evening the clerks of Muggi & Labore came in with many loads and people, women & children chiefly. They say that the Makraka soldiers have joined the soldiers at Muggi & they have all started, last Saturday, for Regaf, with some 500 guns...We heard in the evening that Abdullah Aga Manzal wrote to Selim Aga to send him carriers at once to remove the ammunition from Muggi & all the things there, meanwhile we have had no official letter & we do not know what is happening up North.

On 16 November news came of the utter failure of the attack on Rejaf, mounted from Muggi on the 14th. Many officers were killed, including Hamad Aga, the Major who, despite his connection with the original rebels at Rejaf, had always been a favourite of Jephson's. His wives and children had been taken captive when the Mahdist forces took Rejaf in October, and Jephson thought he may have

become reckless in consequence. He was one of those fatherly looking old negroes with white hair, & I am really grieved I shall not see again his good kind old face...As for the rest of the officers I can only rejoice that they have been killed, for they are some of the worst of the rebels. Ali Aga Dgabor was, I may, say, the worst. Abdul Vehab Effendi was the officer who went & complained to Stanley, & was one of the first promoters of the rebellion. Sheik Bacheet & Selim Aga were two very mischevious Soudanese, & Hassan Effendi Lutvi was a scoundrelly clerk who was always writing against the Pasha—so there are now five enemies out of our path. The truth is the soldiers did not wish to go & fight, but they were forced into it by their officers...

Unfortunately, however, it did not appear that any disaster would galvanize the now demoralized garrisons into concerted action.

What is so maddening is that no amount of disasters will ever teach these people common sense, they will not believe there is any danger until the enemy is actually at the gates, & then they will run away, meantime here are we who can see what will be likely to happen, cooped up like rats in a trap neither allowed to act nor to retire. Of course either Casati or I can retire tomorrow if we please, but without the Pasha, & that we do not intend to do. The steamer came in today so now they are both here but there is no wood ready for either of them so they cannot start, & this is the state of things which goes on even after a crushing defeat. Just before sitting down to luncheon the officers sent over to say they would like to come over & see the Pasha. They came in & after talking for a few minutes on indifferent subjects they began to speak about the real reason for their visit. They said they had decided to do as the Pasha wished & let him go to Wadelai where he would be free to go about as he pleased, but Fadl el Mulla Aga begged he would not conspire with people who would no doubt come to him to turn things upside down, the Pasha said he would not, for after what has happened he wished to have nothing to do with affairs of the country. Fadl el Mulla is awfully afraid of what has happened & fears the Pasha for he knows that at Wadelai & the Southern stations the Pasha has only to hold up his finger & everyone will come over to him. After a lot of talking it was decided we are all to start tomorrow in the big steamer for Wadelai. Sulieman Aga will come up by the return steamer & take us all on to Tunguru—from there it will be easy to reach Stanley when he comes. We owe this step chiefly to Sulieman Aga's influence, & things look much more hopeful for us now. The clerks are of course furious at what the officers have decided to do but as the chief rebel officers have been killed there is no one more to intrigue with. It will be a great relief to leave this place where we have been prisoners for just three months, there have been so many worries & so much unpleasantness all this time. We have to thank the Donagla for our immediate release from here, for the officers are really frightened at this last disaster, they told us that Faratch Aga Ajoke is missing also, but they think he has escaped to Makraka. In the evening I went with the Pasha to Selim Aga's house & the Pasha talked with him a long time. Everyone seemed pleased to see the Pasha out & many people came to greet him. Achmet Effendi Mahmoud went to talk some mischief to Fadl el Mulla Aga, but Sulieman Aga at once interrupted him & drove him out with a stick & said that any clerk who came near would have his head broken, he also said that Fadl el Mulla should leave the station & go back to Fabbo. The Pasha at Wadelai will be free to go & comes as he likes & do just as he pleases.

November 17th. We were all up early this morning & sent our things down to the steamer in good time. The farewell the Pasha received was a triumph over his enemies. The soldiers were marched down to the landing place & the Khedivial hymn was played, they were all drawn up in two lines & saluted as the Pasha passed between them; salutes were fired by the mountain guns & the whole station, with the exception of the five clerks, turned out 'en masse' to greet the Pasha & wish him God speed. Every one seems to breathe more freely now that he is at liberty again & they are no longer afraid of offending the rebel officers. All, nearly, came & kissed his hands & conducted him to the steamer in triumph, his own flag, as governour, was flying at the fore & two flags aft, as before the rebellion. At 7.30 we steamed away from Duffile amid loud spoken expressions of good will from everyone. The steamer has been going very badly all day, there was very little wood ready when we left so we have been obliged to stop for wood but we shall steam all night to make up time.

November 18th. I slept splendidly in the open air last night, I always do when I sleep out, at about one oclock in the night we stopped for an hour at a village called Bora to take in wood. I just woke up for half a minute & then went to sleep again in spite of all the noise of getting in wood. A third time we had to stop for wood this morning, so we did not sight the station of Wadelai till 2.30. On seeing the Pasha's flag flying at the fore every one flocked down to the water's edge; & when at 3 o'clock we steamed up to the landing place, the whole station nearly was assembled & the soldiers were all dressed in white & drawn up for saluting. When we were made fast all the officers clerks, civil servants & artisans flocked on board to greet the Pasha & escorted him with joyful acclamations up to his house in front of which a sheep was killed & we were made to step over its blood for luck. As we entered the compound the old negress, whom I have before mentioned as looking after the women of the station, came running forward & with tears pouring down her cheeks kissed the Pasha's hands & danced before him into the house holding her hands over her head & crying 'Allah be praised', there was something very ludicrous in the airy way in which the old hag danced. The soldiers all marched up before the Pasha's house and saluted, he said a few words to them & then they filed off before him. All the officers, clerks etc then came in & had coffee & after talking to the Pasha & congratulating him on his return here, left. In his private compound there must have been fifty or sixty women at a time who all came to kiss his hands & weep. Every one seems glad to have him back & the utmost contentment prevails, the faithfuls who have stuck to him, inspite of threats etc from the rebels, go about with grinning faces, showing the height of their delight that the bad days are over. The Pasha's return here is decidedly triumphant... The delight of once more being free, after three months semi-imprisonment in the middle of a noisy station, is very great; it is all so quiet here, at Duffile there was nothing to be seen, it was so low lying, here the station is built on the top of a hill & as one sits in ones room one gets a splendid view, through the open door, of the river winding below & the distant hills, with a great rolling grassy plain, dotted over with trees, between. When one has been accustomed to a low lying place for long, it is wonderful what an effect getting to the top of a high hill has on one's spirits & thoughts. I love to go by myself on some mountain & look down from a great height, one seems more or less to leave the littleness of one's nature in the valley below & with the wide view ones thoughts & ideas seem to expand & become elevated, to become freer & better, the Jews always built their altars on high places—this feeling has no doubt been strengthened by the long & miserable time we spent in the thick jungle with no view whatever & the relief one feels at being again able to see something is doubly strong.

November 19th. This morning numbers of people have been coming in to see the Pasha neighbouring chiefs, interpreters & noncommissioned officers, he has also had several sick people to attend to in the station. Kodi Aga, the chief of the station, is very ill with inflamation of the lungs, the Pasha has only just come in time to save him. He kissed the Pasha's hands several times when he went to doctor him & said how delighted he was to see him back again. Casati is laid up with muscular rheumatism in his legs—I can sympathise with him for I was a martyr to it myself at Dufile & used to lie awake night after night, I got it first when I was camping out on Beachy Head in the middle of November & Africa has not improved it...

November 29th. I have been out at some distance from the station & find that there are a good many teal & duck in the swamps just now, but on my return to the station I found myself perfectly covered with ticks, & after my bath my boy took 58 off my legs & feet. They are small & bury their heads in the flesh, it is quite impossible to take them off with the hands, one has to use tweezers. After a day or two, where each tick has been there is a little sore very much inflamed & the irritation of over 50 of these little sores on one's legs almost drives one mad...

The Pasha is turning out all his boxes & is discarding such things as are useless, he came on a letter of Doctor Juncker's in which he writes a good deal about the natives, he says after all the years he has been in Africa he has come to the conclusion that the natives are incapable of improvement, they will never rise, that the only thing to do is to try to improve their condition, that a mild treatment will never answer with them, but that they must be ruled by fear. This is pretty strong, & I do not think true, though perhaps it is partly so, there is just now in Germany a strong feeling against the negroes, which is as unjust in its contempt for them, as the feeling in England is absurd in its admiration for their supposed virtues & capabilities. It seems to me the just estimation of their character lies between the two opinions. The negroes never could become a great people or even a nation capable of governing itself, in the sense in which we understand government, but they could by education & mixing with Europeans become a very much higher & better people than they are at present. Even without contact with civilization certain peoples & tribes have become very much better than their neighbours. For instance the people of Uganda are in their way more civilized than the people of Unyoro, who in their turn are very much higher than the surrounding tribes, whilest the natives on the plains around Kavalli's are certainly higher than the people of Ibwiri, whilest the lowest people we have seen, are the bush natives of the upper Aruwimi. One of the first things a traveller notices when he enters Uganda is the cleaness of the people & their dwellings, as well as the goodness of their roads & the improved cultivation. Their household utensils, jars, baskets etc, are all beautifully made & their bark cloth is fine & in considerable quantities. Unyoro is the same in a lesser degree. The natives round Kavalli's make good houses & wear skins, particularly well cured, with all the hair taken off, except a narrow border which is left for ornamentation, & so the natives descend in the scale until they reach the lowest point, which I should say is reached by the people somewhere about the village of Aveysheba, after which they seem to rise in the social scale till they reach the Bangala on the Congo. Of course in speaking of these people I am only speaking of Central Africa, of the part I have seen. The great cleanliness of the Waganda is in itself a great step towards civilisation. The natives about Aveysheba are, judging from the appearance of the men we killed, rather a small, stunted race, with very villainous looking faces, they are peculiarly dirty looking, have long matted hair & a very unpleasant smell. Their houses are badly made & their cultivation is poor, they are cannibals & use almost exclusively poisoned arrows in warfare, their bows are the smallest I have ever seen, being only 18 inches from horn to horn but the black poison with which the tips of their arrows are encrusted is very fatal & out of all the men who were shot in that district, Stairs was, I think, the only one who recovered; all the rest died of lock jaw. It seems to me from what I have seen & heard—it is only a theory the truth of which I have not investigated very closely—is that taking Aveysheba as the point at which natives are at their lowest point of enlightenment & travelling towards the West along our track, the natives gradually improve until Bangala, after which the natives gradually deteriorate until the coast is reached—of course I do not count the natives who have felt the influence of European civilization. Again starting from Aveysheba & travelling East, the natives gradually improve until Uganda is reached, after which they gradually deteriorate as in the West. The two points therefore where natives have reached the highest state undisturbed by outer influences are two points about 600 miles from the sea, & the point where natives are in the lowest state is situated half way between the two. My idea is that the natives of Central Africa, like the Indians of America, will gradually give way before the approach of the white man, though the process will be immensely slower than it was in America. Natives, there will always be, of course, as there are so many parts of Africa in which a white man cannot live, but the people who will eventually be *the* people of Central Africa will be a race which will spring up from the mixing of black & white blood, & these will be the people who will cultivate the land, trade, & civilize the country & eventually perhaps become a great people—& assuredly they will possess a great & splendid country when it is all opened up to civilization. I know the existence of this mixed race has been deplored in India by many people, but I think European blood would mix better with African than it would with Indian blood & the result would in time be a good one. The Africans are liars, thieves, & cheats, it is true, but only from want of teaching, where as the East Indians are all that & more, & they have, more over, in place of the rollicking happy humour which Africans as a rule possess, a deep seated passion for intrigue & revenge—the Africans are more guileless, their minds are like an unwritten sheet. In talking with the Pasha the other day I mentioned my idea of a half caste nation eventually dominating Central Africa, & he said 'It is perfectly true, what you say is exceedingly likely'. He has always cherished an idea of introducing Chineese into Africa & had a long & interesting correspondence with Gordon on the subject, when he was Governor General, but Gordon whilest admitting the justness of his ideas objected on the plea that the Chinese were the most immoral people under the sun, & he therefore refused to further such a plan. Even Admitting they are very immoral, I think it was a pity he refused, for cheap labour & intelligence are all that are required for the rapid civilization of the country. I had such hopes of the Kavirondo scheme, but alas, that I fear now will never come to pass, this rebellion has made it impossible, unless it is begun under different auspices, the coming of the Donagla, too, would make it harder & could close three of the richest countries—Makraka, Monbuttu & Latooka & I may add Niam Niam[1] also, for no doubt the Donagla will overrun these countries, they will depopulate them by slave hunting & ruin them by exhausting the supply of ivory & by insufficient cultivation. There is no knowing where Madhdism will stop; possibly it will extend South & the movement will be joined by the Zanzibar Arabs of Manyema & so on down the Congo. Kodi Aga sent in a large piece of fish as a present, I never

[1] More correctly, Azande .The early travellers always spoke of the 'Niam-Niam'. The term was sometimes thought to suggest cannibal gusto.

saw any fresh water fish so large, it must have been over 10 ft long & thick in proportion. In the evening in answer to three or four imploring messages I paid a visit to Hawashi Effendi. He seemed very glad to see me & told me he was always alone, nobody ever came to see him—he has only himself to thank for that. However I sat & talked with him a long time, whatever he has done against the Pasha, & he has behaved very badly, he has always been particularly civil & obliging to me...

On 1 December rumours came in of a Mahdist advance from the Bahr el Ghazal direction, into the Makaraka region to within less than three days' march of Wadelai, and a deputation waited on the Pasha. The diary entry for that day contains an outburst from Jephson.

December 1st [1888]...It is true, there is no fathoming Egyptian effrontery, an Egyptian came to the Pasha yesterday & said all the people were greatly frightened at the rumours we have heard & at the non-arrival of the steamers, & wanted to know what was best to be done, he ended up by saying 'of course you are responsible for us all & cannot abandon us; we came from Egypt by the orders of the Government to serve under you & you must look after us'. The Pasha said 'Indeed! you seem to forget that I have a paper in which it is written that the officers have deposed me & no longer desire me to meddle with the affairs of the country or to be their Governour, this paper was written at Duffile & is signed by you all'. 'Oh' said the Egyptian 'that was all nonsense'. 'Nonsense or not I was kept in prison for three months & had I been free & allowed to act, you know perfectly well we never should have been in this predicament,' answered the Pasha, 'so I have absolutely no responsibility'.

Next day, 2 December, they were still waiting for the steamer, and in the afternoon the soldiers staged a demonstration, without their officers, and clamoured for the Pasha's reinstatement. Emin made a speech to them in which he refused to take on the governorship again, but assured them that his advice was always available to Kodi Aga, the station commander. Jephson and Casati were at one in agreeing that the speech was a mistake.

December 2nd...Casati & I groaned together over his speech to the soldiers, as Casati says, he has been a good governor, but he is not & has not been good for the present crisis, to use Casati's words 'il n'a pas de courage', he will not speak out plainly & firmly & say that they must not look to him for anything now, as everything has been taken out of his hands. All through the rebellion it has been the same...When the soldiers fell in in front of the house both Captain Casati & myself implored him not to commit himself in any way to them & he said he had'nt the slightest intention of doing so & was going to speak very firmly to them, but when he began to speak his words were by no means firm & he certainly raised hopes which, as I said before, he had no intention of carrying out unless obliged to do so. He said afterwards he was afraid of offending the soldiers by speaking out too plainly...No doubt in treating with these people it is often necessary to make a compromise, but these are no times now to make compromises, now is the time for plain speaking & very soon, if I'm not very much mistaken, it will be the case of 'sauve qui peut'. If Stanley were here he would very soon bring these people to their correct bearings...

December 3rd. This morning the Pasha has been to Kodi Aga & has told him he will not have any more such demonstrations as yesterday. Kodi Aga complains that people will not leave the station & go to Tunguru when they are ordered even though the carriers are ready to take their goods—from this it may be imagined what state of discipline there is now in the country.

Rumours poured in from the north that all the stations, including Dufilé, had fallen, and Jephson was able to persuade Emin to evacuate Wadelai. The *Advance*, which had brought the expedition up the Congo and had carried Jephson to his first meeting with the Pasha, was broken up.

December 4th... It was with a sore heart that I went down in the evening & unscrewed two of the sections & threw the bolts & spanners far out into the river. The poor old boat had been so useful to us & was still as good as new, I had always had to look after her, to put her together or take her to pieces, or to carry her with my own people when necessary. She had saved us many a weary mile & certainly had once saved the lives of Stanley, Stairs, Parke & I, for had it not been for the boat I never could have got the supply of Indian corn I did when we were starving. There she lies the poor old 'Advance' broken in three pieces on the sands of Wadelai, my three men, even, were sad at seeing her broken up & said 'Ah! she's been a good friend to us all', & Binza made a long lamentation over her—quite a second 'By the waters of Babylon' etc, he praised her powers of going & dilated upon all that she had done for us; he touched pathetically upon what I must feel on being obliged to destroy her after looking after her so long &, as he was pleased to say, managing her so well, he spoke of the Zanzibaris sorrow at not seeing her again & ended up with a moral upon the whole thing, a sort of 'Sic transit gloria mundi'! That boy is a regular character & often makes me laugh at the queer remarks he makes on people & things; he is a regular savage, but gives himself airs of civilisation & looks down with the greatest contempt on people whom he considers inferior to himself in cultivation & manners, he is a good boy however & is willing & ready & has a great idea of being considered a very good servant, he is at times possessed by the devil & has fits of idling & general 'cussedness' & the greatest punishment

I can inflict on him is to send for some one else to do his work...He is of the regular flat nosed negro type of the Niam-Niams, without any more profile than a currant bun has, his face however shows plainly he possesses the most humanizing of all influences—, the capacity of laughter.

Emin's priceless collection of birds was discarded and, hardly less important, his instruments; Jephson had to leave behind him not only his curios and souvenirs, but a number of useful articles in cotton and in wood, and a hoard of tobacco, which he had been saving up for his fellow officers. At the last moment, the soldiers refused to move, but the women and children straggled off in a pitiful procession which is movingly described in the diary.

December 5th. We were up before day break this morning to get everything ready for an early start if possible. The storehouses we[re] opened & all the ammunition was distributed amongst the soldiers, as well as the stores of all descriptions. Women & children came begging to be carried for they said they could not walk, the old women were given donkeys as far as possible, but I doubt many women & children will fall by the way. We got off by seven o'clock & as we left the station we could see a confused line of women & children & baggage stretching ahead for some three miles, all was utter confusion & hurry, some women were hurrying along carrying their goods & dragging little children or goats after them; others were seated mournfully in small groups with their children & loads before them waiting for their husbands or fathers to join them, whilest the noise of people shouting to each other, the crying of the children & the bleating & lowing of cattle & boats made a maddening din. At the last minute the soldiers refused to go, but we went on without them with such few officers & soldiers as were faithful. The whole road was strewn with things which people had taken & found too heavy to carry—the people, some of them, took the queerest things with them; I saw one man carrying in his load the four heavy carved legs of a bed stead; another had a great bunch of ostrich feathers, which he had heard were valuable in Europe; another was toiling along with a heavy cross cut saw; whilest others were carrying heavy round irons for baking bread, & even grinding stones for grinding corn, some of the people, too, took their parrots & one man had a cat in a basket. One saw men with some of the Pasha's thermometers hanging to their belts, they were under the impression that they were a sort of clock by which they could tell the time, it really was laughable only that one felt much more inclined to do the other thing; it is so awfully pathetic to see these poor half savage people toiling along with their loads stuffed with all sorts of the most useless rubbish & dragging or carrying their poor unfortunate little children. At one place we had to cross a broad shallow river with a steep bank on the other side, there the utmost confusion prevailed; the high bank was churned into a black slippery mud & women & children kept falling down & were trampled under foot by the press behind. It was perfectly heartrending to see them & hear their cries for help, I stood on one side & helped such women & children who had fallen to get up the bank & had occasionally to make a plunge amongst the press to save some little child from being trampled under foot; Until tired out & sick with the sight of it I had to hurry on after the Pasha to join the head of the column. People in Europe have a queer idea of what evacuation means in these countries, they say tell one to 'evacuate' just as they would tell one to eat one's dinner & evidently do'nt seem to think that the one is much harder than the other, they do'nt know the time it takes, the work it involves & the general despair of ever moving the people such an order produces, & then when they are got to move, what heart-rending, sickening sights one sees every day & what distress & misery a wholesale evacuation makes. After the river was passed we got on better but had to make frequent halts to allow the last of the women & children to come up. We camped at about 2.30 after having marched about 9 miles & the last of the people came in at 5. On the way one was painfully impressed afresh with the utter incapacity of the Pasha to act in an imergency, he has no firmness & never can give a decisive order he argues & talks with every-one & allows people to discuss his orders before his face—one quite longed to have Stanley here for a few days to reduce the whole people to a state of order & healthy subjection by his firmness. We heard from the last of the column when they got into camp that the steamers had come in to Wadelai & that all the soldiers women & children had returned & many of the people as well & our caravan was reduced to a fifth of its dimensions on leaving the station. Some people said the news was untrue, some said that the steamers contained the Donagla & others said it was the people from Dufile. We have no means of knowing the truth tonight, but shall probably hear all about it tomorrow. If it is the Donagla they will probably come on us in the night—if it is the Dufile people we shall hear by messanger tomorrow, in either case we go on now we have once started. We made our camp in the grass & slept in the open, small rough huts & shelters being made for the women & children; fortunately it is now the dry season. The people were all tired out & the camp was quiet early in the night.

December 6th. We were up early & got off by 6 o'clock, the people went somewhat better than yesterday, but from being unaccustomed to walk, their feet are very blistered & sore. At 9 o'clock we saw a steamer coming after us & thought it was all up with us, it kept up a constant whistling & two of our men fired off their guns, she came to the bank & it turned out that the two steamers had come in yesterday bringing refugees from Dufile, that Dufile had been attacked by the Donagla & after four days fighting the enemy had been repulsed with considerable loss. This accounted for the delay of the steamers, we heard also Fabbo had been evacuated & the people had retired to Dufile, it was the seige of Dufile by the Donagla & the evacuation of Fabbo which had given rise to the native report that both stations were lost. The soldiers thought when they saw the steamers approaching Wadelai that they contained Donagla & had received them with a brisk fire. A letter came from Kodi Aga the chief of Wadelai & from the people who had come up from Dufile begging the Pasha to return, the people were all anxious to make a triumphant demonstration & offer him their congratulations, but after the behaviour of the soldiers yesterday after all their promises, he had had enough of demonstrations, & he decided to go on to Tunguru & make the best of our way to M'swa. Casati & I used all our arguments to get him to go on & not to return, for when he wished to get away when Stanley arrives, it would be the same thing all over again, besides too we heard that the soldiers entered & plundered all our houses directly we left the station, so there is nothing to go back to except vexation & bother for the Pasha. We had a council in a little village at the top of a hill overlooking the river & everyone decided on embarking in the steamer, going to Tunguru & then sending her back with letters. The people as they came straggling up were delighted at the idea of being able to get into the steamer & indeed it was high time for their feet were awfully sore. We embarked on board the steamer & at 10.45 started off for Tunguru...We reached Okello's villages at 4.30 & as we were short of wood the Pasha decided to camp there tonight. We left all the women & children on board the steamer & went up to the villages & camped out in the open. Okello's country is about the prettiest country about; it is just like a great Park...

December 7th. We had big fires going last night & had our dinner, Arab fashion—i.e., eating all out of the same dish with our fingers—by the light of them [*sic*, ? the fires] we sat up smoking our pipes & talking over the news we had heard today & went to bed somewhat late, to thank the Good God we were not caught by the Donagla this time, & to sleep soundly, as one always does in the open. The dew is very heavy at this time of the year & one's mosquito nets were drenched in the morning. Okello's people brought in wood early this morning & he himself came to make his salutations to the Pasha & we got away by eight o'clock. At 11 we got to Boki's villages, where we stopped to take in wood & everyone went over the side for a swim in the clear water of the lake—these people never seem the least afraid of crocodiles; anything they do'nt see they are not afraid of. At 3.30 we steamed up to the station where every one turned out to greet the Pasha & express their contentment at once more seeing him amongst them. The officer from Wadelai in charge of the steamer decided to go back at once in order to lose no time & to reach Wadelai tomorrow, so the Pasha sent letters back to Kodi Aga & Selim Aga & sent one of his boys to try & save some of his things from the wreck—I told him also to look after my things & save what he could. Naturally so many people coming into the station without beds, chairs etc, was rather a tax on the people of the station & people were hurrying about arranging & borrowing until a late hour. Those people who have come with us are:— Osman Effendi Latif & family, Hawashi Effendi, Sultan Aga, Basilli Effendi, Signor Marko & Senor Vita, with all their women & children, some seven or eight clerks with their people & a whole host of minor persons. There is not much grain in the station, but in three or four days we shall start for M'swa, so it does not much signify. Our houses are not very comfortable without our things & I hope the Pasha's boy will be able to save some tables, chairs, lanterns, etc, for us. I do regret the boat terribly, but under the circumstances one was quite justified in destroying it & the council in asking me to do so. I shall not really feel safe until we are at M'swa then if things turn out badly we can take to the mountains & go to Kavalli's & on to Fort Bodo...

December 8th... The fleas last night gave one no rest; they were swarming in my bed when I got up this morning. A letter came in from Shookri Aga saying he was just about to start Mogo off with our letters to Stanley to Kavallis, but we sent a letter telling him to delay sending him for a bit & to wait till we came to M'swa, when we can give Stanley the last news & tell him better how to act...

December 9th. Nothing much happened today the people are all busy getting together a few things in place of those which had to be thrown away, I managed to buy some cotton cloth but it is fearfully expensive. One hears little incidents of the seige of Dufile & of the behaviour of the different people. We heard that the clerks who went & sat up to their necks in the river to hide from the Donagla were Achmet Effendi Mahmoud, the one eyed clerk, Sabri Effendi, Mustapha Effendi Achmet & the chief clerk, these are just about the worst lot of people in the Mudirieh; it is a pity there were not a few hungry crocodiles about at the time. It is evident even yet that people distrust Stanley & the object of his coming, for these same people who hid in the water tried to pursuade the officers to surrender to the Donagla when they appeared before the station, they said it was well to surrender at once, for it was better to surrender to Mahomedans than to infidels like the English. It is impossible to understand the minds of these people; you must be one of them before you can fathom the extraordinary ideas they get into their heads, as Mrs. Poyser[1] says 'you must be a bat to know what the bats are flying after' in the same way one must be an Egyptian

[1] In George Eliot's *Adam Bede*.

to know what Egyptians think of. A good many people have gone back to Wadelai to see if they can save anything from the loot & to bring the wives & children of the officers who were killed in the Regaf affray, here...

December 11th. Today canoes came in from M'swa bringing vegetables & letters from Shookri Aga for the Pasha. In the afternoon I went for a walk but on returning to the station found I was covered with ticks, it is impossible to go out now in the grass without getting covered with them.

December 12th. In the afternoon a sergeant came in from Wadelai & brought a number of letters. Kodi Aga tells the Pasha it is the wish of the officers that great rejoicings should be made in this station to celebrate the victory over the Donagla at Duffile & asks the Pasha to take part in & superintend the rejoicings, this of course he refused to do. Such ceremonies are great nonsense & waste of time, it would be a good deal better if the officers hurried up with the evacuation instead, & kept their energies for that, for the Donagla will most assuredly return after they have received reinforcements & perhaps even before & they will probably find the people still at Dufile. The Pasha's boy who was sent back to Wadelai to try & save what he could from the wreck, writes & sends a list of the things he found in the house on his return. The list is a very small one, for the soldiers were quick in their looting & have left hardly anything, they however left the Pasha's instruments & medicine chest which is something, & also a little salt & some corn. They broke open all the boxes & strewed such things as they did not want about the place. Ibrahim Effendi Elam writes to say that on the return of the Nyanza steamer from Duffile he will come in her here & join the Pasha. We hear that Sulieman Aga, when the Donagla were before Dufile, was preparing to sally out against them when he was set upon by five of the Donagla. He was alone with his boy only, but he killed three men himself & his boy killed one & the last man left fired at him & shattered the bone of his leg. I am very sorry for he would have been a very useful man on the road, far more useful than any of the other officers. I suppose if he goes out he will have to be carried, but it will require at least twelve men every day for he is a great big fellow & is enormously fat & broad. Selim Aga the newly elected Major was abandoned by his men & had to fight his way out of the Donagla with nothing but his sword. Bachet Aga also behaved very well. These are the few exceptional cases of bravery amongst the sea of cowardice of the soldiers & show up all the more plainly in consequence, it is satisfactory to find there are at least two or three men amongst these people who have a little courage & can behave like men occasionally. The captain of the Khedive steamer had his head cut open & one side of his face is so gashed that his teeth are laid bare. The Pasha has decided to remain here until he hears news from Dufile, it is rather annoying, as we are all anxious to get to M'swa from which place we can communicate more easily with Stanley, but it is I think better to remain for a bit, or the people might think we are running away. We are expecting the Nyanza steamer to come in from Dufile tomorrow or the next day.

December 13th & 14th. Nothing has happened, there is nothing going on & no books; the steamer has not yet come in. . .

Casati & I had a long talk yesterday about things in the Mudirieh, & I was glad to find he agreed with me almost entirely on the view I have taken of things here & the events which have happened. One of the things was that Felkin, Juncker & even the Pasha himself have given people in Europe a very wrong idea of things in this province. Felkin has absolutely written falsities, Juncker has not spoken about things he knew were happening in the country, he merely spoke about Emin Pasha's being in great difficulties, & gave people the idea that the difficulties chiefly consisted in difficulties from outside causes, instead of saying that the greatest difficulties were from internal causes, things actually to be feared from his own people. The Pasha wrote about the wonders his people had done in the war in Amadi, & how, after the last food had been eaten, they fought their way out. It was perfectly true, but he did not say how in every case his people had run before the Mahdi's people until the last, when they were surrounded at Rimo & people had been killed & women & children had been taken, in sheer desparation they had fought their way out, he has only told the good of his soldiers & not the immense mass of cowardice & insubordination which they showed before they finally screwed up their courage to fight, the whole story of that war was precisely the same as what has happened now. They do'nt mind seeing their women & children taken from them, but what they ca'nt stand is their stomachs pinching them. Now from the Pasha's letter all Europe thought his soldiers were heroes, it is perhaps natural that he should have written only of their prowess & suppressed their cowardice, still when he says, Mr Stanley thinks this, that & the other, one feels vexed for he has himself contributed to give us a false idea of things here, he has moreover said nothing about one half of his people being in open rebellion against him & many of the others being disaffected in his letters. We were led to believe that either he & his soldiers would follow us out of the country, or that they would receive us with a certain amount of gratitude, accept what we had brought them in the way of ammunition, clothes, etc. &, after perhaps staying a short time with them, we should go on our way to the coast wishing them well & having their good wishes with us also. But we did not expect, nor had anyone given us the slightest reason to expect, that after getting through the dangers & overcoming the difficulties on the road— & their name was legion—that the greatest danger of all awaited us, when we reached this country, in the shape of a plot, formed by the very people we had come to help, to seize & rob us of all that we had & then to turn us adrift. As I said before, Felkin has written absolute falsities, no doubt when he knew the country, things were very different to what they are now, still even at the time he was in the country his account would not have been true, for instance, he gives the number of the Pasha's soldiers as 5,000 bearing guns, whereas the Pasha tells me he never had more than 2,500, & that was counting all the interpreters & armed men who were not soldiers. Felkin gives the population of the Mudireh at 5,000,000, whereas it was from one & a half to two millions. He says the Pasha has taught the people to weave & make boots, it is not true; he probably did all he could to encourage such things, but the industry itself was introduced by such people as had been in the Soudan, at Khartoum & to the north of it. These are only few instances out of the many which I do not recollect. Felkin was very young, I do not think he was more than 24 or 25 when he was in this country, & he took evidently a young man's enthusiastic view of everything,[1] he did not go into the heart of the thing & judged only from the surface, & many of his facts are not correct; It is perhaps natural that he should have taken such an enthusiastic idea of everything here, for I know things were much better in those days, still it is unfortunate for the expedition that he should have been considered such an authority on affairs in Hatalastiva, for it has misled us terribly. Juncker is even more blamable, for he had only left the Province a year before we started on the expedition & he did not a bit make Stanley & people in general understand what a bad & rotten state things were in here & how if Emin Pasha did fall it would probably be owing to his own people. It is when the Pasha says Mr. Stanley & the people in Europe have queer ideas, that I feel angry, for it is only from Felkin's, Juncker's & his own writings that people have taken those ideas. The Pasha still believes in his soldiers in spite of the many evidences they have given him that they are not to be relied upon, they come before him & make protestations, which mean nothing, & he believes them. After the affair at Wadelai when he told the soldiers if he told them to start they must do so at once, & when he was asked to take charge of the people again when we heard Dufile had fallen, he said he would on the condition, that of implicit obedience to his orders, & they all made promises. I told him afterwards they would never start when he told them to do so, he said most emphatically they would do so & that he knew them for 13 years & I only knew them for six months. The result was as I predicted; when we all thought things were at the very worst they deserted him almost to a man, & the first thing they said when the ammunition in the storehouses was divided amongst them, that now they

[1] See Introduction above, p. 44.

had a lot of ammunition they would go on their own hook. The Pasha cannot bear to say 'I have deceived myself'.

In the entry dated 'December 15th 16th 17th,' Jephson recorded the arrival of the steamer, late on the night of the 17th, with wounded from Dufilé aboard. Two of the Pasha's servants came too with what they had been able to save from the wholesale looting at Wadelai—a number of books, some cotton cloth for Jephson and a fine trophy in the shape of an enemy spear captured at Dufilé. The enemy had indeed retreated, but Jephson was by no means sure that this would improve Emin's position. 'Now that the immediate fear of the Donagla has gone the party against the Pasha will again become powerful, though I trust it will never again preponderate', he wrote in this same long diary entry. Recorded too in these dispiriting December days are stories of the Dufilé fighting recounted by Suleiman Aga, who had come on to Tunguru in the hope that the Pasha might save his shattered leg. Jephson was astonished at the way the big Sudanese stood the pain of the probing for bone splinters patiently carried out by Emin, so much more admirable as a doctor than as a Governor.[1] The wound came about from the wild firing of his own soldiers, Suleiman Aga told them, and gave a poor account of his men in the fighting. All they seem to have done with any effect was to murder the captive dervish emissaries at Dufilé; since they believed them immune to ordinary bullets, they had clubbed them to death and thrown them to the crocodiles. 'They are charming people these so called soldiers', wrote Jephson, consoling himself for the dreary human prospect by communing with nature.

Every evening I take a walk along the shore of the lake, there is always a very strong wind in the evening & it is one of the greatest pleasures I have here to start off for a walk along the hard sand at 5.30. I do not generally get back till 7.30 & return home by moonlight. It is splendid to stand on the point & facing SW, down the lake, one sees nothing but water, with a great headland something the shape of Beachy Head, only three times higher, coming down, a great purple mass, sheer into the lake. A steady strong SW wind, warm & yet cool, blows with a force almost amounting to a gale & brings the great waves tumbling in on the flat sandy beach & throws up masses of weeds exactly like the sea. A long narrow spit of sand seperates the lake from great broad shallow lagoons inland, in which there are swarms of duck & geese, storks, ibis, herons, snipe, & various kinds of divers & plover all fishing & bobbing about in the water. It is along this narrow spit, which extends for miles, that I always take my walk with nothing round me but water & wild fowl, there is to me a great charm about it, though people laugh & wonder at my taking the same walk night after night . . .

[1] When, in 1894, Major Thruston, in the service of the Imperial British East Africa Company, was campaigning against Bunyoro, he met with the remnant of Emin Pasha's soldiers, those who had finally deserted under Fadl el Mulla. He asked them what they really felt about the Pasha: 'One officer said that Emin was a good hăkīm but no hăkīm—that is to say, a doctor but not a ruler, and this appeared to be the general opinion' (Thruston, *African Incidents* (London, 1900), p. 168).

Return to Wadelai

The year wore itself out slowly at Tunguru, the easing of the danger from the north reviving old intrigues. The entry for 'December 19th and 20th' records that a council is to be held at Wadelai to discuss, among other things a permanent settlement of Emin's people on the frontier of Unyoro—Kabarega's favourite raiding ground, observes Jephson, and therefore hardly suitable. He tried to make the time pass by calculating how soon Stanley was likely to arrive at Kavalli's and how soon they could make contact. The friendly local chief from M'swa, Mogo, had promised to take their letters to Kavalli's, an eight-day journey, and Jephson kept in constant touch with Shukri Aga. Meanwhile, demoralization had set in and incidents were frequent of the kind he describes in this same entry:

When the next steamer was about to return to Wadelai the clique of clerks brought down loads of corn to send to Wadelai, but there was a sort of mutiny amongst the soldiers who seized the corn & said that after the clerks & Egyptians had got them into all this trouble they were now getting together a stock of corn to take to Wadelai & the soldiers would be left without anything, they therefore seized the corn & said they would plant the officers & go & join the Pasha. Of course it all ended as it always does; the officers very soon pursuaded them into silence & things went on smoothly as before. If one was'nt so angry with them, one wd. find something pathetic in the blind brutish rage of these people who are going to do all sorts of things & then are easily brought down by a few words from the people who are doing their best to ruin them, they have such an immense idea of themselves that a few flattering words soon quiet them & a few goats or cattle are killed for the occasion & given them & they go off delighted, feeling that they are very fine fellows indeed & that they are going to stick up for their rights & are not going to be put upon; they do not in the least see that the clerks are making mere puppets of them—poor fools.

December 24th. The Pasha asked me today to go out & try to get a bird for the Christmas dinner, so I went out early & was fortunate enough to get some birds amongst others a big goose which is to be the 'piece de resistance' for dinner. Our Christmas dinner was today, according to the German custom held to by the Pasha of eating the Christmas dinner on Christmas eve. Casati & Signor Marko dined with us & after dinner we had some hot punch made of spirits of wine, hot water & honey, it wasnt half bad though it had rather a taste of furniture polish, but it was cheering & warm & was a great treat.

The following is the menue of the dinner.

Soup

Fish

Entrees Cutlets a la Hatalastiva. Hotch Potch. Roast Goose
stuffed with Ground nuts. Roast Beef.

316

Legumes	Kolokasias—Balmias—Haricots—Salad.
Entremets	Rice pudding—Banana Fritters—Fried bananas (meaning literally stick jaw, made of flour & honey oil)
Desert	Bananas—Papaws.

This really is a most creditable dinner to get out in the wilds.

December 25th. Christmas day. A most dreary Christmas day with nothing to do. The Pasha is still very seedy—bad chest, no sleep, sulky. Last Christmas day I spent in a shirt & pair of trousers ferrying the expedition across the Ituri river, after having swum across early in the morning to make a raft of banana trees, that Christmas day was, however, a more cheery one than this & Stairs & I were quite gay over our frugal dinner especially when Stairs brought out from the depths of his box a medicine bottle wrapped up in a bundle of rags containing about a gill of whiskey...

December 29th. At 10.30 last night Sulieman Aga died, the Pasha & I were with him in the evening & when the Pasha saw him he told me he could not last long. He was buried this morning. I attended the funeral, but as he was much hated there was a very scanty attendance, no soldiers were present except the fatigue party who dug the grave. The priest refused to say any prayers over his grave & everything had to be done by the Irregulars, these are the men whom he has beaten & ground down more even than his own people, but, they being a braver lot of men than the Regulars, are naturally more generous, so they buried him & had everything done decently...

When I killed the crested crane yesterday its mate flew about uttering the most pitiful cries & even followed the man, at a certain distance, who was carrying the body of its dead companion, this morning it came to the place where the feathers & head had been thrown out & uttered the most mournful cries—one felt like a murderer.

CHAPTER 15

REUNION WITH STANLEY

Book 3 of the diary begins with the New Year of 1889, in the second of the two exercise books Emin had given his friend at M'swa at the beginning of their time together. The month of January was spent on tenterhooks awaiting news of Stanley at the south end of the lake, while in the north the evacuation of the garrisons went on. Dufilé was finally abandoned and left in flames, the Madi and Shuli people harassing the retreating columns as they rose against the powers which had occupied their country. Jephson saw where the present situation would lead.

January 1st [1889]...If Wadelai & this station are evacuated the negroes will attack at once, for none of them like Egyptian rule, moreover directly we evacuate the country all natives who have lived peacibly with the Turks (as these people are called) will be destroyed by Kaba-Regga. It is very hard lines on them, they were forced to be friendly to Egypt & now Egypt is abandoning this country they will be destroyed by Kaba-Regga for having been so. It will be better for them if the Donagla come in, for they much prefer their rule to that of the 'Turks'. It is true the Donagla beat them & make them slaves, but when they make raids they take the natives with them & give them a share of the spoil again too they live with them on terms of comparative intimacy, in spite of their levying grain taxes on them with great irregularity & unfairness. But they much prefer this to the rule of the 'Turks' who are not allowed to ill use them, & levy taxes with comparative fairness & regularity, they seem to understand the irregularity & rough intimacy of the Donagla much better...

It was the season for burning the grasslands, and with his naturalist's eye Jephson noticed how the surviving bushes were stunted to 'merely nasty tempered looking bushes all ugly & twisted from peevishness'. The people too were on edge, and so were the Pasha and his friends. Chief Mogo, who should have left from M'swa for the south with letters for Stanley, was unaccountably missing. The Council was sitting again at Wadelai. Jephson curbed his impatience by getting out of doors as much as possible.

January 5th...I took a walk this evening through some swampy, rushy lagoons towards the mountains to try & get a hippopotamus, we are running short of soap & I want to get a supply of fat for making more, but they are scarce here & I was unable even to see one. 'Hippos' are very fierce here when they are out of water & readily attack a man when wounded. Several people have been fearfully mashed up & some have been killed by them. There were great numbers of crocodiles lying on the sand banks, but they are always very wide awake & plunge sullenly into the stagnant water before one can get a shot at them. These crocodiles of the lake & Nile are I fancy of a different species to those I have seen in confinement in England. These are much larger, heavier beasts & are of a lighter colour, being of a light yellowish green with broad black bands round them. I saw a great many plover and a good number of different kinds of herons, there is one sort one sees pretty frequently in this country & is the largest of the tribe; it is a great bird, of a blackish gray colour with a good deal of dull red on its throat & breast. There are also numbers of goat suckers or nightjars, of a peculiar form. They are large birds with very long wings & from each wing grow two long feathers a small distance apart, the stem of these feathers is quite bare except at the tip where it is shaped like the round tip of a peacock's feather, these feathers are very long & when the bird is flying it has a most peculiar appearance, as if the bird itself were being pursued by small birds which fly round over & under in all directions, the Arabs call the bird 'the father of the air' for this reason. The grass fires are magnificent on the mountains this evening, the whole sky being lighted up; the crackling of the burning grass being heard for miles in the still evening. We are just now experiencing one of the plagues of Egypt—the plague of frogs & or rather of toads, they actually swarm in the station & fill my house. If they kept to the floor I should'nt so much mind, but they climb up on to the tables & shelves and get into everything. If one turns over one's clothes toads hop out, or if one puts one's hand into a basket or bag to take anything out, one's hand encounters a fat cold clammy toad. I have had all the little boys in to collect & destroy them, we got hundreds but the next day they were just as bad as ever...

The country round Tunguru was in a disturbed state: forays to collect corn were resisted, and news from Wadelai was ominous. There was a rumour that Emin, Jephson and Casati had all been sentenced to death by hanging. Shukri Aga sent over from M'swa begging the Pasha to come on to him, where he would not only be safe himself but within three days' march of Kavalli and eventual reunion with Stanley. The Pasha, of course, hesitated; it might call down an attack on M'swa and the deposing of Shukri Aga if he went there, on the other hand Suleiman Aga's death had made the position at Tunguru dangerous. Jephson considered the situation in his diary:

January 10th...I should be inclined to go to M'swa, but as I am generally too hasty I distrust my own judgement & have not in any way tried to persuade the Pasha to go. Naturally of course I look a good deal at what will be best for Stanley & the people, whereas I do not think that enters much into the Pasha's calculations. Stanley has had orders to relieve him & must do it. The Pasha may be right I can only hope it will prove so but I fear...

January 11th...As I expected, the Pasha has decided to remain here yet awhile & see what happens, if we hear of Stanley's arrival we are to start at once the only question is, shall we be able to do so then? However I do not quarrel with his decision; it may be as well to wait yet awhile... The negroes all round are ripe for rebellion & a good deal of anxiety is felt in the station at the position of affairs, & this has been greatly increased by the news we heard yesterday that some of Kaba-Regga's people have crossed the lake & have slaughtered a young girl & a black bullock & have buried them only a few miles from here in Boki's country. This is the recognized method of declaring war against a country & obtains in Unyoro & Uganda. There is not the slightest doubt but that Kaba-Regga's emissaries have been very busy in the country ever since the Pasha's deposition, & now it appears he intends to make war on us, all the negroes will be ready to join him; they would be obliged to even if they did not wish it, but the natives during the last few years have been treated very bady by the soldiers & they will all be ready now to take their revenge...

On 13 January Shukri Aga wrote from M'swa that Stanley was reported only four days from the Lake, on the far side of the Ituri, but next day the entry begins 'Nothing doing' and goes on to describe the day's shooting.

January 21st. I have had an awful day of it with fever, a very sharp attack accompanied by a fearful pain in the side & I couldn't get my breath, however the Pasha was most attentive & gave me medicine & applied mustard plaster & some other doctor's stuff & rubbed & thumped & kneaded my side & in about an hour & a half I was able to breathe naturally again...

January 22nd. No sleep much last night, it was so hot, & I lay awake listening to the trumpetings of a herd of elephants which had approached the station, the second day after the fever one always, nearly, feels miserable; I feel like a broken down cabhorse, utterly gone in the knees.

January 23rd. Another attack of fever came on this morning & lasted till evening, it was a very strong attack & has left me quite nerveless & exhausted...

News filtered through from Wadelai that the officers sitting in Council had fallen out between themselves and next day:

After some very violent scenes amongst the officers & soldiers it has been decided that anyone who wishes to go out can go & those who wish to stay can stay, if this is true it is only what we wished in the first instance, & all this trouble for the last six months has been unnecessary...

On 26 January the long-awaited letters from Stanley came, written from 'Camp at Gaviras one day from Nyanza & I days march from Mazamboni's east'.[1] There were two for Jephson and one for Emin, and they were copied at once into the diary.

My dear Jephson,   January 17th/89

Your letter of Nov 7th/88 with 2 postscripts one dated Nov. 24th the other dated Dec. 18th is to hand and its contents noted.

I will not criticise your letter nor discuss any of its contents. I wish to be brief & promptly act. With that view I present you with a precis of events connected with our journey.

We separated from the Pasha on the 23rd of May last with the understanding that in about two months—you with or without the Pasha would start for Fort Bodo with sufficient porters to take the goods at the fort, & convey them to Nyanza. The Pasha expressed himself anxious to see Mt. Pisgah, & if words may be relied on he was anxious to assist us in his own relief. We somewhat doubted whether his affairs would permit the Pasha's absence, but we were assured you would not remain inactive. It was also understood that the Pasha would erect a small station, on Nyamsassie Island as a provision depot, in order that our expedition might find means of subsistance on our arrival at the Lake.

Eight months have elapsed & not one single promise has been performed. On the other hand we faithful to our promises departed from the Nyanza plain May 25th, arrived at Fort Bodo June 8th—15 days from the Nyanza. Conveying to Lt. Stairs & Capt. Nelson your comforting assurances that you would be there in three months, & giving Stairs & Nelson written permission to evacuate the Fort, & accompany you to Nyanza with the garrison which with the Pasha's soldiers would have made a strong depot of Nyamsassie.

I set out from Fort Bodo on the 16th June to hunt up the Major & his column, alone unaccompanied by any officer. On the 10th August we overtook our courriers who had left Fort Bodo on the 15th Feb. with Stairs. Of the 20 courriers 3 had been killed 2 were so debilitated by the effects of arrow poison that they eventually died, fifteen were left but only 1 has carried. On the morning of Aug. 17th at 10 am we sighted the rear column at Banalya—90 miles (English) from Yambuya—592 miles from the Nyanza, on the 63rd day from Fort Bodo & the 85th day from the Nyanza Plain. The rear column which on our departure from Yambuya numbered 271 all told was a mere wreck. Major Barttelot was dead—had been shot by a gun of one of Tippu Tib's Manyema on the morning of the 21st July just 27 days before my arrival, Mr. Jameson had departed on the 23rd July for Stanley

---

[1] 'Mazamboni's west' in *Emin Pasha*, obviously the correct location.

falls & a letter dated August 12th, five days before my arrival at Banalya states that he was about descending the Congo for Bangala—but the couriers who brought his letter to us stoutly asserted his last intentions were to go down to Banana Point. Mr. Herbert Ward had been sent to Bangala & finally to St. Paul del Loanda! He had returned & reached Bangala with letters & instructions from the committee but was detained there by order of Major Barttelot. Mr. John Rose Troup had been invalided home in Feb/88, so no-one was left with the wreck of the rear column except William Bonny, who is now with me in this camp. 100 Soudanese, Zanzibaris & Somalis had been buried at Yambuya—33 men were left at Yambuya, helpless & dying & 14 of these died later on—26 deserted so that when I saw Bonny & his people the rear column, Zanzibaris, Somalis & Soudanese numbered 94 all told! out of 271! & only 1 officer out of 5! Besides this deplorable record the conditions of the stores was just as bad—Out of 660 loads of 65 lbs each—there remained only 230 loads of 65 lbs weight. All my personal clothing except Hats, boots, flannel jacket a cane & 3 pr drawers had been sent down to Bangala because rumour had stated I was dead & the advance party gone to the dogs—a remnant of 30 however had managed to escape to Ujiji!!!

I sent my despatches to Stanley Falls & thence to Europe & on the 31st August commenced my return towards the Nyanza. Two days before the date stated I was at Fort Bodo—Dec 20th. On Dec. 24th we moved from Fort Bodo towards the Ituri ferry. But as your non arrival at Fort Bodo had left us with a larger number of goods than our own force could carry at one time we had to make double journeys to Fort Bodo & back to the Ituri Ferry but by the 10th January all that remained of the expedition with all its effects were on this side of the Ituri River, encamped ½ mile from the Ferry with abundance of food assured for months. On the 12th January I left Stairs, Nelson, Parke & William at the Ituri Ferry camp with about 150 people all told & started for the lake with 210 people all told to obtain news of the Pasha & yourself. Your absence from the Fort—& the absolute silence respecting you all—made us suspect that serious trouble had broken. Yesterday your letter as above stated came to hand & its contents explained the trouble.

The difficulties I met at Banalya, are repeated today near the Albert Lake & nothing can save us now from being overwhelmed by them but a calm and clear decision. If I had hesitated at Banalya—very likely I should still be there waiting for Jameson & Ward with my own men dying by dozens from sheer inanition. And when I should have started at all I should have found my strength, stores & men exhausted. But the officers were plunged in their own follies, the rear column was wrecked by indecision. Barttelot, Jameson & Ward reaped only what they had sown.

Are the Pasha, Casati & yourself to share the same fate? If you are still victims of indecision—then a long good night to you all—but while I retain my senses—I must save my expedition. You may be saved also if you are wise.

In the 'High Order' of the Khedive dated 1st Feb/87 No 3, to Emin Pasha a translation of which was handed to me I find the following words:

'And since it is our sincerest desire to relieve you with your officers & soldiers from the difficult position you are in our government have made up their mind about the manner by which relief from these troubles may be obtained.

'A mission for the relief has been formed & the command of it given to Mr. Stanley the famous etc. etc., & as he intends to set out on it with all necessary provisions for you so that he may bring you with your officers & men to Cairo by the route he may think proper to take.

'Consequently we have issued this High order to you & it is sent to you by the hand of Mr. Stanley to let you know what has been done. As soon as it reaches you convey my best wishes to the officers & men. And you are at full liberty with regard to your leaving for Cairo or you stay there with officers & men.

'Those who wish to stay there of the officers & men do so on their own responsibility, & they may not expect any assistance from the government.

'Try to understand the contents well & make them well known to all the officers & men that they may be fully aware of what they are going to do.'

It is precisely what the Khedive says, that I wish to say to you. Try & understand all this thoroughly that you may be saved from the effects of indiscretion, which will be fatal to you all if unheeded.

The first installment of relief was handed to Emin Pasha on or about May 1st/88. The second final installment of relief is at this camp with us ready for delivery at any place the Pasha designates or to any person charged by the Pasha to receive it. If the Pasha fails to receive it or to decide what shall be done with it—I must then decide briefly what I must do.

Our second object in coming here was to receive such at our own camp as were disposed to leave Africa—our Expedition has no further business in these regions & will at once retire. Try & understand what all this means. Try & see the utter & final abandonment of all further relief, & the bitter end & fate of those obstinate & misguided people who decline assistance when tendered to them. From May 1st/88 to January/89 are nine months—so long a time to consider a simple proposition of leaving Africa or staying here!

Therefore in the official & formal letter accompanying this explanatory note to you I designate Kavalli's village as the rendezvous where I am willing to receive those who are deserious of leaving Africa—subject of course to any new light thrown upon the complication by a personal interview, or a second letter from you.

And now I address myself to you personally. If you consider yourself still a member of this expedition subject to my orders—then upon receipt of this letter you will at once leave for Kavalli's with such of my men, Binza, & the three Soudanese as are willing to obey you & bring to me the final decision of Emin Pasha, Signor Casati respecting their personal intentions. If I am not at Kavalli's—then stay there & send word by letter by Kavalli's messengers, to M'pinga—Chief of Gavira's who will transmit the same to Mazamboni's—where probably I shall be.

You will understand that it will be a severe strain on Kavalli's resources to maintain us with provisions for longer than 6 days & if you are longer than this period we must retire to Mazamboni's & finally to our camp on the Ituri Ferry. Otherwise we must seize provisions by force & any act of violence would cut off & close native communication, this difficulty might have been avoided had the Pasha followed my suggestion of making a depot at Nyamsassie. The fact that there are provisions at M'swa does not help us at all. There are provisions in Europe also, but unfortunately they are as inaccessible as those of M'swa. We have no boat now to communicate by Lake—& you do not mention what has become of the steamers, the Khedive & Nyanza.

I understand that the Pasha has been deposed & is a prisoner. Who then is to communicate with me respecting what is to be done? I have no authority to receive communications from officers—mutineers. It was Emin Pasha & people I was supposed to relieve. If Emin Pasha was dead then his lawful successor in authority. Emin Pasha being alive I can receive no communication from any other person unless he be designated by the Pasha. Therefore the Pasha, if he be unable to come in person to me at Kavalli's with a sufficient escort of faithful men, or be unable to appoint some person authorized to receive this relief—it will remain for me to destroy the ammunition so laboriously brought here & return home.

You must understand that we are perfectly unable to assist Emin Pasha by force. My people are mere porters incapable of standing before a volley of Remingtons. They have performed their contract with me with a fidelity unexampled, & having brought the boat & goods here, their duty is ended. You have been pleased to destroy the boat & have injured us irreparably by so doing. I presume the two cases of Winchester ammunition left with the Pasha are lost also.

I ought to mention also that the people at the Ituri River Ferry camp are almost all sick & will be unable to move for at least a month.

And also I have brought with me about 100 Manyema—with 42 of whom I have contracted to pay a tusk of ivory to each, for 42 loads they have brought here for Emin Pasha. Therefore to satisfy them I require 42 tusks of ivory to pay them. Please consider how this can be done to their satisfaction. Also consider how we are to be supported by food pending the termination of this eventful part of our journey—if we have to return to the neighbourhood of Kavalli's or the Lake, to await this long deferred decision on the part of the Pasha & his men.

Finally if the Pasha's people are desirous of leaving this part of Africa & settle in some country not far remote from here or anywhere bordering the Nyanza (Victoria) or along the route to Zanzibar—I am perfectly ready to assist, besides escorting those willing to go home to Cairo safely, but I must have clear & definite assertions followed by promptitude according to such orders as I shall give for effecting this purpose, or a clear & definite refusal as we cannot stay here all our lives awaiting people who seem to be not very clear as to what they wish.

Give my best wishes to the Pasha & Signor Casati & I hope & pray that wisdom may guide them both before it is too late. I long to see you my dear fellow & hear from your own lips your story.

Yours very sincerely
Henry M. Stanley

To A J Mounteney Jephson, Esq.
STRICTLY PERSONAL

Kavalli's January 18th/89 3 pm.

My Dear Jephson,

I sent a brief note of news from Mazamboni's the same day I arrived there, with a view to confirm a rumour of our being in the neighbourhood, if any such was afloat, I hear that on arriving here that the note was put into the hands of Mogo who stopped at Kyan-Kondo's who seems to have built his new village on the very spot where we met the Pasha & yourself the day of arrival at the Lake.

I now send 30 rifles & three of Kavalli's men down to the Lake with these letters with urgent instructions that a canoe should set off—& the bearers be rewarded.

I may be able to stay longer than six days here perhaps ten days. I will do my best to prolong my stay here until you arrive without rupture. Our people have a good store of beads & cowries & cloth & I notice that the natives trade very readily which will assist Kavalli's resources in case he gets weary at our prolonged stay.

If you can bring anything in the way of food such as a store of grain or a few head of cattle then of course matters will be smooth for a stay of many days. Some of the Pasha's whiskey would be desirable also as well as a little oil for the whites for cooking.

Be wise be quick & waste no hour of time & bring Binza & your own Soudanese with you. I have read your letters half a dozen times over, but I fail to grasp the situation thoroughly, because in some important details one letter contradicts the others. In one you say the Pasha is a close prisoner— while you are allowed a certain amount of liberty—in the other you say you will come to me as soon as you hear of our arrival here—& 'I trust' you say 'the Pasha will be able to come with me to see you'. All this is not very clear to us who are fresh from the bush. How being prisoner you could leave Tunguru at all I fail to see.

If the Pasha can come send on your arrival at Kyan-Kondos a native courrier to announce the fact & I will dispatch a strong detachment to escort him up here—even to carry him if he needs it.

I feel too exhausted after my 1300 mile march to go down to the Lake again. I hope the Pasha will have a little pity for me. Do'nt be alarmed or uneasy on our account. Nothing hostile can approach us within 12 miles without my knowing it. I am in the midst of a friendly population & if I sound the war note—within four hours I can have 2000 warriors to assist to repel any force disposed for violence. And if it is to be a war of wits—why then—I am ready for the cunningest Arab alive. I said above that I read your letters half a dozen times & my opinion of you varys with each reading. Sometimes I fancy you are half Mahdist, or Arabist, then Eminist I shall be wiser when I see you.

Jameson paid a thousand pounds to accompany us. Well you see he disobeyed orders & we left him to ponder on the things he had done. Ward, you know was very eager to accompany us, but he disobeyed orders & he was left at Bangala a victim to his craving for novel adventures, Barttelot poor fellow, was mad for Kudos, but he has lost his life & all a victim to perverseness.

Now do'nt you be perverse, but obey—& set my order to you as a frontlet between the eyes, & all with God's gracious help will end well.

I want to help the Pasha somehow, but he must help me & credit me. If he wishes to get out of this trouble I am his most devoted servant & friend, but if he hesitates—something rises within me which causes me excessive wonder & perplexity. I could save a dozen Pasha's if they were willing to be saved. I could go on my Knees & implore the Pasha to be sensible in his own care. Wise enough in all conscience in all things else—save his own interest. Be kind & good to him for many virtues but do not you be drawn into that fatal fascination Soudan territory seems to have for all Europeans of late years. as soon as they touch its ground they seem to be drawn into a whirlpool which sucks them in & covers them with its waves. The only way to avoid it is to obey blindly & devotedly unquestioning all orders from the out side.

The committee said relieve Emin Pasha with this ammunition. If he wants to come out the ammunition will enable him to do so. The Khedive said the same thing, & added but if the Pasha & the officers elect to stay—they do so on their own responsibility. Baring said the same thing clear & decided—& here I am after 4100 miles of travel with the last installment of relief. Let him who is authorised to take it take it—Let him who wants to come out of this devouring circle come—I am ready to lend all my strength & wit to assist him. But this time there must be no hesitation—but positive Yea or Nay—& home we go.

> Yours very sincerely
> *Henry M Stanley*

To A M Jephson Esq.,

P.S. Yesterday four letters were brought to me in the midst of a bad attack of fever. Today I am all right & have marched nearer to you by eight miles & it is bright sunshine.

The following is Stanley's letter to the Pasha.

> Camps at M'pinga's long march from Nyanza
> *& 10 miles East of Maʒamboni's.*

To
His Excellency Emin Pasha

> *Governor of Equatorial Province.*

Sir,

I have the honor to inform you that the second installment of relief which this expedition was ordered to convey to you is now in this camp ready for delivery to any person charged to receive it by you. If you prefer that we should deposit it at Kavalli's or at Kyan-Kondo's on the Lake we shall be ready to do so on the receipt of your instructions. The second installment of relief consists of 60 cases Remington Cartridges 26 cases of gunpowder each 45 1lbs weight—4 cases of percussion caps, 4 bales of goods, 1 bale of goods for Signor Casati—a gift from myself—two pieces of blue serge writing paper envelopes, blank books, etc. Having after great difficulty, greater than was anticipated brought relief to you, I am constrained to officially demand from you receipts for the above goods & relief brought to you, & also a definite answer to the question if you propose to accept our escort & assistance to reach Zanzibar—or if Signor Casati proposes to do so, or whether there are any officers or men disposed to accept our safe conduct to the sea. In the latter event I would be obliged to you if you would kindly state how those persons desirous of leaving Africa can be communicated with.

I would respectfully suggest that all persons desirous of leaving with me should proceed to & form camp either at M'sabe or at Kyya-nKondo's on the Lake, with sufficient stores of grain etc to support them one month & that a note should be sent to me to inform me of the same via Kavalli's whence I soon may receive it. The person in charge of the people at this camp will inform me definitely whether the people are ready to accept of our safe conduct & upon being thus informed I shall be pleased to assume all further charge of them.

Here below I beg to present you with an approximate statement of our movements pending the receipt of your answer which is compulsory on us owing to the fact that in the vicinity of the Lake the supply of food is very precarious & uncertain unless seized by force which considering the state of affairs in your province would be highly impolitic.

18th January we shall be at Kavalli's.

19th	,,	Halt	,,
20th	,,	Halt	,,
21st	,,	Halt	,,
22nd	,,	Halt	,,
23rd	,,	Halt	,,
24th	,,	Halt	,,

25th   we shall return to M'pingas 10 miles from Mazambonis.

26th   ,,   to Mazamboni's 10 miles.

27th   ,,   camp 13 miles.

28th   ,,   Kapogiri 12 miles.

29th January we shall return to Stairs camp on the Ituri 12 miles.

20th   ,,   Halt ⎫

31st   ,,   Halt ⎬ for resting the people.

1st February   ,,   Halt ⎭

2nd   We march to Kapogiri 12 miles.

3rd   ,,   to camp   12 miles.

4th   ,,   to Mazamboni's 10 miles.

5th   ,,   to M'pinga's   10 miles.

6th   ,,   to Kavalli's   10 miles.

If at the end of 20 days no news has been heard from you or Mr. Jephson I cannot hold myself responsible for what may happen. We should be glad to stay at Kavalli's if we were assured of food—but a large following cannot be maintained there except by exacting contributions by force which would entirely close our intercourse with the natives & prevent us from being able to communicate with you.

If grain could be landed at KyanKondo's by steamer left in charge of 6 or 7 of your men, I could on being informed of the fact send a detachment of the men to convey it to the plain. It is only the question of food which creates anxiety. Hence you will perceive I am under the necessity of requesting you to be very definite & prompt if you have the power.

If within this period of 20 days you will be able to communicate with me & inform or suggest to me anyway I can make myself useful or lend effective aid I promise to strain every effort to perform service to you. Meanwhile awaiting your answer with great anxiety I am

Your obedient servant
Henry M Stanley

These are the letters; of the letter to the Pasha I say nothing—it is merely an official letter. But his letter to me is in many ways greatly wanting in common sense & I think the way he speaks about the officers of the rear guard is not very pleasant. He seems to forget he told them he would be away at the outside 6 months & in point of fact was gone 14 months, meanwhile these people were left encumbered with loads, unable to move, & the men, from his description, dying like flies, they could have hardly anything moreover to eat. However I reserve my judgement of the whole until I hear the story from Bonny, the sole remaining European of the rear guard. Stanley's stories are never very just in matters of this kind & I suspect there is a good deal more in the real story than meets the eye in his letters. Immediately I had communicated with the Pasha we told Casati of the news & spread it also in the station. Poor Barttelot's death is most tragic & sad, & will create a profound sensation at home where he is fairly well known. Poor fellow he was so bright & full of life & go—indeed the whole story is a very dark one, as dark as any of the many dark stories connected with African travel. Ward's having returned to St Paul de Loanda & set such news (false news) afloat is very bad & will have a very bad effect in Europe. No doubt my people will all consider I'm dead—well I should be no great loss that I know of. Immediately on receiving the letters I sent for Saleh Aga & told him I must have carriers ready to start tomorrow morning for M'swa from which place I shall proceed in canoes to M'sabe & from thence ascend the mountains to Kavalli's there to await Stanley's return from the Ituri river.

In the evening the steamer came in bringing Hawashi Effendi & a lot of clerks & refugees, from Wadelai.

It was decided therefore that I should go in the steamer to M'swa & perhaps to M'sabe in her if the steamers people would take me. We sat up late talking over the awful news Stanley's letters contained & the method of imparting that news.

Jephson left by steamer for M'swa on 28 January, arriving late that evening to be warmly welcomed by Shukri Aga. Here he was held up again by the lack of wood and the reluctance of the steamer's crew to take him on down the lake, and here his heart began to fail him, when a strange and moving incident occurred.

January 29th . . . I was sitting out in the evening before dinner, by myself thinking of their helplessness & ingratitude utterly tired out by trying to arrange things for them & show them what was for their own interest, & I was thinking how unworthy they were to be helped & how utterly devoid of all sense of appreciation of our disinterested wish to help them, when in the dark there was a flutter of a white garment & before I knew where I was a negro woman had prostrated herself on the ground before me & kissed my feet. She had come to thank me for wishing & trying to help the people & as I started tomorrow morning she had come to thank me & prayed that Allah would bless me for coming to help them. She had brought me a small offering for the journey. Before I could prevent it she had again kissed my feet & disappeared leaving me 'planté la' with two clean straw trays on the ground before me. I called my boy & asked who she was but he did not know; nobody had seen her. One of the trays contained some dry kuskussu & 6 fresh eggs, & the other a chicken very nicely cooked & clean but in a common wooden plate which she had tried to hide by piling bread round it. Poor thing, I was awfully touched at her bringing me this little offering no doubt she was some poor woman & she had given me of her best, & woman-like she thought of one's creature comforts. So after all, the people are not as wholly ungrateful as I supposed, but it remained for a woman to show it, probably some poor creature who was accustomed to be beaten & looked on as a mere beast of burden or an inferior animal. I went to bed very tired at an early hour as I must be up at dawn tomorrow to arrange things for the start.

When, on rising early next morning, he saw the steamer far out in the lake making the best of her way back northward to Tunguru (30 January) 'I was too far gone to do more than shrug my shoulders & think this was a fitting climax to all their actions for the last six months'. He got away finally in a canoe on the 31st. On the afternoon of 3 February they passed the old camp at Nsabé and in the evening reached Nyamsassie's island, peopled by a fine-looking tribe of men whose chief occupation was the making of salt. Jephson was disgusted with the arrogance of his soldiers who ordered about these handsome people who cheerfully helped in every way asked of them.

From Nyamsassie's they struck inland, and with the country restless with rumours of invasions from Bunyoro it was difficult to secure carriers to take them to Kavalli's. The entry for 6 February at last reports progress and the eventual reunion with Stanley's men.

February 6th [1889]. Up early this morning to get off in good time so that we should have finished the ascent of the mountains before the sun got very hot, but he who trusts the natives is generally doomed to disappointment & must have an almost inexhaustable stock of patience. Katonza, in spite of his emphatic promises that everything should be ready, came & told me that his people had not yet come in sufficient numbers to permit of his sending carriers with me. I talked with him a long time with a sort of impatient patience & explained to him that he had asked me to lay his story & complaints before Stanley, & if he vexed Stanley by not giving me people at once to carry my loads, he was much less likely to notice his story, so after much talk & many arguments he consented to give me 8 carriers, & I said I would leave three loads with him, & he promised to send them up to me on the morrow when his people came in. Under these conditions I started at 7.30 & I noticed that one of my carriers was a little thin looking woman & she had picked out the heaviest load of all, & yet she kept up with the men & carried her load up the mountains with apparently no great effort. We went gaily along through the lovely park like plain in which great herds of hartbeest, Kudu, & Springbok were feeding it looked all so lovely & ones spirits rose as one ascended the mountains & got into the clear, cool, breezy atmosphere of the tablelands. When we were about three quarters of the way up the mountains & were just taking a rest in the shade by the side of a rushing stream, Masa called out that he saw people with gay coloured clothes descending the winding path in the distance these turned out to be 30 Zanzibaris Stanley had heard from the natives the day before that I had landed & had at once sent his people to fetch me. The Zanzibaris showed great delight at seeing me again; they all came rushing up in their boisterous way with congratulations & words of welcome & Uledi fairly took me in his arms & embraced me. They told me that Stanley was terribly uneasy about my nonappearance & the absence of news & each day became more & more anxious, & had at last decided to send for Stairs & the rest of the expedition—he himself finding there was plenty of food coming in from the natives had remained at Kavalli's since the 18th. It was a very long march & I stopped on the way & had a delicious bathe in a shady stream & had a change of clothes so that I arrived at camp decently dressed. Stanley had all men fallen in to receive me, but as I approached they all broke from the ranks & surrounded me shouting congratulations & shaking hands—it was delightful to be so boisterously welcomed after one had been smarting for many months under the treatment of the Soudanese & Egyptians. Stanley received me in his usual calm way, tempered however by a smile.—I think he was glad to see me. The camp which is close to Kavalli's village is of a good size; the Zanzibaris have built grass huts all round & Stanley's tent is pitched in the middle & a nice little house was built for me close to it. Bonny alone is with Stanley & all the three officers Stairs Nelson & Parke are at the camp on the Ituri with the sick & some loads. I dined with Stanley & we sat up till late exchanging news. I explained as well as I could the position of the Pasha & gave Stanley to understand as is most emphatically the case that the principal obstacle to our rescuing him is himself.

It is impossible to write the story of Stanley's return journey and experiences yet one will have to wait a few days till one can take it all in. There were two letters for me one from Rosanna containing an enclosure from Mary & another. Both envelopes bore the postmark of June 20th/87, that is they were written eighteen months ago but famished as I was for news from home I read & reread them several times.—they were not exactly satisfactory any of them, but one has got so used to disappointment ever since we left England that one hardly now expects anything else. I had also a short note from Stairs saying he had a bag with clothes in it which had been left at Yambuya by me, but apparently many of the clothes had been taken out— & he had also a box of European provisions & amongst them 6 tins of milk I am very glad of this as I shall be able to give them to the Pasha if he comes with us for his little girl—it is just what he wants. It was late when I got to bed dead tired by the very long march I have done today.

Next day Stanley called in all the people and loads from the Ituri, and was planning to collect Emin, when the Pasha's approach was announced. The diary does not say that the party brought the boat, salvaged from Wadelai, as well as the ivory (see *Emin Pasha*, pp. 446–7).

February 13th... Since I have been here Stanley has asked me to have my meals with him a thing I have never known him do before. We were sitting together talking after dinner when a native came in bringing a letter. Stanley tore it open in great excitement & tossed an enclosure over to me, it was from the Pasha who arrived the day before at Were near Nyamsassie Island. He had brought with him Selim Aga (now a Bey) Bilal Aga who fought so well in Dufile, Surore Aga who tried to kill us at Labore & several others Clerks etc. with their wives & children. It appears that Selim Bey receiving my letter he read it out before all the officers & he at once decided to come in the steamer & see Stanley. There were as a matter of course great discussions amongst the officers who wished to go out & those who wished to remain, & the quarrel became violent. But the officers & soldiers were rather alarmed to hear that I had actually got out of the country without their permission & had probably reached Stanley by the time they got the letter so Selim Bey prevailed & a number of officers & people took the steamer bringing with them 60 tusks of ivory to pay Tippoo Tib's carriers & started for Tunguru to consult with the Pasha. On arriving there they all came before him & asked him to go down with them to Stanley. He at first refused but at length said he would go as far as M'swa so he started off with them taking Casati, Vita, Marko & as many people as the steamer would hold with him. After waiting a few days at M'swa the officers again came to him & begged him to accompany them, he asked them in what capacity they wished him to go & they told him as their interpreter upon which he said, that was impossible he could never go in that capacity, so after going away & talking among themselves they came in a body & made their submission & asked him to go as their Governour & on this understanding he consented to go. Shookri Aga was of course delighted at the turn affairs had taken & made great rejoicings in the station. The Pasha then made Selim Aga a Bey (equal to Lieut Colonel) & told him to send him in the names of such officers as had behaved well in the seige of Dufile. On the names being given in he made several promotions & promoted Shookri Aga, on his own account, to the rank of Captain—he was only 2nd Lieut before. After this they all started in the steamer for Were & arrived the day before yesterday. So after all all is well & we shall not have to march to M'swa everything is as we wanted & the ivory is here to pay the carriers. Stanley was delighted with the news & said to me leaning across the table, 'Shake hands on it old fellow we'll be successful after all'. I shook hands most heartily & told him if any one deserved success he did. He told me that on the morrow I must start down with a lot of Zanzibaris & natives & fetch the Pasha & his loads up here at once—it is just what I wish of all things. Stanley then went out & called to the Zanzibaris that he had something to tell them, they all came running up & he told them the news. They all shouted & cheered most tremendously & were delighted with the news & shouted out many complimentary things about 'Bubarika' (that's me) & seemed to put down the success to my door. After talking over things with Stanley I retired to make preparations for an early start tomorrow morning.

February 14th. I started off at about 7 o'clock with 65 Zanzibaris & about the same number of native carriers. Stanley had given me orders to bring up the Pasha & his loads & such officers as wished to come up & consult with him—these officers after consulting with him will return to Wadelai to remain or to bring out their families as the case may be. We got down the

hill in good time but the natives who led us did not seem to know the way
to the Pasha's camp & took us down a very bad mountain road, & then in
a semicircle through the plain, so that we did not arrive at the Pashas camp
till past four after a hot & weary march of 17 miles a great part of which was
mountain road, the result was we arrived footsore, tired & parched with
thirst for there was hardly any water on the way & that only of the filthiest
description—there were herds of antelope of all kinds & numbers of buffaloes & pig but the people were too weary to leave the path to shoot them
& only thought of getting in to camp. On arriving however in spite of their
weariness the Zanzibaris rushed madly into camp shouting at the top of their
voices & went through their usual mad antics expressive of their satisfaction
at seeing the Pasha, they surrounded him shouting out all kinds of welcome
—he stood amongst them laughing & looked very pleased. I could not help
smiling at the faces of the Soudanese soldiers when they saw the antics of the
Zanzibaris they stood looking on with their unsmiling heavy, sullen, brutish
faces, wondering what kind of people these laughing boisterous & apparently
unruly Zanzibaris could be. I felt almost inclined to hug the dear old pasha,
I was so pleased at getting him once more amongst us. I know my own feeling
of intense contentment when I first arrived a few days ago at Stanley's camp.
Sitting out in the evening & seeing all round one the happy, contented faces
of the Zanzibaris hearing their nonsense & laughter all round the camp one
felt what a satisfaction & pleasure it was to be again surrounded by faithful
friends after the months one had only been surrounded & hemmed in by
treachery.—it was this feeling which I was so pleased the Pasha was soon to
share in, a feeling quite unknown to him for many years. The Pasha was
very unwell but cheered up wonderfully at the idea of getting out of the
country. Farida & her nurse were there, & all the officers clerks & people
came up to greet me. The Pasha decided to call all his officers together
tomorrow morning & to ask me to speak to them & get them to decide
upon what they wished to do . . .

It was decided that the Pasha's eight officers were to accompany Jephson to
Kavalli's and arrangements were put in hand for bringing the others later. Demands
for carriers were soon beyond all reason: Casati said he could 'manage' with 80,
Marko asked for 60 and Vita Hassan 50.

February 15th . . . Why at that rate 20,000 carriers would not be sufficient
to take these people to the coast, & we only have about 250 . . . These people
are awfully selfish and helpless & after arranging things with them I became
quite beside myself & had to go out for a walk alone & have a regular good
'damn damn' which relieved my feelings considerably...

February 16th. We were out early this morning to get the loads off. such a confusion & waiting as there was for the loads of the officers & clerks who were coming up with us. Some of the loads were enormously too heavy, others were absurdly light, they are so lazy they will not take the trouble to equalise them. One sees a great load of pots kettles & pans heavy enough for two men to carry, & another basket containing only a lantern & a pipe the two equally divided would make two fair loads, but these people are too lazy to arrange them even. The officers all looked on me with surprise when they saw me giving out the loads to each man with my own hands, they made no attempt whatever to assist me & I felt with an amused feeling that I had fallen 50 per cent in their estimation by doing so—had I sat still & deputed somebody else to do my work they would have respected me... It was now that one felt so indignant when one saw one of our hard worked, patient, faithful Zanzibaris toiling in the sun up the mountain side staggering under the weight of a load belonging to some of these worthless people, & loads of rubbish which will have to be thrown away when we make our final start. Selim Bey, the great fat Soudanese, a sort of perspiring mountain of flesh, rode up the mountain on a small donkey & never got off even at the most precipitous places where one had almost to go up on one's hands & knees, one occasionally got views of him against the sky line which were most ludicrous this huge fat man seated on his small donkey well over the very tail which hung down from directly beneath him & looked as if it belonged to himself. We got up to camp in good time & in the afternoon the Pasha & I bathed & had a clamber over the rocky bed of the stream in search of botanical specimens, the Pasha peering in the most laughable way with his short sighted spectacled eyes into every hole & corner & stumbling about in the most helpless way—why is it scientific men who hunt for birds & bugs are always made so ludicrous by their absurd shortsightedness? We slept in the open & as it was a most exposed spot were awfully cold all night.

February 17th. Some of the natives had run away in the night owing to the unconscionable weight of the officers' & clerks' luggage & as they refused to allow their servants to carry I was obliged to give the loads to my Soudanese soldiers till we got to the top of the mountain, when I was able to get some natives from a neighbouring village. I had told the Pasha to stop at a river about half an hour from Kavallis, & we stopped & bathed & had a change, & all the officers & people belonging to the Pasha put on their best things, we were quite an imposing looking caravan with all the bright clothes & many flags flying. I sent the Pasha on & took charge of the rear guard, I could hear the guns going & the Khedivial hymn played in the distance as the Pasha entered the camp. I came in about half an hour after & found the Pasha & Stanley with all the officers seated in the 'Baraza' which Stanley had built during my absence. Stanley rose & took off his hat

335

to me & received me with great 'empressement' & cordiality before the officers which was highly flattering, he always does that if one is successful, but makes no allowances whatever if one is unsuccessful, however hard the task may have been, & however well one may have toiled for success. The Pasha & his officers were accomodated in such houses as had been built for them the house I had built for Stairs was given to the Pasha & I turned out of my own for some other officers. The Pasha & I went & had breakfast in Stanley's tent, & he came in & talked with us after a bit. In the evening after dinner we all three had a long talk, & in speaking of things that had taken place & relating the story of the last few months, the Pasha told Stanley his ideas on several important points & though he only touched lightly on them & did not tell him everything about them, they were just the very things I had told Stanley of & had dwelt strongly on; everything agreed with what I had said & everything corroborated with what I had written in my report. At every fresh thing Stanley looked at me as much as to say 'you were perfectly right in what you said' I was very glad it happened so, for I know I am hasty & impulsive & often distrust my own judgement in consequence & in this case I had extra reason for feeling hot & angry by reason of the treatment I had received in the country. The Pasha enlarged upon the affair at Labore & told Stanley about it, & Stanley was pleased to say he thought I had been very modest in my description of the affair.

February 18th. At about 10 o'clock the caravan bringing all the loads men & officers from Kandekori, the station on the Ituri, was seen winding over the hills, & in about an hour & a half the head of the column entered the Station. Many of the faces of the Zanzibari I knew, but a good many, chiefly the Yambuyia men, I had forgotten. Most of them looked well, but some of them were perfect skeletons, both of the Zanzibaris, Soudanese, Manuyema & Madis. Poor devils, how I pitied them they marched along in a stolid painful manner & looked up at one with a doglike pitiful look which went to one's heart. Stairs, Nelson & Parke all looked very well. Of course we were very glad to meet again after being separated so long; it will be a real relief to me to have Stairs here again, we always get on so capitally well together. The expedition is entirely reunited & we are all together for the first time since June 28th/87. The officers are not very pleased with Bonny's story of events which happened in the rear guard & do not give credence to a good deal of what he relates, it is certainly peculiar that when he tells his story one is struck by the fact that any grain of sense which is shown in the many senseless councils they held should have invariably come from Bonny —according to his own account—he was never very remarkable for common sense, so one is rather inclined to distrust this evidence. He has stocked his outfit with numbers of things belonging to the other officers such as European provisions, boots, clothes, books, boxes & even Jameson's ammunition & collecting gun, & seems to have been the residuary legatee of all the officers. It is all very strange & one looks at such things askance, for Bonny is in a different position to the rest of us, first of all he is paid for his services, he is only a hospital sergeant & came merely as Parke's assistant, & we do not therefore think it likely that the officers would have given him their things in the way he said they did. Even the Zanzibaris speak about it & say he came with only two small loads & now he has eight. Stanley & the officers are terribly down on him & speak out plainly about him, I myself hardly know what to think; it seems impossible that any man could dare to do the things they accuse him of doing however we can only know what is true when we again see Jameson. The thing which is so bad is that Bonny seems to take such a pleasure in telling all the most dark & disreputable stories of the officers & he has certainly done his best to blacken their character as much as possible, for even were all the stories true—which we all of us doubt—still there is no necessity to repeat them with such pleasure. He says he thinks Barttelot became insane, & he tells a story of his running after a woman & seizing her by the cheek with his teeth, & relates a story of Jameson having bought a slave woman & handed her over to the Manuyema on condition that they would kill & eat her before him. Stories like these are incredible. . . [1]

Trouble mounted over the difficulty of carrying the loads of household goods brought by Emin's people, which had to be manhandled from the lake up the hill to Kavalli's. Stanley's Zanzibaris mutinied on one occasion and, despite his sympathy with them and increasing dislike of the people he had come to rescue, the leader punished them severely and kept them at it. Emin meanwhile hunted birds, plants and butterflies. Farida and her nurse arrived, and on 13 March Hawashi Effendi came in. He was made welcome by Stanley after his imprisonment and ill usage by the mutineers and Jephson gave him the last of the brandy to cheer him up. Shukri Aga arrived on the 15th bringing news of more quarrels and delays at Wadelai, where Selim Bey was collecting a party to join the Pasha. In spite of anxiety, Jephson was still able to enjoy a day out.

March 16th. Stanley & I went up with a party of men and climbed the mountains above the camp, it is splendid to be up so high—5550 feet— everything is so fresh & one gets such magnificent views of the country all round. The flora is very much the same as that of Pusselewa in Ceylon which was almost exactly the same height above the sea, for instance all the

[1] See Introduction above, pp. 57–9, for summary of the disaster of the Rear Column. These stories, incredible as Jephson rightly says, gained no currency though they were repeated by Bonny after the return of the expedition. Tippoo Tib himself formally and completely denied the slander on Jameson.

ravines up there are full of tree ferns & the same sort of creepers as one saw in Ceylon, whereas about here only a few hundred feet lower there is not a tree fern to be seen. It is curious that much the same flora should exist in two places so widely separated & so vastly different to each other. The streams are all clear & very cold it is a luxury to get a drink of such cold clear water. We sat down & rested on a little knoll near the top of the mountains, there were streams & ravines on each side of us overshadowed by great trees & thickets & the birds were singing all round us, it was delightful sitting there with the fresh cool breeze playing about one, taking in great breaths of the pure mountain air & listening to the birds, one could almost imagine one was in England if one shut ones eyes. Our description of what we had seen so excited the Pasha, especially as we brought down the trunk & fronds of a great tree fern, a thing he had never seen before, that he declared he would go up himself the very next day in spite of his bad leg. It was decided in the evening that all of us officers, with the exception of Stanley, who would stay & look after the camp, should start with the Pasha the next day early & should take up a supply of food & have a sort of picnic.

March 17th. Early this morning we all started off each of us taking some little food, but the 'pièce de resistance' being a fat goat which the Pasha took with him & which was to be slaughtered & cooked for us hungry white men when we came in from our researches. When we got up the mountains the Pasha chose a good spot for camping on, a delightful place near a thicket & under the shade of some large trees behind which ran a stream of ice cold water. On his arrival the Pasha established himself with a party of Zanzibaris & Soudanese soldiers whom Stanley had sent up as a body guard. Each of us officers started off accompanied by a Zanzibari, carrying his & our own rifles, to search for things for the Pasha's collection & notes, Stairs to ascend the highest peak & take observations with aneroid & prismatic compass, Parke to collect botanical specimens, Nelson & Bonny to shoot birds, & I to collect butterflies, which is rather mania with me. It was delightful roaming about in these lovely mountains sides, every thing was fresh & cool & new & nearly all round one saw the fertile plain lying hundreds of feet below stretching 70 miles away to the forest line & terminating in the mountain of Imandi (Pisgah) which stands up like a solitary giant & dominates the whole country round. On the other side one could see ridge after ridge of rocky mountains divided from each other by deep ravines lined with thickets & huge trees, which are swarming with life, monkeys, birds, antelope & insects of all sorts abound there far from the abode of man, & live far removed & secure from that great destroyer. If one was of a poetical nature one would certainly drop into poetry among such scenes as these, & be able to describe this beautiful land in fitting language, & the natives too, the Wa-homa or shepherd kings, leading their quiet, peaceful lives among their flocks & herds; living in all simplicity & in happy ignorance of everything belonging to the great world, not knowing what hurry & bustle is, but living as their fathers & grandfathers lived before them, still conserving the manner & customs of the hundreds of generations preceding them, slow to take in new ideas & slower still to act upon them, peacefully passing their days in slow tranquillity, their greatest excitement being the death or marriage of a chief, their own small quarrels or the rumour of an expected raid from Kaberega. A peaceful, happy & trustful people, contented with their lot in the middle of this fertile & rich grazing country, their few acres of corn & sweet potatoes giving them sufficient food & their flock & herds supplying them with milk and clothing—it is such a free & simple life which they lead in the midst of this Arcadia—why was'nt I a poet to describe it properly, such scenes are wasted on a person like me! We each brought in what we had collected to the Pasha who was in his element arranging & classifying his specimens. At midday we had luncheon & I think we astonished the Pasha at the amount of food we were able to consume, five young & vigorous Englishmen coming in with appetites like wolves. In the afternoon we each took a different track & wandered back to camp collecting whatever we saw on the way. The Pasha was very pleased with his day's work, Stairs had made some good observations, Bonny had brought in some rare birds, I had got several new butterflies & we had all brought in numbers of interesting botanical specimens, the arranging of which took the Pasha till late at night, & above all he had seen tree ferns growing in numbers in the ravines—a thing he had never seen before. Shookri Aga & his people returned to the Nyanza this morning & will start off in the steamer for M'swa tomorrow & when Selim Bey & his people have passed he is to evacuate the station & march overland to this place.

March 18th. All the men were fallen in this morning & a general muster made & the people were then divided into three companies, Stanley No 1, Stairs No 2 & Nelson No 3, & I am to have charge of No 1 & look after the men & act as Stanley's 'Aide'. There are a great number of sick, about 40, I should say, who are not able to carry & never have been good for anything & this cuts down our number of able men terribly. We have in all 200 Zanzibaris & 17 Soudanese; of Tippu Tib's Manuyema there are about 50 able men, so that our force is not a large one & we shall not be able to carry the boat, which will be a great pity. We are obliged to carry the loads of ammunition for the Pasha's people as his people are 'soldiers' & will not even carry their own ammunition, which makes it very hard for us who thought that, having brought the relief ammunition to the lake, our work with it was ended, but we shall have to carry it & throw away some of our own loads, when one thinks of these things the devil rises in one's heart against these miserable arrogant people who will do nothing for themselves & expect us to do everything for them. More officers & loads came up from the Lake today & among them Abdul Wahad Effendi & Sulieman Effendi Abderrahim, both of them very good fellows, for Egyptians, there are now very few people down in the camp. The natives now are carrying up all the loads, as Stanley has made an arrangement with them with which they are highly satisfied, something like three weeks ago Stanley sent Stairs out to make a raid on the natives who had not come in to make friends with us & to seize cattle, he went out & brought in 125 in a very few hours, Stanley then sent word to the natives that he wanted loads brought up from the Lake, & told them that for every 5 loads they brought up he would return them a cow. The natives readily agreed to this so a party goes down every day nearly and brings up loads & we return the just proportion of cows to the chiefs to whom they belonged, we have in this way got more than 300 loads brought up for us without any trouble—it is rather hard on the natives but it is the fortune of war, & it does not really matter much as the natives redeem their property by labour & not in goods so that they are none the poorer for the transaction it is one of those high handed acts which African travellers are obliged to resort to & for which the Exeter Hall beauties call them 'pirates' & 'fillibusters', but they are only acts which the natives themselves are quite accustomed to, only that they consider us as far better than their ordinary enemies as we give them the chance of redeeming their cattle without making them any poorer—until now they have never been payed for labour & did not know it had any market value.

It has now been fixed when we are to leave this place. Stanley had a long conversation with the Pasha & told him he wished to start from here by the end of the month, but the Pasha begged yet for 10 days grace so it has been decided that we leave here on April 10th, & the Pasha has given his word to start on that day. We arrived at the Lake in the begining of April/88, & the Pasha got my letter from M'swa on April 17th we shall therefore have given these people exactly a year all but a week to make up their minds about leaving the country or staying where they are, no one can say we have not been patient & given them plenty of time.

The last days at Kavalli's saw the steady worsening of Emin's relations with the expedition, the Pasha begging for more time for his people to come in from Wadelai, Tunguru and M'swa, and Stanley's refusal, backed by his officers, to wait any longer. To enforce his decision, he sent Stairs off on 1 April with Hawashi Effendi and a small caravan, marching west for the expedition's old camp at Mazamboni's, from where the road ran south-east round the flank of the Ruwenzori.

April 2nd [1889]. A few days ago we saw the great snow mountain the natives call Ruanzori for the first time. Last year we only saw what seemed to be a large solitary snow capped mountain, but from this view of it it is one great chain of snow capped peaks extending one over another into the far distance. It was a beautiful sight the great expanse of snow, shining in the sun right in the middle of central tropical Africa. As the sun sank it turned the snow a rosey colour. The whole camp was in great excitement about it & all turned out to look at it. Stanley took observations with the theodolyte which Stairs worked & found it was 73 miles distance & 21,900 feet high. The latter working may be incorrect as Stanley only took a base line of 120 feet & at such a distance the angle would be so small, but when we get some 30 or 40 miles nearer it & take a base line of 2 miles we will be able to get the exact height. If it prove the highest mountain in Africa it will be a tremendous find for the expedition—Killamanjaro is only 18000[1] feet odd. We are all in the greatest excitement about it, particularly Stanley & the Pasha. Stanley intends staying there some days & send us each up with a party to take observations & get geological & botanical specimens. Of course it is possible this mountain may be Gambaragarel, or Gordon Bennet as Stanley called it, or Gordon-Bennet may be a peak in this mountain range, but if Gordon-Bennett is in the right place as Stanley has put it in his map, this mountain range is many miles to the West of it—at any rate all sorts of speculations are rife & we hope to solve them all bye & bye & make a big discovery, it must be a most important one whatever it is.

People dribbled in from the north and packing went on in an atmosphere of increasing tension which culminated on 5 April in the discovery of a plot by the Pasha's Egyptians and Sudanese to seize the expedition's arms and to refuse to march, a conspiracy defeated by Stanley's prompt action.

April 6th. Last night Stanley told me to go over to the Pasha and tell him to send round word that he wished all the Egyptians to assemble in the square at half past seven each with his wives, children, servants & slaves & loads before him. The Pasha said he would pass the word, but he did not know if

---

[1] Kilimanjaro's correct height is 19,565 feet. The highest peak of Ruwenzori is Mount Margherita, 16, 795 feet, one of the summits of Mount Stanley in the central group of the range. See entry for 26 May 1888 for Parke's and Jephson's first sight of the snows of the Ruwenzori. The two peaks which Stanley calls the 'Twin Cones' were later named Mount Emin and Mount Gessi, and are visible in favourable conditions from Lake Albert. They may perhaps be identified, without too much exercise of fancy, with the 'Crophi and Mophi' of Herodotus, between which peaks was said to lie a bottomless lake from which sprang the Nile. *See* Stanley, *IDA*, II, 289 ff.; H. B. Thomas and R. Scott, *Uganda* (London, 1935), 412–14; René Bere, *The way to the Mountains of the Moon* (London, 1966), 124–37.

it would be obeyed, I told him that was not the question, Stanley only asked him to pass the word & if the people refused to comply it was their own look out, but that as a friend I advised them strongly to do as they were told for Stanley was in that state now in which if he were thwarted in any way nothing would stop him & he would proceed to extremities the Pasha said he did not see what more he could do than he had done yesterday, & I told him it was not advisable for him to say or even allow himself to think that yesterday's affair was the utmost Stanley could do he did not yet know the man & of what he was capable.

However in due time this morning all was as he had ordered each had his loads & people in front of his house in spite of the heavy rain which was falling. We went round to each family & took the numbers of people & loads & general particulars. It was piteous to see some families, nothing but little bright eyed children with their fathers being killed in the war there was no one but the negro mothers & slaves to look after them, there was one family of 7 small children whose father was dead; little yellow weazened up children with faces like little old women, how they will ever get along is an enigma; there will be some awful scenes on the way, just as there were in our flight from Wadelai, only that this will be such a long journey that the women & children will fall like flies on the road. One wretched looking Egyptian soldier whose wife had run away from him & left him with their little child was standing by himself with one poor load before him holding his little baby in his arms which was reduced to skin & bone through the desertion of its mother he was trying to protect it from the weather by holding a tattered cloth over its head, there he stood, a forlorn looking figure in the fast falling rain, his worldly possessions representing one small basket & a half starved baby, as we came up to ask of what his household consisted a sense of his utterly forlorn & deserted position seemed to come over him & he could only answer with such a passion of sobbing that one felt an utter brute for even asking him the question; ones heart ached for him, but what can one do; to stay here is to die & I fear to take to the road means death also to his child—at any rate the poor little baby shall have half my share of milk so long as there is any. The man, I find, is a convict sent up here from Egypt for highway robbery, which accounts for his forlorn state. It does not do to see such sights as these, if one sees them it must be with unseeing eyes it is only one of the many small things which add to the miseries & horrors of evacuating a country in Africa—I dread the road on account of the heartbreaking scenes we shall have to go through it is so hard when one sees misery to be obliged to pass by on the other side. The following is a return of the people & loads going with us:

Infants of followers	35
Children of Egyptians	74
Wives of Egyptians	84
Women followers	187
Total of women & children	380
Men	190
Total of Emin Pasha's people	570
Total of our expedition	350
Total in our camp	920

This is under the mark & does not include those Egyptians with their families who have gone on with Stairs, so that the total number of souls will be over a thousand. It will be a long column. I really wonder how we shall get along through an enemies country where all stragglers will be assuredly cut off. . .

April 10th. There were so many carriers this morning that we experienced no difficulty in getting the people off. We started at 7.30 & the people really did not go at all badly, much better than we expected. The caravan looked a tremendous length winding along over the plain, & our cattle greatly added to the length as they straggled along a good deal, the caravan was very gay with flags, & the coloured clothes of Zanzibaris & Egyptian women added to the general brightness, there were over 1,400 people including the native carriers & the whole caravan must have been three miles long,— Raschid my head chief said it was like the story of the flight from Egypt under Moschi (Moses) as they read in the Khoran. Children, donkeys, goats, women, Zanzibaris, Egyptians, Circassians, Greeks, Jews & Nubians all mixed up together formed a regular motley crowd. Nelson looked after the rear guard & I went ahead with my company, before leaving our camp at Kavalli's he burnt the place there were over 200 houses and looking back it seemed a tremendous blaze. We reached M'pingas at about 2.30 & camped on the open plain, leaving a small village near by for the Pasha & his people & Stanley had about 10 cattle slaughtered for our native carriers. In the evening Stanley had all the people fallen in & told us he was going to send Nelson & I on a raid against the Waregga, & that we should start at 3.30 in the night & reach the villages just before day break. The Wa-regga have long been the scourge of the country they are brave & descend constantly from their mountains & take cattle & slaves, they render the path between the friendly settlements of Mazamboni, Usere, Kavalli, M'pinga, Mwiti, Rugudju & M'Guessa quite unsafe for natives to travel along in small parties & are a general nuisance to everybody. We were chiefly to catch people for carriers & to get cattle.

Bribed by the captured cattle, the chiefs supplied carriers, and the caravan marched west to their old camp at Mazamboni's which Stairs had made ready for them...

April 12th. Shookri Aga arrived with two soldiers & three women only. He said that things were in the utmost confusion in the country & that there were four parties one was for going over to the Donagla, one for settling a country west of Tunguru, one for staying where they were, & one—a very small one—for coming with us. Selim Bey was still in Wadelai & in spite of four urgent letters from Shookri Aga had not moved & was still in Wadelai. At last as the time drew on Shookri Aga spoke to his soldiers & told them he intended to start at once for reaching Stanley, with the exception of 10 all refused to accompany him, with these ten men he made his way along the lake shore & reached Kavalli's the evening of the day we left, finding our camp just burnt he decided to start off the next morning, but found that 8 of his 10 soldiers had run away in the night so he reached us with only two men out of his people, the people of whom the Pasha had felt so sure. He told us that Faratch Aga Ajoke & the people who had escaped from Rejaf had made their way from Makraka with two companies of soldiers (?) to Wadelai but finding things in such disorder they had refused to have anything to do with them & had started off the next day for Tunguru, with the avowed intention of reaching us over land—this of course they will never do; we have had sufficient proofs of what these people are capable of. He (Shookri Aga) reports that great disorder exists in Wadelai the officers & soldiers do nothing but drink merrissa & the soldiers (?) are mutinous & fire away their cartridges for mere devilment, that they have now hardly any ammunition left except the 31 boxes we brought them. In fact ruin in every way & from every side stares them in the face & yet they still go on in the same useless quarrels.

Next day desertions were reported from the camp, and that night Stanley fell ill with the same gastritis that so nearly killed him at Fort Bodo and the caravan was obliged to halt for 4 weeks.

The days passed drearily, occupied by raids, of increasing barbarity, on the local people, for food and for captives to act as carriers. The last entry of Book 3 records the increasing weariness and disgust that was overtaking the once hopeful expedition.

April 20th. This morning Stanley told us to count over the slaves, chiefly women & children, whom our people had caught & hand half of them over to the Pasha to give to his people. This Stairs & I did & handed him over 20. We brought them over to the Pasha's house, upon my word it was a most shameful scene & was as bad every bit as the open slave markets that existed in the East till virtuous England set her back up. Orders are however orders & we must obey them in spite of the heartrending scenes & shameless brutality we see in these raids.

CHAPTER 16

LAKE ALBERT TO LAKE EDWARD

25 APRIL–16 JUNE 1889

Book 4 of the diary begins on the eve of departure for the coast. It was written in the second of the two books which Jephson brought out from home.

April 25th. Stanley is now convalescent but poisons himself by the constant doses of Morphine he insists on taking in spite of Parkes protests against it.[1] Parke himself is down with the Billious Remittant fever, a fever which is common on the Congo & terribly fatal, the patient turns the colour of a jaundice patient & vomits constantly, & if the fever is not quickly arrested it carries the patient off in three days. Fortunately he knew what to do & stopped the fever in time. I also have been down with fever for the last four days & am still rather low; it is almost the worst fever I have had for my temperature is constantly up & never goes down to normal. A couple of days ago I was very bad & towards the evening something seemed to rise in my head & press against my brain until in an agony I called for help & then I lost my senses for some time, I was dimly conscious of Stairs holding me up & calling to me & pouring something down my throat, but I felt torpid & unable to move or speak, afterwards I can remember several people round my bed amongst them the Pasha, but the torpor was still on me & I could neither hear nor answer their questions. Later on in the night my senses returned, but I could only lie & groan in speechless agony; my head felt bursting & my body one huge ache.[2] These attacks of fever rather frighten me for one is so powerless under them & each attack seems to get stronger than its predecessor. Africa is a terrible country in the morning one wakes up well & in the evening one is raving in the agonies of fever or some other disorder equally malignant—I have never before gone off my head in sickness & I do'nt like the feeling—shall I ever get home across all this unhealthy East Africa with its fever stricken plains & swamps, though I must say the country we have already passed through is equally unhealthy,

[1] Parke was 'rather in a stew about my morphine, as I have but a few tablets left; and it is the only thing that subdues the paroxysms of agonising pain, from which my patient suffers so terribly' (Parke, p. 412).

[2] 'Mr Mounteney Jephson was so seriously ill in that one night his life was despaired of. He was said to lie in a state of collapse, and our priceless doctor rose from his sick bed and hastened with his men supporting him to the side of his sick comrade, and applied restoratives, and relieved our intense anxieties, and before retiring, he called upon me to relieve my spasms' (Stanley, *IDA*, II, 198).

perhaps more so. It is so maddening to be kept from one's work, particularly when Stanley is ill & I am more wanted. At any rate if fever is to be the end of me, as I fear it will be, I trust it will not let me linger on to be a burden to myself & everyone else, but will be quick & sharp. If I intended to fill up my journal with such things I could write pages & pages on the miseries one suffers stretched on a bed of fever in Africa. Of the intense pains & utter prostration, of the deep dejection & despair which descend on the sufferer, of the hopeless despairing feeling of ever again seeing one's native land, & the home memories which throng up & madden one, until one almost prays for some Merciful Hand to put an end for ever to one's unspeakable misery.

April 26th. Stanley slowly improving—Parke striding away towards recovery & I somewhat better, but still having a good deal of pain & the general feeling of a broken down cab horse. Nelson is also down with Rheumatism. Today we heard a gun fired in camp & on Stairs' running out to find what it was he found that one of Osman Effendi Latiffe's servants—one of these brutal Nubians—had just shot one of the slaves we had caught in one of these raids, through the head, he was one out of three slaves we had handed over to him for helping him to carry his loads, & the servant had shot him because he had not instantly done what he was told—perhaps the poor fellow did not understand.[1] The two other slaves were tied to him with raw cowhide & were trembling & shaking with fear. Osman Effendi himself was quietly eating his dinner apparently undisturbed by the sight of the bloody remains of the unfortunate slave, (his head was split to pieces & his brains splashed over the other two slaves) lying within two yards of him. Stairs took the servant & there was some talk of hanging him, but it was decided not to do so as the Pasha's people are so hard up for carriers he was therefore fixed in a slave yoke & placed under guard with some of the Pasha's other deserters. The scenes in camp now, the constant brutal illtreatment of the slaves by the Pasha's people, is getting beyond anything, & is enough to bring the judgement of destruction & utter annihilation on the expedition. When we were by ourselves no such scenes have ever been seen in our camp, such few natives as the Zanzibaris caught were kindly treated & looked after & soon became content to follow the caravan without any restraint being put upon them—this was in the camp of Stanley who has been called a pirate & freebooter, an adventurer & filibuster. But now that Emin Pasha, who has been represented as one of the champions of Anti Slavery, who is supposed to have kept slavery far from him & his people, has come into our camp, scenes of the most disgraceful cruelty, constant beatings, constant shrieking of women and constant desertions are of daily occurence, while ones heart gets sick & a strong indignation rises in one when one thinks

---

[1] Stanley places this incident on 13 April.

how the sympathies of Europe have been tricked & played with & how we have been duped into giving our best energies towards helping & rescuing a man & his people utterly unworthy of our help or even of our sympathy. Look at the lives we have lost, Major Barttelot & some 450 of our own people, to speak nothing of some hundreds of Manuyema & many hundreds of natives we have killed & whose villages we have destroyed in forcing our way here. Look again at the numbers we shall lose between here & Zanzibar & the natives we shall probably kill. On the other hand what have we done in return for all this? We have Emin Pasha—not alas the Emin Pasha we all imagined him to be—& some 50 Egyptian employés with their wives, concubines, families & slaves, the off scouring & dregs of Cairo & Alexandra. Is what we have got an equivalent to what we have lost? Ten thousand times, no.

April 27th. This afternoon the Pasha came over to Stairs & told him that a soldier had just come to him & told him of a plot existing among his people for the last four days which was to be carried into execution this evening. The whole of the Pasha's people carrying guns & his boy had decided to run away & try & get back to M'swa, they also intended taking with them the Pasha's Madi carriers. The Pasha asked Stairs to come with a party of Zanzibaris & disarm his boys, which he at once did—Shookri Aga had all the soldiers up, some 7 or 8, & disarmed them also, the boys were then tied up & together with the Madis placed under arrest. These desertions are getting very frequent, hardly a day passes but some women or servants run away—some of them are caught & some get clean away, but where they get to no one can tell. These people do nothing to stop the desertions & when remonstrated with & asked why they do not look after their people better, say 'Everything is in the hands of God'. In the evening it was found that Rehan—a servant whom Hawashi Effendi had given Stanley a year ago —had run away taking some women with him, he had also run away with a Remington gun belonging to Stanley.

April 28th. Early this morning the Pasha came over in a very excited mood & said he had made up his mind to put a stop to these frequent intrigues & desertions & he had therefore made up his mind to call a court of enquiry on which his officers would sit—they would enquire into the whole affair of yesterday & declare what judgement the ringleaders should receive, he wished when his officers had sifted the whole thing & decided what punishment the offenders should receive that Stairs would act with him on Stanley's behalf. Stairs said that he would, so the court was called & after sitting all morning it was found that Rehan—who had decamped over night—& two of the Pasha's servants were the ringleaders—one of the servants—this being his third offense of the same kind—was sentenced by the officers to be shot. The Pasha in the morning was loud in his assertions that he would abide by the decision of the court of officers he had called, & hoped that they would pass a sentence of death on whoever they found to be the ringleaders, but Stairs says that when it came to the point the Pasha tried all he could to back out of it, however the decision of the court was laid before the Pasha & Stairs, & the latter of course went to Stanley & asked if he approved of the sentence, Stanley said 'Perfectly' & thought it was the only sentence they could have come to. The Pasha then sent in to ask Stanley to let him have a party of Zanzibaris to shoot the man, but Stanley said he thought it advisable for the Pasha's people to do it themselves as an ill feeling already existed between his & the Pasha's people & he did not wish to make it stronger. The Pasha then declared he had no people who could shoot & so after flogging the ring leaders they were set free. The truth is when it came to the point the Pasha was afraid to act & tried to put the responsibility on Stanley, Stanley did not mind the responsibility, but objected to lending the Zanzibaris, though he afterwards offered some of our Soudanese but the Pasha was glad of any excuse to get out of the affair & said he had decided to flog them only. Stanley was very angry, as were Stairs & the Pasha's officers who had been made such fools of, the Pasha himself was the only person thoroughly satisfied he had kicked up a dust & had had the bugles going for a good half hour; he had called a court of officers, who had sat for five or six hours, & had called in one of Stanley's officers to act with him he had then reversed their judgement & had successfully made fools of the whole lot—what more could he want to complete his self satisfaction? All these little things show us more plainly than a regular written history could the reason of the four years rebellion in the Pasha's country & of his subsequent imprisonment & deposition.

April 29th. Shookri Aga came to Stanley this morning & asked if he would let him have 30 Zanzibaris to accompany him to the Lake where he wished to go in the hope of catching some of the deserters, Stanley who is anxious to get hold of Rehan, who has made immense mischief amongst the Pasha's people, consented & ordered me to send 30 men out of my company with him—they will probably be away five days. I have been building a sort of arbour for Stanley amongst the trees near the tent he is so much better that he is going to sit out tomorrow.

April 30th. Stanley has been sitting out all day & is very much better. We shall be unable to take all the powder & ammunition on from here, so we buried 16 boxes of powder & 28 boxes of Remington ammunition under the mud floor of our house, we did it at night so no one knows anything about it, when we leave we shall burn the house down & so destroy all traces of the earth having been moved. We have been having a great quantity of rain; nearly every night now there is a thunderstorm; it is always so at the beginning of the rainy season. Very little food comes in, Mazamboni is as mean as a man can be, we have given him 60 cattle, a present such as no chief gets in his life time, but he gives us just as little food as he possibly can without coming to an open rupture with Stanley, there is a sort of mean cunning which passes for cleverness with these natives. The other day some of our people & all the Pasha's people were sent to a settlement about an hours march from here, the people are under Mazamboni, but he did not seem to mind it at all & one of his brothers, Katto, even went with our people & looted on his own account—it is impossible to understand these people; they seem to steal from their friends as readily as from their foes. The only thing really to wake Mazamboni up will be to help ourselves to food from his own private plantations & fields. The women come every day & form a little market, bringing in flour, potatoes, bananas etc, the Zanzibaris deal readily with them but how they pay is more than I know; they are tremendous bargainers & seem to enjoy it, the women are nice & pleasant looking, especially the Wakhoma of whom there are a good many.

May 5th [1889]. Stanley is getting on steadily & sits out all day & walks about a bit. So many people have run away that Shookri Aga begged Stanley to let him have 30 Zanzibaris & he returned after 5 days absence having caught Rehani & his slave & several women & children servants of the clerks & officers. Stanley ordered us officers Stairs, Nelson, Parke & I to try him impartially & bring him our verdict. We tried him on the two charges, first of inciting others to desert & second for desertion with a gun belonging to the expedition. After sitting some two hours & calling in numbers of witnesses we found him guilty on both charges, we tried him in the manner of a court martial which is generally considered the fairest & justest trial possible. Stanley at once sentenced him to death which sentence was carried out instantly; he was hanged by the neck till he died.[1] I never saw a man go to his death with such complete sang froid, he did not utter a word nor did his face change in any way; he just walked quietly to the tree & waited till the noose was fixed. I do not think these Nubians feel like other people; they are so impressionless & bestial & never seem to take a thing in; it is all part of the days work even being hung. His death will, I think, make a good impression after the Pasha's vacillating & timid policy. The day before yesterday evening Shookri Aga went with the Pasha's people & about 40 of our Zanzibaris on a raid to catch slaves. Stairs & I were to have gone with our companies, but the Pasha the day before was exasperated with his people & said he did not care a bit about his people getting slaves as they were

---

[1] Stanley puts this incident on 17 April, and says he was strung up and died instantly. Parke gives a different account: he says the rope was rotten and broke, and there was an appreciable delay until a new rope was brought (Parke, pp. 419–20).

behaving so badly, he was moreover, very rude & aggravating to Stairs & I. Now as these raids for slaves were made at the Pasha's earnest entreaty, it angered us very much that we should be going out on these cruel hunts, doing what was an outrage to our feelings as English gentlemen for his sake, & then his turning round & trying, as he did, to put the whole thing on us. We therefore went to Stanley & told him what the Pasha had said to us & further declined to go on such raids any more. He was furious with the Pasha & told us he sympathised with us in every fibre of his body, & expressed his utter contempt for the Pasha's meanness & rudeness. The breach between the two is daily widening; we are very sorry for it but cannot wonder at it; our whole sympathies are with Stanley. It is sad to see the utter downfall & collapse of the ideal the people in Europe had formed of the Pasha's character —'The active champion of the Anti Slavery Party'! 'A brave man fighting bravely against fearful odds & keeping the wolves from his fold'! 'A second Gordon'! And so on. The position is this, the Pasha is continually listening to little paltry stories about his people which are brought to him by—well by his spies; stories of petty intrigues & speeches made about him & remarks about his scandal with the engineer's wife,[1] he listens to them all & broods over them, & refuses to give them a share of the food we send him for his people & does a hundred & one spiteful little things & sends spiteful messages to Stanley about his people, his requiring protection from them & so forth. The people on the other hand are constantly coming to Stanley to complain of the Pasha, which in his state of health irritates him almost to madness, the result is that unpleasant messages are daily passing between them, & we officers are made the carriers of these messages. Stanley is rude to us because he knows we do not deliver his messages as he gives them—we cannot—& the Pasha is very rude to us in his turn when we deliver the messages in a milder form & I really think he believes we add to the rudeness instead of doing all we can to soften Stanley's messages. It is an awfully unpleasant position for us all & we get blamed &, I may say, insulted for doing our best to prevent a regular row. The Pasha is in his way as dangerous a man as Stanley & tries to put one in very nasty positions; only he does it in a

[1] 'April 4 [1889].—Last evening, about 7 p.m., there was a great noise in the camp. Mohammed Effendi, who had been engineer on one of the steamers, worked himself into a desperate temper, because his wife would not return to her marital duties. He used very foul language about the Pasha. After this effusion he came and complained to Mr. Stanley. He told the latter, that the Pasha kept his wife in his house to take care of Ferida (the Pasha's child), and that she would not return to him.' Eventually, after much abuse on all sides, it was agreed that Farida's nurse should stay at the Pasha's house by day and return to her husband at night but, as Parke wrote in his diary, and afterwards published in his book: 'It is well that we have no scandal journal published here: this tyrannical segment of the press would, of course, as *usual*, be absolutely indifferent to the truth or falsehood of the statements' (Parke, p. 399).

meaner & more ungenerous way than Stanley does, & that is saying a good deal. For the last three days I have not gone to see the Pasha I can no longer trust myself to remain quiet under his rudeness.

May 6th. Shookri Aga, the Zanzibaris & the Pasha's people returned today bringing with them numbers of slaves, the Pasha's people must now have over 150 natives they have caught as slaves. Stanley has decided to the great joy of every one that he is sufficiently well to be carried in the 'Kitanda' I have made for him so we start the day after tomorrow. We have now been 28 days in this place & are all deadly sick of it, & the Pasha's people, having nothing to do, intrigue to their hearts' content. We should know nothing about it if the Pasha acted as he should & took no notice of it, but that is impossible for him, & he listens to each story about his people & assails everyone with all sorts of stories & complaints about them. I should not write these things about the Pasha, though God knows I do not describe a tithe of his contemptible behaviour, for if I belittle the Pasha, I belittle the success of the Expedition in only after all rescuing such a poor specimen of a man.

May 7th. Early this morning we gave out 30 rounds of ammunition to each man & saw that the guns & loads were all in order. We gave over 25 Remingtons & 60 rounds of ammunition each to the Pasha's people, but we took the precaution to take out the mainsprings of all their guns which renders them useless & we shall not return them until we get at such a distance that there can be no treachery or desertion—they were awfully disgusted when they found what we had done. I have got all my loads & things ready & have been hard at work all day & in spite of a touch of fever my spirits rise at the thought of again being on the march. In the evening Mazamboni's people came in to dance & later on some natives came in with the news that the small steamer had come to the Lake shore with some of the Pasha's people, they also brought a packet of letters from the people to the Pasha. The chief letter came from three officers & a clerk who said that they had come to the Lake shore with 20 soldiers by order of Selim Bey who had heard that loads had been put on officers' heads, & they had been otherwise illtreated by us & he had therefore sent these people to enquire into the matter, the letter was written in a most impertinent strain. There were several other letters which the officers & clerks in our camp had sent to their friends in Wadelai, these letters had been handed over to the natives nearly a month before with orders to the natives to carry them in canoes to M'swa, but the natives had not done so &, after keeping them all this time, had brought them to the Pasha. They contained all sorts of treasonable things, they were very anxious that Selim Bey should bring two companies of soldiers & then they would have things in their own hands—'we shall be able to obtain what we desire'. The Pasha was very excited by the news & was very afraid that the soldiers & officers on arriving in our camp would shoot at him or endeavour to do him some bodily injury. Stanley sent for Stairs, Parke & I late in the evening & told us all the news; he told us what to do should different circumstances arise. We shall start tomorrow morning as we originally intended & the officers & soldiers will probably catch us up shortly after we arrive in camp, after telling us to be careful not to spread the news about camp & to act as if nothing had happened he dismissed us. Stairs, Parke & Nelson were very much disturbed by the news & suggested all sorts of things which they considered ought to be done. I did not enter the discussion for knowing these people as I do I am quite satisfied nothing will come of it.

May 8th. Started off with fever on me this morning, there was no difficulty in getting the Pasha's people to move in spite of the disturbing news of yesterday, we had thought they might wish to stay for the arrival of the soldiers & officers. Stairs stayed behind & acted as rear guard & burnt the entire camp before leaving. Stanley has told me that my place in the column is always to be in front, so if there is any fighting in future I shall have a good time of it—Nelson & Stairs will take charge of the rear guard on alternate days. The Zanzibaris & everybody were in high spirits at starting for Zanzibar at last & shouting & singing was heard along the whole column as we brushed our way through dewy fields of Indian corn or M'tama. For the first two hours of the march we returned on our old track through Mazamboni's & then we turned off sharp to the left, i.e. to the South, into the unknown country. As we turned South round the shoulder of the mountains we got a beautiful view of Ruanzori with its snows just tinged red by the rays of the early sun, in two minutes the clouds had covered it entirely & we saw it no more that day. The sight of the pure snowy peak seen above the clouds whilst the lower part of the mountain is hidden has a wonderful unearthly & mysterious effect, the pureness & beauty of which is perfectly indescribable, it is no wonder that the Masai, on seeing the peak of Killimanjaro above the clouds, say in a voice of mingled wonder & awe 'It is the abode of God'. We soon reached the large settlement at the foot of the mountains which I had seen on the occasion of our first visit to the Lake, I had been sent out with a party of men to drive the natives from the hills & burn their villages—we were then in the thick of our three days' fight with Mazamboni—& in the early evening I arrived at the last of the mountains & had seen this settlement lying beneath me, but it had been too late to descend into it & I had returned & described it to Stanley as being a settlement with 400 acres of solid cultivation, from the place where I stood however I had only been able to see a part of the settlement. Anything like the beauty of this settlement as we passed through today I never saw, fields of Indian corn & M'tama all about 2 ft high & of the most delicate green alternating with large dark groves of bananas, huge spreading trees chiefly of the fig tribe dotted about here & there making great dark patches of shade, whilst the villages— collections of 5 or 6 huts placed in a circle—had a secluded & peaceful appearance, there was an air of thrift & richness & plenty about the whole settlement such as I have never seen before in Africa, the whole was beautifully watered by numbers of clear cool streams coming down from the mountains. We camped in the far end of it & Stanley said in passing through he had estimated that there were 1,400 acres of solid cultivation. He said he had perfectly remembered the settlement from my description of it 16 months ago & he had even recognized the mountain upon which I must have stood & looked down on it all. After we had been in camp 3 or 4 hours the four officers arrived who had been sent by Selim Bey to speak with the Pasha. They had left the 20 soldiers behind at Mazambonis & had followed us by themselves, their tone was very different from the tone of their letter & they had a piteous tale to tell. They were brought before Stanley & the Pasha acted as Interpreter. It appears that on Selim Bey's return to Wadelai he had not obeyed the Pasha's orders of instantly returning with his family & people, but had gone off on his own hook in the steamers to fetch some people who had been left between Dufile & Wadelai. Whilst he was away Fadl el Mulla Aga, Achmet Aga Dinkane, Abdulla Aga el Apt & Mustapha Effendi Achmet together with Kismallah, the Pasha's former favourite, & some others had left Wadelai in the night taking a good number of soldiers with them & every box of ammunition & were well on their way to Makraka before Selim Bey returned.[1] This is Fadl el Mulla who posed as the saviour of the Province! Selim Bey & his party in terror at their desparate position massed at M'swa, having in their possession only 4 boxes of ammunition. The officers begged for ammunition & prayed that Stanley would give them time to join him. He answered that they had had more than a year now to get ready they had refused his help, had ruined the country, imprisoned & deposed their governor, had ill treated his officer whom he had sent to help them, they had disobeyed orders they had promised to carry out, they had behaved in fact like savages & madmen & now he would not give them a cartridge or wait an hour for them, he would go on marching day by day & if they liked to follow him & try & catch him up they might do so, but he would not alter his plans in the slightest degree for them. They were receiving & answering treacherous letters from the people already in his camp & readily believed the lies they were told, he then dismissed them & told them to go & make enquiries amongst their people, & they would then learn how false had been the information they had received about his ill

---

[1] See pp. 422–4 below for the rest of the story of Selim Bey and Fadl el Mulla.

treatment of the officers. A proclamation was sent through the camp that all those who were discontented & did not wish to come on with us were free to return on the morrow with the officers & soldiers, they were however so horrified by the news they had heard of the position of affairs in the Province that not one expressed a wish to return, they all determined to go on with us into the unknown. Their case desparate & with death staring them in the face, Selim Bey & his people will never be got to move a step to follow us, as soon as the question of moving is mooted there will be a cry of 'who is to carry our goods' & as there will be no Stanley there to teach them that goods must be thrown away they will never move, but will just stay where they are till the ammunition is exhausted, the soldiers will then desert to their own countries & the officers, clerks, etc, will be killed by the natives, the same story will apply to Fadl el Mulla & his party; they could not have a better punishment than being left to themselves.

May 10th. My fever is getting intense & never goes down I can scarcely crawl from camp to camp. Today in camp we heard many guns going & men came in says Kaberegga's men were not far off, they had had a brush with a small party of the Pasha's people & Vakul Casati's pet boy had been killed in the first encounter,[1] Stanley at once sent out mine & Stairs companies, but I was too utterly gone with fever to be able to go much to my disappointment as I had always wanted to meet Kaberegga's people. Stairs & the Zanzibaris returned late in the evening, they had chased Kaberegga's people for miles & had captured a few cattle they had with them, the Wa-unyoro had fled at the first sight of the Zanzibaris advancing against them.

May 27th. A long blank in my journal & almost in my memory—I have been carried from camp to camp more dead than alive, ever since the 10th day after day & night after night I have been lying half senseless wasting with fever which has only just left me, for days & nights my temperature never went down below 105° & I have become a shadow of my former self & am only able to totter along with the help of a stick. Lying awake at night with the fever wasting & burning me up, I had quite made up my mind that I should not get over it, but must die in a night or two. After the first horrified feeling of dying in this miserable country was over, death seemed so easy, it seemed such an easy solution to many difficulties which troubled ones mind about the future, I was neither glad nor sorry but felt perfectly content to die, I made my will,[2] wrote a few short letters, & felt quite ready, the thought of my future after death did not trouble me in the least, I can only describe what I felt as being perfectly resigned to whatever might

---

[1] Stanley calls him 'Captain Casati's faithful servant Okili, for whom Casati entertained deep affection' (Stanley, *IDA*, II, 233).   [2] See p. 182 and Plate 13.

happen, my only regret was that my death would be a great grief to my sisters, especially to Mary who poor thing has enough griefs of her own without my adding to them. Stanley, I knew, would bear witness to my having done my duty to the expedition honestly & loyally throughout & that would be sufficient for my friends. Now that the fever has left me & I am out of danger, though enfeebled & exhausted to the last degree, I feel equally content to live & fight out my difficulties, but I do not feel any great thankfulness or enthusiasm for my recovery. Parke who has been, as he always is, most untiring in his efforts to get one well blames me terribly for the way I have fallen into of looking at it all & will not allow me to speak about it, though he admits I nearly passed the threshold of life & death.[1] However enough about myself. We have crossed the Semliki, a large turbid swift river some 60 to 80 yards wide, running into the Albert Lake, but not discovered by either Mason or Gessi when they circumnavigated the Lake on account of the forest of Ambatch trees growing across the mouth, this is out & away the largest river falling into the Albert & greatly adds to its importance as a feeder, & not a mere reservoir to the waters of the Nile, the river probably has its rise among the chain of mountains in which Ruanzori is situated. The natives on this side of the river offered a strong opposition to our crossing but Uledi & Saa Tato very pluckily swam across the river and captured a canoe the natives were trying to take away, Saa Tato got wounded in the shoulder, but they swam with the canoe back

[1] May 12: 'Mr. Jephson was still an invalid with a fever which varied from 102° to 105°, ever since the 23rd April, and at this time he was in rather an anxious frame of mind. Like myself, he was much shrunk, and we both looked it.' (Stanley, *IDA*, II, 235.)

Parke gives a detailed account of Jephson's illness between 10 and 21 May. On the 10th he records that 'Jephson is very feverish and almost hysterical, having to perform these marches with a temperature of 103° F. or more.' On the 11th: 'Jephson is, I fear, in for a very serious illness; when he arrived in camp...his temperature was 104° F., and he looked very badly. He is naturally of an anxious temperament, although full of work and energy. He now thinks the fever will kill him, as he feels that he is losing his senses; indeed he is bordering on delirium from excessive fever.' 12 May: 'I was up twice last night to see Jephson, who is really in a very serious condition: he does not sleep at all. At 11 p.m. I gave him a large dose of chloral hydrate. His fever commences to rise about 8.30 or 9 a.m. Accordingly, I give him thirty grains of quinine about 5.30 every morning; in spite of this, however, his temperature at 11.30 a.m. was 103° F., and at 4.45 p.m., 104° F. For the last week I have also given him a twenty-fifth of a grain of arsenic, three times a day.'

Similar entries recur, until on 20 May 'Stairs and Jephson are both doing fairly well. The latter takes thirty grains of quinine every morning and evening. It is very heavy marching this, along the Semliki valley, as the ground is very boggy and damp.' On 21 May, Jephson's temperature had been normal for 12 hours, and on 26 May this state of affairs had continued 'for some time, and he is picking up. Poor fellow! he has lately been several times at death's door.' (Parke, pp. 424–33.)

across the river & a party of men with guns at once went across in it drove back the natives—captured two other canoes by which means the whole lot of people—somewhere about 1000, were transported safely across without any accident in less than two days.[1] Whilst the people were being transported about 70 of Kaberegga's people crept up near & had the impertinence to fire a volley at the people crossing, our people made a rush for them & drove them across the country for miles, until in their efforts to escape they dropped cartridges, ammunition & all sorts of things, they got such a scare that they troubled us no more. From the river up to the mountains is all bush & we have been making very slow short marches on account of the Pasha's people who are very bad at getting along, many of them are so ill with Syphillis that they can scarcely walk & will never reach the coast. We are now camped some 10 miles from the foot of the mountains on a high plateau or spur from which we can see miles round, we are about 2,900 ft above sea level, that is about 500 ft above the Lake. The banana plantations are more extensive then any we have ever seen; where ever one looks for miles one can see nothing but bananas; they are in such quantities that the huts are full of ripe bananas & we even find them ripe on the trees.

June 11th [1889]. After a few days of convalescence during which time I was slowly regaining strength another attack of fever came on & brought me down still lower than before, it lasted over a week, but I am now free from it, only I fear to get it again almost immediately, judging from this former experience.[2] On May 29th we heard a good many guns firing in the distance, but imagined it was only the Zanzibaris out looting & foraging, but shortly afterwards a small party came in bringing with them a gun (an old Tower Musket) they said they had come upon people armed with guns & had driven them away & one of them had thrown away his gun. Stanley at once sent out a party of men to find out who they were. We soon heard a tremendous firing about half—three quarters of a mile from camp & not long afterwards Uledi Saadi was brought in with his elbow shattered, he was followed by Khamis Kuyamwye & Farajala, the former has the flesh on the inner side of his arm all torn into a big wound & a bullet had passed through his side but had broken no bones, Farajala's case, poor boy, was hopeless one could see that at once, he was badly shot in different parts of the body & had a wound in the abdomen from which his entrails were protruding. Later on Uledi & some of the other Zanzibaris returned bringing with them

[1] 'The brave fellows were rewarded with $20 worth of cloth on the spot' (Stanley, *IDA*, II, 237).

[2] Parke's entry for 4 June: 'Jephson will surely die if this attack is prolonged much further, and he is obliged to walk owing to the scarcity of carriers.' 7 June: 'Jephson's temperature went up to 106° F. last night. I am very anxious about him; but he is full of pluck, which, in Africa, is worth a great deal more than medicine' (Parke, p. 438).

two of Kilonga-longa's people, those with whom Nelson & Parke stayed.[1]
They had a camp with a party of 50 or 60 guns about 4 hrs distant from our
camp & had been there 20 days, a small party of our men had met some of
the Manyuema & they had fired at each other, each party thinking the other
was Kaberegga's people. On hearing that there were people with guns ahead
they, like us, had sent out a party to reconoitre, but they saw our people
in the distance & hid in the long grass until they were close up & then fired
right into them, with the result of three men badly wounded, one fatally,
for Farajala died that same night, & two or three very slightly. We buried
poor little Farajala next morning. I was very sorry, he was quite a boy &
was such a nice bright civil little chap. We killed three of their people.
Uledi had followed them & found them to be the Manuyema of Ipoto &
had brought two on with him to see Stanley. They brought a present of some
goats & Stanley agreed that the whole thing had been a mistake & that both
parties, having suffered equally, he would think no more about it—the
Manuyema had been very frightened when they heard it was Stanley's people
they had fired into. The next day the chiefs of the Manuyema came in to
pay their respects, they had no news. From the camp we got splendid views
of different peaks in the mountain range & Stanley & Stairs tried to get the
height of some of them but the clouds came up & they remained covered
the whole day. After leaving this camp & avoiding going near the Manuyema
camp we passed along near the foot of the mountains, the country being all
long grass ten feet high. Towards the end of the march we got into very
bad country, hilly jungle the paths going down fearfully steep descents to
the very bottom of great gorges 200 ft deep & then mounting up on the
other side so steeply that in places one almost had to go on one's hands &
knees, and villages were always built on the flat places between two such
gorges & had the natives been inclined to stand they might have made it
very nasty for us, but everywhere they cleared out before us. Here the fever
returned & I had a bad time of it getting up & down these places where it
was perfectly impossible to be carried, after some four days of this sort of
country we got out again into the long grass & camped close to the very
foot of the mountains on the edge of a splendid ravine, a wooded gorge ran
down the mountain & out from the trees leapt a great cascade into the ravine
below—it was a sort of Switzerland. The water was icy cold. Stanley decided
to stay here for four days & send Stairs up the mountain to see how far he
could get, I was to have gone too but I was with high fever & that night
my temperature was 106·7, a height of fever none of us have ever reached
before, besides I was too pulled down & weak even to walk properly. It was
a bitter disappointment to me as I had been looking forward to it for so long

[1] At Ipoto, see pp. 168 ff. above, App. IV, pp. 434–6 below.

& I fear this will be the only chance.[1] Stairs started at about seven in the morning & returned at 3 on the following day. He had managed to get to a height of 11,000 ft above the level of the sea, that was about 7,500 ft above our camp. He had had hard work to get up & he & his 40 men were 30 hrs without water, they slept out in the open in the bitter cold without any fire or covering. He could see the snow above him but had been unable to reach it as he & his men were insufficiently equipped for sleeping a night near the snow line. He brought back a bunch of blackberries, real English ones, he said there were quantities & he & the men had had a splendid feed, he also brought such flowers etc as he saw for the Pasha. Another party had gone out to find the road & returned the next day saying that we should reach the plain in three days. They also reported to have come on three hot springs close together, the springs turned out to be small & having a temperature of 102 Fahrenheit. We passed entirely through jungle the last half of the march & camped in the jungle. A jungle camp on a hot sunny day is very pleasant, nice & cool with a chequered shade, it was so many months that I have camped in the jungle. I had almost forgotten how pleasant it was; it was certainly a great relief after some of the glaring camps we have been in lately. The next day we came out of the jungle into a well cleared country at the very foot of the mountains & here we made friends with the natives. Native clearings of bananas & Indian corn extend up the mountain sides nearly the whole way along to, in some places, considerably over 1500 feet. The same wealth of bananas are round one every where almost as far as one can see, the huts are full of ripe & rotting bananas, & hollowed out tree trunks are in every village evidently in daily use for making banana pombe,

---

[1] Stanley indulges in some heavy sarcasm here; his entry for 3 June includes the following passage:

'Now was the period of exploration, and to make botanical collections. Accordingly I sounded the note to prepare to win immortal renown by scaling the heights of the famous Mountains of the Moon. My strength was so far recovered that I could walk 200 yards. Mr. Jephson regretted to say that the fever had conquered and subdued his sanguine spirit, Captain Nelson was sorry, but really if there was any practical use in climbing such ruthlessly tall mountains—and he took a solemn look at them, and said "No, thanks". Surgeon Parke's life was amid suffering humanity; Mr. Bonny was in bad luck—an obstinate fever had gripped him, and reduced his limbs to mere sticks. Captain Casati smiled mournfully, and seemed to say, "Look at me, and imagine how far I could go". But the Pasha's honour was at stake; he had at all times expressed rapture at the very thought, and this was the critical period in the march of the Expedition, and Stairs took a sly glance at the grim, unconquered heights, and said "I'll go like a shot"...In the morning Stairs departed...but alas! the Pasha had to yield after a thousand feet, and returned to camp, while Stairs held on his way' (Stanley, *IDA*, II, 254).

Stairs's report is printed in full in *In Darkest Africa*, II, 254–8, with a list of 38 plants collected by him and identified by Emin.

there a great numbers of ripe bananas on the trees even along the road, there must be far far more than ever the natives can eat or make drink of, even though this is a populous country.

The mountain range is magnificent; such gigantic, splendid peaks & such fine gorges & spurs, but Stairs told me one can get no idea of its gigantic mass until one is high up on the mountain. Today we skirted along the edge of the mountains & emerged from the long grass at the top of a low hill— saw the most splendid country beneath, it was one huge cultivation, we passed through this & made friends with the natives on the road, & are camped in an open space & have the real open plain with short grass & very few trees lying at our feet at no great distance off, perhaps an hour or two's march.

June 12th. Yesterday evening we got the most magnificent view of the snow mountain, or I should say the mountain range, for the whole of that particular range is covered with snow, which in some places seems to come low down on the mountain which must be a great height. It was a splendid sight & by far the best & nearest view we have got of it. Stanley was most anxious to photograph it but the light was failing & the clouds were rolling up—gradually obscuring it, it is seldom seen for very long & generally at early morning & evening. Stairs has gone out with a party of men to discover a large river lying about 12 to 15 miles from this, the natives describe it as a very large river; it maybe the Semliki or the Ituri, but not very likely the latter—of course it may be a new river altogether. We are now according to the natives, only three days from Muta N'zige[1] & two from Usongora. A great number of natives have been in today & have been questioned closely by Stanley about the countries round. They brought in large quantities of banana pombe which was given out amongst the men. This pombe is not bad; it is infinitely superior to that made with M'tama, but it is sickly sweet & after a short time becomes extremely acid. The mountain has unfortunately been shrouded completely with clouds all day, we have been unable to get a sight of it. We seem now to have got quite on to the open plain again, ever since leaving the 'Semliki' it has been jungle & here & there long grass 12 ft high for a day or so, then jungle again, but our marches have been so short & our stoppages so constant, on account of these Egyptians, that we have been over a month from Mazamboni's, this distance in an ordinary way we would have done in 11 to 12 days. One Circassion clerk died on the road two or three days ago, he had been ailing for a long time in the Pasha's

[1] Muta N'zige was the name given to more than one lake in Central Africa. Baker uses the name, or its variant Luta N'zige, for Lake Albert: Jephson refers here to the lake lying south of the Ruwenzori named 'Albert Edward' by Stanley in 1876 and now known as Lake Edward.

country & the march has done for him, he is only one of the many who must perish by the roadside eventually. The worst of it is so few of the Pasha's people—except the negroes—are sound, the greater part are in a terrible state from Syphillis, these appeared all well & sound when they arrived at Kavallis, but soon after the march began, gangrenous ulcers, swellings, & fearful looking sores broke out amongst those affected with this foul disease, ten of them came up at our last camp to ask Stanley to give the people another three days halt there, so that they might recover themselves a bit, this request was refused the place would not have supported us with food for such a time. One never saw ten more miserable looking people; they had all their sores etc on show to add weight to their request, it reminded me of the maimed, the halt & the blind waiting at the pool of Bethesda for the troubling of the waters. The Pasha seems to get along very well & does himself very comfortably.

June 13th. The natives come & go amongst the Zanzibaris without the slightest signs of timidity, Stanley is ever ready to make friends & do it thoroughly, or if need be to fight & do it thoroughly that's what I like, there are no half measures no little petty compromises, either we make friends if the natives are willing, or we fight them & drive them out of our road, time is lost by making friends & we do'nt get so much food, but on the other hand Stanley gets much information from the natives when they are friendly. We hear that the people just ahead of this country do not cultivate much food but collect salt & sell it to these people for food. The men brought in two days ago a large quantity of fine white salt. In 1876 when Stanley reached the Muta-Nzige he heard a good deal about Usongora from different natives, about the quantities of salt, the springs of hot mud, the cattle & the warlike nature of the Wa-songora, they all said 'Usongora is a wonderful country' & it is this country we are about to enter. We cannot be many days march now from Stanley's old camp on the Muta-Nzige, he then knows the route, but I do not think he has decided what route he will take, whether the eastern or Western shore of the Lake, he will wait & see in what direction the Lake lies. The position of this camp is very fine, it is on the flat summit of a low hill, in front of us stretches the plain, short grass dotted sparsely with trees, it stretches as far as one can see to a low range of hills some 20 miles distant, to the right are solid banana groves stretching right away to the jungle, to the left is the glorious range of mountains ever dominating the whole country round, cool breezes come down from the snows & at night one requires two blankets as the night winds are so piercing. I'm afraid there will be no more chances of trying to get up to the snow, the mountain range which is snow capped lies so much in the centre of the entire range that it would be difficult to get to it unless the exploring party went for some days.

I am always unlucky, I am perfectly well when there is nothing particular to do & then fever comes & prostrates me just when I am wanted. Stanley had all such people of the Pasha as have guns up before him & formed them into a company under Shookri Aga, Nubians, Egyptians, clerks or servants were all included & they are to be always ready to fight or do what he orders when he gives the word. Early in the afternoon Stairs returned he had reached the river which he found at that place to be forty two yards broad with an average depth of ten feet & a current of three miles an hour. From the general appearance of the river, from the direction in which it was running, & from the fact that the water had a brackish taste he had no hesitation in pronouncing it to be the 'Semliki' which was 75 yds where we crossed it forty or fifty miles below & the great numbers of rivers & streams we crossed over all flowing from the mountains to the river are quite enough to account for the difference in breadth. The natives declare the river comes out of Muta Nzige, but of course their reports cannot be considered trustworthy. Stairs reports plenty of food ahead, he says he never before saw such a drunken country every other native who came out to greet him as he passed was half drunk with pombe, there is certainly any amount of banana pombe in the country & very little seems to affect both natives & Zanzibaris, the amount which would make a Zanzibari or a Native quite drunk would have no effect whatever upon me, though I am not able to stand much wine, I never drink pombe of any sort; all native made drinks seem to me to have an unfresh, fusty taste which I find most unpleasant. In the evening we had another of those unpleasant scenes between Stanley & the Pasha which are so regrettable.[1] Shookri Aga's new company, composed of all the Pasha's people who are bearing guns, had orders from Stanley to act as rearguard tomorrow to relieve Nelson & Stairs who always take it on alternate days. In the evening the Pasha came up to Stanley to say he did not want his boys to do duty in the rear guard as he wanted them himself on the road, Stanley, very naturally, remonstrated & said it would be such a bad example to set his people for all would follow suit & all would say they wanted their boys & then the company would collapse. The Pasha knew that Stanley was going to make this arrangement weeks ago & had said it was just the thing, but when it came to the point he wanted Stanley to give all his boys Remington Rifles but did not want to help us. This very naturally angered Stanley for the Pasha never will help him in any way & does all he can to oppose his plans, he never, too, seems to learn wisdom from experience & always says just the very things calculated most to anger Stanley; at any rate high words were running between the two when we officers, in answer to Stanley's

[1] Stanley does not mention this incident in *In Darkest Africa*; Parke records it more briefly as occurring on 16 June (Parke, p. 439).

signal to bring up our companies of Zanzibaris in front of his tent, arrived on the scene, both were in a towering rage & we heard the Pasha shout out as he was going 'I think you had better leave me here, I wish you had never come to help me', & Stanley answered him 'You are a most thankless & ungrateful man'. Of course all we officers felt furious at the Pasha's ungrateful speech, after all those lives have been lost, after all the trouble we have gone through, the time we have given up to hard & unpleasant work & all to help him in answer to his earnest appeals for help to England or rather to the English people.

June 14th. We made a very fair march of about 7½ miles today & camped in a small village half way up a low hill from which we get a splendid view of the plain for miles & a distant view of the 'Semliki' winding like a silver thread through the plain. We passed through great numbers of plantain groves & there was a good deal of Indian corn & beans so that there is plenty of food here. We are now getting near the end of this range of mountains & the range is gradually getting lower & lower; we shall probably follow it right up to the Lake. We passed over a hot stream today in which was a considerable body of water, it must have been very hot at the point where it issued from the mountain side, there was a slight smell of sulphur. The natives are very friendly & readily act as guides. Kaberegga has swept & raided over all this country so that there are no cattle, but we expect to find a good many near the Lake & further on, we have still about 80 cattle & a large number of goats & sheep. Some natives came in late this afternoon & the Pasha questioned them about the river, they called it the 'Ingezi' which was the same name as the natives gave it at the point where Stairs struck it, they said it ran into the Nyanza, but that means nothing as every bit of water of any size is called Nyanza by them. If it does run out of the Muta Nzige it is to be hoped that we shall be able to find the place of its exit & so make the problem a certainty.

June 15th. Shortly after leaving camp we turned to the left over the mountains & had a splendid cold breeze blowing strongly the whole way. The country is much like that round Kavalli's, open country with a few trees dotted about. There were many new flowers I had not seen before, notable amongst them a large thistle with clusters of pink lupin-like flowers, a plant like a pink flox, another like a forget-me-not & quantities of real lemon thyme, the latter smelling most deliciously. The path was good but led up & down hill a good deal, it is wonderful how ones spirits rise when one gets high up & feels the cold breeze blowing round one. We are camped in a small village with extensive banana plantations & Indian corn fields about it. On the crest of the hill ahead are numbers of Candelabra Euphorbia & a good many dracoenas, it is unusual to see the former so high up & in such exposed places hitherto I have only seen them at a much lower altitude & always on hot & sheltered plains. The natives tell us there is no food ahead right up to the lake, there is only salt, tomorrow I believe we camp near a market where quantities of salt is sold; the next day we should reach the Lake. We got a good view of the snow mountain range shortly after leaving camp this morning, I fear there is no chance of anything more being done towards attempting the ascent as we are going further from it every day now. I still continue without fever, thank God,—but Parke still gives me large doses of quinine (10 grs) every morning to prevent any return of it,— & am getting quite strong again, but still fearfully thin & meagre, it will be weeks—even if I continue in good health—before I can get back to my natural state again. We got a magnificent view of the Ruanzori snow mountains this evening through a gap in the hills & Stanley was able to get two photographs of it, the distance was however great & I am afraid the mountains will not come out very distinctly.

June 16th. This morning almost immediately after leaving camp we began to descend the mountains & came down on to a plain much like that below Kavalli's, bordering the Albert Nyanza, except there were much fewer trees & these were almost entirely Euphorbias, we passed two or three villages all of which had cattle Kraals but they had been deserted some days & the cattle driven off by Kaberega's soldiers, our road was good & we got on at a good rate, we crossed a very considerable stream, in fact a small river, running into the Lake. At about 10 o'clock we captured 36 head of cattle— which was a welcome addition to our herd reduced now to about 68 head— these cattle had been captured by Kaberega's soldiers & left by them in charge of some natives whilst they went somewhere up the mountains to make a raid, the cattle were all in very good condition, a great contrast to our poor half starved, over-driven herd reduced to a state of meagreness by want of good grass & being driven along the road too fast every day. We camped in a large village surrounded by three cattle Kraals, capable of taking in over 300 cattle & surrounded by thorns & hedges of Euphorbia planted very closely. Rather a nasty thing happened between Bonny & Nelson.[1] Bonny has been told off by Stanley to look after the cattle & goats, that is his work in the expedition but like everything else he has to do he simply neglects his duty to such an extent that he might just as well not be there at all, for the officers of the rear guard always have to bring the cattle into camp, whilst Bonny merely goes ahead & establishes himself in camp as early as he can without thinking or troubling his head about his work. Nelson therefore reported Bonny's neglect of duty to Stanley but not till after every means had been tried by both himself & Stairs to get Bonny to

[1] Neither Stanley nor Parke records this incident.

look after his work. Bonny was very angry at being reported & a furious scene took [place] in which he said all sorts of evil things about Nelson in a sort of shrill scream—whether true or not I ca'nt say—& finally called Nelson a liar, upon which Nelson struck him & a rather disgraceful struggle took place in Stanley's hut in front of him, the combattants were finally seperated, & Stanley read them both a lecture on the disgrace of two Europeans fighting. It is a great pity such a thing has happened for two Europeans fighting in the middle of Central Africa is not a very creditable thing & is very bad for the Zanzibaris to hear & talk about. Bonny is a most exasperating, low sort of fellow, he is just a sergeant with all the feelings, ideas, & loafing propensities of a typical 'Tommy Atkins' added to this he has an overweening conceit which is quite wonderful seeing that he has absolutely nothing to be conceited about; he has done nothing for the Expedition & is despised by the men. We have treated him much as an equal, being all Europeans together in Africa, & he has come to think that he actually is our equal in every way & so has become spoilt, he is a man none of us have ever liked or trusted, for he is simply dishonest. [1] In the evening we got a view of the lake some four & a half miles distant, but it was so hazy that the whole thing looked more like a mirage than anything real.

[1] The mistrust which Jephson and his brother officers continued to feel where Bonny was concerned is partly explained by incidents such as these, and by his descriptions of life with the Rear Column. (See p. 337 above.)

Bonny's origins were not, however, so plebeian as Jephson suggests. I am indebted to Mr Iain Smith, who, in his researches into the history of the Emin Pasha Relief Expedition, has found among the Barttelot family papers the following information about Bonny in a letter from Major Barttelot to his fiancée Miss Mabel Godman:

'Bonny is a good honest man, but rough, and not a man I could make a close friend of were I shut up for years alone with him...(he) is the queerest specimen you ever saw. A mixture of conceit, bravery and ignorance, born a gentleman, but by circumstances a non-commissioned officer in the Army, he purchased his discharge to come on this expedition. His continual cry is that he is every bit as good as we are, and must be treated the same. Stanley was very down on him, and he was very bitter about it. Since he has been with me I have done all I can for him. He is most useful with the natives and Arabs, of an unchangingly slow temperament, he is just suited to them. He purchases all supplies for us and doctors the sick, for he was in the Army Medical Department. He is in charge also of the Zanzibaris. He is the third man who is going with me, Jameson being the other' (Barttelot to Mabel Godman, Barttelot Papers, 26 May 1888).

CHAPTER 17

THE SALT LAKE
AND THE MARCH THROUGH ANKOLE
AND KARAGWE

17 JUNE–2 AUGUST 1889

June 17th. This morning we started off in an Easterly direction for the head of the lake, a direction almost at right angles to that in which we had seen the Lake last night. The road led through a hot scorched up plain until we reached a large beautiful clear stream taking a large body of water into the Lake, it is evidently one of the rivers which drain the southern slopes of the Ruanzori Range, near this river were very extensive villages & cattle Kraals all surrounded by thick hedges of Euphorbias, perfectly impenetrable. It was in these villages that Kabarega's soldiers had established themselves with the herds of cattle they had taken from the natives all round, but the natives attacked them & obliged them to retire, but they were able to take their stolen cattle with them, we could trace the broad track made by the cattle for miles along the plain; there must have been large numbers of them. These villages had immense stores of salt in them, numbers of great bushel baskets full of a sort of pinkish crystal looking rock salt, but with a slightly soda like taste, after a hot fatiguing march of another hour we came upon a small placid lake lying in a hollow below us, it was a mile long & half a mile broad with apparently no outlet—on the other side of the path,—we were walking on a narrow ridge 50 yds broad, we saw the Muta N'zige—or the Luta-Nzige as the natives here seem to call it—lying like glass beneath us, as one walked along the ridge the two lakes lay on ones right & left hands immediately beneath us, each seeming to be but a stone's throw from the path. It was very hazy but we could distinguish two high rocky islands, the nearest of which was covered with huts, evidently it is a place of refuge for the natives of the main land. We have struck the North West corner of the Lake, but our native guides tell us the lake extends in a long narrow neck to the north & it will take us some days to march round it to the Eastern side opposite here which looks only a few hours march distant, as from here we cannot see the neck of the Lake which runs up a narrow gorge between two cliffs. We passed the ridge dividing the two lakes & camped in a very extensive collection of villages situated rather prettily amongst groups of large Euphorbias, each village & cattle Kraal had its boma of Euphorbias &

bamboos, & each opened into the other by narrow entrances, it was a most bewildering network of bomas & would be a very hard place to take in the face of a determined enemy unless one fired the huts. Here were immense stores of salt lying about in the open, sufficient for the whole caravan of over 1,100 souls many times over, moreover the road for the last two miles was strewn with heaps of salt every few hundred yards, each heap containing perhaps over a peck of rock salt. We found a good deal of Indian corn, Tullaboon, & beans hidden in the grass round the villages, there were also a good many chickens left & my Zanzibaris brought me in some very good eggs. After we had been some two hours in camp 21 canoes were reported approaching the shore from the island, a party was sent down with our interpreter but the natives in the canoes would not believe we were the caravan of white men but thought we were more of Kaberega's people until Stairs went down to the water's edge & showed himself, they then paddled back to their island about half a mile distant but promised to return tomorrow & talk with Stanley. Afterwards several natives came in to see Stanley but I have not heard what information he obtained from the interview. The men who went down to the Lake found great numbers of large packets of salt, each a man's load, hidden in the grass near the water's edge ready for embarkation in the canoes. They also captured two small canoes & a large one; the former were made of planks sewn together like the canoes of Uganda, the large canoe was the ordinary dug-out. All the canoes were badly shaped & very clumsy, but the paddles were neatly & most cleverly made. Stanley's boy caught several large fish with a hook & line, Stanley sent us one; it was very good & fairly firm, one of the fish he caught must have weighed quite 10 lbs. This is a most interesting country; we stay here tomorrow, but there are no cultivations about & there is a scarcity of food which will not admit of our staying more than a day I fear.

June 18th. The mosquitos last night kept the whole camp awake officers & men in despair left their huts & went to sleep, or rather tried to sleep in the open, but with little success; the mosquitos were everywhere, I am the only one of the officers who has mosquito curtains, so I slept soundly all night untroubled by these insect pests. I always put up my mosquito curtains whenever I can, not for the mosquitos for hitherto we have had none, but they are wonderful for keeping off malaria.[1] This morning a party was dispatched to get food in any villages round which were deserted, I sent out my servants & they brought in a quantity of green Indian corn & a large bunch of bananas. Two camps back I warned them to take in a supply of food, for assuredly there would be hunger ahead, but they are so improvident

[1] Jephson, of course, held the contemporary view that malaria was caused by 'bad air', particularly the mist rising from a swamp (see p. 103 above).

& trust to finding food on the road from day to day; the consequence is they arrived here with nothing. We have sent out men with fishing lines & hooks to the Lake & hope to get a supply of fish it is a great treat to us as we have had so little of it. Some of the men brought up some water from the small lake to show me—it is far salter than the sea, & is of a pinkish colour like the colour of the salt here, there are no signs of life whatever in this lake. The water of the big lake, Luta-Nzige has the same unpleasant soda like taste as the water of the Albert Nyanza, but I think it is more salt, though the other officers say not. There are numbers of doves & spur winged plover & quantities of little birds which come down to eat the salt which is scattered about. In the afternoon Stairs & I went down to the small salt lake,[1] the water looks almost like Condy's Fluid it is such a dark crimson colour, the water is very shallow, a man can go out into the water 100 yards from shore & the water will scarcely reach above his ankles, & it is therefore quite hot from the sun & the evaporation must be enormous, the bottom is all black mud with a foetid, sulphurous smell. It is now the dry season & the lake has fallen very low in consequence of the great evaporation & the water falling has left large mud flats bare & exposed, on these the natives have made their salt pans, they enclose a round space thirty feet in diameter with banks of mud & the water of the Lake retiring as the lake falls leaves small shallow ponds the water of which from the action of the sun dries up gradually & leaves a beautifully crystalized encrustation of salt some inch & a half thick all over the bottom of the pond—it is the simplest & most primitive method possible & the salt is splendid, very sharp but with a slightly soda like taste, the top of this deposit is formed entirely of large beautifully clear crystals, & the lower half is opaque & of a very pretty pink coral-like colour. The water in these salt pans is more intensely crimson than the water of the lake & the surface is covered with a coating of salt looking exactly like ice which, when broken, sinks to the bottom, when the water is completely dried up the natives break up the encrustation of salt left & pile it in heaps, pack it neatly with banana leaves & fibre into good sized packages & store it in the huts ready for exportation on the Lake, or for the caravans of natives who come from a distance to trade with them. The amount of salt

---

[1] This was the famous salt lake of Katwe: 'The salt lake at Katwe is astonishing. The visitor comes suddenly upon a cauldron-like hole with a mean diameter of about 2 miles, which is an explosion crater blown through pre-existing deposits of volcanic ashes. It is separated from Lake Edward by a neck of land only some 800 yards wide (on which are the remains of Fort George constructed by Lugard in 1891), yet its level is some 95 feet below that of Lake Edward. Its shallow waters appear in some lights to have a blood-red colour. The better qualities of salt are obtained as crystals or by evaporation, while in a less pure form it is extracted in slabs from the floor of the lake' (Thomas and Scott, *Uganda*, pp. 453–4).

obtained this way is immense, the mud, sticks, bits of rushes, etc which have been covered by the water are stiff with a white coating of salt & as one walks along, the ground crackles under one's feet as if there had been a strong hoar frost there is salt everywhere, the sloping cliffs which enclose one side of the lake are covered with a sort of hoar frost which has a very bitter taste & contains quantities of iron ore, lying about amongst the salt frequently there are bits of a white opaque substance, looking something like chalk, which when touched with the tongue have a bitter acrid taste. I showed a specimen to the Pasha who declared it to be pure sulphate of soda. There are no signs of life in the waters of this salt, dead lake, no shells or fish of any sort, a few melancholy looking spur-winged & gray plover brood along its shores, & here & there a stray black & white Kingfisher is to be seen, but I have not observed any of them feeding upon anything. One side & end of this lake is utterly barren & there are no springs entering the lake[1] & nothing but a sort of stiff stunted looking rush 18 inches in height grows there, the other side & end is clothed all round by a narrow belt of rank vegetation amongst which a few palm trees may be seen growing, the Pasha found a small stream running from the hill side into the lake, but the water has a slightly bitter taste, there are probably small springs all round this side & end of the lake which would account for the vegetation. The Pasha took the height of the surface of the two lakes, the salt lake & the Luta-Nzige & found that the former was some 150 feet below the latter though only about 350 yards distant from it. One of the great things in Africa is the scarcity of salt, & he is considered a rich man who is able to have salt every day. Thus from any place where there is salt it is carried to great distances & dispersed all over the country in most minute quantities, the natives themselves never know where it comes from, thus Kibero in Unyoro supplies the whole of northern Unyoro, Uganda & all the countries to the [indecipherable] & West, but the yield of salt at Kibero[2] is not a hundredth part as great as this, this must be the largest salt producing district in all Central Africa & its salt must be carried to incredible distances, it must supply all Ruanda & the countries to the West & South & must be a great source of wealth to the natives round here. Kaberegga's people have now reached here & will doubtless turn the flow of salt in a great measure to the Eastern countries, but their presence is likely greatly to interfere with the salt trade as the natives can no longer make & sell their salt in the same

[1] Parke states: 'We found one rivulet running into the lake; this is at the Southern extremity, and its waters have a highly sulphurous odour...There is no effluent passing from the lake' (Parke, p. 441).

Parke took a sample of the water home & had it analysed by Sir Charles Cameron at the Royal College of Surgeons, Dublin (*ibid.*).

[2] Kibero has of late years ceased to be of importance as a salt centre.

security as formerly. This lake is most wonderful & I should think will be considered a very important discovery. We hear from the natives that Unyampaka, the point at which Stanley reached the Luta Nzige in 1877 is only three days march from here & there is plenty of food there. Stanley reached this place accompanied by 2500 Waganda lent him as an escort by M'tesa King of Uganda, but on reaching the lake, rumours that the natives were massing in enormous numbers with the intention of attacking them, created such a panic amongst the Waganda that they insisted on retiring & Stanley was obliged to give up his much cherished plan of circumnavigating the Lake. Now after nearly 13 years he is here again & I trust will be able to clear up the mystery of the Muta Nzige.

June 19th. Stanley has gone this morning in a canoe we captured a few days ago to the island where the natives are camped, he will no doubt go round the head of the Lake & perhaps reach the place where the Semliki flows out, & so clear up the long argued question as to whether the Luta Nzige & the Albert Nyanza are connected by a river. The canoe is a good size, but awfully heavy & incapable of going fast. The chief of the island came over to see Stanley & to make friends, he got a present of a handsome silk cloth & a cow. Early in the afternoon Stanley returned; he had only been able to get 7 miles along the East coast, the canoe went so badly. The name of the salt lake is Kehir & the village we are in is Katwa. The Luta-Nzige or Muta-Nzige was found by boiling to be 850 ft above the Albert. A good deal of Indian corn, Tullaboon & beans were found in the village & all hands are making flour in expectation of hunger ahead. When Stanley went down to Lake Kahir yesterday he found a regular bed of fossils in the hill side near the lake; a number of different kinds of teeth & a tusk of ivory. Though Stanley has not been down to the place where the Semliki flows out of the lake he has not a doubt, from the way the river runs, that it does connect the Luta N'zige with the Albert.

June 20th. The road lay today along the shore of the a small lake for some three miles & ran in nearly a due Easterly direction, the plain through which we passed was nearly quite flat & the road was good, everything was dried up & sere & nothing in the shape of trees except Euphorbias were to be seen, the whole plain had a peculiarly desolate & dead look. At about 10 o'clock we came upon some water holes near a large deserted village, but the water except for the Zanzabaris was undrinkable. There were signs of immense numbers of cattle having passed along the road & there were kraals in the villages, but the cattle had all been driven away some days ago by Kabarega's people. After going till 12, the character of the vegetation changed & we came on Acacia trees & scrub. We stopped for lunch at 12 for an hour & Stanley took the sun, & shot a Nile goose, which was feeding in a water hole at a distance of 80 yards, with a Winchester rifle, a very good shot. At about 2.30 we came in sight of the Lake again, & camped in a large village called Hamkongo,[1] or rather a chain of villages, on the Lake shore opposite Irangara island having done a march of 18½ miles, the distance between the main land and the island was only 150 yards. The natives had left the village & had retired to the island we could see numbers of other villages & it was evidently thickly populated, taking with them their sheep, goats & fowls but we found a good deal of Tullaboon corn, Indian corn & beans in the huts—this village is exactly on the Equator. The[re] was a very large hut in the village surrounded by a fine boma containing four other huts & one for cooking, it was evidently the residence of a big chief. The inside of the hut was neatly plastered over with a mixture of clay & cowdung this was painted white & all sorts of hieroglyphics painted in red black & yellow were pictured on this back ground, inside the door was a small raised divan for sitting upon, this was painted in imitation of mosaics in black, red & yellow, in front of the door ran a screen painted in the same style as the inside of the hut. This screen shut off a large room in which there were five beds raised & painted like the divan & covered with clean straw. The door way itself & the porch were marvels of native art, with queer nooks & brackets in the sides; at the entrance were two pillars with plain round capitals, much like the ringed Doric capital, & the posts supporting the roof inside were also plastered over & made to look like pillars, the whole was brilliantly painted in the same three colours & had a most remarkable & pleasing effect, the Pasha said it greatly reminded him of some of the temples at Thebes. We had none of us ever seen anything like it before, all the huts, even of the big chiefs, are the same dark, smoke stained, dirty places only differing from the ordinary huts in point of size, & this seemed like a bit of another country planted in the middle of central Africa. Stanley & the men were equally astonished as ourselves. The hut was of the ordinary behive shape except that it was beautifully made & very lofty.[2] There were numbers of geese surviving unconcernedly close to shore, Stanley had a shot at them with his Winchester Rifle but missed; he however transfixed a sacred Ibis & a heron, who were sitting on a tree together, with one bullet at a distance of 70 yards, the Ibis is very good eating. If any of us had a shot gun we could get a lot of geese & duck but Parke—who is the only officer who brought one—has run out of cartridges.

June 21st. We followed the shores of the lake at a distance of about three

[1] Stanley calls this group of villages 'Mukungu, in Unyampala of Toro, Chief Kassesse, whose name was made familiar to me in January 1876' (*IDA*, II, 319).

[2] Stanley describes the 'hut which the Pasha occupied' as being 20 ft in height and about 21 ft in diameter, with a doorway 6 ft high by 6 ft wide, all ornately decorated (*IDA*, II, 319–20).

miles, this shore seems to be most irregular, all bays & lagoons the consequence was we marched in every direction sometimes we were going East sometimes North & the last part of the road led West. The plain here is narrow & lies between the lake & a chain of mountains of no great height, perhaps 4,000 ft. We passed through a pretty bit of Acacia forest & marched into a village called N'guli situated on a stream called the Mokia, here we found the village burnt & the huts still smoking, the Wanasura had only left the day before & we caught one of them lurking about & put him in chains, but he managed somehow to get away at night, the men got a fair amount of food in the shape of Indian corn & beans, there had been a fine field of half ripe Indian corn but the Wanasura had turned their cattle into it & destroyed it entirely.

June 22nd. Made a fairly good march & camped in a large banana plantation amid very extensive cultivations, here there was food in abundance, hundreds of acres of bananas, fields of standing corn & beans & quantities of dry Indian corn, beans & ripe bananas in the huts, this was one of the best places we had been in for a long time for food, there was enough to keep the caravan of over 1100 people for days & days & all the food was close round us. At about ten o'clock as the head of the column was entering a large growth of high grasses & canes some of the Wanasura who were lying concealed on the other side of a stream which ran through the long grass fired a volley point blank into the faces of the advance party, unfortunately there were a lot of women with the advance party & these at once turned round en masse & rushed in a body completely running over the men behind them who were hastening up, for a minute or two it created quite a panic & everyone threw down their loads until Stanley got the people together & sent my company to attack, we went forward at a steady run crossed the stream & drove the Wanasura up the hills but did not follow them further. We found they had five distinct camps all round a small village with a very fine hut new & painted & arranged like the one I described before, but the Wanasura put fire to it before evacuating & we only arrived to find it in flames. There were quantities of food of different kinds in the camp & the men loaded themselves down with it before leaving. Kabarega's people— the Wanasura as they are called—are the pests & terror of all the countries near & they raid devastate & ruin whole tracts of country carrying off with them hundreds of cattle & goats. Some Wa-homa came into our camp they are magnificent looking men & look—as they claim to be—of royal descent & whose only occupation for countless generations has been tending their flocks & herds, any other other occupation they consider beneath them, they love their cattle & hate to see any of them killed. These people told us the Wanasura had driven away all their cattle & that their people had said it was no good living without them, so they agreed to follow their flocks into captivity for the sake of being allowed to tend them & milk them for the Wanasura rather than live without them—these people are also going to give themselves up to the Wanasura for the sake of being again with their flocks & herds. The more one sees of the Wa-homa the more one likes them, they have such a fine bearing & nice clear cut faces; they make all the flat nosed, thick-lipped natives round look so ill-bred & common. We crossed the Nyamwamba a considerable stream running into the Lake, before camping in this settlement which is called M'ruli, & the country is called M'toro.[1]

June 23rd. Stay here for two days to prepare food as Stanley thinks it likely we may not find much ahead. Some of our people came in late yesterday evening & said they had been out at some distance & had seen numbers of Wanasura passing ahead with their loads on their heads—they were passing on in front of us to get out of our way—Nelson was therefore sent out with a party of 100 guns to go after them, he went all day & returned when it was nearly dark but had been unable to come up with them. This awful sickness of fever continues & one Zanzibari died today—as for the Pasha's people hardly a day passes that some one is not left behind, the water is so bad & nitrous. The country we are passing through is a dried up desolate looking place with here & there a stream, but for the most part the people have to get their water from mud holes, all this time we are marching along the Lake, within a mile or two of it, but we only see it occasionally, a deep haze, which began directly we approached the vicinity of the Lake, has shrouded everything & one can only see a few miles & even then very indistinctly, the haze has a most depressing effect on ones spirits.

June 24th. Our guides, who have been with us for a fortnight, & have been most useful, leave us today, & tomorrow we march without any, Stanley is rather nervous about the food & water supply ahead.

June 25th. Marched 12 miles & camped in a small forest, on the road we passed through two large marshes & much malarious ground, in the various puddles dried up by the sun there was a white powder & on tasting it I found it had a bitter nitrous taste, this taste of nitre is more or less noticible in all the water we drink & is most unwholesome & nauseous. The plain is uninteresting all round, nothing but Euphorbias & we are marching between a low barren burnt up range of mountains & a glaring fever stricken land with perfectly undrinkable water. The water in camp is very bad & fever is raging among the people my boy & my woman servant who carries my food are both down with fever & I have to do most of the tent work myself.

June 26th. The jungle we passed through this morning was full of wild

[1] Stanley gives Buruli in the country of Toro; the latter is the correct modern name of the Province.

date palms nearly all bearing a small yellow fruit, the taste was something like a date but there was nothing on them but the skin & a taste round the stone, these palms are very handsome & form most graceful groups of drooping fronds with the bright yellow fruit standing out well against the green. We crossed a large river 35 yds wide running into the Lake it is called N'songi & has a good large body of water in it & judging from the water mark must in the rainy season carry a considerable amount of water into the Lake. On emerging from the jungle in which were large camps of the Wanasura, only abandoned two or three days before, we saw two Wanasura seated on the top of a hill about half a mile distant, in spite of the distance they fired off their guns at us & ran & my company threw down their loads & Stanley stopped while we gave chase. We very nearly came up with them but they disappeared in some long grass & canes where it was impossible to find them. The column then marched on & we came to large native settlements quite deserted on account of the Wanasura but there were large fields of standing ripe white & red m'tama & sesam, this is the first time we have come on white M'tama grown by the natives. The Wanasura had been lately camping in the villages & had looted all the huts & taken the goats & chickens, we marched through this settlement & camped on a low plateau at the foot of a range of low mountains which lies between us & the Lake. Tonight I am down with high fever. We caught a Wanasura spy near the camp & put him in chains.

June 27th. Remained in camp today. Stairs & a party of men went back to look for some loads & men who had been left behind he found a woman of the Pasha's lying dead by the road pierced [by] the spears of the Wanasura. On reaching the people he was almost immediately fired upon by a large party of Wanasura who had evidently been creeping up in the grass to cut off the stragglers when Stairs party arrived just in time to save them, they chased the Wanasura off & dispersed them & brought the missing people safely into camp. Oh! the indescribable torture & misery of this fever, the lying awake at night racked with pain & the fever consuming one & eating up ones strength & energy.

June 28th. Parke gave me opium last night & I had a better night, but the fever is still on me so I have had to march in the blazing sun in spite of it. Stanley, Parke, Stairs, Bonny & myself are all down with fever, this gives some idea of the unhealthiness of the country Nelson is the only one of us today without fever.[1] Our march was 7 miles in a SE direction, we crossed

[1] Parke's entry for 29 June: 'We marched to day from early morning till 10.15 a.m., and then halted in a banana plantation. Mr. Stanley's temperature is extremely high to-day; Stairs, Jephson, and Bonny are also prostrated by the prevailing disorder; and a very large proportion of our men are entirely unable to carry their loads from this horrid fever, whose presence weighs us all down. Every man's tongue is coated

the M'pango river running into the Lake [Edward]. I never saw any one so knocked over before as Stanley he just threw himself down on the grass & simply lay there before all the men, speechless & powerless to move, as a rule he keeps out of sight of the men as much as possible when he's sick.

June 29th. My fever is gone today, we marched through a dreary scorched up country for about 7 miles & camped near the lake & made friends with the natives, they told us how a canoe had come down from Katwa (the salt village at the head of the Lake) & told them we were good people we did not loot their country & we had driven away the Wanasura & opened up the salt trade again.

June 30th. Marched SSW 3 miles & crossed the Rusango river & camped in a village called Kasunga Nyanza on the edge of the Lake & almost immediately below the mountains where Stanley made his camp in /77, when he was accompanied by the 2500 Waganda & had to turn back, there is now, as then, a deep haze over everything. We are now in the country called Unyampaka, mentioned in Stanley's book. The natives came in & eventually promised to bring us their chief to make friends with us but they are very shy & timid & awfully afraid of us.

July 1st [1889]. Halted in order to let the people get food. It is a great pity Stanley will not be able to circumnavigate the Lake & so put an end to discussion, the thing is he has no boat & there are no canoes sufficiently large or safe to be got in order to take sufficiently large party as would be required for circumnavigation, it is impossible to estimate its size, it is very different to the Albert in this way that its shores all seem low, its banks or at any rate its Eastern bank is most irregular, being a series of bays & coves, & this lake is full of large islands whereas the Albert has high straight shores & no islands, the water of this lake like that of the Albert has a soda like taste but this is more soda like & dirty as well a great contrast to the clear waters of the Albert. There is another difficulty also in getting a place with sufficient food in it to feed this large caravan of 1100 souls for time to be spared in circumnavigating the Lake.[1]

with a white fur, even if he has not an elevated temperature. Emin Pasha's temperature is now normal but he has still the white tongue' (Parke, p. 446).

On 1 July he writes: 'I filled to-day all the quinine bottles belonging to the officers of the Expedition...This ounce bottle must do for each till we reach Zanzibar, as there is no more quinine left' (*ibid.* p. 447).

[1] Stanley records the muster roll of the Pasha's people at this date:

    44 officers, heads of families and clerks
    90 married women and concubines
   107 children
   223 guards, soldiers, orderlies, and servants
    91 followers
   ___
   555   (Stanley, *IDA*, II, 325.)

July 2nd. Halted to see if the Sultan of the district would come in & make friends, he sent friendly messages by his people but seems afraid to come himself. The name of this village is Chikom.

July 3rd. Marched SSW 6 miles, on the way some natives came over from an island & made friends with us & some of them escorted us to a village where we camped. In talking with the Natives Stanley heard Antari the King of Ankori[1] through whose country we want to pass & who at the time he was here before was not of much consequence, has now become a personage & has guns & Waganda & men of Karagwe in his service, he therefore sent for all us officers & laid the case before us, he said we could not pay our way through the country as we had not enough cloth & with the long straggling column we have to protect were not strong enough to fight, there were four roads open to us. One was to return West & reach the forest go South & reach Ujiji, a second to skirt S & go through Ruanda, the third was this Ankori route & the fourth to go North skirt Southern Uganda & cross the Alexandra Nile as quickly as possible. The forest route was rejected as being too long—the fourth route as being too risky with our slow marching column, the second & third routes therefore only were left. Stairs on being asked said he thought the second, the route through Ruanda the best, I declared for the third, viz our proposed route through Ankori, it is the shortest besides I think Stanley's fears are groundless, he himself, I could see, was for the Ankori route but he wished to put the difficulties of the four routes to be chosen from before us. Stanley went on to explain that as we had opened up the salt market again & the people had come down here & given a good account of us & we had fought & driven away the Wanasura, Antari's deadly enemies, he thought we might make sufficient capital out of these facts to enable us to pass through Ankori without our fighting or paying much beyond small presents—the Ankori route therefore was decided on, as I knew it would be when he first laid matters before us. The chiefs were then called & asked if they were ready to fight if necessary & they all said 'Yes', after things had been explained to them—so the 'shauri' ended, as all 'shauris' do, by everyone being brought round to Stanley's way of thinking. The name of the village we are camping in is Chokom & we are now in Ankori & the natives we have made friends with here are Antari's subjects.

July 4th. Marched SSE 7 miles & camped in a village called Kitata, half way up the mountains. We left the Lake behind us, enshrouded as usual in

---

[1] Correctly Ankole, and the King's name is also, and more usually, spelt Ntali. Lugard in 1891 marched through Toro, and entered Ankole hoping to meet Ntali and make a pact with him. Ntali sent his son Birinzi for a blood brotherhood ceremony, rather as Uchunki was later sent to meet Stanley (Lugard, *Rise of our East African Empire*, II, 160). See map, p. 66 above.

a dense haze—I think the Albert Edward Lake will forever be associated in my mind with haze, fever, bad water & papyrus, for we had nothing else the whole time we were on it.[1] As we marched on we gradually came to plantations of bananas in the valleys & sheltered gullys in the mountains & hundreds of natives came up from the villages to see the white men & their caravan—the first that had ever passed through their country. They showed every sign of friendliness & confidence & thanked us for having opened up the salt market—the fact that we have done so will, I'm sure, ensure us a free pass through the country. The natives are fine made men with some Wahoma blood in them & a good many Wahoma mixed amongst them, their spears are beautifully made & are kept bright & sharp with great care, there is no ornamentation about them, they are just well made, strong, stabbing spears, but though the iron is of course soft, European artisans themselves could not make them better. Their bows & arrows are immensely large, when a man is standing up, & one horn of his bow resting on the ground, the bow in some cases reaches a foot above his head, they are of a very queer shape, are strong & strung with twisted gut, the arrows are long & heavy with long iron spear shaped heads in some cases 14 inches long, the arrow itself is somewhat over a yard long & is feathered with three feathers, this is the first time we have seen real feathers used for arrows, hitherto we have seen only leaves or leather. There are comparatively few men carrying bows, & shields are small & rarely seen. It will be extremely difficult for Stanley to give any idea of the size or extent of the Lake or of the outline of its Eastern shore, it is certain, I think, that the Semliki is the only out flow from the Lake, & Baker was, after all, right in calling the Albert a reservoir of the Nile, the fact that a large river like the Semliki runs into the Albert & connects the two lakes greatly adds to the importance of the discovery of the Albert Lake, for it has until now been thought that the Albert added little or no volume of water to the Nile. I am glad Stanley has called the Lake the Albert Edward, for the Prince took such an interest in everything connected with the Expedition, the only one of the Royal family who did.

July 5th. Marched through valleys & gorges in the mountains & reached a settlement called Kiwiga, the natives came in in great numbers & mixed freely with the men, they brought in butter, chickens, tobacco etc to sell, but always wanted cloth which is just what we have'nt got, they ask exorbitant prices for the least little thing & are quite unaccustomed to trade, they think for a little packet of butter, perhaps containing a quarter of a pound, they can get sufficient cloth to cover them from head to foot. The natives however are so friendly that we are now assured of a free passage through

---

[1] Stanley describes graphically the mist and mysterious atmosphere of these regions: 'A suggestion of chaos' is the page heading to *In Darkest Africa*, II, 327.

Ankori. The cold at nights is intense & the men suffer much from coughs & colds which, with them, often develope into pneumonia & is very fatal, the keen wind of the mountains too, meeting one as one reaches the top of a pass in a profuse perspiration, greatly adds to the number of men with bad chests etc, it cuts into one like a knife. There is another thing too which was quite unexpected & unlooked for; on leaving the plain behind & ascending the mountains we at least expected we should have good water, instead of which all the ravines are choked with vast masses of papyrus & the water is scarcely fit to drink, being muddy & strongly impregnated with vegetable matter, one always boils it before drinking but even then it is most unpalatable. This want of good water & the mountain winds keep the fever rate as high as it was on the plain, & as soon as one of us gets over a fever another is struck down. The natives bring in a good deal of pombe & I have taken to drinking it in preference to the muddy dirty ravine water. We have one of the Wanasura we caught in Usongora in chains carrying a load, Stanley showed him to one of the big chiefs & his people & they jeered at & regarded him with looks of intense hate & grasped their spears as if they would like to bury them in him, it was quite wonderful to see their faces, & when he walked away with the other prisoners, the chain clanking after them, the natives laughed with delight, his chance would be a poor one of escaping if he got loose from the chains, he has often tried to escape before, but after this exhibition of hate & fury on the part of the Wa-Ankori, I do not suppose he will make another attempt.

July 6th. Marched right up the mountains through a high pass & almost immediately descended the other side, the mountain being a sort of narrow back-bone only, the descent was fearful & I had fever & my knees gave under me at every painful tedious step I took, I thought we never should get to the bottom, we camped in a large settlement called Busimba, & great numbers of natives came in to see us, I just threw myself down when I got in, for the fever had fast hold of me & I was powerless before it.

July 7th. Remained in camp. Fever. Fever that strikes one down like a sledge hammer & burns into one's very vitals leaving one as nerveless & weak as a child. My God am I not brought low enough yet? Must I die by slow degrees? A quick death is so much easier. I am reduced to mere skin & bone & am an object to look at, my arms & legs are mere skin & bone with the muscles standing out like cords—a study for an anatomist.

July 8th. Remained in camp; fever still consuming one; utterly unable to do anything. In the evening messengers arrived from Antari saying he would not be able to see us & he did not wish us to pass through his village as he had gone to Ruanda. This is of course a lie, these people are awfully afraid of us & it is the custom of Kings in this part of the world to run away &

hide when strangers enter the country; even Kaberega does it. We shall not therefore pass through his village but will go by a shorter road to the river, he bids us go in peace & the people will give us to eat beans, corn, bananas, etc.

July 9th. In the night a violent shivering fit lasting two hours came on & this was succeeded by a profuse perspiration which lasted nearly till morning, it left me utterly done up but carried the fever away & after an hour's sleep I woke without fever & was able to eat before starting on the march. I was just able to crawl along to the next camp high up among the mountains. Seven or eight Waganda came in from Antari, they are some of Mackay's mission people & talk Ki-swahili.[1] They report that 18 months ago a rebellion took place in Uganda—or as they call it Buganda—Mwanga, the King was deposed & took refuge on an island in the Lake near Ukerewe, the Katichiro, the faithful prime minister of M'tesa & Mwanga was deprived of all that he had & after being disgracefully illtreated was killed in his own house by a spear wound, most of the chief men, men whom Stanley knew well in /76 when he visited Uganda, were killed & many less important people were killed & many fled from the country amongst them nearly 2,000 fled to Ankori & sought the protection of Antari, & these men who now came to see us are some of the chiefs of these people & they all talk about Mackay with the greatest respect & admiration. The rebellion was got up by the Mahomedan party who placed a brother of Mwanga, Kiwewa by name, on the throne, but he, refusing to be circumcised, they deposed & placed Keremma, his brother, in his place. Keremma immediately began a course of butchery, killing all whom he supposed unfriendly to him; in short there was quite a 'reign of terror' in Uganda, the English & French Missionaries fled, & only some Arabs, some of whom had instigated the rebellion, were left. This is the story shortly told by the Waganda, no doubt the whole thing has been told in Europe long since. The Waganda accompany us tomorrow on the road. Fever is raging amongst the men in spite of the cold air & height we are now at, we shall never get rid of the fever till we get better water.

July 10th. Led by Waganda & Ankori guides, we marched through the mountains & reached a village on the side of a hill. This country swarms with cattle, every day we pass large herds grazing on the mountain sides, the whole country is however, burnt up: all the watercourses are dry & every thing is like tinder, it is awfully dreary to look at the sere yellow grass with here & there large black patches where the grass has been burned & hardly a tree to be seen. We passed over a stream of a good size, quite a dark brown

[1] They included Samuel and Zachariah, two Waganda Christians who played a prominent part in the Uganda civil wars and subsequent peacemaking under Lugard (*see* Lugard, II, *passim*).

colour from running through the Papyrus swamps, this stream runs into the Kagera which runs into the Alexandra Nile. We have with us three Ankori chiefs acting as guides, & their cheek & impertinence surpasses anything I ever saw in a native, one longs to give them a facer when they come with ridiculous complaints about this & that & shout in one's face, but one is obliged to be friendly with them.

July 11th. Descended the hills & reached the plains, & crossed a large dark brown papyrus stream tasting badly of mud & camped in a very large settlement where there was abundance of food & here for the first time, we got a quantity of peas, dry peas, these are a great find & will be most excellent food on the road. The women here are rather fine looking & quite covered with skins, nicely dressed & bark cloth, some of these women had necklaces of large bright copper bells of a crescent shape which were very pretty. The three Ankori chiefs demanded cloth which Stanley had promised them if they conducted him to the river, Stanley very naturally refused to give it until we had reached the river, the chiefs still insisted & were very impertinent, whereupon a very stormy scene ensued in which Stanley got furious & threatened all sorts of things if they did not lower their tone, the result was the chiefs went off in high dudgeon saying they would not go a step further & Stanley told them he would do without them. One of my men Sangoro Baraka died of fever.

July 12th. Started off without guides & after going for a couple of hours reached a papyrus swamp which Stanley entered, we never had such an experience before, for two hours we were plunging along among the papyrus up to our waists in the muddy foul smelling water with the roots of the papyrus tripping one up at every step & getting entangled in one's feet, after passing through & marching along the hillside we could see the place we should have crossed about a mile higher up where the swamp was only 30 or 40 yds wide. We marched on for an hour & camped in a large settlement. The rear guard did not get in for some hours after us & Nelson, who was in charge, reported that 21 cows & 7 goats had been left in the swamp entirely unable to get on, unfortunately amongst the 21 were all our milch cows so now we shall have no more milk to eat with our porridge in the morning, it will be a great loss, for this tullaboon porridge by itself is most nauseous. Several children were lost in the marsh & the Pasha's people had great difficulty in getting their donkeys through. One has taken a great dose of quinine for fear of fever after breathing the evil smelling malaria-tainted air of the marsh.

July 13th. Halted today & Stanley sent Nelson & Stairs back with their companies to the marsh to kill the cattle & bring on the meat. In the afternoon the companies returned bringing in the meat from 21 cattle, a great pile of

379

meat, which was divided amongst the whole 1100 people. The people came in today bringing small things for sale & I was able to buy a little butter at an exorbitant price, it was a great thing getting it for though we have plenty of food we have nothing with which to make it very palatable & the expedition supplies us with nothing; we just have to forage for our food. Milk is impossible to buy at any price though there are flocks & herds of cattle all round us, the people believe that if they sell their milk to us their cows will run dry, so nothing will induce them to sell a drop. The chief brought in a present of a small amount of milk when we arrived, but it had the strong smoky taste which all milk has when the natives wash the vessel in the cow's urine, indeed it seems this habit obtains in all cases, for I saw a man deliberately squat down in front of my tent & wash his hands in his own urine & during the operation he was talking to one of his friends as if it were all the usual thing.

July 14th. Yesterday the King's brother, who is chief of this part of the country, came in & conducted us to a very good camp where there was abundance of food. The King's brother is a small sharp featured man, dressed in a red cloth, there is nothing to distinguish him from the rest of the people. Our men & some of the Pasha's people got into trouble with the natives and a good deal of flogging took place in camp, one of the Pasha's people was wounded by a spear in the face & one of our Soudanese, not being able to return what he had stolen, was left by Stanley in the natives' hands, but he was afterwards able to arrange it some how; I think his companions clubbed together & made up some present to satisfy the natives.

July 15th & 16th. Down with fever, raging fever, for two days & nights, but this evening the fever has left me after shattering ones whole frame, the violence of these fevers is incredible; one's temperature keeps up at over 105° & never goes down, all the other officers, with the exception of Nelson,[1] have fever now as I do, but my fever always rides higher, perhaps because I am stronger, but I have been more beaten down than any one, for I had that terrible 17 days fever to start with & that had already frightfully reduced my strength. When I got up this evening after this last fever the officers, accustomed as they have become to the sight of wan & emaciated faces, exclaimed at the ghastliness of my appearance, & indeed on looking in the glass I was startled to see what a ghost I had become, my hands are mere claws, hollow eyed, with hollows in my temples & cheek bones prominent, my cheeks fallen in like a toothless old man's & my neck in the last stage of scragginess: I am a most repulsive object. One is in despair; whatever care one takes the fever always returns & after one has regained a little strength

[1] Parke commends Nelson 'as he carefully carries out the prophylactic treatment...' (Parke, p. 458).

falls on one & beats one back again into a worse state than before. It is so hateful to lie there & feel one cannot do one's work & another is doing it instead: one gets perfectly rabid at being rendered useless.

July 17th. Crawled into camp at the top of a hill, but though feeling very weak I somehow feel better & more hopeful, there is no real reason for it; these things come on one suddenly & after weeks of low spirits & melancholy I feel a hopefullness rising in me which makes things look brighter & better & one feels 'perhaps I shall reach home after all'.

July 18th & 19th. Stanley is down with a sharp attack of fever, & we are remaining here in camp for two days. Antari is sending his son to Stanley to make bloodbrotherhood & to exchange gifts, & we are loitering on the road to allow him to come up. One of our chiefs, Umari, was despatched to Antari & has just returned, he describes Antari as an enormously fat old man living on nothing but milk, meat & pombe, his village, to use Umari's term, is 'not bad', he has the ordinary kind of hut only larger than the usual sized ones & enclosed in a large boma with the huts of his family & servants all round. Umari was not much impressed by him.

July 20th. Stanley has recovered from his fever so today we marched a shortish march & camped in a large settlement where the people were friendly & there was lots of food, here we got tomatoes for the first time. The women are very heavily clothed from head to foot in nicely dressed cloth, albeit they are rather greasy from constant wear, their heads are covered with different coloured beads with a long fringe of them hanging down all round their heads, the women as a rule are very fat & are not nice looking, but they are friendly & by no means shy. The country all round has the same barren, rocky, burnt up appearance which is very depressing especially as one knows when one does reach a settlement where there is cultivation there will be only water of the most undrinkable description to be got & even that far off & in small quantities, to look round on this country, merely, makes one thirsty; it is all so burnt up & treeless. Stanley sent me to stop a row between two of our Manuyema chiefs, they were going at it hammer & tongs when I arrived & it was only by taking their sticks & telling them I would use them on both that I got them quiet & I was then able to settle their dispute, which after all was only about a hut. Such quarrels are always dangerous as the Manuyema are so hasty & savage that they are very apt in the heat of passion to use their guns & knives. In the afternoon Antari's son came in, a small boy of about 16 wrapped in a filthy greasy old cloth, a sort of garment one would'nt touch with a long pole.[1] He was carried all the way from his father's village pig-a-back by

[1] Stanley describes Uchunku as 'a sweet faced, gentle looking boy of about thirteen or fourteen years old, a true Mhuma with the Abyssinian features...' (*IDA*, II, 348).

some of his people of whom he had some 40 with him, he was followed by two men, one carrying a jar of pombe & the other a jar of milk. As a present he brought from his father protestations of friendship & two cows—these two make 9 cows we have received from Antari since we have been in his country. The boy—Prince as Stanley calls him!—remained with Stanley for a couple of hours & his followers doing all the talking for him & then retired to his hut, he will come tomorrow morning & make blood brotherhood with Stanley, who seems deeply impressed with the importance of 'the Prince' & intends making the ceremony quite an affair.

July 21st. This morning 'the Prince' brought his people & Stanley & he sat on a mat & after the usual incisions were made in their arms butter was mixed with the blood of each & this was rubbed again into their arms, Stanley's into the boy's & vice versa:[1] the chiefs then made long exhortations to them to be true to each other & to behave well & our chiefs joined in. We had had our companies all drawn up in line & by Stanley's order fired two volleys, after which the Maxim gun was put together & a series of volleys fired, much to the astonishment, fear & amusement of the natives, all of which feelings were mixed up when they heard the guns going & saw the effect on the mountain opposite.

July 22nd. The road lay through the most arid, dried up country. Still there are numerous herds of cattle feeding on the dried up mountain sides, where they get water to drink is a puzzle. At length we came to a long line of settlements the fields of which were full of peas M'tama & Manioc, of the latter there were large quantities, we have not seen it since leaving the bush & the men were very glad to get it once more for a change. We passed through a good many of these settlements & camped in one of the driest & hottest at the foot of a range of mountains to our right, here we got better water than we have had for some time, but where it came from one ca'nt imagine for the whole country as far as one could see was regularly baked up. Stairs, who was in charge of the rearguard reported that two women, native slaves, had been beaten to death by some of the Pasha's people who had simply crushed their heads in in the most barborously brutal manner, when Stairs found them they were just breathing. These are some of the unfortunate people whom Stairs & I caught on the raids we made from Mazamboni's & M'pinga's. They were made at the Pasha's request & the captives were given over to the Pasha's people who tied them together in threes & fours & gave them outrageously heavy loads & drove them along the road. On arriving in camp they were again driven off to fetch wood & water & were never given regular food. Under such treatment, together

---

[1] 'The ceremony was thus relieved of the repulsiveness which accompanies it when performed among the Congo tribes' (Stanley, *IDA*, II, 349).

with constant brutal flogging, it is no wonder that the unfortunate people gradually sank, until at length they were no longer able to fulfil their tasks, it is then that they are beaten savagely & left on the road to struggle & gasp until death comes to relieve them. Such things are common with the Pasha's people who are the most savage, stupid, bestial, useless people that ever the devil invented, God never could have made them, that is if He is the Good God we believe Him to be. And it is we, Stairs & I, who have in a wickedly weak manner carried out the orders given us & captured these unfortunates, why did we not stand up before we did & say 'we will not do this foul wrong', it is a thing I shall always feel remorse for. They say that a soldier should have no conscience but that of his commander, but I cannot altogether look at it in that way. The Manuyema are cruel to their slaves, but when one of the Pasha's people went to Saadi our Manuyema chief with 50 dollars in his hand to buy a slave from him, Saadi indignantly refused him & said he would sooner sell his life than sell a slave to the brutal 'Turks'. This will give some idea of the treatment the slaves of the Pasha's people receive when a half civilised Manuyema will refuse a large sum of money for a slave & in such an indignant manner. The Pasha should do something to stop it, but he is more incapable & impotent than ever, nor do I think he greatly cares, he has lived too long in the Orient (25 years) among Mahomedans to give much thought to such things, they are of daily occurrence & are taken after a bit as a matter of course. Gordon spoke truly when he said a man should return to Europe every three years otherwise his sense of morality (in the broad sense of the word) would gradually adapt itself to that of the country in which he lived. The Pasha is a striking example of the truth of Gordon's remark. Someone defines morality as a tissue to the growth of which a hot climate is not conducive—I think it was Lord Beaconsfield.

July 23rd. A long march through the most arid, blackened plain I have ever seen, to which the very acacias which were pretty freely dotted about seemed to add a fresh desolation, for all their foliage had been burnt & scorched by the grass fires & the ashes lay thick beneath their leafless, shadeless branches. After passing through this & noticing the evidently hostile feelings of the natives in a village on the mountain tops, we at last reached the Alexandra Nile a fine, full, swiftly flowing river about 150 yards broad, making its way through a gorge between the mountain ranges of Ankori & Karagwe, the sight of the water with the narrow green belt of jungle fringing both banks looked most refreshing to us who for nearly 6 weeks had been accustomed only to see swamps or mud holes. We marched about 500 yds up the river & camped on a rocky flat immediately above it. The men threw down their loads on reaching camp & rushed down to drink & revel in the sweet cool water, they had'nt had a wash since we left the

Lake & I simply had to go & drive some of them up with a stick to pitch Stanley's tent. The people dragged behind terribly today & the officers did not reach camp till late in the afternoon & all of them ill, Stairs & Bonny with fever, Parke with bad eyes which nearly made him blind for the time being & Nelson with something else, I had fever, but I had got up a good deal of my strength & was able to fight against it & no one suspected that I had it. The truth is I was so furious at getting it just as we reached the river & I should be particularly wanted that I determined to fight against it & not give way. When the rear guard had come in it was found that one of my men 'London' carrying the iron stock of the Maxim gun & my little Kinyoro boy 'Tumbo' who was with him had not come into camp. London was a fine, strong, fat fellow & a capital carrier & if his load was lost the gun with all the boxes of Maxim ammunition would be rendered useless. My boy 'Tumbo' whose real name is 'Basuri', is a most bright & useful little fellow, he has learnt my ways wonderfully quickly & does the work of the tent remarkably well, I suppose he is about 8 years old, he has one fault, he simply gorges himself with whatever food he can get hold of, he prefers bananas & sweet potatoes, but all is grist that comes to his mill, the result is he has an enormous stomach which is remarkable even in this country where all small children have huge stomachs. One day I called him 'Tumbo' which in Ki-Swahili means stomach, & the men at once took to the name & always called him by it, he is a sort of butt amongst them & they delight in teasing him, he has a regular bull dog face & an awful temper, which by the way he never dares show before me, & if anyone pushes him in the road he turns on them in a fury, the men often do it by way of amusement. I have seen him, when I have been lying ill with fever, & a group of Zanzibaris near my hut were making rather a noise—I have seen him, take up a stick & lay it about their backs & ask them did they not know his master was lying sick in the hut & could'nt stand any noise. He is in short a most useful amusing little fellow & I shall be more than sorry if he is lost. I sent back the faithful Uledi with five men to look for him, the man & the load, but he returned at dark with no tidings of the lost people. He reported however having seen two Manuyema a man & a woman lying dead near the path pierced by a hundred spear wounds—the work of the hostile natives we had seen on the hills in the morning. It appears the woman was tired & had hidden in the grass & let the rear guard go by, her husband who was carrying one of the tents, on reaching camp, put down his load & went back to look for his wife & just as he reached her they were set upon by the natives, who had probably been following her as she trudged wearily after the column & fell upon the pair just as they met, they had taken the man's gun & had horribly mutilated the body of the woman. This is bad news & I'm afraid there is little hope

384

of London & Tumbo having escaped the same fate if they have tried to cross the dangerous bit of country alone.

July 24th. This morning we marched for about an hour to the place where the natives were accustomed to ferry their canoes across to the Karagwe shore. Here we found a good many natives assembled with all their canoes on the other side. They were at first rather unwilling to ferry the expedition until they had consulted their Sultan (7 days march off!) but Stanley managed to induce them to agree to cross us & promised them good presents of cloth in payment. Stanley ordered me to go up to the plateau above to pitch camp, cut a good road down to the portage & then superintend the crossing of the Expedition. The canoes were of the most miserable rotten kind & were so shallow & narrow that they had to be lashed together by means of short poles to keep them from toppling over. Stairs with his company & loads crossed & went to form camp on the other side. Then began the crossing of the Pasha's people, a most troublesome piece of work, but I crossed them in families which, with a plentiful use of tongue & stick, made the work quicker finished. The natives who were ferrying us across declared themselves after two hours work too tired to do any more, so I siezed the canoes & an awful uproar was the result, some of the chief natives rushed up to Stanley's tent to complain but they got little sympathy from him & he told them I had done quite right when the natives were tired to put my own people in their place. We got on much more quickly by ourselves than with the natives who had quarreled & stormed at the way in which the loads were placed in the canoes & would only take two or three at a time, when our men took the management into their hands we put 6 or 7 loads in & everything was done in a more quiet & orderly way. I worked away till dark & got two thirds of the Expedition across by nightfall without any accident. On reaching camp I found that London & his load, & my boy Tumbo had reached camp. Stanley had sent Nelson & his company back in the morning to hunt them up & they had come upon them sitting in a native village not far from our last camp, they had fortunately not tried to cross the dangerous zone. Their explanation was they had lost the road & had gone back to the village & had only arrived a few hours before the search party reached them. Their story is evidently not true, they hid in the grass & let the column go by from sheer laziness, these people are most foolish & never think they may be cut off; it is quite wonderful how many of them have escaped what seemed to us almost certain death.

July 25th. I was down at the river all morning & got the entire expedition crossed by three in the afternoon, after which I crossed myself & reported the work done without a single accident. The camp here in Karagwe is very pretty, on the side of a hill in a grove of Acacias. Thank goodness! another stage of our journey is done & we are past Ankori,[1] Ankori is undoubtedly a fine country & very rich in cattle goats etc, we have never anywhere seen such large & frequent flocks & herds. We have, of course, seen it at its worst when everything is burnt up & there is no water, how on earth the people manage to water their cattle in the dry season is astonishing. No doubt during & immediately after the rains the country looks fine & flourishing, but even in the rains the water cannot be anything else than poisonous owing to the papyrus which chokes every ravine & valley—no country, in my mind, can be called a really good country unless it is thoroughly well watered—what we suffered from bad & insufficient water the whole time we were in Ankori I shall never forget. The people are a fine people, not too hospitable, as the Zanzibaris say—'their heads are too big & they ought to get some medicine', which means they are too uppish & independant & should be taught a lesson by some passing caravan which would chastise them when they got uproarious. It is perfectly true, far removed from any caravan route & unconquered by anyone, they think too much of themselves, we of course could have walked through the country with impunity taking what we wanted, but that is not Stanley's policy, he never fights where there is the slightest chance of making friends with the natives & he is wonderfully patient & long suffering with them,—pirate as he has been called. The spears, bows & arrows of the Wan-Kori are undoubtedly the finest we have yet seen & are always beautifully kept, I may add a word too for the tobacco pipes which are classically shaped, small & beautifully bound with brass or copper wire which gives them a more neat & finished look than the ordinary pipes have.

July 27th. Left camp late & marched up hill & down dale through a country of much the same character as Ankori except that if anything it is more black & burnt up. We saw three rhinosceros feeding on a hill—the first I have seen—Stanley fired at them, but only succeeded in making them gallop off. The people through whose villages we passed were silent but not unfriendly. Camped in a dried up valley where there was bad water, the natives came in from some distant villages.

July 28th. Marched a long march & reached a place called M'utagata, renowned among the surrounding countries for its hot springs. The springs are rather pleasantly situated at the head of a narrow valley which is full of fine forest trees the result of the fertilising effect of the stream which flows from the springs, which consist of three small ponds with the hot water bubbling up in the centre of each, at one place, where the water gushes from a rock, it is impossible to bear one's hand in the hot water. These springs

[1] They were now entering modern Tanzania along part of whose boundary with Uganda runs the Kagera or, as the old travellers called it, the Alexandra Nile.

are supposed by the natives to be a perfect cure for all ills the flesh is heir to, but particularly for ulcers & rheumatism, people, I am told, come from far & near to benefit by the waters & there is usually a large gathering of invalids from the countries round, when we arrived there were not many, not above a dozen.

July 29th. Stayed in camp today to allow the people to bathe which they did almost without ceasing the whole day. Some of the Pasha's people, Shookri Aga & Surore Adam, went out shooting & got a lot of rhinoceroses which seem to be found in great numbers about here, some of our own people went out as well & shot three, so that the camp is well supplied with meat. Shookri Aga came in saying there was a little rhinoceros about two miles off, he had shot the mother but the baby was too wicked to secure & his people were unable to bring it in. Stanley sent me with some of my company to see what I could do. I went down with a lot of men & some rope & found it near a swamp. Immediately we came near it began charging at everyone uttering a constant cry something between grunt & a squeal, but it was decidedly a cry of defiance. He was such an ugly little brute one couldn't help laughing at him. We got his legs tied together over a strong pole & carried him up to camp, he struggled & shouted defiance the whole way, much to the amusement of the whole camp who heard him far off & turned out en masse to see him. We tied a stout rope round his neck & fastened it to a tree & then cut his bonds. He immediately began a perfect chorus of defiant squeals & charged right & left to the extent of the rope amid the roars of laughter from all the people—he was certainly very comical. Afterwards Stanley had his throat cut & the meat divided amongst the officers, which turned out to be very tender & good tasting.

July 30th & 31st and August 1st. Three uninteresting marches, the country burnt up, & blackened & barren, we get a certain amount of food but not much. There are no signs of cattle whatever not even any kraals about the villages—extensive banana cultivations & plenty of good water. We hear that there are now no Arabs left in Kafro, the capital of Karagwe, which we reach tomorrow, there are only two Ki-Swahili speaking traders who depend mainly on the bounty of the King. This is a great disappointment to us all as we were counting on getting a little rice from them & perhaps some coffee & curry powder, besides hearing a little news however old.

August 2nd. After a fairly long march we entered Kafro, a miserable collection of huts surrounded by mountains we found that what we had heard was true, there were no Arabs, the last of them had died & the others had gone away. There were the remains of their tembes & some lime & pomegranate trees & acres of tomatoes growing wild to show that while there they had done what they could in the way of cultivation. There was a sort of Swahili trader there, named [left blank] another named [left blank] but both were very poor & almost entirely dependant on the King for food & lodging. Both were of a low class & had no influence in the country they were neither of them of the slightest use to us during our three days stay at Kafro. On the afternoon a very old fellow called Kiengo came down with a large retinue of wives, daughters, sons & slaves to see Stanley. He had been with Speke & Grant on their expedition to Uganda & had been very useful to them, finally at the request of Rumanika who struck up a great friendship with him he settled in Karagwe & has remained there ever since. He has a regular little village to himself & is rich in cattle & goats, he has numbers of men & guns, & is altogether quite an important person in Karagwe. He showed us a gun which Speke had given him & told us Speke had also given him a telescope, which while it lasted was a wonder to everyone, but it was broken. Poor old fellow he sat on & on in Stanleys tent talking of Speke & Grant & of his former friends among the white men, he was perfectly senile but he showed such pleasure in seeing us & talking about his former life that Stanley was loth to turn him out but let him run on repeating the same things again & again, once when we thought we had got rid of him he announced he was so glad after all these years to be again with Europeans that he found it impossible to tear himself away, so he stayed on till evening pouring out a stream of senile talk, sitting cross legged on his mat with his gourd of pombe before him. Late in the evening he sent us a cow, two sheep & a quantity of milk for a present.[1] The King, who is a lad of about 18 years & is a grandson of Rumanika, Stanley's old friend, sent down to say he would like Stanley to go & see him & he would send him plenty of food, the supply he sent for 1000 people consisted of about 50 bunches of green bananas & a few small baskets of beans. Stanley said he was too old a man to go & see him at his residence about 6 miles from Kafro, but one of his sons would go, so next morning I started off with an escort of 40 men to pay him a visit. The road lay over the mountains some six miles off, there was nothing to indicate we were approaching the King's residence, there were perhaps rather more banana plantations but the population seemed just as sparse as in any other part of the country. About half a mile from the King's boma one of the Swahili traders who accompanied me sent on men to tell the King I was coming & to ask him if he was ready to receive me. I waited for about half an hour in a small kraal, when the messengers returned & said the King was waiting. I was much amused at the serious demeanour

[1] His name was Kiengo. According to Stanley, the old man took a great fancy to Nelson to whom, 'because he bore some resemblance to "Speki", he gave a fat broad-tailed sheep, & the only tax we had to pay was that on our patience while listening to his reminiscences of "Speki" which he was never tired of repeating' (*IDA*, II, 378).

of the Zanzibaris with me they were the pick of No 1, my company, & in
an ordinary way are a noisey, rollicking lot, excellent fellows, but still inclined to sing & shout along the road, today they were as serious as possible
& when we neared the boma they divided & put me in the middle with my
three chiefs Uledi, Rashid & Murabo behind me. When we were about 200
yds from the boma a party of women dressed in the most fantastic way met
us & danced wildly round me, their rattles, drums & pipes making a
deafening noise, they accompanied us to the gate of the outer boma where
we were greeted by a burst of music (?) from the King's band which was
concealed in the trees at the other side of the boma, it was the nearest approach
to music I had yet heard in Africa & in the distance sounded rather well,
the musicians played a kind of tune, the music burst out suddenly & as
suddenly ceased, which had rather a wierd effect especially as the musicians
were unseen. The Zanzibaris conducted me with a slow solemn step through
the first boma which was round & about 100 yds in diameter. The boma &
gateway were formed of trees like sycamores planted so closely together that
it was impossible to see through, the outer boma was like a deserted farm
yard in Autumn. Out of this boma led a shady lane leading to a small boma
in which was the King's divan. The divan was nothing more than a small
hut in the door of which sat or rather crouched, a bright looking youth
clothed in a very dirty greasy piece of coloured cloth. I wished to shake
hands with him but was waved back by his prime minister who asked me to
have my chair placed near him but not to touch him. The King's guard
consisted of some two hundred & 50 men who were all seated in a semi
circle on each side of the hut, all armed with spears—I saw no guns—my
men were all drawn up in line & stood to attention the whole time they evidently thought it all a serious business. I spoke in Ki-swahili to the trader
Khamis who interpreted to the prime minister, who in his turn told the King
what I said, in speaking before the King Khamis went down on his hands
& knees & spoke in a low abject voice which I found very unpleasant. I
stayed about three quarters of an hour talking, I asking about the country
etc & he asking about our guns, he evidently seemed impressed by the long
shining row of guns & asked if all my people were armed like that, he was
highly delighted with my Winchester Rifle &, on my showing him the way
it worked, went into fits of delighted laughter. He & his people seemed
pleased when I asked about the country & readily answered all my questions.
He is a grandson of Rumanika, the King of Karagwe, who was very friendly
to Speke & Grant & afterwards to Stanley, his uncle governs the country
until he is old enough to do so & things, according to Stanley, are not nearly
as nice as they were in Rumanika's time. All I can say is the Kings Krall is
nothing but a collection of dirty miserable huts surrounded by untidy court

yards & the King himself is just like any ordinary native, he lives in the same way & has the same kind of hut to live in, only that it is a little larger. Stanley always accuses me of being a pessimist & a traveller of the Burtonian school who can see but little to admire either in the country or in the character of the natives, he is quite wrong; I simply see things as they are & speak of them as they are, he writes flowery descriptions of King's palaces, court pages etc, of colonels, generals & regiments, of pomp & show, & gives people at home a most false idea. I have no doubt he would have written of the King's Kraal quite differently to the way I have written, there would have been palaces & courtyards, with the King sitting in his divan surrounded by courtiers & generals, with his wives dressed in their court dresses, while a string of clients & courtiers streamed through the palace gates etc, etc, etc—I only saw a dirtily clothed youth seated in the door of a small hut in which were a lot of black sluts, whilest some 250 natives squatted around upon the straw which had spread on the ground for their accomodation, all of them very dirty & had an exceedingly unpleasant smell & thought a great deal of themselves. I think people like Stanley who write in that absurdly exaggerated style do a great deal of harm in Africa, people who do not know their style come out expecting to find all these fine things & go away disappointed. All this talk of Kings & emperors & princes of the royal blood, with their residences, courts & palaces sounds all very fine in books of travel, but it is nothing but bosh & it conveys a very false idea to the people for whose instruction the book is published. As the King had been so mean in sending food Stanley gave me no present to take to him, he evidently seemed to expect a present. After I had taken my leave & had got about a quarter of a mile on the road, a messenger came running after me & said the King wanted my rifle & some ammunition, I told him to tell the King he must ask Stanley & perhaps if he sent in plenty of food, Stanley would give him one. I laughed to my chiefs about the King, his general dirtiness & the wretchedness of his Kraal, but they didnt seem half to like it: they evidently thought it was sacrilege to laugh at so important a person as the King of Karagwe.[1]

[1] Emin writes on 5–11 August: 'Jephson has come back dissatisfied. He looks on all African kings as humbugs and all of us as travelling for an impostor' (Sir John Gray's new translation, kindly shown to me in typescript).

CHAPTER 18

THE LAST LAP

We stayed three days at Kafro[1] during which time we rested & got rid of
the remains of our fevers by eating quantities of tomatoes. We are all getting
up our strength now, we do not get the violent fevers we had in Usongora
& Ankori, & though the country is dried up & burnt black what water we
get is good, the temperature does not seem to have so great a range here,
the nights are not so intensely cold as in Ankori, & that was one of the great
causes of our constant fevers. Please God we'll pull through. Stanley finally
sent the King a present of a Winchester Rifle & 200 rounds of ammunition.
It is now five days to the boundary of Karagwe, the country is up &
down mountains all burnt & blackened & the monotony of the country
is only relieved by the banana groves which are dotted here & there
among the villages. [*7 August*] We passed Kienzie's[2] settlement, a very
flourishing one with quantities of cattle & goats in it, the fields are all
marked out with hedges of milk bush which has a pretty effect, the village
itself is also surrounded by a high hedge of it. Kienzi came out to say good
bye & gave Stanley some beautiful spears & bows & arrows; all his young
men escorted us out of the place with a tremendous noise. This is a tremendous country for lakes & mountains & in the wet season must be very
pretty, on climbing the mountains one constantly comes on a beautiful,
peaceful lake surrounded by hills. The King had given us guides so that we
had to pay for no food, but just took bananas etc. as we wanted them, but
Stanley was very careful & punished the Zanzibaris severely whenever the
natives had reason to complain of them. Our real route to Msalala runs
through Usui, but we hear that the chief of Usui is very extortionate &
demands large hongo (tribute), we hear also that an Arab caravan is on its
way to Karagwe, but has been stopped by the King who has compelled the
Arab to wait in order to get all his cloth from him, he will neither allow him
to proceed on his journey or to return, Stanley has therefore decided to go
by a slightly longer road between Usui & the lake, the people of which are
governed by small chiefs & will not demand hongo. Of course if we chose
we could easily force our way through Usui, but Stanley does not wish to

---

[1] 2 August is the last date given in the diary: the narrative now is continuous until it
peters out on or about October 1889. Dates from *In Darkest Africa* have been inserted
in square brackets.   [2] Kiengo, Speke's old guide; see page 388.

fight. [*10 August*] Near the limit of Karagwe we came on the beautiful lake
of Urigi [Burigi], visited by Speke & Grant, but put down wrong in the
map & is very much larger than they supposed, it winds about among the
mountains & has numerous islands & headlands in it. The water is intensely
blue & there is a narrow beach of bright yellow and all round it & with the
purple mountains in the background & a green plain between it has much the
same appearance as the shores of the Mediteranean. There are numerous
fishing villages along the shores & on the islands, the huts are beehive shaped
& very neatly made of bright yellow straw, these are dotted about on the
slopes among clumps of castor oil & milk bushes & are very picturesque;
here we came upon fields of manioc again. The general name of the country
is Ihangiro, but it is divided up into small states under chiefs, each state
being called by the name of its chief. The natives are friendly, but do not
bring in much food. In a village where we camped some of the men went
out looting, & the natives came in in a body to complain to Stanley, he
sent me out with my company with orders to arrest anyone I found in the
villages, for the chief said our people had killed one man & wounded another.
[*11 August*] I took the natives with me & they recognised Fadl el Mulla,
one of our Nubian soldiers as the man who had shot the natives, I took him
prisoner & went round the villages with the chief & arrested all those people
belonging to us whom I found there. They showed me the dead native & I
picked up a Remington cartridge near him, who had been shot through both
knees & had evidently bled to death; the wounded man I brought back with
me to camp; he was slightly wounded in the throat. All hands were ordered
to fall in & the natives were taken round to identify any man whom they had
seen looting, they recognised several of our Soudanese but none of the
Zanzibaris. It is always either ours or the Pasha's Soudanese who make
mischief with the natives; they are naturally a taciturn, brutish race & with
the smattering of the accursed Turkish education which they all have, they
have about the worst traits in their character which it is possible for a human
being to have. The Zanzibaris are thieves & liars but they are hardworking
& have that joyousness & childlike simplicity of character which redeems
their bad qualities & one is forced to like them, though one swears at them
often, the Soudanese have none of these qualities, but in their place are the
habits & customs of the lowest Turks together with a joyless brutishness
which is most repulsive, they are moreover intensely arrogant, which is a
trait never seen in the simple minded Zanzibari. Fadl el Mulla's gun was
examined & was found to have been just fired off, I produced the exploded
cartridge & all the natives said he was the man who had shot their brother;
this was only one specimen of Fadl el Mulla's conduct throughout the expedition, he has always been most troublesome & insubordinate & lazy & has

been constantly flogged, so Stanley told him he could stand it no longer; he had shot a friendly native & might have caused the caravan to be attacked in consequence, he had always been a source of endless trouble to us & he had also intrigued against the expedition at Kavalli's with the Pasha's people & therefore it was a case of blood for blood & he handed him over to the natives; they rushed at him with yells, bound him & carried him away. The guides tell us the natives will all collect tonight from the villages round & have a feast & drink quantities of pombe, they will have the prisoner bound in their midst & the women will all insult & beat him & when the men have drunk sufficient pombe to madden them, they will rush on him in a body & hew him to pieces. That is their custom. A horrible fate certainly, I cannot conceive a much worse, but it is a fate he has brought on himself & one which he richly deserves. The rest of the men who were found looting all received a sound flogging & peace was restored. These people have to be held with a very firm hand otherwise anarchy, confusion & ruin would be the result. [*13 August*] We left the lake at this point, we had been marching along its shores three days & had not yet reached the end of it, so it is large, we struck East straight for the Victoria Nyanza, whose banks we shall follow as far as M'salala, we should strike the lake slightly to the north of Bumbireh island. We marched east over the mountains & reached a large settlement on the table lands & camped in the middle of it beside a clear stream, there were enormous plantations of bananas & fields of manioc & food of all sorts. The Pasha & his party were somewhat behind the main body of the caravan & a large party of half drunken natives came up & barred the road & threatened with violent gestures to shoot him if he moved another step without paying hongo. They drew a line across the path & dared him to cross it. They had placed arrows in their bows & were getting more & more excited & the Pasha was getting in a terrible funk when fortunately Nelson came up with his company & cleared them out pretty sharp. Stanley was furious & sent for the chief & told him if he & his people wished to be friends let them be so, but if they wished to fight his guns were ready & he would destroy the whole settlement, the chief urged friendship & said that this party of men had come from a village some distance off & were all half drunk, to which Stanley answered it did not matter whether they were drunk or not, that they had threatened his people & if a drunken man entered his camp he would at once shoot him & make war. The chief then harangued his people & warned them to be careful. We stayed here a day the natives brought in abundance of food but were rather cheeky. Numbers of the Pasha's people almost poisoned themselves with eating manioc which if not prepared properly is poisonous especially if eaten raw which they are very fond of doing—there is an immense amount of prussic acid in it. The next day [*15 August*] we reached the country of Kajumah who is the largest chief about here. His is a very fine settlement close to the Lake but sheltered from it by a high range of flat hills. There were beautiful banana groves in all the hollows the best bananas we have ever seen, there was abundance of food & very cheap & lots of honey if we had only had a few doti of cloth to buy it with, but Stanley does not know what we shall find ahead & so will not give us a yard of cloth, he is quite right for we have but twelve bales & do not know how long we may have to make them last. Kajumah was a fine big old man & very patronizing, he was suffering from bad eyes & asked Parke to go up to his Kraal & give him medicine. When Parke arrived he was taken into a Kraal by himself into an empty hut in which Kajumah was waiting for him, he would not allow any of his own people to come in for fear of poison. He told Parke he was sure some one of his people had a spite against him & that his bad eyes were the result of this person's using witch craft, he wanted to have his wise men brought in & a chicken killed in the presence of the man he suspected & if the entrails were red the man was guilty & should be killed & if they were white the man was innocent. Parke persuaded him not to put this test & gave him some medicine with which the old fellow seemed highly satisfied. We stayed here two days & started off with guides supplied by Kajumah with whom we parted excellent friends. After going for an hour we sighted the Nyanza[1] lying immediately beneath us. It is a glorious looking lake. We were a little south of Bumbireh but there were whole chains of islands to the South East & East & to the North East there was a broad stretch of dark blue water & a cool breeze blowing & making the face of the Lake a mass of little crisp waves. The islands were mostly lofty & rugged and formed of a bright yellowish orange stone which contrasted prettily with the blue of the Lake. On some of the islands might be seen fishing villages with bright green acacia trees growing amongst them. We were standing at the edge of some rocky cliffs some two to three hundred feet above the lake which went sheer down to the sandy strand which, with a breadth of about 50 yards, skirted the Lake. [*20 August*] It was a splendid view & we stood for a long time feasting our eyes on it & the wind blew cool & fresh across the great expanse of water & brought the little waves dancing in upon the shore with a cool soothing sound. It seemed as if we were now really & truly getting near home. We hear that all this country has been conquered by Usui but the people here are too far removed from the influence of the King. We could see the lake shore stretching away to the South into the blue distance with broad low headlands stretching away into the lake with a double chain of islands stretching away as far as we could see & our road lay in a fairly straight line across these headlands, so

[1] Lake Victoria.

that each day we marched we were able to camp on the shores of the lake, all day we passed through a sort of open forest with no water & reached the lake again usually at about 12.30 the march being from 10 to 11 miles. The natives were all friendly & beads were given out in order to buy food consisting chiefly of bananas, sweet potatoes & M'tama. The villages here are groups of round huts without palisades, & for the most part surrounded by high hedges of milk bushes; the water was very bad for though we camped on the lake shore nearly every day the papyrus grew so thickly & extended into the lake often as much as a mile so far that we could only get water discoulered with decayed vegetation & tasting horribly of mud. At one village two of my boys Iabia & Tumbo deserted. The former was a Kuku boy from Labore who had been the boy of Rehani who was hung for deser- tion, theft, & inciting others to desert, Stanley had ordered him to enter my service on his master's death[1], he was not a bad sort of boy but had all the nasty ways of the Pasha's people about him & I had never during the three months he was with me taken to him much. Tumbo I was really very sorry to lose, he was the son of the chief of Kibero, & had been taken prisoner when the Pasha's people burnt that place[2] & was afterwards given to me by Shookri Aga, chief of M'swa. He was as bright & sharp as a needle. I had called him Tumbo (Kiswahili for stomach) on account of his insatiable appetite which caused him to have an enormous rotundity of stomach, he was all stomach; his head & legs were small & he had the appearance of Humpty Dumpty in the nursery rhyme books. Kavalli had taken a great fancy to him & asked me to sell him, I told him if the boy wished to stay with him & his people, who were of the same race & spoke the same language as he, I would give him to him, but on the boy's being asked he had put his hand on mine & said 'no I will stay with you', I was rather touched by it & had always made much of him. He was a plucky little chap too & when I was ill & the men were making a noise anywhere near my hut he would take a stick & drive them away, he was much liked by the men & was always teased & chaffed very much by them on account of his tumbo. At Kajuma's a few days back he had gorged himself with raw manioc & had been ill in consequence, & the night before he ran away he said to the other boys in the kitchen 'My master always say in a few more days we shall reach M'salala where there will be rest for the people but he has said it so often that I do'nt believe there is such a place, & I am tired of marching every day' so I suppose the result was Iabia & he laid their heads together & agreed to desert on the road, they left their loads consisting of my plates, knives & forks etc. on the path for the rearguard to pick up & ran away into the forest without taking anything of mine with them. They like a good many other

[1] See above, p. 349   [2] See above, p. 257

people were quite worn out & weary of the everlasting marching every day. After leaving Kadjumah's some six or seven days & passing through a large dried up forest we came into Unyamweze, here the villages were all surrounded by a strong high boma made of the trunks of trees imbedded in the ground to a depth of some four feet, they are immensely strong & but for the want of water the villages would be able to hold out against a large force. There were signs of immense cultivations round these villages but many of them were half deserted & many burned. Eighteen months ago the Waganda had descended on the country & devastated it, driving away immense flocks of cattle & goats & taking great numbers of slaves. Their raid had been followed by another few months after made by the Wa-tuta, a race of people allied to the Zulus, who have devastated a great portion of central Africa & have their head quarters on the Eastern shore of Lake Tanganika, Livingstone speaks of them & of the ruin they have accomplished among the tribes of the Tanganika. The natives here know a little Ki'swahili & the Zanzibaris were overjoyed at hearing their own language again & felt that they were now truly nearing their beloved Zanzibar. It is strange that though we are so near M'salala we should not be able to get any reliable news as to whether there are any Europeans there or if so how many, news travels slowly in this country. Meanwhile we are now pressing on eagerly to M'salala looking forward to getting our letters & papers. Stanley intends to stay there at least ten days to rest the people for we are all completely worn out. The Pasha's people are now marching very well but we have lost immense numbers on the road through desertion & death & are now having to carry a good many of them in hammocks which is very hard on the Zanzibaris. Each day the natives tell us M'salala is five days then the next day they say it is seven & so on until our people almost doubt if there is such a place, even though it has always been placed before their eyes as a haven of rest where all their troubles will cease & where we will be able to get any number of Wnyamwezi porters to carry the extra loads & sick people. After marching five or six days through the driest & most shadeless country we arrived at the station of [blank]. It was built by the French priests who have a station at Bukumbi not far from M'salala & another in Uganda of whom Père Lourdel is the head, they belong to the Algerian Mission of which Cardinal Livigerie is the director. It was most startling on coming out of the forest after months of seperation from civilization to be suddenly without the least warning confronted by a church with a cross over it. [*21 August*] The mission which consisted of a number of buildings very well made & surrounded by a double boma had been abandoned some months before on account of the hostility of the natives, but there were a good number of native & Zanzibari converts still in it.

We camped there for the night & heard from the mission people that Mackays mission was now at a place called Usambiro whose chief is Makolo, he had left M'salala some time & had moved the mission there on account of some difficulties the Missionaries had with the chief of M'salala.[1] Stanley sent off a note in the evening to tell Mackay of our coming, he got the note next morning & must have been considerably astonished as he had not heard of the expedition for months & months & had no idea where we were. Next morning at about 10 o'clock we came across a broad cart road leading into the jungle & in another hour we had reached Usambiro. It is a nicely situated place about a mile from the south west arm of the lake & is surrounded by a boma. [*27 August*] Mackay received us very cordially, he & another missionary, named Deeks, are the only two Europeans there, Stokes an Irish trader with two other missionaries had started only the day before to Uganda where they are going to help M'wanga to reestablish the mission which was destroyed by the Arabs, Mackay sent messengers to recall them, but as they had gone by boat they were unable to communicate with them. [*28 August*] We all arrived in an utterly worn out condition & with scarcely any clothes or boots, though still as keenly interested in our work as ever, we were worn down & tired out by fevers & constant marching, we wanted rest, anything for rest; our nerves were in a state of rack & strain & the slightest sudden noise nearly sent one mad. When we came in there was a musical box playing Auld lang Syne, I could'nt listen to it & had to leave the room; to hear that tune of all others was more than I could bear—I who when I left England did'nt ever suspect I was possessed of nerves. There were no letters or papers for us. Stairs had two, one announcing the death of his father, & another containing the news that his sister whose husband is stationed in Burmah was burnt out of house & home by the Decoits & had had to take refuge in the jungle until she was rescued. Ah! the bitter, bitter disappointment it was to us to hear that all our letters had been stupidly sent on to Uganda & had been destroyed by the Arabs. In our low & depressed state of spirits we imagined all sorts of things happening to our people & news equally bad as that which poor Stairs had received. One got into a morbid desponding state of mind which was unusual & most distressing. From Mackay we heard further news of the German occupation of which before we had heard rumours & of the dangers & difficulties which it caused to all Europeans. Mackay was threatened by an invasion of Arabs from Unyanyembe & had fortified the station strongly in consequence. He had had no papers for over a year & the few letters he had had been smuggled past the Arabs hidden in bags of grain or in the stocks of the runners guns.

[1] Mackay had already been driven out of Buganda by the civil war. See Introduction above, pp. 27, 43.

There were immense numbers of cuttings from the different papers about the expedition—the people at home seem to have lost their heads completely. One paper says we are completely Anihilated & another sends us off with Emin Pasha to fight the Mahdi; a third sends us to found a state East of the Niger, a fourth to found a state in Masai land; a fifth marches us off to Ujiji; a sixth leaves us sticking in a morass somewhere in a forest, & so on through dozens of reports, letters & leading articles all vieing with each other in the utter falseness & improbability of their conjectures. Meantime, while all Europe has been starting all sorts of extraordinary rumours, we have been plodding slowly & doggedly on, not looking to the right or the left neither founding states nor sticking in morasses, but bearing steadily in front of our eyes the things we had undertaken to perform & carrying them out, however slowly & painfully. We hear there are two expeditions out from the East coast in search of us & that the East African Association on the lines of the East India Company is a 'fait accompli'.[1] M'wanga of Uganda is deposed & is now with the help of the Missionaries trying to regain the throne & drive out his brother who has unseated him, he is now established on Sesse island & has all the Uganda canoes with him, he has solicited help from the Missionaries & promises to behave better to them if he regains his throne, but I rather fancy it will be a case of 'The devil was sick, The devil a monk would be, The devil got well the devil a monk was he'. It is a funny thing how seldom missionaries can be got to stick to their own proper work they always go interfering with things which do'nt concern them & invariably get into trouble. We found a large supply of cloth, beads & brass wire had been lying here ready for us for more than a year, & also a large stock of European provisions which were very welcome. Mackay told us there were fifteen priests at the Catholic Mission Ukumbi & that perhaps they might have some clothes which they would let us have, so we wrote over & asked & they answered by sending two of their peres with a large stock

[1] This must refer to Jackson's and Gedge's expedition which is described in the Introduction above, pp. 28–9.

As late as 21 October 1889 the American journalist Thomas Stevens, who had made a sally into East Africa as far as Kilimanjaro, wrote from Zanzibar that 'Stanley seems to have again lapsed into obscurity... We know that he has reached Emin and that Emin's province is fruitful, so that they may well be left in peace to work out together their own salvation. My opinion is that Stanley and Emin are yet together in the Equatorial Province, carrying out the plans of the IBEA Co., and waiting for the Company to make connection with them. The story about Stanley having been to Msalala at the south end of Victoria Nyanza, that was published some time ago, was all moonshine. He has never been south of Uganda, and the stories about his approach to the coast are not worth a moment's consideration' (T. Stevens to Mrs French Sheldon, 21 October 1889, preserved in the R.G.S. Museum). Stevens made another attempt, was arrested by the Germans on the orders of Major Wissmann, but was released and met Stanley on 27 November 1889. (Stanley *IDA*, II,).

of clothes & boots which was eagerly bought up by us. The priests did not lose by the transaction. They brought us quantities of beautiful cabbages, tomatoes lettuces etc from their garden. On the fifth day after our arrival Stanley sent off couriers to the coast with letters & dispatches & I wrote a few, but I was not in the humour for writing & could not write much. Our letters will probably get to the coast about the end of November & telegrams will be sent to the English Consul & Mackinon's people to England. Mackay was expecting his mail to come up in a few days so Stanley said he would wait till it arrived to see what news there was from the coast & to decide on what was best to do if the Arabs were still fighting. We all found Mackay the kindest & best of hosts, he fed us up & left us to do as we pleased, I'm sure we made free with his house & overan everything. He is a very nice & very clever fellow & was educated to be a civil engineer, he builds boats, makes spinning machines for the natives & is universally liked & respected by natives & Europeans, he is clever in everything & teaches his people to be good artisans & does'nt stick too much to proselytizing which is a good thing, we all got on capitally with him, & he seemed to be really sorry when we left. Deeks, his companion, is of the usual type of African Missionary, any amount of zeal but not much common sense, still he was good natured & very civil & we have every reason to be grateful to him for his attention to us—Mackay is of quite a different sort & one would like to see him again. The first 10 days we did nothing but eat & idle & rest & then we began to get anxious to be on the move again so we began a tremendous arranging of loads & giving out of rations of cloth to the Pasha's people to last them to the coast which we should reach in three months after starting from here. We have lost great numbers of the Pasha's people on the road from death & desertion, the people, too, took to selling their children to the natives for cows, goats etc, so that of the people who started from Kavalli's we had only [ ] left when we left Usambiro. We waited till from August 28th to September 16th, & as the mail had not come in by that time, we started off without waiting for it longer.

On September 16th we started off in high spirits for the coast, we had completely got rid of our nerves & were all as eager & strong as ever. I, after being a skeleton, have got as fat as a pig, a perfect bolster & am better than I have ever been before in Africa. Mackay gave us lots of old papers to read, the oldest even of which are read by us with eager interest. The Zanzibaris were all in the wildest spirits at the idea of the final start for Zanzibar, they do'nt yet quite know what to think of the German occupation, but say that the 'Bibi' (the Queen of England) wo'nt allow the Germans to do any harm as she has always been the firm friend of Zanzibar. From Mackay's we took with us 12 or 15 Wanyamwezi porters who will carry our loads as far as

Usorigo where we hope to get more porters from Mitingini, the chief of the country. We started the Pasha's people ahead & left them in charge of Nelson, who with his company camped about 6 miles from Usambiro, whilest Stanley Stairs & I remained with Mackay to give the mail, which we heard was in the neighbourhood, a chance of arriving. All day we waited impatiently but with no result, & next morning we started off with our respective companies to join Nelson. One was really very sorry to say good bye to Mackay, he is such a good fellow, & is embarked, I'm afraid, on such a hopeless affair. One cannot but say that Missionaries do a good work in Africa, but their work is not lasting & if their backs were turned tomorrow, everything would relapse into the old state of things in a very short time & no traces would be left of them except perhaps a few plants which the natives find do well & are adapted to their climate, plants introduced by the missionaries. And yet, though one must admit that the missionaries do a good work, it seems to me to be such a hopeless bolstering up, such a very superficial civilization, the converts do not seem really to understand what they profess to believe; they seem merely to ape the white man & repeat parrot like what he tells them. Before people can do any lasting good they must go to the root of the thing & begin first to alter, or perhaps I should say, to improve the whole social life of the negro, & it seems to me that the only way by which this reform can be carried out is *trade*. For myself I know nothing about trade & in the abstract I dislike it. I hate all the nasty cheap Manchester cottons which are imported into this unfortunate Africa & are greedily bought up by the ignorant natives whose eyes are caught by the base gaudy patterns displayed on the handkerchiefs. I consider that it is a disgrace to an Englishman to manufacture & sell anything so common & tawdry but still the manufacturers have some excuse for the natives will give just as much for common flimsey cloth as they will for real strong serviceable cottons. I think Europeans, & especially Missionaries, make a very great mistake in the way they train the negroes—I put forward my idea merely as a suggestion & with all humility—they seem to try to Europeanise the negro & make him ape European manners, customs & dress, instead of which I think they should leave him a negro but improve the resources they find in the country, it is in their power to make him an enlightened negro capable of thinking, a man who by his mere example would do infinite good to his less enlightened brothers, but they prefer apparently to make a bad European of him, & all the mission boys I have seen are a canting, servile worthless lot, talking a good deal about Jesus Christ, but not liking work. Anything more painfully ludicrous than a native dressed in European clothes & aping European manners & phrases it is difficult to imagine. How much nicer the natives look clothed in their finely made bark cloth or their beautifully dressed skins, instead of the cheap Manchester cottons, why not develop the resources the country has; why not cultivate the fine cotton which grows as freely almost everywhere in Africa & teach the natives how to weave it into cloth themselves, the cloth which the people in the Pasha's country made far surpassed any of the Manchester goods one ever saw in Africa: it was warmer & far stronger. It is the same thing all through; Europeans come out to Africa & seem to depend on Europe for everything they do not seem to understand that the things they find in Africa are probably much better adapted to the country than the things European traders import; they merely want improving & developing. The man who comes out here with the idea of Europeanising Africa will, I am sure, fail. Better have a good negro than a bad European. Therefore I think trade is the only thing to civilize this continent & trade can only be really developped by the making of railways to bridge over the waterless deserts which seperate the unhealthy coast from the rich breezy countrys which lie about the Victoria Nyanza. Let the European trader bring into the country such things as the native cannot make, & let him encourage the native to cultivate the rich soil which lies ready to his hand, & grow corn & rice & tobacco & cotton & whatever the country will grow, in exchange for the European traders goods. The ordinary native is a lazy person & only grows just enough corn etc for the use of himself & his family let him once see that what he grows has a very substantial value, & he will cultivate more, & be more hardworking & thrifty, he will not then be so ready to go to war with his neighbour, he will have more at stake & will therefore avoid fighting & the little petty wars which are the curse of Africa will, with the coming of the railway & the consequent increase of trade, gradually cease. I would in future discourage all large contributions either to the suppression of the slave trade or to the missions, I would rather advise people to look somewhat further ahead & put the money they so lavishly throw away on missions into schemes for railways & trade. It seems to me such an absurd thing for missionaries to be teaching ignorant natives the mysteries of the Holy Trinity when the poor natives do'nt even know how to count three. To return to the caravan after this digression, we started off in high spirits, we had been able to buy a certain amount of clothes from the French Missionaries, Mackay had given us a collection of clothes which belonged to missionaries who had died at the station—it's an ill wind which blows nobody good—& we had a certain amount of European provisions, & tea, coffee & sugar which with care should last us nearly to the coast. The country we were passing through was Usukuma, a fine grain & cattle country—the whole place smelt of cattle— but the people were somewhat boisterous & ill behaved, they had had things too long in their own hands & were accustomed to demand & receive large hongo (tribute) from anyone passing through their country. The French priests & Mackay were loud in their complaints of them & said that it was becoming hardly worth while to bring up caravans of cloth, beads etc. as the Wasukuma demanded such an enormous percentage on everything which passed. [*18 September*] In one place[1] we were obliged to make a demonstration against the natives as they became so troublesome, but Stanley behaved with the utmost patience & forbearance & not a shot was fired. But the very next day the natives became so outrageous that it resulted in a collision & we were at once plunged into war. It happened thus, we were quietly marching along wishing to reach the village of the chief of the country with whom Stanley wanted to transact some business,[2] the natives, who were following the caravan in hundreds, became very insolent & ordered Stanley to camp then & there [*20 September*], this he very naturally refused to do & one man, a chief, became so impertinent that Stanley ordered me to tie him up & to bring him along with us to the chief. This created a great excitement & some men came & struck at Stanley with a spear, upon which they were promptly shot dead & the Zanzibaris who were highly exasperated at the behaviour of the natives, threw down their loads & pursued them like bloodhounds firing right & left among the natives who fled in all directions when they saw that we did not submit tamely to them as other caravans had been accustomed to do & that our guns could speak at the first rush 17 natives were shot down & the whole country was immediately up in arms against us. The Wanyamwezi porters we had taken from Mackay's were so frightened at the turn affairs were taking that they threw down their loads & ran. Stanley swept round a group of rocks upon which hundreds of natives were collected driving everything before him. Stairs & I were left to gather up the loads which had been thrown & to make the best of our way to a place where Stanley had camped about two miles further on. All our chiefs had to pick up the discarded loads & carry them & then there were insufficient men so Stairs & I shouldered a load each & made our way slowly to camp, we had to keep stopping every now & then to make charges at the natives who kept closing in upon us. However we finally reached camp which Stanley had made amongst one of the curious groups of rocks which lie like islands in the flat monotonous country. Here we were at once busily engaged in forming a boma of boughs & thorns round the camp as the natives were collecting in hundreds from all sides & we expected a night attack. By evening we had all in readiness to receive the enemy; the Maxim gun was mounted & in position, & the men were all set to sleep at their posts. Parties of pickets were posted all round the camp some two hundred

[1] Stanley calls this place 'Gengé' (*IDA*, II, 396).
[2] Chief Malissa, of Ikoma (*IDA*, II, 397).

yards distant from the boma. In the night we were turned out several times by the pickets firing at stray natives whom they could see creeping towards the camp by the light of occasional flashes of lightning, however no determined attack was made, though at one time we thought it was imminent & all stood breathlessly at our posts with our teeth clenched & our hearts in our mouths. With the rising sun the natives gathered in hundreds all round & it was considered advisable for the main body to remain in camp while parties went out to punish the natives & drive them away. Stairs was sent out in one direction & I with my company in another to drive off the natives & to burn their villages. One regretted having to burn the villages because they were so pretty & fresh looking, they consist of groups of circular, conical roofed huts, very well made with a sort of basket work plasterd with clay, all round the huts & also forming hedges to the little gardens & fields, are planted milk bushes which are the only green things to be seen at this time of the year in all this burnt up thirsty land where, with the exception of a miserable looking baobab here & there, there are no trees whatever. We drove away the natives & burnt the villages all round, & the men got an immense amount of loot. Towards evening the natives began to mass together in the open, about three quarters of a mile from camp, so the Maxim was directed against them, one man was killed & the natives, in terror of the unusual sound, fled right & left pursued by a party of Zanzibaris who were so infuriated with the natives that they cut the dead man up & slung pieces of him on their guns. The next night passed quietly with but few disturbances. I will mention here that when we were expecting a night attack & the picquets were all on the look out for the enemy, the picquet composed entirely of our Soudanese soldiers was the only one who from sheer funk retired inside the Boma, all the other picquets, composed of Zanzibaris, stuck to their posts. On every occasion our Soudanese have failed us. [*21 September*] On our starting next morning we soon had hundreds of natives following us on either side of the column in a long line sometimes they would mass as if for an attack & we would halt & be ready for them, then as if funking an encounter they would disperse, again they would make a swoop down on the rear guard & try & get at some of our women & children, but they were always repulsed. The Egyptian refugees crowded together in a dense mass, & were defended on each side by a European & a party of Zanzibari sharp shooters who marched along side of them, whilest another European with another party brought up the rear. We had not gone far before the natives began to get rather too bold & gathered in a good big mass in cover of a large village, so Stanley halted the column & sent me with my company to attack the natives & burn their villages, while Nelson with his company swept round & met me from another side. Soon the whole country side was in a blaze, the natives made some attempt to stand but the Zanzibari's blood was up & nothing would stop them now, besides nothing seems to terrify a native so much as the sight of his villages burning, he stands dead silent watching the blaze & makes no attempt to fight. We camped that night near another group of rocks having done a very long march & not being able to stop sooner on account of there being no water. We had not had a single person wounded & we had killed many natives, they cannot stand against the guns, but they are constantly harrassing the column & are ready to take advantage of the least carelessness, so that one is not able to relax one's vigilance for a moment & the noise they make, shouting & blowing horns & beating drums, is very confusing, & the whole thing is fatiguing to the last degree. The next day we did a long march & camped by the dried up bed of a large river in which were dug numerous holes containing a good supply of brackish unpleasant tasting water. The natives had followed us in the same way as before, but after we had been in camp some time natives came towards the camp holding up their hands & making signs of peace, Stanley, ever ready to make peace if the natives desire it, ordered them to be allowed to approach & enter the camp. They came in & told us they wished to make friends, but when some hundreds had gathered in & round the camp they most treacherously attacked us, they killed one man & wounded two others before we recovered from our astonishment but then with one howl the Zanzibaris were after them & there were a great many left dead on the field, the Zanzibaris cut off all their heads & made a pile of them in camp. The man killed was an old fellow named Feraji he was minding the goats & as the natives ran out of the camp pursued by our people old Feraji got speared. I think he was the man of all others in the expedition whom we could best spare, but we are all so intimate & so wrapped up in our people that it is painful to loose even one of the least useful. The next day the natives became very bold & troublesome they gathered on both sides of the caravan in large numbers & apparently took our forbearance for fear, in the distance we could see great herds of cattle, & in desparation Stanley said we must teach these foolish people a lesson & show them that forbearance is not fear, so he ordered me to go & capture some cattle. I have never in Africa seen so many cattle together, the natives had concealed their herds behind a line of villages & when we passed the line we came in sight of vast herds of them: there must have been at least five thousand of them. The natives saw us coming & began madly to drive them away: the cattle put up their tails in a kind of crook & made off followed by the herdsman, who urged them on with stick & voice to their utmost speed a vast cloud of dust seemed to roll across the plain & the cattle disappeared. Not however before we had captured some 200 cattle & about the same number of goats & sheep, just as many as we could drive. We marched on, driving the flocks in front, & entered a different sort of country, a sort of scrubby jungle, however the natives were just as hostile here & we were unable to find water, we camped near some large villages from which the natives had run away there was just enough water in the earthen jars in the huts to keep us going. Here we killed an immense number of sheep & the whole expedition feasted. The next day we marched & marched hopelessly on with no water under a burning, a maddening sun until we reached a large village, here we halted for half an hour & the men rushed off to slake their burning thirst with what water they could find in the huts. After toiling on for some hours we found some wells & camped near them close to a large cluster of rocks from the top of which we took it in turns to keep a look out on the great flat plain all round us. Some of the Pasha's people went out into the villages with a recklessness which nearly cost them their lives, for the natives almost cut them off when fortunately Stanley, who was on the top of the rock, saw what was going to happen & sent out Nelson with a party of men to save them, which was only just accomplished in time. Here we stayed another day & there was again a general slaughter of beasts & the Zanzibaris were again feasted. At night a fearful thunderstorm came on & Stanley's tent was blown down as well as Parke's & Nelson's; Stairs' & mine were the only one's which stood. The whole plain which a few hours ago was dried up & burnt now appeared like a large lake but the ground was so cracked & parched that the water soon subsided & in a few hours no one would have expected there had been rain for days. All day long the natives had been passing in the distance in great numbers & we rather expected on the following day there would be a combined attack on our line of march, but shortly after starting we got into another country, a sort of scrubby jungle, from which we emerged in the afternoon to find ourselves amongst friendly natives. Usukuma must be a beautiful country in the wet season with its thousands upon thousands of acres of cultivated land & its fine grassy plains & herds of sheep & cattle. As we saw it the whole country was one uniform yellow colour, the monotony of which was broken by groups of rocks in the crevices of which numbers of trees, looking something like birches, were growing, these rose like islands from the plain & were sufficiently picturesque as we saw them, but in the rains when they are clothed in green they must be perfectly lovely. The great want in Usukuma in the dry season is the want of water; in the rains there must be abundance but in the dry season there are nothing but water holes or shallow ponds which for the most part yield very muddy saltish water & even then only in small quantities. [*4 October*] After two or three long & weary marches with very little water only, we reached Usongo whose chief is Mityngeni an unusually enlightened Unyamwezi chief & a firm friend of the white man. It is here that Stokes, an Irishman formerly in the Church Missionary Society, has his head quarters[1]. He has a large stockaded camp built for him by Mityngeni. He is at present away in Uganda where he has gone with two missionaries, Gordon & [blank], to help to replace M'wanga on the throne. Here we found a large body of 600 Masai warriors were camped, they had been away to the West on a raiding expedition, & had got together immense herds of cattle & sheep & goats. Owing to the drought they were unable to drive their cattle back to their own country for there was not sufficient water to water their flocks on the way so they were camping in Mityngeni's country with whom they are great friends waiting for the rain to come & fill the ponds & streams. They are a fine race of men with enormous shields painted red & white & huge heavy spears, they have a great number of ear & nose rings, bracelets, anklets, & necklets their hair is plaited up, drawn tight away from the temples & formed into a sort of queue (!) behind, they are fond of covering their heads with a sort of tight skull cap made from the bladder of the cow. They are clothed in skins & have a great many small wooden chains round their necks & they almost always wear sandals made of raw bullock hide. They are tall lanky fellows & are very well described by Thompson who calls them 'regular hobbledy hoys', which is just what they are. These are the first circumcised natives we have yet encountered. We found them very arrogant & rather impertinent but though they were constantly in our camp they gave us no trouble. Stanley wanted to get carriers from Mtyngeni to help us to carry the Pasha's sick people, but unfortunately Mytingeni was just about to make war on his neighbour Simba another Unyamwezi chief who had always been his enemy & said he could not give us any carriers till the war, which was supposed to last four days, was finished. The presence of his friends the Masai, who are great warriors, had emboldened him & he told us he was going to give Simba pepper this time. He was, however, anxious that we should join in the war with him, he had heard of our prowess in Usukuma & learnt with delight how we had punished his old enemies the Wasukuma & was anxious to obtain our services in helping him. We had a good many talks over it but Stanley refused to espouse his cause & said we only fought in self defence & were quite unable to help him. After a day or two he said he would try & give us some porters but that he was by no means sure if he could get them as all the young men wanted to go to the war. We stayed there eight days & eventually got 17 porters under a chief Monoboli. Before we went

[1] C. H. Stokes, an Irishman who worked as a missionary in Buganda and later became a trader. He was charged by the Belgian authorities with smuggling guns across the Free State border and summarily executed by them in 1895. See Jackson, pp. 80–4.

we saw Mityngini, his followers & the Masai all start off for the war. There was an immense concourse of people all gaily dressed & armed to the teeth, the Masai looked very formidable in their war attire with their big head dresses of ostrich feathers—they started off at four in the afternoon & we started off the next day. While we were at Mityngini's courriers came in from Mackay, he had heard of our fighting in Usukuma & sent after us to get news. The courriers had done in five days what we had done in fifteen. They had come along by a different road to our's & had travelled chiefly at night for fear of the natives. At Usongo we also got a letter from a French priest, belonging to the Algerian Mission at Bukumbi at the south end of the Victoria, saying that he Père Giriau, & Père Shintz[1] were desirous to going to the coast with us & availing themselves of our escort & they were coming after us as hard as they could & would catch us up in a few days, meanwhile we went slowly on & they joined us five or six days afterwards. [*17 October*] We are very glad to have them with us it all makes a change in the camp & one can jabber bad French to them which is good exercise. They told us that Mityngini had been very good to them when they passed through his country, he had just returned triumphant having utterly squashed Simba, he had brought back heaps of spoil & had got numbers of women, cattle sheep & goats & he gave Père Giriau quite a small flock of goats to last him to the coast. Père Giriau has cataract coming on & is returning to Europe to have an operation performed, he is a very good natured little fellow & is quite lively in the camp.

After leaving Usongo we arrived in six days at a forest called the 'M'Gunda Makali' it is a forest in which there are no villages & scarcely any water. It is a terrible place so burnt up & parched, it is not exactly a forest but might be called rather a wilderness in which there are great tracts of quivering plains the very sight of which quite takes one's breath away. We had been toiling on parched & dried up, when we came to a great rock in whose shade we camped. Never did I so well understand what is said, I think, in Isaiah,— 'The shadow of a great rock in a weary land'—as an ideal of rest & relief.

---

[1] More correctly, Père Girault and Père Schynse, or Schintz. Stanley describes the two French priests as having overtaken the caravan at Ikungu on 17 October. 'We received them with open arms, we supplied them and their people with meat rations daily to the Coast. We paid their tribute to the Wagogo.' Stanley states that Père Schynse made trouble between him and the Pasha, though his companion 'acknowledged the kindness he received' (*IDA*, II, 405).

Emin found a sympathetic listener in Père Schynse, who reports him as complaining: '"Je suis très reconnaissant à ces messieurs de ce qu'ils ont fait"... "mais j'ai pénétré le but véritable de l'expédition dès mon premier entretien avec Stanley. S'il ne m'a pas fait de proposition directe, j'ai cependant senti tout de suite qu'il y avait là-dessus autre chose que le simple désir de repatrier quelques employés égyptiens"' (Schynse, p. 201).

The last lap

The words came into my mind directly we sighted it & one felt a sort of pleasure in repeating them over & over again to oneself as one actually sat in the shadow of the great rock with the burning weary land all round one. Here a second courrier from Mackay reached us, he was going down to the coast & would accompany us, we got a note or two from him, I got no note myself, but he sent a very kind message to me whom he was pleased to designate 'the friend of Africa & the African'. I had had long talks with him & had felt a pleasure in speaking of my ideas of Africa, it was pleasant to speak to so intelligent a man upon a subject about which one felt very strongly & enthusiastically. I always condemn Stanley's optimistic views as being exceedingly misleading to people who have never been to Africa; on the other hand I equally condemn Burton's pessimistic idea & deny most emphatically the truth of his saying 'The African has neither love, gratitude nor affection'. Baker's views seem to appeal more to my understanding, though he too sometimes offends by talking coarsely about the negro. I was very pleased therefore to see that in talking to Mackay & neither speaking as an optimist or as a pessimist, I had still given the idea that I was a 'friend of Africa & of the African' it is a title I feel very proud to be distinguished by, for I did not in any way disguise from Mackay the fact that I thought there were very many things against Africa & the African, & I by no means blindly praised the one or the other. Mackay, evidently seeing how interested I was in the subject gave me a book called 'Islam, Christianity & the Negro race'; it is written by a Dr Blyden a pure blooded negro, he was ambassador at the Court of St James of the Liberian Republic. I was deeply interested in the book, there is much in it that I do not agree with & will not for a moment admit but on the other hand there is the charm of finding the ideas which have merely floated through one's brain & never been expressed, just written down as one would wish them to be & expressed in just the right words, it sent a sort of glow through one & one read eagerly on & on until the book was finished. At night we had a perfect chorus round the camp & none of us were able to sleep. A Lion was roaring all night & troops of great apes paraded the rocks, one could distinctly hear the patriarch ape laying down the law to the rest of his people, his words being sometimes received with rounds of applause at another time with howls of derision. Melancholy hyaenas cried in the distance & our donkeys brayed to each other in fear & trembling. Never was there such a noisey camp. In passing through this dried up wilderness the fact that we were at least reaching water was revealed to us by seeing in the distance great cool groves of Borrassus Palms. Ah, how lovely their green seemed to us, after having our eyes nearly blinded by the yellow glare, & the very sound of their big fans swishing in the breeze made one feel cool & rested. After passing the M'Gunda Makali

we then again entered the forest. The villages are all built in a large square
with wood & mud all the huts open inward so that there is an unbroken line
of mud walls towards the out side—except where the gate of the village is
these walls are pierced with loopholes for firing through & the villages would
be almost impregnable if held by a determined enemy—the Masai even we
hear will not face a determined enemy when entrenched in one of these
villages or tembes as the Zanzibaris call them. The roofs are flat & covered
with a thick layer of clay. These villages in side a[re] filthily dirty & are
perfect nests of vermin of all kinds. The cultivations round these villages are
very extensive & fairly well cultivated. It being now the dry season there
are no crops but judging from the size of the dry millet or M'tama stalks
left in the ground the crops must be large & well grown. At about this time
the three couriers whom we had sent down to Mpwapwa returned to us,
they brought some official letters to Stanley but none to us there was a letter
from Wissman for the Pasha & a letter from Nicol, Mackinnon's manager
in Zanzibar & some telegrams from the consul. We got all the European
news, the changes in Germany, the princess Louise's marriage with Lord
Fife & several other things but it was a very uninteresting lot of telegrams
& seemed chiefly to relate to strikes at home. Wissman was at Mpwapwa
& took charge of our letters & telegrams down to the coast where they
should arrive somewhere about November the 6th. There was a letter from
Smith the acting consul in Zanzibar in which he detailed different pieces of
news, we were much amused by his beginning 'Queen Victoria still reigns
over England'. Our messenger, Mergain, tells us the Germans treated him
very well & have built a fort of stone at Mpwapwa. A day or two after this
we passed a very large caravan of Wanyamwezi going up country. [*17 October*, Ikungu] There were more than 1,500 porters—they all told was the
Wa'deutch (the Germans) were everything at the coast now, that there
were no more slaves now etc, but one could not get any regular authentic
news from them, one never can. They all amused us by saying to each white
man as they passed 'Guten Morgen'. I suppose they took it from the
Germans, as one passed the caravan one was hailed with by a perfect volley
of Guten Morgens & Yambos.

After travelling for 6 more days through a dried up forest we suddenly
emerged to find the country of Ugogo lying at our feet, a barren waste of
sand which made one blink to look at it, it was, however, evidently very
populous for there were large numbers of Tembe's dotted about, sufficient
to shelter some thousands of people. The Wagogo are supposed to be the
most impertinent people existing, according to Stanley it is impossible to
keep them out of ones tent if you shut the tent door they pull up the side
of the tent & look in that way.

409

EPILOGUE

It is a pity that Mounteney Jephson, after 2 August 1889, gave up the daily entry system in his diary. It permitted the recording of so many incidents, trivial, perhaps, at the time, but which would have helped in the assessment of personal relationships. Yet there was plenty of action—visits to local chiefs and a good deal of fighting, while his observations on the new countries through which the expedition marched would have been of interest. There was, of course, a darker side on which he touched in the book he wrote after his return.

I grieve to say [he writes towards the end of his *Emin Pasha*] that we saw many things on the road between the Albert and the Victoria Lakes, that we should have preferred not to have seen. We were really distressed to see the laden porters belonging to the refugees so cruelly treated by the lazy Egyptians and Soudanese. We could not help being witnesses to many atrocious acts. Then the callousness with which the women of the party were treated, shocked and angered us greatly, so that frequently I and the other officers were compelled to interfere. Poor women, young girls from twelve or thirteen, with ulcered limbs, heated with fever, and footsore, would be seen miles away from the column, loaded down with sheer rubbish, that neither had value nor use for anyone.[1]

And there were other incidents, which perhaps Victorian delicacy restrained him from mentioning, but he used to describe in conversation how the women had to fall out from the march to give birth to their babies, and then hurry on to catch up the column. The white officers were horrified, and used to wait near by and make a cup of tea for the mothers, as there was little more they could do. But their men, including the fathers (where, indeed, these were known) thought the officers were quite demented and roared with laughter at such quixotic action. Though this does not appear in the diary, other distressing incidents are recorded, and it may be that Mounteney became tired of writing about what gave him such pain. Probably too the inevitable reaction was setting in. The great adventure was nearly over, and in the absence of excitement the lassitude engendered by constantly recurring bouts of fever overcame any desire to write regularly. By the end of October they had reached the fringe of civilization and, unfortunately, he evidently felt there was thereafter nothing worth recording.

On 10 November the expedition reached Mpwapwa, where the Germans had established a fort a month previously. On 3 December, as dusk fell, the sound of a distant cannon was heard faintly in the camp. It was the

[1] Jephson, *Emin Pasha*, p. 465.

evening gun at Zanzibar, carried across the sea in the twilight stillness.
At once the Zanzibaris went wild with joy; it was the sound of home to
them.[1]

The following day they arrived at Bagamoyo on the Indian Ocean, and
the great traverse of Africa was completed. There they were entertained to
a banquet that night by Major von Wissman, the representative of the German Government in German East Africa. Towards the end of the meal,
Emin Pasha walked out on to a balcony and fell into the street fourteen feet
below. This unfortunate incident brought the proceedings to an abrupt close.
Emin was taken to hospital in an unconscious condition, and the German
surgeons pronounced that he had fractured the base of his skull. This turned
out to be incorrect, and the damage, though serious, was mainly superficial.

Two days later, 6 December, the expedition embarked for Zanzibar,
leaving Parke behind in case he could be of any help to Emin. The unfortunate Parke had a very unpleasant time, and was treated with studied
discourtesy by the Germans. Then he himself fell ill and had to be conveyed
to hospital in Zanzibar. A few days later Stairs crossed back to Bagamoyo
in the steamer which was to take Emin to Egypt. But the Pasha made the
excuse that he did not feel fit enough to undertake the voyage, and the ship
had to proceed without him.

During this period of Emin's illness, there seems no doubt that the Germans were putting all possible pressure on him to sever his connections with
Britain and Egypt and take service with them. They did what they could to
isolate him from the officers of the expedition by discouraging visits from
them, and their rudeness to Parke was all part of this plan. Its success must
have been largely due to Emin's condition: his fall had caused a further
deterioration in his mental and physical condition and made him more
pliable in their hands, whilst his barely concealed feeling of antipathy towards Stanley added, no doubt, to his readiness to listen.

As a final effort to get him away to Cairo, Mounteney Jephson went over
to Bagamoyo on 28 December and remained with him until the following
day. Parke sent a message to Emin by Jephson that the sea voyage would
be the best thing for his health. But it was to no avail; Emin reiterated that
he could not go. It may be that he had, even as soon as this, been induced
by the Germans to sign some agreement to take service with them. And
Mounteney Jephson, who had succeeded in extricating him from Equatorial
Africa in the face of such infinite difficulties, now failed at Bagamoyo when
it seemed so simple. As they parted, Emin took Mounteney's hand in both
of his and expressed the deepest gratitude for all that he had done on his
behalf. 'You I shall never forget,' he said, 'for you have been my

[1] Stanley, *IDA*, II, 406–11.

companion and friend through those months of our imprisonment together, those months which were the worst of my life.'[1]

From then on Emin's attitude towards Britain and Stanley became one of hostility. The insidious propaganda to which he, in an enfeebled condition, was subjected, had done its work. He stepped down from his pedestal as the heroic ex-Governor of Equatorial Africa, renounced a future in which he was assured of the world's honour and respect, and elected to become an inglorious servant of German East Africa. But he soon quarrelled with his new masters. It was inevitable. His lack of decision must have infuriated his military-minded colleagues, and he does not seem to have impressed the Germans favourably with his administrative ability. The United States newspaper *The Democrat*, of Madison, Wisconsin, published the following article on 27 May 1891, which seems to be his version of the matter:

EMIN PASHA TO RETIRE

Asks to Have a Small Cottage Built for Him at Bagamoyo

Emin Pasha has written from central Africa that his present mission there will be his last. He has asked that a small cottage be built for him at Bagamoyo, on the Indian Ocean, opposite the island of Zanzibar. He says he intends to return to that town and spend the remainder of his days there. Possibly he may change his mind. At the time of writing he was greatly depressed, owing to a letter he had received from Dr. Schmidt, the imperial deputy commissioner, who had censured him for not having observed certain formalities in his reports.

'I should ?[not like]', writes Emin, 'to receive more letters of this sort. I have led the expedition with good success. I have established stations and altogether done more than I was bound to, and instead of recognition I have been censured. No wonder I am vexed.'

He added that he was just about to go to Ruhanda, where no Arab had ever been, and where, he said, there are heaps of ivory. Emin has done one good thing in breaking up the nest of Arab slave hunters who have infested the south shores of Victoria Nyanza for a number of years. They established there a very large station with many buildings, and from their little port they sent expeditions along the shores of the lake to buy ivory and slaves from the natives. They have constantly incited the tribes for hundreds of miles along the lake to engage in slave raids that they might have victims to sell to the Arabs. Their slaves have come from as far north as Uganda.

Emin determined to break up this establishment, and he sent an armed force against it. Several little battles were fought, with some loss on both sides, and finally the Arabs fled southward, leaving several hundreds of slaves behind them. Emin's soldiers found that the slaves were treated with great severity, and that for a year or two past not a few of them had escaped and run away into the forests, preferring to perish there rather than be ill-treated by their cruel masters.

[1] Jephson, *Emin Pasha*, pp. 476–7. For the last days of the expedition from the time they fell in with the Germans until they parted with Emin at Bagamoyo, see *Emin Pasha*, pp. 461–80, and Stanley, *IDA*, II, 406–28.

Epilogue

The Arab power in the Victoria Nyanza region is becoming almost broken up, Emin having dispersed the strongest body of Arab traders in the south, who nearly ruined their country, and driven them north into Usogo, and it is now said that these northern Arabs have formed a juncture with the forces of the mahdi's successor which have taken possession of Emin's old provinces.[1]

But nothing came of Emin's plan to settle down at Bagamoyo. The post referred to in this article was at Bukoba, where Emin had been appointed by the German administration, but piqued by letters such as the one quoted, he left his post to join the German traveller Franz Stuhlmann, who was afterwards to edit Emin's diaries. Their aim seems to have been to cross the Congo region to the Atlantic, and to go by way of Kavalli's with a view to enlisting Selim Bey and those soldiers who had stayed with him. The meeting at Lake Albert in August 1891 was not a happy one, for Selim felt his old governor had deserted him when he marched out of Mazamboni's with Stanley, and in any case Selim was the Khedive's soldier and not minded to take service under the Germans.

The expedition as such faded out with Stuhlmann's return to the coast, and Emin blundered on, half-blind, and by now infirm. In October 1892, he was murdered by Arab slave and ivory traders encountered on the Lindi, a tributary of the Congo, at a place called Kinema.[2]

Emin's daughter Farida was taken to Germany and lived there. It is nice to be able to record that she never forgot Mounteney Jephson, for the warmth of feeling her father entertained for him. Not all Mounteney's acts of kindness to the little girl were recorded in the diary. He told a friend many years afterwards that he had carried her on his back for many miles during the evacuation of the Lake Albert camps. Farida kept in touch with her friend during the years that followed. Her last letter to him, announcing her approaching arrival in London, and hoping to see him, reached him on his deathbed.[3]

For Emin's rescue from Equatorial Africa two British officers and, at a very conservative estimate, three hundred Africans of the expedition had died: and so too did an unknown number of local inhabitants. The five British officers who survived never fully recovered from the effects of fever and privation. Of Emin's people, Stanley recorded that roughly six hundred

---

[1] Cutting from the *Democrat*, 27 May 1891, in the Mallow Castle papers.

[2] This very brief summary of Emin's last days is based on the account in Lugard's *Rise of our East African Empire*, ii, 201–15. Lugard wrote: 'Regarding the history of events in Equatoria subsequent to the departure of Mr. Stanley and Emin Pasha in May 1889, I cannot do better than quote the excellent *résumé* elicited from those of the refugees whom I sent to Egypt, by the authorities there, and published in the "Times" of July 14th, 1892.' The *résumé* is printed on pages 201–6, and the rest of the chapter concerns Lugard's negotiations with Selim.

[3] Letter in Mallow Castle papers.

had left Kavalli's on 10 April 1889. He handed over to the Egyptian authorities in Cairo on 16 January 1890, exactly two hundred and sixty persons, a grim comment on the effects of that long march on men, women and children who were totally unfitted for any form of physical hardship. And, as things turned out, except for Emin himself, they would hardly have fared worse by remaining in Equatorial Africa. So far as the expedition was concerned, however, its objective had been attained. Emin's appeal for help had been nobly answered. But his refusal to leave German East Africa was a shattering anticlimax, and Stanley's success was a Pyrrhic victory to which the whitening bones of so many of his followers, strewn across the breadth of Africa, bore poignant witness.

After the return to Britain, Mounteney recorded three things which kept Stanley's four officers steadfast and comparatively cheerful throughout the period of the expedition, even in its darkest days.

The first was the love and interest we all had in our work. Second, the implicit trust and confidence we have ever had in our leader. And third, and I think not the least, the strong friendship which has always existed between Stairs, Nelson, Parke, and myself. When starvation stared us in the face, when our faithful men fell around us, and when there seemed to be no break in the black cloud which enveloped us, these three influences cheered us on, and prevented our giving in.[1]

Mounteney never forgot those 'faithful men'. In the midst of the honours and compliments so freely meted out to the white officers on their return to Europe, scant mention was made of the part played by the Zanzibaris, whose bravery, loyalty and endurance were among the most important elements which brought the expedition through its ordeal. His sense of fairness prompted him to write to *The Times* on the subject. The following day, 11 April 1890, his letter was referred to at some length in a leading article. The writer agreed that the just claims of the African followers had, in fact, been largely overlooked. On the other points raised in Mounteney's letter, *The Times* seemed somewhat doubtful, particularly his opinion that European interests were perpetually brought forward, while those of the natives, 'the lawful possessors of the country', were scarcely mentioned. The leading article continued—'Mr Jephson seems to presume a degree of ownership of Africa by its negro population which is incompatible with the claims on the continent of any European State or society'. It concluded:

Though there are highlands amidst which Europeans might live and thrive, the mass of Africa is destined to be either negro land or a wilderness. European States and companies which wish to draw wealth from African lordships will have to rely for their gains upon civilized negro industry. If they empty the land of its black people, or suffer it by an evil policy to be emptied, they will commit a most wasteful

[1] Jephson, *Emin Pasha*, p. 459.

and ruinous wickedness. That is the lesson to be gathered from Mr. Jephson's protest of yesterday. The European communities which act wisely and honestly in its spirit will be rewarded by deriving the most gain from their African dominions.

Evidently at that date *The Times* was not prepared to concede that Africa belonged to the Africans.

It would be nice to end here when the mind dwells with admiration and a degree of happiness on Stanley and his four faithful officers. But their stories, after they had returned to England, may be of some interest, though they make sad reading. On arrival home they found they were national heroes; they were feted, lionized and made the recipients of many honours.

Stanley frequently and generously expressed his opinion of his four officers, and they too in their public utterances paid high tribute to their leader. On 30 May a magnificent banquet, given in honour of the officers of the expedition by Americans in London, was the occasion for the presentation to each of them of a massive silver medallion. The Prince of Wales made the presentation. On the one side of each medallion in bas-relief was the head of Stanley, and on the other were the heads of his four officers and beneath was inscribed: 'Never while human nature remains as we know it will there ever be found four gentlemen so matchless for their constancy, devotion to their work, earnest purpose and unflinching obedience to honour and duty. Stanley.' Included in the souvenir menu of the dinner there was a photograph of each officer with his signature and a suitable tribute from Stanley beneath:

Lieut. W. G. Stairs, R.E. 'One of those rare personalities, oftener visible among military men than among civilians, who could obey orders without argument, who could accept a command, and without ado or fuss execute it religiously—Courageous, careful, watchful, diligent and faithful.'

Surgeon T. H. Parke, Army Medical Staff. 'I consider this expedition in nothing happier than in the possession of an unrivalled physician and surgeon, Dr. T. H. Parke, of the A.M.D.—Loyal and devoted services gratuitously [given]—Skilled as a physician, tender as a nurse, gifted with remarkable consideration and sweet patience—Every white officer in the expedition, Emin Pasha, Captain Casati, and the Egyptian officers and all are indebted to him.'

Capt. R. H. Nelson. 'Consistent zeal to duties.—High soldierly qualities, proving to what a pitch of devotion a highly honourable man can carry his ideas of duty.—A devotion to duties, an intelligence to comprehend, an obedience without cavil, a zeal which never flagged to perform and endure whatever task was put before him.'

Mr. A. J. Mounteney Jephson. 'Distinguished by his untiring industry and indefatigable zeal and unique service to the expedition,—devotion and chivalrous kindness to Emin Pasha. An indomitability of spirit, courage, and celerity of movement.—Faithful and obedient.'[1]

[1] A copy of the commemorative album is among the Mallow Castle papers, and also in the Museum of the Royal Geographical Society.

It is a wonder how they stood up to all this entertainment, but they did not do so for long. On 26 June, *The Pall Mall Gazette*, describing the dinner that Sampson, Low & Co., the publishers, gave to Stanley and his officers, reported—'In spite of the weary round of heavy dinners, speeches and hand-shaking the lion of the season looks remarkably fit...Neither Parke, Nelson nor Stairs turned up...But Mr. Jephson was equal to the occasion.' It was not generally realized how much their health had been undermined by their sufferings.

Stanley was married to Dorothy Tennant in Westminster Abbey on 12 July and Stairs, Nelson and Jephson were groomsmen. The honeymoon was spent in the Engadine. The newly married couple asked Mounteney to come out to them there, and when with them he met Sir Richard and Lady Burton. The *Daily Graphic* of 8 October carried an interesting picture of the five of them which is reproduced in Plate 15.

Next year both Stanley and Mounteney Jephson went on a lecture tour to North America. The latter, on the urgent representations of his friends, resting in the Yosemite Valley in California and trying to make headway against frequent attacks of malaria, received a letter from Stairs written on 17 May 1891. He was going to Katanga to work for the King of the Belgians. He ended: 'Good-bye, old man—Heaven grant that we may yet serve together through Africa through forest and plain.'[1] Mounteney was deeply moved by this letter. He wrote to a friend: 'Perhaps I have lingered too long for my peace of mind in this land of sun and flowers...A farewell letter too comes from my old friend Stairs on the eve of his departure for Africa which is a reproach to me for having, contrary to my promise, let him go alone.'[2] To judge by his self-reproach, it would seem that Mounteney did not realize that his health would never again stand up to the rigours of service in Africa. Or perhaps this talk of return to the Dark Continent was just an emotional pipe-dream conjured up by his love of adventure and action, and the deep friendship between these two men engendered by the perilous years they had spent together.

Stairs completed his task in Katanga much more quickly than he had expected. He freed numbers of slaves, built a strong fort at Msiri and concluded treaties with the twelve most important native chiefs. Steaming through Lake Nyasa on the *S.S. Domera*, he wrote to Parke on 19 May 1892 to apprise him that he was on the way home. The only intimation of any ill health was in a postscript to this letter: 'Have had a dose of Typhomalia [*sic*]. Almost died twelve days unconscious well again now'. The abrupt

[1] Stairs to Jephson, 17 May 1891, Mallow Castle papers.
[2] Jephson probably wrote this letter to the novelist and dramatist Hamilton Aidé. It is in the Mallow Castle papers.

ending to the postscript and the shaking hand in which the last words were written belie the optimism of his statement—'well again now'.[1] He died three weeks later at the confluence of the Zambezi and Chinde rivers, a tragic loss to his country.

Six months later Nelson died of dysentery. He was in the service of the Imperial British East Africa Company and in charge of the Kikuyu district of Kenya.

On 7 August 1893, Parke, employed at Netley Hospital with the Army Medical Department, wrote a cheerful letter to Mounteney. In it he asked: 'When shall I see you again?'[2] On 11 September he died suddenly when staying with friends in Scotland. It was only nine months after Nelson's death.

That left only Stanley and Jephson, and less than four years since the end of the Relief Expedition. The loss of their three comrades seemed to draw them ever closer together. In 1896 Stanley had a long and dangerous illness. He pulled through with difficulty, and thereafter had to adopt a reduced tempo of living. Then in the spring of 1904 he fell ill again. On 3 May Dorothy Stanley wrote to Mounteney: 'I cannot trust myself to write much. Mr. Wellcome will tell you all. Now there is no hope of saving my Beloved Husband. He must leave me.'[3]

Stanley died a week later at the age of sixty-three. Mounteney Jephson tried to have the body buried in Westminster Abbey, but he could not obtain the necessary approval. The funeral service was held there, and Mounteney, always an emotional man, confessed afterwards that he nearly broke down during the singing of the well-known lines:

> Time like an ever rolling stream
> Bears all its sons away.

Standing there in the Abbey beside the coffin of his old chief, the realization that he was now the sole survivor of the great enterprise brought anguish to his heart.

Throughout all these years illness dogged Mounteney's footsteps. He longed to return to Africa, and he had plenty of opportunities of doing so. It seems that late in 1890 he applied for government employment there, because in February the following year, while he was lecturing in the United States, the Foreign Office was trying to get in touch with him to offer him a post on the Oil Rivers, as the coastal lands of Nigeria were then called. In September 1891, he and Stanley were invited to Ostend by the King of the Belgians. They spent several days there, and the talk was of the Congo. Soon afterwards the King asked him to lead an expedition to Katanga to

---

[1] Stairs to Parke, 19 May 1892. Mallow Castle papers.
[2] Parke to Jephson, 7 August 1893. Mallow Castle papers.
[3] Lady Stanley to Jephson, 3 May 1904. Mallow Castle papers.

reinforce Stairs with men and supplies. And Sir William Mackinnon, of the Imperial British East Africa Company, offered him the same sort of employment, an expedition to Uganda. But he felt most inclined to fall in with a plan suggested to him by Scott Keltie, of the Royal Geographical Society, and Moberly Bell, editor of *The Times*. This was to travel through Liberia in the steps of Mungo Park, nearly a century earlier, and write articles for the paper descriptive of the country, its peoples and their institutions. But, of course, his health made all such schemes quite impracticable. And it prevented him from accepting the invitation to stand as Unionist candidate for South Aberdeen which A. L. Bruce, Livingstone's son-in-law, sent him in December 1891 at the instigation of Lord Wolmer, the Unionist Whip. He rendered useful services in urging the construction of the Uganda Railway. He used to tell the story how some time afterwards he was sent for by the Prime Minister. 'Uncle Salisbury told me that there was available a pension of £400 a year for some person who was regarded as specially deserving. He asked if it would be any good to me.' Mounteney recalled how he had to gulp back his astonishment and delight, for this was wealth indeed for him in those days. At last he blurted out in some confusion— 'Well, Sir, it certainly is better than a poke in the eye with a blunt stick.' Lord Salisbury laughed: he understood: Mounteney was just too overcome to think of a more appropriate expression to convey the gratitude he felt.

He was employed as Queen's Messenger from 1895 to 1901. But the work was shown to be too much for him when he was discovered unconscious, when in charge of dispatches, in a train on the continent. He was taken to hospital and had to undergo an operation. After he was sufficiently recovered he was given the less strenuous post of Usher at Court. Then, thinking it might benefit his health, Lord Ranfurly, Governor of New Zealand, offered him the appointment of A.D.C., which he accepted gratefully. He went out in 1902, but returned the following year, again seriously ill.

In June 1904, Mounteney married Anna Head, of San Francisco. The story is rather a sad one. He had met her in 1891, when lecturing in the United States. The attraction was mutual and immediate. He wrote to her that she was nothing but 'a little peaky faced girl in a simple frock'. She accepted this meekly! But, he went on, to dance with and talk to her made him insensible to everything except that, to quote his own words, 'a feeling of intense relief had suddenly come to me & taken away the excited discontented feeling of despondency and un-rest which had been with me for so long'.[1] He felt her presence as a cool hand on the brow of a man racked by fever. But Anna's father, Addison Head, was a tough business man. Glamour, in his eyes, went hand in hand with wealth and business acumen:

[1] Letters at Mallow Castle.

African exploration left him cold. He rated Mounteney as a penniless adventurer. He refused to permit them even to become officially engaged, let alone married. And Anna was too loyal and devoted a daughter to defy her father. Mounteney wrote to a friend and expressed the opinion that all would have been well had she done so, and Addison Head would soon have accepted the situation. But delicacy of feeling prevented him from making any real attempt to override her scruples. And so these two remained steadfastly pledged to each other until, on his deathbed in the late spring of 1903, the old man repented of his obduracy and consented to their union. But his stubbornness, for all that it was dictated by what he believed to be his daughter's best interests, had deprived these two people of twelve years of married life. And during all those years that spirit of despondency and unrest, which could so easily have been dispelled by Anna's presence, remained with him never far beneath the surface.

As soon as possible Anna and her mother hurried over to London, where Mounteney lay ill in hospital. His recovery was painfully slow, and it was not until the following summer that he was considered well enough to get married. The wedding took place on 8 June. Stanley's present was a Georgian soup tureen and ladle. On the former was inscribed: TO A. J. MOUNTENEY JEPHSON (BOUBARIKA). One of my Chief Officers throughout the Emin Pasha Relief Expedition. His loyalty and devotion, his unflagging zeal and courage—even in our darkest days—won my admiration and warm affection. Many happy years to him. From H. M. Stanley (Bula Matari). 1904.'

But Stanley had died in May, four weeks before the wedding, and the occasion, which should have been one of so much joy to those two people, who had waited faithfully for each other for so long, was clouded with sorrow.

A son was born in May 1905, to the great delight of Mounteney and Anna. But Mounteney's periods of good health were all too few. However, early in 1908 he must have been better, because there was again some talk of his standing for Parliament. The Duke of Argyle was anxious that he should become a candidate for a Manchester constituency. But it was all of no avail. On 25 April the Duke wrote: 'I am much disturbed to hear of your weakness. I hope you will give your heart full time to recover "its normal" by keeping free of business exertion.'[1] This time, however, it was the beginning of the end, and Mounteney died six months later. The son, the only child, was killed in the Underground Railway accident near Charing Cross on 17 May 1938, aged just thirty-three. He was unmarried.[2]

[1] Letter in Mallow Castle papers.
[2] This account of Mounteney Jephson's later years is summarized from his nephew's family history: M. D. Jephson, *An Anglo-Irish Miscellany*, which is based on the letters and papers at Mallow Castle (chapter XVI, 'A. J. Mounteney Jephson', pp. 268–87).

A brief reference seems desirable to the two other white men who accompanied the expedition through to the end, but were not often mentioned in the diary.

William Bonny was a paid medical assistant, not an officer. He made a bad start to the expedition. As already recorded, he missed the steamer at Tilbury under circumstances which suggest a considerable degree of stupidity. Following his return to the main body with the remnants of the rearguard, he was questioned by Stairs, Nelson and Parke about the tragic events at Yambuya. They were dissatisfied with his account. Mounteney heard the news of Barttelot's death in Stanley's letter to him dated 18 January 1889. Soliloquizing in his diary on the 26th of that month while still at Tunguru, he wrote that he would reserve judgment until he could hear the story from Bonny. But after he had rejoined the main body and questioned Bonny himself, he also seems to have been dissatisfied. And from then on a coolness arose between Bonny and Stanley's four officers which was noticed, and commented upon in the press, after the return to England. Perhaps Bonny had a very poor memory, or was bad at expressing himself. But so unreliable did Mounteney Jephson regard Bonny's account of the rearguard's story that he wrote in the book he published dealing with the period of his imprisonment with Emin: 'The story of that terrible time will never, I fear, be correctly known.'[1] And he wrote this while Bonny was very much alive and well. According to William Hoffmann, who is referred to below, Bonny died in Fulham Workhouse some years before 1907.[2]

This William Hoffmann was the other European; he was Stanley's German servant. Curiously enough, Stanley makes no mention of him in *In Darkest Africa*. Mounteney Jephson refers to him in the diary occasionally and very briefly in connection with his duties to his master, and never by name.

In 1938, he published a book entitled *With Stanley in Africa*. Written some fifty years after the events it purports to record, it somewhat understandably contains certain inaccuracies and questionable statements. However, his story records that he was apprenticed as a boy to a bagmaker in London. He first met Stanley at an hotel in Sackville Street in November 1884 when delivering goods to Mrs French Sheldon, who was later to distinguish herself by her travels in East Africa.[3] Evidently impressed by the lad's bearing and ability to talk French and German fluently, Stanley asked him if he would like to enter his service, and the matter was arranged after details had been settled with Hoffmann's father.

[1] Jephson, *Emin Pasha*, p. 403.
[2] An interesting sidelight on Bonny is contained in a letter from Barttelot to his fiancée Miss Godman, quoted the footnote on p. 364 above.
[3] Dorothy Middleton, *Victorian Lady Travellers* (London, 1965), pp. 90–103.

Soon afterwards, William Hoffmann accompanied Stanley to Berlin for the international conference on the Congo. Towards the end of 1887, he was with him on a lecturing tour in the United States when the telegram appointing Stanley to the leadership of the Relief Expedition arrived from William Mackinnon.

Hoffmann conveys the impression that he was an officer of the expedition and was at times given certain executive duties. But the lack of any mention of him, referred to above, must indicate that this was not the case.

On the journey home from Zanzibar, Hoffmann recounts how Sir Francis de Winton met them at Mombasa and applied to Stanley for his services, in view of his knowledge of conditions in Africa, and that he and Stanley had agreed somewhat reluctantly. He evidently felt that he was able to carry out good work in that appointment because he states in his book: 'Thanks to the ceaseless work of my Chief, Sir Francis, and partly, I think, owing to my own efforts, the slave trade showed a marked decrease in 1890.'[1]

Hoffmann returned to England in 1891, and went at once to see Stanley, who urged him to go to some lonely seaside resort to recuperate from the effects of four years in Africa, and he would pay for his room. Four months later, he recalls that Stanley went to see him and suggested that he should go to the Congo Free State for employment as an interpreter. Hoffmann accepted and signed a contract in Brussels for three years' service in such a capacity. He was back in England by the end of 1894, but returned to the Congo the following April for two years' further employment, spent mainly in operations against the slave-traders. In 1897, Stanley asked him to accompany him to Bulawayo to attend the celebrations to mark the opening of the Cape Town–Bulawayo railway, and Hoffmann quotes Dorothy Stanley's words: 'I am very glad, William, that you are going with my husband. He needs someone to look after him, and he trusts you as he trusts few men.'[2]

After his return from the Congo in 1896, Hoffmann seems to have settled down in London, and he gives a clear indication of close and friendly relations with both Stanley and his wife. It is difficult, therefore, to reconcile this impression with the account of a newspaper reporter's interview with him which appeared in *The Evening News* on 1 July 1907. Hoffmann was in financial difficulties at the time, and is quoted as saying: 'I only wish Stanley were alive today. He would see that I did not want for anything.'[3] But Dorothy Stanley was alive. And so was Mounteney Jephson, who is referred to in the article as the only other white survivor of the expedition and 'a man who is today rich and in a good position', a remark obviously

---

[1] William Hoffmann, *With Stanley in Africa* (London, 1938), p. 176.
[2] Hoffmann, p. 246.
[3] From a cutting in the Mallow Castle papers.

intended as a reproach to him for not having helped. It is therefore difficult to avoid the conclusion that neither of these two people was anxious to help Hoffmann, at any rate at that time.

In the same newspaper article Hoffmann was reported as saying that he had returned from the Congo in 1900, when he 'was compelled to give evidence injurious to the Congo people, and were I to return now it would only be a matter of hours before they put a bullet through me'. Yet in his above-quoted book he describes how he left Cape Town with Stanley by steamer after visiting Bulawayo in 1897, and adds: 'Neither he nor I ever saw Africa again.'[1] So one must conclude, with as much kindness as one can muster, that even in 1907, the date of the newspaper article, Hoffmann's memory was very unreliable. It is not known when he died.

Finally, a short summary of what happened to Emin's troops may be of interest. Two parties of soldiers and clerks with their officers were left behind when Stanley marched out of Mazamboni's on 8 May 1889. Fadl el Mulla, for long the ringleader of the mutiny, retired to the hills above Wadelai with a large number of men and most of the Irregulars. Selim Bey seems to have been in earnest in trying to collect a party to march to the coast, but the distances between the garrisons were too great and the difficulties overcame him, and he was left behind with a smaller following at Kavalli's. Both groups were well supplied with ammunition, having located and dug up the boxes of ammunition which Jephson reports burying before the retreat[2].

Fadl el Mulla consolidated a position at Wadelai and entered into under-hand correspondence with the Mahdist forces once more approaching from the north; these, expecting his cooperation, attacked the garrison. To their surprise, Fadl el Mulla's men repulsed the enemy with severe losses and immediately after slaughtered the Irregulars, of whom, it may be remembered, they had always been suspicious. Disgusted with Fadl el Mulla's double-dealing, but not daring to attack the only senior officer left, some 800 of his men deserted and joined Selim at Kavalli's.

In 1892 a Belgian expedition approached the Congo–Nile watershed from the Free State with a view to extending Leopold's kingdom, the King's interest in Equatoria and the upper Nile valley having by no means declined. They were led by G. F. van Kerckhoven and, after his death in an accident, by Jules Milz. The Belgians attempted to enlist Fadl el Mulla and his men under the Free State flag, and some sort of agreement was arrived at, but it did not work out satisfactorily. Siding first with the Belgians and then accepting overtures from the Mahdist forces, Fadl el Mulla came to a violent end, being killed with at least half his men in a battle near Wadelai against

[1] Hoffmann, p. 258.   [2] See p. 348 above

the Mahdists on 25 January 1894. A remnant of the men escaped, and were taken in charge by the British authorities in Uganda.[1]

Selim and his men had settled down at Kavalli's to await a rescue from the east coast, and this came in 1891 in the person of Major F. D. Lugard, then in the employ of the Imperial British East Africa Company and conducting a campaign for the ending of civil war in Uganda between the Protestants, Catholics, Moslems and pagans. When Lugard came up from the coast to Buganda in the August of 1890 he had with him seventy Sudanese soldiers led by Shukri Aga, lately of M'swa. Shukri and his men had returned to Egypt with Stanley and received their back pay in accordance with the Khedive's letter to the Equatorial garrisons, and had been recruited by Lugard for his work in Buganda. In need of reinforcements, he determined to seek out the remnants of Emin's men left at Lake Albert. Shukri maintained that Selim Bey had always been loyal to the Khedive, and Lugard reported that as they approached Kavalli's after the long march by way of the Salt Lake and the Semliki river, they were met by Sudanese officers and (to quote Lugard himself) 'there was great joy and kissing of my hand... and hand-shaking with Shukri and my Sudanese. Everyone talked at the same time, and congratulated each other, and everyone temporarily became a fool, and smiled extremely, and talked incessantly, as is right and proper on such an occasion.'[2]

Selim had established at Kavalli's, under the chief's friendly protection, a community based on the pattern Emin had taught him in better days. He had about 600 men and an enormous following of women and children, slaves and local tribesmen who had accompanied the contingent from Wadelai which had deserted Fadl el Mulla. Lugard tells us that 'they had brought cotton-seeds with them, and planted and gathered the produce of the fields, and in their own rough looms had woven the cloth from which were made the coats and trousers which they wore. A coinage yet circulated among them, and the Egyptian clerks still wrote the official dispatches sent by Selim to his out-stations and subordinate officers. In short, among all the outward savagery of soldiers dressed in hides, of naked women, and grass huts, there was a noticeable—almost pathetic—attempt to maintain the status they claimed as soldiers of a civilized Government.'[3]

Selim, protesting his loyalty to the Khedive, at first would not consider joining the British under Lugard any more than he had entertained the idea of enlisting with Emin and the Germans only a month before. But when it was explained that the Khedive's permission was to be asked, he consented

[1] See R. O. Collins, *The southern Sudan 1883–1898*, pp. 92–117, for account of Fadl el Mulla's story; also Major A. B. Thruston, *African incidents*, pp. 164–6.
[2] Lugard, II, 201.   [3] Lugard, II, 218.

to accompany Lugard. The whole party, some 8000 souls, moved slowly back to Buganda, a substantial number of Selim's men being posted at the forts built by Lugard in Toro between Lake Albert and the Buganda capital. Selim and about 100 soldiers were enlisted in the chartered company's forces, and served their new masters well, but after Lugard's departure in 1892 Selim became involved in the complicated disputes between the Moslems and the other factions in Buganda civil strife. He openly favoured the Moslem claim for more territory, and was arrested and his garrison disarmed. He was to have been deported, but died on his way to the coast. Lugard maintained that he had been misjudged and hardly treated.[1]

From the Equatorial soldiers left in Toro, a number were eventually enlisted into the forces of the British Protectorate which came into being in April 1893, and the rest were disarmed and disbanded, and settled down in little colonies of their own. The enlisted men were good soldiers, and the mutiny which broke out among them in 1897 was due as much to the hard conditions of service which circumstances forced upon them as to any fault in the men themselves. They were a brave body of men, and history has partly exonerated them.[2]

So much for the people; what of the Equatorial Province itself, the scene of Emin's greatest achievements and deepest humiliations? Equatoria is divided now by the boundary between the modern States of Sudan and Uganda, which crosses the Nile at Nimule at the Fola Rapids, just north of Dufilé, where Jephson spent his three months' imprisonment with Emin, at the mercy of the mutinous garrisons. Emin's stations have almost entirely disappeared. A party of students from London University travelled to Uganda in 1965, with the aim of surveying Emin's forts. The fine buildings at Dufilé where, under the orange and lime trees, gazing through an arch of greenery to the river, 'Baker, Gordon, Gessi, Juncker, Prout and all the celebrities of the Equatorial provinces' had sat with their coffee and cigarettes,[3] have returned to the swamp and the bush. 'The local people', runs the report of the 1965 expedition, 'were at first frightened by our appearance ...and mistook us for the ghosts of the former inhabitants.' Either from fear, or from respect for the ghosts of the past, these local people have not attempted to cultivate the ground where Dufilé stood, and vivid traditions persist—not always accurate, as, for instance, the statement made to these recent visitors that three graves within the area contained the remains of 'Emin, Gordon and Wilton-Jones'.[4]

[1] Lugard, II, 479–80.
[2] Thomas and Scott, pp. 263–5; Thruston, pp. 286–323.
[3] Diary, 14 July 1888, p. 269 above.
[4] Report of Imperial College Exploration Club, *Uganda 1965* (London, 1966).

Epilogue

At Wadelai, the hub of the Province as Jephson knew it, even less remains than at Dufilé. The writer and traveller Alan Moorehead, who covered the ground when writing his book on the White Nile, found no road through the high grass.

It was, then, a matter of some astonishment that a tall and nearly naked African now suddenly jumped up in front of the truck, and pointing with his black finger into the grass ahead, uttered a single, luminous cry: 'Emin Pasha.' No doubt this man's family had been here since Emin's time, and had somehow retained their memory of the name through nearly three-quarters of a century. Clearly, too, he had reasoned that only some business connected with Emin or his ghost could have brought a white man to this outlandish spot. At all events it was both startling and pleasant to be reminded thus of the continuity of things and, sure enough, the green sheen of the river with fields of feathery papyrus on either bank soon broke into view. But where was Wadelai?

A cairn of stones marked the site of the town, and upon it was a plaque with the words:

Wadelai
Egyptian Station 1879–89
Headquarters of Equatoria
Under Emin Pasha

But the town itself had returned almost entirely to the jungle. All that was left of the orderly streets, the brick houses of the officials, the wharves and the gun emplacements, was a heap of reddish rubble hidden under the grass. Even the high walls and the ditch that once surrounded the garrison had fallen in and were now no more than a gentle undulation on the ground.[1]

[1] Moorehead, pp. 357–8.

A. J. MOUNTENEY JEPHSON'S CONTRACT WITH THE EMIN PASHA RELIEF EXPEDITION COMMITTEE

I, Arthur Jermy Mounteney Jephson, agree to accompany the Emin Pacha Relief Expedition and place myself under the command of Mr. H. M. Stanley the leader of the Expedition and to accept any post or position in that Expedition which he may assign to me.

I further agree to serve him loyally and devotedly, to obey all his orders, and to use my utmost endeavours to bring the Expedition to a successful issue.

I also agree to pay the sum of One Thousand Pounds to the credit of the Emin Pacha Relief Expedition at Messrs. Ransome, Bouverie and Sons No. 1 Pall Mall and to pay expenses of my passage from and to England, and to forfeit the above mentioned sum of £1000 if I leave the Expedition through sickness or of my own free will.

For the above I am to receive a due share of the European provisions provided for the Expedition, and also a share of native provisions purchased in the country: also 1 tent, 1 Winchester Rifle, and 1 Revolver, with ammunition for the same.

I also undertake not to publish anything connected with the Expedition or to send any account to the newspapers for six months after the issue of the official publication of the Expedition by the leader or his representative.

ARTHUR JERMY MOUNTENEY JEPHSON

Witnesses   *F. de Winton*
                 William Hoffmann

Approved

Henry M. Stanley

[The words in para. 3 'and to forfeit the above-mentioned sum of £1000 if I leave the Expedition through sickness or of my own free will', were written in after the rest of the clauses had been set out. The original of the contract is among the Jephson family papers at Mallow Castle.]

APPENDIX II

STATEMENT OF THE EMIN PASHA RELIEF FUND

[Appendix D of Stanley, *In Darkest Africa*, II, 461–2.]

RECEIPTS FROM SUBSCRIBERS

	£	s	d
Egyptian Government	14,000	0	0
Sir William Mackinnon, Bart.	3,000	0	0
Peter Mackinnon, Esq.	1,500	0	0
Peter Bonny, Esq., of Dumbarton	1,500	0	0
Baroness Burdett-Coutts	100	0	0
James Sligo Jameson, Esq.	1,000	0	0
Countess de Noailles	1,000	0	0
Gray, Dawes & Co., London	1,500	0	0
J. Mackinnon, Esq.	450	0	0
H. T. Younger, Esq., of Benmore	500	0	0
Duncan MacNeil, Esq.	1,050	0	0
Alexander L. Bruce, Esq., Edinburgh	750	0	0
James F. Hutton, Esq., Manchester	250	0	0
Royal Geographical Society	1,000	0	0
W. Burdett-Coutts, Esq.	400	0	0
J. M. Hall, Esq.	375	0	0
N. MacMichael, Esq.	375	0	0
J. Siltzer, Esq.	100	0	0
Sir Thomas Fowell Buxton	250	0	0
Col. J. A. Grant	100	0	0
W. P. Alexander, Esq.	250	0	0
A. F. Walter, Esq., of the *Times*	500	0	0

Received from newspapers on account of letters from
H. M. Stanley:

	£	s	d
Daily News, London	£500	0	0
Standard, London	250	0	0
Daily Telegraph, London	200	0	0
Manchester Guardian	200	0	0
Scotsman, Edinburgh	200	0	0

	£	s	d
	1,350	0	0

carried forward

Appendix II

brought forward

H. M. Stanley, refund of cash received from Beyts & Co., Suez	597	4	1
Eastern Telegraph Co., refund of half rates on Zanzibar Telegrams	167	4	6
Interest on deposits, Ransom & Co.	171	6	4
Gray, Dawes & co., refund of Transport	489	0	11
B. Edgington, refund from bills	5	6	10
Messrs. S. Allnatt	3	0	0
Rev. S. Stephenson	2	2	0
African Trading Company (sale of Stores)	152	12	2
Gray, Dawes & Co., amount refunded	30	15	2
Lord Kinnaird	100	0	0
Sampson Low, Marston, Searle & Rivington, Limited	250	0	0
	£33,268	12	0

Appendix II

	£	s	d
Transport and Travelling Expenses	7,202	3	5
Stores	5,046	8	4
Expedition Equipment	2,307	15	7
Wages advanced to Porters	2,027	15	4
Salaries and Commissions	636	16	8
Telegrams	518	18	0
Insurance	30	2	10
Medical Attendance	96	4	9
Special Messenger to Khartoum	65	0	0
Two drafts drawn in Africa for Goods	225	0	0
Petty expenses in London	97	14	10
Eastern Telegraph Co.	35	4	1
Printing	1	7	9
Petty Cash	10	0	0
Wages of Soudanese (Suez Draft)	1,200	0	0
Edinburgh Draft	0	5	0
William Bonny's balance of Salary	242	0	0
Captain Nelson's Expenses	30	9	4
Passage, Stairs and Jephson	44	13	6
Expenses on 'Katoria' and 'Rewa'	24	11	2
Smith, Mackenzie & Co's Draft for Payment of Expedition	6,066	18	10
1st Donation to Lieut. W. G. Stairs	400	0	0
1st Donation to A. Mounteney Jephson, Esq.	400	0	0
1st Donation to Capt. R. H. Nelson	400	0	0
1st Donation to Surgeon T. H. Parke	400	0	0
1st Donation to William Bonny, Esq.	200	0	0
	£27,709	9	5

To contributions to Widows and Orphans of deceased
Zanzibaris   10,000 rupees

LETTERS TO EMIN FROM THE KHEDIVE OF EGYPT AND HIS PRIME MINISTER NUBAR PASHA; AND LETTER FROM STANLEY TO EMIN'S SOLDIERS

The letters addressed to Emin Pasha by the Khedive of Egypt and by his Prime Minister, Nubar Pasha, are printed in Jephson, *Emin Pasha*, pages 45–8. Stanley's letter to the soldiers is on pages 48–50. The letters are first referred to in full in the entry for 22 June 1887 when Jephson read them to the garrison at Tunguru.

To His Excellency Mehmed Emin,
Mudir of Hatalastiva

Some time ago I commended you for your bravery and for the stand you and your officers and soldiers made, and for your victory over the adversities which beset you, I have rewarded you by conferring upon you the exalted rank of a general, and I have confirmed every promotion you have conferred on your officers, and have informed you of all this by my sovereign letter of November 29th, 1886, No. 31. And most certainly this letter reached you, together with the post forwarded by our Prime Minister, His Excellency Nubar Pasha. I am very pleased with your good behaviour and with whatever you have done, you, your officers and soldiers, and therefore my Government has busied itself with the means to extricate you, and save you if possible from the straits in which you find yourself. And now there has been constituted a force, under the direction of Mr. Stanley, the famous savant, who is known in all parts of the world for his great qualities and pre-eminence as a traveller. This Expedition is now ready to start for you, and with it whatever you are in need of in the way of provisions of every description, to bring you, your officers and soldiers, to Egypt, by the road Mr. Stanley considers is most preferable and easiest to march on. Therefore I command you, by this my order, sent by the hands of Mr. Stanley, to make known to you all these things, that after the arrival of this you will communicate them to your officers and soldiers, and read before them my Sovereign greetings with the intention to inform them of this. At the same time I give to you, to your officers and soldiers, full liberty to rest where you are, or to do your best to come out with the Expedition which is now sent to you. Our Government has decided to pay you and all the employés, officers and soldiers, all the appointments and allowances due to you. If, however, any one, officer or soldier, wishes to rest in the country, he is free to do so, but he does so on his own responsibility, and must not in future expect any assistance from this Government. And now make them understand all this distinctly, and communicate it word for word to all your officers and soldiers in order that every one may make up his mind. This is our Sovereign Order.

MOHAMMED TEWFIK

Eight Jumad Owel, 1304

To His Excellency Mehmed Emin Pasha,
Governor of the Equatorial Province

I have sent you by means of the English Consulate at Zanzibar, a letter from our August Sovereign, by which he thanks you for the bravery and courage shown by you, your officers and soldiers, by which he commends you for your gallantry, perseverance and victory over the adversities which beset you, and by which he expressed his appreciation of you, and conferred on you the exalted rank of a general, and confirmed the promotions and rewards you have conferred on your officers. At the same time I informed you that an Expedition would be sent out; and now this Expedition has been constituted under the direction of Mr. Stanley, who will hand you this letter, and this Expedition is now ready to start to you...for Egypt by the road which seems best to Mr. Stanley...Our August Sovereign gives you, your officers and soldiers who are with you, full liberty...to be able to come back with the Expedition which is now sent to you. But you must understand and make it understood at the same time by all your officers, soldiers and others, that if any one wishes to stay in the country where he is now, he is free to do so, but he will do it on his own responsibility, and need not expect the slightest assistance from this Government in future. And this is what our August Sovereign wishes you to make distinctly understood to any one wishing to stay there. There is no need to inform you that we will pay you, your officers, soldiers and civil servants, the wages and allowances due to you, in consequence of our August Master's having confirmed all your ranks. This is all, and I hope Mr. Stanley will find you in good health and safe. This is my sincere wish and what I wish you all. Written 9th Jumah Owel, 1304, corresponding to Feb. 2nd, 1887. No. 2.

NUBAR

(i.e. President of the Council of Ministers)

The blanks in Nubar's letters were owing to some parts of the letter being erased by damp.

It will be seen from these letters that no direct order was given to Emin or his people to leave the Province, nor was any promise of employment given to them when they reached Egypt. The letter of Nov. 29th, 1886, which the Khedive speaks of in his letter, never reached Emin.

The following is Stanley's address to the soldiers:

Soldiers of Emin Pasha

After a long journey from Zanzibar, I have at last reached your Nyanza, and seen your Pasha. I have come expressly at the command of the Khedive Tewfik, to lead you out of this country and show you the way to Egypt. For you must know that the river el Abiad is closed, that Khartoum is in the hands of the followers of Mohammed Achmet, that the great Pasha Gordon and all his people were killed over three years ago, and that the country and river between Wady Halfa and the Bahr Ghazal is occupied by your enemies and by the rebels.

Four times have the Khedive and your friends made attempts to help you. First Gordon Pasha was sent to Khartoum to bring you all home, but before he could safely leave Khartoum, that city was taken and he himself killed.

Next, the English soldiers came near to Khartoum to try and help Gordon Pasha, but they were four days too late, for Gordon was dead and Khartoum was lost.

Next came Dr. Fischer, by way of the Nyanza of Uganda, but he found too many enemies in the path, and returned home and died.

Next came Dr. Lenz, by way of the Congo, but he could not find men enough to carry his goods, and he also went home.

I tell you these things to prove to you that you have not been forgotten in Egypt. No, the Khedive and his vizier Nubar Pasha have always kept you in mind though they could not reach you. They have heard from your Pasha, by way of Uganda, how bravely you have held to your posts, and how staunch you have been to your duties as soldiers.

Therefore they sent me to tell you this, and to say to you that you are well remembered and that your reward is awaiting you. At the same time, the Khedive says that if you think the road is too long, or are afraid of the journey, that you may stay here, but if you do so you are no longer his soldiers, and that your pay stops at once, and that if any trouble befall you hereafter you are not to expect any help from him. Should you decide to obey him and follow me to Egypt, I am to show you the way to Zanzibar, and there put you on board a steamer, and take you to Suez, and thence to Cairo, and that your pay continues until you arrive in Egypt, and that all promotions made here will be secured to you, and all rewards promised you here will be paid in full.

I send one of my officers, Mr. Jephson, to read to you this message, and that you may know that he comes from me I lend him my sword. I now go back a little way to collect all my people and goods, and bring them here. After a few months—Inshallah—I shall return to hear what you have to say. If you say, 'Let us go to Egypt', I will then show you a safe road, and will accompany you and not leave you until you stand before the Khedive. If you say, 'We shall not leave this country', then I will bid you farewell and return to Egypt with my own people, and give the Khedive your answer.

May God have you in his safe keeping.

This is from your good friend,

STANLEY

APPENDIX IV

SURGEON T. H. PARKE'S REPORT TO STANLEY OF CONDITIONS AT THE ARAB CAMP AT IPOTO FROM 28 OCTOBER 1887 TO 23 JANUARY 1888

The report is copied into Jephson's diary following the entry for 8 February 1888; it is also printed in Stanley, *IDA*, I, 338–40. Jephson dates the letter '17th Feb./88', which may be the date on which he copied it; there is no other entry between the 8th and 19th. Stanley gives 8 February 1888, the date on which Parke and Nelson arrived at Fort Bodo.

From Surgeon T. H. Parke Army Medical Dept in medical charge E.P.R. Expedtn
To H. M. Stanley Esq. Commanding Emin Pasha Relief Expedtn

Fort Bodo
17th Feb. /88

Sir

I have the honour to forward this report for your information. In compliance with your orders dated 24th Oct/87 I remained at the Manyema camp to take charge of invalids & Impedimenta left there on your departure 28th Oct/87 up to the time the Relief party arrived 23 Jan/88. Of those invalids you left in camp seven were sufficiently recoovered to send on with Capt Jephson 7th November, those remaining were increased in number by the arrival of Capt Nelson his two boys & two men 3rd Nov also the chief Omari & nine men who were found in a starving condition in the bush by Chilongalonga & brought by him to camp 9th January, this made a total of One sick officer & 38 invalids remaining in camp. Of this number Capt Nelson & 16 men left with relief party, eleven men were away on safari (foraging, A.M.J.) looking for food & therefore remain at Manyema camp, & 11 deaths occured, this extremely high mortality will no doubt astonish you especially as it was entirely due to starvation except in two instances only. From the time you left the Manyema camp until our departure 26th January the chiefs gave little or no food to either officers or men, those men who were sufficiently strong to do a good days work sometimes got as many as 10 heads of corn per man but as the working men were not constantly employed their average ration of corn was about 3 per day, those invalids who were unable to work of whom there were many received no food from the chiefs & were therefore obliged to count on Mboya (herbs). Remembering the wretched & debilitated condition of all these men both from privation & disease you will readily understand that the heartless treatment of the Manyema chiefs was sufficient to cause an even greater mortality. The men were badly housed & their scanty clothing consisted of about ½ yd of native bark cloth as they sold their own clothes for food, they experienced not only the horror of starvation but were cruelly & brutally treated by the Manyema who drove them to commit theft by withholding food & then scored their backs with rods, & in one case speared a man to death, for stealing. Capt Nelson arrived in a very weak condition requiring good food & careful treatment. He visited the chiefs & made them handsome presents of articles costing about £75 with a view to win their sympathy, however they continued to give little or no food to officers or men, they said no arrangement had been made for provisioning Capt Nelson & any food they sent to me was entirely of their own generosity, as no arrangement had been made by you. I asked them to let me see the written agreement between you & them, which they did, also another document written in Arabic charater which I could not read. In their agreement with you I saw that they had promised to provision the officers & men whom you would leave. I appealled to them & remonstrated with them, nevertheless they supplied less & less food until finally they refused to give any on the plea that they had none. The height of their generosity would be reached when they would send two or three cups of Indian meal to feed Capt Nelson myself & two boys until the next donation would turn up in 6 or 7 days afterwards, during the last 7 weeks we did not receive any food whatever from the chiefs. Owing to their refusal to give us food we were obliged to sell first our own clothes, then some of Emin Pasha's clothing & eight rifles belonging to the Expedition to provide ourselves & boys with food. I repeatedly reminded Assimaili (the Chief) of the conversation he had with you in your tent the night before you left the camp when he promised to look after & care for the officers & men whom you left in camp. Although the chiefs had no food to supply according to their agreement yet they always had plenty to sell, their object being to compel us to sell the arms & ammunition for food. I sent you a complete list of effects left in my charge by Capt Jephson 7th Nov, all of which were correct when the relief party arrived with the following exceptions viz 2 boxes Remington ammunition & one rifle which were stolen by a Zanzibari (Saraboko) & I believe sold to the Manyema chiefs. The following effects were left at camp under the care of Chilongalonga who gave a receipt for them. viz 1 shield Maxim gun, 1 bag native curios, 1 portmanteau, 2 boxes Remington ordinary, 1 tent & poles complete, 47 Remington rifles.—Several attempts were made to steal the arms, boxes etc.

28-2

On the night of Nov 7th the hut in which the baggage was stored was set on fire with a view to taking everything with a rush in the confusion caused by the fire. However their design was frustrated as Capt Nelson who was awake & saw the blaze gave the alarm just in time for ourselves & boys to put out the fire before it got to the baggage. I then had the tents pitched according to your directions not being able to do so earlier as I had no assistance. All the rifles ammunition, boxes etc were packed in the tents one of which was occupied by Capt Nelson & the other by myself. Every effort was made to prevent things being stolen, nevertheless even Capt Nelsons blankets were taken by a thief who got under the tent from behind. On another occasion I heard a noise at my tent door in the early morning & jumping out of bed quickly, I found a box of ammunition 10 yds off which had just been taken from my tent, the thief escaped in the dark. On the night of Jan 9th I heard a noise outside my tent & suspecting a thief I crept out noiselessly to the back where I caught Kamaroui a Zanzibari in the act of stealing a rifle through a hole which he had cut in the tent. For this offence I flogged him severely. Many cases of stealing corn by the Zanzibaris were brought up by the chiefs & in every case where there was proof the Zanzibaris were punished. The people, their manners & surroundings were of the lowest order & owing to the mounds of fecal matter & decomposing vegetation which were allowed to collect on the paths & close to their dwellings the place was a hotbed of disease. Capt Nelson was confined to his bed from sickness for over two months & I got blood poisoning followed by erysipelas which kept me in bed for over 5 weeks. During our illness the chiefs paid us frequent visits but always with a view to covet something they saw in our tents. Their avarice was unbounded & they made agreements one day only to be broken the next. After the arrival of Chilongalonga & his force of about 400 including women children & slaves, food became really scarce therefore the Manyema were obliged to send out large Safari to bring food, the eleven Zanzibaris who were absent accompanied these Safari in search of food & had not returned when I left the Manyema camp with the relief party. The starvation was so great just before we left that the native slaves seized one of their comrades who had gone some distance from the camp to draw water cut him in pieces & ate him. In conclusion I may mention that Capt Nelson & myself did everything we could to preserve a good feeling with the Manyema chiefs & people & we parted on friendly terms. I have the honour to be

yrs obediently

T. H. PARKE (Surgn A.M.S.)

SELECT BIBLIOGRAPHY

ANSTEY, R. T. *Britain and the Congo in the 19th century.* London, 1962.

BAKER, J. N. L. 'Sir Richard Burton and the Nile sources.' *English Historical Review,* LIX (1944), 48–61.

BAKER, SAMUEL WHITE. *Albert Ny'anza, Great basin of the Nile.* London, 1866. *Ismailia.* 2 vols. London, 1874.

BARTTELOT, SIR W. G. (ed.). *The life of Edmund Musgrave Barttelot from his letters and diary.* London, 1890.

BERE, RENÉ. *The way to the Mountains of the Moon.* London, 1966.

BOURNE, H. R. FOX. *The other side of the Emin Pasha Relief Expedition.* London, 1891.

BRIDGES, R. C. 'The R.G.S. and the African Exploration Fund, 1876–80.' *Geographical Journal,* CXXIX (1963), 25–35.
'John Hanning Speke and the R.G.S.' *Uganda Journal,* XXVI (1962), 23–43.

BRODE, HEINRICH. *Tippoo-Tib: the story of his career in Central Africa.* Transl. H. Havelock. London, 1907.

CASATI, CAPT. GAETANO. *Ten years in Equatoria and the return with Emin Pasha.* Transl. Mrs J. R. Clay and I. W. Savage Landor. 2 vols. London, 1891.

CEULEMANS, PÈRE P. *La question arabe et le Congo (1883–1892).* Brussels, 1959.

COLLINS, R. O. *The southern Sudan 1893–1898: the struggle for control.* New Haven and London, 1962.

COUPLAND, SIR REGINALD. *The exploitation of East Africa, 1856–1890; the slave trade and the scramble.* London, 1939.

CROMER, LORD. *Modern Egypt.* 2 vols. London, 1908.

Dictionary of National Biography.

GRAY, SIR JOHN. 'Stanley *versus* Tippoo Tib.' *Tanganyika Notes and Records,* XVIII (1944), 11–27.
'The diaries of Emin Pasha: Extracts, I–XII.' *Uganda Journal,* XXV–XXXI (1961–7).

GRAY, RICHARD. *History of the southern Sudan 1839–1889.* London, 1961.

HOFFMANN, WILLIAM. *With Stanley in Africa.* London, 1938.

IMPERIAL COLLEGE EXPLORATION SOCIETY. *Uganda 1965* (report). London, 1966.

JACKSON, SIR FREDERICK. *Early days in East Africa.* London, 1930.

JAMESON, J. S. *Story of the Rear Column of the Emin Pasha Relief Expedition.* Ed. Mrs J. S. Jameson. London, 1890.

JEPHSON, A. J. MOUNTENEY. *Emin Pasha and the Rebellion at the Equator.* London. 1890.
Stories told in an African forest. London, 1892.

JEPHSON, MAURICE DENHAM. *An Anglo-Irish miscellany: some records of the Jephsons of Mallow.* Dublin, 1964.

JOHNSTON, SIR HARRY. *The Nile Quest.* London, 1903.

JUNKER, WILHELM. *Travels in Africa (1875–1886)*. Transl. A. H. Keane. 3 vols. London, 1890–2.

LIVINGSTONE, DAVID. *Missionary travels and researches in South Africa*. London, 1857.
Last Journals. Ed. Horace Waller. 2 vols. London, 1874.

LUGARD, FREDERICK DEALTRY. *The rise of our East African Empire*. 2 vols. London, 1893.

MAURICE, ALBERT (ed.). *H. M. Stanley: Unpublished letters*. Brussels, 1955 (French); Edinburgh, 1959 (English).

MOOREHEAD, ALAN. *The White Nile*. London, 1960.

OLIVER, ROLAND, and MATHEW, GERVASE (eds.). *History of East Africa*, vol. I. London, 1963.

PARKE, T. H. *My personal experiences in Equatorial Africa as medical officer of the Emin Pasha Relief Expedition*. London, 1891.

PERHAM, MARJORIE, and SIMMONS, J. *African discovery: an anthology*. London, 1942.

ROBINSON, R., GALLAGHER, J., with DENNY, A. *Africa and the Victorians: the official mind of imperialism*. London, 1961.

SANDERSON, G. N. *England, Europe and the Upper Nile*. Edinburgh, 1966.

SCHWEINFURTH, GEORG. *The Heart of Africa*. 2 vols. London, 1873.
(ed.) *Emin Pasha in Central Africa, being a collection of his letters and journals*. Transl. Mrs R. W. Felkin. London, 1888.

SCHWEITZER, GEORG. *Emin Pasha, his life and work*. Translation of the same author's *Emin Pascha* (Berlin, 1898) with the addition of an Introduction by R. W. Felkin. London, 1898.

SCHYNSE, A. *A travers l'Afrique avec Stanley et Émin Pacha: journal de voyage du Père Schynse*. Paris, 1890.

SIMPSON, D. H. 'A bibliography of Emin Pasha.' *Uganda Journal*, XXIV, 2 (1960), 138–65.

SLADE, RUTH. *King Leopold's Congo*. London, 1962.

SPEKE, J. H. *What led to the discovery of the source of the Nile*. Edinburgh, 1864.
Journal of the discovery of the source of the Nile. Edinburgh, 1863.

STANLEY, LADY D. (ed.). *The autobiography of Sir Henry Morton Stanley, G.C.B.* London, 1909.

STANLEY, HENRY MORTON. *Through the Dark Continent*. 2 vols. London, 1877.
The Congo, and the Founding of its Free State. 2 vols. London, 1885.
In Darkest Africa. 2 vols. London, 1890.

STANLEY, RICHARD, and NEAME, ALAN. *The exploration diaries of H. M. Stanley*. London, 1962.

STUHLMANN, FRANZ (ed.). *Die Tagebücher von Dr. Emin Pascha*. 5 vols. Brunswick: Westermann, 1916–27.

THOMAS, H. B. 'Mohammed Biri.' *Uganda Journal*, XXIV (1960), 123–6.

THOMAS, H. B., and SCOTT, R. *Uganda*. London, 1935.

THRUSTON, A. B. *African Incidents*. London, 1900.

TROUP, J. ROSE. *With Stanley's rear column*. London, 1890.

TURNBULL, COLIN. *Wayward servants: the two worlds of the African pygmies*. London, 1966.

Select bibliography

WARD, HERBERT. *My life with Stanley's Rear Guard.* London, 1891.

WAUTERS, A.-J. *Stanley au secours d'Émin Pacha.* Brussels and Paris, 1890.

WERNER, J. R. *A visit to Stanley's Rear Guard at Major Barttelot's camp on the Aruwimi with an account of river-life on the Congo.* Edinburgh, 1891.

WHITE, J. P. 'The Sanford Exploring Expedition.' *Journal of African History*, VIII, 2 (1967), 291–302.

WRIGHT, JOHN KIRTLAND. *Human Nature in Geography.* Belknap Press of Harvard University Press, 1966.

MANUSCRIPT SOURCES

Archives of the Jephson family at Mallow Castle, Co. Cork, Eire, contain correspondence, press-cuttings, etc., which throw light on the part played by A. J. Mounteney Jephson in the relief of Emin Pasha. They also cover the period after the expedition's return, and contain many letters from Stanley, Parke, Stairs, and from others interested in the expedition. These papers have been gone through thoroughly.

The Mackinnon Papers in the School of Oriental and African Studies, University of London, include many letters and memoranda, account books, etc., throwing light on the expedition. They have been consulted but not exhaustively perused.

The Archives of the Royal Geographical Society, London, contain a few marginal references to the expedition, and have been consulted.

INDEX

Abdullah Aga Manzal, commanding Muggi, 273, 274, 275, 292, 300

Abdullah Vaap Effendi, 257, 287, 300

Abyssinia, *see* Ethiopia

Aden, 71, 74

Advance, EPRE steel boat, Jephson put in charge of, 3; on lower Congo, 55–6, 81–95 *passim*; crossing of Inkissi river in, 88–9; on upper Congo, 55–6, 96–111 *passim*; on Aruwimi, 112–71 *passim*; dismantled at Ipoto, 56, 182, 184; fetched from Ipoto to Fort Bodo by Stairs, 57, 222–4; carried to L. Albert, 233–42; crossing of Ituri in, 233–4; launched on L. Albert, 57, 242–4; transported from Dufilé to Wadelai, 285; broken up at Wadelai, 307; retrieved and brought to Nsabé, 332 n.; abandoned, 339

Africa, 'scramble' for, 8, 9–34 *passim*; *see also* France, Great Britain, Germany, Leopold II, Portugal

African Association, 15

Albert, Lake, v, 6, 25, 29, 38, 40, 49, 50, 59, 111, 129, 144 n., 149, 195, 200, 202, 203, 205, 218, 220, 227, 231 n., 232, 235, 291, 351, 352, 359 n., 363, 367, 374; position in Nile system, 10, 16, 17, 18, 19, 355, 369, 376; Baker's and Gordon's advance to, 11, 12; Emin's concentration on, 38, 39; Junker's escape across, 41; Ipoto, 82½ miles from, 171; EPRE's first visit to, December 1887, 56, 206–15; EPRE's 2nd visit to, April 1888, 48, 57, 242–56; journey on, to fetch Emin, 57, 242–50; Jephson's further journey on, with Emin to Wadelai, 257–64; Jephson revisits Tunguru on, 286–9; flight from Wadelai, and halt at Tunguru on, 308–30; Tunguru to M'swa, by way of, 330–2; EPRE's 3rd visit to, January–May 1889, 59, 332–44; Emin returns to, from Wadelai, 413

Ali Aga Djabor, 275, 283, 284, 293, 300

Alur, L. Albert tribe, 266

Amadi, 15, 40

Ankole, 49, 51, 60, 375, 377, 378, 379, 383, 386, 399

Anstey, R. T., 48

Anti-slavery movement, 22, 43, 61, 286, 346, 350

Arabi, Colonel, 13, 24, 39, 257, 260

Arabs, penetration of Africa by, 16, 25, 26, 31, 34–8, 42–3, 51, 77–9; Expedition's contacts with, 56, 57, 115, 125, 144, 147, 148–51, 155, 157, 158, 167, 169–75 *passim*, 180–4 *passim*, 194, 225, 434–6; *see also* Manuyema, Tippu Tib

Arthington, Robert, 52

Aruwimi, river, 43, 51, 54, 56, 101, 102, 103, 106–11 *passim*, 112, 117, 119, 138, 141–2, 149, 153, 158, 188, 243, 249, 304

Ashanti War, 1873, 18, 45

Assimaili, *see* Ismailia

Aveysheba, 135, 304

Azande (or Niam-Niam) tribe, 288 n., 305, 308

Bacheet Aga, commanding Kirri, 273, 274, 275, 283, 292, 298, 300

Bagamoyo, 60, 411, 412

Bahr el Ghazal, 14, 15, 18, 39, 40, 288, 306, 432

Baker, J. R., 207 n.

Baker, Florence (Lady), 10, 11, 17, 206–7, 261 n., 266, 267

Baker, Sir Samuel, explores Nile system, 8, 17, 18, 19, 129 n., 206–7, 376; as Governor of Equatoria, 10, 11, 35, 39, 212 n., 250–1, 261, 269, 424; invasion of and retreat from Bunyoro, 25, 293 n.; reprieves Faratch Aga, 261 n., 267; views on Africa, 408

Baker, V. E., 261 n.

Banana Point, 31, 32, 79

Bangala, 54, 58, 100, 103–4, 304, 321, 326

Bari tribe, 6, 11, 16, 273, 277, 296

Baring, Sir Evelyn (Lord Cromer), 14 n., 46, 53, 62, 327

Baroko, Zanzibari, 137, 140, 154, 166, 224, 225

Barttelot, Edmund Musgrave, his letters and diary, vi; joins EPRE, 52, 67, 70;

Index

Faratch Aga, 261, 266, 267, 283, 301, 344

Felkin, Dr Robert, his correspondence with Emin quoted from, 12–13, 38, 41, 42, 61; first meeting with Emin, 44; leads movement to rescue Emin, 44, 45; draws up agreement between Mackinnon and Emin, 47–8; disappointment of, at failure of EPRE, 63; article by, in *Graphic*, 249; Farida's guardian, 290; Jephson's resentment with, 313–14

Ferhani, Zanzibari, executes war dance on leaving Yambuya, 112

Fetteh, Zanzibari, 202, 208, 235, 236

Fischer, Dr, 44, 432

Fola Rapids, 11, 424

Fort Bodo, 56, 57, 59, 221–31 *passim*; 192, 321, 322, 344

France in Africa, 24, 26, 30, 31, 32

Gavira, alias Mpinga, chief of the Bira, 56, 205, 243, 244, 320, 324, 327, 328, 343, 382

Gedge, Ernest, 27, 28, 29, 45, 49, 50 n., 398 n.

Germany in Africa, 22–4, 25, 27, 46, 71, 409, 410, 411; and relief of Emin, 29

Gessi, Romolo, 11, 19, 39, 269, 288, 341 n., 355, 424

Girault, Père, 407

Gladstone, Rt Hon. W. E., 14, 22, 43, 274

Godman, Miss Mabel, 364 n., 420 n.

Gondokoro, 10, 16, 17, 129, 261

Gordon, General Charles, 8, 73, 75, 212, 260, 274, 278, 286, 288, 294, 295, 305, 350, 383, 406; Governor of Equatoria, 11–12, of the Sudan, 12; at Khartoum, 14–15, 24; relations with Buganda, 25–6, with King Leopold, 14, 30, 32

Grant, James Augustus, 17; explores Nile sources, 25, 26; at Brussels Geographical Conference, 30; rescues Stanley's servant from Fenchurch Street, 67; memories of, in Karagwe, 388–9, 392; contribution to EPRE, 427

Gray, Sir John, vi, viii, 37 n., 59 n., 61 n., 390 n.

Gray, Richard, 43 n.

Great Britain in Africa, dominating influence, 20; anti-slavery campaign, 20; relations with Zanzibar, 20–3; challenged by Germany, 23–4; Anglo-

German agreement, 24–5, 36, 50; interest in Buganda, 26–9; interest in Congo, 32; on L. Tanganyika, 35; official attitude of, to Mackinnon, 22, 46, 47; *see also* Great Britain in Egypt, Germany in Africa, Portugal in Africa

Great Britain in Egypt, occupation of, 13, 24; clash with France over, 13, 24; involvement in Sudan, 13, 14, 24, 43; limited interest in EPRE, 46, 53

Grenfell, Rev. George, 37

Hamad Aga, Major, 1st Btn. Rejaf, 266, 267, 275, 281, 292, 293, 300

Hannington, Bishop James, 27, 46

Hassan, Vita, Emin's apothecary, 40, 41, 42, 249, 264, 283, 287, 288, 289, 311, 333; demands excessive number of carriers, 293, 334

Hawashi Effendi, commanding Dufilé, 39, 270, 347; entertains Jephson to dinner, 271; imprisoned by mutineers, 281–2; accused of malpractices, 283–4, 289, 290; goods of, plundered, 295; leaves for Wadelai, 299; visited by Jephson, 306; accompanies Jephson to Tunguru, 311, 330; arrives at Kavalli's, 337; leaves Kavalli's with Stairs, 340

Head, Addison, 418, 419

Head, Anna (Mrs A. J. Mounteney Jephson), *see* Jephson, Mrs A. J. M.

Henry Reed, American mission steamer, 52, 94, 95, 96, 97, 98–9, 100, 101, 102, 110

Herodotus, 16, 17, 25, 341

Hicks Pasha, 13, 14

Hoffmann, William, 69, 228, 322, 420–2, 426

Holmwood, Fred, Acting Consul at Zanzibar, 46, 49, 53, 54, 72, 73, 246, 250

Hore, Captain E. C., 35

Hutton, J. F., 32, 45, 46, 48, 427

Ibrahim Aga, commanding Emin's 'Irregulars' (or Danaqla), 39, 63, 312, 422

Ibwirri, 192, 195, 311, 321

Ihuru river (Epulu), 230

Illness and accidents on the march: dysentery, 79, 84, 148, 288; fever, 91–2, 107, 111–14, 123, 135, 145, 187–9, 219–20,

3; rebellion, 275–97 *passim*; mutiny at Laboré, 278–90; imprisoned at Dufilé, 282–5; moves to Wadelai, 285–6, Tunguru, 287–8; return to Dufilé, 289–97; return to Wadelai on hearing of Mahdist advance, 298–307; breaks up *Advance*, 307; deplores Emin's vacillations, 306; leads evacuation of Wadelai, 308–11; discusses situation with Casati, 313–14; criticizes Junker and Felkin, 314; letters from Stanley, 321–9; rejoins Stanley, 331; expedition reunited, 336; picnic with Emin, 338–9; appointed aide to Stanley in No. 1 company for return, 339; involved in disputes between Emin and Stanley, 337–44; return journey, L. Albert to L. Edward, 345–64 *passim*; very ill, 354–8; distrust of Bonny, 364; through Ankoe and Karagwe, 365–90 *passim*; visit from Kiengo, Speke's old servant, 388; embassy to Chief of Karagwe, Rumanika's grandson, 388–90; Karagwe to Bagamoyo, 391–409 *passim*; impressions of Zanzibaris, 224, 226, 331–2, 334–5, 346, 382–3, 392, 403, 414; with Mackay at Usambiro, 397–9; march for the coast, 399; views on missions, 400–1; views on Africa's future, 305, 401–2; called by Mackay 'the friend of Africa', 408; return to Zanzibar, 410–12; kindly farewell of Emin to, 411; friendship with Farida, 413; with other officers, 5, 185, 414; Stanley's tribute to, 415; later friendship with Stanley, 417; failing health, 417; appointed Queen's Messenger, 418; marriage to Anna Head, 418–19; birth of son, 419; death, 419

Jephson, Mrs A. J. M., 418, 419

Jephson, Desmond, 419

Jephson, Brig. M. D., v, vi, viii, 419 n.

Johnston, Keith, 23

Junker, Dr Wilhelm, explores Congo–Nile watershed, 18, 142; with Emin in Equatoria, 39, 249, 269, 303, 424; escapes with news of Emin, 41, 42, 43, 424; views on position in Equatoria, 49, 53, 61, 69, 210, 313, 314; meets EPRE at Suez, 68, 69; Jephson's servant Binza formerly in service of, 247; Jephson's resentment with, 313–14

Kabarega, king of Bunyoro, relations with Buganda, 10; relations with Europeans, 10, 11; relations with Egypt, 11, 12; relations with Emin, 27, 41, 42, 43, 246, 250, 257, 320; EPRE and, 45, 210, 237, 240, 242, 264, 265, 354, 356, 362, 363, 365, 369, 371; Jephson's observations on, 316, 318, 339, 368, 378; *see also* Buganda, Bunyoro, Mutesa

Kagera, or Alexandra Nile, 60, 375, 379, 383, 386 n.

Kamrasi, king of Bunyoro (d. 1869), 10, 11

Karagwe, 26, 49, 51, 61, 375, 385, 387, 388, 389, 390, 391, 392

Karam Allah, Mahdist general, 15

Karema, L. Tanganyika, 30, 31, 41

Kasongo, 36, 37, 79 n.

Katonza's, L. Albert, 208, 331

Katwe, the Salt Lake, 365–9, 374

Kavalli, L. Albert chief, character of, 241; his lake-shore village, 171, 210, 211, 212, 232, 239, 242; his hill village (Kavalli's) EPRE base, 3, 57, 203, 206, 242 n., 298, 311, 316, 323, 324, 325, 326, 327, 328, 329, 331, 332, 334, 335, 337, 340, 360, 362, 363, 393; EPRE departure from, 60, 342–4, 399, 414; Selim Aga remains at, 29, 413, 422

Kavirondo, L. Victoria, 28, 45, 48, 49, 50 n., 57, 262, 264, 305

Kenya, 23, 24

Kenya, Mount, 16

Kerckhoven, G. F. van, 422

Khamis, Arab trader at Ipoto, 168, 170, 173, 182, 190–2, 193, 194

Khamis Aga, commanding Chor Ayu, 272

Khamis Parry, Zanzibari headman, 159, 174, 187, 193, 228

Khartoum, 10, 11, 12, 13, 14, 15, 17, 20, 24, 26, 35, 39, 43, 70, 73, 75, 264, 269, 276, 278, 281, 282, 293, 294, 295, 296, 298, 299, 314, 432

Khedive steamer, 11, 42, 212, 250, 251, 283, 287, 324

Kibero, L. Albert, 41, 42, 210, 212, 213, 232, 257, 368, 394

Kiengo, Speke's old guide, 388, 391

Kilimanjaro, Mount, 16, 23, 24, 256, 262, 341, 352, 398 n.

Kilonga-Longa, Arab trader, 35, 56, 168, 222, 230, 357, 436

Index

Kingsley, Mary, 126

Kirk, Sir John, British Consul at Zanzibar, 20, 34, 50 n., 70, 72; signs anti-slavery agreement with Sultan, 21, 22; deplores German penetration of East Africa, 23; retires, 1886, 24, 46, 70, 72; relations with Arabs, 35; *see also* Zanzibar

Kirri, Equatoria station, 11, 12, 274, 275, 292

Kodi Aga, commanding Wadelai, 268, 283, 286, 287, 299, 303, 305, 306, 307, 310, 311, 312

Kordofan province, 13

Krapf, Rev. Ludwig, 16

Kwamouth, 96, 98

Laboré, 12, 40, 273, 277, 283, 295, 298, 332, 395; letters read at, 278; mutiny breaks out at, 279–81

Lado, Equatoria garrison, 11, 12, 15, 38, 39, 40, 44, 61, 269, 294

Lamu, 71

Lander, John and Richard, 15

Lavigerie, Cardinal, 26, 396

Lenda river, 153, 173

Lenz, Oscar, 44, 432

Leopold II, king of the Belgians, vii, 14, 22, 36, 73, 94, 102, 417; founds International African Association, 22, 30–2; enters the Congo, 32–4, 37; appoints Tippu Tib Governor of Stanley Falls, 38; relations with Mackinnon, 30, 46, 48; interest in EPRE, 51, 52, 57, 83; relations with Stanley, 31, 33, 51; interest in Emin, 48, 57

Leopoldville, 33, 54, 92, 93, 94, 96, 100, 102, 109, 110

Livingstone, David, 8, 9, 17, 18, 20, 21, 25, 35, 208 n., 396, 418

Lobo, Fr. Jeronimo, 16

Lourdel, Père, 27, 29, 396

Lualaba river, 17, 18, 31, 35, 37, 79 n.

Lugard, Frederick Dealtry (Lord Lugard), 29, 40, 367 n., 378 n., 423, 424

Lupton, Frank, 11, 12, 14, 15

Lur tribe, *see* Alur

Mackay, Alexander, pioneer missionary in Buganda, 26–7, 378; Emin's contacts with, 41, 42, 61; retires south of L. Victoria, 27, 28 n., 43, 60; receives EPRE

at Usambiro, 397, 400, 402; calls Jephson 'friend of Africa', 6, 408; Jephson's opinion of, 400

Mackinnon, Sir William, 399, 418, 421, 427; interest in East Africa, 22, 23, 27, 28, 30, 47, 49; in West Africa, 32; relations with King Leopold, 30, 46, 48; sponsorship of EPRE, 45, 46, 47, 49, 427

Madi tribe, 253, 254, 259, 260, 273, 335, 347

Mahdi, the (Mohammed Ahmed Ibn el-Seyyid), v, 13, 14, 15, 34, 40, 41, 51, 264, 313, 398, 432

Mahdist forces in Equatoria, 40, 60, 294, 295, 296, 300, 306, 309, 310, 312, 315, 422–3

Mahomed Effendi, leader of mutiny from Makaraka, 275, 281

Makaraka country, 15, 61, 260, 274, 275, 281, 296, 301, 306, 344

Mallow Castle, Co. Cork, v, vi, viii, 1, 7 n., 169 n., 207 n., 416–21 nn.

Mangbetu country, 249, 260, 283, 288

Manning, Olivia, vi

Manuyema, people and region, 36, 55, 79, 150, 347, 383; at Ipoto, 165, 168, 169–82, 210, 219, 220, 222, 225, 230, 305, 321, 357, 434–6; Rear Column porters, 53, 55, 58, 325, 336, 337, 339, 381, 384

Manyanga, 81, 82, 83, 85, 277

Marco, Signor, 40, 266, 285, 289, 311, 316, 333, 334

Masailand, and the Masai, 23, 25, 28, 45, 50, 352, 398, 407, 409

Mason, Col. A. M., 11, 12, 18, 208, 212, 355

Matadi, 54, 80

Matakos, Congo currency, 100, 105, 130, 132, 151, 181, 203

Mazamboni, Lake Albert chief, hostile to EPRE, 56, 203; EPRE makes friends with, 237, 238, 324, 326, 327, 328, 340; EPRE camps with on return journey, 60, 342, 344, 349, 351, 353, 382; EPRE march away from, 352, 359, 422

Medical treatment: vaccination refused by Jephson, 71; of arrow wounds, 136, 194, 235; of tetanus, 140; amputation, 142; use of brandy, 168; of 'forced march' tablets, 168; of quinine, 187, 355, 374, 379; of Stanley at Fort Bodo, 228; of Suleiman Aga by Emin, 315; of

448

Medical treatment (*cont.*)
Jephson by Emin, 320; use of morphine, 345, opium, 373; of fever, 373–4
Mehemet Ali, 10, 16
Mengo, 28, 29
Milz, Jules, 422
Mirambo, Unyamwezi chief, 34
Missions: in East Africa, 16; Protestant, in Buganda, 26–7, 29, 42, 44, 46, 378; R.C., in Buganda, 26–7, 29, 378, 396; in the Congo, 37, 52, 96; disputes with, over Congo steamers, 37, 94–5; French, in Unyamwezi, 396, 401, 407; EPRE arrives at Mackay's retreat, south of L. Victoria, 396, 397; Jephson's views on, 399, 400; *see also* Mackay, A., Schynse, A.
Mogo, L. Albert chief, 244, 257, 311, 316, 318, 326
Mohammed Biri, Arab trader, 41, 42, 43
Moorehead, Alan, 425
Mouvement Géographique, Le, vii, 50
Mpinga, *see* Gavira (alternative names)
Mpwapwa, 409, 410
Msalala, 27, 42, 262, 391, 395, 296, 397
M'swa, Equatoria garrison on L. Albert, 38, 39, 57, 60, 213, 245, 254, 256, 257, 283, 287, 288, 290, 298, 310, 311, 312, 316, 318, 319, 320, 324, 329, 333, 339, 340, 347, 353, 395, 423
Muggi, Equatoria garrison on Nile, 11, 12, 273, 275, 277, 283, 284, 292, 295, 298, 299, 300
Munia Pembe, Zanzibari headman, 121, 122, 159, 230, 231
Murabo, Zanzibari headman, 120, 155, 243 n., 389; marches out of Yambuya 'a sight to behold', 112; describes Stanley, 248
Muta N'zige, 129, 147, 208, 262, 359 n., 360, 362, 365, 367, 369
Mutesa, king of Buganda (d. 1884), relations with Bunyoro, 10; relations with Europeans, 10, 11, 26, 44, 369; relations with Egypt, 12; importance of in African history, 25, 26, 27; death of, 27; mentioned by Jephson, 378; *see also* Buganda, Bunyoro, Kabarega
Mwanga, king of Buganda, succeeds Mutesa, 27, 28; persecutes Christians, 27, 43, 378, 397; detains Junker, 42; and

relief of Emin, 45, 46; deposed, 398, 406
Nachtigal, Dr Gustav, 30
Nelson, Captain Robert H., officer of Advance Column, vi, 5, 55; called 'Pandalamona' by Zanzibaris, 6; joins EPRE, 52, 67; on voyage out, 70, 76, 77; on upper Congo, 96, 98, 108, 111; on march from Yambuya, 119, 122, 123, 131, 133, 138, 139, 140, 142, 143, 146, 147, 150, 156; contracts psoriasis and goes lame, 154–5, 157; left at Starvation Camp, 56, 159, 170 n.; rescued by Jephson, 171–82; left at Ipoto, 56, 183–5, 192, 194, 207, 211, 357, 434–6; rejoins expedition at Fort Bodo, 57, 222–5; left at Fort Bodo, 228, 231, 232; 321; at Ituri Camp, 322, 332; rejoins expedition at Kavalli's, 336, 338; at Mazamboni's, 343, 346; on march to Bagamoyo, 339, 352, 358 n., 361, 372, 373, 379, 380 n., 384, 385, 388 n., 393, 400, 405; quarrel with Bonny, 363–4; Stanley's report on, 415; at Stanley's wedding, 416; employed by I.B.E.A., 417; death of, 417
Nepoko river, 56, 142, 172, 177, 249
Ngeliamah, Congo chief at Stanley Pool, 92, 93
Nile, river, 10, 13, 23, 34, 43, 49, 206, 283, 319, 341, 376, 424, 425; 'Nile Quest', 9, 15–19, 25, 26, 376; slave trade on, 20, 35; Equatoria garrisons on, 11–12, 39, 424–5; Mahdi rising on, 13
Nile, Alexandra, *see* Kagera
Nile, Blue, 16, 17
Noailles, Hélène, Comtesse de, 2, 3, 4, 5, 182, 217, 250, 427
Nsabé, L. Albert, 251, 252, 257, 263, 328, 329
Ntali (Antari), Ankole chief, 375, 377, 378, 380, 381
Nubar Pasha, 42; letter to Emin's garrisons, 53, 262, 267, 284, text of, 431
Nuer Aga, 26–7
Nyamsassie, L. Albert, 239, 240, 241, 242, 243, 244, 249, 321, 324, 330, 331
Nyangwe, 35, 37, 79 n.
Nyanza, steamer, 11, 212, 251 n, 298, 312, 313, 324, 351
Nyasa, Lake, 18, 20, 22, 23, 34, 35, 73